Pro Oracle SQL

Karen Morton

Kerry Osborne

Robyn Sands

Riyaj Shamsudeen

Jared Still

Pro Oracle SQL

ISBN-13 (pbk): 978-1-4302-3228-5

ISBN-13 (electronic): 978-1-4302-3229-2

Printed and bound in the United States of America 9 8 7 6 5 4 3 2 1

Trademarked names, logos, and images may appear in this book. Rather than use a trademark symbol with every occurrence of a trademarked name, logo, or image we use the names, logos, and images only in an editorial fashion and to the benefit of the trademark owner, with no intention of infringement of the trademark.

The use in this publication of trade names, trademarks, service marks, and similar terms, even if they are not identified as such, is not to be taken as an expression of opinion as to whether or not they are subject to proprietary rights.

President and Publisher: Paul Manning
Lead Editor: Jonathan Gennick
Technical Reviewers: Christopher Beck, Iggy Fernandez, and Bernard Lopuz
Editorial Board: Steve Anglin, Mark Beckner, Ewan Buckingham, Gary Cornell,
    Jonathan Gennick, Jonathan Hassell, Michelle Lowman, Matthew Moodie, Duncan Parkes,
    Jeffrey Pepper, Frank Pohlmann, Douglas Pundick, Ben Renow-Clarke, Dominic
    Shakeshaft, Matt Wade, Tom Welsh
Coordinating Editor: Anita Castro
Copy Editor: Mary Behr
Compositor: Lynn L'Heureux
Indexer: Julie Grady
Artist: April Milne
Cover Designer: Anna Ishchenko

Distributed to the book trade worldwide by Springer Science+Business Media, LLC., 233 Spring Street, 6th Floor, New York, NY 10013. Phone 1-800-SPRINGER, fax (201) 348-4505, e-mail orders-ny@springer-sbm.com, or visit www.springeronline.com.

For information on translations, please e-mail rights@apress.com, or visit www.apress.com.

Apress and friends of ED books may be purchased in bulk for academic, corporate, or promotional use. eBook versions and licenses are also available for most titles. For more information, reference our Special Bulk Sales–eBook Licensing web page at www.apress.com/info/bulksales.

The information in this book is distributed on an "as is" basis, without warranty. Although every precaution has been taken in the preparation of this work, neither the author(s) nor Apress shall have any liability to any person or entity with respect to any loss or damage caused or alleged to be caused directly or indirectly by the information contained in this work.

Contents at a Glance

Contents

About the Authors

 **KAREN MORTON** is a consultant and educator specializing in application optimization in both shoulder-to-shoulder consulting engagements and classroom settings. She is a Senior DBA Performance and Tuning Specialist for Fidelity Information Services. For over 20 years, Karen has worked in information technology. Starting as a mainframe programmer and developer, she has been a DBA, a data architect, and now is a researcher, educator, and consultant. Having used Oracle since the early 90s, she began teaching others how to use Oracle over a decade ago.

Karen is a frequent speaker at conferences and user groups, an Oracle ACE, and a member of the OakTable network (an informal association of "Oracle scientists" that are well known throughout the Oracle community). She blogs at karenmorton.blogspot.com.

 **KERRY OSBORNE** began working with Oracle (version 2) in 1982. He has worked as both a developer and a DBA. For the past several years, he has been focused on understanding Oracle internals and solving performance problems. He is an OakTable member and is the author of an upcoming Apress book on Exadata. Kerry is a frequent speaker at Oracle conferences. Mr. Osborne is also a co-founder of Enkitec, an Oracle-focused consulting company headquartered in Dallas, Texas. He blogs at kerryosborne.oracle-guy.com.

ROBYN SANDS is a software engineer for Cisco Systems, where she designs and develops embedded Oracle database products for Cisco customers. She has been working with Oracle since 1996, and has extensive experience in application development, large system implementations, and performance measurement. Robyn began her work career in industrial and quality engineering, and has combined her prior education and experience with her love of data by searching for new ways to build database systems with consistent performance and minimal maintenance requirements. She is a member of the OakTable network and a co-author of *Expert Oracle Practices: Oracle Database Administration from the Oak Table* (Apress, 2010). Robyn occasionally posts random blog entries at adhdocddba.blogspot.com.

RIYAJ SHAMSUDEEN is the principal DBA and President of OraInternals, a performance/recovery/E-Business consulting company. He specializes in RAC, performance tuning, and database internals. He frequently blogs about these technology areas in his blog orainternals.wordpress.com. He is also a regular presenter in US and international conferences. He is a proud member of OakTable network and an Oracle ACE. He has 19 years of experience using Oracle technology products and 18 years as an Oracle DBA/Oracle Applications DBA.

JARED STILL has been wrangling Oracle databases for longer than he cares to remember. During that time he has learned enough about SQL to realize that there will always be more to learn about SQL. He believes that everyone that queries an Oracle database should gain enough mastery of the SQL language that writing effective queries should become second nature. He participation as a co-author of Pro Oracle SQL is one way to help others achieve that goal. When Jared isn't managing databases, he likes to tinker with and race fast cars.

About the Technical Reviewers

CHRISTOPHER BECK has a degree in computer science from Rutgers University and has been working with multiple DBMSs for more than 19 years. He has spent the last 15 years as an Oracle employee where he is currently a Master Principal Technologist focusing on core database technologies. He is a co-inventor of two U.S. Patents on software methodologies that were the basis for what is now known as Oracle Application Express. Chris has reviewed other Oracle books including *Expert One-On-One* (Peer Information, 2001) and *Expert Oracle Database Architecture* (Apress, 2005), both by Tom Kyte, and is himself the co-author of two books, *Beginning Oracle Programming* (Apress, 2003) and *Mastering Oracle PL/SQL* (Apress, 2004). He resides in Northern Virginia with his wife Marta and 4 children; when not spending time with them, he can usually be found wasting time playing video games or watching Serie A football.

IGGY FERNANDEZ has a rich history of working with Oracle Database in many capacities. He is the author of *Beginning Oracle Database 11g Administration* (Apress, 2009) and the editor of the *NoCOUG Journal*. He writes a regular column called "The SQL Corner" for the *NoCOUG Journal* and regularly speaks on SQL topics at Oracle conferences. He has a lot of opinions but is willing to change them when confronted with fresh facts. His favorite quote is *"A foolish consistency is the hobgoblin of little minds, adored by little statesmen and philosophers and divines. Speak what you think now in hard words, and tomorrow speak what tomorrow thinks in hard words again, though it contradict everything you said today."* (Ralph Waldo Emerson, *Self-Reliance and Other Essays.*)

■**BERNARD LOPUZ** has been a senior technical support analyst at Oracle Corporation since 2001, and he is an Oracle Certified Professional (OCP). Before he became an Oracle DBA, he was a programmer developing Unisys Linc and Oracle applications, as well as interactive voice response (IVR) applications such as telephone banking voice-processing applications. Bernard was coauthor of the *Linux Recipes for Oracle DBAs* (Apress, 2008) and technical reviewer of two other books, namely, *Oracle RMAN Recipes* (Apress, 2007) and *Pro Oracle Database 11g Administration* (Apress, 2010). He has a bachelor's degree in computer engineering from the Mapúa Institute of Technology in Manila, Philippines. Bernard was born in Iligan, Philippines, and now resides in Ottawa, Canada, with his wife, Leizle, and daughters, Juliet and Carol. Aside from tinkering with computers, Bernard is a soccer and basketball fanatic.

Acknowledgments

I want to thank my fellow authors for all their hard work. This book is the result of many hours of your personal time and I appreciate every minute you spent to produce this excellent work. I'd also like to thank my family who graciously supported me during the long hours I had my nose stuck in my computer working. Your encouragement to take on this project was the main reason I decided to do so. Thanks for always believing in me.

Karen Morton

I'd like to dedicate this work to my family. My wife Jill and my kids Jordan, Jacob, Noah, and Lindsey have put up with me while I sat around with a far off look in my eyes (usually I wondering why my Mac wouldn't apply the right fonts to my examples). Seriously though, anyone who writes a book sacrifices a lot of time to do so. Writers undertake these projects for various reasons, but it is their choice. The people that care about them, though, also end up sacrificing a lot, through no fault of their own. So I am thankful for my family and the patience they have shown with me and for even occasionally pretending to be mildly interested in what I writing about.

Kerry Osborne
Enkitec
blog: kerryosborne.oracle-guy.com

Thank you to the Oracle community in general and the OakTable network specifically for all the support and encourage over the years. Your examples motivated me to continue to learn, and the information you shared made it possible.

Robyn Sands

I dedicate this book to my lovely wife Nisha Riyaj.

Riyaj Shamsudeen

My portion of this book is dedicated to my wife Carla. She patiently tolerated the many late nights I spent in the home office, creating example SQL queries and writing text to explain them. Without her support I just couldn't do this.

I have spent a large portion of my DBA career working as a lone DBA, without a team of DBA peers to call on when needed. The online Oracle communities in their many forms have filled that void nicely. In particular, I would like to acknowledge those that participate in the Oracle-L mailing list at `www.freelists.org/list/oracle-l`. Though this is now considered an old fashioned form of social media, the members of the Oracle-L community are quite knowledgeable and always willing to share their expertise. Much of what I have learned has been through participation in this forum.

Jared Still

CHAPTER 1

■ ■ ■

Core SQL

Karen Morton

Whether you're relatively new to writing SQL or you've been writing it for years, learning to write "good" SQL is a process that requires a strong foundation knowledge of core syntax and concepts. This chapter provides a review of the core concepts of the SQL language and its capabilities along with descriptions of the common SQL commands with which you should already be familiar. For those of you who have worked with SQL previously and have a good grasp on the basics, this will be a brief refresher, and it will prepare you for the more detailed treatment of SQL we'll cover in the chapters ahead. If you're a new SQL user, you may want to read *Beginning Oracle SQL* first to make sure you're comfortable with the basics. Either way, Chapter 1 is intended to "level set" you with a whirlwind tour of the five core SQL statements and provide a quick review of the tool we'll be using to execute SQL, SQL*Plus.

The SQL Language

The SQL language was originally developed in the 1970s by IBM and called Structured English QUEry Language, or SEQUEL. The language was based on the model for relational database management systems (RDBMS) developed by E.F. Codd in 1969. The acronym was later shortened to SQL due to a trademark dispute. In 1986, ANSI adopted SQL as a standard, and in 1987, ISO did so as well. A piece of not-so-common knowledge is that the official pronunciation of the language was declared to be "ess queue ell" by ANSI. Most people, including me, still use the *sequel* pronunciation just because it flows a bit easier linguistically.

The purpose of SQL is to simply provide an interface to the database, in our case, Oracle. Every SQL statement is a command, or instruction, to the database. It differs from other programming languages like C and Java in that it is intended to process data in sets, not individual rows. The language also doesn't require that you provide instructions on how to navigate to the data—that happens transparently under the covers. But, as you'll see in the chapters ahead, knowing about your data and how and where it is stored can be very important if you want to write efficient SQL in Oracle.

While there are minor differences in how vendors (like Oracle, IBM and Microsoft) implement the core functionality of SQL, the skills you learn in one database will transfer to another. You will be able to use basically the same SQL statements to query, insert, update, and delete data and create, alter, and drop objects regardless of the database vendor.

Although SQL is the standard for use with various RDBMS, it is not particularly relational in practice. I'll expand on this a bit later in the book; I would also recommend that you read C.J. Date's book entitled *SQL and Relational Theory* for a more detailed review. Keep in mind that the SQL language doesn't always follow the relational model precisely—it doesn't implement some elements of the relational model at all while implementing other elements improperly. The fact remains that since SQL is based on this model you must not only understand SQL but you must understand the relational model as well in order to write SQL as correctly and efficiently as possible.

Interfacing to the Database

Numerous ways have been developed over the years for transmitting SQL to a database and getting results back. The native interface to the Oracle database is the Oracle Call Interface (OCI). The OCI powers the queries that are sent by the Oracle kernel internally to the database. You use the OCI anytime you use one of Oracle's tools like SQL*Plus or SQL Developer. Various other Oracle tools like SQL*Loader, Data Pump, and Real Application Testing (RAT) use OCI as well as language specific interfaces such as Oracle JDBC-OCI, ODP.Net, Oracle Precompilers, Oracle ODBC, and the Oracle C++ Call Interface (OCCI) drivers.

When you use programming languages like COBOL or C, the statements you write are known as Embedded SQL statements and are preprocessed by a SQL preprocessor before the application program is compiled. Listing 1-1 shows an example of a SQL statement that could be used within a C/C++ block.

Listing 1-1. *Embedded SQL Statement Used Within C/C++ Block*

```
{
        int a;
        /* ... */
        EXEC SQL SELECT salary INTO :a
                    FROM hr.employees
                    WHERE employee_id = 108;
        /* ... */
        printf("The salary is %d\n", a);
        /* ... */
}
```

Other tools, like SQL*Plus and SQL Developer, are interactive tools. You enter and execute commands, and the output is displayed back to you. Interactive tools don't require you to explicitly compile your code before running it. You simply enter the command you wish to execute. Listing 1-2 shows an example of using SQL*Plus to execute a statement.

Listing 1-2. *Using SQL*Plus to Execute a SQL Statement*

```
SQL> select  salary
  2  from    hr.employees
  3  where   employee_id = 108;

        SALARY
---------------
         12000
```

In this book, we'll use SQL*Plus for our example listings just for consistency, but keep in mind that whatever method or tool you use to enter and execute SQL statements, everything ultimately goes through the OCI. The bottom line is that the tool you use doesn't matter, the native interface is the same for all.

Review of SQL*Plus

SQL*Plus is a command line tool provided with every Oracle installation regardless of platform (Windows, Unix). It is used to enter and execute SQL commands and to display the resulting output in a text-only environment. The tool allows you to enter and edit commands, save and execute commands individually or via script files, and display the output in nicely formatted report form. To start SQL*Plus you simply start sqlplus from your host's command prompt.

Connect to a Database

There are multiple ways to connect to a database from SQL*Plus. Before you can connect however, you will likely need to have entries for the databases you will need to connect to entered in the $ORACLE_HOME/network/admin/tnsnames.ora file. Two common ways are to supply your connection information when you start SQL*Plus, as shown in Listing 1-3; the other is to use the SQL*Plus connect command after SQL*Plus starts, as shown in Listing 1-4.

Listing 1-3. *Connecting to SQL*Plus from the Windows Command Prompt*

```
E:\pro_oracle_sql>sqlplus hr@ora11r2

SQL*Plus: Release 11.2.0.1.0 - Production on Sun Jun 6 11:22:24 2010

Copyright (c) 1982, 2010, Oracle.  All rights reserved.
Enter password:

Connected to:
Oracle Database 11g Enterprise Edition Release 11.2.0.1.0 - Production
With the Partitioning, OLAP and Data Mining and Real Appliation Testing
options

SQL>
```

To start SQL*Plus without being prompted to login to a database, you can start SQL*Plus with the /nolog option.

Listing 1-4. *Connecting to SQL*Plus and Logging into the Database from The SQL> Prompt*

```
E:\pro_oracle_sql>sqlplus /nolog

SQL*Plus: Release 11.2.0.1.0 - Production on Sun Jun 6 11:22:24 2010

Copyright (c) 1982, 2010, Oracle.  All rights reserved.

SQL> connect hr@ora11r2
Enter password:
Connected.
SQL>
```

Configuring the SQL*Plus environment

SQL*Plus has numerous commands that allow you to customize the working environment and display options. Listing 1-5 shows the SQL*Plus commands available after entering the SQL*Plus help index command at the SQL> prompt.

Listing 1-5. *SQL*Plus Command List*

```
SQL> help index

Enter Help [topic] for help.

@                COPY             PAUSE                    SHUTDOWN
@@               DEFINE           PRINT                    SPOOL
/                DEL              PROMPT                   SQLPLUS
ACCEPT           DESCRIBE         QUIT                     START
APPEND           DISCONNECT       RECOVER                  STARTUP
ARCHIVE LOG      EDIT             REMARK                   STORE
ATTRIBUTE        EXECUTE          REPFOOTER                TIMING
BREAK            EXIT             REPHEADER                TTITLE
BTITLE           GET              RESERVED WORDS (SQL)     UNDEFINE
CHANGE           HELP             RESERVED WORDS (PL/SQL)  VARIABLE
CLEAR            HOST             RUN                      WHENEVER OSERROR
COLUMN           INPUT            SAVE                     WHENEVER SQLERROR
COMPUTE          LIST             SET                      XQUERY
CONNECT          PASSWORD         SHOW
```

The set command is the primary command used for customizing your environment settings. Listing 1-6 shows the help text for the set command.

Listing 1-6. *SQL*Plus SET Command*

```
SQL> help set

 SET
 ---

 Sets a system variable to alter the SQL*Plus environment settings
 for your current session. For example, to:
     -   set the display width for data
     -   customize HTML formatting
     -   enable or disable printing of column headings
     -   set the number of lines per page

 SET system_variable value
```

where system_variable and value represent one of the following clauses:

```
APPI[NFO]{OFF|ON|text}
ARRAY[SIZE] {15|n}
AUTO[COMMIT] {OFF|ON|IMM[EDIATE]|n}
AUTOP[RINT] {OFF|ON}
AUTORECOVERY {OFF|ON}
AUTOT[RACE] {OFF|ON|TRACE[ONLY]}
    [EXP[LAIN]] [STAT[ISTICS]]
BLO[CKTERMINATOR] {.|c|ON|OFF}
CMDS[EP] {;|c|OFF|ON}
COLSEP {_|text}
CON[CAT] {.|c|ON|OFF}
COPYC[OMMIT] {o|n}
COPYTYPECHECK {ON|OFF}
DEF[INE] {&|c|ON|OFF}
DESCRIBE [DEPTH {1|n|ALL}]
    [LINENUM {OFF|ON}] [INDENT {OFF|ON}]
ECHO {OFF|ON}
EDITF[ILE] file_name[.ext]
EMB[EDDED] {OFF|ON}
ERRORL[OGGING] {ON|OFF}
    [TABLE [schema.]tablename]
    [TRUNCATE] [IDENTIFIER identifier]

ESC[APE] {\|c|OFF|ON}
ESCCHAR {@|?|%|$|OFF}
EXITC[OMMIT] {ON|OFF}
FEED[BACK] {6|n|ON|OFF}
FLAGGER {OFF|ENTRY|INTERMED[IATE]||FULL} TAB {ON|OFF}
FLU[SH] {ON|OFF}
HEA[DING] {ON|OFF}
HEADS[EP] {||c|ON|OFF}
INSTANCE [instance_path|LOCAL]
LIN[ESIZE] {80|n}
LOBOF[FSET] {1|n}
LOGSOURCE [pathname]
LONG {80|n}
LONGC[HUNKSIZE] {80|n}
MARK[UP] HTML [OFF|ON]
    [HEAD text] [BODY text] [TABLE text]
    [ENTMAP {ON|OFF}]
    [SPOOL {OFF|ON}]
    [PRE[FORMAT] {OFF|ON}]
SQL>
```

```
NEWP[AGE] {1|n|NONE}
       NULL text
NUMF[ORMAT] format
NUM[WIDTH] {10|n}
PAGES[IZE] {14|n}
         PAU[SE] {OFF|ON|text}
RECSEP {WR[APPED]|EA[CH]|OFF}
RECSEPCHAR {_|c}
SERVEROUT[PUT] {ON|OFF}
         [SIZE {n | UNLIMITED}]
         [FOR[MAT]  {WRA[PPED] |
                WOR[D_WRAPPED] |
            TRU[NCATED]}]
SHIFT[INOUT] {VIS[IBLE] |
                     INV[ISIBLE]}
SHOW[MODE] {OFF|ON}
         SQLBL[ANKLINES] {OFF|ON}
SQLC[ASE] {MIX[ED] |
         LO[WER] | UP[PER]}
SQLCO[NTINUE] {> | text}
SQLN[UMBER] {ON|OFF}
SQLPLUSCOMPAT[IBILITY]
                {x.y[.z]}
SQLPRE[FIX] {#|c}
SQLP[ROMPT] {SQL>|text}
SQLT[ERMINATOR] {;|c|ON|OFF}
SUF[FIX] {SQL|text}

         TERM[OUT] {ON|OFF}
         TI[ME] {OFF|ON}
TIMI[NG] {OFF|ON}
TRIM[OUT] {ON|OFF}
         TRIMS[POOL] {OFF|ON}
         UND[ERLINE] {-|c|ON|OFF}
VER[IFY] {ON|OFF}
             WRA[P] {ON|OFF}
XQUERY {BASEURI text|
         ORDERING{UNORDERED|
ORDERED|DEFAULT}|
         NODE{BYVALUE|BYREFERENCE|
         DEFAULT}|
         CONTEXT text}
```

Given the number of commands available, you can easily customize your environment to best suit you. One thing to keep in mind is that the set commands aren't retained by SQL*Plus when you exit/close the tool. Instead of typing in each of the set commands you want to apply each time you use SQL*Plus, you can create a file named login.sql. There are actually two files which SQL*Plus reads by default each time you start it. The first is glogin.sql and it can be found in the directory $ORACLE_HOME/sqlplus/admin. If this file is found, it is read and the statements it contains are executed. This will allow you to store the SQL*Plus commands and SQL statements that customize your experience across SQL*Plus sessions.

After reading glogin.sql, SQL*Plus looks for the login.sql file. This file must exist in either the directory from which SQL*Plus was started or in a directory included in the path the environment variable SQLPATH points to. Any commands in login.sql will take precedence over those in glogin.sql. Since 10g, Oracle reads both glogin.sql and login.sql each time you either start SQL*Plus or execute the connect command from within SQL*Plus. Prior to 10g, the login.sql script was only executed when SQL*Plus started. The contents of a common login.sql file are shown in Listing 1-7.

Listing 1-7. *A Common login.sql File*

```
SET LINES 3000
Sets width of display line (default 80 characters)
SET PAGES 1000
Sets number of lines per page (default 14 lines)
SET TIMING ON
Sets display of elapsed time (default OFF)
SET NULL <null>
Sets display of nulls to show <null> (default empty)
SET SQLPROMPT '&_user@&_connect_identifier> '
Sets the prompt to show connected user and instance
```

Note the use of the variables _user and _connect_identifier in the SET SQLPROMPT command. These are two examples of predefined variables. You may use any of the following predefined variables in your login.sql file or in any other script file you may create:

- _connect_identifier
- _date
- _editor (This variable specifies the editor which is started when you use the edit command.)
- _o_version
- _o_release
- _privilege
- _sqlplus_release
- _user

Executing Commands

There are two types of commands that can be executed within SQL*Plus: SQL statements and SQL*Plus commands. The SQL*Plus commands shown in Listing 1-5 and 1-6 are specific to SQL*Plus and can be used for customizing the environment and executing commands that are specific to SQL*Plus, like

DESCRIBE and CONNECT. Executing a SQL*Plus command requires only that you type the command at the prompt and hit Enter. The command is automatically executed. On the other hand, in order to execute SQL statements, you must use a special character to indicate you wish to execute the entered command. You may use either a semi-colon (;) or a forward slash (/). A semi-colon may be placed directly at the end of the typed command or on a following blank line. The forward slash must be placed on a blank line in order to be recognized. Listing 1-8 shows how these two execution characters are used.

Listing 1-8. *Execution Character Usage*

```
SQL>select empno, deptno from scott.emp where ename = 'SMITH' ;
     EMPNO     DEPTNO
---------- ----------
      7369         20
SQL>select empno, deptno from scott.emp where ename = 'SMITH'
  2 ;
     EMPNO     DEPTNO
---------- ----------
      7369         20
SQL>select empno, deptno from scott.emp where ename = 'SMITH'
  2 /
     EMPNO     DEPTNO
---------- ----------
      7369         20
SQL>select empno, deptno from scott.emp where ename = 'SMITH'
  2
SQL>/
     EMPNO     DEPTNO
---------- ----------
      7369         20
SQL>select empno, deptno from scott.emp where ename = 'SMITH'/
  2
SQL>l
  1* select empno, deptno from scott.emp where ename = 'SMITH'/
SQL>/
select empno, deptno from scott.emp where ename = 'SMITH'/
                                                         *
ERROR at line 1:
ORA-00936: missing expression
```

Notice the fifth example that puts the / at the end of the statement. The cursor moves to a new line instead of executing the command immediately. Then, if you press Enter again, the statement is entered into the SQL*Plus buffer but not executed. In order to view the contents of the SQL*Plus buffer, the list command is used (abbreviated to only l). If you then attempt to execute the statement in the buffer using /, which is how the / command is intended to be used, you get an error. That's because you had typed in the / on the end of the SQL statement line originally. The / is not a valid SQL command and thus causes an error when the statement attempts to execute.

Another way to execute commands is to place them in a file. You can produce these files with the text editor of your choice outside of SQL*Plus or you may invoke an editor directly from SQL*Plus using the EDIT command. The EDIT command will either open a named file or create a file if it doesn't exist. The file must be in the default directory or you must specify the full path. To set the editor to one of your choice, you simply set the predefined _editor variable using the following command: define _editor='/<full path>/myeditor.exe'. Files with the extension of .sql will execute without having to include the extension and can be ran using either the @ or START command. Listing 1-9 shows the use of both commands.

Listing 1-9. *Executing .sql Script Files*

```
SQL> @list_depts
    DEPTNO DNAME          LOC
---------- -------------- -------------
        10 ACCOUNTING     NEW YORK
        20 RESEARCH       DALLAS
        30 SALES          CHICAGO
        40 OPERATIONS     BOSTON
SQL>
SQL> start list_depts
DEPTNO DNAME          LOC
---------- -------------- -------------
        10 ACCOUNTING     NEW YORK
        20 RESEARCH       DALLAS
        30 SALES          CHICAGO
        40 OPERATIONS     BOSTON
SQL>
SQL>l
  1* select * from scott.dept
SQL>
```

SQL*Plus has many features and options—way too many to cover here. For what we'll need in this book, this brief overview should suffice. However, the Oracle documentation provides guides for SQL*Plus usage and there are numerous books, including *Beginning Oracle SQL*, that go into more depth if you're interested.

The Five Core SQL Statements

The SQL language contains many different statements. In your professional career you may end up using just a small percentage of what is available to you. But isn't that the case with almost any product you use? I once heard a statistic quoted stating that most people use 20 percent or less of the functionality available in the software products or programming languages they regularly use. I don't know if that's actually true or not, but in my experience, it seems fairly accurate. I have found the same basic SQL statement formats in use within most applications for almost 20 years. Very few people ever use everything SQL has to offer—and often improperly implement those they do use frequently. Obviously, we will not be able to cover all the statements and their options found in the SQL language. This book is intended to provide you deeper insight into the most commonly used statements and help you learn to apply them more effectively.

In this book, we will examine five of the most frequently used SQL statements. These statements are SELECT, INSERT, UPDATE, DELETE, and MERGE. Although we'll address each of these core statements in some fashion, the focus will be primarily on the SELECT statement. Developing a good command of these five statements will provide a strong foundation for your day-to-day work with the SQL language.

The SELECT Statement

The SELECT statement is used to retrieve data from one or more tables or other database objects. You should already be familiar with the basics of the SELECT statement so instead of reviewing the statement from that beginner point of view, I wanted to review how a SELECT statement processes logically. You should have already learned the basic clauses that form a common SELECT statement, but in order to build the foundation mindset you'll need to write well-formed and efficient SQL consistently, you need to understand how SQL processes.

How a query statement is processed logically may be quite different from its actual physical processing. The Oracle cost-based optimizer (CBO) is responsible for generating the actual execution plan for a query and we will cover what the optimizer does, how it does it, and why in the chapters ahead. For now, note that the optimizer will determine how to access tables and in which order to process them, and how to join multiple tables and apply filters. The logical order of query processing occurs in a very specific order. However, the steps the optimizer chooses for the physical execution plan can end up actually processing the query in a very different order. Listing 1-10 shows a query stub containing the main clauses of a SELECT statement with step numbers assigned to each clause in the order it is logically processed.

Listing 1-10. *Logical Query Processing Order*

```
5       SELECT   <column list>
1       FROM            <source object list>
1.1     FROM            <left source object> <join type>
                 JOIN <right source object> ON <on predicates>
2       WHERE           <where predicates>
3       GROUP BY        <group by expression(s)>
4       HAVING          <having predicates>
6       ORDER BY        <order by list>
```

You should notice right away that SQL differs from other programming languages in that the first written statement (the SELECT) is not the first line of code that is processed; the FROM clause is processed first. Note that I have shown two different FROM clauses in this listing. The one marked as 1.1 is provided to show the difference when ANSI syntax is used. It may be helpful to imagine that each step in the processing order creates a temporary dataset. As each step is processed, the dataset is manipulated until a final result is formulated. It is this final result set of data that the query returns to the caller.

In order to walk through each part of the SELECT statement in more detail, you'll use the query in Listing 1-11 that returns a result set containing a list of female customers that have placed more than four orders.

Listing 1-11. *Female Customers Who Have Placed More Than Four Orders*

```
SQL> select c.customer_id, count(o.order_id) as orders_ct
  2  from oe.customers c
  3  join oe.orders o
  4  on c.customer_id = o.customer_id
  5  where c.gender = 'F'
  6  group by c.customer_id
  7  having count(o.order_id) > 4
  8  order by orders_ct, c.customer_id
  9  /
CUSTOMER_ID  ORDERS_CT
-----------  ----------
        146          5
        147          5
```

The FROM Clause

The FROM clause lists the source objects from which data is selected. This clause can contain tables, views, materialized views, partitions or subpartitions, or may specify a subquery that identifies objects. If multiple source objects are used, this logical processing phase also applies each join type and ON predicates (shown as step 1.1). You'll cover join types in more detail later but note that as joins are processed, they occur in the following order:

1. Cross join, also called a Cartesian product
2. Inner join
3. Outer join

In the example query in Listing 1-11, the FROM clause lists two tables: customers and orders. They are joined on the customer_id column. So, when this information is processed, the initial dataset that will be produced by the FROM clause will include rows where the customer_id matches in both tables. The result set will contain 105 rows at this point. To verify this is true, simply execute only the first four lines of the example query as shown in Listing 1-12.

Listing 1-12. *Partial Query Execution Through the FROM Clause Only*

```
SQL> select c.customer_id cust_id, o.order_id ord_id, c.gender
  2  from oe.customers c
  3  join oe.orders o
  4  on c.customer_id = o.customer_id;

CUST_ID ORD_ID G  CUST_ID ORD_ID G   CUST_ID ORD_ID G
------- ------ -  ------- ------ -   ------- ------ -
    147   2450 F      101   2430 M       109   2394 M
    147   2425 F      101   2413 M       116   2453 M
    147   2385 F      101   2447 M       116   2428 M
    147   2366 F      101   2458 M       116   2369 M
    147   2396 F      102   2431 M       116   2436 M
```

148	2451 M	102	2414 M	117	2456 M
148	2426 M	102	2432 M	117	2429 M
148	2386 M	102	2397 M	117	2370 M
148	2367 M	103	2437 F	117	2446 M
148	2406 M	103	2415 F	118	2457 M
149	2452 M	103	2433 F	118	2371 M
149	2427 M	103	2454 F	120	2373 M
149	2387 M	104	2438 F	121	2374 M
149	2368 M	104	2416 F	122	2375 M
149	2434 M	104	2355 F	123	2376 F
150	2388 M	104	2354 F	141	2377 M
151	2389 M	105	2439 F	143	2380 M
152	2390 M	105	2417 F	144	2445 M
153	2391 M	105	2356 F	144	2422 M
154	2392 F	105	2358 F	144	2382 M
155	2393 M	106	2441 M	144	2363 M
156	2395 F	106	2418 M	144	2435 M
157	2398 M	106	2359 M	145	2448 M
158	2399 M	106	2381 M	145	2423 M
159	2400 M	107	2442 F	145	2383 M
160	2401 M	107	2419 F	145	2364 M
161	2402 M	107	2360 F	145	2455 M
162	2403 M	107	2440 F	119	2372 M
163	2404 M	108	2443 M	142	2378 M
164	2405 M	108	2420 M	146	2449 F
165	2407 M	108	2361 M	146	2424 F
166	2408 F	108	2357 M	146	2384 F
167	2409 M	109	2444 M	146	2365 F
169	2411 F	109	2421 M	146	2379 F
170	2412 M	109	2362 M	168	2410 M

105 rows selected.

■**NOTE** I formatted the result of this output manually to make it fit nicely on the page. The actual output was displayed over 105 separate lines.

The WHERE Clause

The WHERE clause provides a way to conditionally limit the rows emitted to the query's final result set. Each condition, or predicate, is entered as a comparison of two values or expressions. The comparison will match (evaluate to TRUE) or it will not match (evaluate to FALSE). If the comparison is FALSE, then the row will not be included in the final result set.

I need to digress just a bit to cover an important aspect of SQL related to this step. Actually, the possible values of a logical comparison in SQL are TRUE, FALSE, and UNKNOWN. The UNKNOWN value occurs when a null is involved. Nulls compared to anything or nulls used in expressions evaluate to null, or UNKNOWN. A null represents a missing value and can be confusing due to inconsistencies in how nulls are treated within different elements of the SQL language. We'll address how nulls effect the execution of SQL statements throughout the book, but I didn't want to ignore mentioning the topic at this point. What I stated previously is still basically true, that comparisons will either return TRUE or FALSE. What you'll find is that when a null is involved in a filter comparison, it is treated as if it were FALSE.

In our example, there is a single predicate used to limit the result to only females who have placed orders. If you review the intermediate result after the FROM clause was processed (see Listing 1-12), you'll note that only 31 of the 105 rows were placed by female customers (gender = 'F'). Therefore, after the WHERE clause is applied, the intermediate result set would be reduced from 105 down to 31 rows.

After the WHERE clause is applied, the detailed result set is ready. Note that I use the phrase "detailed result set." What I mean is the rows that satisfy your query requirements are now available. Other clauses may be applied (GROUP BY, HAVING) that will aggregate and further limit the final result set that the caller will receive, but it is important to note that at this point, all the data your query needs to compute the final answer is available.

The WHERE clause is intended to restrict, or reduce, the result set. The less restrictions you include, the more data your final result set will contain. The more data you need to return, the longer the query will take to execute.

The GROUP BY Clause

The GROUP BY clause aggregates the filtered result set available after processing the FROM and WHERE clauses. The selected rows are grouped by the expression(s) listed in this clause to produce a single row of summary information for each group. You may group by any column of any object listed in the FROM clause even if you don't intend to display that column in the list of output columns. Conversely, any non-aggregate column in the select list must be included in the GROUP BY expression.

There are two additional operations that can be included in a GROUP BY clause: ROLLUP and CUBE. The ROLLUP operation is used to produce subtotal values. The CUBE operation is used to produce cross-tabulation values. If you use either of these operations, you'll get more than one row of summary information. Both of these operations will be discussed in detail in Chapter 7: Advanced Grouping.

In the example query, the requested grouping is by customer_id. This means that there will only be one row for each distinct customer_id. Of the 31 rows that represent the females who have placed orders that have made it through the WHERE clause processing, there are 11 distinct customer_id values, as shown in Listing 1-13.

Listing 1-13. *Partial Query Execution Through the GROUP BY Clause*

```
SQL> select c.customer_id, count(o.order_id) as orders_ct
  2  from oe.customers c
  3  join oe.orders o
  4  on c.customer_id = o.customer_id
  5 where gender = 'F'
  6 group by c.customer_id;

CUSTOMER_ID  ORDERS_CT
-----------  ----------
        156           1
        123           1
        166           1
```

```
           154               1
           169               1
           105               4
           103               4
           107               4
           104               4
           147               5
           146               5
11 rows selected.
```

You'll notice that the output from the query, while grouped, is not ordered. The display makes it appear as though the rows are ordered by order_ct, but this is more coincidence and not guaranteed behavior. This is an important item to remember: the GROUP BY clause does not insure ordering of data. If you want the list to display in a specific order, you have to specify an ORDER BY clause.

The HAVING Clause

The HAVING clause restricts the grouped summary rows to those where the condition(s) in the clause are TRUE. Unless you include a HAVING clause, all summary rows are returned. The GROUP BY and HAVING clauses are actually interchangeable positionally; it doesn't matter which one comes first. However, it seems to make more sense to code them with the GROUP BY first since GROUP BY is logically processed first. Essentially, the HAVING clause is a second WHERE clause that is evaluated after the GROUP BY occurs and is used to filter on grouped values.

In our example query, the HAVING clause, HAVING COUNT(o.order_id) > 4, limits the grouped result data of 11 rows down to 2. You can confirm this by reviewing the list of rows returned after the GROUP BY is applied, as shown in Listing 1-13. Note that only customers 146 and 147 have placed more than four orders. The two rows that make up the final result set are now ready.

The SELECT List

The SELECT list is where the columns included in the final result set from your query are provided. A column can be an actual column from a table, an expression, or even the result of a SELECT statement, as shown in Listing 1-14.

Listing 1-14. *Example Query Showing Select List Alternatives*

```
SQL> select c.customer_id, c.cust_first_name||' '||c.cust_last_name,
  2  (select e.last_name from hr.employees e where e.employee_id = c.account_mgr_id)
acct_mgr)
  3  from oe.customers c;


  CUSTOMER_ID CUST_NAME                                        ACCT_MGR
--------------- --------------------------------------------- --------------
          147 Ishwarya Roberts                                 Russell
          148 Gustav Steenburgen                               Russell
...
```

```
        931 Buster Edwards                        Cambrault
        981 Daniel Gueney                         Cambrault
319 rows selected.
```

When another SELECT statement is used to produce the value of a column, the query must return only one row and one column value. These types of subqueries are referred to as scalar subqueries. While this can be very useful syntax, keep in mind that the scalar subquery will be executed once for each row in the result set. There are optimizations available that may eliminate some duplicate executions of the subquery, but the worse case scenario is that each row will require this scalar subquery to be executed. Imagine the possible overhead involved if your result set had thousands, or millions, of rows! We'll review scalar subqueries later in the book and discuss how to use them optimally.

Another option you may need to use in the SELECT list is the DISTINCT clause. The example doesn't use it, but I wanted to mention it briefly. The DISTINCT clause causes duplicate rows to be removed from the data set produced after the other clauses have been processed.

After the select list is processed, you now have the final result set for your query. The only thing that remains to be done, if it is included, is to sort the result set into a desired order.

The ORDER BY Clause

The ORDER BY clause is used to order the final set of rows returned by the statement. In this case, the requested sort order was to be by orders_ct and customer_id. The orders_ct column is the value computed using the COUNT aggregate function in the GROUP BY clause. As shown in Listing 1-13, there were two customers that each placed more than four orders. Since each customer placed five orders, the order_ct is the same, so the second ordering column determines the final display order. As shown in Listing 1-15, the final sorted output of the query is a two row data set ordered by customer_id.

Listing 1-15. *Example Query Final Output*

```
SQL> select c.customer_id, count(o.order_id) as orders_ct
  2  from oe.customers c
  3  join oe.orders o
  4  on c.customer_id = o.customer_id
  5  where c.gender = 'F'
  6  group by c.customer_id
  7  having count(o.order_id) > 4
  8  order by orders_ct, c.customer_id
  9  /
CUSTOMER_ID  ORDERS_CT
-----------  ----------
        146          5
        147          5
```

When ordered output is requested, Oracle must take the final set of data after all other clauses have been processed and sort them as specified. The size of the data that needs to be sorted is important. When I say size, I mean total bytes of data that is in the result set. To estimate the size of the data set, you multiply the number of rows by the number of bytes per row. The bytes per row are determined by summing the average column lengths of each of the columns in the select list.

The example query requests only the `customer_id` and `orders_ct` column values in the select list. Let's use 10 as our estimated bytes per row value. I'll show you in Chapter 6 where to find the optimizer's estimate for this value. So, given that we only have two rows in the result set, the sort size is actually quite small, approximately 20 bytes. Remember that this is only an estimate, but the estimate is an important one.

Small sorts should be accomplished entirely in memory while large sorts may have to use temporary disk space to complete the sort. As you can likely deduce, a sort that occurs in memory will be faster than a sort that must use disk. Therefore, when the optimizer estimates the effect of sorting data, it has to consider how big the sort is in order to adjust how to accomplish getting the query result in the most efficient way. In general, consider sorts as a fairly expensive overhead to your query processing time, particularly if the size of your result set is large.

The INSERT Statement

The `INSERT` statement is used to add rows to a table, partition, or view. Rows can be inserted in either a single-table or multi-table method. A single-table insert will insert values into one row of one table by either explicitly specifying the values or by retrieving the values using a subquery. The multi-table insert will insert rows into one or more tables and will compute the row values it inserts by retrieving the values using a subquery.

Single-table Inserts

The first example in Listing 1-16 illustrates a single-table insert using the values clause. Each column value is explicitly entered. The column list is optional if you include values for each column defined in the table. However, if you only want to provide values for a subset of the columns, you must specify the column names in the column list. A good practice is to include the column list regardless of whether or not you specify values for all the columns. Doing so acts to self-document the statement and also can help reduce possible errors that might happen in the future should someone add a new column to the table.

Listing 1-16. *Single-Table Insert*

```
SQL> insert into hr.jobs (job_id, job_title, min_salary, max_salary)
  2   values ('IT_PM', 'Project Manager', 5000, 11000) ;

1 row created.

SQL> insert into scott.bonus (ename, job, sal)
  2   select ename, job, sal * .10
  3   from scott.emp;

14 rows created.
```

The second example illustrates an insert using a subquery. This is a very flexible option for inserting rows. The subquery can be written to return one or more rows. Each row returned will be used to supply column values for the new rows to be inserted. The subquery can be as simple or complex as needed to satisfy your needs. In this example, we use the subquery to compute a 10% bonus for each employee based on their current salary. The bonus table actually has four columns, but we only populate three of them with this insert. The comm column isn't populated with a value from the subquery and we do not include it in the column list. Since we don't include this column, the value for that column will be null. Note that if the comm column had a not null constraint, you would have gotten a constraint error and the statement would have failed.

Multi-table Inserts

The multi-table insert example in Listing 1-17 illustrates how rows returned from a single subquery can be used to insert rows into more than one table. We start with three tables: small_customers, medium_customers, and large_customers. We'd like to populate these tables with customer data based on the total amount of orders a customer has placed. The subquery sums the order_total column for each customer and then the insert conditionally places a row in the proper table based on whether the customer is considered to be small (less than $10,000 of total orders), medium (between $10,000 and $99,999.99), and large (greater than or equal to $100,000).

Listing 1-17. *Multi-Table Insert*

```
SQL> select * from small_customers ;

no rows selected

SQL> select * from medium_customers ;

no rows selected

SQL> select * from large_customers ;

no rows selected

SQL> insert all
  2    when sum_orders < 10000 then
  3    into small_customers
  4    when sum_orders >= 10000 and sum_orders < 100000 then
  5    into medium_customers
  6    else
  7    into large_customers
  8    select customer_id, sum(order_total) sum_orders
  9    from oe.orders
 10    group by customer_id ;

47 rows created.

SQL> select * from small_customers ;
```

```
CUSTOMER_ID SUM_ORDERS
----------- ----------
        120        416
        121       4797
        152     7616.8
        157     7110.3
        160      969.2
        161        600
        162        220
        163        510
        164       1233
        165       2519
        166        309
        167         48
```

12 rows selected.

SQL> select * from medium_customers ;

```
CUSTOMER_ID SUM_ORDERS
----------- ----------
        102    69211.4
        103    20591.4
        105    61376.5
        106    36199.5
        116      32307
        119    16447.2
        123    11006.2
        141    38017.8
        142    25691.3
        143    27132.6
        145    71717.9
        146    88462.6
        151      17620
        153    48070.6
        154      26632
        155    23431.9
        156      68501
        158    25270.3
        159    69286.4
        168      45175
        169    15760.5
        170      66816
```

22 rows selected.

```
SQL> select * from large_customers ;
CUSTOMER_ID SUM_ORDERS
----------- ----------
        101   190395.1
        104   146605.5
        107   155613.2
        108   213399.7
        109   265255.6
        117   157808.7
        118   100991.8
        122   103834.4
        144   160284.6
        147   371278.2
        148   185700.5
        149   403119.7
        150   282694.3

13 rows selected.
```

Note the use of the ALL clause following the INSERT keyword. When ALL is specified, the statement will perform unconditional multi-table inserts. This means that each WHEN clause is evaluated for each row returned by the subquery regardless of the outcome of a previous condition. Therefore, you need to be careful about how you specify each condition. For example, if I had used WHEN sum_orders < 100000 instead of the range I specified, the medium_customers table would have included the rows that were also inserted into small_customers.

You should specify the FIRST option to cause each WHEN to be evaluated in the order it appears in the statement and to skip subsequent WHEN clause evaluations for a given subquery row. The key is to remember which option, ALL or FIRST, best meets your needs and then use the one most suitable.

The UPDATE Statement

The UPDATE statement is used to change the column values of existing rows in a table. The syntax for this statement is composed of three parts: UPDATE, SET, and WHERE. The UPDATE clause specifies the table to update. The SET clause specifies which columns are changed and the modified values. The WHERE clause is used to conditionally filter which rows will be updated. It is optional and if it is omitted, the update operation will be applied to all rows of the specified table.

Listing 1-18 demonstrates several different ways an UPDATE statement can be written. First, I create a duplicate of the employees table called employees2, then I execute several different updates that accomplish basically the same task: the employees in department 90 are updated to have a 10% salary increase and, in the case of Example 5, the commission_pct column is also updated. Following are the different approaches taken:

Example 1: Update a single column value using an expression.

Example 2: Update a single column value using a subquery.

Example 3: Update single column using subquery in WHERE clause to determine which rows to update.

Example 4: Update a table using a SELECT statement to define the table and column values.

Example 5: Update multiple columns using a subquery.

Listing 1-18. *UPDATE Statement Examples*

```
SQL> -- create a duplicate employees table
SQL> create table employees2 as select * from employees ;
Table created.

SQL> -- add a primary key
SQL> alter table employees2
  1   add constraint emp2_emp_id_pk primary key (employee_id) ;

Table altered.

SQL> -- retrieve list of employees in department 90
SQL> select employee_id, last_name, salary
  2   from employees where department_id = 90 ;

   EMPLOYEE_ID LAST_NAME                          SALARY
--------------- ------------------------- ----------------
           100 King                                24000
           101 Kochhar                             17000
           102 De Haan                             17000

3 rows selected.

SQL> -- Example 1: Update a single column value using an expression

SQL> update employees2
  2   set salary = salary * 1.10 -- increase salary by 10%
  3   where department_id = 90 ;

3 rows updated.

SQL> commit ;

Commit complete.
```

```
SQL> select employee_id, last_name, salary
  2  from employees2 where department_id = 90 ;

EMPLOYEE_ID LAST_NAME  SALARY
----------- ---------- ------
        100 King        26400    -- previous value 24000
        101 Kochhar     18700    -- previous value 17000
        102 De Haan     18700    -- previous value 17000

3 rows selected.

SQL> -- Example 2: Update a single column value using a subquery

SQL> update employees
  2  set salary = (select employees2.salary
  3                  from employees2
  4                 where employees2.employee_id = employees.employee_id
  5                   and employees.salary != employees2.salary)
  6  where department_id = 90 ;

3 rows updated.

SQL> select employee_id, last_name, salary
  2  from employees where department_id = 90 ;

    EMPLOYEE_ID LAST_NAME                        SALARY
--------------- ------------------------- ---------------
            100 King                               26400
            101 Kochhar                            18700
            102 De Haan                            18700

3 rows selected.

SQL> rollback ;

Rollback complete.

SQL> -- Example 3: Update single column using subquery in
SQL> -- WHERE clause to determine which rows to update

SQL> update employees
  2  set salary = salary * 1.10
  3  where department_id in (select department_id
  4                            from departments
  5                           where department_name = 'Executive') ;

3 rows updated.
```

```
SQL> select employee_id, last_name, salary
  2  from employees
  3  where department_id in (select department_id
  4                                from departments
  5                                where department_name = 'Executive') ;

    EMPLOYEE_ID LAST_NAME                          SALARY
--------------- ------------------------- ---------------
            100 King                                26400
            101 Kochhar                             18700
            102 De Haan                             18700

3 rows selected.

SQL> rollback ;

Rollback complete.

SQL> -- Example 4: Update a table using a SELECT statement
SQL> -- to define the table and column values

SQL> update (select e1.salary, e2.salary new_sal
  2            from employees e1, employees2 e2
  3            where e1.employee_id = e2.employee_id
  4              and e1.department_id = 90)
  5  set salary = new_sal;

3 rows updated.

SQL> select employee_id, last_name, salary, commission_pct
  2  from employees where department_id = 90 ;

    EMPLOYEE_ID LAST_NAME                          SALARY COMMISSION_PCT
--------------- ------------------------- --------------- ---------------
            100 King                                26400
            101 Kochhar                             18700
            102 De Haan                             18700

3 rows selected.

SQL> rollback ;

Rollback complete.

SQL> -- Example 5: Update multiple columns using a subquery
```

```
SQL> update employees
  2  set (salary, commission_pct) = (select employees2.salary, .10 comm_pct
  3                    from employees2
  4                    where employees2.employee_id = employees.employee_id
  5                    and employees.salary != employees2.salary)
  6  where department_id = 90 ;

3 rows updated.
SQL> select employee_id, last_name, salary, commission_pct
  2  from employees where department_id = 90 ;

   EMPLOYEE_ID LAST_NAME                         SALARY COMMISSION_PCT
--------------- ------------------------- --------------- ---------------
           100 King                               26400             .1
           101 Kochhar                            18700             .1
           102 De Haan                            18700             .1

3 rows selected.

SQL> rollback ;

Rollback complete.

SQL>
```

The DELETE Statement

The DELETE statement is used to remove rows from a table. The syntax for this statement is composed of three parts: DELETE, FROM, and WHERE. The DELETE keyword stands alone. Unless you decide to use a hint, which we'll discuss later, there are no other options associated with the DELETE keyword. The FROM clause identifies the table from which rows will be deleted. As the examples in Listing 1-19 demonstrate, the table can be specified directly or via a subquery. The WHERE clause provides any filter conditions to help determine which rows are deleted. If the WHERE clause is omitted, the delete operation will delete all rows in the specified table.

Listing 1-19 demonstrates several different ways a DELETE statement can be written. Note that I am using the employees2 table created in Listing 1-18 for these examples. Here are the different delete methods that you'll see:

Example 1: Delete rows from specified table using a filter condition in the WHERE clause.

Example 2: Delete rows using a subquery in the FROM clause.

Example 3: Delete rows from specified table using a subquery in the WHERE clause.

Listing 1-19. *DELETE Statement Examples*

```
SQL> select employee_id, department_id, last_name, salary
  2  from employees2
  3  where department_id = 90;
```

```
    EMPLOYEE_ID    DEPARTMENT_ID LAST_NAME                      SALARY
--------------- --------------- ------------------------- ---------------
            100              90 King                             26400
            101              90 Kochhar                          18700
            102              90 De Haan                          18700

3 rows selected.
SQL> -- Example 1: Delete rows from specified table using
SQL> -- a filter condition in the WHERE clause
SQL> delete from employees2
  2  where department_id = 90;

3 rows deleted.

SQL> select employee_id, department_id, last_name, salary
  2  from employees2
  3  where department_id = 90;

no rows selected

SQL> rollback;

Rollback complete.

SQL> select employee_id, department_id, last_name, salary
  2  from employees2
  3  where department_id = 90;

    EMPLOYEE_ID    DEPARTMENT_ID LAST_NAME                      SALARY
--------------- --------------- ------------------------- ---------------
            100              90 King                             26400
            101              90 Kochhar                          18700
            102              90 De Haan                          18700

3 rows selected.

SQL> -- Example 2: Delete rows using a subquery in the FROM clause
SQL> delete from (select * from employees2 where department_id = 90);

3 rows deleted.

SQL> select employee_id, department_id, last_name, salary
  2  from employees2
  3  where department_id = 90;

no rows selected
```

```
SQL> rollback;

Rollback complete.

SQL> select employee_id, department_id, last_name, salary
  2   from employees2
  3   where department_id = 90;
   EMPLOYEE_ID   DEPARTMENT_ID LAST_NAME                         SALARY
--------------- --------------- ------------------------- ---------------
           100              90 King                              26400
           101              90 Kochhar                           18700
           102              90 De Haan                           18700

3 rows selected.

SQL> -- Example 3: Delete rows from specified table using
SQL> -- a subquery in the WHERE clause
SQL> delete from employees2
  2   where department_id in (select department_id
  3                             from departments
  4                             where department_name = 'Executive');

3 rows deleted.

SQL> select employee_id, department_id, last_name, salary
  2   from employees2
  3   where department_id = 90;

no rows selected

SQL> rollback;

Rollback complete.

SQL>
```

The MERGE Statement

The MERGE statement is a single command that combines the ability to update or insert rows into a table by conditionally deriving the rows to be updated or inserted from one or more sources. It is most frequently used in data warehouses to move large amounts of data but its use is not limited to only data warehouse environments. The big value-add this statement provides is that you have a convenient way to combine multiple operations into one. This allows you to avoid issuing multiple INSERT, UPDATE, and DELETE statements. And, as you'll see later in the book, if you can avoid doing work you really don't have to do, your response times will likely improve.

The syntax for the MERGE statement is:

```
MERGE <hint>
INTO <table_name>
USING <table_view_or_query>
ON (<condition>)
WHEN MATCHED THEN <update_clause>
DELETE <where_clause>
WHEN NOT MATCHED THEN <insert_clause>
[LOG ERRORS <log_errors_clause> <reject limit <integer | unlimited>];
```

In order to demonstrate the use of the MERGE statement, Listing 1-20 shows how to create a test table and then appropriately insert or update rows into that table based on the MERGE conditions.

Listing 1-20. *MERGE Statement Example*

```
SQL> create table dept60_bonuses
  2  (employee_id        number
  3  ,bonus_amt          number);

Table created.

SQL> insert into dept60_bonuses values (103, 0);

1 row created.

SQL> insert into dept60_bonuses values (104, 100);

1 row created.

SQL> insert into dept60_bonuses values (105, 0);

1 row created.

SQL> commit;

Commit complete.

SQL> select employee_id, last_name, salary
  2  from employees
  3  where department_id = 60 ;

    EMPLOYEE_ID LAST_NAME                         SALARY
    --------------- ------------------------- ----------------
            103 Hunold                          9000
            104 Ernst                           6000
            105 Austin                          4800
```

```
          106 Pataballa                          4800
          107 Lorentz                            4200

5 rows selected.

SQL> select * from dept60_bonuses;
     EMPLOYEE_ID        BONUS_AMT
--------------- ---------------
           103               0
           104             100
           105               0

3 rows selected.

SQL> merge into dept60_bonuses b
  2  using (
  3    select employee_id, salary, department_id
  4    from employees
  5    where department_id = 60) e
  6  on (b.employee_id = e.employee_id)
  7  when matched then
  8    update set b.bonus_amt = e.salary * 0.2
  9     where b.bonus_amt = 0
 10    delete where (e.salary > 7500)
 11  when not matched then
 12    insert (b.employee_id, b.bonus_amt)
 13    values (e.employee_id, e.salary * 0.1)
 14    where (e.salary < 7500);

4 rows merged.

SQL> select * from dept60_bonuses;

     EMPLOYEE_ID        BONUS_AMT
--------------- ---------------
           104             100
           105             960
           106             480
           107             420

4 rows selected.

SQL> rollback;

Rollback complete.

SQL>
```

The MERGE accomplished the following:

- Two rows were inserted (employee_ids 106 and 107).
- One row was updated (employee_id 105).
- One row was deleted (employee_id 103).
- One row remained unchanged (employee_id 104).

Without the MERGE statement, you would have had to write at least three different statements to complete the same work.

Summary

As you can tell from the examples shown so far, the SQL language offers many alternatives that can produce the same result set. What you may have also noticed is that each of the five core statements can utilize similar constructs, like subqueries. The key is to learn which constructs are the most efficient under various circumstances. We'll cover how to do that later in the book.

If you had any trouble following the examples in this chapter, make sure to take the time to review either *Beginning Oracle SQL* or the *SQL Reference Guide* in the Oracle documentation. The rest of the book will assume you are comfortable with the basic constructs for each of the five core SQL statements: SELECT, INSERT, UPDATE, DELETE, and MERGE.

CHAPTER 2

■ ■ ■

SQL Execution

Karen Morton

You likely learned the mechanics of writing basic SQL in a relatively short period of time. Over the course of a few weeks or few months, you became comfortable with the general statement structure and syntax, how to filter, how to join tables, and how to group and order data. But, how far beyond that initial level of proficiency have you traveled? Writing complex SQL that executes efficiently is a skill that requires you to move beyond the basics. Just because your SQL gets the job done doesn't mean it does the job well.

In this chapter, I'm going to raise the hood and look at how SQL executes from the inside-out. I'll discuss basic Oracle architecture and introduce the cost-based query optimizer. You'll learn how and why the way you formulate your SQL statements affects the optimizer's ability to produce the most efficient execution plan possible. You may already know what to do, but understanding how SQL execution works will help you help Oracle accomplish the results you need in less time and with fewer resources required.

Oracle Architecture Basics

The SQL language is seemingly easy enough that you can learn to write simple SQL statements in fairly short order. But, just because you can write SQL statements that are functionally correct (i.e. produce the proper result set), that doesn't mean you've accomplished the task in the most effective and efficient way.

Moving beyond basic skills requires a deeper understanding of that skill. For instance, when I learned to drive, my father taught me the basics. We walked around the car and discussed the parts of the car that he thought were important to be aware of as the driver of the vehicle. We talked about the type of gas I should put in the car, the proper air pressure the tires should have, and the importance of getting regular oil changes. Being aware of these things would help make sure the vehicle would be in good condition when I wanted to drive it.

He then taught me the mechanics of driving. I learned how to start the engine, shift gears, increase and decrease my speed, use the brake, use turn signals, and so on. But, what he didn't teach me was specifically how the engine worked, how to change the oil myself, or anything else other than what I needed to do to allow me to safely drive the vehicle from place to place. If I needed for my car to do anything outside of what I learned, I'd have to take it to a professional mechanic.

This isn't a bad thing. Not everyone needs to have the skills and knowledge of a professional mechanic just to drive a car. But the analogy applies to anyone who writes SQL. You can learn the basics and be able to get your applications from place to place. But, without extending your knowledge, I don't believe you'll ever be more than an everyday driver. To really get the most out of SQL, you need to understand how it does what it does. That means you need to understand the basics of the underlying architecture on which the SQL you write will execute.

Figure 2-1 depicts how most people view the database when they first learn to write SQL. It is simply a black box to which they direct SQL requests to and get data back from. The "machinery" inside the database is a mystery.

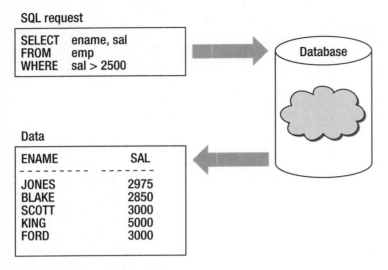

Figure 2-1. *Using SQL and the database*

The term "Oracle database" is typically used to refer to both the files, stored on disk, where data resides and the memory structures used to manage those files. In reality, the term "database" belongs to the data files and the term "instance" belongs to the memory structures. An instance consists of the system global area (SGA) and a set of background processes. Each user connection to the database is managed via a client process. Client processes are associated with server processes which are each allocated their own private memory area called the program, or process, global area (PGA). Figure 2-2 shows the Oracle Instance and Database diagram as found in the *Oracle Concepts Guide*.

Don't get overwhelmed by how complex this looks. The *Oracle Concepts Guide* goes into detail about each of the elements you see in Figure 2-1. I think it's a great idea for everyone who will use Oracle to read the *Oracle Concepts Guide*. But for our purposes, I want to limit the discussion to a few key areas that will help you understand how SQL operates. Specifically, I want to review two areas of the SGA, the shared pool (specifically, the library cache within the shared pool) and the database buffer cache. Later in the book, I'll also discuss some particulars about the PGA, but I'm going to keep our review limited to the SGA for now. Note that these discussions will present a fairly broad picture. As I said, I don't want to overwhelm you, but I do think this is critical information to get a grasp on before you go any further.

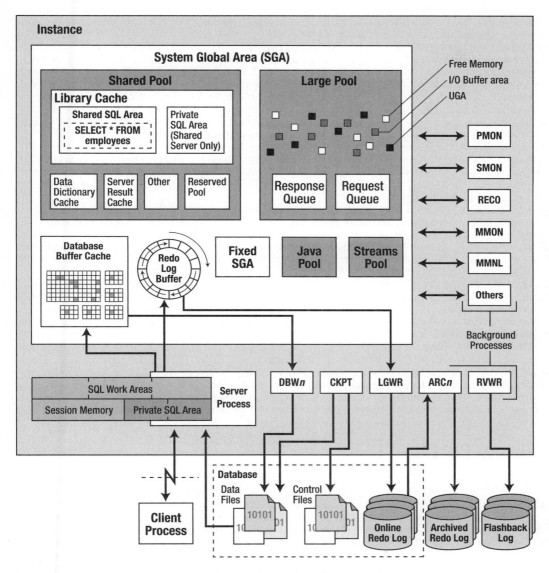

Figure 2-2. *Oracle instance and database diagram from the Oracle Concepts Guide*

SGA – The Shared Pool

The shared pool is one of the most critical memory components particularly when it comes to how SQL executes. The way you write SQL doesn't just effect the individual SQL statement itself. The combination of all SQL that executes against the database has a tremendous effect on overall performance and scalability due to how it affects the shared pool.

The shared pool is where Oracle caches program data. Every SQL statement executed will have its parsed form stored in the shared pool. The area within the shared pool where statements are stored is called the library cache. Even before any statement is parsed, Oracle will check the library cache to see if that same statement already exists there. If it does exist, then Oracle will retrieve and use the cached information instead of going through all the work to parse the same statement again. The same thing goes for any PL/SQL code you run. The really nifty part is that no matter how many users may want to execute the same SQL statement, Oracle will typically only parse that statement once and share it among all users who want to use it. Maybe you can see where the shared pool gets its name.

SQL statements you write aren't the only things stored in the shared pool. The system parameters Oracle uses will be stored in the shared pool as well. In an area called the dictionary cache, Oracle will also store information about all the database objects. In general, Oracle stores pretty much everything you could think of in the shared pool. As you can imagine, that makes the shared pool a very busy and important memory component.

Since the memory area allocated to the shared pool is finite, statements that originally get loaded may not stay there for very long as new statements are executed. A Least Recently Used (LRU) algorithm regulates how objects in the shared pool are managed. To borrow an accounting term, it's similar to a FIFO (First In First Out) system. The basic idea is that statements that are used most frequently and most currently are what are retained. Unlike a straight FIFO method, how frequently the same statements are used will effect how long they remain in the shared pool. If you execute a SELECT statement at 8 A.M.and then execute the same statement again at 4 P.M., the parsed version that was stored in the shared pool at 8 A.M. may not still be there. Depending on the overall size of the shared pool and how much activity it has between 8 A.M. and 4 P.M., as Oracle needs space to store the latest information throughout the day, it will simply reuse older areas and overlay newer information into them. But, if you execute a statement every few seconds throughout the day, the frequent reuse will cause Oracle to retain that information over something else that may have originally been stored later than your statement but hasn't been executed frequently, or at all, since it was loaded.

One of the things you need to keep in mind as you write SQL is that in order to use the shared pool most efficiently, statements need to be shareable. If every statement you write is unique, you basically defeat the purpose of the shared pool. The less shareable it is, the more effect you'll see to overall response times. I'll show you exactly how expensive parsing can be in the next section.

The Library Cache

The first thing that must happen to every SQL statement you execute is that it must be parsed and loaded into the library cache. The library cache, as mentioned earlier, is the area within the shared pool that holds previously parsed statements. Parsing involves verifying the statement syntax, validating objects being referred to, and confirming user privileges on the objects. If those checks are passed, the next step is for Oracle to see if that same statement has been executed previously. If it has, then Oracle will grab the stored information from the previous parse and reuse it. This type of parse is called a *soft* parse. If the statement hasn't previously been executed, then Oracle will do all the work to develop the execution plan for the current statement and then store it in the cache for later reuse. This type of parse is called a *hard* parse.

Hard parses require Oracle to do a lot more work than soft parses. Every time a hard parse occurs, Oracle must gather all the information it needs before it can actually execute the statement. In order to get the information it needs, Oracle will execute a bunch of queries against the data dictionary. The easiest way to see what Oracle does during a hard parse is to turn on extended SQL tracing, execute a statement and then review the trace data. Extended SQL tracing captures every action that occurs so not only will you see the statement you execute, but you'll see every statement that Oracle must execute as well. Since I haven't covered the details of how tracing works and how to read a trace file, I'm not going to show the detailed trace data. Instead, Table 2-1 provides the list of system tables that were queried during a hard parse of select * from employees where department_id = 60.

Table 2-1. *System Objects Queried During Hard Parse*

Tables	#Queries	Purpose
access$	1	Permissions used by a dependent object against its parent
ccol$	10	Constraint column-specific data
cdef$	3	Constraint-specific definition data
col$	1	Table column-specific data
dependency$	1	Interobject dependencies
hist_head$	12	Histogram header data
histgrm$	3	Histogram specifications
icol$	6	Index columns
ind$, ind_stats$	1	Indexes, index statistics
obj$	8	Objects
objauth$	2	Table authorizations
seg$	7	Mapping of all database segments
syn$	1	Synonyms
tab$, tab_stats$	1	Tables, table statistics
user$	2	User definitions

In total, there were 59 queries against system objects executed during the hard parse. The soft parse of the same statement did not execute any queries against the system objects since all that work was done during the initial hard parse. The elapsed time for the hard parse was .060374 seconds while the elapsed time for the soft was was .000095 seconds. So, as you can see, soft parsing is a much more desirable alternative to hard parsing. Don't ever fool yourself into thinking hard parsing doesn't matter. As you can see, it does!

Identical Statements

In order for Oracle to determine if a statement has been previously executed, it will check the library cache for the identical statement. You can see what statements are currently stored in the library cache by querying the v$sql view. This view lists statistics on the shared SQL area and contains one row for each child of the original SQL text entered. Listing 2-1 shows three different executions of a query against the employees table followed by a query against v$sql showing information about the three queries that have been stored in the library cache.

Listing 2-1. *Queries Against Employees and v$sql Contents*

```
SQL> select * from employees where department_id = 60;

    EMPLOYEE_ID FIRST_NAME           LAST_NAME                 EMAIL        ...
--------------- -------------------- ------------------------- ----------- ...
            103 Alexander            Hunold                    AHUNOLD      ...
            104 Bruce                Ernst                     BERNST       ...
            105 David                Austin                    DAUSTIN      ...
            106 Valli                Pataballa                 VPATABAL     ...
            107 Diana                Lorentz                   DLORENTZ     ...

SQL> SELECT * FROM EMPLOYEES WHERE DEPARTMENT_ID = 60;

    EMPLOYEE_ID FIRST_NAME           LAST_NAME                 EMAIL        ...
--------------- -------------------- ------------------------- ----------- ...
            103 Alexander            Hunold                    AHUNOLD      ...
            104 Bruce                Ernst                     BERNST       ...
            105 David                Austin                    DAUSTIN      ...
            106 Valli                Pataballa                 VPATABAL     ...
            107 Diana                Lorentz                   DLORENTZ     ...

SQL> select /* a_comment */ * from employees where department_id = 60;

    EMPLOYEE_ID FIRST_NAME           LAST_NAME                 EMAIL        ...
--------------- -------------------- ------------------------- ----------- ...
            103 Alexander            Hunold                    AHUNOLD      ...
            104 Bruce                Ernst                     BERNST       ...
            105 David                Austin                    DAUSTIN      ...
            106 Valli                Pataballa                 VPATABAL     ...
            107 Diana                Lorentz                   DLORENTZ     ...


SQL> select sql_text, sql_id, child_number, hash_value, address, executions
  2  from v$sql where upper(sql_text) like '%EMPLOYEES%';

SQL_TEXT                     SQL_ID        CHILD_NUMBER HASH_VALUE ADDRESS  EXECUTIONS
---------------------------- ------------- ------------ ---------- -------- ----------
select * from employees      0svc967bxf4yu            0 3621196762 67197BC4          1
 where department_id = 60
SELECT * FROM EMPLOYEES      cq7t1xq95bpm8            0 2455098984 671A3034          1
 WHERE DEPARTMENT_ID = 60
select /* a_comment */ *     2dkt13j0cyjzq            0 1087326198 671A2E18          1
 from employees
 where department_id = 60
```

Although all three statements return the exact same result, Oracle considers them to be different. This is because when a statement is executed, Oracle first converts the string to a hash value. That hash value is used as the key for that statement when it is stored in the library cache. As other statements are executed, their hash values are compared to the existing hash values to find a match.

So, why would these three statements produce different hash values, even though they return the same result? It's because the statements are not exactly identical. Lower case text is different from upper case text. Adding a comment into the statement makes it different from the statements that don't have a comment. Any differences will cause a different hash value for the statement and cause Oracle to hard parse the statement.

This is why using bind variables instead literals in your SQL statements is so important. When you use a bind variable, Oracle will be able to share the statement even as you change the values of the bind variables, as shown in Listing 2-2.

Listing 2-2. *The Effect of Using Bind Variables on Parsing*

```
SQL> variable v_dept number
SQL> exec :v_dept := 10
SQL> select * from employees where department_id = :v_dept;

    EMPLOYEE_ID FIRST_NAME           LAST_NAME                 EMAIL         ...
    --------------- -------------------- ------------------------- ----------- ...
            200 Jennifer             Whalen                    JWHALEN       ...

1 row selected.

SQL> exec :v_dept := 20

PL/SQL procedure successfully completed.

SQL> select * from employees where department_id = :v_dept;

    EMPLOYEE_ID FIRST_NAME           LAST_NAME                 EMAIL         ...
    --------------- -------------------- ------------------------- ----------- ...
            201 Michael              Hartstein                 MHARTSTE      ...
            202 Pat                  Fay                       PFAY          ...

2 rows selected.

SQL> exec :v_dept := 30

PL/SQL procedure successfully completed.

SQL> select * from employees where department_id = :v_dept;

    EMPLOYEE_ID FIRST_NAME           LAST_NAME                 EMAIL         ...
    --------------- -------------------- ------------------------- ----------- ...
            114 Den                  Raphaely                  DRAPHEAL      ...
            115 Alexander            Khoo                      AKHOO         ...
            116 Shelli               Baida                     SBAIDA        ...
```

```
          117 Sigal              Tobias              STOBIAS     ...
          118 Guy                Himuro              GHIMURO     ...
          119 Karen              Colmenares          KCOLMENA    ...

6 rows selected.

SQL> select sql_text, sql_id, child_number, hash_value, address, executions
  2    from v$sql where sql_text like '%v_dept';

SQL_TEXT                        SQL_ID        CHILD_NUMBER  HASH_VALUE  ADDRESS   EXECUTIONS
------------------------------  ------------- ------------  ----------- --------  ----------
select * from employees         72k66s55jqk1j            0  1260079153  6726254C           3
  where department_id = :v_dept

1 row selected.
```

Notice how there is only one statement stored in the library cache with three executions. If I had executed the queries using the literal values (10, 20, 30), there would have been three different statements. Always keep this in mind and try to write SQL that takes advantage of bind variables and uses exactly the same SQL. The less hard parsing that is required will mean your applications will perform better and be more scalable.

One last mechanism that is important to understand is something called a latch. A latch is a type of lock that Oracle must acquire in order to read information stored in the library cache as well as other memory structures. Latches protect the library cache from becoming corrupted by concurrent modifications by two sessions or by one session trying to read information that is being modified by another one. Prior to reading any information from the library cache, Oracle will acquire a latch that will then cause all other sessions to have to wait until that latch is released before they can acquire the latch and do the work they need to complete.

Latches, unlike typical locks, are not queued. In other words, if Oracle attempts to acquire a latch on the library cache in order to check to see if the statement you are executing already exists, it will check to see if the latch is available. If the latch is available, it will acquire the latch, do the work it needs to, then release the latch. However, if the latch is already in use, Oracle will do something called *spinning*. Think of spinning like a kid in the backseat of a car that asks "Are we there yet?" over and over and over. Oracle will basically iterate in a loop and continue to check to see if the latch is available. During this time, Oracle is actively using CPU to do these checks, but your query is actually "on hold" and not really doing anything until the latch can be acquired.

If the latch is not acquired after spinning for a while (Oracle will spin up to the number of times indicated by the _spin_count hidden parameter, which is set to 2000 by default), then the request will be halted temporarily and your session will have to get in line behind other sessions that need to use the CPU. It must wait its turn to use the CPU again in order to check to see if the latch is available. This iterative process will continue until the latch can be acquired. You don't just get in line and wait on the latch to become available, so it's entirely possible that another session can acquire the latch while your session is waiting in line to get back on the CPU to check the latch again. As you can imagine, this could be quite time-consuming if many sessions all need to acquire the latch concurrently.

The main thing to remember is that latches are serialization devices. The more frequently Oracle needs to acquire a latch, the more likely it is that contention will occur, and the longer you'll have to wait. The effects on performance and scalability can be dramatic. So, writing your code in such a way as to require fewer latches (i.e. less hard parsing) is critical.

SGA – The Buffer Cache

The buffer cache is one of the largest components of the SGA. It stores database blocks after they have been read from disk or before they are written to disk. A block is the smallest unit that Oracle will work with. Blocks contain rows of table data or index entries, and some blocks will contain temporary data for sorts. The key thing to remember is that Oracle must read blocks in order to get to the rows of data needed to satisfy a SQL statement. Blocks are typically either 4KB, 8KB, or 16KB in size, although the only restricting factor to the size of a block depends on your operating system.

Each block has a certain structure. Within the block there are a few areas of block overhead that contain information about the block itself that Oracle uses to manage the block. There is information that indicates the type of block it is (table, index, etc.), a bit of information about transactions against the block, the address where the block physically resides on the disk, information about the tables that store data in the block, and information about the row data contained in the block. The rest of the block contains the actual data or free space where new data can be stored. There's more detail about how the buffer cache can be divided into multiple pools and have varying block sizes, but I'm going to keep it simple for this discussion and just consider one big default buffer pool with a single block size.

At any given time, the blocks in the buffer cache will either be *dirty*, which means they have been modified and need to be written into a physical location on disk, or *not dirty*. In the discussion on the shared pool, I mentioned the Least Recently Used (LRU) algorithm employed by Oracle to manage the information there. The buffer cache also uses a LRU list to help Oracle know which blocks are most recently used in order to know how to make room for new blocks as needed. Besides just the LRU list, Oracle maintains a *touch count* for each block in the buffer cache. This count indicates how frequently a block is used; blocks with higher touch counts will remain in the cache longer than those with lower touch counts.

Also like in the shared pool, latches must be acquired to verify if blocks are in the buffer cache and to update the LRU information and touch counts. One of the ways you can help Oracle use less latches is to write your SQL in such a way that it accesses the fewest blocks possible when trying to retrieve the rows needed to satisfy your query. I'll discuss how you can do this throughout the rest of the book, but for now, keep in mind that if all you think about when writing a SQL statement is getting the functionally correct answer, you may write your SQL in such a way that it inefficiently access blocks and therefore uses more latches than needed. The more latches required, the more chance for contention and the more likely your application will be less responsive and less scalable.

Executing a query whose blocks are not in the buffer cache requires Oracle to make a call to the operating system to retrieve those blocks and then place them in the buffer cache before returning the result set to you. In general, any block that contains rows that will be needed to satisfy a query must be present in the buffer cache. When Oracle determines that a block already exists in the buffer cache, such access is referred to as a *logical* read. If the block must be retrieved from disk, it is referred to as a *physical* read. As you can imagine, since the block is already in memory, response times to complete a logical read is faster than physical reads. Listing 2-3 shows the differences between executing the same statement multiple times under three scenarios. First, the statement is executed after clearing both the shared pool and the buffer cache. This means that the statement will be hard parsed, and the blocks that contain the data to satisfy the query (and all the queries from the system objects to handle the hard parse) will have to be physically read from disk. The second example shows what happens if only the buffer cache is cleared. The final example shows what happens if both the shared pool and buffer cache are populated.

Listing 2-3. *Hard Parsing and Physical Reads vs. Soft Parsing and Logical Reads*

```
SQL> alter system set events 'immediate trace name flush_cache';

System altered.

SQL> alter system flush shared_pool;

System altered.

SQL> set autotrace traceonly statistics
SQL>
SQL> select * from employees where department_id = 60;

5 rows selected.


Statistics
----------------------------------------------------------
        951  recursive calls
          0  db block gets
        237  consistent gets
         27  physical reads
          0  redo size
       1386  bytes sent via SQL*Net to client
        381  bytes received via SQL*Net from client
          2  SQL*Net roundtrips to/from client
          9  sorts (memory)
          0  sorts (disk)
          5  rows processed

SQL> set autotrace off
SQL>
SQL> alter system set events 'immediate trace name flush_cache';

System altered.

SQL> set autotrace traceonly statistics
SQL>
SQL> select * from employees where department_id = 60;

5 rows selected.
```

```
Statistics
----------------------------------------------------------
          0  recursive calls
          0  db block gets
          4  consistent gets
          2  physical reads
          0  redo size
       1386  bytes sent via SQL*Net to client
        381  bytes received via SQL*Net from client
          2  SQL*Net roundtrips to/from client
          0  sorts (memory)
          0  sorts (disk)
          5  rows processed

SQL> select * from employees where department_id = 60;

5 rows selected.


Statistics
----------------------------------------------------------
          0  recursive calls
          0  db block gets
          4  consistent gets
          0  physical reads
          0  redo size
       1386  bytes sent via SQL*Net to client
        381  bytes received via SQL*Net from client
          2  SQL*Net roundtrips to/from client
          0  sorts (memory)
          0  sorts (disk)
          5  rows processed

SQL> set autotrace off
```

You can see from the statistics that when a query is executed and does only a soft parse and finds the blocks in the buffer cache, the work done is at a minimum. Your goal should always be to develop code that will promote reusability in both the shared pool and buffer cache.

Query Transformation

Prior to the development of the execution plan, a step called *query transformation* occurs. This step happens just after a query is checked for syntax and permissions and just before the optimizer computes cost estimates for the various plan operations it considers when determining the final execution plan. In other words, transformation and optimization are two different tasks.

After your query passes the syntactical and permissions checks, the query enters the transform phase in a set of query blocks. A query block is defined by the keyword SELECT. For example, select

* from employees where department_id = 60 has a single query block. However, select * from employees where department_id in (select department_id from departments) has two query blocks. Each query block is either nested within another or interrelated to another in some way. The way the query is written determines the relationships between query blocks. It is the query transformer's main objective to determine if changing the way the query is written will provide a better query plan.

Make sure you caught that last sentence. The query transformer can, and will, rewrite your query. This is something you may have never realized. What you write may not end up being the exact statement for which the execution plan is developed. Many times this is a good thing. The query transformer knows how the optimizer deals with certain syntax and will do everything it can to render your SQL in a way that helps the optimizer to come up with the best, most efficient execution plan. However, the fact that what you write can be changed may mean that a behavior you expected, particularly the order in which certain parts of the statement occur, doesn't happen the way you intended. Therefore, you really need to understand how query transformation works so that you can make sure to write your SQL properly to get the behaviors you intend.

The query transformer may change the way you originally formulated your query as long as the change does not affect the result set. Any change that might cause the result set to differ from the original query syntax will not be considered. The change that is most often made is to transform separate query blocks into straight joins. For example, this statement

```
select * from employees where department_id in (select department_id from departments)
```

will likely be transformed into this statement

```
select e.* from employees e, departments d where e.department_id = d.department_id
```

The result set doesn't change, but the execution plan choices for the transformed version would be better from the optimizer's point of view.

Once you learn what to look for, you can usually tell by looking at the execution plan if a transformation occurs. You can also execute your query using the NO_QUERY_TRANSFORMATION hint and compare the execution plan from this query with the plan from the query without the hint. If the two plans are not the same, the differences can be attributed to query transformation. When using the hint, all query transformations with the exception of predicate pushing (which I'll review shortly) will be prohibited.

There are several basic transformations that can be applied to a given query:

- View merging
- Subquery unnesting
- Predicate pushing
- Query rewrite with materialized views

View Merging

As the name implies, view merging is a transformation that expands views, either in-line views or stored views, into separate query blocks that can either be analyzed separately or that can be merged with the rest of the query to form a single overall execution plan. Basically, the statement is rewritten without the view. A statement like select * from my_view would be rewritten as if you had simply typed in the view source. View merging usually occurs when the outer query block's predicate contains:

- a column that can be used in an index within another query block.

- a column that can be used for partition pruning within another query block.

- a condition that limitis the rows returned from one of the tables in a joined view.

Most people believe that a view will always be treated as a separate query block and will always have its own subplan and be executed prior to joining to other query blocks. That is not true due to the actions of the query transformer. The truth is that sometimes views will be analyzed separately and have their own subplan, but more often than not, merging views with the rest of the query provides a greater performance benefit. For example, the following query might use resources quite differently depending on whether or not the view is merged:

```
select *
from   orders o,
       (select sales_rep_id
              from orders
       ) o_view
where  o.sales_rep_id = o_view.sales_rep_id(+)
and    o.order_total > 100000;
```

Listing 2-4 shows the execution plans for this query when view merging occurs and when it doesn't. Notice the plan operations chosen and the A-Rows count (actual rows retrieved in that step of the plan) in each step.

Listing 2-4. *View Merging Plan Comparison*

```
-- View merging occurs
```

```
-------------------------------------------------------------------------
| Id  | Operation          | Name           | Starts | E-Rows | A-Rows |
-------------------------------------------------------------------------
|   1 |  NESTED LOOPS OUTER|                |      1 |    413 |     31 |
|*  2 |   TABLE ACCESS FULL| ORDERS         |      1 |     70 |      7 |
|*  3 |   INDEX RANGE SCAN | ORD_SALES_REP_IX |    7 |      6 |     26 |
-------------------------------------------------------------------------

Predicate Information (identified by operation id):
---------------------------------------------------

   2 - filter("O"."ORDER_TOTAL">100000)
   3 - access("O"."SALES_REP_ID"="SALES_REP_ID")
       filter("SALES_REP_ID" IS NOT NULL)
```

```
-- View merging does not occur

-----------------------------------------------------------------
| Id | Operation            | Name   | Starts | E-Rows | A-Rows |
-----------------------------------------------------------------
|* 1 | HASH JOIN OUTER      |        |      1 |    413 |     31 |
|* 2 |  TABLE ACCESS FULL   | ORDERS |      1 |     70 |      7 |
|  3 |  VIEW                |        |      1 |    105 |    104 |
|  4 |   TABLE ACCESS FULL  | ORDERS |      1 |    105 |    104 |
-----------------------------------------------------------------

Predicate Information (identified by operation id):
---------------------------------------------------

   1 - access("O"."SALES_REP_ID"="O_VIEW"."SALES_REP_ID")
   2 - filter("O"."ORDER_TOTAL">100000)
```

Did you notice how in the second, non-merged plan, the view is handled separately? The plan even indicates the view was kept "as is" by showing the VIEW keyword in line 3 of the plan. By treating the view separately, a full scan of the orders table occurs before it is joined with the outer orders table. But, in the merged version, the plan operations are merged into a single plan instead of keeping the in-line view separate. This results in a more efficient index access operation being chosen and requires fewer rows to be processed (26 vs 104). This example uses small tables, so imagine how much work would occur if you had really large tables involved in the query. The transformation to merge the view makes the plan perform more optimally overall.

The misconception that an in-line or normal view will be considered first and separately from the rest of the query often comes from our education about execution order in mathematics. Let's consider the following examples:

```
6 + 4 / 2 = 8
(6 + 4) / 2 = 5
```

The parenthesis in the second example cause the addition to happen first, whereas in the first example the division would happen first based on the rules of precedence order. We are trained to know that when we use parenthesis, that action will happen first. But the SQL language doesn't follow the same rules that mathematical expressions do. Using parenthesis to set a query block apart from another does not in any way guarantee that block will be executed separately or first. If you have written your statement to include an in-line view because you intend for that view to be considered separately, you may need to add the NO_MERGE hint to that query block to prevent it from being rewritten. As a matter of fact, using the NO_MERGE hint is how I was able to produce the non-merged plan in Listing 2-4. With this hint, I was able to tell the query transformer that I wanted the o_view query block to be considered independently from the outer query block. The query using the hint actually looked like this:

```
select *
from    orders o,
        (select /*+ NO_MERGE */ sales_rep_id
              from orders
        ) o_view
where   o.sales_rep_id = o_view.sales_rep_id(+)
and     o.order_total > 100000;
```

There are some conditions that, if present, will also prevent view merging from occurring. If a query block contains analytic or aggregate functions, set operations (such as UNION, INTERSECT, MINUS), an ORDER BY clause, or uses ROWNUM, view merging will be prohibited or limited. Even if some of these conditions are present, you can force view merging to take place by using the MERGE hint. If you force view merging to occur by using the hint, you must make sure that the query result set is still correct after the merge. If view merging was not going to occur, it was likely due to the fact that the merge might cause the query result to be different. By using the hint, you are indicating the merge will not affect the answer. Listing 2-5 shows a statement with an aggregate function that does not view merge and how the use of a MERGE hint can force view merging to occur.

Listing 2-5. *The MERGE Hint*

```
SQL> SELECT e1.last_name, e1.salary, v.avg_salary
  2      FROM employees e1,
  3        (SELECT department_id, avg(salary) avg_salary
  4           FROM employees e2
  5           GROUP BY department_id) v
  6      WHERE e1.department_id = v.department_id AND e1.salary > v.avg_salary;

...

38 rows selected.

Execution Plan
----------------------------------------------------------
Plan hash value: 2695105989
```

Id	Operation	Name	Rows	Bytes	Cost (%CPU)	Time
0	SELECT STATEMENT		17	697	8 (25)	00:00:01
* 1	HASH JOIN		17	697	8 (25)	00:00:01
2	VIEW		11	286	4 (25)	00:00:01
3	HASH GROUP BY		11	77	4 (25)	00:00:01
4	TABLE ACCESS FULL	EMPLOYEES	107	749	3 (0)	00:00:01
5	TABLE ACCESS FULL	EMPLOYEES	107	1605	3 (0)	00:00:01

```
Predicate Information (identified by operation id):
---------------------------------------------------
1 - access("E1"."DEPARTMENT_ID"="V"."DEPARTMENT_ID")
        filter("E1"."SALARY">"V"."AVG_SALARY")
```

```
SQL> SELECT /*+ MERGE(v) */ e1.last_name, e1.salary, v.avg_salary
  2     FROM employees e1,
  3       (SELECT department_id, avg(salary) avg_salary
  4          FROM employees e2
  5          GROUP BY department_id) v
  6     WHERE e1.department_id = v.department_id AND e1.salary > v.avg_salary;

...

38 rows selected.

Execution Plan
-----------------------------------------------------------
Plan hash value: 3553954154
```

```
-------------------------------------------------------------------------------
| Id  | Operation           | Name      | Rows | Bytes | Cost (%CPU)| Time     |
-------------------------------------------------------------------------------
|   0 | SELECT STATEMENT    |           |  165 | 5610  |    8  (25)| 00:00:01 |
|*  1 |  FILTER             |           |      |       |           |          |
|   2 |   HASH GROUP BY     |           |  165 | 5610  |    8  (25)| 00:00:01 |
|*  3 |    HASH JOIN        |           | 3296 | 109K  |    7  (15)| 00:00:01 |
|   4 |     TABLE ACCESS FULL| EMPLOYEES |  107 | 2889  |    3   (0)| 00:00:01 |
|   5 |     TABLE ACCESS FULL| EMPLOYEES |  107 |  749  |    3   (0)| 00:00:01 |
-------------------------------------------------------------------------------
```

```
Predicate Information (identified by operation id):
---------------------------------------------------

   1 - filter("E1"."SALARY">SUM("SALARY")/COUNT("SALARY"))
   3 - access("E1"."DEPARTMENT_ID"="DEPARTMENT_ID")
```

    View merging behavior is controlled by the hidden parameter _complex_view_merging that defaults to TRUE in version 9 and above. Starting in version 10, transformed queries are reviewed by the optimizer and the costs of both the merged and non-merged plans are evaluated. The optimizer will then choose the plan that is the least costly.

Subquery Unnesting

Subquery unnesting is similar to view merging in that just like a view a subquery is represented by a separate query block. The main difference between mergeable views and subqueries that can be unnested is location: Subqueries located within the WHERE clause are reviewed for unnesting by the transformer. The most typical transformation is to convert the subquery into a join. If a subquery isn't unnested, a separate subplan will be generated for it and executed in an order within the overall plan that allows for optimal execution speed.

    When the subquery is not correlated, the transformed query is very straightforward, as shown in Listing 2-6.

Listing 2-6. *Unnesting Transformation of an Uncorrelated Subquery*

```
SQL> set autotrace traceonly explain
SQL>
SQL> select * from employees where department_id in (select department_id from departments);

Execution Plan
----------------------------------------------------------
Plan hash value: 169719308

--------------------------------------------------------------------------------
| Id  | Operation            | Name        | Rows  | Bytes | Cost (%CPU)| Time     |
--------------------------------------------------------------------------------
|   0 | SELECT STATEMENT     |             |   106 |  7632 |     3   (0)| 00:00:01 |
|   1 |  NESTED LOOPS        |             |   106 |  7632 |     3   (0)| 00:00:01 |
|   2 |   TABLE ACCESS FULL  | EMPLOYEES   |   107 |  7276 |     3   (0)| 00:00:01 |
|*  3 |   INDEX UNIQUE SCAN  | DEPT_ID_PK  |     1 |     4 |     0   (0)| 00:00:01 |
--------------------------------------------------------------------------------

Predicate Information (identified by operation id):
---------------------------------------------------

   3 - access("DEPARTMENT_ID"="DEPARTMENT_ID")
```

The subquery in this case is simply merged into the main query block and converted to a table join. The query plan is derived as if the statement were written as follows:

```
select e.*
from    employees e, departments d
where   e.department_id = d.department_id
```

Using the NO_UNNEST hint, I could have forced the query to be optimized as written, which would mean that a separate subplan would be created for the subquery (as shown in Listing 2-7).

Listing 2-7. *Using the NO_UNNEST Hint*

```
SQL> select employee_id, last_name, salary, department_id
  2  from    employees
  3  where   department_id in
  4              (select /*+ NO_UNNEST */department_id
  5                  from departments where location_id > 1700);

Execution Plan
----------------------------------------------------------
Plan hash value: 4233807898
```

```
--------------------------------------------------------------------------------
| Id  | Operation                     | Name         | Rows  | Bytes | Cost (%CPU)| Time     |
--------------------------------------------------------------------------------
|   0 | SELECT STATEMENT              |              |   10  |  190  |  14   (0)| 00:00:01 |
|*  1 |  FILTER                       |              |       |       |          |          |
|   2 |   TABLE ACCESS FULL           | EMPLOYEES    |  107  | 2033  |   3   (0)| 00:00:01 |
|*  3 |   TABLE ACCESS BY INDEX ROWID | DEPARTMENTS  |    1  |    7  |   1   (0)| 00:00:01 |
|*  4 |    INDEX UNIQUE SCAN          | DEPT_ID_PK   |    1  |       |   0   (0)| 00:00:01 |
--------------------------------------------------------------------------------

Predicate Information (identified by operation id):
---------------------------------------------------

   1 - filter( EXISTS (SELECT /*+ NO_UNNEST */ 0 FROM "HR"."DEPARTMENTS"
           "DEPARTMENTS" WHERE "DEPARTMENT_ID"=:B1 AND "LOCATION_ID">1700))
   3 - filter("LOCATION_ID">1700)
   4 - access("DEPARTMENT_ID"=:B1)
```

The main difference between the plans is that without query transformation, a FILTER operation is chosen instead of a NESTED LOOPS join. I'll discuss both of these operations in detail in Chapters 3 and 6, but for now just note that the FILTER operation typically represents a less efficient way of accomplishing a match, or join, between two tables. You can see that the subquery remains intact if you look at the Predicate Information for step 1. What happens with this "as is" version is that for each row in the employees table, the subquery must execute using the employees table department_id column as a bind variable for comparison with the list of department_ids returned from the execution of the subquery. Since there are 107 rows in the employees table, the subquery will execute once for each row. That's not precisely what happens due to a nice optimization feature Oracle uses called *subquery caching*, but hopefully you can see that executing the query for each row isn't as efficient as joining the two tables. I'll discuss the details of these operations and review why the choice of a NESTED LOOPS join is more efficient than the FILTER operation in the chapters ahead.

The subquery unnesting transformation is a bit more complicated when a correlated subquery is involved. In this case, the correlated subquery is typically transformed into a view, unnested, and then joined to the table in the main query block. Listing 2-8 shows an example of subquery unnesting of a correlated subquery.

Listing 2-8. *Unnesting Transformation of a Correlated Subquery*

```
SQL> select outer.employee_id, outer.last_name, outer.salary, outer.department_id
  2  from employees outer
  3  where outer.salary >
  4     (select avg(inner.salary)
  5         from employees inner
  6        where inner.department_id = outer.department_id)
  7  ;

Execution Plan
----------------------------------------------------------
Plan hash value: 2167610409
```

```
-------------------------------------------------------------------------------
| Id  | Operation            | Name      | Rows | Bytes | Cost (%CPU)| Time     |
-------------------------------------------------------------------------------
|   0 | SELECT STATEMENT     |           |   17 |  765  |   8  (25)| 00:00:01 |
|*  1 |  HASH JOIN           |           |   17 |  765  |   8  (25)| 00:00:01 |
|   2 |   VIEW               | VW_SQ_1   |   11 |  286  |   4  (25)| 00:00:01 |
|   3 |    HASH GROUP BY     |           |   11 |   77  |   4  (25)| 00:00:01 |
|   4 |     TABLE ACCESS FULL| EMPLOYEES |  107 |  749  |   3   (0)| 00:00:01 |
|   5 |   TABLE ACCESS FULL  | EMPLOYEES |  107 | 2033  |   3   (0)| 00:00:01 |
-------------------------------------------------------------------------------

Predicate Information (identified by operation id):
---------------------------------------------------

   1 - access("DEPARTMENT_ID"="OUTER"."DEPARTMENT_ID")
       filter("OUTER"."SALARY">"VW_COL_1")
```

Notice in this example how the subquery is transformed into an in-line view, then merged with the outer query and joined. The correlated column becomes the join condition and the rest of the subquery is used to formulate an inline view. The rewritten version of the query would look something like this:

```
select outer.employee_id, outer.last_name, outer.salary, outer.department_id
  from employees outer,
          (select department_id, avg(salary) avg_sal
             from employees
           group by department_id) inner
 where outer.department_id = inner.department_id
```

Subquery unnesting behavior is controlled by the hidden parameter _unnest_subquery that defaults to TRUE in version 9 and above. This parameter is specifically described as controlling unnesting behavior for correlated subqueries. Just like with view merging, starting in version 10, transformed queries are reviewed by the optimizer, and the costs are evaluated to determine whether or not an unnested version would be the least costly.

Predicate Pushing

Predicate pushing is used to apply the predicates from a containing query block into a non-mergeable query block. The goal is to allow an index to be used or allow for other filtering of the data set earlier in the query plan rather than later. In general, it is always a good idea to filter out rows that aren't needed as soon as possible. Always think: filter early.

A real life example where the downside of filtering late is readily apparent is moving to another city. Let's say you are moving from Portland, Oregon to Jacksonville, Florida. If you hire a moving company to pack and move you—and they charge by the pound—it wouldn't be a very good idea to realize that you really didn't need or want 80% of the stuff that was moved. If you'd just taken the time to check out everything before the movers packed you up in Portland, you could have saved yourself a lot of money!

That's the idea with predicate pushing. If a predicate can be applied earlier by pushing it into a non-mergeable query block, there will be less data to carry through the rest of the plan. Less data means less work. Less work means less time. Listing 2-9 shows the difference between when predicate pushing happens and when it doesn't.

Listing 2-9. *Predicate Pushing*

```
SQL> set autotrace traceonly explain
SQL>
SQL> SELECT e1.last_name, e1.salary, v.avg_salary
  2    FROM employees e1,
  3      (SELECT department_id, avg(salary) avg_salary
  4         FROM employees e2
  5        GROUP BY department_id) v
  6   WHERE e1.department_id = v.department_id
  7     AND e1.salary > v.avg_salary
  8     AND e1.department_id = 60;

Execution Plan
----------------------------------------------------------
Plan hash value: 2684380651
```

```
--------------------------------------------------------------------------------------
| Id  | Operation                      | Name              | Rows | Bytes | Cost (%CPU)|
--------------------------------------------------------------------------------------
|   0 | SELECT STATEMENT               |                   |    1 |    41 |    3   (0)|
|*  1 |  TABLE ACCESS BY INDEX ROWID   | EMPLOYEES         |    1 |    15 |    1   (0)|
|   2 |   NESTED LOOPS                 |                   |    1 |    41 |    3   (0)|
|   3 |    VIEW                        |                   |    1 |    26 |    2   (0)|
|   4 |     HASH GROUP BY              |                   |    1 |     7 |    2   (0)|
|   5 |      TABLE ACCESS BY INDEX ROWID| EMPLOYEES        |    5 |    35 |    2   (0)|
|*  6 |       INDEX RANGE SCAN         | EMP_DEPARTMENT_IX |    5 |       |    1   (0)|
|*  7 |    INDEX RANGE SCAN            | EMP_DEPARTMENT_IX |    5 |       |    0   (0)|
--------------------------------------------------------------------------------------
```

```
Predicate Information (identified by operation id):
---------------------------------------------------

   1 - filter("E1"."SALARY">"V"."AVG_SALARY")
   6 - access("DEPARTMENT_ID"=60)
   7 - access("E1"."DEPARTMENT_ID"=60)

SQL> SELECT e1.last_name, e1.salary, v.avg_salary
  2    FROM employees e1,
  3      (SELECT department_id, avg(salary) avg_salary
  4         FROM employees e2
  5        WHERE rownum > 1            -- rownum prohibits predicate pushing!
  6        GROUP BY department_id) v
  7   WHERE e1.department_id = v.department_id
  8     AND e1.salary > v.avg_salary
  9     AND e1.department_id = 60;
```

Execution Plan

Plan hash value: 3834222907

```
--------------------------------------------------------------------------------
| Id  | Operation                    | Name              | Rows | Bytes | Cost (%CPU)|
--------------------------------------------------------------------------------
|   0 | SELECT STATEMENT             |                   |    3 |   123 |    7  (29)|
|*  1 |  HASH JOIN                   |                   |    3 |   123 |    7  (29)|
|   2 |   TABLE ACCESS BY INDEX ROWID| EMPLOYEES         |    5 |    75 |    2   (0)|
|*  3 |    INDEX RANGE SCAN          | EMP_DEPARTMENT_IX |    5 |       |    1   (0)|
|*  4 |   VIEW                       |                   |   11 |   286 |    4  (25)|
|   5 |    HASH GROUP BY             |                   |   11 |    77 |    4  (25)|
|   6 |     COUNT                    |                   |      |       |           |
|*  7 |      FILTER                  |                   |      |       |           |
|   8 |       TABLE ACCESS FULL      | EMPLOYEES         |  107 |   749 |    3   (0)|
--------------------------------------------------------------------------------
```

Predicate Information (identified by operation id):

```
   1 - access("E1"."DEPARTMENT_ID"="V"."DEPARTMENT_ID")
       filter("E1"."SALARY">"V"."AVG_SALARY")
   3 - access("E1"."DEPARTMENT_ID"=60)
   4 - filter("V"."DEPARTMENT_ID"=60)
   7 - filter(ROWNUM>1)
```

Notice step 6 of the first plan. The WHERE department_id = 60 predicate was pushed into the view, allowing the average salary to only be determined for one department. When the predicate is not pushed, as shown in the second plan, the average salary must be computed for every department. Then, when the outer query block and inner query blocks are joined, all the rows that are not department_id 60 get thrown away. You can tell from the Rows estimates as well as by the cost of the second plan that the optimizer realizes that having to wait to apply the predicate requires more work and therefore is a more expensive and time-consuming operation.

I used a little trick to stop predicate pushing in this example that I want to point out. The use of the rownum pseudocolumn in the second query (I added the predicate WHERE rownum > 1) acted to prohibit predicate pushing. As a matter of fact, rownum not only prohibits predicate pushing but it prohibits view merging as well. Using rownum is like adding the NO_MERGE and NO_PUSH_PRED hints to the query. In this case, it allowed me to point out the ill effects that occur when predicate pushing doesn't happen, but I also want to make sure you realize that using rownum will affect the choices the optimizer has available when determining the execution plan. Be careful when you use rownum–it will make any query block it appears in both non-mergeable and unable to have predicates pushed into it.

Other than through the use of rownum or a NO_PUSH_PRED hint, predicate pushing will happen without any special action on your part. And that's just what you want! While there may be a few corner cases where predicate pushing might be less advantageous, those cases are few and far between. So, make sure to check execution plans to ensure predicate pushing happens as expected.

Query Rewrite with Materialized Views

Query rewrite is a transformation that occurs when a query, or a portion of a query, has been saved as a materialized view and the transformer can rewrite the query to use the precomputed materialized view data instead of executing the current query. A materialized view is like a normal view except that the query has been executed and its result set has been stored in a table. What this does is to precompute the result of the query and make it available whenever the specific query is executed. That means that all the work to determine the plan, execute it, and gather up all the data has already been done. So, when the same query is executed again, there is no need to go through all that effort again.

The query transformer will match a query with available materialized views and then rewrite the query to simply select from the materialized result set. Listing 2-10 walks through creating a materialized view and how the transformer would rewrite the query to use the materialized view result set.

Listing 2-10. *Query Rewrite with Materialized Views*

```
SQL> set autotrace traceonly explain
SQL>
SQL> SELECT p.prod_id, p.prod_name, t.time_id, t.week_ending_day,
  2         s.channel_id, s.promo_id, s.cust_id, s.amount_sold
  3  FROM   sales s, products p, times t
  4  WHERE  s.time_id=t.time_id  AND s.prod_id = p.prod_id;

Execution Plan
----------------------------------------------------------
Plan hash value: 1109402314
```

Id	Operation	Name	Rows	Bytes	Cost (%CPU)	Pstart	Pstop
0	SELECT STATEMENT		918K	65M	485 (17)		
* 1	HASH JOIN		918K	65M	485 (17)		
2	TABLE ACCESS FULL	TIMES	1826	29216	15 (0)		
* 3	HASH JOIN		918K	51M	453 (14)		
4	TABLE ACCESS FULL	PRODUCTS	72	2160	3 (0)		
5	PARTITION RANGE ALL		918K	25M	434 (11)	1	28
6	TABLE ACCESS FULL	SALES	918K	25M	434 (11)	1	28

```
Predicate Information (identified by operation id):
---------------------------------------------------

   1 - access("S"."TIME_ID"="T"."TIME_ID")
   3 - access("S"."PROD_ID"="P"."PROD_ID")
SQL>
SQL> set autotrace off
```

```
SQL>
SQL> CREATE MATERIALIZED VIEW sales_time_product_mv
  2    ENABLE QUERY REWRITE AS
  3    SELECT p.prod_id, p.prod_name, t.time_id, t.week_ending_day,
  4           s.channel_id, s.promo_id, s.cust_id, s.amount_sold
  5    FROM   sales s, products p, times t
  6    WHERE  s.time_id=t.time_id  AND s.prod_id = p.prod_id;
SQL>
SQL> set autotrace traceonly explain
SQL>
SQL> SELECT p.prod_id, p.prod_name, t.time_id, t.week_ending_day,
  2           s.channel_id, s.promo_id, s.cust_id, s.amount_sold
  3    FROM   sales s, products p, times t
  4    WHERE  s.time_id=t.time_id  AND s.prod_id = p.prod_id;

Execution Plan
----------------------------------------------------------
Plan hash value: 1109402314
```

Id	Operation	Name	Rows	Bytes	Cost (%CPU)	Pstart	Pstop
0	SELECT STATEMENT		918K	65M	485 (17)		
* 1	HASH JOIN		918K	65M	485 (17)		
2	TABLE ACCESS FULL	TIMES	1826	29216	15 (0)		
* 3	HASH JOIN		918K	51M	453 (14)		
4	TABLE ACCESS FULL	PRODUCTS	72	2160	3 (0)		
5	PARTITION RANGE ALL		918K	25M	434 (11)	1	28
6	TABLE ACCESS FULL	SALES	918K	25M	434 (11)	1	28

```
Predicate Information (identified by operation id):
---------------------------------------------------

   1 - access("S"."TIME_ID"="T"."TIME_ID")
   3 - access("S"."PROD_ID"="P"."PROD_ID")

Note
-----
   - dynamic sampling used for this statement

SQL>
SQL> SELECT /*+ rewrite(sales_time_product_mv) */
  2           p.prod_id, p.prod_name, t.time_id, t.week_ending_day,
  3           s.channel_id, s.promo_id, s.cust_id, s.amount_sold
  4    FROM   sales s, products p, times t
  5    WHERE  s.time_id=t.time_id  AND s.prod_id = p.prod_id;
```

```
Execution Plan
----------------------------------------------------------
Plan hash value: 663088863

--------------------------------------------------------------------------------
| Id  | Operation                  | Name                | Rows  | Bytes | Cost (%CPU)|
--------------------------------------------------------------------------------
|   0 | SELECT STATEMENT           |                     | 909K|   95M|  1935    (3)|
|   1 |   MAT_VIEW REWRITE ACCESS FULL| SALES_TIME_PRODUCT_MV |  909K|   95M|  1935    (3)|
--------------------------------------------------------------------------------

Note
-----
   - dynamic sampling used for this statement
```

In order to keep the example simple, I used a REWRITE hint to turn on the query rewrite transformation. You can enable query rewrite to happen automatically as well. But as you notice in the example, when the rewrite does occur, the plan simply shows a full access on the materialized view instead of the entire set of operations required to produce the result set originally. As you can imagine, the time savings can be substantial for complicated queries with large results sets, particularly if the query contains aggregations. For more information on query rewrite and materialized views, refer to *The Oracle Data Warehousing Guide* where you'll find an entire chapter on advanced query rewrite.

Determining the Execution Plan

When a hard parse occurs, Oracle will determine which execution plan is best for the query. An execution plan is simply the set of steps that Oracle will take to access the objects used by your query and return the data that satisfies your query's question. In order to determine the plan, Oracle will gather and use lots of information, as you've already seen. One of the key pieces of information that Oracle will use to determine the plan is statistics. Statistics can be gathered on objects, such as tables and indexes; system statistics can be gathered as well. System statistics provide Oracle data about average speeds for block reads and much more. All this information is used to help Oracle review different scenarios for how a query could execute and to determine which of these scenarios is likely to result in the best performance.

Understanding how Oracle determines execution plans will not only help you write better SQL but will help you to understand how and why performance is affected by certain execution plan choices. After Oracle verifies the syntax and permissions for a SQL statement, it uses the statisics information it collects from the data dictionary to compute a *cost* for each operation and combination of operations that could be used in order to get the result set your query needs. Cost is an internal value Oracle uses to compare different plan operations for the same query to each other with the lowest costed option being considered best. For example, a statement could be executed using a full table scan or an index. Using the statistics, parameters, and other information, Oracle determines which method will result in the fastest execution time.

Since Oracle's main goal in determining an execution plan is to choose a set of operations that will result in the fastest response time possible for the SQL statement being parsed, the more accurate statistics are, the more likely Oracle will be to compute the best execution plan. In the chapters ahead, I'll review details about the various access methods and join methods available and how to review execution plans in detail. For now, I want to make sure you understand what statistics are, why they're important, and how to review them for yourself.

The optimizer is the code path within the Oracle kernel that is responsible for determining the optimal execution plan for a query. So, when I talk about statistics, I'm talking about how the optimizer uses statistics. I use the script named st-all.sql to display statistics for the employees table, as shown in Listing 2-11. I'll use this information to discuss how statistics are used by the optimizer.

Listing 2-11. *Statistics for the Employees Table*

```
SQL> @st-all
Enter the owner name: hr
Enter the table name: employees
====================================================================================
  TABLE STATISTICS
====================================================================================
Owner          : hr
Table name     : employees
Tablespace     : example
Partitioned    : no
Last analyzed  : 06/21/2010 17:27:14
Degree         : 1
# Rows         : 107
# Blocks       : 5
Empty Blocks   : 0
Avg Space      : 0
Avg Row Length : 68
Monitoring?    : yes
Status         : valid


====================================================================================
  COLUMN STATISTICS
====================================================================================
Name            Null?  NDV  # Nulls  # Buckets  AvgLen  Lo-Hi Values
====================================================================================
commission_pct   Y      7    72        1          2      .1 | .4
department_id    Y     11     1       11          3      10 | 110
email            N    107     0        1          8      ABANDA | WTAYLOR
employee_id      N    107     0        1          4      100 | 206
first_name       Y     91     0        1          7      Adam | Winston
hire_date        N     98     0        1          8      06/17/1987 | 04/21/2000
job_id           N     19     0       19          9      AC_ACCOUNT | ST_MAN
last_name        N    102     0        1          8      Abel | Zlotkey
manager_id       Y     18     1       18          4      100 | 205
phone_number     Y    107     0        1         15      011.44.1343.329268 | 650.509.4876
salary           Y     57     0        1          4      2100 | 24000
```

```
=============================================================================================
  INDEX INFORMATION
=============================================================================================

Index Name          BLevel Leaf Blks #Rows Dist Keys LB/Key DB/Key ClustFactor Uniq?
-----------------   ------ --------- ----- --------- ------ ------ ----------- -----
EMP_DEPARTMENT_IX      0          1   106        11      1      1           7 NO
EMP_EMAIL_UK          0          1   107       107      1      1          19 YES
EMP_EMP_ID_PK         0          1   107       107      1      1           2 YES
EMP_JOB_IX            0          1   107        19      1      1           8 NO
EMP_MANAGER_IX        0          1   106        18      1      1           7 NO
EMP_NAME_IX           0          1   107       107      1      1          15 NO

Index Name           Pos# Order Column Name
-----------------   ---------- ----- ------------------------------
emp_department_ix        1 ASC   department_id

emp_email_uk             1 ASC   email

emp_emp_id_pk            1 ASC   employee_id

emp_job_ix               1 ASC   job_id

emp_manager_ix           1 ASC   manager_id

emp_name_ix              1 ASC   last_name
```

The first set of statistics shown in Listing 2-11 is table statistics. These values can be queried from the all_tables view (or dba_tables or user_tables as well). The next section lists column statistics and can be queried from the all_tab_cols view. The final section lists index statistics and can be queried from the all_indexes and all_ind_columns views.

Just like statistics in baseball, the statistics the optimizer uses are intended to be predictive. For example, if a baseball player has a batting average of .333, you'd expect that he'd get a hit about 1 out of every 3 times. That won't always be true, but it is an indicator that most people rely on. Likewise, the optimizer relies on the num_distinct column statistic to compute how frequently values within a column will occur. By default, the assumption is that any value will occur in the same proportion as any other value. If you were looking at the num_distinct statistic for a column named color and it was set to 10, it means that the optimizer is going to expect there to be 10 possible colors and that each color would be present in one tenth of the total rows of the table.

So, let's say that the optimizer was parsing the following query:

```
select * from widgets where color = 'BLUE'
```

The optimizer could choose to read the entire table (TABLE ACCESS FULL operation) or it could choose to use an index (TABLE ACCESS BY INDEX ROWID). But how does it decide which one is best? It uses statistics. I'm just going to use two statistics for this example. I'll use the statistic that indicates the number of rows in the widgets table (num_rows = 1000) and the statistic that indicates how many distinct values are in the color column (num_distinct = 10). The math is quite simple in this case:

```
Number of rows query should return =  (1 / num_distinct) x num_rows
   = (1 / 10) x 1000
   = 100
```

If you think about it for a second, it makes perfect sense. If there are 1000 rows in the table and there are 10 distinct colors present in the table, then if your query only wants rows where the color is blue, you'll be asking for only one tenth of the data, or 100 rows. This computed value is called *selectivity*. By dividing the number of distinct values into 1, you will determine how selectivity any single value is. Easy, right?

Well, as you can imagine, the computations do get more complex, but I hope this simple example helps you see how the optimizer is doing nothing more than some fairly straightforward calculations. No rocket science…really! But, as you can see, even something so simple can be dramatically affected if the values used aren't accurate.

What if, at the time the optimizer parsed this query, the statistics were out of date or missing? For example, let's say that instead of indicating there were 1000 rows and 10 colors, the statistics showed 100 rows in the table and 1 color. Using these values, the number of rows the query should return would be computed to be 100 (1 / 1 x 100). The number of rows is the same as our original computation, but is it really the same? No, it's very different. In the case of the first calcuation, the optimizer would have assumed 10% of 1000 rows were returned while in the second case the 100 rows returned represent all the rows in the table (at least according to the statistics). Can you see how this would influence the optimizer's decision about what operation to choose to retrieve the data?

Understanding the importance of statistics will help you know how to identify performance problems that are not necessarily related to the way you wrote the SQL but instead rooted in issues with the statistics. You could have done everything right, but if the statistics are wrong or inaccurate enough that they don't accurately reflect the reality of your data, you need to be able to pinpoint that quickly—and not spend hours or days trying to fix a code problem that really isn't a code problem.

But just to keep you from getting too happy that you've now got a way to point the finger of blame away from yourself, let me show you an example of how you can write SQL in such a way that the optimizer can't use the statistics properly. In this case, you write a very simple query as follows:

```
select * from car_purchases where manufacturer = 'Ford' and make = 'Focus'
```

The query uses a table containing information about car purchases for all American model cars. For the sake of this example, let's assert that each make of car is only produced by one manufacturer. That means that only Ford will have a Focus. So, what's the problem with the way this query is written? It will certainly return the correct result set, but that's not the only question that needs to be answered. You also need to determine if the optimizer will be able to accurately understand the data given this query formulation. So, let's look at the statistics:

```
num_rows (car_purchases):  1,000,000
num_distinct (manufacturer): 4
num_distinct (make):  1000
```

Since there are two different conditions (or predicates) to apply, you need to first figure out the selectivities of each one by itself. The selectivity of manufacturer would be 1/4 or .25. The selectivity of make would be 1/1000 or .001. Since the predicates are combined with an AND, the two selectivities will be multiplied together to get the correct overall selectivity for both combined. So, the final selectivity would be .00025 (.25 x .001). That means the optimizer will determine that the query will return 250 rows (.00025 X 1,000,000).

Remember that I started by asserting that only one manufacturer would produce a certain make of car. That means that since none of the other three manufacturers could have possibily produced a Focus, the calculation that includes the selectivity for manufacturer is flawed. The truth is that we know all Focus model vehicles have to be manufacturered by Ford. Including the condition where manufacturer = 'Ford' reduces the overall selectivity by 25%. In this case, the true selectivity should have been only the selectivity for the model column alone. If just that predicate had been written, then the selectivity would have been 1/1000 or .001, and the optimizer would have computed that 1,000 rows would be returned by the query instead of 250. That means the answer the optimizer came up with was "off" by a factor of 4. You may look at the difference between 250 and 1,000 and think "so what's the big deal; that's not that far off, is it?" Let's go back to the baseball example and apply this same logic to see if it stands out more to you. If a player normally has a .333 average and you were to tack on another meaningless condition that would require you to multiply his average by .25 as well, what happens? All of a sudden, the high-paid professional athlete looks like a sandlot wanna-be with an average of .083 (.333 x .25)!

Numbers can change everything—and not just in baseball. The calculations the optimizer makes will drastically affect the choice of execution plan operations. Those choices can make the difference between response times of a few seconds to response times of several hours. In this particular example, you get to see what happens when the optimizer doesn't know something that you do. All the optimizer can do is to plug in the statistics values and come up with an answer. If you know something about your data that the optimizer can't know, make sure you code your SQL accordingly and don't lead the optimizer astray.

Executing the Plan and Fetching Rows

After the optimizer determines the plan and stores it in the library cache for later reuse, the next step is to actually execute the plan and fetch the rows of data that satisfy your query. I'm going to cover much more on plan operations and how to read and understand execution plan output in the chapters ahead, but for now, let's talk about what happens after the plan is chosen.

An execution plan is just a set of instructions that tell Oracle which access method to use for each table object and which order and join method to use to join multiple table objects together. Each step in the plan produces a row source that is then joined with another row source until all objects have been accessed and joined. As rows are retrieved that satisfy the query, they must be returned from the database to the application. For result sets of any size, the rows that need to be returned will very likely not all be passed to the application in a single roundtrip. Packets of data will be transmitted from the database and across the network until all rows ultimately arrive back to the user/requestor.

When you execute a query, what appears to you to be a single response consisting of the rows that satisfy your query is really a series of calls executed independently. Your query will complete PARSE, BIND, EXEC and FETCH steps in order to complete. One or more FETCH calls will occur for a query that each return a portion of the rows that satisfy the query. Figure 2-3 shows the steps that actually occur "under the covers" when a SELECT statement is executed.

The network roundtrip between the client and the database for each call will contribute to the overall response time of the statement. There will be only one of each type of database call except for FETCH. As previously mentioned, Oracle will need to execute as many FETCH calls as necessary to retrieve and return all the rows required to satisfy your query.

A single FETCH call will access one or more blocks of data from the buffer cache. Each time a block is accessed, Oracle will take rows from the block and return them to the client in one roundtrip. The number of rows that are returned is a configurable setting called *arraysize*. The arraysize is the number of rows that will be transmitted in a single network roundtrip, if possible. If the size of the rows is too large to fit in a single packet, Oracle will break up the rows into multiple packets, but even then, only a single FETCH call will be needed to provide the specified number of rows.

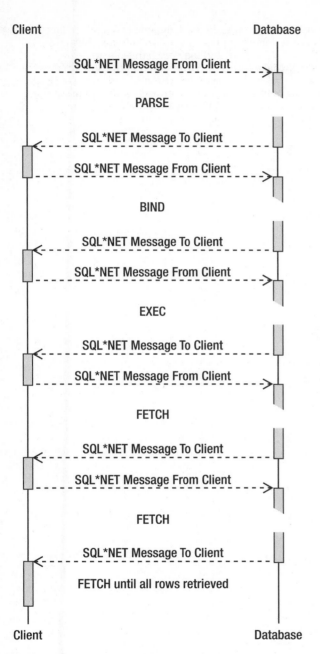

Figure 2-3. *Under the covers of a SELECT statement execution*

The arraysize setting is set programmatically; how it is accomplished will depend on which calling application environment you use. In SQL*Plus, where the default arraysize is 15, you change the arraysize setting using the command SET ARRAYSIZE n. The JDBC default is 10 and may be changed using ((OracleConnection)conn).setDefaultRowPrefetch (n). Make sure to discover your application's arraysize setting and increase it as necessary. The benefit to having a larger arraysize is two-fold: reduction of FETCH calls and reduction of network roundtrips. It may not seem like much, but the impact can be quite stunning. Listing 2-12 demonstrates how logical reads for the same query are reduced by simply changing the arraysize. Note that logical reads are labeled as consistent gets in the autotrace output.

Listing 2-12. *How Arraysize Setting Affects Logical Reads*

```
SQL> set arraysize 15
SQL>
SQL> set autotrace traceonly statistics
SQL>
SQL> select * from order_items ;

Statistics
----------------------------------------------------------
          0  recursive calls
          0  db block gets
         52  consistent gets
          0  physical reads
          0  redo size
      18815  bytes sent via SQL*Net to client
        865  bytes received via SQL*Net from client
         46  SQL*Net roundtrips to/from client
          0  sorts (memory)
          0  sorts (disk)
        664  rows processed

SQL>
SQL> set arraysize 45
SQL> /

Statistics
----------------------------------------------------------
          0  recursive calls
          0  db block gets
         22  consistent gets
          0  physical reads
          0  redo size
      15026  bytes sent via SQL*Net to client
        535  bytes received via SQL*Net from client
         16  SQL*Net roundtrips to/from client
          0  sorts (memory)
          0  sorts (disk)
        664  rows processed
```

Even for this small result set of 664 rows, the difference that increasing the arraysize setting produces is clearly visible. I increased the setting from 15 to 45 and reduced the logical reads from 52 to 22 and reduced the number of network roundtrips from 46 to 16! This change had nothing to do with the SQL statement and everything to do with how Oracle was able to access and return the rows to you. This is just one more example of how understanding how things work can help you help Oracle use less resources and time to do what you ask of it.

SQL Execution – Putting It All Together

Now that I've covered the details, I'm ready to put the whole picture of how a SQL statement executes together. Figure 2-4 shows the steps that are involved when a SQL statement executes.

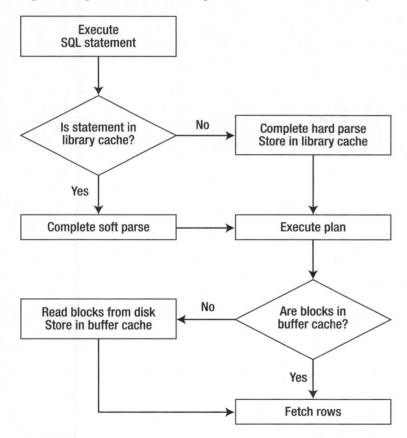

Figure 2-4. *Overview of steps that occur when a SQL statement is executed*

This is a simplified view, but it encapsulates the view of the process. From a big picture perspective, every query must complete PARSE, EXECUTE and FETCH steps. DML statements (INSERT, UPDATE, DELETE) will only need to parse and execute. In addition to these steps, statements that use bind variables will also include a step to read the bind values as part of the parse component.

Summary

Understanding how SQL executes will enable you to write it more effectively. The optimizer is at the heart of every SQL statement you write; writing SQL with the optimizer in mind will help you more than you can imagine. On this point, I'll ask you to trust me for now. I can assure you that understanding the optimizer has been one of the most beneficial pieces of knowledge I've gained. So, don't get frustrated if you're itching to just start looking at syntax and specific SQL code. What you'll end up with by the end of this journey will be well worth it.

At this point, I hope you feel more comfortable with at least some of the key parts of Oracle's architecture that are involved in the execution of the SQL you send to the database. You should also have a flavor for the power of statistics and how they are used by the optimizer. It is outside the scope of this book to go into more detail about this topic, but I'd highly recommend picking up Jonathan Lewis' *Cost-Based Oracle Fundamentals* if you really want to take a deep dive into this subject matter. The more you know, the better equipped you'll be to write SQL that works with the optimizer and not against it.

In the chapter ahead, I'm going to cover the access and join methods the optimizer can choose and review numerous examples of how and why the optimizer does what it does. What I've covered so far has built the foundation for what I'll cover next and each chapter will continue to add to the foundation. The goal is to shed some light on the black box into which you've been throwing SQL and to help you develop an enriched perspective on the importance of what's under the covers of Oracle, in particular the optimizer, and how to properly interact with it.

Access and Join Methods

Karen Morton

The optimizer must determine how to access the data your SQL statements require. You formulate your statement and the optimizer, during a hard parse, will figure out which operations should provide the data in the most effective way possible. Using statistics as the primary guide, the optimizer will compute the cost of the possible alternatives to first access data and then join multiple tables to get the final result set. The more you understand about the different access and join methods the optimizer will consider, the more likely you will be to formulate your SQL to help the optimizer make the best choices. And, when the operation chosen by the optimizer doesn't provide the performance you need, you can more accurately determine which operations would be more suited to produce the response times you want.

After your SQL statement's expressions and conditions are evaluated and any query transformation that might help it more accurately develop the execution plan are complete, the next step in the development of the execution plan is for the optimizer to determine which method of accessing the data will be best. In general, there are only two basic ways to access data: either via a full scan or an index scan. During a full scan (which, by the way, can be a full table scan or a fast full index scan) multiple blocks are read in a single IO operation. Index scans first scan index leaf blocks to retrieve specific rowids and then hand those rowids to the parent table access step to retrieve the actual row data. These accesses are performed via single block reads. If there are additional filters that need to be applied to the data after the table access step, the rows will pass through that filter before being included in the final result set from that step.

The access method that is chosen for a table is used to determine the join methods and join orders that will be used in the final plan. So, if the access method chosen for a table is suboptimal, the likelihood that the whole plan is faulty is high. As discussed in Chapter 2, statistics play a vital role in how accurate the optimizer is in determining the best method. Along with representative statistics, the optimizer will use your query to figure out how much data you are requesting and which access method will provide that data as quickly as possible. Each table in the query will first be evaluated independently from the others to determine its optimal access path. In the next sections, I'll review each of the access methods in detail.

Full Scan Access Methods

When full scanning an object, all the blocks associated with that object must be retrieved and processed to determine if rows in a block match your query's needs. Remember that Oracle must read an entire block into memory in order to get to the row data stored in that block. So, when a full scan occurs, there are actually two things the optimizer (and you) needs to consider: how many blocks must be read and how much data in each block will be thrown away. The idea I want you to grab on to at this point is that the decision as to whether a full scan is the right choice isn't just based on how many rows your query will return. There have been many "rules of thumb" published that state things like "if your query will retrieve more than x% of rows from the table, then a full scan should be chosen." There's more to the decision than just that ROT (Rule Of Thumb = ROT) and I don't want you to get stuck on a rule that limits the consideration that should be given to the choice.

I'm not saying the theory behind the rule of thumb doesn't make logical sense. I'm just saying that it isn't everything that must be considered. In a case where the query will return a very high percentage of rows, the likelihood that a full scan should be use is certainly high, but the trouble with a generalized rule is that the percentage of rows chosen is somewhat arbitrary. Over the years, I've seen this rule published in various books, articles, and forums with percentages varying from 20% to 70%. Why should it change?

How Full Scan Operations are Chosen

At this point, now that I've briefly discussed the problem with generalizing how full table scans are chosen, I can continue with the rest of the story. It's not just about rows, it's also about blocks and about throwaway. The combination of all of these pieces of information may lead to a conclusion that it makes sense to do a full scan even when the percentage of rows is quite small. On the other hand, a full scan may not be chosen even when a large percentage of the rows are returned. Let's walk through an example in Listing 3-1 showing how even when a small percentage of rows satisfies the query, the optimizer may choose a full table scan plan. First, two tables are created that contain the exact same 10,000 rows. Next, the execution plans for the same query against each table are shown. Notice how even though the query returns 100 rows (only 1% of the total data), a full scan plan can be chosen.

Listing 3-1. *Creating Two Test Tables*

```
SQL> create table t1 as
  2  select  trunc((rownum-1)/100) id,
  3          rpad(rownum,100) t_pad
  4  from    dba_source
  5  where   rownum <= 10000;

Table created.

SQL> create index t1_idx1 on t1(id);

Index created.

SQL> exec dbms_stats.gather_table_stats(user,'t1',method_opt=>'FOR ALL COLUMNS SIZE
1',cascade=>TRUE);

PL/SQL procedure successfully completed.
```

```
SQL> create table t2 as
  2  select  mod(rownum,100) id,
  3          rpad(rownum,100) t_pad
  4  from    dba_source
  5  where   rownum <= 10000;

Table created.

SQL> create index t2_idx1 on t2(id);

Index created.

SQL> exec dbms_stats.gather_table_stats(user,'t2',method_opt=>'FOR ALL COLUMNS SIZE
1',cascade=>TRUE);

PL/SQL procedure successfully completed.
```

Both tables will have 10,000 rows. The id columns in both tables will have 100 rows for each value between 0 and 99. So, in terms of the data content, the tables are identical. However, notice that for t1, the id column was populated using the expression trunc((rownum-1)/100) while for t2 the id column was populated using mod(rownum,100). Figure 3-1 shows how the rows might be stored physically in the table's data blocks.

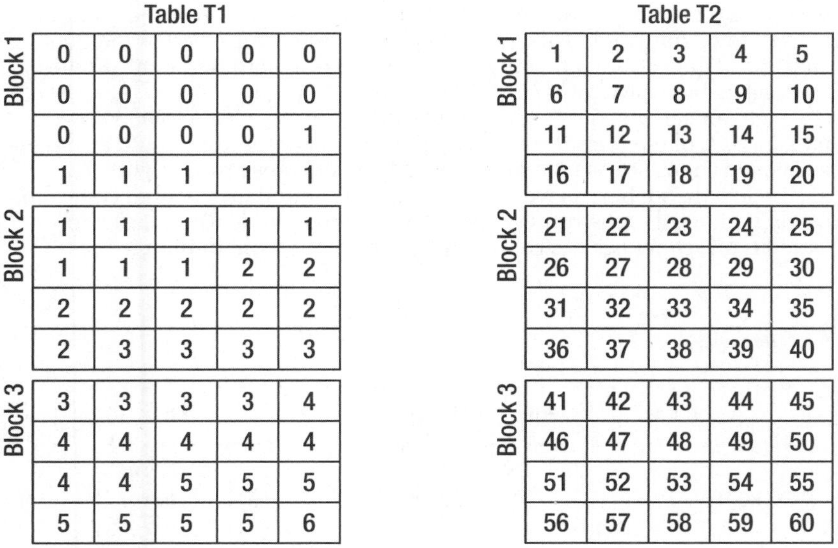

Table T1

0	0	0	0	0
0	0	0	0	0
0	0	0	0	1
1	1	1	1	1
1	1	1	1	1
1	1	1	2	2
2	2	2	2	2
2	3	3	3	3
3	3	3	3	4
4	4	4	4	4
4	4	5	5	5
5	5	5	5	6

(Block 1: rows 1–4, Block 2: rows 5–8, Block 3: rows 9–12)

Table T2

1	2	3	4	5
6	7	8	9	10
11	12	13	14	15
16	17	18	19	20
21	22	23	24	25
26	27	28	29	30
31	32	33	34	35
36	37	38	39	40
41	42	43	44	45
46	47	48	49	50
51	52	53	54	55
56	57	58	59	60

(Block 1: rows 1–4, Block 2: rows 5–8, Block 3: rows 9–12)

Figure 3-1. *Diagram of random vs. sequentially stored row values*

Given what you just inserted, you'd expect to get a result set of 100 rows if you executed a query for any single value of either table. You know how many rows you should get because you just created the tables yourself. But, how could you get an idea of what the tables contained and how those rows were stored otherwise? One way is to run a query and use the COUNT aggregate function, as shown in Listing 3-2.

Listing 3-2. *Count(*) Queries Against Tables T1 and T2*

```
SQL> select count(*) ct from t1 where id = 1 ;

           CT
---------------
          100

1 row selected.

SQL> select count(*) ct from t2 where id = 1 ;

           CT
---------------
          100

1 row selected.
```

Notice that, as expected, you get 100 rows from both tables. If it is reasonable to query actual data to determine the result set sizes, this is a great way to know what to expect from your query. For each table involved in the query you write, you can execute individual queries that apply the predicates for that table and count the number of rows returned. This will help you estimate which access method will likely be best suited for your final query. But, knowing row counts is only part of the information you need. Now, you need to go back to how the data is stored.

Out of 10,000 total rows in each table, if you query for a single value (where id = 1), you know you'll get back 100 rows. That's just 1% of the total rows. Given that small percentage, you'd also then likely expect that the optimizer would choose to use the index on id to access those rows, right? That certainly seems like a logical conclusion, but here is where knowing how your data is stored comes in. If your data is stored sequentially with most of the rows where id = 1 stored physically in just a few blocks, like is the case with table t1, this conclusion is correct, as shown in the explain plan in Listing 3-3.

Listing 3-3. *EXPLAIN PLAN for Query Against T1*

```
-------------------------------------------------------------------------------------
| Id  | Operation                   | Name    | Rows  | Bytes | Cost (%CPU)| Time     |
-------------------------------------------------------------------------------------
|   0 | SELECT STATEMENT            |         |   100 | 10300 |     3   (0)| 00:00:01 |
|   1 |  TABLE ACCESS BY INDEX ROWID| T1      |   100 | 10300 |     3   (0)| 00:00:01 |
|*  2 |   INDEX RANGE SCAN          | T1_IDX1 |   100 |       |     1   (0)| 00:00:01 |
-------------------------------------------------------------------------------------

Predicate Information (identified by operation id):
---------------------------------------------------
   2 - access("ID"=1)
```

So, wouldn't you expect the query against t2 to do exactly the same thing since it will return the same 100 rows? As you can see from the explain plan shown in Listing 3-4, that is not the case at all.

Listing 3-4. *EXPLAIN PLAN for Query Against T2*

```
-------------------------------------------------------------------------
| Id  | Operation          | Name  | Rows  | Bytes | Cost (%CPU)| Time     |
-------------------------------------------------------------------------
|   0 | SELECT STATEMENT   |       |   100 | 10300 |    39   (3)| 00:00:01 |
|*  1 |   TABLE ACCESS FULL| T2    |   100 | 10300 |    39   (3)| 00:00:01 |
-------------------------------------------------------------------------

Predicate Information (identified by operation id):
---------------------------------------------------
   1 - filter("ID"=1)
```

Why didn't the optimizer make the same plan choice for both queries? It's because of *how* the data is stored in each table. The query against table t1 will require that Oracle access only a few blocks to get the 100 rows needed to satisfy the query. Therefore, the index costs out to be the most attractive option. But, the query against table t2 will end up having to read practically every block in the table to get the same 100 rows since the rows are physically scattered throughout all the table blocks. The optimizer calculates that the time to read every block in the table using an index would likely be more than just reading all the blocks in the table using a full table scan and simply throwing away rows that aren't needed from each block. Retrieving the rows from an index would require approximately 200 block accesses. I'll discuss why it's 200 in the next section when I cover index scans. So, the query against t2 will use a TABLE ACCESS FULL operation instead of an index.

This demonstration shows you that there can be differences in the optimizer's plan choices based on how the data is stored. While knowing this may not necessarily make a difference in how you end up writing a query, it can make a difference in how you determine if the performance of the query will meet your SLAs. If you kept seeing a full table scan plan operation, you may think you needed to change or hint your query to force the use of the index. But, doing so might make performance worse in the long term. If you don't understand how the data is stored, you can make poor decisions about what should happen when your query executes.

Full Scans and Throwaway

Always remember that whether or not a full scan will be an effective choice depends on the number of blocks that will need to be read as much as on how many rows will end up in the final result set. How the data is stored plays an important role in the decision, as demonstrated in this example. However, the other key factor in whether or not a full scan is an effective choice is throwaway. Throwaway rows are those rows that are checked against a filter predicate and don't match the filter and are thus rejected from the final result set.

In the previous example, the full table scan operation would have to check all 10,000 rows in the table and throw away 9,900 of them to end up with the final result set of 100 rows. The check on each row is simply the filter predicate on id = 1 (seen in Listing 3-4 in the Predicate Information section for step 1). In order to execute this filter, the CPU will be utilized for each check. That means that while the number of blocks accessed will be limited, there will be quite a bit of CPU resources used to complete the filter checks for each row. The use of the CPU will be factored into the cost of the full scan.

As the number of blocks accessed and the amount of throwaway increases, the more costly the full scan will become. Listing 3-5 is a simple query to show the number of rows and number of blocks for table T2 in your example. Based on the number of blocks shown, the full table scan would access approximately 164 blocks.

Listing 3-5. *Rows and Blocks Statistics for Tables T1 and T2*

```
SQL> select table_name, num_rows, blocks from user_tables where table_name = 'T2' ;

TABLE_NAME                        NUM_ROWS        BLOCKS
------------------------------    ------------    ------------
T2                                    10000           164

1 rows selected.
```

Over time, as rows are added to the table and the table grows larger, the cost of throwing away so many rows would increase enough to cause the optimizer to switch to an index scan operation instead. The point where the optimizer decides to switch over may not necessarily be the point where you achieve optimal performance. You can use hints to force the optimizer to use an index and test to see at what point it might make more sense to use an index, and if the optimizer doesn't choose that path, you can consider using hints or SQL profiles to help. Chapter 16 will cover using hints and profiles so you'll be prepared to use them if you ever need to do so.

Full Scans and Multiblock Reads

Another thing you need to know about full scans is how blocks are read. A full scan operation makes multiblock reads. This means that a single IO call will request several blocks instead of just one. The number of blocks requested will vary and can actually range anywhere from one to the number of blocks specified in the db_file_multiblock_read_count parameter. For example, if the parameter is set to 16 and there are 160 blocks in the table, there could be only 10 calls made to get all the blocks.

I say that only 10 calls *could* be made because of the following limitations on multiblock read calls. Oracle will read db_file_multiblock_read_count blocks unless reading the full number of blocks

- causes Oracle to have to read blocks that cross an extent boundary. In this case, Oracle will read the blocks up to the extent boundary in one call, then issue another call to read the remainder.

- means a block already in the buffer cache would be read again as part of the multiblock read. Oracle will simply read the blocks up to those not already in memory, then issue another read call that skips those blocks to read the rest. This could mean that a multiblock read might only read one block at a time. For example, let's say the multiblock read count was 16 and the range of blocks to be read was between block number 1 and 16. If the even numbered blocks had already been placed into the buffer cache, individual single block reads would be done for each odd numbered block in that range. In that case, 8 read calls would be made—one for each block in that range not already in the buffer cache.

- would exceed an operating system limit for multiblock read sizes. This is dependent on your operating system so it can vary.

Full Scans and the Highwater Mark

A final point of note regarding full table scans is that as the multiblock read calls for the scan are made, Oracle will read blocks up to the highwater mark in the table. The highwater mark marks the last block in the table that has ever had data written to it. To be technically correct, this is actually called the low highwater mark. For your purposes, the low highwater mark is what I'll be discussing and I'll refer to it generically as the highwater mark. For a more detailed discussion, please see the Oracle documentation.

When rows are inserted into a table, blocks are allocated and the rows are placed in the blocks. Figure 3-2 shows how a table might look after a large insert to populate the table.

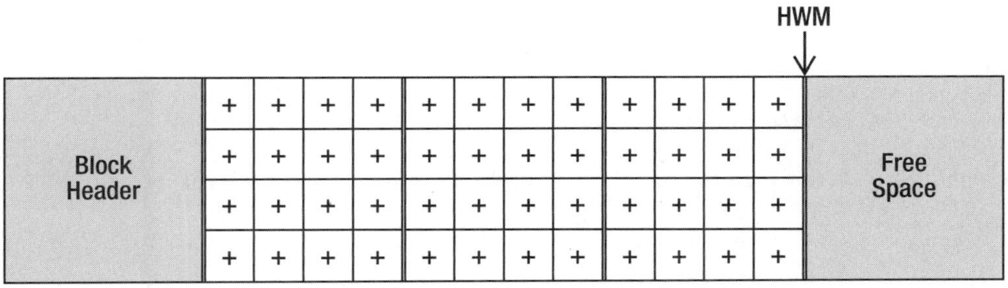

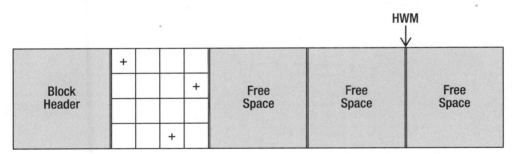

Figure 3-2. *Blocks allocated to a table with rows indicated with a +*

Over the course of normal operations, rows are deleted from the blocks. Figure 3-3 shows how the table might look after a large number of rows have been deleted from the table.

Figure 3-3. *The blocks after rows have been deleted. The HWM remains unchanged.*

Even though almost all the rows have been deleted and some blocks have actually become totally unused, the highwater mark remains the same. When a full scan operation occurs, all blocks up to the highwater mark will be read in and scanned, even if they are empty. This means that many blocks that don't need to be read because they are empty will still be read. Listing 3-6 shows an example of how highwater mark doesn't change, even if all the rows in the table are deleted.

Listing 3-6. *Highwater Mark*

```
SQL> -- List number of allocated blocks (table has 800,000 rows)
SQL> -- The highwater mark is the last block containing data.
SQL> -- While this query doesn't specifically show the HWM, it gives you an idea.
SQL>
SQL> select blocks from user_segments where segment_name = 'T2';

        BLOCKS
---------------
         12288

1 row selected.

SQL> -- List how many blocks contain data
SQL>
SQL> select count(distinct (dbms_rowid.rowid_block_number(rowid))) block_ct from t2 ;

      BLOCK_CT
---------------
         12122

1 row selected.

SQL> -- List the lowest and highest block numbers for this table
SQL>
SQL> select min(dbms_rowid.rowid_block_number(rowid)) min_blk,
max(dbms_rowid.rowid_block_number(rowid)) max_blk from t2 ;

       MIN_BLK         MAX_BLK
--------------- ---------------
       1302492         1386248

1 row selected.

SQL> -- Check the space usage in the table
SQL> get space_usage.sql
  1  declare
  2      l_tabname         varchar2(30) := '&1';
  3      l_fs1_bytes number;
  4      l_fs2_bytes number;
  5      l_fs3_bytes number;
  6      l_fs4_bytes number;
  7      l_fs1_blocks number;
  8      l_fs2_blocks number;
  9      l_fs3_blocks number;
 10      l_fs4_blocks number;
```

```
11    l_full_bytes number;
12    l_full_blocks number;
13    l_unformatted_bytes number;
14    l_unformatted_blocks number;
15  begin
16    dbms_space.space_usage(
17        segment_owner     => user,
18        segment_name      => l_tabname,
19        segment_type      => 'TABLE',
20        fs1_bytes         => l_fs1_bytes,
21        fs1_blocks        => l_fs1_blocks,
22        fs2_bytes         => l_fs2_bytes,
23        fs2_blocks        => l_fs2_blocks,
24        fs3_bytes         => l_fs3_bytes,
25        fs3_blocks        => l_fs3_blocks,
26        fs4_bytes         => l_fs4_bytes,
27        fs4_blocks        => l_fs4_blocks,
28        full_bytes        => l_full_bytes,
29        full_blocks       => l_full_blocks,
30        unformatted_blocks => l_unformatted_blocks,
31        unformatted_bytes  => l_unformatted_bytes
32    );
33    dbms_output.put_line('0-25% Free   = '||l_fs1_blocks||' Bytes = '||l_fs1_bytes);
34    dbms_output.put_line('25-50% Free  = '||l_fs2_blocks||' Bytes = '||l_fs2_bytes);
35    dbms_output.put_line('50-75% Free  = '||l_fs3_blocks||' Bytes = '||l_fs3_bytes);
36    dbms_output.put_line('75-100% Free = '||l_fs4_blocks||' Bytes = '||l_fs4_bytes);
37    dbms_output.put_line('Full Blocks  = '||l_full_blocks||' Bytes = '||l_full_bytes);
38* end;
SQL>
SQL> @space_usage T2
0-25% Free   = 0 Bytes = 0
25-50% Free  = 0 Bytes = 0
50-75% Free  = 0 Bytes = 0
75-100% Free = 16 Bytes = 131072
Full Blocks  = 12121 Bytes = 99295232

PL/SQL procedure successfully completed.

SQL> -- Note that most blocks are full
SQL> -- A full table scan would have to read all the blocks (12137 total)
SQL>
SQL> -- Delete all the rows from the table
SQL> delete from t2 ;

800000 rows deleted.
```

```
SQL>
SQL> commit ;

Commit complete.

SQL> -- Check the space usage after all rows are deleted
SQL> @space_usage T2
0-25% Free    = 0 Bytes = 0
25-50% Free   = 0 Bytes = 0
50-75% Free   = 0 Bytes = 0
75-100% Free  = 12137 Bytes = 99426304
Full Blocks   = 0 Bytes = 0

PL/SQL procedure successfully completed.

SQL> -- Note that blocks are now free but the same space is still consumed
SQL> -- A full table scan would still read 12137 blocks
SQL> -- List number of blocks (table has 0 rows)
SQL> select blocks from user_segments where segment_name = 'T2';

        BLOCKS
---------------
         12288

1 row selected.

SQL> -- List how many blocks contain data
SQL> select count(distinct (dbms_rowid.rowid_block_number(rowid))) block_ct from t2 ;

       BLOCK_CT
---------------
              0

1 row selected.

SQL> -- Execute a full table scan and note the consistent gets (logical block reads)
SQL>
SQL> set autotrace traceonly
SQL> select * from t2 ;

no rows selected
```

```
Execution Plan
-----------------------------------------------------------
Plan hash value: 1513984157

---------------------------------------------------------------------------
| Id | Operation         | Name | Rows | Bytes | Cost (%CPU)| Time     |
---------------------------------------------------------------------------
|  0 | SELECT STATEMENT  |      |   1  |   65  | 2674   (1)| 00:00:33 |
|  1 |  TABLE ACCESS FULL| T2   |   1  |   65  | 2674   (1)| 00:00:33 |
---------------------------------------------------------------------------
Statistics
-----------------------------------------------------------
          0  recursive calls
          0  db block gets
      12148  consistent gets
      11310  physical reads
          0  redo size
        332  bytes sent via SQL*Net to client
        370  bytes received via SQL*Net from client
          1  SQL*Net roundtrips to/from client
          0  sorts (memory)
          0  sorts (disk)
          0  rows processed

SQL> set autotrace off
SQL>

SQL> -- Truncate the table to deallocate the space and reset the HWM
SQL> truncate table t2 ;

Table truncated.

SQL> -- Check the space usage after table is truncated
SQL> @space_usage T2
0-25% Free   = 0 Bytes = 0
25-50% Free  = 0 Bytes = 0
50-75% Free  = 0 Bytes = 0
75-100% Free = 0 Bytes = 0
Full Blocks  = 0 Bytes = 0

PL/SQL procedure successfully completed.

SQL> -- Note that the space has been deallocated
SQL>
SQL> -- List number of blocks (table has 0 rows and all space recovered)
SQL> select blocks from user_segments where segment_name = 'T2';
```

```
        BLOCKS
---------------
              8
```

1 row selected.

```
SQL> set autotrace traceonly
SQL> select * from t2 ;
```

no rows selected

Execution Plan

Plan hash value: 1513984157

```
-------------------------------------------------------------------------
| Id  | Operation          | Name | Rows  | Bytes | Cost (%CPU)| Time     |
-------------------------------------------------------------------------
|   0 | SELECT STATEMENT   |      |     1 |    65 |  2674   (1)| 00:00:33 |
|   1 |  TABLE ACCESS FULL | T2   |     1 |    65 |  2674   (1)| 00:00:33 |
-------------------------------------------------------------------------
```

Statistics

```
          0  recursive calls
          0  db block gets
          3  consistent gets
          0  physical reads
          0  redo size
        332  bytes sent via SQL*Net to client
        370  bytes received via SQL*Net from client
          1  SQL*Net roundtrips to/from client
          0  sorts (memory)
          0  sorts (disk)
          0  rows processed
```

SQL> set autotrace off

I hope this example illustrates that even when a full table scan is the "right" plan operation choice, the overhead of reading additional empty blocks can mean performance takes a significant hit. For tables that are frequently loaded and unloaded (using DELETE instead of TRUNCATE), you may discover that response time suffers. This occurs often with tables that are used for ETL or any form of load/process/unload activity. Now that you know how full scan behavior can be affected, you will be able to diagnose and correct related performance problems more easily.

Index Scan Access Methods

If you have a book about U.S. Presidents and want to find information on Jimmy Carter, you could start on the first page and visually scan each page until you came to the section of the book about Carter. However, it would take a lot of time to do that scan so you might find it more expedient to look up Carter in the book's index. Once you have the page number, you can go directly to that location. An index scan operation is conceptually similar to using an index in a book.

The default index type is a B-tree index and is the only type I am going to discuss in this chapter. Indexes are created on one or more table columns or column expressions and store the column values along with a rowid. There are other pieces of information stored in the index entry, but for your purposes you're only going to concern yourselves with the column value and the rowid. The rowid is a pseudocolumn that uniquely identifies a row within a table. It is the internal address of a physical table row and consists of an address that points to the data file that contains the table block that contains the row and the address of the row within the block that leads directly to the row itself. Listing 3-7 shows how to decode the rowid into a readable form.

Listing 3-7. *Decoding rowid*

```
SQL> column filen format a50 head 'File Name'
SQL>
SQL> select  e.rowid ,
  2              (select file_name
  3                  from dba_data_files
  4                where file_id = dbms_rowid.rowid_to_absolute_fno(e.rowid, user, 'EMP'))
filen,
  5              dbms_rowid.rowid_block_number(e.rowid) block_no,
  6              dbms_rowid.rowid_row_number(e.rowid) row_no
  7      from  emp e
  8    where  e.ename = 'KING' ;

ROWID              File Name                                            BLOCK_NO   ROW_NO
------------------ -------------------------------------------------- --------- --------
AAANprAAEAAAWVvAAI C:\ORACLE\PRODUCT\11.2.0\ORADATA\DB\USERS01.DBF       91503        8

1 row selected.
```

As you can see, the rowid points to the exact location of a particular row. Therefore, when an index is used to access a row, all that happens is that a match is made on the access criteria provided in the predicate, then the rowid is used to access the specific file/block/row of data. Block accesses made via an index scan are made using single-block reads. That makes sense when you consider how the rowid is used. Once the index entry is read, only the single block of data identified by that rowid is retrieved; once it is retrieved, only the row specified by the rowid is accessed.

What this means is that for each row that will be retrieved via an index scan, at least two block accesses will be required: at least one index block and one data block. If your final result set contains 100 rows and those 100 rows are retrieved using an index scan, there would be at least 200 block accesses required. I keep saying "at least" because depending on the size of the index, Oracle may have to access several index blocks initially in order to get to the first matching column value needed.

Index Structure

An index is logically structured, as shown in Figure 3-4. Indexes are comprised of one or more levels of branch blocks and a single level of leaf blocks. Branch blocks hold information about the range of values contained in the next level of branch blocks and are used to search the index structure to find the needed leaf blocks. The *height* of an index is the number of branch levels between the initial branch block (referred to as the root block) and the leaf blocks. The leaf blocks contain the indexed values and the rowid for each in sorted order as mentioned previously.

If you start with a newly created, empty table and create an index on that table, the index consists of one, empty block. In this case, the single block acts as both a root block and a leaf block. The height of the index will be 1. There is another statistic called *blevel* that represents the number of branch levels present in an index. In this case, the blevel would be 0.

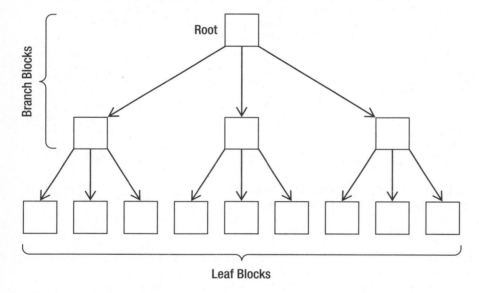

Figure 3-4. *Logical view of an index structure*

As new rows are added to the table, new index entries are added to the block, and it will fill to the point where additional entries won't fit. At this point, Oracle will allocate two new index blocks and place all the index entries into these two new leaf blocks. The previously filled single root block is now replaced with pointers to the two new blocks. The pointers are made up of the Relative Block Address (RBA) to the new index blocks and a value indicating the lowest indexed value (i.e. lowest in sorted order) found in the referenced leaf block. With this information in the root block, Oracle can now search the index to find specific leaf blocks that hold a requested value. At this point, the index now has a height of 2 and a blevel of 1.

Over time, as more rows are inserted into the table, index entries are added into the two leaf blocks that were just created. As these leaf blocks fill up, Oracle will add one leaf block and allocate the index entries between the full and new leaf blocks. Every time a leaf block fills up and splits, a new pointer for this new leaf block will be added to the root block. Eventually, the root block will fill up and the process repeats with the root being split into two new branch blocks. When this split occurs, the height of the index will increase to 3 and the blevel to 2.

At this point, as new index entries are made, the leaf blocks will fill and split, but instead of a new pointer being added to the root block, the pointer will be added to the corresponding branch block. Eventually the branch blocks will fill and split. It is at this point that a new entry gets added to the root block. As this process continues, eventually the root block will fill up and split increasing the height of the index once again. Just remember that the only time the height of an index increases is when the root block splits. For that reason, all leaf blocks will always be at the same distance from the root block. This is why you'll hear the term *balanced* used in regard to Oracle B-tree indexes. Indexes are guaranteed to remain height-balanced.

Why go through all this detail? Understanding how an index structure is created and maintained will help you understand how the various types of index scans work. Now that you have an understanding of how indexes are structured, you're ready to discover how the different index scans traverse that structure to retrieve row data that your query needs.

Index Scan Types

There are several different types of index scans but each share some common ground in how they must traverse the index structure to access the leaf block entries that match the values being searched. First, the root block of the index is accessed with a single block read. The next step is to read a branch block. Depending on the height of the index, one or more branch blocks may need to be read. Each read is for a separate single block. Finally, the first index leaf block that contains the start of the index entries needed is read. If the height of an index is 4, to get to the leaf block needed, 4 single block reads will be performed. At this point, the rowid for the first matching index value in the leaf block is read and used to make a single block read call to retrieve the table block where the entire row resides. Therefore, in this example, to retrieve a single row from a table using an index, Oracle would have to read 5 blocks: 4 index blocks and 1 table block.

The various index scan types you will review are index range scan, index unique scan, index full scan, index skip scan, and index fast full scan. An index fast full scan is actually more like a full table scan, but since they are scans against an index structure I'll cover them in this section.

Before I review the different scan types, I want to point out a very important index statistic called *clustering factor*. The clustering factor statistic of an index helps the optimizer generate the cost of using the index and is a measure of how well ordered the table data is as related to the indexed values. Recall that index entries are stored in sorted order while table data is stored in random order. Unless an effort has been made to specifically load data into a table in a specific order, you are not guaranteed where individual rows of data will end up. For example, rows from the orders table that share the same order_date may not all reside in the same blocks. They are likely to be scattered randomly across the blocks in the table.

The clustering factor of an index indicates to the optimizer if data rows containing the same indexed values will be located in the same or a small set of contiguous blocks, or if rows will be scattered across numerous table blocks. Figure 3-5 shows how the rows might be stored physically in the table's data blocks.

In the diagram showing table T1, you see how rows containing the value 2 were loaded into the same block. But, in table T2, rows with a value of 2 are not loaded in contiguous blocks. In this example, an index on this column for table T1 would have a lower clustering factor. Lower numbers that are closer to the number of table blocks are used to indicate highly ordered, or clustered, rows of data based on the indexed value. The clustering factor for this column in table T2, however, would be higher and typically closer to the number of rows in the table. Listing 3-8 shows the clustering factor statistic for each of these two tables.

Table T1

Block 1				
0	0	0	0	0
0	0	0	0	0
0	0	0	0	1
1	1	1	1	1

Block 2				
1	1	1	1	1
1	1	1	2	2
2	2	2	2	2
2	3	3	3	3

Block 3				
3	3	3	3	4
4	4	4	4	4
4	4	5	5	5
5	5	5	5	6

Table T2

Block 1				
1	2	3	4	5
6	7	8	9	10
11	12	13	14	15
16	17	18	19	20

Block 2				
21	22	23	24	25
26	27	28	29	30
31	32	33	34	35
36	37	38	39	40

Block 3				
41	42	43	44	45
46	47	48	49	50
51	52	53	54	55
56	57	58	59	60

Figure 3-5. *Diagram of random vs. sequentially loaded row values*

Listing 3-8. *Index clustering_factor*

```
SQL> select t.table_name||'.'||i.index_name idx_name,
  2          i.clustering_factor, t.blocks, t.num_rows
  3     from user_indexes i, user_tables t
  4    where i.table_name = t.table_name
  5      and t.table_name in ('T1','T2')
  6    order by t.table_name, i.index_name;

IDX_NAME         CLUSTERING_FACTOR      BLOCKS        NUM_ROWS
---------------  -----------------  ---------------  ---------------
T1.T1_N1                       152              164            10000
T2.T2_N1                     10000              164            10000

2 rows selected.
```

As demonstrated earlier in this chapter (see Listings 3-3 and 3-4), the optimizer would choose an index scan when querying table T1 but a full table scan when querying table T2. The clustering_factor was the key piece of information that helped the optimizer make that decision.

So, while clustering factor is a statistic associated with an index, it is computed by looking at the blocks of data in the table. When computing clustering factor, Oracle will do something similar to what is shown in Listing 3-9.

Listing 3-9. *Computing Index clustering_factor*

```
SQL> select t.table_name||'.'||i.index_name idx_name,
  2          i.clustering_factor, t.blocks, t.num_rows
  3    from all_indexes i, all_tables t
  4   where i.table_name = t.table_name
  5     and t.table_name = 'EMPLOYEES'
  6     and t.owner = 'HR'
  7     and i.index_name = 'EMP_DEPARTMENT_IX'
  8   order by t.table_name, i.index_name;

IDX_NAME                          CLUSTERING_FACTOR BLOCKS NUM_ROWS
-------------------------------   ----------------- ------ --------
EMPLOYEES.EMP_DEPARTMENT_IX                       7      5      107

1 row selected.
SQL> select department_id, last_name, blk_no,
  2          lag (blk_no,1,blk_no) over (order by department_id) prev_blk_no,
  3          case when blk_no != lag (blk_no,1,blk_no) over (order by department_id)
  4                  or rownum = 1
  5               then '***   +1'
  6               else null
  7          end cluf_ct
  8    from (
  9    select department_id, last_name,
 10           dbms_rowid.rowid_block_number(rowid) blk_no
 11     from hr.employees
 12    where department_id is not null
 13    order by department_id
 14    );

DEPARTMENT_ID LAST_NAME        BLK_NO PREV_BLK_NO CLUF_CT
------------- ---------------- ------ ----------- -------
           10 Whalen              84          84 ***   +1
           20 Hartstein           84          84
           20 Fay                 84          84
           30 Raphaely            88          84 ***   +1
           30 Colmenares          88          88
...
           30 Himuro              88          88
           40 Mavris              84          88 ***   +1
           50 OConnell            84          84
           50 Grant               84          84
           50 Weiss               88          84 ***   +1
           50 Fripp               88          88
           50 Kaufling            88          88
...
```

70	Baer	84	88 ***	+1
80	Bates	88	84 ***	+1
80	Smith	88	88	
100	Sciarra	88	88	
110	Gietz	84	88 ***	+1
110	Higgins	84	84	

106 rows selected.

As I mentioned, this isn't precisely how the clustering factor is computed, but this query can help you see how it is done in general terms. Note that I deleted some of the output rows for brevity, but left enough of the output so you could see where the block number for the row changed from the previous row's block number. Clustering factor is computed by adding one to a counter each time the block number for the current row is different from the previous row. In this example, that happens seven times. What this number is supposed to represent is seven *different* table blocks that hold data for this table. As you can see from the output, there are really only two blocks that contain data (block numbers 84 and 88). In reality, the clustering factor isn't exactly accurate. In this case, it is off by a factor of 3.5.

Although most of the time this inaccuracy in the way clustering_factor is computed won't make enough difference to cause the optimizer to over-cost the index enough to prevent it from being chosen, it is possible that situation could occur. If the optimizer doesn't choose the index you expect, it may choose another index that can satisfy the predicate that contains similar columns. In these situations, you may need to do a careful analysis of the indexes you have created to see if there is a way to consolidate several indexes into a single compound index. Do not make the mistake of rebuilding the index thinking it will help "fix" the clustering_factor. As I have demonstrated here, the clustering_factor is related to the table data, not the index. So, rebuilding the index won't have any effect on it.

On the other hand, if you start to consider rebuilding the table to improve the clustering_factor, proceed with caution. Tables typically have numerous indexes. You can't rebuild the table to make the order match one index without causing it to be less ordered by other columns. So, a rebuild may help in relation to one index but hurt others. Also, rebuilding tables is typically a time-consuming and resource-intensive process. Just because you rebuild the table in a particular order today doesn't mean it's going to stay in that order over time as rows are inserted, updated, and deleted. As you proceed through the rest of the book, you'll learn enough to understand when clustering_factor may be part of a problem and you'll likely be able to find ways to adjust for it if needed.

■**NOTE** In each of the following examples that explain plan output, the output has been edited; I've removed the Time column for brevity.

Index Unique Scan

An index unique scan is chosen when a predicate contains a condition using a column defined with a UNIQUE or PRIMARY KEY index. These types of indexes guarantee that only one row will ever be returned for a specified value. In this cases, the index structure will be traversed from root to leaf block to a single entry, retrieve the rowid, and use it to access the table data block containing the one row. The

TABLE ACCESS BY INDEX ROWID step in the plan indicates the table data block access. The number of block accesses required will always be equal to the height of the index plus one unless there are special circumstances like the row is chained or contains a LOB that is stored elsewhere. Listing 3-10 shows an example query that will produce an index unique scan plan.

Listing 3-10. *Index Unique Scan*

```
SQL> set autotrace traceonly explain
SQL>
SQL> select * from hr.employees where employee_id = 100;

Execution Plan
----------------------------------------------------------
Plan hash value: 1833546154

--------------------------------------------------------------------------------
|Id  | Operation                    | Name          | Rows  | Bytes | Cost (%CPU)|
--------------------------------------------------------------------------------
|  0 | SELECT STATEMENT             |               |     1 |    82 |     2  (0)|
|  1 |  TABLE ACCESS BY INDEX ROWID | EMPLOYEES     |     1 |    82 |     2  (0)|
|* 2 |   INDEX UNIQUE SCAN          | EMP_EMP_ID_PK |     1 |       |     1  (0)|
--------------------------------------------------------------------------------

Predicate Information (identified by operation id):
---------------------------------------------------

   2 - access("EMPLOYEE_ID"=100)
```

Index range scan

An index range scan is chosen when a predicate contains a condition that will return a range of data. The index can be unique or non-unique as it is the condition that determines whether or not multiple rows will be returned or not. The conditions specified can use operators such as <, >, LIKE, BETWEEN and even =. In order for a range scan to be selected, the range will need to be fairly selective. The larger the range, the more likely a full scan operation will be chosen instead. Listing 3-11 shows an example of a query that will produce an index range scan plan.

Listing 3-11. *Index Range Scan*

```
SQL> set autotrace traceonly explain
SQL>
SQL> select * from hr.employees where department_id = 60 ;

Execution Plan
----------------------------------------------------------
Plan hash value: 2056577954
```

```
---------------------------------------------------------------------------------
| Id  | Operation                    | Name             | Rows | Bytes | Cost (%CPU)|
---------------------------------------------------------------------------------
|   0 | SELECT STATEMENT             |                  |    5 |  340  |   2   (0)|
|   1 |  TABLE ACCESS BY INDEX ROWID | EMPLOYEES        |    5 |  340  |   2   (0)|
|*  2 |   INDEX RANGE SCAN           | EMP_DEPARTMENT_IX|    5 |       |   1   (0)|
---------------------------------------------------------------------------------

Predicate Information (identified by operation id):
---------------------------------------------------

   2 - access("DEPARTMENT_ID"=60)
```

A range scan will traverse the index structure from the root block to the first leaf block containing an entry matching the specified condition. From that starting point, a rowid will be retrieved from the index entry and the table data block will be retrieved (TABLE ACCESS BY INDEX ROWID). After the first row is retrieved, the index leaf block will be accessed again and the next entry will be read to retrieve the next rowid. This back-and-forth between the index leaf blocks and the data blocks will continue until all the matching index entries have been read. Therefore, the number of block accesses required will include the number of branch blocks in the index (this can be found using the blevel statistic for the index) plus the number of index entries that match the condition multiplied by two. You have to multiply by two because each retrieval of a single row in the table will require that the index leaf block be accessed to retrieve the rowid and then the table data block will be accessed using that rowid. Therefore, if the example returned 5 rows and the blevel was 3, the total block accesses required would (5 rows x 2) + 3 = 13.

If the range of entries matching the condition is large enough, it is likely that more than one leaf block will have to be accessed. When that is the case, the next leaf block needed can be read using a pointer stored in the current leaf block that leads to the next leaf block (there's also a pointer to the previous leaf block). Since these pointers exist, there is no need to go back up to the branch block to determine where to go next.

When an index range scan is chosen, the predicate information in the plan will show the condition used to access the index. In the example, step 2 in the plan has an asterisk beside it. This is an indicator that predicate information for that step is listed below the plan. In that section, you see an entry showing that the index entry access was determined using the condition DEPARTMENT_ID = 60.

There are cases when predicates that you might think should use index range scans do not. For example, if you use a LIKE operator with a condition that starts with a wildcard such as '%abc', the optimizer will not choose a range scan on an index for that column because the condition is too broad. Another similar case is when you have a predicate that uses a column that isn't the leading column in a compound index. In that case, as I'll discuss shortly, it is more likely for an index skip scan to be chosen instead.

One final nuance of an index range scan that I'd like to note is the ability of an ascending ordered index (the default) to return rows in descending sorted order. The optimizer may choose to use an index to access rows via an index even if a full scan might be warranted. This may occur when the query includes an ORDER BY clause on a column that is indexed. Since the index is stored in sorted order, reading rows using the index will mean the rows are retrieved in sorted order and the need to do a separate sort step can be avoided. But, what if the ORDER BY clause is requested in descending order? Since the index is stored in ascending order, the index couldn't be used for a descending order request, could it? Listing 3-12 shows an example of this behavior and the special range scan operation used to handle it.

Listing 3-12. *An Index Range Scan Used to Avoid a Sort*

```
SQL> set autotrace traceonly explain
SQL>
SQL> select * from hr.employees
  2    where department_id in (90, 100)
  3    order by department_id  desc;

Execution Plan
----------------------------------------------------------
Plan hash value: 3707994525
```

Id	Operation	Name	Rows	Bytes	Cost (%CPU)
0	SELECT STATEMENT		9	612	2 (0)
1	INLIST ITERATOR				
2	TABLE ACCESS BY INDEX ROWID	EMPLOYEES	9	612	2 (0)
* 3	INDEX RANGE SCAN DESCENDING	EMP_DEPARTMENT_IX	9		1 (0)

```
Predicate Information (identified by operation id):
---------------------------------------------------

   3 - access("DEPARTMENT_ID"=90 OR "DEPARTMENT_ID"=100)
       filter("DEPARTMENT_ID"=90 OR "DEPARTMENT_ID"=100)
```

In this case, the index entries are actually read in reverse order to avoid the need for a separate sort.

Index Full Scan

An index full scan is chosen under several conditions including: when there is no predicate but the column list can be satisfied through an index on a column, the predicate contains a condition on a non-leading column in an index, or the data can be retrieved via an index in sorted order and save the need for a separate sort step. Listing 3-13 shows an example of each of these cases.

Listing 3-13. *Index Full Scan Examples*

```
SQL> set autotrace traceonly explain
SQL> select email from hr.employees ;

Execution Plan
----------------------------------------------------------
Plan hash value: 2196514524
```

```
-------------------------------------------------------------
| Id | Operation          | Name         | Rows | Bytes | Cost (%CPU)|
-------------------------------------------------------------
|  0 | SELECT STATEMENT   |              |  107 |  856  |   1   (0)|
|  1 |  INDEX FULL SCAN   | EMP_EMAIL_UK |  107 |  856  |   1   (0)|
-------------------------------------------------------------
```

```
SQL>
SQL> select first_name, last_name from hr.employees
  2  where first_name like 'A%' ;

Execution Plan
-------------------------------------------------------------
Plan hash value: 2228653197
```

```
-------------------------------------------------------------
| Id | Operation          | Name         | Rows | Bytes | Cost (%CPU)|
-------------------------------------------------------------
|  0 | SELECT STATEMENT   |              |   3  |  45   |   1   (0)|
|* 1 |  INDEX FULL SCAN   | EMP_NAME_IX  |   3  |  45   |   1   (0)|
-------------------------------------------------------------
```

```
Predicate Information (identified by operation id):
---------------------------------------------------

   1 - access("FIRST_NAME" LIKE 'A%')
       filter("FIRST_NAME" LIKE 'A%')
```

```
SQL> select * from hr.employees order by employee_id ;

Execution Plan
-------------------------------------------------------------
Plan hash value: 2186312383
```

```
-----------------------------------------------------------------------
| Id | Operation                   | Name         | Rows | Bytes | Cost (%CPU)|
-----------------------------------------------------------------------
|  0 | SELECT STATEMENT            |              |  107 | 7276  |   3   (0)|
|  1 |  TABLE ACCESS BY INDEX ROWID| EMPLOYEES    |  107 | 7276  |   3   (0)|
|  2 |   INDEX FULL SCAN           | EMP_EMP_ID_PK|  107 |       |   1   (0)|
-----------------------------------------------------------------------
```

```
SQL> select * from hr.employees order by employee_id desc ;

Execution Plan
-------------------------------------------------------------
Plan hash value: 2761389396
```

```
-----------------------------------------------------------------------
| Id  | Operation                    | Name          | Rows  | Bytes | Cost (%CPU)|
-----------------------------------------------------------------------
|   0 | SELECT STATEMENT             |               |   107 |  7276 |    3   (0)|
|   1 |  TABLE ACCESS BY INDEX ROWID | EMPLOYEES     |   107 |  7276 |    3   (0)|
|   2 |   INDEX FULL SCAN DESCENDING | EMP_EMP_ID_PK |   107 |       |    1   (0)|
-----------------------------------------------------------------------
```

An index full scan operation will scan every leaf block in the index structure, read the rowids for each entry, and retrieve the table rows. Every leaf block is accessed. This is often more efficient than doing a full table scan as the index blocks will contain more entries than the table blocks will, therefore fewer overall blocks may need to be accessed. In cases where the columns needed to satisfy the column list are all present as part of the index entry, the table access step is avoided as well. This means that choosing an index full scan operation will be more efficient than reading all the table blocks.

You may have noticed in the last example that the index full scan operation also has the ability to read in descending order to avoid the need for a separate descending ordered sort request. There is another optimization for index full scans. This optimization occurs when a query requests the minimum or maximum column value and that column is indexed. Listing 3-14 shows an example of this operation choice.

Listing 3-14. *Index Full Scan Min/Max Optimization*

```
SQL> set autotrace traceonly explain
SQL> select min(department_id) from hr.employees ;

Execution Plan
----------------------------------------------------------
Plan hash value: 613773769
```

```
-----------------------------------------------------------------------
| Id  | Operation                 | Name             | Rows  | Bytes | Cost (%CPU)|
-----------------------------------------------------------------------
|   0 | SELECT STATEMENT          |                  |     1 |     3 |    3   (0)|
|   1 |  SORT AGGREGATE           |                  |     1 |     3 |           |
|   2 |   INDEX FULL SCAN (MIN/MAX)| EMP_DEPARTMENT_IX |   107 |   321 |           |
-----------------------------------------------------------------------
```

```
SQL> select max(department_id) from hr.employees ;

Execution Plan
----------------------------------------------------------
Plan hash value: 613773769
```

```
--------------------------------------------------------------------------------
| Id  | Operation                   | Name             | Rows  | Bytes | Cost (%CPU)|
--------------------------------------------------------------------------------
|   0 | SELECT STATEMENT            |                  |     1 |     3 |     3  (0)|
|   1 |  SORT AGGREGATE             |                  |     1 |     3 |           |
|   2 |   INDEX FULL SCAN (MIN/MAX) | EMP_DEPARTMENT_IX |  107 |   321 |           |
--------------------------------------------------------------------------------
```

SQL> select min(department_id), max(department_id) from hr.employees ;

Execution Plan

Plan hash value: 1756381138

```
---------------------------------------------------------------------
| Id  | Operation           | Name      | Rows  | Bytes | Cost (%CPU)|
---------------------------------------------------------------------
|   0 | SELECT STATEMENT    |           |     1 |     3 |     3  (0)|
|   1 |  SORT AGGREGATE     |           |     1 |     3 |           |
|   2 |   TABLE ACCESS FULL | EMPLOYEES |   107 |   321 |     3  (0)|
---------------------------------------------------------------------
```

SQL> select (select min(department_id) from hr.employees) min_id,
  2   (select max(department_id) from hr.employees) max_id
  3   from dual
  4

Execution Plan

Plan hash value: 2189307159

```
--------------------------------------------------------------------------------
| Id  | Operation                   | Name             | Rows  | Bytes | Cost (%CPU)|
--------------------------------------------------------------------------------
|   0 | SELECT STATEMENT            |                  |     1 |       |     2  (0)|
|   1 |  SORT AGGREGATE             |                  |     1 |     3 |           |
|   2 |   INDEX FULL SCAN (MIN/MAX) | EMP_DEPARTMENT_IX |  107 |   321 |           |
|   3 |  SORT AGGREGATE             |                  |     1 |     3 |           |
|   4 |   INDEX FULL SCAN (MIN/MAX) | EMP_DEPARTMENT_IX |  107 |   321 |           |
|   5 |  FAST DUAL                  |                  |     1 |       |     2  (0)|
--------------------------------------------------------------------------------
```

As the example shows, when a MIN or MAX aggregate is requested, the optimizer can choose a special optimized version of the index full scan operation. In these special cases, when the index is used to quickly retrieve the minimum value, it will be the first entry in the first index leaf block; when it retrieves the maximum value, it will be the last entry in the last index leaf block. This makes perfect sense as the index is stored in sorted order so the minimum and maximum values have to be at either end of the first and last leaf blocks. But the really great part is that in these special cases, the index full scan isn't really a full scan—it is a scan of only root block, one or more branch blocks, and first or last leaf blocks. This means that finding these values is very fast and very low cost in terms of the number of block accesses required. While the index full scan operation title may make it seem a bit confusing as index full scans typically read all the index leaf blocks, this optimization is a nice win in terms of performance.

I did include an example of where the query included both a MIN and a MAX aggregate, and as you may have noticed, the optimizer chose to do a full table scan with a sort instead of the nice optimized index full scan operation. While I think this is a short-coming in the way the optimizer handles this situation, there is a fairly easy way to get the same optimized behavior. Just code the two queries separately. In this way, you get the benefits of the optimization.

Index Skip Scan

An index skip scan is chosen when the predicate contains a condition on a non-leading column in an index and the leading columns are fairly distinct. In earlier releases of Oracle, if a predicate used a column that wasn't the leading column in an index, the index couldn't be chosen. This behavior changed in Oracle version 9 with the introduction of the *index skip scan*. A skip scan works by logically splitting a multi-column index into smaller subindexes. The number of logical subindexes is determined by the number of distinct values in the leading columns of the index. Therefore, the more distinct the leading columns are, the more logical subindexes would need to be created. If too many subindexes would be required, the operation won't be as efficient as simply doing a full scan. However, in the cases where the number of subindexes needed would be smaller, the operation can be many times more efficient than a full scan as scanning smaller index blocks can be more efficient than scanning larger table blocks. Listing 3-15 shows an example of an index skip scan plan (Note: For this example, I used a copy of the hr.employees table which had nearly 28,000 rows).

Listing 3-15. *Index Skip Scan Examples*

```
SQL> create index emp_jobfname_ix on employees(job_id, first_name, salary);

Index created.

SQL> set autotrace traceonly
SQL>
SQL> select * from employees where first_name = 'William';

Execution Plan
----------------------------------------------------------
Plan hash value: 3440948136
```

```
---------------------------------------------------------------------------------
| Id  | Operation                    | Name            | Rows | Bytes | Cost (%CPU)|
---------------------------------------------------------------------------------
|   0 | SELECT STATEMENT             |                 |    1 |    82 |    21   (0)|
|   1 |  TABLE ACCESS BY INDEX ROWID | EMPLOYEES       |    1 |    82 |    21   (0)|
|*  2 |   INDEX SKIP SCAN            | EMP_JOBFNAME_IX |    1 |       |    20   (0)|
---------------------------------------------------------------------------------
```

Predicate Information (identified by operation id):
----

   2 - access("FIRST_NAME"='William')
       filter("FIRST_NAME"='William')

Statistics
----
          0 recursive calls
          0 db block gets
         50 consistent gets
          0 physical reads
          0 redo size
       2362 bytes sent via SQL*Net to client
        392 bytes received via SQL*Net from client
          3 SQL*Net roundtrips to/from client
          0 sorts (memory)
          0 sorts (disk)
         23 rows processed

SQL> select /*+ full(employees) */ * from employees where first_name = 'William';

23 rows selected.

Execution Plan

Plan hash value: 1445457117

| Id | Operation | Name | Rows | Bytes | Cost (%CPU)| Time |

| 0 | SELECT STATEMENT | | 1 | 82 | 84   (2)| 00:00:02 |
|* 1 | TABLE ACCESS FULL | EMPLOYEES | 1 | 82 | 84   (2)| 00:00:02 |

Predicate Information (identified by operation id):
----

   1 - filter("FIRST_NAME"='William')

```
Statistics
----------------------------------------------------------
          0  recursive calls
          0  db block gets
        376  consistent gets
          0  physical reads
          0  redo size
       2735  bytes sent via SQL*Net to client
        392  bytes received via SQL*Net from client
          3  SQL*Net roundtrips to/from client
          0  sorts (memory)
          0  sorts (disk)
         23  rows processed

SQL> -- How many distinct values of job_id?
SQL> select count(distinct job_id) ct from employees ;

           CT
---------------
           19
```

In this example, the leading column of the index, job_id, has 19 distinct values. Using an index skip scan to access the 23 rows that match the condition (first_name = 'William'), there are 50 consistent gets (logical block accesses). However, if a full table scan is used, 376 blocks are accessed. As you can see, the skip scan is much more efficient. What happened was that the index was logically divided into 19 subindexes and each subindex was scanned for a match for first_name = 'William'. For this index scan type, just keep in mind that the fewer distinct values the leading column (or columns) have, the fewer logical subindexes will be needed and therefore the fewer total block accesses required.

Index Fast Full Scan

An index fast full scan is more like a full table scan than like other index scan types. When an index fast full scan operation is chosen, all the index blocks are read using multiblock reads. This type of scan is chosen as an alternative to a full table scan when all the columns needed to satisfy the query's column list are included in the index and at least one column in the index has the NOT NULL constraint. In this case, the data is accessed from the index instead of having to access table blocks. Unlike other index scan types, the index fast full scan cannot be used to avoid a sort since the blocks are read using unordered multiblock reads. Listing 3-16 shows an example of an index fast full scan plan.

Listing 3-16. *Index Fast Full Scan*

```
SQL> alter table hr.employees modify (email null) ;

Table altered.

SQL> set autotrace traceonly explain
SQL> select email from hr.employees ;
```

```
Execution Plan
------------------------------------------------------------
Plan hash value: 1445457117


--------------------------------------------------------------------
| Id  | Operation        | Name      | Rows  | Bytes | Cost (%CPU)|
--------------------------------------------------------------------
|   0 | SELECT STATEMENT |           |   107 |   856 |    3   (0)|
|   1 |  TABLE ACCESS FULL| EMPLOYEES |   107 |   856 |    3   (0)|
--------------------------------------------------------------------

SQL> set autotrace off
SQL>
SQL> alter table hr.employees modify (email not null) ;

Table altered.

SQL> set autotrace traceonly explain
SQL> select email from hr.employees ;

Execution Plan
------------------------------------------------------------
Plan hash value: 2196514524


----------------------------------------------------------------------
| Id  | Operation         | Name         | Rows  | Bytes | Cost (%CPU)|
----------------------------------------------------------------------
|   0 | SELECT STATEMENT  |              |   107 |   856 |    1   (0)|
|   1 |  INDEX FULL SCAN  | EMP_EMAIL_UK |   107 |   856 |    1   (0)|
----------------------------------------------------------------------
```

This example demonstrates how the index fast full scan operation relies on the NOT NULL constraint in order to be chosen. Without the constraint, a full scan operation is chosen instead.

Join Methods

If there are multiple tables in your query, after the optimizer determines the access methods most appropriate for each of the tables, the next step is to determine the way the tables can best be joined together and the proper order in which to join them. Anytime you have multiple tables in the FROM clause, you will have a join. Tables relationships are defined with a condition in the WHERE clause. If no condition is specified, the join will be implicitly defined such that each row in one table will be matched with every row in the other table. This is called a Cartesian join and I will discuss it in further detail later in this section.

Joins occur between pairs of tables or row sources. When multiple tables exist in the FROM clause, the optimizer will determine which join operation is most efficient for each pair. The join methods are: nested loops joins, hash joins, sort-merge joins, and Cartesian joins. Each join method has specific conditions to which it is best suited. For each pair, the optimizer must also determine the order in which the tables are joined. Figure 3-6 shows a diagram of how a query with four tables might be joined.

Notice that after the first pair of tables is joined, the next table is joined to the resulting row source from the first join. After that join is made, the next table is joined to that row source. This continues until all tables have been joined.

Each join method will have two children. The first table accessed is typically called the driving table and the second table is called the inner or driven-to table. The optimizer determines the driving table by using the statistics and the filter conditions in the WHERE clause to calculate how many rows will be returned from each table. The table with the smallest estimated size (in terms of blocks, rows, and bytes) will typically be the driving table. This is true particularly if the optimizer can determine that one of the tables will return at most one row based on a UNIQUE or PRIMARY KEY constraint. These tables are placed first in the join. Tables with outer join operators (which I'll discuss later) must come after the table to which it is joined. Other than these two specific cases, the join order of the other tables is evaluated based on their computed selectivities based on the optimizer's calculations using available table, column, and index statistics.

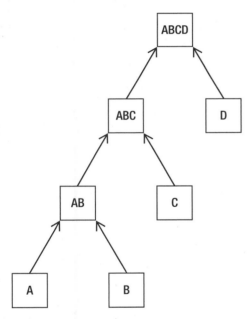

Figure 3-6. *Join order example diagram*

Nested Loops Joins

Nested loops joins use each row of the query result reached through one access operation to drive into another table. These joins are typically most effective if the result set is limited in size and indexes are present on the columns used for the join. With nested loops, the cost of the operation is based on reading each row of the outer row source and joining it with the matching row of the inner row source.

A nested loops join is, as its name implies, a loop inside a loop. The outer loop is basically a query against the driving table that uses only the conditions from the WHERE clause that pertain to that table. As rows pass the outer conditional check and are confirmed to match the request, they are passed into the second inner loop one at a time. Each row is then checked to see if it matches the joined-to table based on the join column. If the row matches this second check, it is then passed on to the next step in the plan or is included in the final result set if no further steps are present.

These kinds of joins are quite robust in that they use very little memory. Since row sets are built one row at a time, there is little overhead required. For that reason, they are actually good for huge result sets except for the fact that building a huge result set one row at a time can take quite a long time. That's why I mentioned earlier that nested loops are typically best when the result sets are smaller. The primary measurement for nested loops is the number of block accesses required to prepare the final result set.

Let's take a simple query and break it down into how the nested loop join would be processed.

```
select empno, ename, dname, loc
from emp, dept
where emp.deptno = dept.deptno
```

This query would be processed as if it were written like the following pseudocode:

```
for each row in (select empno, ename, deptno from emp) loop
        for (select dname, loc from dept where deptno =      outer.deptno) loop
            If match then pass the row on to the next step
            If inner join and no match then discard the row
            If outer join and no match set inner column values to null
                    and pass the row on to the next step
        end loop
end loop
```

Listing 3-17 shows the plan for this query.

Listing 3-17. *Nested Loops*

```
SQL> set autotrace traceonly explain
SQL>
SQL> select empno, ename, dname, loc
  2  from emp, dept
  3  where emp.deptno = dept.deptno;

Execution Plan
----------------------------------------------------------
Plan hash value: 351108634
```

Id	Operation	Name	Rows	Bytes	Cost (%CPU)
0	SELECT STATEMENT		14	462	4 (0)
1	NESTED LOOPS		14	462	4 (0)
2	TABLE ACCESS FULL	EMP	14	182	3 (0)
3	TABLE ACCESS BY INDEX ROWID	DEPT	1	20	1 (0)
* 4	INDEX UNIQUE SCAN	PK_DEPT	1		0 (0)

```
Predicate Information (identified by operation id):
---------------------------------------------------

   4 - access("EMP"."DEPTNO"="DEPT"."DEPTNO")
```

The plan shows the nested loops method with the emp table as the driving table and the dept table as the inner (or driven-to) table. With a nested loops plan, the first table listed after the NESTED LOOPS operation is the driving table. That table will be accessed via the method chosen for it. In this case, it is a full table scan on emp. That means that all the blocks in the emp table are read using multiblock reads, then each row is accessed one at a time, and the deptno (the join column) is passed to the inner loop query against the dept table. For an inner join, each row where there is a match on the dept table's deptno column, the row will be returned. For an outer join, each row from emp will be returned and null values will be used to populate the columns from dept.

If you're wondering why the emp table was chosen as the driving table, just take a second to think about the query. The query is asking for all rows where there is a match between the two tables on deptno. In my test, the emp table did not have an index on deptno so the only way it could be accessed was with a full table scan. Since the way a nested loops join works is to process the inner join for each row of the outer table, if the dept table had been the driving table, for every row in dept a full table scan on emp would have occurred. On the other hand, driving the join with the emp table means that only one full table scan is needed, and since there is an index on deptno in the dept table (it's the primary key), the inner loop can directly access the row it needs from dept. Listing 3-18 shows the comparison of the autotrace statistics output for both join orders.

Listing 3-18. *Nested Loops Join Order Comparison*

```
SQL> set autotrace traceonly statistics
SQL>
SQL> select empno, ename, dname, loc
  2  from scott.emp, scott.dept
  3  where emp.deptno = dept.deptno;

Statistics
----------------------------------------------------------
          0  recursive calls
          0  db block gets
         24  consistent gets
          0  physical reads
          0  redo size
        999  bytes sent via SQL*Net to client
        381  bytes received via SQL*Net from client
          2  SQL*Net roundtrips to/from client
          0  sorts (memory)
          0  sorts (disk)
         14  rows processed

SQL> select /*+ ordered use_nl (dept emp) */ empno, ename, dname, loc
  2  from scott.dept, scott.emp
  3  where emp.deptno = dept.deptno;
```

```
Statistics
----------------------------------------------------
          0  recursive calls
          0  db block gets
         37  consistent gets
          0  physical reads
          0  redo size
        853  bytes sent via SQL*Net to client
        381  bytes received via SQL*Net from client
          2  SQL*Net roundtrips to/from client
          0  sorts (memory)
          0  sorts (disk)
         14  rows processed
```

I had to use hints (hints will be covered later in the book) to force the optimizer to choose a plan with the dept table as the driving table. Notice that when the join is driven by dept, the logical reads (consistent gets) are higher than when the join is driven by the emp table. So, the optimizer made the correct join order choice by choosing to lead with emp. One of the keys to optimizing performance is to make sure that only work that needs to happen is done. The extra work (i.e. extra logical reads) that would have occurred if the dept table had been the driving table was avoided with this join order choice.

Sort-Merge Joins

Sort-merge joins read the two tables to be joined independently, sorts the rows from each table (but only those rows that meet the conditions for the table in the WHERE clause) in order by the join key, and then merges the sorted rowsets. The sort operations are the expensive part for this join method. For large row sources that won't fit into memory, the sorts will end up using temporary disk space to complete. This can be quite memory and time-consuming to complete. But once the rowsets are sorted, the merge happens quickly. To merge, the database alternates down the two lists, compares the top rows, discards rows that are earlier in the sort order than the top of the other list, and only returns matching rows.

Let's use the same query used earlier and break it down into how the sort-merge join would be processed.

```
select empno, ename, dname, loc
from emp, dept
where emp.deptno = dept.deptno
```

This query would be processed as if it were written like the following pseudocode:

```
select empno, ename, deptno from emp order by deptno

select dname, loc, deptno from dept order by deptno

compare the rowsets and return rows where deptno in both lists match

for an outer join, compare the rowsets and return all rows from the first list

setting column values for the other table to null
```

Listing 3-19 shows the plan for this query.

Listing 3-19. *Sort-Merge Join*

```
SQL> select /*+ ordered */ empno, ename, dname, loc
  2  from scott.dept, scott.emp
  3  where emp.deptno = dept.deptno;
```

```
---------------------------------------------------------------------------
| Id  | Operation                    | Name    | Rows  | Bytes | Cost (%CPU)|
---------------------------------------------------------------------------
|   0 | SELECT STATEMENT             |         |    14 |   462 |    6  (17)|
|   1 |  MERGE JOIN                  |         |    14 |   462 |    6  (17)|
|   2 |   TABLE ACCESS BY INDEX ROWID| DEPT    |     4 |    80 |    2   (0)|
|   3 |    INDEX FULL SCAN           | PK_DEPT |     4 |       |    1   (0)|
|*  4 |   SORT JOIN                  |         |    14 |   182 |    4  (25)|
|   5 |    TABLE ACCESS FULL         | EMP     |    14 |   182 |    3   (0)|
---------------------------------------------------------------------------
```

```
Predicate Information (identified by operation id):
---------------------------------------------------

   4 - access("EMP"."DEPTNO"="DEPT"."DEPTNO")
       filter("EMP"."DEPTNO"="DEPT"."DEPTNO")
```

I used the same query as before but had to force the plan with an ordered hint. Notice how the plan operations show a MERGE JOIN operation followed by an index access on the dept table and a SORT JOIN operation of a full table scan on the emp table. The first thing to note is the use of the index scan on dept. In this case, the optimizer chose to read the table data from the index since the index would return the data in sorted order. That means a separate sort step could be avoided. The emp table was full scanned and required a separate sort step since there was no index on deptno that could be used. After both rowsets were ready and in sorted order, they were merged together.

A sort-merge join will access the blocks needed and then do the work to sort and merge them in memory (or by using temp disk space if there isn't enough memory). So, when you do a comparison of logical reads for a sort-merge join to a nested loops join, particularly for a query against a larger row source, you will likely find that there are more block accesses required for the nested loops join. Does that mean that the sort-merge is a better choice? It depends. You have to take into account all the work required to complete the sort and merge steps and realize that work may end up taking much more time than doing more block accesses might.

Sort-merge joins are typically best suited to queries that have limited data filtering and return lots of rows. They are also often a better choice if there are no suitable indexes that can be used to access the data more directly. Finally, a sort-merge is often the best choice when the join is an inequality. For example, a join condition of WHERE table1.column1 between table2.column1 and table2.column2 would be a candidate for a sort-merge. As you'll see in the next section, a hash join is not possible for such a join; if the row sources are large, the sort-merge will likely be the only viable choice.

Hash Joins

Hash joins, like sort-merge joins, first reads the two tables to be joined independently and applies the criteria in the WHERE clause. Based on table and index statistics, the table that is determined to return the fewest rows will be hashed in its entirety into memory. This hash table includes all the row data for that table and is loaded into hash buckets based on a randomizing function that converts the join key to a hash value. As long as there is enough memory available, this hash table will reside in memory. However, if there is not enough memory available, the hash table may be written to temp disk space.

The next step is for the other larger table to be read and the hash function is applied to the join key column. That hash value is then used to probe the smaller in memory hash table for the matching hash bucket where the row data for the first table resides. Each bucket has a list (represented by a bitmap) of the rows in that bucket. That list is checked for matches with the probing row. If a match is made, the row is returned; otherwise it is discarded. The larger table is read only once and each row is checked for a match. This is different from the nested loops join where the inner table is read multiple times. So really in this case, the larger table is the driving table as it is read only once and the smaller hashed table is probed many times. Unlike a nested loops join plan, however, the tables are listed in the plan output with the smaller hashed table first and the larger probe table second.

Let's use the same query used earlier and break it down into how the hash join would be processed.

```
select empno, ename, dname, loc
from emp, dept
where emp.deptno = dept.deptno
```

This query would be processed as if it were written like the following pseudocode:

```
determine the smaller row set, or in the case of an outer join,
    use the outer joined table

select dname, loc, deptno from dept

hash the deptno column and build a hash table

select empno, ename, deptno from emp

hash the deptno column and probe the hash table

if match made, check bitmap to confirm row match

if no match made, discard the row
```

Listing 3-20 shows the plan for this query.

Listing 3-20. *Hash Join*

```
---------------------------------------------------------------
| Id  | Operation          | Name | Rows  | Bytes | Cost (%CPU)|
---------------------------------------------------------------
|   0 | SELECT STATEMENT   |      |    14 |   462 |    7  (15)|
|*  1 |  HASH JOIN         |      |    14 |   462 |    7  (15)|
|   2 |   TABLE ACCESS FULL| DEPT |     4 |    80 |    3   (0)|
|   3 |   TABLE ACCESS FULL| EMP  |    14 |   182 |    3   (0)|
---------------------------------------------------------------
```

```
Predicate Information (identified by operation id):
---------------------------------------------------

   1 - access("EMP"."DEPTNO"="DEPT"."DEPTNO")
```

In the hash join plan, the smaller hash table is listed first and the probe table is listed second. Keep in mind that the decision as to which table is smallest depends not just on the number of rows but the size of those rows as well, since the entire row must be stored in the hash table.

Hash joins are considered more preferable when the row sources are larger and the result set is larger as well. Also, if one of the tables in the join is determined to always return the same row source, a hash join would be preferable since it would only access that table once. If a nested loops join was chosen in that case, the row source would be accessed over and over again, requiring more work than a single independent access. Finally, if the smaller table can fit in memory, a hash join may be favored.

Blocks are accessed for hash joins similar to how they are accessed for a sort-merge join. The blocks needed to build the hash table will be read and then the rest of the work will be done against the hashed data stored in memory (from temp disk space if there isn't enough memory). So, when you do a comparison of logical reads for a hash join to a sort-merge join, the block accesses will be approximately identical. But the logical reads as compared to a nested loops join will be less since the blocks are read once and either placed into memory (for the hash table) where they are then accessed or only read once (for the probe table).

Hash joins are only possible if the join is an equi-join. As mentioned previously, a sort-merge join can be used to handle joins specified with an inequality condition. The reason why hash joins can't be chosen unless the join is an equi-join is that the matches are made on hashed values and it doesn't make sense to consider hashed values in a range. Listing 3-21 demonstrates how a computed hash value doesn't necessarily correspond to the key value being hashed (in terms of its numeric value, in this case).

Listing 3-21. *Hash Values*

```
SQL> select distinct deptno,
  2         ora_hash(deptno,1000) hv
  3    from scott.emp
  4   order by deptno;

        DEPTNO              HV
--------------- ---------------
             10             547
             20             486
             30             613
SQL>
SQL> select deptno
  2     from
  3   (
  4   select distinct deptno,
  5         ora_hash(deptno,1000) hv
  6    from scott.emp
  7   order by deptno
  8   )
  9   where hv between 100 and 500;
```

```
        DEPTNO
---------------
            20
SQL>
SQL> select distinct deptno,
  2          ora_hash(deptno,1000,50) hv
  3    from scott.emp
  4    order by deptno;

        DEPTNO              HV
--------------- ---------------
            10             839
            20             850
            30             290
SQL>
SQL> select deptno
  2     from
  3   (
  4   select distinct deptno,
  5          ora_hash(deptno,1000,50) hv
  6    from scott.emp
  7    order by deptno
  8   )
  9    where hv between 100 and 500;

        DEPTNO
---------------
            30
```

I used the ora_hash function to demonstrate how a hash value might be generated. The ora_hash function takes up to three parameters: an input value of any base type, the maximum hash bucket value (the minimum value is zero), and a seed value (also defaults to zero). So, for example, ora_hash(10,1000) will return an integer value between zero and 1000.

In the two examples, I use the default seed in the first and a seed value of 50 for the second. Notice how the hash values for each deptno are quite different in each query. So when I try to query a range of hash values for each, I get a different result. However, in both cases, if I was simply querying a range of the column values, I could easily formulate what I wanted and be assured of always getting the right answer. This example is a bit forced, but I wanted to give you a visual on hash value comparisons so you could better understand why they don't work with inequality joins.

Cartesian Joins

Cartesian joins occur when all the rows from one table are joined to all the rows of another table. Therefore, the total number of rows resulting from the join equals the number of rows from one table (A) multiplied by the number of rows in the other table (B) such that A x B = total rows in the result set. Cartesian joins often occur when a join condition is overlooked or left out such that there isn't a specified join column so the only operation possible is to simply join everything from one row source to everything from the other.

Let's use the same query used earlier, but leave off the WHERE clause, and break it down into how the Cartesian join would be processed.

```
select empno, ename, dname, loc
from emp, dept
```

This query would be processed as if it were written like the following pseudocode:

```
determine the smaller table

select dname, loc from dept

select empno, ename from emp

for each row in dept match it to every row in emp retaining all rows
```

Listing 3-22 shows the plan for this query.

Listing 3-22. *Cartesian Join*

```
---------------------------------------------------------------------
| Id | Operation            | Name | Rows | Bytes | Cost (%CPU)|
---------------------------------------------------------------------
|  0 | SELECT STATEMENT     |      |   56 | 1568  |    9   (0)|
|  1 |  MERGE JOIN CARTESIAN|      |   56 | 1568  |    9   (0)|
|  2 |   TABLE ACCESS FULL  | DEPT |    4 |   72  |    3   (0)|
|  3 |   BUFFER SORT        |      |   14 |  140  |    6   (0)|
|  4 |    TABLE ACCESS FULL | EMP  |   14 |  140  |    2   (0)|
---------------------------------------------------------------------
```

Notice the rows estimates in the plan and how the final row estimate is the product of the rows from the two tables (4 x 14 = 56). What you end up with in this case is likely a result set that has a whole lot more rows than you want or intended to have. When plans aren't checked properly while developing SQL, Cartesian joins may end up causing the result set to appear to have numerous duplicate rows. And, unfortunately, the first thing many people will do is to add a distinct operator to the SQL. This has the effect of getting rid of the duplicates so that the result set is correct, but at a significant cost. The duplicates shouldn't have been there in the first place but since they're there, adding distinct will cause a sort to occur and then all the duplicates will be eliminated. That's a lot of wasted work. So, make sure to always verify the plan for Cartesian joins if you end up with unexpected duplicate rows in your result set before you simply add distinct out of hand.

One thing you'll notice about the Cartesian join plan is the presence of the BUFFER SORT operation. This isn't really a sort but since Oracle is joining every row to every row, using the buffer sort mechanism to copy the blocks from the second row source out of the buffer cache and into private memory has the benefit of not requiring the same blocks in the buffer cache to be revisited over and over. These revisits would require a lot more logical reads and would also create more opportunity for contention on these blocks in the buffer cache. So, buffering the blocks into a private memory area can be a much more efficient way to accomplish the repeated join.

Outer Joins

An outer join returns all rows from one table and only those rows from the joined table where the join condition is met. Oracle uses the + character to indicate an outer join. The + is placed in parentheses on the side of the join condition with the table where only rows that match is located. As I've indicated in each of the join method overviews, outer joins will require that the outer joined table be the driving table. This can mean that join orders that might be more optimal will not be used. So, use outer joins properly with care since their use has implications related to performance of the overall plan.

Listing 3-23 shows an example of how outer joins work. In the example, you have been asked to produce a count of how many customers have placed between $0 and $5000 in orders.

Listing 3-23. *Outer Join*

```
SQL> -- Query to show customers with total orders between $0 and $5000
SQL> select c.cust_last_name, nvl(sum(o.order_total),0) tot_orders
  2    from customers c, orders o
  3   where c.customer_id = o.customer_id
  4   group by c.cust_last_name
  5  having nvl(sum(o.order_total),0) between 0 and 5000
  6   order by c.cust_last_name ;

CUST_LAST_NAME            TOT_ORDERS
-------------------- ----------------
Alexander                        309
Chandar                          510
George                           220
Higgins                          416
Kazan                           1233
Sen                             4797
Stern                          969.2
Weaver                           600

8 rows selected.

SQL> -- To produce just a count, modify the query slightly
SQL> select count(*) ct
  2    from
  3  (
  4  select c.cust_last_name, nvl(sum(o.order_total),0) tot_orders
  5    from customers c, orders o
  6   where c.customer_id = o.customer_id
  7   group by c.cust_last_name
  8  having nvl(sum(o.order_total),0) between 0 and 5000
  9   order by c.cust_last_name
 10  );
```

```
          CT
---------------
          8
```

1 row selected.

```
SQL> -- What about customers who haven't placed orders (they would have $0 order amount)?
SQL> -- Change the query to an outer join to include customers without orders
SQL> select count(*) ct
  2    from
  3  (
  4  select c.cust_last_name, nvl(sum(o.order_total),0) tot_orders
  5    from customers c, orders o
  6   where c.customer_id = o.customer_id(+)
  7   group by c.cust_last_name
  8  having nvl(sum(o.order_total),0) between 0 and 5000
  9   order by c.cust_last_name
 10  );
```

```
          CT
---------------
         140
```

1 row selected.

```
SQL> set autotrace traceonly explain
SQL> /
```

```
Execution Plan
----------------------------------------------------------
Plan hash value: 3042670853
```

Id	Operation	Name	Rows	Bytes	Cost (%CPU)
0	SELECT STATEMENT		1		5 (20)
1	SORT AGGREGATE		1		
2	VIEW		1		5 (20)
* 3	FILTER				
4	HASH GROUP BY		1	22	5 (20)
5	NESTED LOOPS OUTER		319	7018	4 (0)
6	VIEW	index$_join$_002	319	3828	3 (0)
* 7	HASH JOIN				
8	INDEX FAST FULL SCAN	CUSTOMERS_PK	319	3828	1 (0)
9	INDEX FAST FULL SCAN	CUST_LNAME_IX	319	3828	1 (0)
10	TABLE ACCESS BY INDEX ROWID	ORDERS	1	10	1 (0)
* 11	INDEX RANGE SCAN	ORD_CUSTOMER_IX	2		0 (0)

```
Predicate Information (identified by operation id):
---------------------------------------------------

   3 - filter(NVL(SUM("O"."ORDER_TOTAL"),0)>=0 AND NVL(SUM("O"."ORDER_TOTAL"),0)<=5000)
   7 - access(ROWID=ROWID)
  11 - access("C"."CUSTOMER_ID"="O"."CUSTOMER_ID"(+))
       filter("O"."CUSTOMER_ID"(+)>0)
```

The example shows how the original answer wasn't exactly correct without using an outer join. Since customers who haven't yet placed orders would not have rows in the order table, they would not be included in the query result set. Changing the query to be an outer join will cause those customers to be included. Also notice the plan operation on line 5 that specifies the NESTED LOOPS OUTER. Outer joins can be used with any join method (nested loops, hash, sort-merge) and will be denoted with the word OUTER at the end of the normal operation name.

As mentioned earlier, the use of the (+) operator to denote an outer join is Oracle-specific syntax. The same thing can be accomplished using ANSI join syntax as well, as shown in Listing 3-24.

Listing 3-24. *Outer Join Using ANSI Join Syntax*

```
SQL> select count(*) ct
  2      from
  3  (
  4  select c.cust_last_name, nvl(sum(o.order_total),0) tot_orders
  5    from customers c
  6         left outer join
  7         orders o
  8         on (c.customer_id = o.customer_id)
  9   group by c.cust_last_name
 10  having nvl(sum(o.order_total),0) between 0 and 5000
 11   order by c.cust_last_name
 12  );

        CT
---------------
        140
```

1 row selected.

With ANSI syntax, you simply use the keywords LEFT OUTER JOIN. This indicates that the table on the left (i.e. the first table listed) is the one that you want to have all rows included even if a match on the join condition isn't found. You could use RIGHT OUTER JOIN if you wanted to have all rows from orders included even if there was no match in customers.

When you use the Oracle (+) operator, you have some limitations that do not exist if you use ANSI syntax. Oracle will throw an error if you attempt to outer join the same table to more than one other table. The error message you get is "ORA-01417: a table may be outer joined to at most one other table". With ANSI syntax, there is no limit on the number of tables to which a single table can be outer-joined.

Another limitation of Oracle's outer join syntax is that it doesn't support full outer joins. A full outer join will join two tables from left-to-right and right-to-left. Records that join in both directions are output once to avoid duplication. To demonstrate a full outer join, Listing 3-25 shows the creation of two tables that contain a small subset of common data but have some data that is only present in the single table. The full outer join will return all the rows from both tables that match plus the rows that are unique to each table.

Listing 3-25. *Full Outer Join Using ANSI Join Syntax*

```
SQL> create table e1 as select * from emp where deptno in (10,20);

Table created.

SQL> create table e2 as select * from emp where deptno in (20,30);

Table created.

SQL> select e1.ename, e1.deptno, e1.job
  2         ,e2.ename, e2.deptno, e2.job
  3  from   e1
  4         full outer join
  5         e2
  6         on (e1.empno = e2.empno);
```

ENAME	DEPTNO	JOB	ENAME	DEPTNO	JOB
SMITH	20	CLERK	SMITH	20	CLERK
JONES	20	MANAGER	JONES	20	MANAGER
SCOTT	20	ANALYST	SCOTT	20	ANALYST
ADAMS	20	CLERK	ADAMS	20	CLERK
FORD	20	ANALYST	FORD	20	ANALYST
CLARK	10	MANAGER			
MILLER	10	CLERK			
			TURNER	30	SALESMAN
			BLAKE	30	MANAGER
			ALLEN	30	SALESMAN
			WARD	30	SALESMAN
			MARTIN	30	SALESMAN
			JAMES	30	CLERK

```
13 rows selected.

SQL> set autotrace traceonly explain
SQL> /
```

```
Execution Plan
-----------------------------------------------------------
Plan hash value: 3117905978

---------------------------------------------------------------------------
| Id  | Operation            | Name | Rows  | Bytes | Cost (%CPU)| Time     |
---------------------------------------------------------------------------
|   0 | SELECT STATEMENT     |      |    11 |   572 |  13    (8)| 00:00:01 |
|   1 |  VIEW                |      |    11 |   572 |  13    (8)| 00:00:01 |
|   2 |   UNION-ALL          |      |       |       |           |          |
|*  3 |    HASH JOIN OUTER   |      |     7 |   448 |   7   (15)| 00:00:01 |
|   4 |     TABLE ACCESS FULL| E1   |     7 |   245 |   3    (0)| 00:00:01 |
|   5 |     TABLE ACCESS FULL| E2   |    11 |   319 |   3    (0)| 00:00:01 |
|*  6 |    HASH JOIN ANTI    |      |     4 |   100 |   7   (15)| 00:00:01 |
|   7 |     TABLE ACCESS FULL| E2   |    11 |   231 |   3    (0)| 00:00:01 |
|   8 |     TABLE ACCESS FULL| E1   |     7 |    28 |   3    (0)| 00:00:01 |
---------------------------------------------------------------------------

Predicate Information (identified by operation id):
---------------------------------------------------

   3 - access("E1"."EMPNO"="E2"."EMPNO"(+))
   6 - access("E1"."EMPNO"="E2"."EMPNO")
```

Note that rows from both tables appear in the output, even if they do not have a match in the opposite table. This is what a full outer join does and can be useful when partial datasets need to be joined. As you can see from the plan, the full outer join actually executed two separate query blocks (one HASH JOIN OUTER and one HASH JOIN ANTI) and appended the results with UNION ALL.

Using the plan from the ANSI full outer join example, you could write an equivalent statement using Oracle's syntax that would result in the same final result set. Listing 3-26 shows how the statement would be coded.

Listing 3-26. *Oracle Equivalent Syntax for Full Outer Join Functionality*

```
SQL> select e1.ename, e1.deptno, e1.job,
  2          e2.ename, e2.deptno, e2.job
  3  from    e1,
  4          e2
  5  where   e1.empno (+) = e2.empno
  6  union
  7  select e1.ename, e1.deptno, e1.job,
  8          e2.ename, e2.deptno, e2.job
  9  from    e1,
 10          e2
 11  where   e1.empno = e2.empno (+);
```

```
ENAME            DEPTNO JOB         ENAME            DEPTNO JOB
---------- --------------- --------- ---------- --------------- ---------
ADAMS                 20 CLERK      ADAMS                 20 CLERK
CLARK                 10 MANAGER
FORD                  20 ANALYST    FORD                  20 ANALYST
JONES                 20 MANAGER    JONES                 20 MANAGER
MILLER                10 CLERK
SCOTT                 20 ANALYST    SCOTT                 20 ANALYST
SMITH                 20 CLERK      SMITH                 20 CLERK
                                    ALLEN                 30 SALESMAN
                                    BLAKE                 30 MANAGER
                                    JAMES                 30 CLERK
                                    MARTIN                30 SALESMAN
                                    TURNER                30 SALESMAN
                                    WARD                  30 SALESMAN

13 rows selected.

SQL> set autotrace traceonly explain
SQL> /

Execution Plan
----------------------------------------------------------
Plan hash value: 3941775845
```

```
--------------------------------------------------------------------------
| Id  | Operation            | Name | Rows  | Bytes | Cost (%CPU)| Time     |
--------------------------------------------------------------------------
|   0 | SELECT STATEMENT     |      |    18 |   756 |    15  (60)| 00:00:01 |
|   1 |  SORT UNIQUE         |      |    18 |   756 |    15  (60)| 00:00:01 |
|   2 |   UNION-ALL          |      |       |       |            |          |
|*  3 |    HASH JOIN OUTER   |      |    11 |   462 |     7  (15)| 00:00:01 |
|   4 |     TABLE ACCESS FULL| E2   |    11 |   231 |     3   (0)| 00:00:01 |
|   5 |     TABLE ACCESS FULL| E1   |     7 |   147 |     3   (0)| 00:00:01 |
|*  6 |    HASH JOIN OUTER   |      |     7 |   294 |     7  (15)| 00:00:01 |
|   7 |     TABLE ACCESS FULL| E1   |     7 |   147 |     3   (0)| 00:00:01 |
|   8 |     TABLE ACCESS FULL| E2   |    11 |   231 |     3   (0)| 00:00:01 |
--------------------------------------------------------------------------

Predicate Information (identified by operation id):
---------------------------------------------------

   3 - access("E1"."EMPNO"(+)="E2"."EMPNO")
   6 - access("E1"."EMPNO"="E2"."EMPNO"(+))
```

You may have noticed that the Oracle equivalent plan is just a bit different from the ANSI plan. Oracle uses two outer joins, one in each direction, which is exactly what you asked it to do. So you could use Oracle syntax to accomplish a full outer join, but the ANSI syntax is certainly more straightforward. Also keep in mind that full outer joins can be quite costly in terms of the amount of resources required to execute. Always be careful to understand the implications of coding such queries and note the performance implications.

Summary

The optimizer must make a few key choices when determining the execution plan for any SQL statement. First, the best way to access each table used in the statement has to be determined. There are basically two choices: an index or a full table scan. Each access method works differently to access the blocks containing the row data your SQL statement needs. Once the optimizer chooses the access methods, the join methods have to be selected. Tables will be joined together in pairs with the row source from one join result being used to join to another table until all the tables are joined to produce the final result set.

Understanding how each access and join method works can help you write your SQL so that the optimizer can make the most efficient choices. Being able to review the execution plans, understand the operations chosen, and how those operations work will also help you notice areas where performance problems might occur. Once again, knowing what is under the hood will help you write better, faster SQL.

SQL is About Sets

Karen Morton

One of the most difficult transitions to make in order to become highly proficient at writing SQL well is to shift from thinking procedurally to thinking declaratively (or in sets). It is often hardest to learn to think in sets if you've spent time working with virtually any programming language. If this is the case for you, you are likely very comfortable with constructs such as IF-THEN-ELSE, WHILE-DO, LOOP-END LOOP, and BEGIN-END. These constructs support working with logic and data in a very procedural, step-by-step, top-down type approach. The SQL language is not intended to be implemented from a procedural point of view, but from a set-oriented one. The longer it takes you to shift to a set-oriented point of view, the longer it will be before you are truly proficient at writing SQL that is functionally correct and also highly optimized to perform well.

In this chapter, you're going to explore common areas where you may need to shift your procedural way of thinking to non-procedural. You'll begin to understand how to work with sets of data elements versus sequential steps. You'll also look at several specific set operations (UNION, INTERSECT, MINUS) and how nulls affect set-thinking.

Thinking in Sets

As a fun way to help you start thinking in sets, I'm going to review one of my favorite games, SET. You can play it online at www.setgame.com/puzzle/set.htm where a new SET puzzle is posted every day. The SET game is a puzzle that uses cards with four features on them: colors, symbols, shadings, and the number of symbols. The colors are red, green, or purple. Symbols can be squiggles, diamonds, or ovals. Shadings can be solid, striped, or outlined. As for numbers, each card has one, two, or three symbols on it. There is only one rule to make a SET. A SET is three cards in which each individual feature is either all the same on each card or all different on each card. So, an example of a valid SET would be three cards that all have the same symbol (diamonds, for example), all three cards have two symbols, all three cards were different colors, and all three cards had solid shading. Any combination where all the cards have the same feature or different features makes a SET. The object is to find a SET in twelve cards. Once a SET is found, those three cards are removed and three more are added. In the online version, there will always be six SETs in the layout of twelve cards and your goal is to find all six.

Figure 4-1 shows a 12 card layout where you should be able to find six SETs. The letter in the upper left of each box indicates color (R = red, G = green, P = purple). Give it a try.

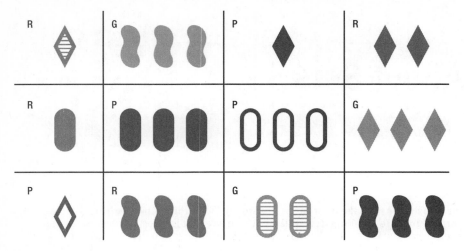

Figure 4-1. *A valid SET*

The solution grid is at the end of this chapter (no cheating!). I'll give you the first set to get you started: Row 1 Column 2 (solid green squiggles), Row 3 Column 2 (solid red squiggles) and Row 3 Column 4 (solid purple squiggles). This game forces you to think in sets. There's no other way to play. If you find it hard to make a SET, I'll bet you'll find it harder to think in sets when writing SQL. Writing SQL works under the same premise (set-thinking is a must!); it's just a different game. Now that you're warmed up to think in sets, let's look at several ways to switch procedural thinking to set thinking.

Moving from Procedural to Set-based Thinking

The first thing you need to do is to stop thinking about process steps that handle data one row at a time. If you're thinking one row at a time, your thinking will use phrases like "for each row do x" or "while value is y do x." Try to shift this thinking to use phrases like "for all." A simple example of this is adding numbers. When you think procedurally, you think of adding the number value from one row to the number value from another row until you've added all rows together. Thinking of summing all rows is different. As I said, that's a very simple example, but the same shift in thinking applies to situations that aren't as obvious.

For example, if I asked you to produce a list of all employees who spent the same number of years in each job they held within the company during their employment, how would you do it? If you think procedurally, you would want to look at each job position, compute the number of years that position was held, and compare it to the number of years any other positions were held. If the number of years don't match, then you'd reject the employee from the list. That approach might lead to a query that uses a self-join like this:

```
select distinct employee_id
  from job_history j1
 where not exists
                (select null
                   from job_history j2
                  where j2.employee_id = j1.employee_id
                    and round(months_between(j2.start_date,j2.end_date)/12,0) <>
                        round(months_between(j1.start_date,j1.end_date)/12,0) )
```

On the other hand, if you look at the problem from a set-based point of view, you might write the query by accessing the table only once, grouping rows by employee, and filtering the result to retain only those employees whose minimum years in a single position match their maximum years in a single position like this:

```
select employee_id
  from job_history
 group by employee_id
having min(round(months_between(start_date,end_date)/12,0)) =
    max(round(months_between(start_date,end_date)/12,0))
```

Listing 4-1 shows the execution of each of these alternatives. You can see that the set-based approach uses fewer logical reads and has a more concise plan.

Listing 4-1. *Procedural vs Set-based Approach*

```
SQL> set autotrace on
SQL>
SQL> select distinct employee_id
  2      from job_history j1
  3    where not exists
  4                (select null
  5                   from job_history j2
  6                  where j2.employee_id = j1.employee_id
  7                    and round(months_between(j2.start_date,j2.end_date)/12,0) <>
  8                        round(months_between(j1.start_date,j1.end_date)/12,0) );

    EMPLOYEE_ID
---------------
            102
            201
            114
            176
            122

Execution Plan
----------------------------------------------------------
Plan hash value: 1261305189
```

107

```
-------------------------------------------------------------------------------
| Id  | Operation                      | Name             | Rows  | Bytes | Cost (%CPU)|
-------------------------------------------------------------------------------
|   0 | SELECT STATEMENT               |                  |     7 |   140 |    14   (8)|
|   1 |  HASH UNIQUE                   |                  |     7 |   140 |    14   (8)|
|*  2 |   FILTER                       |                  |       |       |            |
|   3 |    TABLE ACCESS FULL           | JOB_HISTORY      |    10 |   200 |     3   (0)|
|*  4 |    TABLE ACCESS BY INDEX ROWID | JOB_HISTORY      |     1 |    20 |     2   (0)|
|*  5 |     INDEX RANGE SCAN           | JHIST_EMPLOYEE_IX|     1 |       |     1   (0)|
-------------------------------------------------------------------------------

Predicate Information (identified by operation id):
---------------------------------------------------

   2 - filter( NOT EXISTS (SELECT /*+ */ 0 FROM "JOB_HISTORY" "J2" WHERE
              "J2"."EMPLOYEE_ID"=:B1 AND ROUND(MONTHS_BETWEEN(INTERNAL_FUNCTION("J2".
              "START_DATE"),INTERNAL_FUNCTION("J2"."END_DATE"))/12,0)<>ROUND(MONTHS_B
              ETWEEN(:B2,:B3)/12,0)))
   4 - filter(ROUND(MONTHS_BETWEEN(INTERNAL_FUNCTION("J2"."START_DATE"),INTERNAL_
              FUNCTION("J2"."END_DATE"))/12,0)<>ROUND(MONTHS_BETWEEN(:B1,:B2)/12,0))
   5 - access("J2"."EMPLOYEE_ID"=:B1)


Statistics
----------------------------------------------------------
          0  recursive calls
          0  db block gets
         27  consistent gets
          0  physical reads
          0  redo size
        482  bytes sent via SQL*Net to client
        381  bytes received via SQL*Net from client
          2  SQL*Net roundtrips to/from client
          0  sorts (memory)
          0  sorts (disk)
          5  rows processed

SQL> select employee_id
  2    from job_history
  3   group by employee_id
  4  having min(round(months_between(start_date,end_date)/12,0)) =
  5         max(round(months_between(start_date,end_date)/12,0));
```

```
        EMPLOYEE_ID
        ---------------
                102
                114
                122
                176
                201
```

Execution Plan

Plan hash value: 1551509957

```
---------------------------------------------------------------------------------------
| Id  | Operation                     | Name              | Rows  | Bytes | Cost (%CPU)|
---------------------------------------------------------------------------------------
|   0 | SELECT STATEMENT              |                   |     1 |    20 |     2   (0)|
|*  1 |  FILTER                       |                   |       |       |            |
|   2 |   SORT GROUP BY NOSORT        |                   |     1 |    20 |     2   (0)|
|   3 |    TABLE ACCESS BY INDEX ROWID| JOB_HISTORY       |    10 |   200 |     2   (0)|
|   4 |     INDEX FULL SCAN           | JHIST_EMPLOYEE_IX |    10 |       |     1   (0)|
---------------------------------------------------------------------------------------
```

Predicate Information (identified by operation id):

```
   1 - filter(MIN(ROUND(MONTHS_BETWEEN(INTERNAL_FUNCTION("START_DATE"),INTERNAL_FUNCTION
        ("END_DATE"))/12,0))=MAX(ROUND(MONTHS_BETWEEN(INTERNAL_FUNCTION("START_DATE")
                        ,INTERNAL_FUNCTION("END_DATE"))/12,0)))
```

Statistics

```
          0  recursive calls
          0  db block gets
          4  consistent gets
          0  physical reads
          0  redo size
        482  bytes sent via SQL*Net to client
        381  bytes received via SQL*Net from client
          2  SQL*Net roundtrips to/from client
          0  sorts (memory)
          0  sorts (disk)
          5  rows processed
```

The key is to start thinking in terms of completed results, not process steps. Look for group characteristics and not individual steps or actions. In set-based thinking, everything exists in a state defined by the filters or constraints applied to the set. You don't think in terms of process flow but in terms of the state of the set. Figure 4-2 shows a comparison between a process flow diagram and a nested sets diagram to illustrate my point.

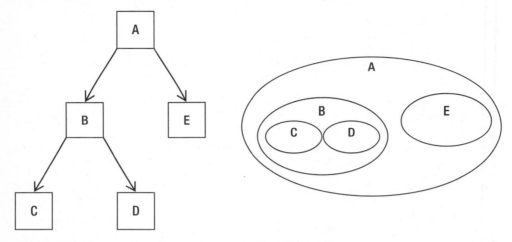

Figure 4-2. *A process flow diagram vs a nested set diagram*

The process flow diagram implies the result set (A) is achieved through a series of steps that build upon one another to produce the final answer. B is built by traversing C and D, and then A is built by traversing B and E. However, the nested sets diagram views A as a result of a combination of sets.

Another common but erroneous way of thinking is to consider tables to be ordered sets of rows. Just think of how you typically see table contents listed. They're shown in a grid or spreadsheet-type view. However, a table represents a set, and a set has no order. Showing tables in a way that implies a certain order can be confusing. Remember from Chapter 2 that the ORDER BY clause is applied last when a SQL statement is executed. SQL is based on set theory and since sets have no predetermined order to its rows, order has to be applied separately after the rows that satisfy the query result have been extracted from the set. Figure 4-3 shows a more correct way to depict the content of tables that doesn't imply order.

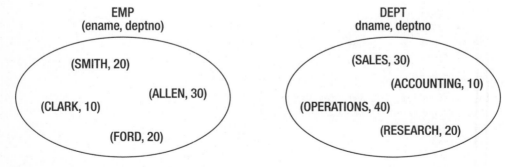

Figure 4-3. *The emp and dept sets*

It may not seem important to make these seemingly small distinctions in how you think, but these small shifts are fundamental to correctly understanding SQL. Let's look at an example of writing a SQL statement taking both a procedural thinking approach and a set-based approach to help clarify the distinctions between the two.

Procedural vs Set-based Thinking: An Example

In this example, the task is to compute an average number of days between orders for a customer. Listing 4-2 shows one way to do it from a procedural thinking approach. To keep the example output shorter, I'm going to only work with one customer, but I could easily convert this to handle all customers.

Listing 4-2. *Procedural Thinking Approach*

```
SQL> -- Show the list of order dates for customer 102
SQL> select customer_id, order_date
  2  from orders
  3  where customer_id = 102 ;

  CUSTOMER_ID ORDER_DATE
--------------- -------------------------------
          102 19-NOV-99 06.41.54.696211 PM
          102 14-SEP-99 11.53.40.223345 AM
          102 29-MAR-99 04.22.40.536996 PM
          102 14-SEP-98 09.03.04.763452 AM
SQL>
SQL> -- Determine the order_date prior to the current row's order_date
SQL> select customer_id, order_date,
  2             lag(order_date,1,order_date)
  3             over (partition by customer_id order by order_date)
  4             as prev_order_date
  5  from orders
  6  where customer_id = 102;

  CUSTOMER_ID ORDER_DATE                       PREV_ORDER_DATE
--------------- ------------------------------- -------------------------------
          102 14-SEP-98 09.03.04.763452 AM     14-SEP-98 09.03.04.763452 AM
          102 29-MAR-99 04.22.40.536996 PM     14-SEP-98 09.03.04.763452 AM
          102 14-SEP-99 11.53.40.223345 AM     29-MAR-99 04.22.40.536996 PM
          102 19-NOV-99 06.41.54.696211 PM     14-SEP-99 11.53.40.223345 AM
SQL>
SQL> -- Determine the days between each order
SQL> select trunc(order_date) - trunc(prev_order_date)  days_between
  2  from
```

```
  3  (
  4  select customer_id, order_date,
  5             lag(order_date,1,order_date)
  6             over (partition by customer_id order by order_date)
  7             as prev_order_date
  8  from orders
  9  where customer_id = 102
 10  );


   DAYS_BETWEEN
---------------
             0
           196
           169
            66
SQL>
SQL> -- Put it together with an AVG function to get the final answer
SQL> select avg(trunc(order_date) - trunc(prev_order_date))  avg_days_between
  2  from
  3  (
  4  select customer_id, order_date,
  5             lag(order_date,1,order_date)
  6             over (partition by customer_id order by order_date)
  7             as prev_order_date
  8  from orders
  9  where customer_id = 102
 10  );


AVG_DAYS_BETWEEN
----------------
          107.75
```

This looks pretty elegant, doesn't it? In this example, I've executed several queries one-by-one to show you how my thinking, followed a step-by-step procedural approach to writing the query. Don't worry if you're unfamiliar with the use of the analytic function LAG; analytic functions are covered in Chapter 8. Briefly, what I've done is to read each order row for customer 102 in order by order_date and, using the LAG function, look back at the prior order row to get its order_date. Once I have both dates, the date for the current row's order and the date for the previous row's order, it's a simple matter to subtract the two to get the days between. Lastly, I use the average aggregate function to get my final answer.

You can tell that this query is built following a very procedural approach. The best giveaway to knowing the approach is the way I can walk through several different queries to show how the final result set was built. I could see the detail as I went along. When you're thinking in sets, you'll find that you don't really care about each individual element. Listing 4-3 shows the query written using a set-based thinking approach.

Listing 4-3. *Set-based Thinking approach*

```
SQL> select (max(trunc(order_date)) - min(trunc(order_date))) / count(*) as avg_days_between
  2  from orders
  3  where customer_id = 102 ;

AVG_DAYS_BETWEEN
----------------
          107.75
```

How about that? I really didn't need anything fancy to solve the problem. All I needed to compute the average days between orders was the total duration of time between the first and last order and the number of orders placed. I didn't need to go through all that step-by-step thinking as if I was writing a program that would read the data row-by-row and compute the answer. I just needed to shift my thinking to consider the problem in terms of the set of data as a whole.

I am not completely discounting the procedural approach. There may be times when you have to take that approach to get the job done. However, I want to encourage you to shift your thinking: start by searching for a set-based approach and move towards a more procedural approach only when and to the degree needed. By doing this, you will likely find that you can come up with simpler, more direct, and often better performing solutions.

Set Operations

Oracle supports four set operators: UNION, UNION ALL, MINUS, and INTERSECT. Set operators combine the results from two or more SELECT statements to form a single result set. This differs from joins in that joins are used to combine columns from each joined table into one row. The set operators compare completed rows between the input queries and return a distinct set of rows. The exception to this is the use of UNION ALL, which returns all rows from both sets, including duplicates. UNION returns a result set from all input queries with no duplicates. MINUS returns distinct rows that appear in the first input query result but not in the subsequent ones. INTERSECT returns the distinct rows that appear in all input queries.

All queries that are used with set operators must conform to the following conditions:

- All input queries must retrieve the same number of columns.

- The data types of each column must match the corresponding column (by order in the column list) for each of the other input queries. It is possible for data types to not match directly but only if the data types of all input queries can be implicitly converted to the data types of the first input query.

- The ORDER BY clause may not be used in the individual queries and may only be used at the end of the query where it will apply to the entire result of the set operation.

- Column names are derived from the first input query.

Each input query is processed separately and then the set operator is applied. Finally, the ORDER BY is applied to the total result set if one is specified. When using UNION and INTERSECT, the operators are commutative (i.e. the order of the queries doesn't matter). However, when using MINUS, the order is important since this set operation uses the first input query result as the base for comparison to other results. All set operations except for UNION ALL will require that the result set go through a sort/distinct process that will mean additional overhead to process the query. If you know that no duplicates will ever exist, or you don't care if duplicates are present, make sure to use UNION ALL.

UNION and UNION ALL

UNION and UNION ALL are used when the results of two, or more, separate queries needs to be combined to provide a single final result set. Figure 4-4 uses Venn diagrams to show how the result set for each type could be visualized.

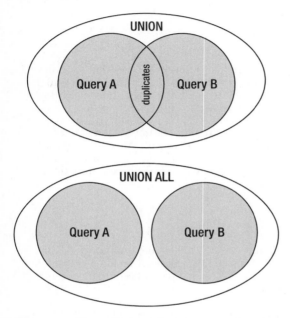

Figure 4-4. *Venn diagram for UNION and UNION ALL result sets*

The UNION set operation will return the results of both queries but will remove duplicates while the UNION ALL will return all rows including duplicates. As mentioned previously, in cases where you need to eliminate duplicates, use UNION. But when you either don't care if duplicates exist or don't expect duplicates to occur, choose UNION ALL. Using UNION ALL has a less resource intensive footprint than using UNION since UNION ALL will not have to do any processing to remove duplicates. This processing can be quite expensive in terms of both resources and response time to complete. Prior to Oracle version 10, a sort operation was used to remove duplicates. Beginning with version 10, an option to use a HASH UNIQUE operation to remove duplicates is available. The HASH UNIQUE doesn't sort but uses hash value comparisons instead. I mention this to make sure you realize that even if the result set appears to be in sorted order, it will not be guaranteed to be sorted unless you explicitly include an ORDER BY clause. Listing 4-4 shows examples of using UNION and UNION ALL.

Listing 4-4. *UNION and UNION ALL Examples*

```
SQL> CREATE TABLE table1 (
  2    id_pk INTEGER NOT NULL PRIMARY KEY,
  3    color VARCHAR(10) NOT NULL);
SQL> CREATE TABLE table2 (
  2    id_pk INTEGER NOT NULL PRIMARY KEY,
  3    color VARCHAR(10) NOT NULL);
SQL> CREATE TABLE table3 (
  2    color VARCHAR(10) NOT NULL);
SQL> INSERT INTO table1 VALUES (1, 'RED');
SQL> INSERT INTO table1 VALUES (2, 'RED');
SQL> INSERT INTO table1 VALUES (3, 'ORANGE');
SQL> INSERT INTO table1 VALUES (4, 'ORANGE');
SQL> INSERT INTO table1 VALUES (5, 'ORANGE');
SQL> INSERT INTO table1 VALUES (6, 'YELLOW');
SQL> INSERT INTO table1 VALUES (7, 'GREEN');
SQL> INSERT INTO table1 VALUES (8, 'BLUE');
SQL> INSERT INTO table1 VALUES (9, 'BLUE');
SQL> INSERT INTO table1 VALUES (10, 'VIOLET');
SQL> INSERT INTO table2 VALUES (1, 'RED');
SQL> INSERT INTO table2 VALUES (2, 'RED');
SQL> INSERT INTO table2 VALUES (3, 'BLUE');
SQL> INSERT INTO table2 VALUES (4, 'BLUE');
SQL> INSERT INTO table2 VALUES (5, 'BLUE');
SQL> INSERT INTO table2 VALUES (6, 'GREEN');
SQL> COMMIT;
SQL>
SQL> select color from table1
  2  union
  3  select color from table2;

COLOR
----------
BLUE
GREEN
ORANGE
RED
VIOLET
YELLOW

6 rows selected.

SQL> select color from table1
  2  union all
  3  select color from table2;
```

```
COLOR
----------
RED
RED
ORANGE
ORANGE
ORANGE
YELLOW
GREEN
BLUE
BLUE
VIOLET
RED
RED
BLUE
BLUE
BLUE
GREEN

16 rows selected.

SQL> select color from table1;

COLOR
----------
RED
RED
ORANGE
ORANGE
ORANGE
YELLOW
GREEN
BLUE
BLUE
VIOLET

10 rows selected.

SQL> select color from table3;

no rows selected

SQL> select color from table1
  2  union
  3  select color from table3;
```

```
COLOR
----------
BLUE
GREEN
ORANGE
RED
VIOLET
YELLOW

6 rows selected.

SQL> -- The first query will return a differen number of columns than the second
SQL> select * from table1
  2  union
  3  select color from table2;
select * from table1
*
ERROR at line 1:
ORA-01789: query block has incorrect number of result columns
```

These examples demonstrate the UNION of two queries. Keep in mind that you can have multiple queries that are unioned together.

MINUS

MINUS is used when the result of the first input query are used as the base set from which the other input query result sets are subtracted to end up with the final result set. The use of MINUS has often been used instead of using NOT EXISTS (anti-join) queries. The problem being solved is something like "I need to return the set of rows that exists in row source A but not in row source B." Figure 4-5 uses a Venn diagram to show how the result set for this operation could be visualized.

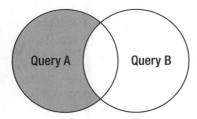

Figure 4-5. *Venn diagram for MINUS result sets*

Listing 4-5 shows examples of using MINUS.

Listing 4-5. *MINUS Examples*

```
SQL> select color from table1
  2  minus
  3  select color from table2;

COLOR
----------
ORANGE
VIOLET
YELLOW

3 rows selected.

SQL> -- MINUS queries are equivalent to NOT EXISTS queries
SQL> select distinct color from table1
  2  where not exists (select null from table2 where table2.color = table1.color) ;

COLOR
----------
ORANGE
VIOLET
YELLOW

3 rows selected.

SQL>
SQL> select color from table2
  2  minus
  3  select color from table1;

no rows selected

SQL> -- MINUS using an empty table
SQL> select color from table1
  2  minus
  3  select color from table3;

COLOR
----------
BLUE
GREEN
ORANGE
RED
VIOLET
YELLOW

6 rows selected.
```

INTERSECT

INTERSECT is used to return a distinct set of rows that appear in all input queries. The use of INTERSECT has often been used instead of using EXISTS (semi-join) queries. The problem being solved is something like "I need to return the set of rows from row source A only if a match exists in row source B." Figure 4-6 uses a Venn diagram to show how the result set for this operation could be visualized.

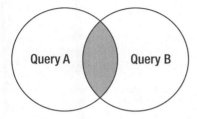

Figure 4-6. *Venn diagram for INTERSECT result sets*

Listing 4-6 shows examples of using INTERSECT.

Listing 4-6. *INTERSECT Examples*

```
SQL> select color from table1
  2  intersect
  3  select color from table2;

COLOR
----------
BLUE
GREEN
RED

3 rows selected.

SQL> select color from table1
  2  intersect
  3  select color from table3;
no rows selected
```

Sets and Nulls

You often hear the term *null value*, but in truth, a null isn't a value at all. A null is, at best, a marker. I always think of null as meaning "I don't know." The SQL language handles nulls in unintuitive ways—at least from my point of view; results from their use are often not what I would expect in terms of real world functionality.

IS THE TERM "NULL VALUE" WRONG?

Strictly speaking, a null is not a value, but rather the absence of a value. However, the term "null value" is in wide use. Work in SQL long enough, and you'll surely encounter someone who will pontificate on how wrong it is to use the term "null value."

But is it really wrong to use the term "null value?"

If you find yourself on the receiving end of such a lecture, feel free to argue right back. The term "null value" is widely used in both the ANSI and ISO editions of the SQL standard. "Null value" is an official part of the description of the SQL language, and thus is fair game for use when discussing the language.

Keep in mind, though, that there is a distinction to be drawn between the SQL language and relational theory. A really picky person can argue for the use of "null value" when speaking of SQL, and yet argue against that very same term when speaking of relational theory upon which SQL is loosely based.

NULLs and Unintuitive Results

Listing 4-7 shows a simple query for which I'd expect a certain result set but end up with something different than my expectations. I'd expect that if I queried for the absence of a specific value, and no matches were found, including when the column contained a null, that Oracle would return that row in the result set.

Listing 4-7. *Examples using NULL*

```
SQL> -- select all rows from emp table
SQL> select * from scott.emp ;
```

EMPNO	ENAME	JOB	MGR	HIREDATE	SAL	COMM	DEPTNO
7369	SMITH	CLERK	7902	17-DEC-80	800		20
7499	ALLEN	SALESMAN	7698	20-FEB-81	1600	300	30
7521	WARD	SALESMAN	7698	22-FEB-81	1250	500	30
7566	JONES	MANAGER	7839	02-APR-81	2975		20
7654	MARTIN	SALESMAN	7698	28-SEP-81	1250	1400	30
7698	BLAKE	MANAGER	7839	01-MAY-81	2850		30
7782	CLARK	MANAGER	7839	09-JUN-81	2450		10
7788	SCOTT	ANALYST	7566	19-APR-87	3000		20
7839	KING	PRESIDENT		17-NOV-81	5000		
7844	TURNER	SALESMAN	7698	08-SEP-81	1500	0	30
7876	ADAMS	CLERK	7788	23-MAY-87	1100		20
7900	JAMES	CLERK	7698	03-DEC-81	950		30
7902	FORD	ANALYST	7566	03-DEC-81	3000		20
7934	MILLER	CLERK	7782	23-JAN-82	1300		10

```
14 rows selected.
```

```
SQL> -- select only rows with deptno of 10, 20, 30
SQL> select * from scott.emp where deptno in (10, 20, 30) ;

    EMPNO ENAME      JOB           MGR HIREDATE     SAL   COMM  DEPTNO
    ------ ---------- --------- ------- --------- ------ ------ -------
     7369 SMITH      CLERK        7902 17-DEC-80    800            20
     7499 ALLEN      SALESMAN     7698 20-FEB-81   1600    300     30
     7521 WARD       SALESMAN     7698 22-FEB-81   1250    500     30
     7566 JONES      MANAGER      7839 02-APR-81   2975            20
     7654 MARTIN     SALESMAN     7698 28-SEP-81   1250   1400     30
     7698 BLAKE      MANAGER      7839 01-MAY-81   2850            30
     7782 CLARK      MANAGER      7839 09-JUN-81   2450            10
     7788 SCOTT      ANALYST      7566 19-APR-87   3000            20
     7844 TURNER     SALESMAN     7698 08-SEP-81   1500      0     30
     7876 ADAMS      CLERK        7788 23-MAY-87   1100            20
     7900 JAMES      CLERK        7698 03-DEC-81    950            30
     7902 FORD       ANALYST      7566 03-DEC-81   3000            20
     7934 MILLER     CLERK        7782 23-JAN-82   1300            10

13 rows selected.

SQL> -- select only rows with deptno not 10, 20, 30
SQL> select * from scott.emp where deptno not in (10, 20, 30) ;

no rows selected

SQL> -- select only rows with deptno not 10, 20, 30 or null
SQL> select * from scott.emp where deptno not in (10, 20, 30)
  2        or deptno is null;

    EMPNO ENAME      JOB           MGR HIREDATE     SAL   COMM  DEPTNO
    ------ ---------- --------- ------- --------- ------ ------ -------
     7839 KING       PRESIDENT        17-NOV-81   5000

1 row selected.
```

This listing demonstrates what is frustrating to me about nulls: they don't get included unless explicitly specified. In my example, 13 of the 14 rows in the table have deptno 10, 20, or 30. Since there are 14 total rows in the table, I'd expect a query that asked for rows that did not have a deptno of 10, 20, or 30 to then show the remaining 1 row. But I'd be wrong to expect that as you can see from the results of that query. If I explicitly include the condition to also include where deptno is null, I get the full list of employees that I had expected.

I realize what I'm doing when I think this way is to consider nulls to be "low values." I suppose it's the old COBOL programmer in me that remembers the days when LOW-VALUES and HIGH-VALUES were used. I also suppose that my brain wants to make nulls equate with an empty string. But, no matter what my brain wants to make of them, nulls are nulls. Nulls do not participate in comparisons. Nulls can't be added, subtracted, multiplied, or divided by anything. If they are, the return value is null. Listing 4-8 demonstrates this fact about nulls and how they participate in comparisons and expressions.

Listing 4-8. *NULLs in Comparisons and Expressions*

```
SQL> select * from scott.emp where deptno is null ;

    EMPNO ENAME      JOB          MGR HIREDATE     SAL   COMM  DEPTNO
   ------- ---------- --------- ------- --------- ------ ------ -------
     7839 KING       PRESIDENT      17-NOV-81   5000

1 row selected.

SQL>
SQL> select * from scott.emp where deptno = null ;

no rows selected

SQL> select sal, comm, sal + comm as tot_comp
  2  from scott.emp where deptno = 30;

     SAL   COMM        TOT_COMP
   ------ ------ ---------------
     1600    300            1900
     1250    500            1750
     1250   1400            2650
     2850
     1500      0            1500
      950

6 rows selected.
```

So, when my brain wants rows with a null deptno to be returned in the query from the Listing 4-7 above, I have to remind myself that when a comparison is made to a null, the answer is always "I don't know." It would be the same as you asking me if there was orange juice in *your* refrigerator and me answering "I don't know." You might have orange juice there or you might not, but I don't know. So I couldn't answer in any different way and be truthful.

The relational model is based on two-valued logic (TRUE, FALSE), but the SQL language allows three-valued logic (TRUE, FALSE, UNKNOWN). And this is where the problem comes in. With that third value in the mix, your SQL will return the "correct" answer as far as how three-valued logic considers the comparison, but the answers may not be correct in terms of what you'd expect in the real world. In the example above, the answer of no rows selected is correct in that since one deptno column contains a null, you can't know one way or the other if the column might possibly be something other than 10, 20, or 30. To answer truthfully, the answer has to be UNKNOWN. It's just like me knowing whether or not you have orange juice in your refrigerator!

So you have to make sure you keep the special nature of nulls in mind when you write SQL. If you're not vigilant to watch out for nulls, you'll very likely have SQL that returns the wrong answer. At least it will be wrong as far as the answer you *expect*.

NULL Behavior in Set Operations

Set operations treat nulls as if they were able to be compared using equality checks. This is an interesting, and perhaps unexpected, behavior given the previous discussion. Listing 4-9 shows how nulls are treated when used in set operations.

Listing 4-9. *NULLs and Set Operations*

```
SQL> select null from dual
  2  union
  3  select null from dual
  4  ;

N
-


1 row selected.

SQL> select null from dual
  2  union all
  3  select null from dual
  4  ;

N
-



2 rows selected.

SQL> select null from dual
  2  intersect
  3  select null from dual;

N
-


1 row selected.

SQL> select null from dual
  2  minus
  3  select null from dual;

no rows selected
```

```
SQL> select 1 from dual
  2  union
  3  select null from dual;

          1
--------------
          1


2 rows selected.

SQL> select 1 from dual
  2  union all
  3  select null from dual;

          1
--------------
          1


2 rows selected.

SQL> select 1 from dual
  2  intersect
  3  select null from dual ;

no rows selected

SQL> select 1 from dual
  2  minus
  3  select null from dual ;

          1
--------------
          1


1 row selected.
```

In the first example, when you have two rows with nulls that are unioned, you only end up with one row. That implies that the two rows were equal to one another and therefore when the union was processed, the duplicate row was excluded. As you noticed, the same is true for how the other set operations behave. So keep in mind that set operations treat nulls as equals.

NULLs and GROUP BY and ORDER BY

Just like in set operations, the GROUP BY and ORDER BY clauses process nulls as if they were able to be compared using equality checks. You'll notice that with both grouping and ordering, nulls are always placed together just like known values. Listing 4-10 shows an example of how nulls are handled in the GROUP BY and ORDER BY clauses.

Listing 4-10. *NULLs and GROUP BY and ORDER BY*

```
SQL> select comm, count(*) ctr
  2  from scott.emp
  3  group by comm ;

COMM               CTR
------ ---------------
                    10
  1400               1
   500               1
   300               1
     0               1

5 rows selected.

SQL> select comm, count(*) ctr
  2  from scott.emp
  3  group by comm
  4  order by comm ;

COMM               CTR
------ ---------------
     0               1
   300               1
   500               1
  1400               1
                    10

5 rows selected.

SQL> select comm, count(*) ctr
  2  from scott.emp
  3  group by comm
  4  order by comm
  5  nulls first ;

COMM               CTR
------ ---------------
                    10
     0               1
   300               1
   500               1
  1400               1

5 rows selected.
```

```
SQL> select ename, sal, comm
  2  from scott.emp
  3  order by comm, ename ;

ENAME        SAL   COMM
---------- ------ ------
TURNER       1500      0
ALLEN        1600    300
WARD         1250    500
MARTIN       1250   1400
ADAMS        1100
BLAKE        2850
CLARK        2450
FORD         3000
JAMES         950
JONES        2975
KING         5000
MILLER       1300
SCOTT        3000
SMITH         800

14 rows selected.
```

The first two examples show the behavior of nulls within a GROUP BY clause. Since the first query returned the result in what appeared to be descending sorted order by the comm column, I wanted to issue the second query to make a point that I made earlier in the book: the only way to ensure order is to use an ORDER BY clause. Just because the first query result appeared to be in a sorted order didn't mean it was. When I added the ORDER BY clause in the second query, the null group moved to the bottom. In the last ORDER BY example, note that the nulls are displayed last. That's not because nulls are considered to be "high values." It's because the default for ordered sorting is to place nulls last. If you want to display nulls first, you simply add the clause NULLS FIRST after your ORDER BY clause as shown in the third example.

NULLs and Aggregate Functions

This same difference of the treatment of nulls with some operations like set operations, grouping and ordering, also applies to aggregate functions. When nulls are present in columns that have aggregate functions such as SUM, COUNT, AVG, MIN, or MAX applied to them, they are removed from the set being aggregated. If the set that results is empty, then the aggregate returns a null.

An exception to this rule involves the use of the COUNT aggregate function. The handling of nulls depends on if the COUNT function is formulated using a column name or a literal (like * or 1). Listing 4-11 demonstrates how aggregate functions handle nulls.

Listing 4-11. *NULLs and Aggregate Functions*

```
SQL> select count(*) row_ct, count(comm) comm_ct,
  2          avg(comm) avg_comm, min(comm) min_comm,
  3          max(comm) max_comm, sum(comm) sum_comm
  4   from scott.emp ;

  ROW_CT  COMM_CT AVG_COMM MIN_COMM MAX_COMM SUM_COMM
-------- -------- -------- -------- -------- --------
      14        4      550        0     1400     2200

1 row selected.
```

Notice the difference in the value for COUNT(*) and COUNT(comm). Using * produces the answer of 14, which is the total of all rows, while using comm produces the answer of 4, which is only the number of non-null comm values. You can also easily verify that nulls are removed prior to the computation of AVG, MIN, MAX, and SUM since all the functions produce an answer. If nulls hadn't been removed, the answers would have all been null.

Summary

Thinking in sets is a key skill to master in order to write SQL that is easier to understand and that will typically perform better than SQL written from a procedural approach. When you think procedurally, you attempt to force the SQL language, which is non-procedural, to function in ways it shouldn't need to function.

In this chapter, you reviewed these two approaches and discussed how to begin to shift your thinking from procedural to set-based. As you proceed through the rest of the book, work to keep a set-based approach in mind. If you find yourself thinking row-by-row in a procedural fashion, stop and check yourself. The more practice you give yourself, the easier it will become.

Lastly, early in the chapter I promised to show the solution to the puzzle in Figure 4-1. You can see that solution now, in Figure 4-7. Here's a detailed explanation:

SET 1: All have three symbols, all symbols are squiggles, all symbols are solid, all symbols are different colors

SET 2: All symbols are red, all symbols are different shapes, all symbols are solid, all have different number of symbols

SET 3: All symbols are ovals, all symbols are different colors, all symbols have different fill, all have different number of symbols

SET 4: All symbols are diamonds, all symbols are different colors, all symbols are solid, all have different number of symbols

SET 5: All symbols have different shape, all symbols are different colors, all symbols have different fill, all have different number of symbols

SET 6: All symbols have different shape, all symbols are different colors, all symbols are solid, all have three symbols

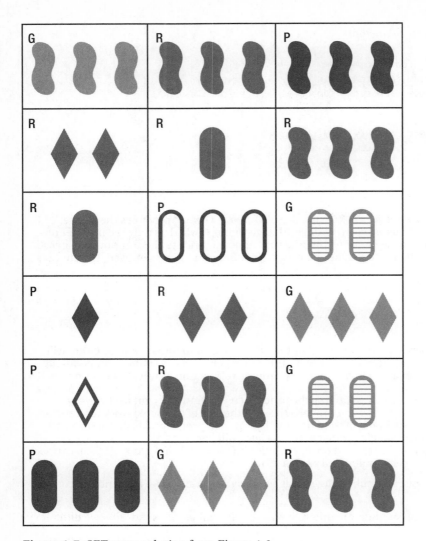

Figure 4-7. *SET game solution from Figure 4-1*

CHAPTER 5

■ ■ ■

It's About the Question

Karen Morton

"It's not about the query, it's about the question." That's one of my favorite sayings when it comes to writing SQL. Regardless of your level of proficiency, writing SQL well is as much about questions as it is about queries.

There are many ways that questions play an important role when writing SQL. First, understanding the question behind the query is often more important than the query syntax itself. If you start with the question the SQL is intended to answer, you will be more likely to think through and understand how to best formulate the query to get the desired result. Second, it is critical to be able to ask good questions to clarify what the SQL is intended to do and to gather all the pertinent information you'll need to write SQL that is not only functionally correct, but efficient as well. Finally, you must be able to create well-formed logical expressions that help answer the questions behind the SQL.

In this chapter, I'll cover how to go about ferreting out all the information you need to write the query in the best way possible. The way you do it is by asking good questions. Regardless of whether you are writing a new SQL statement or modifying an existing one, questions are the heart of the process.

Asking Good Questions

Asking good questions is an intellectual habit. Habits don't form overnight. Long ago, I read that it takes between 21 and 28 days to form a new habit. However, a 2009 research study published in the *European Journal of Social Psychology*[1] suggests that forming new habits actually takes an average of 66 days; however, the more complex a behavior is, the longer it takes for that behavior to become a habit. So, if you're not already in the habit of asking good questions, it's important to understand that learning to do so will take specific effort on your part to gain proficiency.

You may be wondering what any of this has to do with writing SQL. I believe knowing how to ask good questions, and even more specifically, knowing how to ask questions that will allow you to determine the correct question your SQL statement is intended to answer, is a crucial habit you'll need to form if you really want to elevate your SQL skills to the next level.

In order to write any SQL statement, begin with a question you need to answer. The answer will be a result set comprised from one or more rows of data from the tables in your database. As a starting point, you may be given the answer being sought in the form of a sample report or screen display. At other times, you'll be given a more complete specification for what the query needs to deliver. You shouldn't

---

[1] See www3.interscience.wiley.com/journal/122513384/abstract?CRETRY=1&SRETRY=0, www.telegraph.co.uk/health/healthnews/5857845/It-takes-66-days-to-form-a-habit.html, and www.spring.org.uk/2009/09/how-long-to-form-a-habit.php.

be surprised when I tell you that you'll get weak query specifications more often than you'll get strong, detailed ones. No matter how much information you are given about the queries you need to write, you need to make sure that you ask good questions that ensure you have everything you need to write SQL that does what it is supposed to—and does it quickly and efficiently.

The Purpose of Questions

Questions help you clarify the request and help you probe assumptions that either you or the requestor may hold. Questions can also help you to gather evidence and work out the implications or consequences of implementing code in certain ways. Questions are gold. Well, I suppose you could say that the answers are the gold, but questions are the tools you need to mine the gold.

In order to ask questions that will get you the information you need to write functionally correct and optimally performing SQL, you must be able to properly formulate your questions. Regardless of how much you know, or think you know, about what you've been asked to code, it can be helpful to start with a blank slate and ask questions as if you know nothing. By doing so, you are more likely to reach greater levels of detail and avoid making assumptions.

Many people think that asking questions makes them appear ignorant. I think that questions are a magic tool. Asking intelligent, well-crafted questions will cause people to think. And when someone thinks, the door is open for new ideas, new answers, and new possibilities to emerge. When you ask a person a question, particularly a person who wants something from you, you are letting them know that you care about what they want and that you want to service their request in the best way possible. Keeping silent out of a fear of looking dumb has more potential to backfire. If you don't ask questions and then deliver something that doesn't satisfy the request effectively, you'll call more negative attention to yourself than asking questions ever could.

I want to point out that you should ask questions even if you ask them only to yourself. As odd as that may sound, if you happen to be in a situation where there is no good resource at your disposal, you'll still need to ask questions and get answers. The answers will have to come from research you do, but if you start by preparing a good list of questions, you will be able to direct your research more clearly.

Categories of Questions

There are many categorizations of questions. Typically, questions will be categorized primarily as open or closed. The category you choose depends on whether or not you want a longer, detailed answer or a short, limited answer.

Open questions are intended to open a dialogue and help you engage in a conversation. Answers to open questions usually provide more detail and can't be answered with a simple yes or no. Questions that begin with "What," "How," "Who," "When," and "Why" are open questions. Just be careful when asking "Why" questions as they may come across as confrontational. Remember that your questions should be intended to help you get all the detail you need but not put anyone on the defensive. For example, asking "Why would anyone ever choose to do it that way?" has a very different feeling than "What rationale prompted that choice?" does. Even if you discover something questionable, or just plain wrong, you can provide feedback directly and may not need to use "Why" questions very often.

Most of the time, your questions will be aimed at digging out facts. Objective open questions ask for specific information and tend to be answered with facts. However, you must take care to make sure you are getting facts and not opinions. Formulating a question subjectively by asking someone what they think about something will elicit a response that is more subjective. The difference can be a critical one.

Some open questions are intended to get responses to help you get ideas, particularly ideas about actions you should take. These are problem-solving questions. These types of questions are great to aid in brainstorming different approaches to take. Your colleagues are great people sources for the answers to these types of questions. Once you've got the detail you need, don't hesitate to bounce things off other developers. They'll often offer solutions you never would have thought of otherwise.

The two most common types of questions you should ask when developing SQL are objective and problem-solving questions. Here are a few examples:

- What is the data model and is a data dictionary or ERD available?

- How have other related queries, if any, been written?

- Who is the subject matter expert for this application?

- What are the response time requirements for this query?

- How would you implement the request?

- What steps should I take next?

- What resources would you suggest I review?

If you just need a yes or no response or just a short answer, closed questions will best suit that purpose. Questions that begin with "Are," "Can," "Did," or "Do" will elicit short, direct responses. These types of questions should not be ambiguous. You want to make sure you ask the question so that you don't end up getting a long response if all you really wanted was a yes or no. These kinds of questions are intended to prevent or inhibit long discussions.

Closed questions can be separated into three types: identification, selection, and yes/no. When you use an identification type question, you want to know a specific answer but don't provide choices. A selection type question provides a list of two or more choices. The yes/no type asks for a simple yes or no response only.

To demonstrate the differences between these three types, I'll ask the same question in 3 different ways:

- Identification: What kind of table is employees?

- Selection: Is the employees table a heap table or an IOT?

- Yes/No: Is the employees table a heap table?

Of these types, the selection type is the one you will need to formulate most carefully. In this example, I provided only two selections: heap and IOT. But what if the table was a clustered table type? If you don't include that option in the selection list, you could end up getting a Yes/No answer to the original question. The person answering the question might (rudely) answer with a simple "No." Then you'd have to follow up with an identification question to get the answer you need.

Selecting the right type of question is almost as important as the question itself. You want to get the details needed as expeditiously as possible. So, remember to use closed questions if you want to keep answers short and open questions if you want to open up a discussion and get more detail. The most common mistake is asking a closed question when you really want more detail. For example, "Will you tell me about the project?" is technically a closed question that should return a yes or no answer. Most people have learned to provide a polite response (with detail) even when asked the wrong type of question. But it is truly your responsibility to ask the correct type and style of question to make it easier for the responder to provide you with the appropriate answer.

Questions about the Question

Developing new queries is usually easier than trying to modify a query that someone else has already written. This is because when you write a brand new query, you don't have to worry about interpreting the meaning of someone else's code. But, what you do have to worry about is the query specification. Whether it's detailed or not, it's your job to make sure you code the SQL to deliver the answer to the question you've been handed.

Let's walk through an example of how this process might work. I'll play the role of business user and you play the role of application developer. My request is for you to write a query that provides a list of employees who have held more than one job in the company. I'd like the output to display only the employee_id and a count of how many total jobs they've held. Listing 5-1 shows the query you create to satisfy my request.

Listing 5-1. *List of Employees Who Have Held Multiple Jobs*

```
SQL> select employee_id, count(*) job_ct
  2  from job_history
  3  group by employee_id
  4  having count(*) > 1;

   EMPLOYEE_ID        JOB_CT
--------------- ---------------
           101             2
           176             2
           200             2

3 rows selected.
```

That was pretty simple, right? You complete your testing and deliver this code. However, I quickly come back to you and say it's wrong. The list is missing some employees who have held more than one job. I had been manually producing this list previously and know that the following list of employees should be displayed: 101, 102, 114, 122, 176, 200, and 201.

What went wrong? This seemed like a fairly simple query, didn't it? It went wrong because the solution was developed without any questions being asked. By not asking questions, you made some assumptions (whether you realized it or not). The assumptions you made caused you to write the query as you did. The way you wrote the query didn't provide the result I was expecting. Admittedly, I could have helped you out more by giving you a more detailed specification or providing you with the expected result set initially. Regardless of the quality of the query specification you have, never forget that it is your job to ferret out the details and make sure you develop code that specifically answers the real question being asked.

Let's start over. The query specification I provided asked you to write a query that provides a list of employees who have held more than one job in the company, displaying the employee_id and a count of how many total jobs they've held. While at first glance, the query request seems straightforward, the apparent simplicity hides several nuances that you won't be aware of unless you ask some questions. The following list includes a few questions that you might have asked to help clarify the request:

- Should the query consider the employee's current job as part of the count or only jobs held other than the current position?

- Where is the data that will satisfy the request stored, i.e. in one table or several?

- What is the data model and can I get a copy of the data dictionary or an ERD (entity relationship diagram) if one exists?

- Is there an expected typical size of the result set?

- How is the data stored?

- Must this query meet any response time SLA (service level agreement)?

- How frequently will the query execute?

If you receive a request from a business user, it might not be feasible to ask them all of these questions. Asking a business user about which tables contain the data they want or if you could get a copy of the ERD might be answered with blank stares as those things aren't typically in the domain of the business user's knowledge. It is important to note whether the request for the query is coming from an application user or an application technical architect. Many of these questions can only be answered by someone with an understanding of the application from the technical perspective. Therefore, learn who the "go to" people are when you need to get detailed technical information. This may be the DBA, the data architect, or perhaps a developer that initially worked on other code in this particular application. Over time, you'll build the knowledge you need to determine many of these answers for yourself, but it's always good to know who the subject matter experts are for any application you support.

Getting answers to the first three questions are the most important, initially. You must know more than just a description of what the query needs to ask for. Being as familiar as possible with the data model is the starting point. When writing the original query, an assumption was made that the only table containing information needed to satisfy the query was the job_history table. If you had asked the first three questions, you'd have found out that the job_history table is truly a history table; it only contains historical data, not current data. The employees table contains a job_id column that holds the employee's current position information. Therefore, in order to determine how many positions an employee has held, you need to get their current job from the employees table and their previous jobs from the job_history table.

With this information, you might rewrite the query as shown in Listing 5-2.

Listing 5-2. *The Rewritten Employee Jobs Query*

```
SQL> select employee_id, count(*) job_ct
  2  from
  3  (
  4  select e.employee_id, e.job_id
  5  from employees e
  6  union all
  7  select j.employee_id, j.job_id
  8  from job_history j
  9  )
 10  group by employee_id
 11  having count(*) > 1;
```

```
    EMPLOYEE_ID              JOB_CT
    ---------------   ---------------
            102                    2
            201                    2
            101                    3
            114                    2
            200                    2
            176                    2
            122                    2
```

`7 rows selected.`

It looks like the answer is correct now. It's at this point that the answers to the next questions come into play. Knowing what to ask for is certainly important and the first three questions helped me describe the data the query needed to return. Most people would stop here. However, knowing *how* to get the data I'm after is just as important. This is contrary to what most of us are taught about relational databases in general. In one of my college courses on relational database management systems, I was taught that SQL is used to access data. There is no requirement that I need to know anything about where or how the data is stored or how the RDBMS processes a SQL statement in order to access that data. In other words, SQL is used to describe what will be done, not how it will be done.

The reality is that knowing how your data is stored and accessed is just as important as describing the data your query retrieves. Let's say you need to book a trip from Washington, DC to Los Angeles, CA. You call your travel agent to handle the booking for you. If the only information you provide to the agent is your departure and arrival cities and that you want the least expensive fare possible, what could happen? Well, it's possible that the least expensive fare involves leaving at 5:30 A.M. from Washington, DC then making stopovers in Atlanta, Chicago and Dallas before finally connecting into Los Angeles at midnight (Los Angeles time, which means it would be 3 A.M. in DC time). Would that be OK with you? Probably not. Personally, I'd be willing to pay extra to get a direct flight from DC to Los Angeles. Think about it. If you could get a direct flight leaving from DC at 8 A.M. and arriving into Los Angeles at 10 A.M., wouldn't it be worth quite a bit to you versus making multiple stopovers and spending nearly a full day to complete the trip? And what if the direct flight only cost 10% more than nightmare flight? Your original request to book the least expensive fare didn't include any conditions under which you'd be willing to pay more. So, your request was satisfied but you probably won't be happy with the outcome.

Knowing how the data is stored and how it *should* be accessed will ensure that your query not only returns the correct answer, but does so as quickly and efficiently as possible. That's why questions like "How big is the typical expected result set?", "How is the data stored?", and "How fast and how frequently does it need to execute?" must be asked. Without those answers, your query may get the correct answer but still be a failure due to poor performance. Simply getting the right result isn't enough. To be successful, your query must be *right* and it must be *fast*.

Questions about Data

I hope at this point you agree that you do need to concern yourself with how data is stored and how it should be accessed. Where do you find this information? The database can give you most of the answers you need by executing a few simple queries. Once you have this data, you then need to determine how data should be accessed. This comes from understanding how the various access and join methods work and when it is appropriate to use each. I've already covered access and join methods, so you've got the information you need to help you there. But how do you discover how the data is stored? Let's walk through the questions you need to ask and queries you can execute to get the answers.

As a first step, try to think like the optimizer would. The optimizer needs statistics and instance parameter values to be able to compute a plan. Therefore, it's a good idea for you to put yourself in the optimizer's place and gather the information that will help to formulate the execution plan. You should always seek out the answers to the following questions about the data:

- Which tables will be needed to gather all the data required?

- Are any of the tables partitioned, and if so, how are the partitions defined?

- What columns are in each table?

- What indexes are available in each table?

- What are the statistics for each table, column, and index?

- Are there histograms on any of the columns?

Statistics help the optimizer paint a picture of how the various ways of accessing and joining data will perform. You can know what the optimizer knows. All you need to be able to do is query the information from the data dictionary. One thing to keep in mind when you're reviewing statistics is that statistics may or may not accurately represent your data. If the statistics are stale, missing, or poorly collected, it's possible that they paint the wrong picture. The optimizer can only know what the statistics tell it. You, on the other hand, have the ability to determine if the statistics make sense. For example, if a date column in one of your tables has a high value of six months ago, you can quickly see that and know that rows exist with current date values. That visual inspection can help you determine if statistics need to be updated. But you can't know these kinds of things unless you look. A key question you must always ask is whether or not the statistics accurately represent your data. Listing 5-3 uses a single script named st-all.sql (previously used in Chapter 2) to answer each of the questions listed above in one simple script. It gives you a single source to review to verify how representative the available statistics really are.

Listing 5-3. *Getting All the Statistics Information You Need*

```
SQL> @st-all
Enter the owner name: sh
Enter the table name: sales
================================================================================
   TABLE STATISTICS
================================================================================
Owner         : sh
Table name    : sales
Tablespace    : EXAMPLE
Partitioned   : yes
Last analyzed : 09/03/2010 20:17:03
Sample size   : 918843
Degree        : 1
# Rows        : 918843
# Blocks      : 1769
Empty Blocks  : 0
```

```
Avg Space    : 0
Avg Row Length: 29
Monitoring?  : yes

==============================================================================
  PARTITION INFORMATION
==============================================================================

 Part# Partition Name      Sample Size        # Rows         # Blocks
 ------ ---------------  ---------------  ---------------  ---------------
     1 SALES_1995       .                            0                0
     2 SALES_1996       .                            0                0
     3 SALES_H1_1997    .                            0                0
     4 SALES_H2_1997    .                            0                0
     5 SALES_Q1_1998             43687           43687               90
...
    28 SALES_Q4_2003    .                            0                0


 Part# Partition Name  Partition Bound
 ------ ---------------  ---------------------------------------------------------
     1 SALES_1995       TO_DATE(' 1996-01-01 00:00:00', 'SYYYY-MM-DD HH24:MI:SS', ...
     2 SALES_1996       TO_DATE(' 1997-01-01 00:00:00', 'SYYYY-MM-DD HH24:MI:SS', ...
     3 SALES_H1_1997    TO_DATE(' 1997-07-01 00:00:00', 'SYYYY-MM-DD HH24:MI:SS', ...
     4 SALES_H2_1997    TO_DATE(' 1998-01-01 00:00:00', 'SYYYY-MM-DD HH24:MI:SS', ...
     5 SALES_Q1_1998    TO_DATE(' 1998-04-01 00:00:00', 'SYYYY-MM-DD HH24:MI:SS', ...
...
    28 SALES_Q4_2003    TO_DATE(' 2004-01-01 00:00:00', 'SYYYY-MM-DD HH24:MI:SS', ...

==============================================================================
  COLUMN STATISTICS
==============================================================================

Name          Null? NDV    Density   # Nulls  # Bkts  AvgLen  Lo-Hi Values
============================================================================
amount_sold   N     3586   .000279   0        1       5       6.4 | 1782.72
channel_id    N     4      .250000   0        1       3       2 | 9
cust_id       N     7059   .000142   0        1       5       2 | 101000
prod_id       N     72     .000001   0        72      4       13 | 148
promo_id      N     4      .000001   0        4       4       33 | 999
quantity_sold N     1      1.000000  0        1       3       1 | 1
time_id       N     1460   .000685   0        1       8       01/01/1998 00:00:00 |
                                                             12/31/2001 00:00:00
```

```
===========================================================================
   HISTOGRAM STATISTICS      Note: Only columns with buckets containing > 5% are shown.
===========================================================================


PROMO_ID (4 buckets)
1 97%


===========================================================================
   INDEX INFORMATION
===========================================================================


Index Name                              Dstnct  Lf/Blks Dt/Blks Cluf Unq? Type Part?
                     BLevel Lf Blks # Rows  Keys   /Key    /Key
-------------------- ------- ------- ------ ------ ------- ------- ----- ---- ---- -----
SALES_CHANNEL_BIX       1      47      92     4      11      23      92 NO   BITM YES
SALES_CUST_BIX          1     475   35808  7059      1       5   35808 NO   BITM YES
SALES_PROD_BIX          1      32    1074    72      1      14    1074 NO   BITM YES
SALES_PROMO_BIX         1      30      54     4      7      13      54 NO   BITM YES
SALES_TIME_BIX          1      59    1460  1460      1       1    1460 NO   BITM YES


Index Name                      Pos# Order Column Name
----------------------------- ---------- ----- --------------------------------
sales_channel_bix                 1 ASC   channel_id

sales_cust_bix                    1 ASC   cust_id

sales_prod_bix                    1 ASC   prod_id

sales_promo_bix                   1 ASC   promo_id

sales_time_bix                    1 ASC   time_id


===========================================================================
   PARTITIONED INDEX INFORMATION
===========================================================================


Index: SALES_CHANNEL_BIX
                                       Dst LfBlk DtBlk
Part# Partition Name  BLevel LfBlks # Rows Keys /Key  /Key CluF Partition Bound
----- --------------- ------ ------ ------ ---- ----  ---- ---- --------------------
    1 SALES_1995          0      0      0     0     0      0    0 TO_DATE('1996-01-01...
    2 SALES_1996          0      0      0     0     0      0    0 TO_DATE('1997-01-01...
    3 SALES_H1_1997       0      0      0     0     0      0    0 TO_DATE('1997-07-01...
```

137

```
     4 SALES_H2_1997        0       0       0     0     0      0      0 TO_DATE('1998-01-01...
     5 SALES_Q1_1998        1       2       5     4     1      1      5 TO_DATE('1998-04-01...
...
    28 SALES_Q4_2003        0       0       0     0     0      0      0 TO_DATE('2004-01-01...

Index: SALES_CUST_BIX

     1 SALES_1995           0       0       0     0     0      0      0 TO_DATE('1996-01-01...
     2 SALES_1996           0       0       0     0     0      0      0 TO_DATE('1997-01-01...
     3 SALES_H1_1997        0       0       0     0     0      0      0 TO_DATE('1997-07-01...
     4 SALES_H2_1997        0       0       0     0     0      0      0 TO_DATE('1998-01-01...
     5 SALES_Q1_1998        1      28    3203  3203     1      1   3203 TO_DATE('1998-04-01...
...
    28 SALES_Q4_2003        0       0       0     0     0      0      0 TO_DATE('2004-01-01...

Index: SALES_PROD_BIX

     1 SALES_1995           0       0       0     0     0      0      0 TO_DATE('1996-01-01...
     2 SALES_1996           0       0       0     0     0      0      0 TO_DATE('1997-01-01...
     3 SALES_H1_1997        0       0       0     0     0      0      0 TO_DATE('1997-07-01...
     4 SALES_H2_1997        0       0       0     0     0      0      0 TO_DATE('1998-01-01...
     5 SALES_Q1_1998        1       2      60    60     1      1     60 TO_DATE('1998-04-01...
...
    28 SALES_Q4_2003        0       0       0     0     0      0      0 TO_DATE('2004-01-01...

Index: SALES_PROMO_BIX

     1 SALES_1995           0       0       0     0     0      0      0 TO_DATE('1996-01-01...
     2 SALES_1996           0       0       0     0     0      0      0 TO_DATE('1997-01-01...
     3 SALES_H1_1997        0       0       0     0     0      0      0 TO_DATE('1997-07-01...
     4 SALES_H2_1997        0       0       0     0     0      0      0 TO_DATE('1998-01-01...
     5 SALES_Q1_1998        0       1       3     2     1      1      3 TO_DATE('1998-04-01...
...
    28 SALES_Q4_2003        0       0       0     0     0      0      0 TO_DATE('2004-01-01...

Index: SALES_TIME_BIX

     1 SALES_1995           0       0       0     0     0      0      0 TO_DATE('1996-01-01...
     2 SALES_1996           0       0       0     0     0      0      0 TO_DATE('1997-01-01...
     3 SALES_H1_1997        0       0       0     0     0      0      0 TO_DATE('1997-07-01...
     4 SALES_H2_1997        0       0       0     0     0      0      0 TO_DATE('1998-01-01...
     5 SALES_Q1_1998        1       3      90    90     1      1     90 TO_DATE('1998-04-01...
...
```

```
27 SALES_Q3_2003        0    0    0    0    0    0    0 TO_DATE('2003-10-01...
28 SALES_Q4_2003        0    0    0    0    0    0    0 TO_DATE('2004-01-01...
```

With this information, you can answer almost any question about the data. It is best if these statistics are from your production database where the SQL you are writing will be executed. If your development database doesn't have a copy of the production statistics, it's a good idea to request that the production stats be imported into the development database so that the optimizer is formulating plans based on information that is as close to production as possible. Even if the data doesn't match, remember that it's the statistics that the optimizer uses to determine the plan.

Now that you've obtained the statistics, you can use the information to ask, and answer, questions about what you'd expect the optimizer to do with your SQL. For example, if you were writing a query that needed to return all sales data for a specified customer (cust_id), you might want to know how many rows the optimizer will estimate the query to return. With the statistics information you have queried, you could compute the number of rows estimated to be returned by the query to be 130 (918,843 total rows x 1/7,059 distinct values). You can see that there is an index on cust_id, so the proper access operation to use to satisfy the query should be the SALES_CUST_BIX index. When you execute the query, you can verify this operation is selected by checking the execution plan.

In Chapter 3, I discussed the index statistic called *clustering factor*. This statistic helps the optimizer compute how many blocks of data will be accessed. Basically, the closer the clustering factor is to the number of blocks in the table, the fewer the estimated number of blocks to be accessed when using the index will be. The closer the clustering factor is to the number of rows in the table, the greater the estimated number of blocks will be. The fewer blocks to be accessed, the lower the cost of using that index and the more likely it is that the optimizer will choose that index for the plan. Therefore, you can check this statistic to determine how favorable the index will appear. Listing 5-4 shows the clustering factor statistics for the SALES table.

Listing 5-4. *Index clustering_factor*

```
SQL> select t.table_name||'.'||i.index_name idx_name,
  2          i.clustering_factor, t.blocks, t.num_rows
  3     from user_indexes i, user_tables t
  4    where i.table_name = t.table_name
  5      and t.table_name = 'SALES'
  6    order by t.table_name, i.index_name;
```

IDX_NAME	Clustering Factor	# Blocks	# Rows
SALES.SALES_CHANNEL_BIX	92	1769	918843
SALES.SALES_CUST_BIX	35808	1769	918843
SALES.SALES_PROD_BIX	1074	1769	918843
SALES.SALES_PROMO_BIX	54	1769	918843
SALES.SALES_TIME_BIX	1460	1769	918843

```
5 rows selected.
```

In this case, the clustering factors for all of the indexes for the SALES table have a low value (i.e. closer to the number of blocks in the table). That is a good indication that when the optimizer computes the cost of using these indexes, they will not be weighted too heavily based on the estimated number of blocks they will return if used.

In addition to using statistics, you can execute actual queries against the tables to get an idea of the data and number of rows that will be accessed or returned from a single table. Regardless of how complex a statement is, you can do just what the optimizer would do and break the statement down into single table accesses. For each table involved, simply execute one or more queries to count and review the data that would be returned using the filter conditions your SQL will use. As discussed previously, always think "divide and conquer." Breaking a statement down into small increments will help you understand how best to put it together in the most efficient way to arrive at the final result.

Building Logical Expressions

Once you understand the question that the statement you are writing needs to answer, you have to be able to build the SQL to provide the answer. There are often many possible ways to express the same predicate logic. Being able to formulate the conditions in a way that is easy to read and efficient requires you to think in ways you may not be used to. Remember when I discussed the idea of thinking in sets versus thinking procedurally in Chapter 4? There is a similar thought-shift that you may need to make in order to be able to build predicates for your SQL statements most efficiently.

The key is to learn some good Boolean logic techniques so that you don't have to rely on only one way to express conditional logic. You may find that using Boolean logic expressions will always produce the most efficient plan operation choices (make sure to test alternatives thoroughly), but it's good to know how to formulate different alternatives so you aren't stuck with a single way to do things.

When I say conditional logic, I mean an expression something like "if X then Y" where X and Y are both conditions. In a WHERE clause, you might want to have a condition like if :GetAll <> 1 then empno = :empno. In other words, if the value of the input bind variable named :GetAll is 1, then you want to return all rows, but if :GetAll is not 1, then only return rows where empno is equal to the :empno bind variable supplied. A WHERE clause to express this logic might be coded like this:

```
WHERE empno = CASE WHEN :GetAll <> 1 THEN :empno ELSE empno END
```

This logic works, but is a bit counterintuitive to me. Why would you even want to check empno = empno? There are other problems with this kind of formulation as well. If you need to check multiple columns, then you'll need multiple CASE statements. Plus, if empno is null, this check will fail, or at the very least give you a result you didn't expect.

The key is to change this expression to use a regular Boolean expression that uses only AND, OR, and NOT so that your "if X then Y" condition is translated to "(Not X) or Y". This becomes:

```
WHERE (:GetAll = 1) OR (empno = :empno)
```

What you are covering with this expression is that if :GetAll = 1, then you don't even want to bother with checking any more of the expression. Always remember that when using an OR condition, if one condition evaluates to TRUE, then the whole expression is TRUE. There is no need to even check the remaining expression. This "short-circuit" mechanism can save time by not requiring some of the code path to be evaluated. That means you'll not burn as many CPU cycles over all. Only if the first condition that the optimizer chooses to test evaluates to FALSE would the other expression need to be evaluated.

Although you're not looking at expressions involving ANDed conditions in these examples, you can apply similar thinking to the use of ANDed predicates. When using an AND condition, if the first condition evaluates to FALSE, then the whole expression is FALSE. There is no need to evaluate the second expression since both conditions must evaluate to TRUE for the whole condition to be TRUE. So, when you're using AND conditions, it's a good idea to write the condition so the expression that is most likely to evaluate to FALSE is placed first. Doing so allows the second expression evaluation to be short-circuited with similar savings as noted when placing a TRUE expression first in an OR condition.

A similar way of approaching this type of conditional expression is to use a single bind variable instead of two. In this case, you could say "if X is not null then Y = X". This becomes:

```
WHERE empno = NVL(:empno, empno)
```

This is basically the same as writing the CASE expression from the earlier example and could be converted to:

```
WHERE (:empno is null) OR (empno = :empno)
```

In both of these cases, the optimizer may have a bit of a dilemma with determining the optimal plan. The reason is that if the binds you use cause the comparison to end up returning all rows, then the plan operation best suited for that would likely be a full table scan. However, if you specify binds that end up limiting the result set, an index scan might be best. Since you're using bind variables, each time you execute the query, the input bind values could change. So, the optimizer has to choose a plan that will cover both situations. Most likely, you'll end up with a full table scan. Listing 5-5 demonstrates each of the scenarios I have covered and shows the execution plan output for each.

Listing 5-5. *Different Methods to Express Conditional Logic*

```
SQL> variable empno number
SQL> variable getall number
SQL>
SQL> exec :empno := 7369;

PL/SQL procedure successfully completed.

SQL>
SQL> exec :getall := 1;

PL/SQL procedure successfully completed.

SQL>
SQL> select /* opt1 */ empno, ename from emp
  2  where empno = CASE WHEN :GetAll <> 1 THEN :empno ELSE empno END;

     EMPNO ENAME
---------------- ----------
      7369 SMITH
      7499 ALLEN
      7521 WARD
      7566 JONES
      7654 MARTIN
      7698 BLAKE
      7782 CLARK
```

```
                    7788  SCOTT
                    7839  KING
                    7844  TURNER
                    7876  ADAMS
                    7900  JAMES
                    7902  FORD
                    7934  MILLER

14 rows selected.

SQL>
SQL> @pln opt1

PLAN_TABLE_OUTPUT
------------------------------------------------------------------------------------------
SQL_ID  gwcmrzfqf8cu2, child number 0
-------------------------------------
select /* opt1 */ empno, ename from emp where empno = CASE WHEN :GetAll
<> 1 THEN :empno ELSE empno END

Plan hash value: 3956160932

-------------------------------------------------------------------------
| Id  | Operation          | Name | Starts | E-Rows | A-Rows | Buffers |
-------------------------------------------------------------------------
|   0 | SELECT STATEMENT   |      |    1 |        |     14 |      8 |
|*  1 |  TABLE ACCESS FULL | EMP  |    1 |      1 |     14 |      8 |
-------------------------------------------------------------------------

Predicate Information (identified by operation id):
---------------------------------------------------

   1 - filter("EMPNO"=CASE  WHEN (:GETALL<>1) THEN :EMPNO ELSE "EMPNO" END )


19 rows selected.

SQL>
SQL> select /* opt2 */ empno, ename from emp
  2  where (:GetAll = 1) OR (empno = :empno);
```

```
     EMPNO ENAME
--------------- ----------
      7369 SMITH
      7499 ALLEN
      7521 WARD
      7566 JONES
      7654 MARTIN
      7698 BLAKE
      7782 CLARK
      7788 SCOTT
      7839 KING
      7844 TURNER
      7876 ADAMS
      7900 JAMES
      7902 FORD
      7934 MILLER

14 rows selected.

SQL>
SQL> @pln opt2

PLAN_TABLE_OUTPUT
-------------------------------------------------------------------------------------------
SQL_ID  0yk6utwur2fbc, child number 0
-------------------------------------
select /* opt2 */ empno, ename from emp where (:GetAll = 1) OR (empno =
:empno)

Plan hash value: 3956160932

---------------------------------------------------------------------
| Id  | Operation          | Name | Starts | E-Rows | A-Rows | Buffers |
---------------------------------------------------------------------
|   0 | SELECT STATEMENT   |      |      1 |        |     14 |       8 |
|*  1 |  TABLE ACCESS FULL | EMP  |      1 |      1 |     14 |       8 |
---------------------------------------------------------------------

Predicate Information (identified by operation id):
---------------------------------------------------

   1 - filter(("EMPNO"=:EMPNO OR :GETALL=1))


19 rows selected.
```

```
SQL>
SQL> exec :getall := 0;

PL/SQL procedure successfully completed.

SQL>
SQL> select /* opt3 */ empno, ename from emp
  2  where empno = CASE WHEN :GetAll <> 1 THEN :empno ELSE empno END;

        EMPNO ENAME
--------------- ----------
         7369 SMITH

1 row selected.

SQL>
SQL> @pln opt3

PLAN_TABLE_OUTPUT
--------------------------------------------------------------------------------------
SQL_ID  bfmz26532svu1, child number 0
---------------------------------------
select /* opt3 */ empno, ename from emp where empno = CASE WHEN :GetAll
<> 1 THEN :empno ELSE empno END

Plan hash value: 3956160932

-------------------------------------------------------------------------
| Id  | Operation          | Name  | Starts | E-Rows | A-Rows | Buffers |
-------------------------------------------------------------------------
|   0 | SELECT STATEMENT   |       |      1 |        |      1 |       8 |
|*  1 |  TABLE ACCESS FULL | EMP   |      1 |      1 |      1 |       8 |
-------------------------------------------------------------------------

Predicate Information (identified by operation id):
---------------------------------------------------

   1 - filter("EMPNO"=CASE  WHEN (:GETALL<>1) THEN :EMPNO ELSE "EMPNO" END )


19 rows selected.
```

```
SQL>
SQL> select /* opt4 */ empno, ename from emp
  2  where (:GetAll = 1) OR (empno = :empno);

         EMPNO ENAME
--------------- ----------
          7369 SMITH

1 row selected.

SQL>
SQL> @pln opt4

PLAN_TABLE_OUTPUT
--------------------------------------------------------------------------------
SQL_ID  aqp35x47gpphj, child number 0
-------------------------------------
select /* opt4 */ empno, ename from emp where (:GetAll = 1) OR (empno =
:empno)

Plan hash value: 3956160932

-----------------------------------------------------------------------
| Id  | Operation          | Name | Starts | E-Rows | A-Rows | Buffers |
-----------------------------------------------------------------------
|   0 | SELECT STATEMENT   |      |      1 |        |      1 |       8 |
|*  1 |  TABLE ACCESS FULL| EMP  |      1 |      1 |      1 |       8 |
-----------------------------------------------------------------------

Predicate Information (identified by operation id):
---------------------------------------------------

   1 - filter(("EMPNO"=:EMPNO OR :GETALL=1))


19 rows selected.

SQL>
SQL> select /* opt5 */ empno, ename from emp
  2  where empno = NVL(:empno, empno);
```

```
           EMPNO ENAME
---------------- ----------
            7369 SMITH

1 row selected.

SQL>
SQL> @pln opt5

PLAN_TABLE_OUTPUT
----------------------------------------------------------------------------------
SQL_ID  605p3gyjbw82b, child number 0
---------------------------------------
select /* opt5 */ empno, ename from emp where empno = NVL(:empno, empno)

Plan hash value: 1977813858
```

Id	Operation	Name	Starts	E-Rows	A-Rows	Buffers
0	SELECT STATEMENT		1		1	2
1	CONCATENATION		1		1	2
* 2	FILTER		1		0	0
3	TABLE ACCESS BY INDEX ROWID	EMP	0	14	0	0
* 4	INDEX FULL SCAN	PK_EMP	0	14	0	0
* 5	FILTER		1		1	2
6	TABLE ACCESS BY INDEX ROWID	EMP	1	1	1	2
* 7	INDEX UNIQUE SCAN	PK_EMP	1	1	1	1

```
Predicate Information (identified by operation id):
---------------------------------------------------

   2 - filter(:EMPNO IS NULL)
   4 - filter("EMPNO" IS NOT NULL)
   5 - filter(:EMPNO IS NOT NULL)
   7 - access("EMPNO"=:EMPNO)


27 rows selected.
```

```
SQL>
SQL> select /* opt6 */ empno, ename from emp
  2  where (:empno is null) OR (:empno = empno);

        EMPNO ENAME
--------------- ----------
         7369 SMITH

1 row selected.

SQL>
SQL> @pln opt6

PLAN_TABLE_OUTPUT
-------------------------------------------------------------------------------------
SQL_ID  gng6x7nrrrhy9, child number 0
-------------------------------------
select /* opt6 */ empno, ename from emp where (:empno is null) OR
(:empno = empno)

Plan hash value: 3956160932

----------------------------------------------------------------------
| Id  | Operation          | Name | Starts | E-Rows | A-Rows | Buffers |
----------------------------------------------------------------------
|   0 | SELECT STATEMENT   |      |      1 |        |      1 |       8 |
|*  1 |  TABLE ACCESS FULL | EMP  |      1 |      2 |      1 |       8 |
----------------------------------------------------------------------

Predicate Information (identified by operation id):
---------------------------------------------------

   1 - filter((:EMPNO IS NULL OR "EMPNO"=:EMPNO))
SQL>
SQL> exec :empno := null;

PL/SQL procedure successfully completed.

SQL>
SQL> select /* opt7 */ empno, ename from emp
  2  where empno = NVL(:empno, empno);
```

```
     EMPNO ENAME
--------------- ----------
      7369 SMITH
      7499 ALLEN
      7521 WARD
      7566 JONES
      7654 MARTIN
      7698 BLAKE
      7782 CLARK
      7788 SCOTT
      7839 KING
      7844 TURNER
      7876 ADAMS
      7900 JAMES
      7902 FORD
      7934 MILLER

14 rows selected.

SQL>
SQL> @pln opt7

PLAN_TABLE_OUTPUT
----------------------------------------------------------------------------------------
SQL_ID  83dydzdzbn5zh, child number 0
-------------------------------------
select /* opt7 */ empno, ename from emp where empno = NVL(:empno, empno)

Plan hash value: 1977813858
```

Id	Operation	Name	Starts	E-Rows	A-Rows	Buffers
0	SELECT STATEMENT		1		14	4
1	CONCATENATION		1		14	4
* 2	FILTER		1		14	4
3	TABLE ACCESS BY INDEX ROWID	EMP	1	14	14	4
* 4	INDEX FULL SCAN	PK_EMP	1	14	14	2
* 5	FILTER		1		0	0
6	TABLE ACCESS BY INDEX ROWID	EMP	0	1	0	0
* 7	INDEX UNIQUE SCAN	PK_EMP	0	1	0	0

```
Predicate Information (identified by operation id):
---------------------------------------------------

   2 - filter(:EMPNO IS NULL)
   4 - filter("EMPNO" IS NOT NULL)
   5 - filter(:EMPNO IS NOT NULL)
   7 - access("EMPNO"=:EMPNO)


27 rows selected.

SQL>
SQL> select /* opt8 */ empno, ename from emp
  2  where (:empno is null) OR (:empno = empno);

          EMPNO ENAME
--------------- ----------
           7369 SMITH
           7499 ALLEN
           7521 WARD
           7566 JONES
           7654 MARTIN
           7698 BLAKE
           7782 CLARK
           7788 SCOTT
           7839 KING
           7844 TURNER
           7876 ADAMS
           7900 JAMES
           7902 FORD
           7934 MILLER

14 rows selected.

SQL>
SQL> @pln opt8
```

```
PLAN_TABLE_OUTPUT
---------------------------------------------------------------------------------
SQL_ID  4zvrcjd586tt6, child number 0
-------------------------------------
select /* opt8 */ empno, ename from emp where (:empno is null) OR
(:empno = empno)
Plan hash value: 3956160932


--------------------------------------------------------------------------
| Id  | Operation         | Name | Starts | E-Rows | A-Rows | Buffers |
--------------------------------------------------------------------------
|   0 | SELECT STATEMENT  |      |    1 |        |   14 |       8 |
|*  1 |  TABLE ACCESS FULL| EMP  |    1 |      2 |   14 |       8 |
--------------------------------------------------------------------------

Predicate Information (identified by operation id):
---------------------------------------------------

   1 - filter((:EMPNO IS NULL OR "EMPNO"=:EMPNO))
```

For the first two examples where there are two bind variables, you'll notice that the optimizer chooses a full table scan operation in both cases. But, notice what happens when you use only a single variable in the second set of examples. In the second case, the optimizer uses a CONCATENATION plan for the NVL predicate and full table scan for the Boolean expression. The CONCATENATION plan is the best in this case as it will work such that when the bind variable is null, the plan will execute the INDEX FULL SCAN operation to get all the rows; when the bind variable is not null, the plan will execute the INDEX UNIQUE SCAN operation to get just the one row that is needed. That way, both options use an optimal execution path.

In this case, the Boolean logic didn't give you the best plan so it's good to know several alternative ways to formulate the predicate so you can work to achieve the best possible plan. With that in mind, you could actually have written the query as shown in Listing 5-6.

Listing 5-6. *Using a UNION ALL to Handle Conditional Logic*

```
SQL> select /* opt9 */ empno, ename from emp
  2  where :empno is null
  3  union all
  4  select empno, ename from emp
  5  where :empno = empno;

       EMPNO ENAME
--------------- ----------
        7369 SMITH

1 row selected.
```

```
SQL>
SQL> @pln opt9

PLAN_TABLE_OUTPUT
--------------------------------------------------------------------------------
SQL_ID  ab0juatnpc5ug, child number 0
-------------------------------------
select /* opt9 */ empno, ename from emp where :empno is null union all
select empno, ename from emp where :empno = empno

Plan hash value: 2001993376


----------------------------------------------------------------------------------
| Id  | Operation                    | Name   | Starts | E-Rows | A-Rows | Buffers |
----------------------------------------------------------------------------------
|   0 | SELECT STATEMENT             |        |      1 |        |      1 |       2 |
|   1 |  UNION-ALL                   |        |      1 |        |      1 |       2 |
|*  2 |   FILTER                     |        |      1 |        |      0 |       0 |
|   3 |    TABLE ACCESS FULL         | EMP    |      0 |     14 |      0 |       0 |
|   4 |    TABLE ACCESS BY INDEX ROWID| EMP   |      1 |      1 |      1 |       2 |
|*  5 |     INDEX UNIQUE SCAN        | PK_EMP |      1 |      1 |      1 |       1 |
----------------------------------------------------------------------------------


Predicate Information (identified by operation id):
---------------------------------------------------

   2 - filter(:EMPNO IS NULL)
   5 - access("EMPNO"=:EMPNO)
```

Similar to the CONCATENATION plan, in this case you get a plan where two separate sub-plans are unioned together to get the result. If the bind variable is null, you'll get a full scan operation and will get all rows returned. When the bind variable is not null, you'll get the unique index scan and return only the one row needed. The FILTER operation acts to determine if the first sub-plan should be executed or not. Notice the predicate information section where step 2 shows filter(:EMPNO IS NULL) indicating that only if the bind is null will the operation actually happen.

In general, you'll find that the optimizer will be able to make better plan operation choices when AND conditions are used. As covered earlier, this is because an OR condition means that there could be two different possible operations that could be used based on how the expression evaluates. With an AND condition, it is more likely that only a single choice, or at least choices that are not opposite in nature, will be considered. So, if you can figure out a way to formulate your predicates to use ANDed conditions solely, you may find that the SQL produces more efficient plans and even is easier to maintain.

Also, if you are writing SQL statements inside a larger code body, like in a PL/SQL procedure, use conditional constructs in the language and don't put that logic in the SQL. The simpler you can make your SQL, and the fewer conditions that have to be handled in the statement directly, the less complexity the optimizer will need to sort through to determine an optimal plan.

Summary

Questions are an important part of the process of writing good SQL. You begin by understanding the question the SQL needs to answer, then you follow up by asking questions about the data to formulate a SQL statement that is functionally correct as well as optimized for performance. The ability to ask good questions is an intellectual habit that must be developed over time. The more you work to ask questions that clarify and enhance your understanding of what you need to do, the greater your skills as a writer of high-quality, high-performing SQL will become.

■ ■ ■

SQL Execution Plans

Karen Morton

You've seen quite a few execution plans in the first chapters of this book, but in this chapter I'm going to go into detail about how to produce and read plans correctly. I've built the foundation of knowledge you need to understand the most common operations you'll see used in execution plans, but you need to put that knowledge into practice.

By the end of this chapter, I want you to feel confident that you can break down even the most complex execution plan and understand how any SQL statement you write is being executed. With the prevalence of development tools such as SQL Developer, SQL Navigator, and TOAD (just to name a few), that can produce explain plan output, it is fairly easy to generate explain plans. What isn't as easy is to get execution plans. You may be wondering what the difference is between an explain plan and an execution plan. As you'll see throughout this chapter, there can be a significant difference.

I'll walk through the differences between explain plan output and actual execution plan information. You'll learn how to compare the estimated plans with the actual plans and how to interpret any differences that are present. This is "where the rubber meets the road," as race car drivers would say.

Explain Plans

The EXPLAIN PLAN statement is used to display the plan operations chosen by the optimizer for a SQL statement. The first thing I want to clarify is that when you have EXPLAIN PLAN output, you have the estimated execution plan that *should be* used when the SQL statement is actually executed. You do not have the actual execution plan and its associated rowsource execution statistics. You have estimates only—not the real thing. Throughout this chapter, I will make the distinction between actual and estimated plan output by referring to estimated information as *explain plan output* and terming actual information as *execution plan output*.

Using Explain Plan

When using EXPLAIN PLAN to produce the estimated execution plan for a query, the output will show:

- Each of the tables referred to in the SQL statement.

- The access method used for each table.

- The join methods for each pair of joined row sources.

- An ordered list of all operations to be completed.

- A list of predicate information related to steps in the plan.
- For each operation, the estimates for number of rows and bytes manipulated by that step.
- For each operation, the computed cost value.
- If applicable, information about partitions accessed.
- If applicable, information about parallel execution.

Listing 6-1 shows the explain plan output produced for a query that joins five tables.

Listing 6-1. *EXPLAIN PLAN Example*

```
SQL> explain plan for
  2  select e.last_name || ', ' || e.first_name as full_name,
  3         e.phone_number, e.email, e.department_id,
  4         d.department_name, c.country_name, l.city, l.state_province,
  5         r.region_name
  6    from hr.employees e, hr.departments d, hr.countries c,
  7         hr.locations l, hr.regions r
  8   where e.department_id = d.department_id
  9     and d.location_id = l.location_id
 10     and l.country_id = c.country_id
 11     and c.region_id = r.region_id;

Explained.

SQL>
SQL> select * from table(dbms_xplan.display);

PLAN_TABLE_OUTPUT
--------------------------------------------------------------------------------
Plan hash value: 2498281325
```

Id	Operation	Name	Rows	Bytes	Cost (%CPU)
0	SELECT STATEMENT		106	11872	13 (16)
* 1	HASH JOIN		106	11872	13 (16)
* 2	HASH JOIN		27	1917	10 (20)
3	NESTED LOOPS		27	1539	6 (17)
4	MERGE JOIN		27	1134	6 (17)
5	TABLE ACCESS BY INDEX ROWID	DEPARTMENTS	27	513	2 (0)
6	INDEX FULL SCAN	DEPT_LOCATION_IX	27		1 (0)

```
|*  7 |       SORT JOIN            |                |  23 |  529 |   4  (25)|
|   8 |        TABLE ACCESS FULL   | LOCATIONS      |  23 |  529 |   3   (0)|
|*  9 |       INDEX UNIQUE SCAN    | COUNTRY_C_ID_PK|   1 |   15 |   0   (0)|
|  10 |     TABLE ACCESS FULL      | REGIONS        |   4 |   56 |   3   (0)|
|  11 |   TABLE ACCESS FULL        | EMPLOYEES      | 107 | 4387 |   3   (0)|
-----------------------------------------------------------------------------
```

Predicate Information (identified by operation id):

```
   1 - access("E"."DEPARTMENT_ID"="D"."DEPARTMENT_ID")
   2 - access("C"."REGION_ID"="R"."REGION_ID")
   7 - access("D"."LOCATION_ID"="L"."LOCATION_ID")
       filter("D"."LOCATION_ID"="L"."LOCATION_ID")
   9 - access("L"."COUNTRY_ID"="C"."COUNTRY_ID")
```

```
SQL> set autotrace traceonly explain
SQL>
SQL> l
  1  select e.last_name || ', ' || e.first_name as full_name,
  2                 e.phone_number, e.email, e.department_id,
  3                 d.department_name, c.country_name, l.city, l.state_province,
  4                 r.region_name
  5          from hr.employees e, hr.departments d, hr.countries c,
  6               hr.locations l, hr.regions r
  7          where e.department_id = d.department_id
  8            and d.location_id = l.location_id
  9            and l.country_id = c.country_id
 10*           and c.region_id = r.region_id
SQL> /
```

Execution Plan

Plan hash value: 2498281325

```
---------------------------------------------------------------------------
| Id  | Operation            | Name    | Rows | Bytes | Cost (%CPU)|
---------------------------------------------------------------------------
|   0 | SELECT STATEMENT     |         |  106 | 11872 |   13  (16)|
|*  1 |  HASH JOIN           |         |  106 | 11872 |   13  (16)|
|*  2 |   HASH JOIN          |         |   27 |  1917 |   10  (20)|
|   3 |    NESTED LOOPS      |         |   27 |  1539 |    6  (17)|
|   4 |     MERGE JOIN       |         |   27 |  1134 |    6  (17)|
```

| 5 |	TABLE ACCESS BY INDEX ROWID|	DEPARTMENTS	|	27 |	513 |	2	(0)|
| 6 |	INDEX FULL SCAN	| DEPT_LOCATION_IX |	27 |		1	(0)|
|* 7 |	SORT JOIN	|	23 |	529 |	4	(25)|
| 8 |	TABLE ACCESS FULL	| LOCATIONS	|	23 |	529 |	3	(0)|
|* 9 |	INDEX UNIQUE SCAN	| COUNTRY_C_ID_PK	|	1 |	15 |	0	(0)|
| 10 |	TABLE ACCESS FULL	| REGIONS	|	4 |	56 |	3	(0)|
| 11 |	TABLE ACCESS FULL	| EMPLOYEES	|	107 |	4387 |	3	(0)|

```
-------------------------------------------------------------------------------

Predicate Information (identified by operation id):
---------------------------------------------------

   1 - access("E"."DEPARTMENT_ID"="D"."DEPARTMENT_ID")
   2 - access("C"."REGION_ID"="R"."REGION_ID")
   7 - access("D"."LOCATION_ID"="L"."LOCATION_ID")
       filter("D"."LOCATION_ID"="L"."LOCATION_ID")
   9 - access("L"."COUNTRY_ID"="C"."COUNTRY_ID")
```

For this example, I used both the EXPLAIN PLAN command and the SQL*Plus AUTOTRACE command to generate the explain plan output. Using AUTOTRACE automates the steps to generate a plan so that all you have to do is turn on AUTOTRACE (using the TRACEONLY EXPLAIN option) and execute a query. The plan is generated and the output is displayed all in one step. When using this method to generate a plan, neither the EXPLAIN PLAN command nor the TRACEONLY EXPLAIN option actually executes the query. It only generates the plan that is estimated to be executed. The development tool you use (SQL Developer, TOAD, etc.) should also have an option to generate explain plans. I may be a bit old fashioned, but I find the text output often easier to read than the semi-graphical trees some of these common development tools use. I don't particularly need or care to see any little graphical symbols so I'm very happy with text output without any of the extra icons and such. But, don't feel you have to generate explain plans using these methods if you prefer to use your tool.

The information you see in explain plan output is generated by the EXPLAIN PLAN command and stored in a table named PLAN_TABLE by default. The AUTOTRACE command calls the display function from the supplied package named dbms_xplan to format the output automatically; you have to manually execute the query when using EXPLAIN PLAN (I'll discuss dbms_xplan in more detail shortly). For reference, Listing 6-2 shows the table description for the Oracle 11R2 PLAN_TABLE.

Listing 6-2. *PLAN_TABLE*

```
SQL> desc plan_table
 Name                            Null?    Type
 ------------------------------- -------- ------------------
 STATEMENT_ID                             VARCHAR2(30)
 PLAN_ID                                  NUMBER
 TIMESTAMP                                DATE
 REMARKS                                  VARCHAR2(4000)
 OPERATION                                VARCHAR2(30)
 OPTIONS                                  VARCHAR2(255)
 OBJECT_NODE                              VARCHAR2(128)
```

OBJECT_OWNER	VARCHAR2(30)
OBJECT_NAME	VARCHAR2(30)
OBJECT_ALIAS	VARCHAR2(65)
OBJECT_INSTANCE	NUMBER(38)
OBJECT_TYPE	VARCHAR2(30)
OPTIMIZER	VARCHAR2(255)
SEARCH_COLUMNS	NUMBER
ID	NUMBER(38)
PARENT_ID	NUMBER(38)
DEPTH	NUMBER(38)
POSITION	NUMBER(38)
COST	NUMBER(38)
CARDINALITY	NUMBER(38)
BYTES	NUMBER(38)
OTHER_TAG	VARCHAR2(255)
PARTITION_START	VARCHAR2(255)
PARTITION_STOP	VARCHAR2(255)
PARTITION_ID	NUMBER(38)
OTHER	LONG
OTHER_XML	CLOB
DISTRIBUTION	VARCHAR2(30)
CPU_COST	NUMBER(38)
IO_COST	NUMBER(38)
TEMP_SPACE	NUMBER(38)
ACCESS_PREDICATES	VARCHAR2(4000)
FILTER_PREDICATES	VARCHAR2(4000)
PROJECTION	VARCHAR2(4000)
TIME	NUMBER(38)
QBLOCK_NAME	VARCHAR2(30)

I'm not going to review every column listed but I wanted to provide a table description from which you can do further study if you desire. You'll find more information in the Oracle documentation.

The columns from the PLAN_TABLE shown in the explain plan output in Listing 6-1 are only a few of the columns from the table. One of the nice things about the dbms_xplan.display function is that it has the intelligence built in so that it will display the appropriate columns based on the specific plan generated for each SQL statement. For example, if the plan used partition operations, the PARTITION_START, PARTITION_STOP, and PARTITION_ID columns would appear in the display. The ability of dbms_xplan.display to automatically determine the columns that should be shown is a super feature that beats using the old do-it-yourself query against the PLAN_TABLE hands down.

The columns shown in the display for the example query plan are: ID, OPERATION, OPTIONS, OBJECT_NAME, CARDINALITY, BYTES, COST, TIME (this was included but elided in order to save space), ACCESS_PREDICATES, and FILTER_PREDICATES. These are the most typical display columns. Table 6-1 provides a brief definition of each of these common columns.

Table 6-1. *Most Commonly Used PLAN_TABLE Columns*

Column	Description
ID	Unique number assigned to each step.
OPERATION	Internal operation performed by the step.
OPTIONS	Additional specification for the operation column (appended to OPERATION).
OBJECT_NAME	Name of the table or index.
CARDINALITY	Estimated rows accessed by the operation.
BYTES	Estimated bytes accessed by the operation.
COST	Weighted cost value for the operation as determined by the optimizer.
TIME	Estimated elapsed time in seconds for the operation.
ACCESS_PREDICATES	Conditions used to locate rows in an access structure (typically an index).
FILTER_PREDICATES	Conditions used to filter rows after they have been accessed.

One of the columns from the PLAN_TABLE that is not displayed in the plan display output when using the dbms_xplan.display function is the PARENT_ID column. Instead of displaying this column value, the output is indented to provide a visual cue for the parent-child relationships within the plan. I think it would be helpful to include the PARENT_ID column value as well for clarity, but you'll have to write your own query against the PLAN_TABLE to produce the output to include that column if you want it. I created a simple query that I use to display the PARENT_ID for each step and keep it handy for cases when the plan is complicated enough that the visual indentions are harder to line up and follow. I still use the indentation but limit it to a single space per level. Listing 6-3 shows using this for the same query executed for Listing 6-1.

Listing 6-3. *Displaying the PARENT_ID*

```
SQL>select id, parent_id,
  2         lpad(' ',level) || operation || ' ' || options || ' ' ||
  3          object_name as operation
  4    from plan_table
  5    start with id = 0
  6    connect by prior id = parent_id ;

     ID  PARENT_ID OPERATION
---------- ---------- ------------------------------------------------
      0              SELECT STATEMENT
      1          0   HASH JOIN
      2          1    HASH JOIN
      3          2     NESTED LOOPS
```

```
 4        3        MERGE JOIN
 5        4          TABLE ACCESS BY INDEX ROWID DEPARTMENTS
 6        5            INDEX FULL SCAN DEPT_LOCATION_IX
 7        4          SORT JOIN
 8        7            TABLE ACCESS FULL LOCATIONS
 9        3          INDEX UNIQUE SCAN COUNTRY_C_ID_PK
10        2        TABLE ACCESS FULL REGIONS
11        1        TABLE ACCESS FULL EMPLOYEES
```

The PARENT_ID is helpful as operations in a plan are easiest to read if you keep in mind the parent-child relationships involved in the plan. Each step in the plan will have from zero to two children. If you break the plan down into smaller chunks of parent-child groupings, it will make it easier for you to read and understand.

In the example plan, you have operations with 0, 1, and 2 children. A full table scan operation, for example, doesn't have any children. See the line for ID=8 in Listing 6-3. Another example of an operation with zero children is line 6. If you glance down the PARENT_ID column, you'll notice that neither steps 6 nor 8 show up. This means that these operations do not depend on any other operation in order to complete. Both operations are children of other operations, however, and will pass the data they access to their parent step. When an operation has no children, the rows (CARDINALITY column in the PLAN_TABLE) estimate shown represents the number of rows that a single iteration of that operation will acquire. This can be a bit confusing when the operation is providing rows to an iterative parent. For example, step 9 is an index unique scan operation which shows a row estimate of 1 row (see listing 6-1). But the estimate doesn't indicate the total number of rows accessed in that step. The total is determined by the parent operation. I'll delve into this is more detail shortly.

The parent steps for steps 6 and 8—steps 5 and 7—are examples of single child operations. In general, operations with only one child can be divided into three categories:

- **Working operations** receive a row set from the child operation and manipulate it further before passing it on to its parent.
- **Pass-thru operations** act simply as a pass-thru and don't alter or manipulate the data from the child in any way. They basically serve to identify an operation characteristic. The VIEW operation is a good example of a pass-thru operation.
- **Iterative operations** indicate that there are multiple executions of the child operation. You'll typically see the word ITERATOR, INLIST, or ALL in these types of operation names.

Both step 5 and step 7 are working operations. They take the row sets from their children (steps 6 and 8) and do some additional work. In step 5, the rowids returned from the index full scan are used to retrieve the DEPARTMENT table data blocks. In step 7, the rows returned from the full scan of the LOCATIONS table are sorted in order by the join column.

Finally, operations that have two children operate either iteratively or in succession. When the parent type is iterative, the child row sources are accessed such that for each row in row source A, B is accessed. For a parent operation that works on the children in succession, the first child row source is accessed followed by an access of the second row source. Join types such as NESTED LOOPS and MERGE JOIN CARTESIAN are iterative, as is the FILTER operation. All other operations with two children will work in succession on their child row sources.

The reason for this review is to highlight the importance of learning to take a "divide and conquer" approach to reading and understanding plan output. The larger and more complicated a plan looks, the harder it often is to find the key problem areas. If you learn to look for parent-child relationships in the plan output and narrow your focus to smaller chunks of the plan, you'll find it much easier to work with what you see.

Understanding How EXPLAIN PLAN can Miss the Mark

One of the most frustrating things about EXPLAIN PLAN output is that it may not always match the plan that is used when the statement is actually executed. There are three things to keep in mind about using EXPLAIN PLAN that make it susceptible to producing plan output that won't match the actual execution plan:

- EXPLAIN PLAN produces plans based on the environment at the moment you use it.

- EXPLAIN PLAN doesn't consider the datatype of bind variables (all binds are VARCHAR2).

- EXPLAIN PLAN doesn't "peek" at bind variable values.

For these reasons, it is very possible that EXPLAIN PLAN will produce a plan that won't match the plan that is produced when the statement is actually executed. Listing 6-4 demonstrates the second point about bind variable datatypes.

Listing 6-4. *EXPLAIN PLAN and Bind Variable Datatypes*

```
SQL>-- Create a test table where primary key column
SQL>-- is string datatype
SQL>create table regions2
  2  (region_id  varchar2(10) primary key,
  3   region_name varchar2(25));

Table created.

SQL>
SQL>-- Insert rows into the test table
SQL>insert into regions2
  2  select * from regions;

4 rows created.

SQL>
SQL>-- Create a variable and set its value
SQL>variable regid number
SQL>exec :regid := 1

PL/SQL procedure successfully completed.

SQL>
SQL>-- Turn on autotrace explain plan
SQL>set autotrace traceonly explain
```

```
SQL>
SQL>-- Execute query and get explain plan
SQL>select /* DataTypeTest */ *
  2  from regions2
  3  where region_id = :regid;

Execution Plan
----------------------------------------------------------
Plan hash value: 3821806520

-------------------------------------------------------------------------------
| Id  | Operation                    | Name          | Rows  | Bytes | Cost (%CPU)|
-------------------------------------------------------------------------------
|   0 | SELECT STATEMENT             |               |     1 |    21 |     1   (0)|
|   1 |  TABLE ACCESS BY INDEX ROWID | REGIONS2      |     1 |    21 |     1   (0)|
|*  2 |   INDEX UNIQUE SCAN          | SYS_C0011282  |     1 |       |     1   (0)|
-------------------------------------------------------------------------------

Predicate Information (identified by operation id):
---------------------------------------------------

   2 - access("REGION_ID"=:REGID)

SQL>
SQL>set autotrace off
SQL>
SQL>-- Execute query again
SQL>select /* DataTypeTest */ *
  2  from regions2
  3  where region_id = :regid;

REGION_ID  REGION_NAME
---------- -------------------------
1          Europe

SQL>
SQL>-- Review the actual execution plan
SQL>-- This script uses dbms_xplan.display_cursor
SQL>@pln DataTypeTest
```

```
PLAN_TABLE_OUTPUT
-----------------------------------------------------------------------------------------
SQL_ID  2va424cgs3sfb, child number 0
------------------------------------
select /* DataTypeTest */ * from regions2 where region_id = :regid

Plan hash value: 670750275

-----------------------------------------------------------------------
| Id  | Operation          | Name     | Starts | E-Rows | A-Rows | Buffers |
-----------------------------------------------------------------------
|   0 | SELECT STATEMENT   |          |    1 |        |    1 |      8 |
|*  1 |  TABLE ACCESS FULL | REGIONS2 |    1 |     1 |    1 |      8 |
-----------------------------------------------------------------------

Predicate Information (identified by operation id):
---------------------------------------------------

   1 - filter(TO_NUMBER("REGION_ID")=:REGID)

Note
-----
   - dynamic sampling used for this statement (level=2)
```

Did you notice how the EXPLAIN PLAN output indicated that the primary key index would be used but the actual plan really used a full table scan? The reason why is clearly shown in the Predicate Information section. In the explained plan output, the predicate is "REGION_ID"=:REGID, but in the actual plan, the predicate shows TO_NUMBER("REGION_ID")=:REGID. This demonstrates how EXPLAIN PLAN doesn't consider the datatype of a bind variable and assumes all bind variables are string types. For the EXPLAIN PLAN, the datatypes were considered to be the same (both strings). However, the datatypes were considered when the plan was prepared for the actual execution of the statement and Oracle implicitly converted the string datatype for the REGION_ID column to a number to match the bind variable datatype (NUMBER). This is expected behavior in that when datatypes being compared don't match, Oracle will always attempt to convert the string datatype to match the non-string datatype. By doing so in this example, the TO_NUMBER function caused the use of the index to be disallowed. This is another expected behavior to keep in mind: the predicate must match the index definition exactly or else the index will not be used.

If you were testing this statement in your development environment and used the explain plan output to confirm that the index was being used, you'd be wrong. From the explain plan output, it would appear that the plan was using the index as you would expect, but when the statement was actually executed, performance would likely be unsatisfactory due to the full table scan that really would occur.

Another issue with using explain plan output as your sole source for testing is that you never get a true picture of how the statement uses resources. Estimates are just that—estimates. To really confirm the behavior of the SQL and to make intelligent choices about whether or not the statement will provide optimal performance, you need to look at actual execution statistics. I'll cover the details of how to capture and interpret actual execution statistics shortly.

Reading the Plan

Before I dive further into capturing actual execution plan data, I want to make sure you are comfortable with reading a plan. I've already discussed the importance of the PARENT_ID column in making it easier for you to break a long, complex plan down into smaller, more manageable sections. Breaking a plan down into smaller chunks will help you read it, but you need to know how to approach reading a whole plan from start to finish.

There are three ways that will help you read and understand any plan: 1) learn to identify and separate parent-child groupings, 2) learn the order in which the plan operations execute, and 3) learn to read the plan in narrative form. I have learned to do these three things so that when I look at a plan, my eye moves through the plan easily and I notice possible problem areas quickly. It can be frustrating and a bit slow at first, but given time and practice, it will become second nature.

The first place to start is with execution order. The plan is displayed in order by the sequential ID of operations. However, the order in which each operation executes isn't accomplished in a precise top-down fashion. Using the visual cues of the indentation of the operations, you can quickly scan a plan and look for the operations that are the most indented. The operation that is most indented is actually the first operation that will be executed. If there are multiple operations at that same level, the operations are executed in a top-down order.

For reference, I'm going to re-list the example plan here in Listing 6-5 so that you don't have to flip back a few pages to the original example in Listing 6-1.

Listing 6-5. *EXPLAIN PLAN Example (Repeated)*

```
---------------------------------------------------------------------------------------
| Id  | Operation                      | Name           | Rows  | Bytes | Cost (%CPU)|
---------------------------------------------------------------------------------------
|   0 | SELECT STATEMENT               |                |   106 | 11872 |   13  (16)|
|*  1 |  HASH JOIN                     |                |   106 | 11872 |   13  (16)|
|*  2 |   HASH JOIN                    |                |    27 |  1917 |   10  (20)|
|   3 |    NESTED LOOPS                |                |    27 |  1539 |    6  (17)|
|   4 |     MERGE JOIN                 |                |    27 |  1134 |    6  (17)|
|   5 |      TABLE ACCESS BY INDEX ROWID| DEPARTMENTS   |    27 |   513 |    2   (0)|
|   6 |       INDEX FULL SCAN          | DEPT_LOCATION_IX |  27 |       |    1   (0)|
|*  7 |      SORT JOIN                 |                |    23 |   529 |    4  (25)|
|   8 |       TABLE ACCESS FULL        | LOCATIONS      |    23 |   529 |    3   (0)|
|*  9 |     INDEX UNIQUE SCAN          | COUNTRY_C_ID_PK |   1 |    15 |    0   (0)|
|  10 |    TABLE ACCESS FULL           | REGIONS        |     4 |    56 |    3   (0)|
|  11 |   TABLE ACCESS FULL            | EMPLOYEES      |   107 |  4387 |    3   (0)|
---------------------------------------------------------------------------------------

Predicate Information (identified by operation id):
---------------------------------------------------

   1 - access("E"."DEPARTMENT_ID"="D"."DEPARTMENT_ID")
   2 - access("C"."REGION_ID"="R"."REGION_ID")
   7 - access("D"."LOCATION_ID"="L"."LOCATION_ID")
       filter("D"."LOCATION_ID"="L"."LOCATION_ID")
   9 - access("L"."COUNTRY_ID"="C"."COUNTRY_ID")
```

At a glance, you can see that lines 6 and 8 are the most deeply indented. Line 6 will execute first and pass the rowids from the index full scan to its parent (line 5). Line 8 will execute next and pass its row source to its parent (line 7). Steps will continue to execute from most indented to least indented with each step passing row source data to its parent until all steps complete. In order to help see the execution order more clearly, Listing 6-6 executes a query similar to the query used in Listing 6-3 that reads from the PLAN_TABLE and orders the output in execution order.

Listing 6-6. *Plan Operations Displayed in Execution Order*

```
SQL>select id, parent_id, operation
  2  from (
  3  select level lvl, id, parent_id, lpad(' ',level) || operation || ' ' || options
  4             || ' ' || object_name as operation
  5    from plan_table
  6    start with id = 0
  7    connect by prior id = parent_id
  8  )
  9  order by lvl desc, id;

        ID  PARENT_ID OPERATION
---------- ---------- --------------------------------------------------
         6          5          INDEX FULL SCAN DEPT_LOCATION_IX
         8          7          TABLE ACCESS FULL LOCATIONS
         5          4          TABLE ACCESS BY INDEX ROWID DEPARTMENTS
         7          4          SORT JOIN
         4          3         MERGE JOIN
         9          3          INDEX UNIQUE SCAN COUNTRY_C_ID_PK
         3          2        NESTED LOOPS
        10          2         TABLE ACCESS FULL REGIONS
         2          1       HASH JOIN
        11          1        TABLE ACCESS FULL EMPLOYEES
         1          0      HASH JOIN
         0                 SELECT STATEMENT
```

I often use an analogy between parent-child relationships in a plan and real life parent-child relationships. A real child doesn't just spontaneously combust into being; a parent is required to "instantiate" the child into being. But, like most any parent will tell you, one of the greatest things about kids is that (sometimes) you can get them to do work for you. This applies to parent-child operations in a plan. The child takes direction from its parent and goes to do a piece of work. When the child completes that work, it reports back to the parent with the result. So, even though an index operation occurs before its parent (for example, step 6 executes before its parent in step 5), the child wouldn't have meaning or existence without its parent. This is why it's important to always keep the parent-child relationships in mind as it helps make sense of the execution order.

One of the most helpful sections of the explained output is the section named Predicate Information. In this section, the ACCESS_PREDICATES and FILTER_PREDICATES columns are displayed. These columns are associated with a line (denoted by the ID column) in the list of plan operations. You'll notice that for each plan operation that has an access or filter predicate associated with it, there is an asterisk (*) next to the ID. When you see the asterisk, you know to look for that ID number in the Predicate Information section to see which predicate (condition in the WHERE clause) was related to that operation. Using this information you can confirm that columns were correctly (or not) used for index access and also to determine where a condition was filtered.

Filtering late is a common performance inhibitor. For example, if you wanted to move a pile of 100 rocks from the front yard to your back yard but only needed rocks that weighed 5-10 pounds, would you want to move all 100 rocks and then remove the ones you needed, or would you simply want to carry the ones that were the correct weight? In general, you'd want to only take the rocks you need, right?

Using the filter predicate information can help you verify that unneeded rows are filtered out of your result set as early as possible in the plan. Just like it wouldn't make much sense to carry a whole bunch of extra rocks to the back yard, it wouldn't make much sense to carry rows through a whole set of plan operations that ultimately will not be included in the final result set. You will use the filter information to verify that each condition is applied as early in the plan as possible. If a filter is applied too late, you can adjust your SQL or take other steps (like verifying statistics are up to date) to ensure your plan isn't working harder than it needs to.

Finally, learning to read the plan as if it were a narrative can be extremely helpful. For many people, converting the set of plan operations into a paragraph of text can facilitate understanding how the plan executes better than any other method. Let's convert your example plan into a narrative and see if it makes it easier for you to read and understand. The following paragraph is a sample narrative for the example plan.

> *In order to produce the result set for this SELECT statement, rows from the DEPARTMENTS table will be accessed utilizing a full scan of the index on the DEPARTMENTS.LOCATION_ID column. Using a full scan of the LOCATIONS table, rows will be retrieved and sorted by LOCATION_ID and then merged with the rows from DEPARTMENTS to produce a joined result set of matching rows containing both DEPARTMENTS and LOCATIONS data. This row set, which I'll call DEPT_LOC, will be joined to the COUNTRIES table and will iteratively match one row from DEPT_LOC using the COUNTRY_ID to find a matching row in COUNTRIES. This result set, which I'll call DEPT_LOC_CTRY, now contains data from DEPARTMENTS, LOCATIONS, and COUNTRIES and will be hashed into memory and matched with the REGIONS table data using the REGION_ID. This result set, DEPT_LOC_CTRY_REG, will be hashed into memory and matched with the EMPLOYEES table using the DEPARTMENT_ID to produce the final result set of rows.*

To produce this narrative, I simply walk through the steps of the plan in execution order and write out the description of the steps and how they link (join) to each other. I progress through each set of parent-child operations until all the steps are complete. You may find that creating a narrative helps you grasp the overall plan with a bit more clarity. For more complex plans, you may find that breaking out just a few key portions of the whole plan and writing it out in narrative form will help you better understand the flow of operations. The key is to use the narrative to help make better sense of the plan. If you find it harder to do this, then just stick with the plan as it is. But, taking time to learn to convert a plan into a narrative form is a good skill to learn as it can help you describe what your query is doing in a way that doesn't require anyone even looking at plan output. It's similar to giving verbal directions on how to get to the nearest shopping mall. You don't necessarily have to have the map to be able to get from point A to point B.

Execution Plans

The actual execution plan for a SQL statement is produced when a statement is executed. After the statement is hard parsed, the plan that is chosen is stored in the library cache for later reuse. The plan operations can be viewed by querying V$SQL_PLAN. V$SQL_PLAN has basically the same definition as the PLAN_TABLE except that it has several columns that contain the information on how to identify and find the statement in the library cache. These additional columns are: ADDRESS, HASH_VALUE, SQL_ID, PLAN_HASH_VALUE, CHILD_ADDRESS, and CHILD_NUMBER. You can find any SQL statement using one or more of these values.

Viewing Recently Generated SQL

Listing 6-7 shows a query against V$SQL for recently executed SQL for the SCOTT user and the identifying values for each column.

Listing 6-7. *V$SQL Query to Get Recently Executed SQL*

```
SQL>select /* recentsql */ sql_id, child_number, hash_value, address, executions, sql_text
  2    from v$sql
  3   where parsing_user_id = (select user_id
  4                              from all_users
  5                             where username = 'SCOTT')
  6     and command_type in (2,3,6,7,189)
  7     and UPPER(sql_text) not like UPPER('%recentsql%')
  8  /

SQL_ID        CHILD_NUMBER HASH_VALUE ADDRESS  EXECUTIONS SQL_TEXT
------------- ------------ ---------- -------- ---------- --------------------
g5wp7pwtq4kwp            0  862079893 3829AE54          1 select * from emp
1gg46m60z7k2p            0 2180237397 38280AD0          1 select * from bonus
4g0qfgmtb7z70            0 4071881952 38281D68          1 select * from dept

3 rows selected.
```

After connecting as user SCOTT, you execute the three queries shown. Then, when you run the query against V$SQL, you can see that they are now loaded into the library cache and each has identifiers associated with it. The SQL_ID and CHILD_NUMBER columns contain the identifying information that you'll use most often to retrieve a statement's plan and execution statistics.

Viewing the Associated Execution Plan

There are several ways to view the execution plan for any SQL statement that has been previously executed and still remains in the library cache. The easiest way is to use the dbms_xplan.display_cursor function. Listing 6-8 shows how to use dbms_xplan.display_cursor to show the execution plan for the most recently executed SQL statement.

Listing 6-8. *Using dbms_xplan.display_cursor*

```
SQL>select /*+ gather_plan_statistics */ empno, ename from scott.emp where ename = 'KING' ;

     EMPNO ENAME
---------- ----------
      7839 KING
SQL>
SQL>set serveroutput off
SQL>select * from table(dbms_xplan.display_cursor(null,null,'ALLSTATS LAST'));

PLAN_TABLE_OUTPUT
-------------------------------------------------------------------------------------------
SQL_ID  2dzsuync8upv0, child number 0
-------------------------------------
select empno, ename from scott.emp where ename = 'KING'

Plan hash value: 3956160932


---------------------------------------------------------------------------------
| Id  | Operation         | Name | Starts | E-Rows | A-Rows |   A-Time   | Buffers |
---------------------------------------------------------------------------------
|   0 | SELECT STATEMENT  |      |      1 |        |      1 |00:00:00.01 |       8 |
|*  1 |  TABLE ACCESS FULL| EMP  |      1 |      1 |      1 |00:00:00.01 |       8 |
---------------------------------------------------------------------------------

Predicate Information (identified by operation id):
---------------------------------------------------

   1 - filter("ENAME"='KING')
```

First, note the use of the gather_plan_statistics hint in the query. In order to capture rowsource execution statistics for the plan, you must tell Oracle to gather this information as the statement executes. The rowsource execution statistics include the number of rows, number of consistent reads, number of physical reads, number of physical writes, and the elapsed time for each operation on a row. This information can be gathered using this hint on a statement-by-statement basis, or you can set the STATISTICS_LEVEL instance parameter to ALL. Capturing these statistics does add some overhead to the execution of a statement and so you may not want to have it "always on." The hint allows you to use it when you need to—and only for the individual statements you choose. The presence of this hint collects the information and shows it in the Starts, A-Rows, A-Time, and Buffers columns. Listing 6-9 shows how the plan output would appear if you didn't use the hint (or set the parameter value to ALL).

Listing 6-9. *Using dbms_xplan.display_cursor without the gather_plan_statistics hint*

```
SQL>select ename from scott.emp where ename = 'KING' ;

ENAME
----------
KING

SQL>select * from table(dbms_xplan.display_cursor(null,null,'ALLSTATS LAST'));

PLAN_TABLE_OUTPUT
--------------------------------------------------------------------------------
SQL_ID  dgvds8td66zvk, child number 1
-------------------------------------
select ename from scott.emp where ename = 'KING'

Plan hash value: 3956160932

-------------------------------------------
| Id  | Operation        | Name | E-Rows |
-------------------------------------------
|   0 | SELECT STATEMENT |      |        |
|*  1 |  TABLE ACCESS FULL| EMP |     1 |
-------------------------------------------

Predicate Information (identified by operation id):
---------------------------------------------------

   1 - filter("ENAME"='KING')

Note
-----
   - Warning: basic plan statistics not available. These are only collected when:
       * hint 'gather_plan_statistics' is used for the statement or
       * parameter 'statistics_level' is set to 'ALL', at session or system level
```

As you can see, a Note is displayed indicating that the plan statistics aren't available and tells you what to do to collect them.

Collecting the Plan Statistics

The plan operations shown when no plan statistics are available is essentially the same as the output from EXPLAIN PLAN. To get to the heart of how well the plan worked, you need the plan's rowsource execution statistics. These values tell you what actually happened for each operation in the plan. This data is pulled from the V$SQL_PLAN_STATISTICS view. This view links each operation row for a plan to a row of statistics data. A composite view named V$SQL_PLAN_STATISTICS_ALL contains all the columns from V$SQL_PLAN plus the columns from V$SQL_PLAN_STATISTICS as well as a few additional columns containing information about memory usage. Listing 6-10 describes the V$SQL_PLAN_STATISTICS_ALL view columns.

Listing 6-10. *The V$SQL_PLAN_STATISTICS_ALL View Description*

```
SQL>desc v$sql_plan_statistics_all
Name                            Null?    Type
------------------------------- -------- --------------------
ADDRESS                                  RAW(4)
HASH_VALUE                               NUMBER
SQL_ID                                   VARCHAR2(13)
PLAN_HASH_VALUE                          NUMBER
CHILD_ADDRESS                            RAW(4)
CHILD_NUMBER                             NUMBER
TIMESTAMP                                DATE
OPERATION                                VARCHAR2(30)
OPTIONS                                  VARCHAR2(30)
OBJECT_NODE                              VARCHAR2(40)
OBJECT#                                  NUMBER
OBJECT_OWNER                             VARCHAR2(30)
OBJECT_NAME                              VARCHAR2(30)
OBJECT_ALIAS                             VARCHAR2(65)
OBJECT_TYPE                              VARCHAR2(20)
OPTIMIZER                                VARCHAR2(20)
ID                                       NUMBER
PARENT_ID                                NUMBER
DEPTH                                    NUMBER
POSITION                                 NUMBER
SEARCH_COLUMNS                           NUMBER
COST                                     NUMBER
CARDINALITY                              NUMBER
BYTES                                    NUMBER
OTHER_TAG                                VARCHAR2(35)
PARTITION_START                          VARCHAR2(64)
PARTITION_STOP                           VARCHAR2(64)
PARTITION_ID                             NUMBER
OTHER                                    VARCHAR2(4000)
DISTRIBUTION                             VARCHAR2(20)
CPU_COST                                 NUMBER
IO_COST                                  NUMBER
TEMP_SPACE                               NUMBER
ACCESS_PREDICATES                        VARCHAR2(4000)
```

FILTER_PREDICATES	VARCHAR2(4000)
PROJECTION	VARCHAR2(4000)
TIME	NUMBER
QBLOCK_NAME	VARCHAR2(30)
REMARKS	VARCHAR2(4000)
OTHER_XML	CLOB
EXECUTIONS	NUMBER
LAST_STARTS	NUMBER
STARTS	NUMBER
LAST_OUTPUT_ROWS	NUMBER
OUTPUT_ROWS	NUMBER
LAST_CR_BUFFER_GETS	NUMBER
CR_BUFFER_GETS	NUMBER
LAST_CU_BUFFER_GETS	NUMBER
CU_BUFFER_GETS	NUMBER
LAST_DISK_READS	NUMBER
DISK_READS	NUMBER
LAST_DISK_WRITES	NUMBER
DISK_WRITES	NUMBER
LAST_ELAPSED_TIME	NUMBER
ELAPSED_TIME	NUMBER
POLICY	VARCHAR2(10)
ESTIMATED_OPTIMAL_SIZE	NUMBER
ESTIMATED_ONEPASS_SIZE	NUMBER
LAST_MEMORY_USED	NUMBER
LAST_EXECUTION	VARCHAR2(10)
LAST_DEGREE	NUMBER
TOTAL_EXECUTIONS	NUMBER
OPTIMAL_EXECUTIONS	NUMBER
ONEPASS_EXECUTIONS	NUMBER
MULTIPASSES_EXECUTIONS	NUMBER
ACTIVE_TIME	NUMBER
MAX_TEMPSEG_SIZE	NUMBER
LAST_TEMPSEG_SIZE	NUMBER

The columns containing the pertinent statistics information that relates to the output from dbms_xplan.display_cursor all begin with the prefix LAST_. When you use the format option of ALLSTATS LAST, the plan shows these column values for each row in the plan. So, for each operation, you will know exactly how many rows it returned (LAST_OUTPUT_ROWS is shown in the A-Rows column), how many consistent reads occurred (LAST_CR_BUFFER_GETS is shown in the Buffers column), how many physical reads occurred (LAST_DISK_READS is shown in the Reads column), and number of times a step was executed (LAST_STARTS is shown in the Starts column). There are several other columns that will display depending on the operations that take place, but these are the most common.

The dbms_xplan.display_cursor call signature is

```
FUNCTION DISPLAY_CURSOR RETURNS DBMS_XPLAN_TYPE_TABLE
Argument Name                    Type                    In/Out Default?
------------------------------   --------------------    ------ --------
SQL_ID                           VARCHAR2                IN     DEFAULT
CURSOR_CHILD_NO                  NUMBER(38)              IN     DEFAULT
FORMAT                           VARCHAR2                IN     DEFAULT
```

In the example from Listing 6-8, the three parameters used were SQL_ID => null, CURSOR_CHILD_NO => null, and FORMAT => ALLSTATS LAST. The use of nulls for the SQL_ID and CURSOR_CHILD_NO parameters indicates that the plan for the last executed statement should be retrieved. Therefore, you should be able to execute a statement, then execute

```
select * from table(dbms_xplan.display_cursor(null,null,'ALLSTATS LAST'));
```

This will give you the plan output as shown in Listing 6-8.

■**CAUTION** You may have noticed that I executed the SQL*Plus command SET SERVEROUTPUT OFF before executing the call to dbms_xplan.display_cursor. This is a slight oddity that might catch you off-guard if you don't know about it. Whenever you execute a statement and SERVEROUTPUT is ON, a call to dbms_output is implicitly executed. If you don't turn SERVEROUTPUT OFF, then the last statement executed will be this dbms_output call. Using nulls for the first two parameters will not give you the SQL statement you executed, but instead will attempt to give you the plan for the dbms_output call. Simply turning this setting OFF will stop the implicit call and ensure you get the plan for your most recently executed statement.

Identifying SQL Statements for Later Plan Retrieval

If you want to retrieve a statement that was executed in the past, you can retrieve the SQL_ID and CHILD_NUMBER from V$SQL as demonstrated in Listing 6-7. To simplify finding the correct statement identifiers, especially when I'm testing, I add a unique comment that identifies each statement I execute. Then, whenever I want to grab that plan from the library cache, all I have to do is query V$SQL to locate the statement text that includes the comment I used. Listing 6-11 shows an example of this and the query I use to subsequently find the statement I want.

Listing 6-11. *Using a Comment to Uniquely Identify a SQL Statement*

```
SQL>select /* KM-EMPTEST1 */
  2        empno, ename
  3    from emp
  4   where job = 'MANAGER' ;
```

```
       EMPNO ENAME
---------- ----------
       7566 JONES
       7698 BLAKE
       7782 CLARK

SQL>select sql_id, child_number, sql_text
  2  from v$sql
  3  where sql_text like '%KM-EMPTEST1%';

SQL_ID        CHILD_NUMBER SQL_TEXT
------------- ------------ --------------------------------------------
9qu1dvthfcqsp            0 select /* KM-EMPTEST1 */      empno, ename
                           from emp where job = 'MANAGER'
a7nzwn3t522mt            0 select sql_id, child_number, sql_text from
                           v$sql where sql_text like '%KM-EMPTEST1%'

SQL>select * from table(dbms_xplan.display_cursor('9qu1dvthfcqsp',0,'ALLSTATS LAST'));

PLAN_TABLE_OUTPUT
--------------------------------------------------------------------------------------
SQL_ID  9qu1dvthfcqsp, child number 0
-------------------------------------
select /* KM-EMPTEST1 */      empno, ename  from emp where job =
'MANAGER'

Plan hash value: 3956160932

--------------------------------------------------------------------------------
| Id  | Operation         | Name | Starts | E-Rows | A-Rows |   A-Time   | Buffers |
--------------------------------------------------------------------------------
|   0 | SELECT STATEMENT  |      |      1 |        |      3 |00:00:00.01 |       8 |
|*  1 |  TABLE ACCESS FULL| EMP  |      1 |      3 |      3 |00:00:00.01 |       8 |
--------------------------------------------------------------------------------

Predicate Information (identified by operation id):
---------------------------------------------------

   1 - filter("JOB"='MANAGER')
```

You'll notice that when I queried V$SQL, two statements showed up. One was the SELECT statement I was executing to find the entry in V$SQL and one was the query I executed. While this set of steps gets the job done, I find it easier to automate the whole process into a single script. In that script, I find the statement I want in V$SQL by weeding out the query I'm running to find it and also by ensuring that I find the most recently executed statement that uses my identifying comment. Listing 6-12 shows the script I use in action.

Listing 6-12. *Automating Retrieval of an Execution Plan for any SQL Statement*

```
SQL>select /* KM-EMPTEST2 */
  2          empno, ename
  3    from emp
  4    where job = 'CLERK' ;

    EMPNO ENAME
---------- ----------
     7369 SMITH
     7876 ADAMS
     7900 JAMES
     7934 MILLER

SQL>
SQL>get pln.sql
  1   SELECT xplan.*
  2   FROM
  3     (
  4     select max(sql_id) keep
  5            (dense_rank last order by last_active_time) sql_id
  6          , max(child_number) keep
  7            (dense_rank last order by last_active_time) child_number
  8      from v$sql
  9      where upper(sql_text) like '%&1%'
 10        and upper(sql_text) not like '%FROM V$SQL WHERE UPPER(SQL_TEXT) LIKE %'
 11      ) sqlinfo,
 12      table(DBMS_XPLAN.DISPLAY_CURSOR(sqlinfo.sql_id, sqlinfo.child_number, 'ALLSTATS
LAST')) xplan
 13* /

SQL>@pln KM-EMPTEST2

PLAN_TABLE_OUTPUT
-----------------------------------------------------------------------------------SQL_ID
bn37qcafkwkt0, child number 0
-------------------------------------
select /* KM-EMPTEST2 */        empno, ename    from emp  where job =
'CLERK'
```

Plan hash value: 3956160932

```
--------------------------------------------------------------------------------
| Id  | Operation        | Name | Starts | E-Rows | A-Rows |   A-Time   | Buffers |
--------------------------------------------------------------------------------
|   0 | SELECT STATEMENT |      |     1  |        |      4 |00:00:00.01 |       8 |
|*  1 |  TABLE ACCESS FULL| EMP |     1  |     3  |      4 |00:00:00.01 |       8 |
--------------------------------------------------------------------------------
```

Predicate Information (identified by operation id):
----

   1 - filter("JOB"='CLERK')

This script will return the execution plan associated with the most recently executed SQL statement that matches the pattern you enter. As I mentioned, it is easier to find a statement if you've made an effort to use a comment to identify it, but it will work to find any string of matching text you enter. However, if there are multiple statements with matching text, this script will only display the most recently executed statement matching the pattern. If you want a different statement, you'll have to issue a query against V$SQL such as the one in Listing 6-11 and then feed the correct SQL_ID and CHILD_NUMBER to the dbms_xplan.display_cursor call.

Understanding DBMS_XPLAN in Detail

The DBMS_XPLAN package is supplied by Oracle and can be used to simplify the retrieval and display of plan output, as I have demonstrated. In order to use all the procedures and functions in this package fully, you'll need to have privileges to certain fixed views. A single grant on SELECT_CATALOG_ROLE will ensure you have access to everything you need, but at a minimum, you should have select privileges for VSQL, VSQL_PLAN, V$SESSION and V$SQL_PLAN_STATISTICS_ALL in order to properly execute just the display and display_cursor functions. In this section, I want to cover a few more details about the use of this package and, in particular, the format options for the display and display_cursor functions.

The dbms_xplan package has grown since it first appeared in Oracle version 9. At that time, it contained only the display function. In Oracle 11 release 2, the package includes 21 functions, although only six of them are included in the documentation. These functions can be used to display not only explain plan output, but plans for statements stored in the AWR (Automatic Workload Repository), SQL tuning sets, cached SQL cursors, and SQL plan baselines. The five main table functions used to display plans from each of these areas are:

- DISPLAY
- DISPLAY_CURSOR
- DISPLAY_AWR
- DISPLAY_SQLSET
- DISPLAY_SQL_PLAN_BASELINE

These five table functions all return the DBMS_XPLAN_TYPE_TABLE type, which is made up of 300 byte strings. This type accommodates the variable formatting needs of each table function to display the plan table columns dynamically as needed. The fact that these are table functions means that in order to call them you must use the TABLE function to cast the return type properly when used in a SELECT statement. A table function is simply a stored PL/SQL function that behaves like a regular query to a table would. The benefit is that you can write code in the function that performs transformations to data before it is returned in the result set. In the case of queries against the PLAN_TABLE or V$SQL_PLAN, the use of a table function makes it possible to do all the dynamic formatting needed to output only the columns pertinent for a given SQL statement instead of having to try and create multiple queries to handle different needs.

Each of the table functions accepts a FORMAT parameter as input. The FORMAT parameter controls what information is included in the display output. The following is a list of documented values for this parameter:

- BASIC displays only the operation name and its option.
- TYPICAL displays the relevant information and variably displays options like partition and parallel usage only when applicable. This is the default.
- SERIAL is the same as TYPICAL but always excludes parallel information.
- ALL displays the maximum amount of information in the display.

In addition to the basic format parameter values, there are several additional more granular options that can be used to customize the default behavior of the base values. You can specify multiple keywords separated by a comma or a space and use the prefix of a plus sign (+) to indication inclusion or a minus sign (-) to indicate exclusion of that particular display element. All of these options will display the information only if relevant. The following is a list of optional keywords:

- ADVANCED shows the same as ALL plus the Outline section and the peeked binds section.
- ALIAS shows the Query Block Name/Object Alias section.
- ALL shows the Query Block Name/Object Alias section, the predicate section, and the column projection section.
- ALLSTATS* is equivalent to IOSTATS LAST.
- BYTES shows the estimated number of bytes.
- COST is the cost information computed by the optimizer.
- IOSTATS* show IO statistics for executions of the cursor.
- LAST* shows only the plan statistics for the last execution of the cursor (the default is ALL and is cumulative).
- MEMSTATS* shows the memory management statistics for memory intensive operation like hash-joins, sorts, or some bitmap operators.
- NOTE shows the Note section.
- OUTLINE shows the Outline section (set of hints that will reproduce the plan).
- PARALLEL shows parallel execution information.
- PARTITION shows partition pruning information.

- PEEKED_BINDS shows bind variable values.

- PREDICATE shows the predicate section.

- PROJECTION shows the column projection section (which columns have been passed to their parent by each line and the size of those columns).

- REMOTE shows distributed query information.

The keywords followed by an asterisk are not available for use with the DISPLAY function as they utilize information from V$SQL_PLAN_STATISTICS_ALL that only exists after a statement has been executed. Listing 6-13 shows several examples of the various options in use.

Listing 6-13. *Display Options Using the FORMAT Parameter*

```
SQL> explain plan for
  2   select * from emp e, dept d
  3   where e.deptno = d.deptno
  4   and e.ename = 'JONES' ;

Explained.

SQL> select * from table(dbms_xplan.display(format=>'ALL'));

PLAN_TABLE_OUTPUT
---------------------------------------------------------------------------------------------
Plan hash value: 3625962092
```

Id	Operation	Name	Rows	Bytes	Cost (%CPU)	Time
0	SELECT STATEMENT		1	59	4 (0)	00:00:01
1	NESTED LOOPS					
2	NESTED LOOPS		1	59	4 (0)	00:00:01
* 3	TABLE ACCESS FULL	EMP	1	39	3 (0)	00:00:01
* 4	INDEX UNIQUE SCAN	PK_DEPT	1		0 (0)	00:00:01
5	TABLE ACCESS BY INDEX ROWID	DEPT	1	20	1 (0)	00:00:01

```
Query Block Name / Object Alias (identified by operation id):
-------------------------------------------------------------

   1 - SEL$1
   3 - SEL$1 / E@SEL$1
   4 - SEL$1 / D@SEL$1
   5 - SEL$1 / D@SEL$1
```

Predicate Information (identified by operation id):

```
   3 - filter("E"."ENAME"='JONES')
   4 - access("E"."DEPTNO"="D"."DEPTNO")
```

Column Projection Information (identified by operation id):

```
   1 - (#keys=0) "E"."EMPNO"[NUMBER,22], "E"."ENAME"[VARCHAR2,10],
       "E"."JOB"[VARCHAR2,9], "E"."MGR"[NUMBER,22], "E"."HIREDATE"[DATE,7],
       "E"."SAL"[NUMBER,22], "E"."COMM"[NUMBER,22], "E"."DEPTNO"[NUMBER,22],
       "D"."DEPTNO"[NUMBER,22], "D"."DNAME"[VARCHAR2,14], "D"."LOC"[VARCHAR2,13]
   2 - (#keys=0) "E"."EMPNO"[NUMBER,22], "E"."ENAME"[VARCHAR2,10],
       "E"."JOB"[VARCHAR2,9], "E"."MGR"[NUMBER,22], "E"."HIREDATE"[DATE,7],
       "E"."SAL"[NUMBER,22], "E"."COMM"[NUMBER,22], "E"."DEPTNO"[NUMBER,22],
       "D".ROWID[ROWID,10], "D"."DEPTNO"[NUMBER,22]
   3 - "E"."EMPNO"[NUMBER,22], "E"."ENAME"[VARCHAR2,10], "E"."JOB"[VARCHAR2,9],
       "E"."MGR"[NUMBER,22], "E"."HIREDATE"[DATE,7], "E"."SAL"[NUMBER,22],
       "E"."COMM"[NUMBER,22], "E"."DEPTNO"[NUMBER,22]
   4 - "D".ROWID[ROWID,10], "D"."DEPTNO"[NUMBER,22]
   5 - "D"."DNAME"[VARCHAR2,14], "D"."LOC"[VARCHAR2,13]
```

```
SQL> select empno, ename from emp e, dept d
  2  where e.deptno = d.deptno
  3  and e.ename = 'JONES' ;

     EMPNO ENAME
---------- ----------
      7566 JONES

1 row selected.

SQL> select * from table(dbms_xplan.display_cursor(null,null,format=>'ALLSTATS LAST -COST -
BYTES'));

PLAN_TABLE_OUTPUT
--------------------------------------------------------------------------------------------
SQL_ID  3mypf7d6npa97, child number 0
-------------------------------------
select empno, ename from emp e, dept d where e.deptno = d.deptno and
e.ename = 'JONES'
```

Plan hash value: 3956160932

```
-----------------------------------------------------------------------------------
| Id  | Operation        | Name | Starts | E-Rows | A-Rows |   A-Time    | Buffers | Reads |
-----------------------------------------------------------------------------------
|   0 | SELECT STATEMENT |      |    1   |        |    1   |00:00:00.03  |      8  |    6  |
|*  1 |  TABLE ACCESS FULL| EMP |    1   |    1   |    1   |00:00:00.03  |      8  |    6  |
-----------------------------------------------------------------------------------
```

Predicate Information (identified by operation id):
----

   1 - filter(("E"."ENAME"='JONES' AND "E"."DEPTNO" IS NOT NULL))

SQL> variable v_empno number
SQL> exec :v_empno := 7566 ;

PL/SQL procedure successfully completed.

SQL> select * from emp where empno = :v_empno ;

```
    EMPNO ENAME      JOB          MGR HIREDATE         SAL       COMM     DEPTNO
---------- ---------- --------- ---------- --------- ---------- ---------- ----------
     7566 JONES      MANAGER      7839 02-APR-81     3272.5                      20
```

1 row selected.

SQL> select * from table(dbms_xplan.display_cursor(null,null,format=>'+PEEKED_BINDS'));

PLAN_TABLE_OUTPUT

SQL_ID 9q17w9umt58m7, child number 0
----
select * from emp where empno = :v_empno

Plan hash value: 2949544139

```
---------------------------------------------------------------------------
| Id | Operation                   | Name   | Rows | Bytes | Cost (%CPU)| Time     |
---------------------------------------------------------------------------
|  0 | SELECT STATEMENT            |        |      |       | 1 (100)|          |
|  1 |  TABLE ACCESS BY INDEX ROWID| EMP    |    1 |    39 | 1   (0)| 00:00:01 |
|* 2 |   INDEX UNIQUE SCAN         | PK_EMP |    1 |       | 0   (0)|          |
---------------------------------------------------------------------------
```

Peeked Binds (identified by position):
----

   1 - :V_EMPNO (NUMBER): 7566

Predicate Information (identified by operation id):
----

   2 - access("EMPNO"=:V_EMPNO)

```
SQL> select /*+ parallel(d, 4) parallel (e, 4) */
  2  d.dname, avg(e.sal), max(e.sal)
  3  from dept d, emp e
  4  where d.deptno = e.deptno
  5  group by d.dname
  6  order by max(e.sal), avg(e.sal) desc;
```

```
DNAME             AVG(E.SAL)      MAX(E.SAL)
--------------    ---------------    ---------------
SALES             1723.3333333333            3135
RESEARCH                  2392.5            3300
ACCOUNTING        3208.3333333333            5500
SQL> select * from table(dbms_xplan.display_cursor(null,null,'TYPICAL -BYTES -COST'));
```

PLAN_TABLE_OUTPUT

SQL_ID gahr597f78j0d, child number 0

```
select /*+ parallel(d, 4) parallel (e, 4) */ d.dname, avg(e.sal),
max(e.sal) from dept d, emp e where d.deptno = e.deptno group by
d.dname order by max(e.sal), avg(e.sal) desc
```

Plan hash value: 3078011448

```
-------------------------------------------------------------------------------
| Id  | Operation              | Name     | Rows |  TQ   |IN-OUT| PQ Distrib  |
-------------------------------------------------------------------------------
|   0 | SELECT STATEMENT       |          |      |       |      |             |
|   1 |  PX COORDINATOR        |          |      |       |      |             |
|   2 |   PX SEND QC (ORDER)   | :TQ10004 |    4 | Q1,04 | P->S | QC (ORDER)  |
|   3 |    SORT ORDER BY       |          |    4 | Q1,04 | PCWP |             |
|   4 |     PX RECEIVE         |          |    4 | Q1,04 | PCWP |             |
|   5 |      PX SEND RANGE     | :TQ10003 |    4 | Q1,03 | P->P | RANGE       |
|   6 |       HASH GROUP BY    |          |    4 | Q1,03 | PCWP |             |
|   7 |        PX RECEIVE      |          |   14 | Q1,03 | PCWP |             |
|   8 |         PX SEND HASH   | :TQ10002 |   14 | Q1,02 | P->P | HASH        |
|*  9 |          HASH JOIN BUFFERED |     |   14 | Q1,02 | PCWP |             |
|  10 |           PX RECEIVE   |          |    4 | Q1,02 | PCWP |             |
|  11 |            PX SEND HASH| :TQ10000 |    4 | Q1,00 | P->P | HASH        |
|  12 |             PX BLOCK ITERATOR |   |    4 | Q1,00 | PCWC |             |
|* 13 |              TABLE ACCESS FULL| DEPT |  4 | Q1,00 | PCWP |             |
|  14 |           PX RECEIVE   |          |   14 | Q1,02 | PCWP |             |
|  15 |            PX SEND HASH| :TQ10001 |   14 | Q1,01 | P->P | HASH        |
|  16 |             PX BLOCK ITERATOR |   |   14 | Q1,01 | PCWC |             |
|* 17 |              TABLE ACCESS FULL| EMP |  14 | Q1,01 | PCWP |             |
-------------------------------------------------------------------------------
```

Predicate Information (identified by operation id):

```
   9 - access("D"."DEPTNO"="E"."DEPTNO")
  13 - access(:Z>=:Z AND :Z<=:Z)
  17 - access(:Z>=:Z AND :Z<=:Z)
```

Using Plan Information for Solving Problems

Now that you know how to access the various bits of information, what do you do with them? The plan information, particularly the plan statistics, helps you confirm how the plan is performing. You can use the information to determine if there are any trouble spots, so you can then adjust the way the SQL is written, add or modify indexes, or even use the data to support a need to update statistics or adjust instance parameter settings.

If, for example, there is a missing or sub-optimal index, you can see that in the plan. Listing 6-14 shows two examples: one shows how to determine an index is missing and the other shows how to determine if an index is sub-optimal.

Listing 6-14. *Using Plan Information to Determine Missing and Sub-Optimal Indexes*

```
SQL> -- Example 1: sub-optimal index
SQL>
SQL> select /* KM1 */ job_id, department_id, last_name
  2  from employees
  3  where job_id = 'SA_REP'
  4  and department_id is null ;

JOB_ID      DEPARTMENT_ID LAST_NAME
---------- --------------- -------------------------
SA_REP      .               Grant
SQL>
SQL> @pln KM1

PLAN_TABLE_OUTPUT
--------------------------------------------------------------------------------
SQL_ID  cdqaq2k8dvvma, child number 0
-------------------------------------
select /* KM1 */ job_id, department_id,
last_name from employees where job_id = 'SA_REP' and department_id is
null

Plan hash value: 1019430118save
```

```
---------------------------------------------------------------------------------------
| Id | Operation                    | Name        | Starts | E-Rows | A-Rows | Buffers |
---------------------------------------------------------------------------------------
|  0 | SELECT STATEMENT             |             |    1   |        |    1   |    4   |
|* 1 |  TABLE ACCESS BY INDEX ROWID | EMPLOYEES   |    1   |    1   |    1   |    4   |
|* 2 |   INDEX RANGE SCAN           | EMP_JOB_IX  |    1   |   30   |   30   |    2   |
---------------------------------------------------------------------------------------
```

```
Predicate Information (identified by operation id):
---------------------------------------------------

   1 - filter("DEPARTMENT_ID" IS NULL)
   2 - access("JOB_ID"='SA_REP')

SQL>
SQL> create index emp_job_dept_ix on employees (department_id, job_id) compute statistics ;
```

```
SQL>
SQL> select /* KM2 */ job_id, department_id, last_name
  2  from employees
  3  where job_id = 'SA_REP'
  4  and department_id is null ;

JOB_ID      DEPARTMENT_ID LAST_NAME
---------- --------------- -------------------------
SA_REP        .             Grant
SQL>
SQL> @pln KM2

PLAN_TABLE_OUTPUT
---------------------------------------------------------------------------------------
SQL_ID  b4wnf48g9pgzy, child number 0
-------------------------------------
select /* KM2 */ job_id, department_id, last_name from employees where
job_id = 'SA_REP' and department_id is null

Plan hash value: 798439539
```

Id	Operation	Name	Starts	E-Rows	A-Rows	Buffers
0	SELECT STATEMENT		1		1	2
1	TABLE ACCESS BY INDEX ROWID	EMPLOYEES	1	1	1	2
* 2	INDEX RANGE SCAN	EMP_JOB_DEPT_IX	1	1	1	1

```
Predicate Information (identified by operation id):
---------------------------------------------------

   2 - access("DEPARTMENT_ID" IS NULL AND "JOB_ID"='SA_REP')
       filter("JOB_ID"='SA_REP')

SQL> -- Example 2: missing index
SQL>
SQL> select /* KM3 */ last_name, phone_number
  2  from employees
  3  where phone_number = '650.507.9822';
```

```
LAST_NAME                PHONE_NUMBER
------------------------ --------------------
Feeney                   650.507.9822
SQL>
SQL> @pln KM3

PLAN_TABLE_OUTPUT
---------------------------------------------------------------------------
SQL_ID  8vzwg0vkrjp8r, child number 0
--------------------------------------
select /* KM3 */ last_name, phone_number from employees where
phone_number = '650.507.9822'

Plan hash value: 1445457117

---------------------------------------------------------------------------
| Id | Operation         | Name      | Starts | E-Rows | A-Rows | Buffers |
---------------------------------------------------------------------------
|  0 | SELECT STATEMENT  |           |    1   |        |    1   |    7    |
|* 1 |  TABLE ACCESS FULL| EMPLOYEES |    1   |    1   |    1   |    7    |
---------------------------------------------------------------------------

Predicate Information (identified by operation id):
---------------------------------------------------

   1 - filter("PHONE_NUMBER"='650.507.9822')

SQL> column column_name format a22 heading 'Column Name'
SQL> column index_name heading 'Index Name'
SQL> column column_position format 999999999 heading 'Pos#'
SQL> column descend format a5 heading 'Order'
SQL> column column_expression format a40 heading 'Expression'
SQL>
SQL> break on index_name skip 1
SQL>
SQL> -- Check current indexes
SQL>
SQL> select  lower(b.index_name) index_name, b.column_position,
  2              b.descend, lower(b.column_name) column_name
  3  from      all_ind_columns b
  4  where     b.table_owner = 'HR'
```

```
  5   and         b.table_name = 'EMPLOYEES'
  6   order by b.index_name, b.column_position, b.column_name
  7   /
```

```
Index Name                          Pos# Order Column Name
------------------------------ ---------- ----- -----------------
emp_department_ix                      1 ASC   department_id

emp_email_uk                           1 ASC   email

emp_emp_id_pk                          1 ASC   employee_id

emp_job_dept_ix                        1 ASC   department_id
                                       2 ASC   job_id

emp_job_ix                             1 ASC   job_id

emp_manager_ix                         1 ASC   manager_id

emp_name_ix                            1 ASC   last_name
                                       2 ASC   first_name
```

```
SQL> -- Create new index on phone_number
SQL>
SQL> create index emp_phone_ix on employees (phone_number) compute statistics ;
SQL>
SQL> select /* KM4 */ last_name, phone_number
  2   from employees
  3   where phone_number = '650.507.9822';
```

```
LAST_NAME                 PHONE_NUMBER
------------------------- --------------------
Feeney                    650.507.9822
SQL>
SQL> @pln KM4
```

```
PLAN_TABLE_OUTPUT
--------------------------------------------------------------------------------
SQL_ID  3tcqa5jqsyzm0, child number 0
-------------------------------------
select /* KM4 */ last_name, phone_number from employees where
phone_number = '650.507.9822'
```

Plan hash value: 1086981517

```
---------------------------------------------------------------------------
| Id  | Operation                    | Name         | Starts | E-Rows | A-Rows | Buffers |
---------------------------------------------------------------------------
|   0 | SELECT STATEMENT             |              |   1    |        |   1    |    3    |
|   1 |  TABLE ACCESS BY INDEX ROWID | EMPLOYEES    |   1    |   1    |   1    |    3    |
|*  2 |   INDEX RANGE SCAN           | EMP_PHONE_IX |   1    |   1    |   1    |    2    |
---------------------------------------------------------------------------
```

Predicate Information (identified by operation id):
----

   2 - access("PHONE_NUMBER"='650.507.9822')

In each of these examples, there are two keys to look for. I've made these examples short and simple to keep the output easy to view, but regardless of how complex the plan is, the way to spot a missing or sub-optimal index is to look for 1) a TABLE ACCESS FULL operation with a filter predicate that shows a small A-Rows value (i.e. small as in comparison to the total rows in the table) and 2) an index scan operation with a large A-Rows value as compared to the parent TABLE ACCESS BY INDEX ROWID A-Rows value.

In the first example, the index chosen is the EMP_JOB_IX index. The predicate contains two conditions: one for JOB_ID and one for DEPARTMENT_ID. Since the index is only a single-column index on JOB_ID, the index operation will return all rowids for rows with a JOB = 'SA_REP' and then hand those rowids to the parent step. The parent TABLE ACCESS BY INDEX ROWID step will retrieve all of these rows (there are 30) and then apply the filter condition for DEPARTMENT_ID IS NULL. The end result is that only 1 row matches the entire predicate. So, for this example, 97% of the rows were thrown away (29 out of 30).

This example is small, but imagine the additional overhead required if this query was accessing a very large table. By simply adding the DEPARTMENT_ID column to the index, the index scan operation will be able to return rowids that match the entire predicate. After adding the index, you can see how both the index scan and the table access step both have an A-Rows value of 1. In other words, the parent didn't have to do any work to retrieve rows that it ultimately threw away.

The second example, where no index exists on the column used in the predicate, the optimizer has no other choice except to choose a full table scan operation. But, as you can see from the A-Rows value, only 1 row was returned. Once again, the ill effects are minimal in this example since the table is so small. However, you should always watch out for full table scans that return a very small number of rows. The bigger the table becomes, the slower the query will become as more and more blocks have to be accessed to compare to the filter condition only to be thrown away.

In both cases, the main thing to watch out for is excess throw away. The more blocks that have to be accessed to check filter conditions on rows that will ultimately not be included in the result set, the poorer the performance will become. You may not even notice it if data volume is low in the beginning, but the larger the tables become, the more effect accessing unneeded blocks will have on response time.

Another way plan information can help you is by making it easy to spot when statistics might be out of date. Listing 6-15 shows an example of how plan information can point out stale statistics.

Listing 6-15. *Using Plan Information to Determine When Statistics May Be Out of Date*

```
SQL> -- Check current column statistics (collected at 100%)
SQL>
SQL> select column_name, num_distinct, density
  2  from user_tab_cols
  3  where table_name = 'MY_OBJECTS' ;
```

Column Name	NUM_DISTINCT	DENSITY
OWNER	29	.03448275862069
OBJECT_NAME	44245	.00002260142389
SUBOBJECT_NAME	161	.00621118012422
OBJECT_ID	72588	.00001377638177
DATA_OBJECT_ID	7748	.00012906556531
OBJECT_TYPE	44	.02272727272727
CREATED	1418	.00070521861777
LAST_DDL_TIME	1480	.00067567567568
TIMESTAMP	1552	.00064432989691
STATUS	1	1
TEMPORARY	2	.5
GENERATED	2	.5
SECONDARY	2	.5
NAMESPACE	21	.04761904761905
EDITION_NAME	0	0

```
SQL> -- Execute query for object_type = 'TABLE'
SQL>
SQL> select /* KM7 */ object_id, object_name
  2  from my_objects
  3* where object_type = 'TABLE';
...
365056 rows selected.

SQL> @pln KM7


PLAN_TABLE_OUTPUT
--------------------------------------------------------------------------------
SQL_ID  7xphu2p2m9hdr, child number 0
-------------------------------------
select /* KM7 */ object_id, object_name from my_objects where
object_type = 'TABLE'
```

Plan hash value: 2785906523

```
--------------------------------------------------------------------------------------
| Id  | Operation                    | Name          | Starts | E-Rows | A-Rows | Buffers |
--------------------------------------------------------------------------------------
|   0 | SELECT STATEMENT             |               |    1   |        |  365K  |  55697  |
|   1 |  TABLE ACCESS BY INDEX ROWID | MY_OBJECTS    |    1   |  1650  |  365K  |  55697  |
|*  2 |   INDEX RANGE SCAN           | OBJECT_TYPE_IX |   1   |  1650  |  365K  |  26588  |
--------------------------------------------------------------------------------------
```

Predicate Information (identified by operation id):
----

   2 - access("OBJECT_TYPE"='TABLE')

```
SQL> -- Compare statistic to actual
SQL>
SQL> select num_rows
  2  from dba_tables
  3  where table_name = 'MY_OBJECTS';

     NUM_ROWS
--------------
        72588

1 row selected.

SQL> select count(*)
  2  from my_objects ;

     COUNT(*)
--------------
       434792

1 row selected.

SQL> -- Update statistics
SQL>
SQL> exec dbms_stats.gather_table_stats(user,'MY_OBJECTS',estimate_percent=>100,
cascade=>true,method_opt=>'FOR ALL COLUMNS SIZE 1');

PL/SQL procedure successfully completed.
```

```
SQL> select /* KM8 */ object_id, object_name
  2  from my_objects
  3* where object_type = 'TABLE';
...
365056 rows selected.

SQL> @pln KM8

PLAN_TABLE_OUTPUT
-------------------------------------------------------------------------------------------
SQL_ID  2qq7ram92zc85, child number 0
-------------------------------------
select /* KM8 */ object_id, object_name from my_objects where
object_type = 'TABLE'

Plan hash value: 2785906523


-------------------------------------------------------------------------------------------
| Id  | Operation                   | Name          | Starts | E-Rows | A-Rows | Buffers |
-------------------------------------------------------------------------------------------
|   0 | SELECT STATEMENT            |               |    1   |        |  365K  |  54553  |
|   1 |  TABLE ACCESS BY INDEX ROWID| MY_OBJECTS    |    1   |  9882  |  365K  |  54553  |
|*  2 |   INDEX RANGE SCAN          | OBJECT_TYPE_IX|    1   |  9882  |  365K  |  25444  |
-------------------------------------------------------------------------------------------


Predicate Information (identified by operation id):
---------------------------------------------------

   2 - access("OBJECT_TYPE"='TABLE')

SQL> -- Collect histogram statistics
SQL>
SQL> exec dbms_stats.gather_table_stats(user,'MY_OBJECTS',estimate_percent=>100,
cascade=>true,method_opt=>'FOR ALL COLUMNS SIZE AUTO');

PL/SQL procedure successfully completed.

SQL> select /* KM9 */ object_id, object_name
  2  from my_objects
  3* where object_type = 'TABLE';
...
365056 rows selected.
```

```
SQL> @pln KM9

PLAN_TABLE_OUTPUT
--------------------------------------------------------------------------------
SQL_ID  dbvrtvutuyp6z, child number 0
-------------------------------------
select /* KM9 */ object_id, object_name from my_objects where
object_type = 'TABLE'

Plan hash value: 880823944


---------------------------------------------------------------------------
| Id  | Operation          | Name       | Starts | E-Rows | A-Rows | Buffers |
---------------------------------------------------------------------------
|   0 | SELECT STATEMENT   |            |    1 |        |   365K|   30000 |
|*  1 |  TABLE ACCESS FULL| MY_OBJECTS |    1 |    365K|   365K|   30000 |
---------------------------------------------------------------------------


Predicate Information (identified by operation id):
---------------------------------------------------

   1 - filter("OBJECT_TYPE"='TABLE')
```

In this example, the optimizer initially computed that only 1650 rows would be returned by the query for OBJECT_TYPE = 'TABLE'. This was due to the fact that the statistics had been computed prior to the addition of a few hundred thousand rows. When the plan was chosen, the optimizer didn't have the updated information and it selected a plan using an index scan on the object_type index based on the old statistics. However, in reality, there were over 474,000 total rows in the table and over 365,000 of them matched the filter criteria. So, you collected statistics and executed the query again. This time the estimate went up to 9882 rows, but that's still an incorrect estimate as compared to the actual rows returned.

What happened? You collected fresh statistics and even used a 100% estimate, so everything should be correct, right? Well, the problem was that you didn't collect histogram statistics that would tell the optimizer about the heavy skew in the distribution of values of the object_type column. You needed to use a method_opt parameter that would collect histograms. So, you did the collection again and this time used method_opt=>'FOR ALL COLUMNS SIZE AUTO'. This setting allows Oracle to properly collect a histogram on the object_type column. Now when you executed the query, the estimate is right on target and you get full table scan plan instead. In this case, the full scan operation is the best choice as the query returns nearly 80% of all the rows in the table and a full scan will access fewer blocks than an index scan plan would.

Summary

There is a wealth of information contained in plan output for every SQL statement. In this chapter, you have reviewed how plan output can be obtained using EXPLAIN PLAN to get only estimated information or obtained after executing the statement and extracting the plan information from the library cache using DBMS_XPLAN. At times, you may only be able to use EXPLAIN PLAN output, particularly if a query is very long-running and it is not easy or possible to wait to execute the query and get its actual execution data. However, in order to have the best information possible from which to make decisions about indexing, query syntax changes, or the need to update statistics or parameter settings, the use of actual plan execution statistics is the way to go.

I covered some of the ways you can use plan information to help diagnose and solve performance problems for a SQL statement. By carefully reviewing plan output, you can uncover sub-optimal or missing indexes and determine if statistics are stale and need to be updated. Utilizing the knowledge you've gained about the various plan operations for accessing and joining data and understanding how to read and effectively use plan information, you are equipped to not only solve problems quickly and efficiently when they arise, but to verify the characteristics and performance footprint of any SQL statement so that you can write well-behaved SQL from the start.

CHAPTER 7

■ ■ ■

Advanced Grouping

Jared Still

The GROUP BY clause is a venerable member of the SQL statement family. After learning basic SELECT statements, it is one of first specialized parts of SQL that many practitioners cut their teeth on when learning to create aggregations from raw data and transform that data into useful information.

Before I get too deeply into the use of GROUP BY, this would be a good time provide some information about the test environment. All SQL in this chapter was prepared using the Oracle 11.2.0.1 64 bit version on Windows 7. The database account I used has DBA privileges. Using an account with DBA privileges simplifies the use of dbms_xplan.display_cursor, using data from other accounts, and selecting data from system views. I would recommend that if you do the same, do so in a database strictly used for testing.

Much of the test data is provided by Oracle and can be setup on your database by running the scripts found in ORACLE_HOME/demo/schema and ORACLE_HOME/sqlplus/demo directories. The familiar SCOTT schema is included in the demo directory, along with the HR , SH, and other demo accounts. Where it makes sense to create test data to more clearly explain concepts, I will do so. For more complex examples, the built-in test data may be used. At times the examples may seem trivial. These examples are constructed with the purpose of demonstrating the results of different facets of the GROUP BY clause, without any requirement to focus needlessly on the values in the output. While there are many excellent examples based on financial data throughout the Oracle documentation, these examples are sometimes difficult to follow as too much attention is focused on the output values rather than how they were obtained.

The execution plans seen in the SQL examples were generated by the script showplan_last.sql, which is using the DBMS_XPLAN.DISPLAY_CURSOR procedure to generate the output. The code for that script is seen in Listing 7-1. You may have noticed that most of the SQL statements shown include the hint /*+ gather_plan_statistics */. This tells the optimizer to gather statistics for use by DBMS_XPLAN. The results of execution plans may be edited to fit the page, so the results may appear somewhat different when you execute the showplan_last.sql script.

Listing 7-1. *showplan_last.sql*

```
-- showplan_last.sql
set pause off
set verify off
set trimspool on
set line 200 arraysize 1
clear break
clear compute
-- serveroutput must be OFF for dbms_xplan.display_cursor to work.
-- but do not turn it off here, or the SET statemeent will be the 'last' cursor
```

```
select *
from table(dbms_xplan.display_cursor( null,null,'TYPICAL LAST'));
```

Now, let's learn about GROUP BY before moving on to its advanced functions.

Basic GROUP BY Usage

If you needed to know the number of employees in each department of your company, you might use SQL such as that in Listing 7-2 because it will produce one row of output for each row in the DEPT table plus a count of the employees from each department. The output includes the OPERATIONS department, which does not have any employees. This row would not have appeared in the output from a standard JOIN, so the LEFTOUTER JOIN statement was used to include rows from the DEPT table that did not have any matching rows in the EMP table.

Listing 7-2. *Basic GROUP BY*

```
1   select d.dname, count(empno) empcount
2   from scott.dept d
3   left outer join scott.emp e on d.deptno = e.deptno
4   group by d.dname
5   order by d.dname;
```

```
DNAME            EMPCOUNT
--------------   ----------
ACCOUNTING              3
OPERATIONS              0
RESEARCH                5
SALES                   6
```

4 rows selected.

The columns used in the GROUP BY must match the set of columns in the SELECT statement upon which no aggregation functions are used. In Listing 7-2, for example, there are two columns in the SELECT list, deptno and empno. The COUNT() function is used to perform aggregation on the EMPNO column so that the total number of employees in each department can be determined. The only other column in the SELECT list, deptno, must then be included in the GROUP BY clause.

Failure to include the correct columns will result in an error condition as seen in Listing 7-3.

Listing 7-3. *GROUP BY Columns Requirement*

```
1   select d.dname, count(empno) empcount
2   from scott.emp e
3   join scott.dept d on d.deptno = e.deptno
4   order by d.dname;
select d.dname, count(empno) empcount
       *
ERROR at line 1:
ORA-00937: not a single-group group function
```

There is a very important point you need to understand about GROUP BY: although the output of a SELECT statement that includes a GROUP BY clause may always appear to be sorted, you cannot expect GROUP BY to always return your data in sorted order. If the output must be sorted, you must use an ORDER BY clause. This has always been the case with Oracle, and this behavior has been documented since at least Oracle 7.0.

While the sorting behavior of GROUP BY is not specifically mentioned in the Oracle 7 documentation, there was little room for doubt when the 9i documentation was published, which specifically states that GROUP BY does not guarantee the order of the result set.

Listing 7-4 provides a good example of GROUP BY not returning results in sorted order. Notice that the data is not sorted. The only way to guarantee sorted data is by including the ORDER BY clause, which must follow the GROUP BY clause.

Listing 7-4. *GROUP BY Not Sorted*

```
1   select deptno, count(*)
2   from emp
3   group by deptno;

    DEPTNO    COUNT(*)
---------- ----------
        30          6
        20          5
        10          3


3 rows selected.
```

The GROUP BY clause may just be one of the most under-appreciated workhorses of all the SELECT clauses. It is quite easy to take it for granted, as once you understand how to include it in a SELECT statement, it is quite easy to use. Perhaps a better appreciation for just how much work it does (and how much work it saves you from doing) can be gained by trying to write the SELECT statement in Figure 7-2 without using the GROUP BY clause. There are likely many different methods by which this can be done.

Think for just a moment how you might go about writing that SELECT statement. One such attempt was made by your intrepid author, and this attempt can be seen in Listing 7-5. This is not SQL that most people would care to maintain. As you can see, it does create nearly the same output as that found in Listing 7-2. In addition to being somewhat convoluted, you must ask yourself, "What will happen when a new department is added to the DEPT table?"

The answer to that question, of course, is that you will then need to modify the SQL statement in Listing 7-5 to accommodate the change in the data. While it would be possible use dynamic SQL to duplicate the functionality of the SQL to cope with changes to the DEPT table data, doing so would create a piece of SQL that is even more difficult to follow and even harder to maintain.

Listing 7-5. *Convoluted SQL*

```
1   select /*+ gather_plan_statistics */
2   distinct dname, decode(
3       d.deptno,
4       10, (select count(*) from emp where deptno= 10),
5       20, (select count(*) from emp where deptno= 20),
6       30, (select count(*) from emp where deptno= 30),
7       (select count(*) from emp where deptno not in (10,20,30))
```

```
 8  ) dept_count
 9  from (select distinct deptno from emp) d
10  join dept d2 on d2.deptno = d.deptno;
```

```
DNAME          DEPT_COUNT
-------------- ----------
SALES                   6
ACCOUNTING              3
RESEARCH                5
```

3 rows selected.

22:19:51 MORIARTY - jkstill@jks1 SQL> @showplan_last

PLAN_TABLE_OUTPUT

```
-----------------------------------------------------------------------------------------
| Id  | Operation                       | Name     | Rows | Bytes | Cost (%CPU)| Time     |
-----------------------------------------------------------------------------------------
|   0 | SELECT STATEMENT                |          |      |       |   7 (100)|            |
|   1 |  SORT AGGREGATE                 |          |    1 |     3 |          |            |
|*  2 |   TABLE ACCESS FULL             | EMP      |    5 |    15 |   3   (0)| 00:00:01   |
|   3 |    SORT AGGREGATE               |          |    1 |     3 |          |            |
|*  4 |     TABLE ACCESS FULL           | EMP      |    5 |    15 |   3   (0)| 00:00:01   |
|   5 |      SORT AGGREGATE             |          |    1 |     3 |          |            |
|*  6 |       TABLE ACCESS FULL         | EMP      |    5 |    15 |   3   (0)| 00:00:01   |
|   7 |        SORT AGGREGATE           |          |    1 |     3 |          |            |
|*  8 |         TABLE ACCESS FULL       | EMP      |    4 |    12 |   3   (0)| 00:00:01   |
|   9 | HASH UNIQUE                     |          |    9 |   144 |   7  (29)| 00:00:01   |
|  10 |  MERGE JOIN                     |          |   14 |   224 |   6  (17)| 00:00:01   |
|  11 |   TABLE ACCESS BY INDEX ROWID   | DEPT     |    4 |    52 |   2   (0)| 00:00:01   |
|  12 |    INDEX FULL SCAN              | PK_DEPT  |    4 |       |   1   (0)| 00:00:01   |
|* 13 |   SORT JOIN                     |          |   14 |    42 |   4  (25)| 00:00:01   |
|  14 |    TABLE ACCESS FULL            | EMP      |   14 |    42 |   3   (0)| 00:00:01   |
-----------------------------------------------------------------------------------------
```

In addition to greatly simplifying the SQL that must be written, the GROUP BY clause eliminates unnecessary IO in the database. Take another look at Listing 7-5. You will see that a full table scan was performed on the EMP table five times. If you think that seems rather excessive, you are on the right track. Listing 7-6 shows the same SQL as executed in Listing 7-2, this time including the execution plan statistics. There is still a full table scan taking place against the EMP table, but only once—not five times as in the convoluted SQL in Listing 7-5.

Listing 7-6. *GROUP BY Execution Plan*

```
1  select /*+ gather_plan_statistics */
2     d.dname
3     , count(empno) empcount
4  from scott.emp e
```

```
5  join scott.dept d on d.deptno = e.deptno
6  group by d.dname
7  order by d.dname;
```

```
DNAME          EMPCOUNT
-------------- ----------
ACCOUNTING            3
RESEARCH             5
SALES                6
```

3 rows selected.

PLAN_TABLE_OUTPUT

```
-------------------------------------------------------------------------
| Id  | Operation                     | Name    | Starts | E-Rows | A-Rows |
-------------------------------------------------------------------------
|  0  | SELECT STATEMENT              |         |   1    |        |   3    |
|  1  |  SORT GROUP BY                |         |   1    |   4    |   3    |
|  2  |   MERGE JOIN                  |         |   1    |  14    |  14    |
|  3  |    TABLE ACCESS BY INDEX ROWID| DEPT    |   1    |   4    |   4    |
|  4  |     INDEX FULL SCAN           | PK_DEPT |   1    |   4    |   4    |
|* 5  |    SORT JOIN                  |         |   4    |  14    |  14    |
|  6  |     TABLE ACCESS FULL         | EMP     |   1    |  14    |  14    |
-------------------------------------------------------------------------
```

Predicate Information (identified by operation id):

```
  5 - access("D"."DEPTNO"="E"."DEPTNO")
      filter("D"."DEPTNO"="E"."DEPTNO")
```

HAVING Clause

Results generated by GROUP BY may be restricted by the criteria found in the HAVING clause. The HAVING clause is quite versatile, resembling the WHERE clause in the conditions that may be used. Functions, operators, and subqueries may all be used in the HAVING clause. Listing 7-7 shows a query that will return all departments that have hired at least five employees since the beginning of the first full year after hiring began.

That the HAVING operation is executed after all data has been fetched can be seen as the FILTER in step 1 of the execution plan shown in Listing 7-7. Notice that an operator, a function, and subqueries have all been used in the HAVING clause.

Listing 7-7. *HAVING Clause*

```
1  select /*+ gather_plan_statistics */
2     d.dname
3   , trunc(e.hiredate,'YYYY') hiredate
```

```
  4      , count(empno) empcount
  5    from scott.emp e
  6    join scott.dept d on d.deptno = e.deptno
  7    group by d.dname, trunc(e.hiredate,'YYYY')
  8    having
  9      count(empno) >= 5
 10      and trunc(e.hiredate,'YYYY') between
 11        (select min(hiredate) from scott.emp)
 12        and
 13        (select max(hiredate) from scott.emp)
 14    order by d.dname;
```

```
DNAME           HIREDATE             EMPCOUNT
--------------  -------------------  ----------
SALES           01/01/1981 00:00:00         6
```

1 row selected.

PLAN_TABLE_OUTPUT
```
-------------------------------------------------------------------------------
| Id | Operation                     | Name     | Starts | E-Rows | A-Rows |
-------------------------------------------------------------------------------
|  0 | SELECT STATEMENT              |          |    1 |        |      1 |
|* 1 |  FILTER                       |          |    1 |        |      1 |
|  2 |   SORT GROUP BY               |          |    1 |    1 |      6 |
|  3 |    MERGE JOIN                 |          |    1 |   14 |     14 |
|  4 |     TABLE ACCESS BY INDEX ROWID| DEPT    |    1 |    4 |      4 |
|  5 |      INDEX FULL SCAN          | PK_DEPT  |    1 |    4 |      4 |
|* 6 |     SORT JOIN                 |          |    4 |   14 |     14 |
|  7 |      TABLE ACCESS FULL        | EMP      |    1 |   14 |     14 |
|  8 |   SORT AGGREGATE              |          |    1 |    1 |      1 |
|  9 |    TABLE ACCESS FULL          | EMP      |    1 |   14 |     14 |
| 10 |   SORT AGGREGATE              |          |    1 |    1 |      1 |
| 11 |    TABLE ACCESS FULL          | EMP      |    1 |   14 |     14 |
-------------------------------------------------------------------------------
```

Predicate Information (identified by operation id):
```
---------------------------------------------------
```

```
   1 - filter((COUNT(*)>=5 AND TRUNC(INTERNAL_FUNCTION("E"."HIREDATE"),'fmyyyy')>= AND
             TRUNC(INTERNAL_FUNCTION("E"."HIREDATE"),'fmyyyy')<=))
   6 - access("D"."DEPTNO"="E"."DEPTNO")
       filter("D"."DEPTNO"="E"."DEPTNO")
```

37 rows selected.

"New" GROUP BY Functionality

At times, it's necessary to write SQL that appears as unruly as the convoluted example in Listing 7-5 so that the desired output can be obtained. The need for writing such unwieldy SQL has become much less frequent due to the advanced functionality Oracle has included in SQL the past few years. Much of what will be covered in this chapter is not actually new; it has been available for quite some time.

You can start exploring some of the advanced grouping functionality in the Oracle database by experimenting with the CUBE and ROLLUP extensions to GROUP BY, and the GROUPING function. It takes a little effort to get started, as the benefits of newer functionality are not always clear until you spend some time learning to use them.

CUBE Extension to GROUP BY

The CUBE extension is not exactly a newcomer to Oracle. It was first introduced in Oracle 8i in 1999. When used with a GROUP BY clause, it will cause all possible combinations of the elements included in the arguments to CUBE to be considered for each row. This operation will generate more rows than actually exist in the table[1].

Let's look at an example that generates all possible combinations of FIRST_NAME and LAST_NAME for each row in the HR.EMPLOYEES table. The CUBE function was intended for use in generating cross-tab reports with lots of numbers and dollar signs. When trying to understand new functionality, I find it helps to dumb down the SQL a bit so I can see what's going on without getting distracted with subtotals.

Examine Listing 7-8 to see the results of using CUBE as described with the HR.EMPLOYEES table. You will see that there are three rows returned for most employees. In other words, there are 301 rows returned, even though there are only 107 rows in the table.

Listing 7-8. *CUBE Operation on HR.EMPLOYEES*

```
SQL> set autotrace on statistics

    1  with emps as (
    2    select /*+ gather_plan_statistics */
    3           last_name
    4         , first_name
    5    from hr.employees
    6    group by cube(first_name,last_name)
    7  )
    8  select rownum
    9    , last_name
   10    , first_name
   11  from emps;

   ROWNUM LAST_NAME                FIRST_NAME
---------- ------------------------ --------------------
        1
        2                           Ki
        3                           TJ
```

---

[1] If there are no rows in the table, GROUP BY CUBE() will return 0 rows.

```
        4                    Den
        5                    Guy
        6                    Lex
        7                    Pat
...
      231 Vargas
      232 Vargas            Peter
      233 Whalen
      234 Whalen            Jennifer
      235 De Haan
      236 De Haan           Lex
      237 Everett
      238 Everett           Britney
...

301 rows selected.

Statistics
----------------------------------------------------
      759  recursive calls
        0  db block gets
      188  consistent gets
        9  physical reads
        0  redo size
     5990  bytes sent via SQL*Net to client
      557  bytes received via SQL*Net from client
        5  SQL*Net roundtrips to/from client
        7  sorts (memory)
        0  sorts (disk)
      301  rows processed
```

PLAN_TABLE_OUTPUT

Id	Operation	Name	Starts	E-Rows	A-Rows
0	SELECT STATEMENT		1		301
1	COUNT		1		301
2	VIEW		1	107	301
3	SORT GROUP BY		1	107	301
4	GENERATE CUBE		1	107	428
5	SORT GROUP BY NOSORT		1	107	107
6	INDEX FULL SCAN	EMP_NAME_IX	1	107	107

Table 7-1 shows why there are three rows returned for each name pair. For each LAST_NAME, FIRST_NAME pair, CUBE will substitute NULL for each element in turn. The rows generated by CUBE are referred to in the Oracle documentation as superaggregate rows, which are recognizable by the NULL values placed in the columns being operated in. The results described in Table 7-1 appear in the output in Listing 7-8 due to the GROUP BY CUBE(FIRST_NAME,LAST_NAME) operation.

Table 7-1. *CUBE Operation*

First Name	Last Name
Vance	Jones
Vance	NULL
NULL	Jones

Did you notice that the first row returned in Listing 7-8 contained NULL for both LAST_NAME and FIRST_NAME? When considering all possible combinations of a pair of arguments to CUBE, as seen in Listing 7-8, there is a combination of (NULL, NULL) that is returned for each row in the GENERATE CUBE operation. These 428 rows are then processed by the SORT GROUP BY operation, which removes all but one of the NULL pair of columns to produce the final 301 rows to satisfy the query.

Knowing how CUBE operates, you can predict how many rows should be created when using GROUP BY CUBE. Listing 7-9 shows that the number of rows returned can be predicted by adding together the count for three different distinct combinations of names, and adding 1 to that to account for the null pair.

Listing 7-9. *Predicting CUBE Return Rows*

```
 1  with counts as (
 2     select
 3              count(distinct first_name) first_name_count
 4            , count(distinct last_name) last_name_count
 5            , count(distinct(first_name||last_name)) full_name_count
 6     from hr.employees
 7  )
 8  select
 9     first_name_count
10   , last_name_count
11   , full_name_count
12   , first_name_count + last_name_count + full_name_count + 1 total_count
13  from counts;

FIRST_NAME_COUNT LAST_NAME_COUNT FULL_NAME_COUNT TOTAL_COUNT
---------------- --------------- --------------- -----------
              91             102             107         301
```

1 row selected.

You can simulate the operation of CUBE by using SQL to reproduce the steps taken by the database, both to see how the operation works and to see just how much work the database is saving you by using GROUP BY CUBE.

By examining the execution plan shown in Listing 7-8, you can see that the SORT GROUP BY NOSORT operation (step 5) returns 107 rows to the GROUP BY CUBE operation (step 4), which in turn generates 428 rows. Why are 428 rows generated? Listing 7-10 shows that 428 is the expected number of rows if all combinations of LAST_NAME and FIRST_NAME are generated. The GROUP BY then reduces the output to 301 rows, just as the CUBE extension did, but with an important difference: the manual method of UNION ALL and GROUP BY employed in Listing 7-10 required three full scans of the EMP_NAME_IX index and one full scan of the EMP_EMAIL_UK index. Contrast this to the single full scan of the EMP_NAME_IX index in Listing 7-8 as performed by the GROUP BY extension.

The CUBE extension didn't just reduce the SQL required to generate the same data as the UNION ALL and GROUP BY combination did, it also reduced the number of full index scans from four to one. The optimizer chose to use index EMP_EMAIL_UK rather than the EMP_NAME_IX index, resulting in 10 physical reads rather than the nine seen in Listing 7-8. Using the small data set in the Oracle demo schemas does not cause a large difference in execution time for the example queries. With large data sets, however, the effect of using four INDEX FULL SCAN operations rather than just one would be quite obvious.

Listing 7-10. *Generate CUBE Rows with UNION ALL*

```
1   with emps as (
2      select last_name, first_name from hr.employees
3   ) ,
4   mycube as (
5     select last_name, first_name from emps
6     union all
7     select last_name, null first_name from emps
8     union all
9     select null last_name, first_name from emps
10    union all
11    select null last_name, null first_name from emps
12  )
13  select /*+ gather_plan_statistics */ *
14  from mycube
15  group by last_name, first_name;
```

```
LAST_NAME                 FIRST_NAME
------------------------  --------------------
Atkinson                  Mozhe
Bissot                    Laura
Grant                     Kimberely
...
301 rows selected.


Statistics
------------------------------------------------------------
        759  recursive calls
          0  db block gets
        191  consistent gets
         10  physical reads
          0  redo size
       5477  bytes sent via SQL*Net to client
        557  bytes received via SQL*Net from client
          5  SQL*Net roundtrips to/from client
          6  sorts (memory)
          0  sorts (disk)
        301  rows processed
```

```
PLAN_TABLE_OUTPUT
-------------------------------------------------------------------------
| Id  | Operation          | Name          | Starts | E-Rows | A-Rows |
-------------------------------------------------------------------------
|   0 | SELECT STATEMENT   |               |    1   |        |    301 |
|   1 |  HASH GROUP BY     |               |    1   |   428  |    301 |
|   2 |   VIEW             |               |    1   |   428  |    428 |
|   3 |    UNION-ALL       |               |    1   |        |    428 |
|   4 |     INDEX FULL SCAN| EMP_NAME_IX   |    1   |   107  |    107 |
|   5 |     INDEX FULL SCAN| EMP_NAME_IX   |    1   |   107  |    107 |
|   6 |     INDEX FULL SCAN| EMP_NAME_IX   |    1   |   107  |    107 |
|   7 |     INDEX FULL SCAN| EMP_EMAIL_UK  |    1   |   107  |    107 |
-------------------------------------------------------------------------
```

Putting CUBE To Work

When teaching us a new word in fourth grade English class, Mrs. Draper would say, "Now use it in a sentence." Much like that, you now need to put the CUBE extension to practical use. It was fun to see what is doing and just how much work it saves you, but now you need to see its practical use.

When using the GROUP BY clause to perform aggregations, you've probably written several similar SQL statements—just so you could see the aggregations based on different sets of columns, much like what is seen in Listing 7-10. You already know that the CUBE extension can eliminate a lot of work in the database, so let's now put it to "real world" practice, using the test demo test data created earlier.

The SALES_HISTORY schema contains sales data for the years 1998 – 2001. You need to provide a report to satisfy the following request: "Please show me all sales data for the year 2001. I would like to see sales summarized by product category, with aggregates based on 10-year customer age ranges, income levels, as well as summaries broken out by income level regardless of age group, and by age group regardless of income levels."

Your task probably seems daunting at first, but you know all the data is available. You will need to build a query using the COSTS, CUSTOMERS, PRODUCTS, SALES, and TIMES tables. (Now would be a good time to put this book down and try your hand at building such a query.) Perhaps you will create a query like the one in Listing 7-11, as it is a common type of solution for such a request. Prior to the introduction of the CUBE extension, Listing 7-11 is style of query that would be needed to satisfy the request.

Looking at Listing 7-11, you will find four separate queries joined by the UNION ALL operator. These queries are labeled Q1-Q4. The output from the query includes a QUERY_TAG column so that the results from each separate query can clearly be identified in the output. The customer is happy; the output is exactly the output asked for. The query can also be easily changed to report on data for any year.

The operations folks that run the Data Center, however, are not so happy with this new report. When you take a look at the query statistics for the SQL, you can understand why they may not hold this report in high regard. Maybe it's the 10521 physical reads that concerns them. If the query were run only once, this would not be problem, but the marketing folks are running this query multiple times daily to report on different years, trying to discover sales trends, and it is causing all sorts of havoc as IO rates and response times increase for other users of the database.

Now you see that there are four table scans taking place in the execution plan. The factored subquery tsales allows the optimizer to create a temporary table that can then be used by all the queries in the gb subquery, but the use of UNION ALL makes it necessary to do four full table scans on that table, resulting in a lot of database IO.

Listing 7-11. *UNION ALL Query of Sales Data*

```
 1  with tsales as (
 2  select /*+ gather_plan_statistics */
 3      s.quantity_sold
 4      , s.amount_sold
 5      , to_char(mod(cust_year_of_birth,10) * 10 ) || '-' ||
 6        to_char((mod(cust_year_of_birth,10) * 10 ) + 10) age_range
 7      , nvl(c.cust_income_level,'A: Below 30,000') cust_income_level
 8      , p.prod_name
 9      , p.prod_desc
10      , p.prod_category
11      , (pf.unit_cost * s.quantity_sold)  total_cost
12      , s.amount_sold - (pf.unit_cost * s.quantity_sold)  profit
13    from sh.sales s
14    join sh.customers c on c.cust_id = s.cust_id
15    join sh.products p on p.prod_id = s.prod_id
16    join sh.times t on t.time_id = s.time_id
17    join sh.costs pf on
18      pf.channel_id = s.channel_id
19      and pf.prod_id = s.prod_id
20      and pf.promo_id = s.promo_id
21      and pf.time_id = s.time_id
22    where  (t.fiscal_year = 2001)
23  )
24  , gb as (
25    select -- Q1 - all categories by cust income and age range
26      'Q1' query_tag
27      , prod_category
28      , cust_income_level
29      , age_range
30      , sum(profit) profit
31    from tsales
32    group by prod_category, cust_income_level, age_range
33    union all
34    select -- Q2 - all categories by cust age range
35      'Q2' query_tag
36      , prod_category
37      , 'ALL INCOME' cust_income_level
38      , age_range
39      , sum(profit) profit
40    from tsales
41    group by prod_category, 'ALL INCOME', age_range
42    union all
```

```
43   select -- Q3 - all categories by cust income
44     'Q3' query_tag
45     , prod_category
46     , cust_income_level
47     , 'ALL AGE' age_range
48     , sum(profit) profit
49   from tsales
50   group by prod_category, cust_income_level, 'ALL AGE'
51   union all
52   select -- Q4 - all categories
53     'Q4' query_tag
54     , prod_category
55     , 'ALL INCOME' cust_income_level
56     , 'ALL AGE' age_range
57     , sum(profit) profit
58   from tsales
59   group by prod_category, 'ALL INCOME', 'ALL AGE'
60   )
61   select *
62   from gb
63 order by prod_category, profit;
```

QUERY TAG	PRODUCT CATEGORY	INCOME LEVEL	AGE RANGE	PROFIT
...				
Q2	Hardware	K: 250,000 - 299,999	ALL AGE	$26,678.00
Q2	Hardware	L: 300,000 and above	ALL AGE	$28,974.28
Q1	Hardware	F: 110,000 - 129,999	70-80	$30,477.16
Q2	Hardware	J: 190,000 - 249,999	ALL AGE	$43,761.47
Q2	Hardware	B: 30,000 - 49,999	ALL AGE	$53,612.04
Q2	Hardware	A: Below 30,000	ALL AGE	$55,167.88
Q2	Hardware	I: 170,000 - 189,999	ALL AGE	$57,089.05
Q2	Hardware	C: 50,000 - 69,999	ALL AGE	$76,612.64
Q3	Hardware	ALL INCOME	60-70	$85,314.04
Q3	Hardware	ALL INCOME	10-20	$90,849.87
Q3	Hardware	ALL INCOME	0-10	$92,207.47
Q3	Hardware	ALL INCOME	50-60	$93,811.96
Q3	Hardware	ALL INCOME	80-90	$95,391.82
Q2	Hardware	H: 150,000 - 169,999	ALL AGE	$95,437.74
Q3	Hardware	ALL INCOME	40-50	$97,492.51
Q3	Hardware	ALL INCOME	20-30	$101,140.69
Q2	Hardware	D: 70,000 - 89,999	ALL AGE	$102,940.44
Q3	Hardware	ALL INCOME	30-40	$102,946.85
Q3	Hardware	ALL INCOME	90-100	$110,310.69
Q2	Hardware	G: 130,000 - 149,999	ALL AGE	$112,688.64
Q3	Hardware	ALL INCOME	70-80	$117,920.88

Q2	Hardware	E: 90,000 - 109,999	ALL AGE	$135,154.59
Q2	Hardware	F: 110,000 - 129,999	ALL AGE	$199,270.01
Q4	Hardware	ALL INCOME	ALL AGE	$987,386.78

...
714 rows selected.
Elapsed: 00:00:14.53

Statistics

```
    18464  recursive calls
     4253  db block gets
    22759  consistent gets
    10521  physical reads
     4216  redo size
    25086  bytes sent via SQL*Net to client
      601  bytes received via SQL*Net from client
        9  SQL*Net roundtrips to/from client
      174  sorts (memory)
        0  sorts (disk)
      714  rows processed
```

PLAN_TABLE_OUTPUT

Id	Operation	Name	Starts	E-Rows	A-Rows
0	SELECT STATEMENT		1		714
1	TEMP TABLE TRANSFORMATION		1		714
2	LOAD AS SELECT		1		0
* 3	HASH JOIN		1	17116	258K
4	TABLE ACCESS FULL	PRODUCTS	1	72	72
* 5	HASH JOIN		1	17116	258K
* 6	HASH JOIN		1	17116	258K
* 7	TABLE ACCESS FULL	TIMES	1	304	364
8	PARTITION RANGE AND		1	82112	259K
* 9	HASH JOIN		4	82112	259K
10	TABLE ACCESS FULL	COSTS	4	82112	29766
11	TABLE ACCESS FULL	SALES	4	918K	259K
12	TABLE ACCESS FULL	CUSTOMERS	1	55500	55500
13	SORT ORDER BY		1	16	714
14	VIEW		1	16	714
15	UNION-ALL		1		714
16	HASH GROUP BY		1	3	599
17	VIEW		1	17116	258K
18	TABLE ACCESS FULL	SYS_TEMP_0FD9D6620_8BE55C	1	17116	258K
19	HASH GROUP BY		1	4	60
20	VIEW		1	17116	258K
21	TABLE ACCESS FULL	SYS_TEMP_0FD9D6620_8BE55C	1	17116	258K

```
|  22|      HASH GROUP BY      |                          |  1 |     4 |   50 |
|  23|        VIEW             |                          |  1 | 17116 |  258K|
|  24|          TABLE ACCESS FULL |SYS_TEMP_0FD9D6620_8BE55C|  1 | 17116 |  258K|
|  25|      HASH GROUP BY      |                          |  1 |     5 |    5 |
|  26|        VIEW             |                          |  1 | 17116 |  258K|
|  27|          TABLE ACCESS FULL |SYS_TEMP_0FD9D6620_8BE55C|  1 | 17116 |  258K|
--------------------------------------------------------------------------------
```

Thinking back on your earlier experiment with CUBE, you know that multiple queries each doing a GROUP BY and joined by UNION ALL can be replaced with one query using GROUP BY with the CUBE extension. This is due to the requirement to create summaries based on all possible combinations of the CUST_INCOME_LEVEL and AGE_RANGE columns output from the tsales subquery. The CUBE extension can accomplish the same result, but with less code and less database IO.

While the difference in IO rate and timing in that earlier experiment was not very significant, you will see that when used with larger data sets, the difference can be substantial. Listing 7-12 shows the query after it has been modified to use the CUBE extension to GROUP BY. After running the new query, the first thing you look at are the statistics and the execution plan. Removing the entire gb subquery and using GROUP BY CUBE on the output from the tsales subquery reduced physical IO from 10521 physical reads to 2169, nearly a factor of 5. That alone is enough to recommend the use of CUBE; the fact that it results in much less SQL to write is a bonus.

Listing 7-12. *Replace UNION ALL with CUBE*

```
1  with tsales as (
2  select /*+ gather_plan_statistics */
3      s.quantity_sold
4      , s.amount_sold
5      , to_char(mod(cust_year_of_birth,10) * 10 ) || '-' ||
6        to_char((mod(cust_year_of_birth,10) * 10 ) + 10) age_range
7      , nvl(c.cust_income_level,'A: Below 30,000') cust_income_level
8      , p.prod_name
9      , p.prod_desc
10     , p.prod_category
11     , (pf.unit_cost * s.quantity_sold)  total_cost
12     , s.amount_sold - (pf.unit_cost * s.quantity_sold)  profit
13     from sh.sales s
14     join sh.customers c on c.cust_id = s.cust_id
15     join sh.products p on p.prod_id = s.prod_id
16     join sh.times t on t.time_id = s.time_id
17     join sh.costs pf on
18       pf.channel_id = s.channel_id
19       and pf.prod_id = s.prod_id
20       and pf.promo_id = s.promo_id
21       and pf.time_id = s.time_id
22     where  (t.fiscal_year = 2001)
23  )
24  select
25     'Q' || decode(cust_income_level,
26         null,decode(age_range,null,4,3),
```

```
27         decode(age_range,null,2,1)
28       ) query_tag
29     , prod_category
30     , cust_income_level
31     , age_range
32     , sum(profit) profit
33   from tsales
34   group by prod_category, cube(cust_income_level,age_range)
35   order by prod_category, profit;
```

QUERY TAG	PRODUCT CATEGORY	INCOME LEVEL	AGE RANGE	PROFIT
...				
Q2	Hardware	K: 250,000 - 299,999		$26,678.00
Q2	Hardware	L: 300,000 and above		$28,974.28
Q1	Hardware	F: 110,000 - 129,999	70-80	$30,477.16
Q2	Hardware	J: 190,000 - 249,999		$43,761.47
Q2	Hardware	B: 30,000 - 49,999		$53,612.04
Q2	Hardware	A: Below 30,000		$55,167.88
Q2	Hardware	I: 170,000 - 189,999		$57,089.05
Q2	Hardware	C: 50,000 - 69,999		$76,612.64
Q3	Hardware		60-70	$85,314.04
Q3	Hardware		10-20	$90,849.87
Q3	Hardware		0-10	$92,207.47
Q3	Hardware		50-60	$93,811.96
Q3	Hardware		80-90	$95,391.82
Q2	Hardware	H: 150,000 - 169,999		$95,437.74
Q3	Hardware		40-50	$97,492.51
Q3	Hardware		20-30	$101,140.69
Q2	Hardware	D: 70,000 - 89,999		$102,940.44
Q3	Hardware		30-40	$102,946.85
Q3	Hardware		90-100	$110,310.69
Q2	Hardware	G: 130,000 - 149,999		$112,688.64
Q3	Hardware		70-80	$117,920.88
Q2	Hardware	E: 90,000 - 109,999		$135,154.59
Q2	Hardware	F: 110,000 - 129,999		$199,270.01
Q4	Hardware			$987,386.78
...				

```
714 rows selected.
Elapsed: 00:00:08.98


Statistics
----------------------------------------------------------
    17901  recursive calls
        0  db block gets
     5935  consistent gets
```

```
  2169  physical reads
   260  redo size
 24694  bytes sent via SQL*Net to client
   601  bytes received via SQL*Net from client
     9  SQL*Net roundtrips to/from client
   174  sorts (memory)
     0  sorts (disk)
   714  rows processed
```

PLAN_TABLE_OUTPUT

Id	Operation	Name	Starts	E-Rows	A-Rows
0	SELECT STATEMENT		1		714
1	SORT ORDER BY		1	2251	714
2	SORT GROUP BY		1	2251	714
3	GENERATE CUBE		1	2251	2396
4	SORT GROUP BY		1	2251	599
* 5	HASH JOIN		1	17116	258K
6	VIEW	index$_join$_004	1	72	72
* 7	HASH JOIN		1		72
8	INDEX FAST FULL SCAN	PRODUCTS_PK	1	72	72
9	INDEX FAST FULL SCAN	PRODUCTS_PROD_CAT_IX	1	72	72
* 10	HASH JOIN		1	17116	258K
* 11	HASH JOIN		1	17116	258K
* 12	TABLE ACCESS FULL	TIMES	1	304	364
13	PARTITION RANGE AND		1	82112	259K
* 14	HASH JOIN		4	82112	259K
15	TABLE ACCESS FULL	COSTS	4	82112	29766
16	TABLE ACCESS FULL	SALES	4	918K	259K
17	TABLE ACCESS FULL	CUSTOMERS	1	55500	55500

Eliminate NULLs with the GROUPING() Function

There seems to be a problem with the output from the new query seen in Listing 7-12. While the numbers match the earlier query that used the UNION ALL operator, some of the rows have NULL values for the CUST_INCOME_LEVEL and AGE_RANGE rows, and one row has a NULL in both of these columns. You saw this type of result earlier in Table 7-1 as an expected part of the operation of CUBE. When generating the combinations of all columns included in the arguments to CUBE, a NULL value will be generated n-1 times for each column, where n is the number of columns in the list. In the example query, there are two columns, so you can expect to see a NULL value for CUST_INCOME_LEVEL generated once for each distinct value of AGE_RANGE. The same rule applies to the AGE_RANGE column.

These NULL values[2] can be a problem if there are rows in the data that have NULL values for either of these columns. How do you discern between NULLs in the data and NULLs inserted by the CUBE extension? The GROUPING() function was introduced in Oracle 8i, and it may be used to identify these superaggregate rows. The expression used as an argument to the GROUPING() function must match an expression that appears in the GROUP BY clause. For example, write decode(grouping(age_range),1,'ALL AGE',age_range) age_range to detect whether age_range is null due to a row generated by CUBE, or whether it is null due to a row in the database. The value returned will be a 1 if the current row is a superaggregate row generated by CUBE, and a 0 for all other cases.

When used in combination with a CASE expression or the DECODE() function, the NULL values in superaggregate rows can be replaced with values that are useful in a report. In this case, the DECODE() appears to be a better choice due to simplicity and the fact that there are only two possible return values for the GROUPING() function. Listing 7-13 shows show how GROUPING() was used to modify the SQL found in Listing 7-12. The relevant before and after parts of the SQL are shown, along with the output. Now the report is easier to read, and superaggregate NULLs are discernable from NULLs occurring in the data.

Listing 7-13. *GROUPING() Function*

Without GROUPING():

```
27     , cust_income_level
28     , age_range
```

With GROUPING():

```
27     -- either CASE or DECODE() works here. I prefer DECODE() for this
28     , case grouping(cust_income_level)
29         when 1 then 'ALL INCOME'
30         else cust_income_level
31       end cust_income_level
32     , decode(grouping(age_range),1,'ALL AGE',age_range) age_range
```

QUERY TAG	PRODUCT CATEGORY	INCOME LEVEL	AGE RANGE	PROFIT
...				
Q2	Hardware	K: 250,000 - 299,999	ALL AGE	$26,678.00
Q2	Hardware	L: 300,000 and above	ALL AGE	$28,974.28
Q1	Hardware	F: 110,000 - 129,999	70-80	$30,477.16
Q2	Hardware	J: 190,000 - 249,999	ALL AGE	$43,761.47
Q2	Hardware	B: 30,000 - 49,999	ALL AGE	$53,612.04
Q2	Hardware	A: Below 30,000	ALL AGE	$55,167.88
Q2	Hardware	I: 170,000 - 189,999	ALL AGE	$57,089.05
Q2	Hardware	C: 50,000 - 69,999	ALL AGE	$76,612.64
Q3	Hardware	ALL INCOME	60-70	$85,314.04
Q3	Hardware	ALL INCOME	10-20	$90,849.87

---

[2] The NVL() function is used to provide a default value for sh.customers.cust_income_level so that output of examples may be easier to compare.

Q3	Hardware	ALL INCOME	0-10	$92,207.47
Q3	Hardware	ALL INCOME	50-60	$93,811.96
Q3	Hardware	ALL INCOME	80-90	$95,391.82
Q2	Hardware	H: 150,000 - 169,999	ALL AGE	$95,437.74
Q3	Hardware	ALL INCOME	40-50	$97,492.51
Q3	Hardware	ALL INCOME	20-30	$101,140.69
Q2	Hardware	D: 70,000 - 89,999	ALL AGE	$102,940.44
Q3	Hardware	ALL INCOME	30-40	$102,946.85
Q3	Hardware	ALL INCOME	90-100	$110,310.69
Q2	Hardware	G: 130,000 - 149,999	ALL AGE	$112,688.64
Q3	Hardware	ALL INCOME	70-80	$117,920.88
Q2	Hardware	E: 90,000 - 109,999	ALL AGE	$135,154.59
Q2	Hardware	F: 110,000 - 129,999	ALL AGE	$199,270.01
Q4	Hardware	ALL INCOME	ALL AGE	$987,386.78

Extending Reports with GROUPING()

Another use of GROUPING() is in the HAVING clause, where it can be used to control which aggregation levels appear in the output. The report seen in previous examples creates about five pages of output, which may be more than the customer cares to see. By using the GROUPING() function, these aggregations can be condensed to roll up the totals for either or all of the columns used in the CUBE extension. Several variations of GROUPING() have been used to modify the previous SQL. The modifications and resulting output are shown in Listing 7-14.

Examining the data in Listing 7-14 you can see that applying GROUPING() to the CUST_INCOME_LEVEL column created aggregates from all AGE_RANGE values to be accumulated across all income levels. Doing so for the AGE_RANGE column had similar effects, with totals aggregated for all values of INCOME_LEVEL without regard to the value of AGE_RANGE. Including all of the columns from the CUBE extension as arguments to the GROUPING() function will cause the aggregations to be condensed to a single row, similar to what could be done with SUM(PROFIT) and a simple GROUP BY PROD_CATEGORY. Using the CUBE extension, however, allows simple changes to the HAVING clause to create several different reports.

Listing 7-14. *GROUPING() in the HAVING Clause*

CUST_INCOME_LEVEL

```
35   group by prod_category, cube(cust_income_level,age_range)
36      having grouping(cust_income_level)=1
```

QUERY TAG	PRODUCT CATEGORY	INCOME LEVEL	AGE RANGE	PROFIT
Q3	Hardware	ALL INCOME	60-70	$85,314.04
Q3	Hardware	ALL INCOME	10-20	$90,849.87
Q3	Hardware	ALL INCOME	0-10	$92,207.47

...

```
Q4      Hardware                        ALL INCOME        ALL AGE      $987,386.78
```

AGE_RANGE

```
35  group by prod_category, cube(cust_income_level,age_range)
36    having grouping(age_range)=1
```

```
QUERY                                                     AGE
TAG     PRODUCT CATEGORY              INCOME LEVEL         RANGE          PROFIT
------  ---------------------------  --------------------  --------  ---------------
Q2      Hardware                     K: 250,000 - 299,999 ALL AGE       $26,678.00
Q2      Hardware                     L: 300,000 and above ALL AGE       $28,974.28
Q2      Hardware                     J: 190,000 - 249,999 ALL AGE       $43,761.47
...
Q4      Hardware                     ALL INCOME           ALL AGE      $987,386.78
```

CUST_INCOME_LEVEL, AGE_RANGE

```
35  group by prod_category, cube(cust_income_level,age_range)
36    having grouping(cust_income_level)=1 and grouping(age_range)=1
```

```
QUERY                                                     AGE
TAG     PRODUCT CATEGORY              INCOME LEVEL         RANGE          PROFIT
------  ---------------------------  --------------------  --------  ---------------
Q4      Electronics                  ALL INCOME           ALL AGE      $838,994.19
Q4      Hardware                     ALL INCOME           ALL AGE      $987,386.78
Q4      Peripherals and Accessories  ALL INCOME           ALL AGE    $1,751,079.16
Q4      Photo                        ALL INCOME           ALL AGE    $1,570,866.04
Q4      Software/Other               ALL INCOME           ALL AGE      $873,603.25
```

Extending Reports With GROUPING_ID()

The GROUPING_ID() function is relatively new compared to the GROUPING() function, having been introduced in Oracle 9i, and is somewhat similar to the GROUPING() function. Whereas GROUPING() evaluates the expression and returns a 0 or 1, the GROUPING_ID() function evaluates an expression, determines which, if any, of the columns in its arguments are being used to generate a superaggregate row, creates a bit vector, and returns that value as an integer.

Perhaps it would be simpler to see how GROUPING_ID() works with an example. The SQL in Listing 7-15 first creates a single row consisting of two columns, BIT_1 and BIT_0, with values of 1 and 0 respectively. The subquery cubed uses GROUP BY CUBE to generate four rows from the single row of input. The GROUPING_ID() function returns the decimal value of the bit vector that represents the actions of CUBE to the current row. The first two uses of the GROUPING() function then create a 1 or 0 based on the actions of CUBE on the row. These will be used to create a bit vector in the final output. The next two GROUPING() functions then create values displayed in the final output indicating which column that CUBE is currently working on. The final output displays the decimal bit vector, as well as a binary representation of the vector. As would be expected with two binary digits, there are four rows of output.

Listing 7-15. *GROUPING_ID() Bit Vector*

```
1   with rowgen as (
2     select 1 bit_1, 0 bit_0
3     from dual
4   ),
5   cubed as (
6     select
7       grouping_id(bit_1,bit_0) gid
8       , to_char(grouping(bit_1)) bv_1
9       , to_char(grouping(bit_0)) bv_0
10      , decode(grouping(bit_1),1,'GRP BIT 1') gb_1
11      , decode(grouping(bit_0),1,'GRP BIT 0') gb_0
12    from rowgen
13    group by cube(bit_1,bit_0)
14  )
15  select
16    gid
17    , bv_1 || bv_0 bit_vector
18    , gb_1
19    , gb_0
20  from cubed
21  order by gid;
```

```
    BIT     GROUPING  GROUPING
GID VECTOR  BIT 1     BIT 0
---- ------ --------- ---------
  0 00
  1 01                GRP BIT 0
  2 10      GRP BIT 1
  3 11      GRP BIT 1 GRP BIT 0

4 rows selected.
```

So, what good is it? You already know how to use GROUPING() to control output via the HAVING clause, why learn another way? Those are fair questions when you consider that the examples in Listing 7-14 can already create the wanted output.

In the interest of database efficiency, a single GROUPING_ID() call can be used to replace all of the different HAVING GROUPING() clauses from Listing 7-14. The GROUPING() function is limited in its ability to discriminate rows, as it can return only a 0 or 1. Since the GROUPING_ID() function returns a decimal value based on a bit vector, it can easily be used to make many different comparisons without any changes to the SQL.

Why should you care about changing comparisons without changing the SQL? If you are building an application based on the sales history examples, the user may be given four choices of output, and any one or more of them may be chosen. The user choices can be used as inputs to a single SQL statement that uses HAVING GROUPING_ID(), rather than multiple SQL statements based on different combinations of HAVING GROUPING(), so it requires less parsing of SQL by the database. It will also result in fewer SQL statements to execute, less IO, and less memory usage.

Just as using CUBE eliminated multiple SQL statements joined by UNION ALL, GROUPING_ID() can eliminate multiple SQL statements in your application. The choices given to the user will be as follows:

ALL DATA– Display all income level and age range aggregations

ALL AGE– Aggregate all age ranges together

ALL INCOME– Aggregate all income levels together

SUMMARY – Summary only

The application, a SQL*Plus script in this case, will assign to variables values corresponding to the user's choices. The SQL statement, in turn, will evaluate those variables via HAVING GROUPING_ID() to output the requested rows. Listing 7-16 simulates the choices a user might make and demonstrates how to use these inputs in the SQL. In the example, the only rows to be output will be those that are aggregates of all income levels regardless of age group (ALL_AGE) and the summary columns for each product category (ALL_AGE and ALL_INCOME_LEVEL). This is accomplished by setting N_AGE_RANGE and N_SUMMARY to 2 and 4, respectively. These values correspond to the bit vector generated by the GROUPING_ID() function found in the HAVING clause.

As used in the HAVING clause, 1 is added to the value generated by GROUPING_ID(). This is to enable some consistency in setting the values of the variables that control the output. Without adding 1 to the value, the N_ALL_DATA variable would be set to 0 to enable output, and some other value, such as -1 to disable it. Increasing this comparison values by 1 makes it possible to consistently use 0 as a value to disable output.

Listing 7-16. *GROUPING_ID() To Control Report Output*

```
SQL> variable N_ALL_DATA number
SQL> variable N_AGE_RANGE number
SQL> variable N_INCOME_LEVEL number
SQL> variable N_SUMMARY number
SQL>
SQL> begin
  2    -- set values to 0 to disable
  3    :N_ALL_DATA     := 0; -- 1 to enable
  4    :N_AGE_RANGE    := 2; -- 2 to enable
  5    :N_INCOME_LEVEL := 0; -- 3 to enable
  6    :N_SUMMARY      := 4; -- 4 to enable
  7  end;
  8  /

  1  with tsales as (
  2  select /*+ gather_plan_statistics */
  3      s.quantity_sold
  4    , s.amount_sold
  5    , to_char(mod(cust_year_of_birth,10) * 10 ) || '-' ||
  6      to_char((mod(cust_year_of_birth,10) * 10 ) + 10) age_range
  7    , nvl(c.cust_income_level,'A: Below 30,000') cust_income_level
  8    , p.prod_name
  9    , p.prod_desc
 10    , p.prod_category
```

```
11      , (pf.unit_cost * s.quantity_sold)  total_cost
12      , s.amount_sold - (pf.unit_cost * s.quantity_sold)  profit
13    from sh.sales s
14    join sh.customers c on c.cust_id = s.cust_id
15    join sh.products p on p.prod_id = s.prod_id
16    join sh.times t on t.time_id = s.time_id
17    join sh.costs pf on
18      pf.channel_id = s.channel_id
19      and pf.prod_id = s.prod_id
20      and pf.promo_id = s.promo_id
21      and pf.time_id = s.time_id
22    where  (t.fiscal_year = 2001)
23  )
24  select
25    'Q' || to_char(grouping_id(cust_income_level,age_range)+1) query_tag
26    , prod_category
27    , decode(grouping(cust_income_level),1,'ALL INCOME',cust_income_level)
cust_income_level
28    , decode(grouping(age_range),1,'ALL AGE',age_range) age_range
29    , sum(profit) profit
30  from tsales
31  group by prod_category, cube(cust_income_level,age_range)
32    having grouping_id(cust_income_level,age_range)+1
33      in(:N_ALL_DATA,:N_AGE_RANGE,:N_INCOME_LEVEL,:N_SUMMARY)
34  order by prod_category, profit;
```

QUERY TAG	PRODUCT CATEGORY	INCOME LEVEL	AGE RANGE	PROFIT
...				
Q2	Hardware	K: 250,000 - 299,999	ALL AGE	$26,678.00
Q2	Hardware	L: 300,000 and above	ALL AGE	$28,974.28
Q2	Hardware	J: 190,000 - 249,999	ALL AGE	$43,761.47
...				
Q2	Hardware	E: 90,000 - 109,999	ALL AGE	$135,154.59
Q2	Hardware	F: 110,000 - 129,999	ALL AGE	$199,270.01
Q4	Hardware	ALL INCOME	ALL AGE	$987,386.78
...				

65 rows selected.

To be fair, it is possible to achieve the same results using the GROUPING() function, but it requires several tests to be placed in the HAVING clause. The queries of sample sales history data include only two columns in the CUBE arguments. The total number of tests required in the HAVING clause is four, as GROUPING() clause will return either a 1 or a 0, so there are two possible values for each of your columns, resulting in four tests. That doesn't seem too bad, but consider what happens when there three columns: the number of tests goes up to nine. The number of tests required will be 2^n where n is the number of columns or expressions in arguments to CUBE.

Listing 7-17 shows the HAVING clause as it might appear using GROUPING() rather than GROUPING_ID(). This approach would soon become unwieldy if there were many arguments required for the CUBE extension. The four separate tests shown should not be too much trouble to maintain. However, if the number of column in the CUBE arguments goes up from two to three, there will then be nine tests. This is not code that lends itself well to maintenance.

Listing 7-17. *Using GROUPING() instead of GROUPING_ID()*

```
32 having  -- bin_to_num() requires 9i+
33   ( bin_to_num(grouping(cust_income_level), grouping(age_range))+1 = :N_ALL_DATA)
34   or ( bin_to_num(grouping(cust_income_level), grouping(age_range))+1 = :N_AGE_RANGE)
35   or ( bin_to_num(grouping(cust_income_level), grouping(age_range))+1 = :N_INCOME_LEVEL)
36   or ( bin_to_num(grouping(cust_income_level), grouping(age_range))+1 = :N_SUMMARY)
```

EXPERIMENT WITH GROUPING() AND GROUPING_ID()

As an exercise, modify the code from Listing 7-16 so that it adds another column to the arguments to CUBE. Then modify the call to GROUPING_ID() in the HAVING clause to work with the new column. This will require a new variable as well in the PL/SQL block.

After you have that working, replace the GROUPING_ID() call with all the tests needed to accomplish the same output control with GROUPING(). Do you like the results? Is this code that you would like to maintain?

GROUPING SETS and ROLLUP()

There is yet another method that may be used to obtain the results seen in the previous two examples. The GROUPING SETS() extension to GROUP BY made its debut with Oracle 9i. The entire GROUP BY … HAVING clause of the previous example can be replaced with GROUP BY GROUPING SETS(). However, just because you can do something doesn't mean you should. Let's look at example to understand just why you may not want to use GROUPING SETS(). Lines 31–33 in Listing 7-16 can be replaced by lines 31–36 in Listing 7-18.

Listing 7-18. *GROUPING SETS()*

```
1  with tsales as (
2  select /*+ gather_plan_statistics */
3      s.quantity_sold
4      , s.amount_sold
5      , to_char(mod(cust_year_of_birth,10) * 10 ) || '-' ||
6        to_char((mod(cust_year_of_birth,10) * 10 ) + 10) age_range
7      , nvl(c.cust_income_level,'A: Below 30,000') cust_income_level
8      , p.prod_name
9      , p.prod_desc
10     , p.prod_category
```

```
11      , (pf.unit_cost * s.quantity_sold)  total_cost
12      , s.amount_sold - (pf.unit_cost * s.quantity_sold)  profit
13   from sh.sales s
14   join sh.customers c on c.cust_id = s.cust_id
15   join sh.products p on p.prod_id = s.prod_id
16   join sh.times t on t.time_id = s.time_id
17   join sh.costs pf on
18     pf.channel_id = s.channel_id
19     and pf.prod_id = s.prod_id
20     and pf.promo_id = s.promo_id
21     and pf.time_id = s.time_id
22   where  (t.fiscal_year = 2001)
23  )
24  select
25    'Q' || to_char(grouping_id(cust_income_level,age_range)+1) query_tag
26    , prod_category
27    , decode(grouping(cust_income_level),1,'ALL INCOME',cust_income_level)
cust_income_level
28    , decode(grouping(age_range),1,'ALL AGE',age_range) age_range
29    , sum(profit) profit
30  from tsales
31  group by prod_category, grouping sets(
32    rollup(prod_category), -- sub total by product category
33    (cust_income_level),  -- aggregate by category and income levels only
34    (age_range),          -- aggregate by category and age only
35    (cust_income_level,age_range) -- aggregates by category, all age and income
36  )
37  --having group_id() < 1
38 order by prod_category, profit;
```

QUERY TAG	PRODUCT CATEGORY	INCOME LEVEL	AGE RANGE	PROFIT
...				
Q2	Software/Other	E: 90,000 - 109,999	ALL AGE	$124,416.04
Q2	Software/Other	F: 110,000 - 129,999	ALL AGE	$169,482.11
Q4	Software/Other	ALL INCOME	ALL AGE	$873,603.25
Q4	Software/Other	ALL INCOME	ALL AGE	$873,603.25

756 rows selected.

The output shown in Listing 7-18 is similar to that seen when the SQL from Listing 7-16 is executed with all of the output categories enabled. That is a major difference between using GROUP BY CUBE HAVING GROUPING_ID() and GROUP BY GROUPING SETS. The former may be used to easily modify the output simply by setting variables to the correct values, while output from the latter cannot be modified except by modifying or dynamically generating the SQL. Modifying the SQL means there will be more code to maintain and more resources consumed in the database. Dynamically generating the SQL is, well, usually just not a good idea if it can be avoided: it will consume more database resources, and it is much harder to troubleshoot when problems arise.

As mentioned previously, the output in Listing 7-18 is similar to that in Listing 7-16, but not the same. The last two lines of the output shown are duplicates. Sometimes the GROUPING_SETS() extension can cause duplicates to appear in the output. In this case, the duplicates are caused by the ROLLUP(PROD_CATEGORY) line. You can prove that to yourself by removing ROLLUP() from the code in Listing 7-18 and rerunning it. The duplicate lines will no longer appear. However, the totals for each Product Category will no longer appear either. The solution is to use the GROUP_ID() function to identify those duplicate rows, and insert it into a HAVING clause.

The HAVING clause can be seen commented out in Listing 7-18. If you uncomment it and then re-run the script, the output will appear as expected without the duplicate rows. Interestingly, if the ROLLUP(PROD_CATEGORY) line is replaced with (NULL), the HAVING clause can be removed, and the output will appear as expected.

The ROLLUP() extension to GROUP BY can also be used by itself to create running subtotals that would otherwise require multiple queries joined by UNION ALL. Suppose that someone from the Sales Department asked you to create a report showing totals of all purchases by customers whose last name begins with "Sul." In addition, there need to be subtotals for each year by customer, each product category by customer, and a grand total of all sales. This kind of task is easily handled by ROLLUP(). Listing 7-19 shows one way to write a query to satisfy that request.

Notice that the DECODE() and GROUPING() functions are again used to indicate subtotal rows. Also, the grand total is forced to appear at the end of the report by the use of GROUPING(M.CUST_NAME). As the only time this value will be > 0 is when the total for all customers is calculated, the grand total appears at the end of the report as expected.

Listing 7-19. *ROLLUP() Subtotals*

```
1  with mysales as (
2    select
3      c.cust_last_name ||',' || c.cust_first_name cust_name
4      , p.prod_category
5      , to_char(trunc(time_id,'YYYY'),'YYYY') sale_year
6      , p.prod_name
7      , s.amount_sold
8    from sh.sales s
9    join sh.products p on p.prod_id = s.prod_id
10   join sh.customers c on c.cust_id = s.cust_id
11   where c.cust_last_name like 'Sul%'
12   --where s.time_id = to_date('01/01/2001','mm/dd/yyyy')
13  )
14  select
15    decode(grouping(m.cust_name),1,'GRAND TOTAL',m.cust_name) cust_name
16    , decode(grouping(m.sale_year),1,'TOTAL BY YEAR',m.sale_year) sale_year
17    , decode(grouping(m.prod_category),1,'TOTAL BY CATEGORY',m.prod_category) prod_category
18    , sum(m.amount_sold) amount_sold
19  from mysales m
20  group by rollup(m.cust_name, m.prod_category, m.sale_year)
21  order by grouping(m.cust_name), 1,2,3;
```

CUSTOMER	SALE_YEAR	PRODUCT CATEGORY	AMT SOLD
...			
Sullivan,Rue	1998	Peripherals and Accessories	$259.90
Sullivan,Rue	1998	Software/Other	$19.59
Sullivan,Rue	2000	Electronics	$2,213.30
Sullivan,Rue	2000	Hardware	$1,359.06
Sullivan,Rue	2000	Peripherals and Accessories	$1,169.94
Sullivan,Rue	2000	Photo	$331.33
Sullivan,Rue	2000	Software/Other	$933.87
Sullivan,Rue	TOTAL BY YEAR	Electronics	$2,213.30
Sullivan,Rue	TOTAL BY YEAR	Hardware	$1,359.06
Sullivan,Rue	TOTAL BY YEAR	Peripherals and Accessories	$1,429.84
Sullivan,Rue	TOTAL BY YEAR	Photo	$331.33
Sullivan,Rue	TOTAL BY YEAR	Software/Other	$953.46
Sullivan,Rue	TOTAL BY YEAR	TOTAL BY CATEGORY	$6,286.99
GRAND TOTAL	TOTAL BY YEAR	TOTAL BY CATEGORY	$86,994.89

68 rows selected.

GROUP BY Restrictions

Your study of GROUP BY would be incomplete without considering what it cannot do. The list of restrictions placed on GROUP BY is not very long. The restrictions are listed in the Oracle 11.2 SQL Language Reference for Oracle 11.2. For example:

- LOB columns, nested tables, or arrays may not be used as part of a GROUP BY expression.

- Scalar subquery expressions are not allowed.

- Queries cannot be parallelized if the GROUP BY clause references any object type columns.

SQL queries were constructed to demonstrate the first two restrictions as shown in Listing 7-20 and 7-21. The error messages clearly show that LOB columns and scalar subqueries cannot be used as part of GROUP BY clause.

Listing 7-20. *GROUP BY Restrictions – LOB Not Allowed*

```
SQL> @l_7_2
  1  with lobtest as (
  2     select to_clob(d.dname ) dname
  3     from scott.emp e
  4     join scott.dept d on d.deptno = e.deptno
  5  )
  6  select l.dname
  7  from lobtest l
  8* group by l.dname
group by l.dname;
         *
```

```
      ERROR at line 8:
ORA-00932: inconsistent datatypes: expected - got CLOB
```

Listing 7-21. *GROUP BY Restrictions – Scalar Subquery Not Allowed*

```
  1  select d.dname, count(empno) empcount
  2  from scott.emp e
  3  join scott.dept d on d.deptno = e.deptno
  4  group by (select dname from scott.dept d2 where d2.dname = d.dname)
  5  order by d.dname;
  group by (select dname from scott.dept d2 where d2.dname = d.dname);
                *
      ERROR at line 4:
ORA-22818: subquery expressions not allowed here
```

The final restriction listed appears to be a documentation error. Evidence for that can be seen in Listing 7-22 where the GROUP BY on an OBJECT datatype is being executed in parallel, contrary to what the documentation states. The member function match in the dept_location type body is used to compare the value for city, and this in turn is used by GROUP BY to group employees by CITY. Should you need to create aggregations based on data in an OBJECT column, you can certainly do so as of Oracle 11.1.0.7. Testing has shown that the GROUP BY of Listing 7-22 will not be executed in parallel in Oracle 11.1.0.6.

Listing 7-22. *GROUP BY on Object Column in Parallel*

```
SQL> create type dept_location_type
  2  as object
  3  (
  4      street_address      VARCHAR2(40)
  5    , postal_code         VARCHAR2(10)
  6    , city                VARCHAR2(30)
  7    , state_province      VARCHAR2(10)
  8    , country_id          CHAR(2)
  9    , order member function match (e dept_location_type) return integer
 10  );
 11  /

Type created.

SQL>
SQL> create or replace type body dept_location_type
  2  as order member function match (e dept_location_type) return integer
  3  is
  4    begin
  5      if city < e.city then
  6        return -1;
  7      elsif city > e.city then
  8        return 1;
  9      else
 10        return 0;
```

```
 11     end if;
 12    end;
 13  end;
 14  /

Type body created.

SQL>
SQL> create table deptobj
  2  as
  3  select d.deptno,d.dname
  4  from scott.dept d;
Table created.
SQL> alter table deptobj add (dept_location dept_location_type);
Table altered.
SQL> update deptobj set dept_location =
  2     dept_location_type('1234 Money St', '97401','Eugene', 'OR', 'US')
  3  where deptno=20;
1 row updated.
SQL> update deptobj set dept_location =
  2     dept_location_type('459 Durella Street', '97463','Oakridge', 'OR', 'US')
  3  where deptno=40;
1 row updated.
SQL> update deptobj set dept_location =
  2     dept_location_type('12642 Rex Rd', '97006','Beavertown', 'OR', 'US')
  3  where deptno=10;
1 row updated.
SQL> update deptobj set dept_location =
  2     dept_location_type('9298 Hamilton Rd', '97140','George', 'WA', 'US')
  3  where deptno=30;
1 row updated.

1 commit;
Commit complete.
PL/SQL procedure successfully completed.

  1  select /*+ gather_plan_statistics parallel(e 2)*/
  2     d.dept_location, count(e.ename) ecount
  3  from scott.emp e, deptobj d
  4  where e.deptno = d.deptno
  5  group by dept_location
  6  order by dept_location;
```

```
DEPT_LOCATION(STREET_ADDRESS, POSTAL_CODE, CITY, STATE_PROVI      ECOUNT
--------------------------------------------------------------   ------
DEPT_LOCATION_TYPE('1234 Money St', '97401', 'Eugene', 'OR', 'US')     5
DEPT_LOCATION_TYPE('12642 Rex Rd', '97006', 'Beavertown','OR','US')    3
DEPT_LOCATION_TYPE('9298 Hamilton Rd', '97140', 'George','WA','US')    6
3 rows selected.
```

```
PLAN_TABLE_OUTPUT
```

Id	Operation	Name	Starts	E-Rows	A-Rows
0	SELECT STATEMENT		1		3
1	PX COORDINATOR		1		3
2	PX SEND QC (ORDER)	:TQ10002	0	14	0
3	SORT GROUP BY		0	14	0
4	PX RECEIVE		0	14	0
5	PX SEND RANGE	:TQ10001	0	14	0
6	HASH GROUP BY		0	14	0
* 7	HASH JOIN		0	14	0
8	BUFFER SORT		0		0
9	PX RECEIVE		0	4	0
10	PX SEND BROADCAST	:TQ10000	0	4	0
11	TABLE ACCESS FULL	DEPTOBJ	1	4	4
12	PX BLOCK ITERATOR		0	14	0
* 13	TABLE ACCESS FULL	EMP	0	14	0

Summary

Oracle has provided some excellent tools for the SQL practitioner in the form of extensions to the GROUP BY clause. Not only do they reduce code, they improve database efficiency. They do, however, take some dedication and practice to learn how best to use them. The introduction here to advanced grouping features is by no means comprehensive. Most of these features can be combined for many different effects, far more than is practical to include in a book. Please endeavor to make use of these features in your own applications and continue to experiment with them based on what you have learned here.

CHAPTER 8

■ ■ ■

Analytic Functions

Riyaj Shamsudeen

Online Analytic Processing (OLAP) queries perform multi-dimensional aggregation and are useful in business decision-making processes in areas such as sales, marketing, and business intelligence. Fast execution is important for OLAP queries as key decisions hinge on the outcome of OLAP queries and reports.

Although conventional SQL statements can be used to implement OLAP queries, these statements usually result in multiple self-joins, leading to poorly performing queries. In addition, multi-dimensional analysis usually requires aggregation at various levels, and both aggregated and non-aggregated rows must be returned. In the case of conventional SQL statements, fetching the aggregated and non-aggregated values in the same row usually results in a multitude of self-joins.

Analytic function is a new class of functions introduced in Oracle Database version 9i and enhanced in the later releases of Oracle Database. These functions provide the ability to reference values across rows, multi-level aggregation, and granular control of sort order in a subset of data. In contrast to grouping functions, analytic functions do not aggregate a result set into fewer rows.

With the use of analytic functions, you can fetch both aggregated and non-aggregated values without any self-joins. Consider that fetching the salary of an employee, with average salary by department and average salary by location in the same row, would require multiple self-joins to employees table. Analytic functions can be used to write this query without any self-joins.

Analytic functions are sometimes termed as *window functions*. Analytic functions perform calculations within a subset of result set related to the current row by some means. That subset can be termed the *window*.

Example Data

To begin your investigation of the analytic SQL functions, you will create a denormalized fact table using the script in Listing 8-1. All the tables in this chapter refer to the objects in SH Schema supplied by Oracle Corporation Example scripts.

■**NOTE** To install the Example schema, software can be downloaded from `http://download.oracle.com/otn/solaris/oracle11g/R2/solaris.sparc64_11gR2_examples.zip` for the 11gR2 Solaris platform. Refer to the Readme document in the unzipped software directories for installation instructions. Zip files for other platforms and versions are also available at this Oracle web site.

Listing 8-1. *Denormalized sales_fact Table*

```
drop table sales_fact;
CREATE table sales_fact AS
SELECT country_name country,country_subRegion region, prod_name product,
       calendar_year year, calendar_week_number week,
       SUM(amount_sold) sale,
       sum(amount_sold*
         ( case
                 when mod(rownum, 10)=0 then 1.4
                 when mod(rownum, 5)=0 then 0.6
                 when mod(rownum, 2)=0 then 0.9
                 when mod(rownum,2)=1 then 1.2
                 else 1
           end )) receipts
FROM sales, times, customers, countries, products
WHERE sales.time_id = times.time_id AND
sales.prod_id = products.prod_id AND
sales.cust_id = customers.cust_id AND
customers.country_id = countries.country_id
GROUP BY
country_name,country_subRegion, prod_name, calendar_year, calendar_week_number;

function1 (argument1, argument2,..argumentN)
   over ([partition-by-clause] [order-by-clause] [windowing-clause])
```

Anatomy of Analytic Functions

Analytic functions have three basic components: partitioning-clause, order-by-clause, and the windowing clause. Basic syntax of an analytic function is:

```
function1 (argument1, argument2,..argumentN)
   over ([partition-by-clause] [order-by-clause] [windowing-clause])
```

Function1 is the analytic function to call which accepts zero or more arguments. The partitioning clause groups the rows by partitioning column values. All rows with the same value for the partitioning column are grouped as a data partition.

Operationally, rows are sorted by the partitioning columns and partitioned into data partitions. For example, the SQL clause partition by product, country partitions the data using the Product and Country columns. Rows are sorted by both Product and Country columns and grouped into one partition for each combination of product and country.

The order-by clause sorts the rows in a data partition by a column or expression. In an analytic SQL statement, the position of a row in the data partition is important and it is controlled by the order-by clause. Rows are sorted by the sort columns within a data partition. Since the partitioning clause sorts the rows by the partitioning columns, you actually end up with one sort that includes columns specified in the partitioning clause and order-by clause.

Sort order can be specified as ascending or descending order. Nulls can be specified to sort to the top or bottom in a data partition using the clause NULLS FIRST or NULLS LAST.

The windowing clause specifies the subset of rows on which the analytic function operates. This window can be dynamic and is aptly termed a *sliding window*. You can specify the top and bottom boundary condition of the sliding window using the window specification clause. Syntax for the window specification clause is:

```
[ROWS | RANGE] BETWEEN <Start expr> AND <End expr>

Whereas
<Start expr> is [UNBOUNDED PRECEDING | CURRENT ROW | n PRECEDING | n FOLLOWING]
<End expr> is [UNBOUNDED FOLLOWING | CURRENT ROW | n PRECEDING | n FOLLOWING]
```

The keyword PRECEDING specifies the top boundary condition, and the clause FOLLOWING or CURRENT ROW specifies the bottom boundary condition for the window. A sliding window provides the ability to compute complex metrics with ease. For example, you can compute the running sum of the Sale column by the clause rows between unbounded preceding and current row. In this example, the top row in the window is the first row in the current partition and the bottom row in the window is the current row.

■**NOTE** The windowing clause is not supported by all analytic functions.

Analytic functions may not be nested. But a nesting effect can be achieved by placing the encompassing SQL statement in an inline view, and then applying analytic functions outside the view. Analytic functions can be used in deeply nested inline views, too.

List of Functions

The following section tabulates the analytic functions for easy reference.

Table 8-1. *Analytic Functions*

Sl. No	Function	Description
1	Lag	To access prior row in a partition or result set.
2	Lead	To access later row in a partition or result set
3	First_value	To access first row in a partition or result set.
4	Last_value	To access last row in a partition or result set.
5	Nth_value	To access any arbitrary row in a partition or result set.
6	Rank	To rank the rows in a sort order. Ranks are skipped in the case of ties.

continued

Table 8-1. *Continued*

Sl. No	Function	Description
7	Dense_rank	To rank the rows in a sort order. Ranks are not skipped in the case of ties.
8	Row_number	To sort the rows and add unique number to each row. This is a non-deterministic function.
9	Ratio_to_report	To compute the ratio of value to the report.
10	Percent_rank	To compute the rank of value normalized to a value between 0 and 1.
11	Percentile_cont	To retrieve the value matching with the specified percent_rank. Reverse of percent_rank function.
12	Percentile_dist	To retrieve the value matching with the specified percent_rank. Assumes discreet distribution model.
13	Ntile	To group rows in to units.
14	Listagg	To convert column values from different rows in to a list format.

Aggregation Functions

Aggregation functions can operate in analytic mode or conventional non-analytic mode. Aggregation functions in non-analytic mode reduce the result set to fewer rows. However, in analytic mode, aggregation functions do not reduce the result set. Further, the aggregation functions can fetch both aggregated and non-aggregated columns in the same row. Aggregation functions in analytic mode provide the ability to aggregate data at different levels without any need for a self-join.

Analytic functions are useful in writing complex report queries aggregating data at different levels. Consider a demographic market analysis report for a product, a favorite among advertising executives, which requires sales data to be aggregated at myriad levels such as age, gender, store, district, region, and country. Aggregation functions in the analytic mode can be effectively utilized to implement this market analysis report with ease. Analytic functions will markedly improve the clarity and performance of the SQL statements, compared to its non-analytic counterparts.

Let's review the example in the Listing 8-2. The SQL statement is calculating the running of sum of Sale column from the beginning of the year for a product, country, region, and year combination. The clause partition by product, country, region, year specifies the partition columns. Within the data partition, rows are sorted by the Week column using the clause order by week.

In Listing 8-2, the SQL is calculating the running of sum of Sale column, so the analytic function must operate on window of rows from the beginning of the year to the current week. That goal is achieved by the windowing clause rows between unbounded preceding and current row. The sum(sale) function calculates the sum of Sale column values over this window of rows. Since the rows are sorted by the Week column, the sum function is operating over a set of rows from the beginning of the year until the current week.

Listing 8-2. *Running Sum of Sale Column*

```
1   select  year, week,sale,
2      sum (sale) over(
3             partition by product, country, region, year
4             order by week
5             rows between unbounded preceding and current row
6                ) running_sum_ytd
7    from sales_fact
8    where country in ('Australia')  and product ='Xtend Memory'
9*   order by product, country,year, week
/
```

YEAR	WEEK	SALE	RUNNING_SUM_YTD
...			
2000	49	42.38	3450.85
2000	50	21.19	3472.04
2000	52	67.45	3539.49
2001	1	92.26	92.26
2001	2	118.38	210.64
2001	3	47.24	257.88
2001	4	256.70	514.58
...			

Notice in the output of Listing 8-2, column Running_sum_ytd is the output of the sum function in the analytic mode. The column value resets at the onset of the new year 2001. Since year is also a partitioning column, so a new partition starts with each new year.

When a new year begins, the window slides to the next data partition, and the sum function begins aggregating from Week 1. Implementing this functionality with a conventional SQL statement would lead multiple self-joins and/or costly column level sub queries.

Aggregate Function Over An Entire Partition

In some cases, analytic functions might need to be applied over all rows in a given data partition. For example, computing the maximum value of the Sale column for the entire year would require a window encompassing every row in the data partition. In the Listing 8-3, you use the SQL clause rows between unbounded preceding and unbounded following to specify that the MAX function applies to all rows in a data partition. The key difference between Listing 8-2 and Listing 8-3 is that the clause unbounded following specifies the window size to include all rows in a data partition.

Listing 8-3. *Maximum of Sale Column*

```
1   select  year, week,sale,
2      max (sale) over(
3             partition by product, country, region ,year
4             order by week
5             rows between unbounded preceding and unbounded following
6                ) Max_sale
7    from sales_fact
```

```
8     where country in ('Australia')  and product ='Xtend Memory'
9*    order by product, country,year, week
/
YEAR WEEK      SALE     MAX_SALE
----- ---- ---------- ----------------

...
2000   44    135.24       246.74
2000   45     67.62       246.74
2000   46    246.74       246.74
...
2000   50     21.19       246.74
2000   52     67.45       246.74
2001    1     92.26       278.44
2001    2    118.38       278.44
...
```

Granular Window Specifications

Window specification can be more granular, too. Let's say that you want to calculate the Maximum of Sale column for a five week window period encompassing two weeks prior to the current week, the current week, and the two weeks following the current week. You can do that using the clause rows between 2 preceding and 2 following.

In the Listing 8-4, for week 36, the maximum value for the Sale column in the 5 week window is 178.52. For week 37, the maximum value for the Sale column in the 5 week window is 118.41. You can see those values in the MAX_WEEKS_5 column of the output.

Listing 8-4. *Maximum of Sale Column for a Span of Five Weeks Window*

```
1    select  year, week,sale,
2       max (sale) over(
3             partition by product, country, region ,year
4             order by week
5             rows between 2 preceding and 2 following
6             ) max_weeks_5
7    from sales_fact
8    where country in ('Australia')  and product ='Xtend Memory'
9*   order by product, country,year, week
/
YEAR WEEK      SALE MAX_WEEKS_5
---- ---- ---------- -----------

...
2000   34    178.52      178.52
2000   35     78.82      178.52
2000   36    118.41      178.52
2000   37    117.96      118.41
2000   38     79.36      118.41
...
```

Default Window Specification

The default windowing clause is `rows between unbounded preceding and current row`. If you do not explicitly specify a window, you'll get the default window. It is a good approach to specify this clause explicitly to avoid ambiguities.

Lead and Lag

Lag and lead functions provide inter-row referencing ability. Lag provides the ability to access prior row in the result set. The lead function allows access to later row in the result set.

In retail industry, *same-store sales* is a metric calculated to measure an outlet's performance, usually sales data compared to the same quarter last year. With normalized data model, this metric calculation would require accessing another row as the Sale column values for current and prior years are stored in different rows. Using the powerful inter-row referencing ability of lead and lag functions, this metric can be calculated with ease.

Another example is percentage increase or decrease calculations requiring access to the prior or following row. This calculation can be optimally written using lead and lag functions, too.

Syntax and Ordering

As discussed earlier, data in analytic SQL is partitioned on a partitioning column. Fetching a prior row is a position-dependant operation, and the order of the rows in a data partition is important in maintaining logical consistency. Within a data partition, rows are sorted with an order by clause to control the position of a row in the result set. Syntax for the lag function is:

```
lag (expression, offset, default ) over (partition-clause order-by-clause)
```

Lead and lag functions do not support windowing clause. Only `partition-by` and `order` by clauses are supported with these two functions.

Example 1: Returning a Value from Prior Row

Let's say that you need to fetch the sales quantity for the current week and prior week in the same row. Your requirement indicates an inter-row reference, and this in turn necessitates a need for a self-join in a non-analytic SQL statement. However, the lag function provides this inter-row reference without a self-join.

Listing 8-5 uses `lag(sale,1,sale)` to retrieve the Sale column value from one row prior in the result set. The clause `order by year, week` specifies the column sort order in each data partition. Since the rows are ordered by the columns Year and Week, the function `lag(sale,1,sale)` is retrieving the sale column value from the prior row, which is the Sale column value from the prior week (assuming no gaps in the week Column). For example, refer to the row where Year=1998 and week=3. For that row, the lag function is retrieving the Sale column value from the prior row where Year=1998 and week=2. Notice that analytic function does not specify the partitioning column in the clause `lag(sale,1,sale)`. It is implicitly referring to the current partition.

Listing 8-5. *Lag Function*

```
col product format A30
col country format A10
col region format A10
col year format 9999
col week format 99
col sale format 999999.99
col receipts format 999999.99
set lines 120 pages 100
1 select  year, week,sale,
2    lag(sale,1,sale) over(
3          partition by product, country, region
4          order by year, week
5      ) prior_wk_sales
6  from sales_fact
7  where country in ('Australia')  and product ='Xtend Memory'
8  order by product, country,year, week
9 /
```

```
YEAR WEEK       SALE PRIOR_WK_SALES
---- ---- ---------- ---------------
1998    1      58.15          58.15
1998    2      29.39          58.15
1998    3      29.49          29.39
...
1998   52      86.38          58.32
1999    1      53.52          86.38
1999    3      94.60          53.52
```

The third argument in the lag function specifies a default value and it is optional. If the analytic function refers to a non-existent row, then a null is returned. That's the default behavior, which you can modify by specifying some other return value in the third argument. For example, consider the row with Year=1998 and Week=1. That is the first row in its data partition. In that row's case, the lag function is accessing a non-existing prior row. Because the third argument to lag is Sale, the lag function will return the current row's Sale value when the referenced row does not exist.

Understanding that Offset is in Rows

It is possible to access any row within a data partition by specifying a different offset. In Listing 8-6, the lag function is using an offset of 10 to access prior tenth row. Output also shows that at row with Year=2001 and Week=52, the lag function is accessing the tenth prior row in the result set, which is for the week=40. Notice that Lag (sale,10,sale) is *not* accessing the week=42 by subtracting 10 from the current week column value of 52; rather, this clause is accessing tenth prior row in the partition. In this case, the tenth prior row is the row with a Week column value equal to 40.

This issue is tricky, as usually data gaps are not detected in the development environment. But in the production environment, this problem manifests itself as a bug. If there are gaps in the data, as in this example, you have a few options: populate dummy values for the missing rows or use the model clause discussed in Chapter 9.

Listing 8-6. *Lag Function with Offset of 10*

```
1 select  year, week,sale,
2   lag(sale,10,sale) over(
3         partition by product, country, region
4         order by year, week
5   ) prior_wk_sales_10
6 from sales_fact
7 where country in ('Australia')  and product ='Xtend Memory'
8 order by product, country,year, week
9 /
```

```
YEAR WEEK       SALE PRIOR_WK_SALES_10
----- ---- ---------- -----------------
2001   38     139.00            139.28
2001   39     115.57             94.48
2001   40      45.18            116.85
2001   41      67.19            162.91
...
2001   49      45.26             93.16
2001   50      23.14               139
2001   51     114.82            115.57
2001   52      23.14             45.18
```

Example 2: Returning a Value from an Upcoming Row

The lead function is similar to the lag function, except that the lead function accesses later rows in the ordered result set. For example, in the Listing 8-7, the clause lead(sale, 1,sale) is accessing a later row in the ordered result set.

Listing 8-7. *Lead Function*

```
1   select  year, week,sale,
2     lead(sale, 1,sale) over(
3           partition by product, country, region
4           order by year, week
5     ) prior_wk_sales
6    from sales_fact
7    where country in ('Australia')  and product ='Xtend Memory'
8*   order by product, country,year, week
```

```
YEAR WEEK       SALE PRIOR_WK_SALES
---- ---- ---------- --------------
2000   31      44.78         134.11
2000   33     134.11         178.52
2000   34     178.52          78.82
2000   35      78.82         118.41
...
```

The `partition-by` clause can be used to specify different partition boundaries and the `order-by` clause can be used to alter the sorting order within a partition. With effective choice of partitioning and order by columns, any row in a result set can be accessed.

First_value & Last_value

`First_value` and `last_value` functions are useful in calculating the maximum and minimum values in an ordered result set. The `first_value` function retrieves the column value from the first row in a window of rows, and the `last_value` function retrieves the column value from the last row in that window. Queries generating reports such as *Top Store by Sales for a product and market segment* are classic use cases for these analytic functions. Usually, store details and sales amounts would be shown in the report together for the store with maximum value in the Sale column. With proper partition-clause specification, the `first_value` function can be used retrieve these values in an optimal manner. Essentially, any report calculating maximum and minimum values can utilize `first_value` and `last_value` functions.

Power of `first_value` and `last_value` functions emanates from the support for partitioning and windowing clauses. Multi-level aggregation can be implemented concisely using the partitioning clause. For example, if the goal is to fetch the rows with maximum or minimum column values aggregated at different levels such as country, product, or region from the Sales table, then implementing the multi-level aggregation is akin to deciding the columns to include in the partitioning clause.

Utilizing windowing clause, you can define sliding dynamic window for these functions to operate. This window can be defined to include just a few prior and/or later rows or every row in a data partition. Specifically, queries computing metrics such as *maximum sales so far* can be implemented using these functions. As the window can be defined to be a sliding window, these two functions can be used to answer questions such as *Which store had maximum sales in the past three weeks?, Which product had maximum returns in the last two weeks,* etc.

Syntax for the `first_value` function is:

```
first_value(expression) over (partition-clause order-by-clause windowing-clause)
```

In Listing 8-8, the clause `partition by product, country, region, year` is partitioning the rows using the specified partitioning columns. The rows are sorted in a descending order on the Sale column values by the clause `order by sale desc`.

The top and bottom boundary condition of the window is specified by the clause `rows between unbounded preceding and unbounded following`. In this example, you are retrieving the top sales value at a level of Product, Country, Region, and Year columns and hence, the window includes all rows in a data partition.

Operationally, data is sorted by Product, Country, Region, Year, and Sale columns. Sorting order for the Sale column is descending order, though. The first row in every data partition will have the highest value for the Sale column due to descending sort order specification of the Sale column. So, the `first_value(sale)` clause is fetching the maximum Sale column value in the data partition.

In addition to fetching the maximum column value, you might want to fetch other columns from that top row. For example, you might want to fetch the Year and Week column value in which the maximum sale occurred. In conventional SQL statement, implementing this would result in a join and subquery. But, with analytic functions it is simpler to fetch other attributes from that top row too. Hence, the `first_value(week)` clause, with other parts of the analytic function kept the same as the `first_value(sale)`, will fetch the Week column value associated with that top row.

Example: First_value to Calculate Maximum

In Listing 8-8 output, the Top_sale_year column is an aggregated column calculating the maximum value of the Sale column. The Sale column is non-aggregated column. Both aggregated and not-aggregated column values are fetched in the same row without a self join.

Aggregation can be performed at a different level with a different partitioning clause. For example, to compute the maximum value at product, country, and region level, the partitioning clause would be partition by product, country, region.

Listing 8-8. *First_value Function*

```
1    select  year, week,sale,
2       first_value (sale) over(
3             partition by product, country, region ,year
4             order by sale desc
5             rows between unbounded preceding and unbounded following
6          ) top_sale_value,
7       first_value (week) over(
8             partition by product, country, region ,year
9             order by sale desc
10            rows between unbounded preceding and unbounded following
11         ) top_sale_week
12    from sales_fact
13    where country in ('Australia')  and product ='Xtend Memory'
14*   order by product, country,year, week;
```

YEAR	WEEK	SALE	TOP_SALE_VALUE	TOP_SALE_WEEK
2000	49	42.38	246.74	46
2000	50	21.19	246.74	46
2000	52	67.45	246.74	46
2001	1	92.26	278.44	16
2001	2	118.38	278.44	16
2001	3	47.24	278.44	16
2001	4	256.70	278.44	16

Example: Last_value to Calculate Minimum

Similarly, you can use last_value function to calculate minimum or maximum values. The last_value function fetches the column values from the last row in a window of rows. For example, if you want to calculate the minimum Sale column value, then you could use the combination of the clause Last_value(sale) and the clause order by sale desc sorting order. The clause order by sale desc will sort the rows by Sale column values in a descending order, and the clause Last_value(sale) will fetch the Sale column value from the last row. Listing 8-9 provides an example for last_value function usage.

Listing 8-9. *last_value Function*

```
1    select  year, week,sale,
2       last_value (sale) over(
3              partition by product, country, region ,year
4              order by sale desc
5              rows between unbounded preceding and unbounded following
6           ) low_sale
7    from sales_fact
8    where country in ('Australia')  and product ='Xtend Memory'
9*   order by product, country,year, week
```

```
YEAR WEEK       SALE   LOW_SALE
----- ----  ---------- ------------
...
2000   49      42.38       19.84
2000   50      21.19       19.84
2000   52      67.45       19.84
2001    1      92.26       22.37
2001    2     118.38       22.37
2001    3      47.24       22.37
...
```

Granular control of window specification can be effectively utilized to produce complex reports. For example, the clause rows between 10 preceding and 10 following is specifying a window of 21 rows to calculate maximum or minimum value.

Null values are handled by the clause [RESPECT NULLS|IGNORE NULLS]. Clause RESPECT NULLS is the default, and the first_value function returns the null value if the column value in the first row is null, by default. If the clause IGNORE NULLS is specified, then the first_value function returns the first non-null column value in a window of rows.

Other Analytic Functions

Oracle Database implements a great many other analytic functions. Some of those more commonly used are described in the following subsections. The functions that follow are the ones that should be on your short list of good functions to know about.

Nth_value (11gR2)

While first_value and last_value functions provide the ability to fetch the first or last row in an ordered result set, it is not quite straightforward to fetch any arbitrary row with these functions. In fact, fetching the second row using either the first_value or last_value function is a complex task.

Oracle Database Version 11gR2 introduced another analytic function: nth_value, which is a generalization of first_value and first_value functions. Using nth_valuefunction, you can fetch any row in the ordered result set, not just first or last values. The first_value function can be written as nth_value (column_name, 1).

In statistics analysis, outliers can occur in the head or tail of the result set. In some cases, it might be important to ignore first_value or first_value in an ordered result set and fetch the value from the next row. The second value in a result set can be fetched using the nth_value function passing two as the offset to the function.

The nth_value function also supports windowing clauses. As discussed earlier, a windowing clause provides the ability to implement sliding dynamic window. This, in turn, effectively allows you to write simple queries to answer complex questions such as *Which store had second highest Sales in a span of 12 weeks for a product?*

Syntax for the nth_value function is:

```
NTH_VALUE (measure, n ) [ FROM FIRST| FROM LAST] [RESPECT NULLS|IGNORE NULLS]
        OVER (partitioning-clause order-by-clause windowing-clause)
```

The first argument to the nth_value function is the column name, and the second argument is the offset in a window. For example, the clause nth_value(sale, 2) is accessing the second row in a window. In the Listing 8-10, the SQL statement is fetching the Week column value with the second highest Sale column value at product, country, region, and year level. The second row in this result set is the row with second highest value for the Sale column since the rows are sorted by Sale column in the descending order. The clause partition by product, country, region, year is specifying the partitioning columns.

Listing 8-10. *Nth Value*

```
1  select year, week, sale,
2    nth_value ( sale, 2) over (
3     partition by product,country, region, year
4     order by sale desc
5     rows between unbounded preceding and unbounded following
6    ) sale_2nd_top
7  from sales_fact
8  where country in ('Australia') and product='Xtend Memory'
9* order by product, country , year, week

    YEAR       WEEK       SALE SALE_2ND_TOP
---------- ---------- ---------- ------------
...
    2000       49      42.38       187.48
    2000       50      21.19       187.48
    2000       52      67.45       187.48
    2001        1      92.26       256.7
    2001        2     118.38       256.7
    2001        3      47.24       256.7
...
```

For the nth_value function, clauses FROM FIRST and RESPECT NULLS are the defaults. If the clause FROM FIRST is specified, then the nth_value function finds the offset row from the beginning of the window. The clause RESPECT NULLS returns null values if the column contains null values in the offset row.

With an ability to specify a windowing clause, the nth_value function is quite powerful in accessing an arbitrary row in the result set or in a partition.

Rank

The rank function returns the position of a row, as a number, in an ordered set of rows. If the rows are sorted by columns, then the position of a row in a window reflects the rank of the value in that window of rows. In the case of a tie, rows with equal value will have the same rank and the ranks are skipped, leaving gaps in the rank values. This means that two rows can have the same rank, and the ranks are not necessarily consecutive.

The rank function is useful to compute the top or bottom N rows. For example, a query to find the top 10 weeks by sales quantity is a typical retail industry data warehouse query. Such a query will greatly benefit from the use of rank. If you need to write any query that computes top or bottom N-elements of a result set, use the rank or dense_rank function.

The rank function is also useful in finding inner-N rows. For example, if the goal is to fetch rows from 21 through 40 sorted by sales, then you can use the rank function in a subquery with a predicate between 21 and 40 filtering 20 inner rows.

Syntax for the rank function is:

```
rank() over (partition-clause order-by-clause)
```

In the Listing 8-11, you calculate the top 10 rows by sale for a Product, Country, Region, and Year column values. The clause partition by product, country, region, week is specifying the partitioning columns and the rows are sorted by Sale column descending order in that data partition using the order by Sale desc clause. The rank function is calculating the rank of the row in that data partition. This SQL is wrapped inside an inline view, and then a predicate of sales_rank <=10 is applied to fetch the top ten weeks by Sale column.

Also, notice that the windowing clause is not applicable in the rank functions and the rank function is applied over all the rows in a data partition.

Listing 8-11. *Use of Rank Function: Top 10 Sales Weeks*

```
 1  select * from (
 2   select  year, week,sale,
 3     rank() over(
 4             partition by product, country, region ,year
 5             order by sale desc
 6                ) sales_rank
 7   from sales_fact
 8   where country in ('Australia')  and product ='Xtend Memory'
 9   order by product, country,year, week
10  ) where sales_rank<=10
11* order by 1,4
```

```
YEAR WEEK      SALE SALES_RANK
---- ----  --------- ----------
...
2001   16   278.44            1
2001    4   256.70            2
2001   21   233.70            3
2001   48   182.96            4
2001   30   162.91            5
2001   14   162.91            5
```

```
2001   22     141.78          7
2001   43     139.58          8
...
```

The rank function assigns same rank in case of ties. In the output of Listing 8-11, notice that there are two rows with a sales rank of 5, as the Sale column value is 162.91 for these two rows. Also, notice that next rank is 7, not 6. In a nutshell, the rank function skips the ranks if there are ties. Number of rank values skipped equals to number of rows with tied values. If there have been ties for three rows, then the next rank will be 8.

Dense_rank

Dense_rank is a variant of the rank function. The difference between the rank and dense_rank functions is that the dense_rank function does not skip the ranks in case of ties. As discussed in the earlier section, the dense_rank function is useful in finding top, bottom, or Inner N rows in a result set. In the Listing 8-12, the dense_rank function is used instead of rank function. Note that rank column for the week=22 is 6 in the Listing 8-12 and it is 7 in the Listing 8-11.

The dense_rank function is useful in the queries where the ranks need to be consecutive. For example, ranks may not be skipped in a query to compute the top 10 students in a class roster. On the other hand, the rank function is useful where the ranks need not be consecutive.

Listing 8-12. *dense_rank Function*

```
1  select * from (
2   select   year, week,sale,
3      dense_rank() over(
4            partition by product, country, region ,year
5            order by sale desc
6               ) sales_rank
7    from sales_fact
8    where country in ('Australia')  and product ='Xtend Memory'
9    order by product, country,year, week
10  ) where sales_rank<=10
11* order by 1,4
/
YEAR WEEK       SALE SALES_RANK
----- ---- ---------- ----------
 2001   16     278.44          1
 2001    4     256.70          2
 2001   21     233.70          3
 2001   48     182.96          4
 2001   14     162.91          5
 2001   30     162.91          5
 2001   22     141.78          6
```

Sort order for nulls can be controlled by the NULLS FIRST or NULLS LAST clause in the dense_rank function. NULLS LAST is the default for ascending sort order, and NULLS FIRST is the default for the descending sort order. In the Listing 8-12, descending sort order is used and the default NULLS FIRST clause is in effect. Rows with null values will have a rank of 1 in this case.

Row_number

The row_number function assigns a unique number for each row in the ordered result set. If the partitioning clause is specified, then each row is assigned a number unique within a data partition, based upon its position in the sort order in that partition. If the partitioning clause is not specified, then each row in the result set is assigned a unique number.

The row_number function is also useful to fetch top, bottom, or Inner N queries, similar to rank and dense_rank functions. Even though the rank, dense_rank, and row_number functions have similar functionality, there are subtle differences between them. One is that the row_number function does not allow windowing clauses.

Syntax for the row_number function is:

```
Row_number() over (partition-clause order-by-clause)
```

The row_number function is a non-deterministic function. The value of the row_number function is undetermined if two rows have same value in a data partition. For example, in the Listing 8-13, rows with column values of 19, 8, 12, and 4 have same value of 46.54 in the Sale column. The row_number function returns values of 31, 32, 34, and 33 respectively for these rows, in the example output. But the result could just as easily be 34, 31, 32, 33 or 32, 34, 31, 33. In fact, you might get different results with execution of the query. On the contrary, rank and dense_rank functions are deterministic and will always return consistent values if a query is re-executed.

Listing 8-13. *row_number Function*

```
1    select  year, week,sale,
2      row_number() over(
3             partition by product, country, region ,year
4             order by sale desc
5               ) sales_rn,
6      rank() over(
7             partition by product, country, region ,year
8             order by sale desc
9               ) sales_rank
10     from sales_fact
11     where country in ('Australia')  and product ='Xtend Memory'
12*    order by product, country,year,sales_rank

YEAR WEEK        SALE  SALES_RN SALES_RANK
----- ---- ---------- ---------- ----------
...
 2000   19      46.54         31         31
 2000    8      46.54         32         31
 2000   12      46.54         34         31
 2000    4      46.54         33         31
...
```

Ratio_to_report

The analytic function `ratio_to_report` calculates the ratio of a value to the sum of values in the data partition. If the partitioning clause is not specified, this function calculates the ratio of a value to the sum values in the whole result set. This analytic function is very useful in calculating ratios at various levels without a need for self-joins.

`Ratio_to_report` is useful in computing the percentage of a value compared to the total value in a report. For example, consider a sales report of a product in a retail chain. Each outlet in the retail chain contributed to the total sum of sales computed for that product, and knowing what percentage of sales is generated from an outlet is quite useful for market trend analysis. `Ratio_to_report` allows you to compute the percentage easily. Further, this ratio can be calculated at various levels such as district, region, and country. Essentially, data can be diced and sliced at various ways for market trend analysis.

In the Listing 8-14, the SQL statement is computing two ratios: Sales_ratio_yr is computed at product, country, region, and year level and the ratio sales_ratio_prod is computed at the product, country, and region level. Ratio_to_report function returns a ratio and it is multipled by 100 to compute percentage.

The `ratio_to_report(sale) over( partition by product, country, region, year)` clause calculates the ratio of Sale column value to the sum of Sale column values in a data partition, partitioned by the columns Product, Country, Region, and Year. The next clause `ratio_to_report(sale) over( partition by product, country, region)` is different as the Year column is not included in the partitioning columns. So, the ratio is calculated for all years.

The `ratio_to_report` function will return a null value if the expression or column specified in the function returns null values. But other null values in the data partition will be handled as either zero values or empty strings, similar to aggregation functions.

Listing 8-14. *ratio_to_report Function*

```
1  select  year, week,sale,
2  trunc(100*
3         ratio_to_report(sale) over(partition by product, country, region ,year)
4         ,2) sales_yr,
5  trunc(100*
6         ratio_to_report(sale) over(partition by product, country, region)
7         ,2) sales_prod
8  from sales_fact
9  where country in ('Australia')  and product ='Xtend Memory'
10 order by product, country,year, week
/
```

YEAR	WEEK	SALE	SALES_YR	SALES_PROD
2000	1	46.70	1.31	.35
2000	3	93.41	2.63	.7
2000	4	46.54	1.31	.35
2000	5	46.70	1.31	.35
2000	7	70.80	2	.53
2000	8	46.54	1.31	.35

...

Percent_rank

The percent_rank function returns the rank of a value in a data partition, expressed as a fraction between 0 and 1. Percent_rank is calculated as (rank -1)/(N-1) whereas N is the number of elements in the data partition if the partitioning clause is specified or the total number of rows in the result set if the partitioning clause is not specified. The percent_rank function is useful to compute the relative standing of a value in a result set, as a percentile.

   This relative rank can be calculated relative to a partition or the whole result set. For example, computing the sales percentile of a retail outlet in a district or region helps find the top performing outlets or the worst performing outlet.

   In Listing 8-15, you calculate the top fifty sale percentile by year using the percent_rank function. The clause percent_rank() over(partition by product, country, region , year order by sale desc) calculates the percent rank of the Sale column in a data partition defined by the partitioning columns Product, Country, Region, and Year. Rows are ordered by the Sale column in descending order. Function output is multiplied by 100 to compute percentile.

Listing 8-15. *percent_rank Function*

```
1  select * from (
2  select  year, week,sale,
3     100 * percent_rank() over(
4            partition by product, country, region , year
5            order by sale desc
6            ) pr
7    from sales_fact
8    where country in ('Australia')  and product ='Xtend Memory'
9  ) where pr <50
10* order by year, sale desc
```

YEAR	WEEK	SALE	PR
2001	16	278.44	.00
2001	4	256.70	2.27
2001	21	233.70	4.55
2001	48	182.96	6.82
...			

Percentile_cont

The percentile_cont function is useful to compute the interpolated values, such as the median household income per region or city. The percentile_cont function takes a probability value between 0 and 1 and returns an interpolated percentile value that would equal the percent_rank value with respect to the sort specification. In fact, percentile_cont function performs inverse of percent_rank function and it is easier to understand the percentile_cont function in conjunction with the output of percent_rank function.

   The percentile_cont function retrieves the column value matching (or interpolated) with the percent_rank of the argument. For example, the clause percentile_cont(0.25) retrieves the value that has percent_rank of 0.25, assuming matching sort order for these two functions. Another example is computing the median household income in a city or region. The median value will have a percent_rank of 0.5 by the definition of *median value*. The clause percentile_cont(0.5) will return the median value as the `percentile_cont` function is calculating the value with a `percent_rank` of 0.5. In fact, median function is a specific case of the `percentile_cont` function with a default value of 0.5.

Nulls are ignored by the function. This function does not support windowing clauses either. Syntax for the `percentile_cont` function is:

```
Percentile_cont(expr) within group (sort-clause)
     over (partition-clause order-by-clause)
```

The syntax for the `percentile_cont` function is slightly different from the analytic functions discussed so far. A new clause `within group (order by sale desc)` replaces the order-by clause, and it is functionally same as specifying an order-by clause. In Listing 8-16, the clause `percentile_cont (0.5)` `within group (order by sale desc) over( partition by product, country, region , year)` is calling the `percentile_cont` function and passing a probability value of 0.5. Sort order is defined by the clause `within group (order by sale desc)`. The partition-by clause `over( partition by product, country, region , year)` is specifying the partitioning columns.

Listing 8-16 shows the output of `percent_rank` in a side-by-side comparison to that from `percentile_cont`, with a similar partition-by clause and order-by clause. Notice that for the column values year=2001 and week=5, the Sale column value is 93.44 and the `percent_rank` of that value is 0.5. Essentially, value of 93.44 is occurring with a `percent_rank` of 0.5 in the descending order of Sale column values in that data partition. In a nutshell, the value of 93.44 is a median value and thus the `percent_rank` is 0.5. Hence the `percent_rank` function with an argument of 0.5 returns a value of 93.44.

Further, note that the output row for the column values with year=2000. There is no Sale column value with a `percent_rank` matching exactly to 0.5 in the data partition. If there is no value matching exactly, then the `percentile_cont` function computes an interpolated value using the nearest values. Note that there is a row in that data partition with a `percent_rank` of 0.48 for the Sale column value of 79.36 and the next row in that sort order has a `percent_rank` of 0.51 for the Sale column value of 78.82. Since the specified `percent_rank` of 0.5 is between 0.48 and 0.51, the `percentile_cont` function interpolated these two corresponding Sale column values 79.36 and 78.82 and calculated `percentile_cont (0.5)` as 79.09, an average of those two Sale column values. Values are averaged as this function assumes continuous distribution.

Notice that output rows are not sorted in the Listing 8-16. Reason is that, even though there is an order-by clause specified in the analytic function specification (line 3 and line 7), there is no order-by clause in the main body of the query. Should you need rows to be sorted, you need to specify sorting order explicitly in the main body of the query also.

Listing 8-16. *The percentile_cont Function*

```
1  select  year, week,sale,
2     percentile_cont (0.5)  within group
3        (order by sale desc)
4        over( partition by product, country, region , year ) pc,
5     percent_rank () over (
6             partition by product, country, region , year
7             order by sale desc ) pr
8    from sales_fact
9*   where country in ('Australia')  and product ='Xtend Memory'

YEAR WEEK      SALE       PC        PR
---- ----  ---------- ---------- ----------
...
2001  27     94.48       93.44 .454545455
```

2001	46	93.58	93.44	.477272727
2001	5	93.44	93.44	.5
2001	37	93.16	93.44	.522727273
2001	9	92.67	93.44	.545454545
...				
2000	40	89.56	79.09	.435897436
2000	28	88.96	79.09	.461538462
2000	38	79.36	79.09	.487179487
2000	35	78.82	79.09	.512820513
2000	7	70.80	79.09	.538461538
2000	15	70.47	79.09	.564102564
...				

Percentile_disc

The percentile_disc function is functionally similar to percentile_cont except that the percentile_cont function uses a continuous distribution model and the percentile_disc function assumes a discrete distribution model. As discussed in the earlier section, when there is no value matching exactly with the specified percent_rank, then the percentile_cont (0.5) computes an average of two nearest values. In contrast, the percentile_disc function retrieves the value with a percent_rank just greater than the passed argument, in the case of ascending order. In the case of descending order, the percentile_cont function retrieves the value that has a percent_rank just smaller than the passed argument.

In Listing 8-17, the percentile_cont function is replaced by two calls to the percentile_disc function. The first call to the function starting in line 2 specifies descending sort order, and the next call in line 4 specifies no sort order, so it defaults to ascending sort order. In both calls to the percentile_disc function, an argument of 0.5 is passed. As there is no row with a percent_rank of 0.5, the percentile_disc function with the descending sort order specification returns a value of 79.36, as this value has a percent_rank of 0.48 just below the specified argument 0.5. For the ascending order, this function returns a value of 78.82 as this value has a percent_rank of 0.51—just above 0.5.

Listing 8-17. *The percentile_disc Function*

```
1     select  year, week,sale,
2     percentile_disc (0.5)  within group (order by sale desc)
3       over( partition by product, country, region , year ) pd_desc,
4     percentile_disc (0.5)  within group (order by sale )
5       over( partition by product, country, region , year ) pd_asc,
6     percent_rank () over (
7             partition by product, country, region , year
8             order by sale desc ) pr
9     from sales_fact
10*   where country in ('Australia')  and product ='Xtend Memory'
```

YEAR	WEEK	SALE	PD_DESC	PD_ASC	PR
2000	3	93.41	79.36	78.82	.41025641
2000	40	89.56	79.36	78.82	.435897436
2000	28	88.96	79.36	78.82	.461538462
2000	38	79.36	79.36	78.82	.487179487
2000	35	78.82	79.36	78.82	.512820513
2000	7	70.80	79.36	78.82	.538461538
2000	15	70.47	79.36	78.82	.564102564
2000	45	67.62	79.36	78.82	.58974359
2000	52	67.45	79.36	78.82	.615384615

NTILE

The NTILE function divides an ordered set of rows in a data partition, groups them in to buckets, and assigns a unique group number to each group. This function is useful in statistical analysis. For example, if you want to remove the outliers (values that are outside the norm), you can group them in the top or bottom buckets and eliminate those values from the statistical analysis. Oracle Database statistics collection packages also use NTILE functions to calculate histogram boundaries. In statistical terminology, the NTILE function creates equi-width histograms.

The number of buckets is passed as the argument to this analytic function. For example, ntile(100) will group the rows into 100 buckets, assigning an unique number for each bucket. This function does not support windowing clauses, however.

In the Listing 8-18, you split a data partition into 10 buckets using the clause ntile (10). Rows are sorted by the Sale column in the descending order. The NTILE function groups rows into buckets with each bucket containing equal number of rows. Since the rows are sorted by the Sale column values in descending order, rows with lower group numbers have higher Sale column value. Outliers in the data can be easily removed with this technique.

There may be a row count difference of at most 1 between the buckets if the rows can not be divided equally. In this example, rows for the year= 2001 is divided in to 10 buckets, each bucket having 5 rows, but the last bucket 10 has only 4 rows.

Listing 8-18. *NTILE Function*

```
1  select  year, week,sale,
2     ntile (10) over(
3            partition by product, country, region , year
4            order by sale desc
5            ) group#
6     from sales_fact
7* where country in ('Australia')  and product ='Xtend Memory'
```

YEAR	WEEK	SALE	GROUP#
2001	16	278.44	1
2001	4	256.70	1
2001	21	233.70	1

2001	48	182.96	1
2001	14	162.91	1
...			
2001	52	23.14	9
2001	50	23.14	10
2001	6	22.44	10
2001	23	22.38	10
2001	18	22.37	10

The NTILE function is useful in real world applications such as dividing total work among N parallel processes. Let's say you have ten parallel processes; you can divide the total work in to10 buckets and assign each bucket to a process.

Stddev

The stddev function can be used to calculate standard deviation among a set of rows in a data partition or in the result set if no partitioning clause is specified. This function calculates the standard deviation, defined as square root of variance, for a data partition specified using a partitioning clause. If partitioning clause is not specified, this function calculates the stddev for all rows in the result set.

In the Listing 8-19, the clause stddev (sale) is calculating the stddev on Sale column among the rows in a data partition. Partitioning clause partition by product, country, region, year specifies the partitioning columns. The windowing clause rows between unbounded preceding and unbounded following specifies the window as all rows in that data partition. Essentially, this SQL is calculating the standard deviation on Sale column amongst all rows in a data partition.

Standard deviation can be calculated at coarser or granular level by specifying appropriate partition-by clause and windowing clause.

Listing 8-19. *STDDEV Function*

```
1  select  year, week,sale,
2     stddev (sale) over(
3            partition by product, country, region , year
4            order by Sale desc
5            rows between unbounded preceding and unbounded following
6            ) stddv
7     from sales_fact
8     where country in ('Australia')  and product ='Xtend Memory'
9* order by year, week
```

```
YEAR WEEK      SALE     STDDV
----- ----  ---------- ----------
...
2000   50      21.19 49.8657423
2000   52      67.45 49.8657423
2001    1      92.26 59.1063592
2001    2     118.38 59.1063592
2001    3      47.24 59.1063592
...
```

There are various other statistics functions that can be used to calculate statistical metrics; for example, `stddev_samp` calculates the cumulative sample standard deviation, `stddev_pop` calculates the population standard deviation, etc. Detailed discussion about various statistics functions is out of the scope of this book, however.

Listagg

Oracle Database version 11gR2 introduced another analytic function, the `Listagg` function, which is very useful in string manipulation. This analytic function provides the ability to convert column values from multiple rows in to a list format. For example, if you want to concatenate all the employee names in a department, then you can use this function to concatenate all names in to a list.

Syntax for this function is of the format:

```
Listagg (string, separator ) within group (order-by-clause)
    Over (partition-by-clause )
```

Syntax for the `Listagg` function uses the clause `within group (order-by-clause)` to specify sorting order. This clause is similar to `order-by` clause in other analytic functions. The first argument to this function is the string or column name to concatenate. The second argument is the separator for the values. In the Listing 8-20, the partitioning clause is not specified and rows are ordered by the Country column in the descending order. The output shows that country names are converted to a list separated by comma. Note that `Listagg` function does not support windowing clauses.

Listing 8-20. LISTAGG *Function*

```
1  select listagg (country, ',')
2    within group (order by country desc)
3  from (
4    select distinct country from sales_fact
5    order by country
6* )

LISTAGG(COUNTRY,',')WITHINGROUP(ORDERBYCOUNTRYDESC)
---------------------------------------------------------------
United States of America,United Kingdom,Turkey,Spain,Singapore,
Saudi Arabia,Poland,New Zealand, Japan,Italy,Germany,France,
Denmark,China,Canada,Brazil,Australia,Argentina
```

Performance Tuning

Analytic functions are very useful in tuning complex SQL statements. Inter-row referencing, aggregation at multiple levels, and nth-row access are a few of the important features analytic functions provide. For example, a typical query fetching both aggregated and non-aggregated rows must perform a self-join. In a data warehouse environments, due to the sheer size of the tables involved, these self-joins can be cost prohibitive.

The efficiency that analytics bring to the table often makes them useful tools in rewriting queries that do not perform well. In turn, however, you can sometimes face the need to tune an analytic function. To that end, there are some useful things to know about analytic functions and execution plans, analytics and predicates, and strategies for indexing.

Execution Plans

Analytic function introduces few new operations in the SQL execution plan. Presence of the keywords WINDOW SORT indicate that the SQL statement utilizes an analytic function. In this section, I will review the mechanics of analytic function execution.

Listing 8-21 shows a typical execution plan of a SQL statement. Execution of this plan starts at step 4 and works its way outwards to step 1:

4. Table SALES_FACT is accessed using Full Table Scan access path.

3. Filter predicates on Product, Country, Region, and Year column are applied filtering required rows.

2. Analytic functions are applied over the filtered rows from the step 3.

1. Predicate on Week column applied after the execution of these analytic functions.

■**NOTE** The Cost Based Optimizer does not assign or calculate a cost for analytic functions (as of 11gR2). The cost of the SQL statement is calculated without considering the cost of analytic functions.

Listing 8-21. *Execution Plan*

```
-------------------------------------------------------------------
| Id  | Operation            | Name          | Rows  | Bytes | Cost (%CPU)|
-------------------------------------------------------------------
|   0 | SELECT STATEMENT     |               |     5 |   290 |   581   (3)|
|*  1 |  VIEW                | MAX_5_WEEKS_VW |    5 |   290 |   581   (3)|
|   2 |   WINDOW SORT        |               |     5 |   330 |   581   (3)|
|*  3 |    TABLE ACCESS FULL| SALES_FACT    |     5 |   330 |   580   (3)|
-------------------------------------------------------------------

Predicate Information (identified by operation id):
---------------------------------------------------
   1 - filter("WEEK"<14)
   3 - filter("PRODUCT"='Xtend Memory' AND "COUNTRY"='Australia' AND
              "REGION"='Australia' AND "YEAR"=2000)
```

Predicates

Predicates must be applied on the tables as early as possible to reduce the result set for better performance. Rows must be filtered earlier so that analytic functions are applied to relatively fewer rows. Predicate safety is an important consideration in executing analytic functions as not all predicates can be applied beforehand.

In the Listing 8-22, a view called max_5_weeks_vw is defined and a SQL statement is accessing the view with the predicates on Country, Product, Region, Year, and Week columns. The execution plan shows that the following filter predicates are applied in step 3:

```
filter((("PRODUCT"='Xtend Memory' AND "COUNTRY"='Australia'
AND "REGION"='Australia' AND "YEAR"=2000))
```

However, the predicate "WEEK"<14 is not applied in step 3, and is only applied in step 1, indicating that the predicate is applied after executing the analytic functions in step 2's WINDOW SORT step. All supplied predicates except that on the Week column were pushed into the view. Filtering of those predicates then took place before executing the analytic functions.

Predicates on partitioning columns are applied before executing analytic functions, as generally speaking, predicates on partitioning column can be pushed safely into the view. But columns in the order-by-clause of the analytic function syntax can't be pushed safely as the inter-row references need access to other rows in the same partitions, even if those rows are not returned in the final result set.

Listing 8-22. *Predicates*

```
 create or replace view max_5_weeks_vw as
   select  country , product, region, year, week,sale,
   max (sale) over(
          partition by product, country, region ,year
          order by year, week
          rows between 2 preceding and 2 following
           ) max_weeks_5
  from sales_fact
/
1  select year, week, sale, max_weeks_5 from  max_5_weeks_vw
2    where country in ('Australia')  and product ='Xtend Memory' and
3    region='Australia' and year= 2000 and week <14
4*   order by year, week
/
-------------------------------------------------------------
| Id  | Operation          | Name          | E-Rows |
-------------------------------------------------------------
|   0 | SELECT STATEMENT   |               |        |
|*  1 |   VIEW             | MAX_5_WEEKS_VW |     5 |
|   2 |    WINDOW SORT     |               |      5 |
|*  3 |     TABLE ACCESS FULL| SALES_FACT  |      5 |
-------------------------------------------------------------

Predicate Information (identified by operation id):
---------------------------------------------------
   1 - filter("WEEK"<14)
   3 - filter((("PRODUCT"='Xtend Memory' AND "COUNTRY"='Australia' AND
            "REGION"='Australia' AND "YEAR"=2000))
```

Indexes

A good strategy for index selection is to match the predicates applied on the table access step. As discussed in the earlier section, predicates on partitioning columns are pushed into the view and these predicate are applied before executing the analytic functions. So, it's probably a better approach to index the partitioning columns if the SQL statements are using those predicates.

In the Listing 8-23, a new index is added on the columns Country and Product. Step 4 in the execution plan shows that index-based access is used. The predicate Information section shows that predicates on all four partitioning columns were applied at step 4 and step 3 before executing analytic function. But the predicate on Week column was applied much later in the execution plan at step 1. So, in this case, adding Week column to the index is not useful as the predicates are not applied until after the analytic function execution completes.

Listing 8-23. *Predicates and Indices*

```
create index sales_fact_i1 on  sales_fact( country, product);

1  select year, week, sale, max_weeks_5 from  max_5_weeks_vw
2    where country in ('Australia')  and product ='Xtend Memory' and
3    region='Australia' and year= 2000 and week <14
4*   order by year, week
/
```

```
---------------------------------------------------------------------
| Id  | Operation                     | Name           | E-Rows |
---------------------------------------------------------------------
|   0 | SELECT STATEMENT              |                |        |
|*  1 |  VIEW                         | MAX_5_WEEKS_VW |      5 |
|   2 |   WINDOW SORT                 |                |      5 |
|*  3 |    TABLE ACCESS BY INDEX ROWID| SALES_FACT     |      5 |
|*  4 |     INDEX RANGE SCAN          | SALES_FACT_I1  |    147 |
---------------------------------------------------------------------

Predicate Information (identified by operation id):
---------------------------------------------------

   1 - filter("WEEK"<14)
   3 - filter(("REGION"='Australia' AND "YEAR"=2000))
   4 - access("COUNTRY"='Australia' AND "PRODUCT"='Xtend Memory') fs
```

Advanced topics

A few advanced topics about the analytic functions are worthy of discussion. I will discuss topics such as dynamic analytic statements, nesting of analytic functions, parallelism, and PGA size.

Dynamic SQL

A common question about the analytic SQL statement is whether a bind variable can be used in place of partitioning or sorting columns. No. If you want the flexibility to modify the partitioning or sorting columns dynamically, you need to use dynamic SQL statements. Static analytic SQL statements can not change the partitioning or sorting columns.

If your goal is to modify the partitioning columns dynamically, then consider creating a packaged procedure to capture the logic in the procedure. In the Listing 8-24, the procedure Analytic_dynamic_ prc accepts a string to be used as partitioning columns. A SQL statement is constructed using the arguments passed and executed dynamically using Execute immediate syntax. Result of the analytic statement is fetched into an array and printed using a call to dbms_output package.

In the first call, the analytic_dynamic_prc passes the string product, country, region as the first argument and the columns in this list are used as the partitioning columns. The second call to the procedure uses the string product, country, region, year to use a different list of columns for the partitioning-clause.

Note that this procedure is given as an example and as such may not be construed as a production-ready code.

Listing 8-24. *Dynamic SQL Statement*

```
create or replace procedure
  analytic_dynamic_prc ( part_col_string varchar2, v_country varchar2, v_product varchar2)
is
  type numtab is table of number(18,2) index by binary_integer;
  l_year numtab;
  l_week numtab;
  l_sale numtab;
  l_rank numtab;
  l_sql_string  varchar2(512) ;
begin
 l_sql_String :=
 'select * from (
   select  year, week,sale,
     rank() over(
      partition by '||part_col_string ||'
           order by sale desc
             ) sales_rank
    from sales_fact
    where country in (' ||chr(39) || v_country || chr(39) || ' )  and
          product ='  || chr(39) || v_product || chr(39) ||
          ' order by product, country,year, week
    ) where sales_rank<=10
    order by 1,4';
  execute immediate l_sql_string bulk collect into  l_year, l_week, l_sale, l_rank;
  for  i  in 1 .. l_year.count
   loop
        dbms_output.put_line ( l_year(i) ||' |' || l_week (i) ||
                          '|'|| l_sale(i) || '|' || l_rank(i) );
   end loop;
```

```
 end;
/

exec analytic_dynamic_prc ( 'product, country, region','Australia','Xtend Memory');
...
1998 |48|172.56|9
2000 |46|246.74|3
2000 |21|187.48|5
2000 |43|179.12|7
2000 |34|178.52|8
2001 |16|278.44|1
2001 |4|256.7|2
exec analytic_dynamic_prc ( 'product, country,region, year','Australia','Xtend Memory');

1998 |48|172.56|1
1998 |10|117.76|2
1998 |18|117.56|3
1998 |23|117.56|3
1998 |26|117.56|3
1998 |38|115.84|6
1998 |42|115.84|6
...
```

Nesting Analytic Functions

Analytic functions can not be nested, but a nesting effect can be achieved with the use of subqueries. For example, the clause lag(first_value(column,1),1) is syntactically incorrect. Subqueries can be used to create a nesting effect, as you'll see below.

Suppose your goal is to fetch the maximum Sale column value for the year and the prior year in the same row; if so, then analytic functions lag and first_value can be used in the subqueries to write a SQL statement. In Listing 8-25, inner subquery is fetching the Year and Week Sale column value in which the maximum sale occurred, in addition to fetching the maximum Sale column value for that year. The lag function in the outer query retrieves the prior Year Maximum Sale column value.

Notice that the partitioning clause is different between lag and first_value functions. Analytic function first_value is computing the top Sale row in a partition specified by the partitioning columns product, country, region, year whereas the lag is fetching the first row from the prior year specifying only sorting-clause: order by year desc.

With multi-level nesting of analytic functions, complex goals can be implemented concisely using the analytic functions.

Listing 8-25. *Nesting Analytic Functions*

```
select  year, week, top_sale_year,
   lag( top_sale_year) over ( order by year desc) prev_top_sale_yer
from (
 select distinct
    first_value ( year) over (
        partition by product, country, region ,year
```

```
         order by sale desc
         rows between unbounded preceding and unbounded following
    ) year,
   first_value ( week) over (
         partition by product, country, region ,year
         order by sale desc
         rows between unbounded preceding and unbounded following
    ) week,
   first_value (sale) over(
         partition by product, country, region ,year
         order by sale desc
         rows between unbounded preceding and unbounded following
    ) top_sale_year
  from sales_fact
  where country in ('Australia')  and product ='Xtend Memory'
)
  order by year, week
/


YEAR WEEK TOP_SALE_YEAR PREV_TOP_SALE_YER
----- ---- ------------- -----------------
1998   48      172.56         148.12
1999   17      148.12         246.74
2000   46      246.74         278.44
2001   16      278.44
```

Parallelism

By specifying a parallel hint in the SQL statement or by setting parallelism at the object level, analytic functions can be parallelized. If you have huge amount of data that needs to be processed using analytic functions, parallelism is a good choice. A SQL statement using multi-level nesting also can benefit from parallelism.

Listing 8-26 shows the execution plan for the query in the Listing 8-25 using parallelism. In the execution plan, there are two WINDOW operations as the SQL statement has nested the lag and first_value analytic functions.

Optimal distribution of rows between the PQ slaves is critical to maintain functional correctness and that is automatically handled by Oracle database.

Listing 8-26. *Parallelism*

```
------------------------------------------------------
Id  | Operation                      | Name
------------------------------------------------------
 0  | SELECT STATEMENT               |
 1  |   SORT ORDER BY                |
 2  |    WINDOW BUFFER               |
 3  |     PX COORDINATOR             |
```

```
   4 |       PX SEND QC (ORDER)        | :TQ10003
   5 |         SORT ORDER BY           |
   6 |        PX RECEIVE               |
   7 |         PX SEND RANGE           | :TQ10002
   8 |          VIEW                   |
   9 |           HASH UNIQUE           |
  10 |            PX RECEIVE           |
  11 |             PX SEND HASH        | :TQ10001
  12 |             WINDOW SORT         |
  13 |              PX RECEIVE         |
  14 |               PX SEND HASH      | :TQ10000
  15 |                PX BLOCK ITERATOR|
* 16 |                 TABLE ACCESS FULL| SALES_FACT
```

PGA size

Most operations associated with the analytic functions are performed in the Program Global Area (PGA) of the process. So, for optimal performance it is important to have a big enough memory area so that programs can execute analytic functions without spilling to the disk. This is very analogous to a Sort operation. If the Sort operation spills to the disk due to a lower value of the memory size, then the performance of the Sort operation will not be optimal. Similarly, the execution performance of analytic functions will suffer if the operation spills to the disk.

Database initialization parameter PGA_AGGREGATE_TARGET (PGAT) controls the cumulative maximum size of the PGA. By default, a serial process can allocate a PGA up to the maximum size of 5% of PGAT value. For parallel processes, the limit is up to 30% of PGAT. It is essential to keep PGAT to a bigger value to improve the performance of analytic functions.

Organizational Behavior

The hardest thing about analytic functions is the organizational resistance to change. Developers and database administrators are comfortable writing SQL statements using conventional syntax. Using analytic syntax will not come easy. However, these developers and database administrators need to embrace the change. Another plus: use of analytic functions forces one to think in terms of sets.

Oracle Corporation releases new features in every major release of Oracle Database. We need to harness the new features to write more efficient and concise SQL statements. Proper training for these new features is also essential and hopefully, this chapter provided an insight in to analytic functions.

When you start writing SQL statement utilizing the analytic functions, start with simpler SQL statement. Then add more complexity to meet the goal.

Summary

Complex SQL statements can be written using analytic functions concisely. Understanding analytic function provides you whole new way of thinking, analytically speaking. The ability to reference another row combined with partitioning and windowing clause allows you to simplify complex SQL statements. Many performance issues can be resolved rewriting the SQL statement using analytic functions. You may find resistance from developers and DBAs alike when it comes to using analytic functions, and that resistance can be easily overcome by showing the performance improvements with analytic functions.

CHAPTER 9

■ ■ ■

The Model Clause

Riyaj Shamsudeen

The Model clause introduced in the Oracle Database version 10g provides an elegant method to replace the spreadsheet. With the Model clause, it is possible to utilize powerful features such as aggregation, parallelism, and multi-dimensional, multi-variate analysis in SQL statements. If you enjoy working with Excel spreadsheets to calculate formulas, you will enjoy working with the Model clause, too.

In situations where the amount of data to be processed is small, the inter-row referencing and calculating power of the spreadsheet is sufficient to accomplish the task at hand. However, scalability of such a spreadsheet as a data warehouse application is limited and cumbersome. For example, spreadsheets are generally limited to two or three dimensions, and creating spreadsheets with more dimensions is a manually intensive task. Also, as the amount of data increases, the execution of formulas slows down in a spreadsheet. Furthermore, there is an upper limit on the number of rows in a spreadsheet workbook.

Since the Model clause is an extension to the SQL language application. the Model clause is highly scalable, akin to the Oracle database's scalability. Multi-dimensional, multi-variate calculations over millions of rows, if not billions of rows, can be implemented easily with the Model clause, unlike with spreadsheets. Also, many database features such as object partitioning and parallel execution can be used effectively with the Model clause, thereby further improving scalability.

Aggregation of the data is performed inside the RDBMS engine, avoiding costly round-trip calls as in the case of the third party datawarehouse tools. Scalability is further enhanced by out-of-the-box parallel processing capabilities and query rewrite facilities.

The key difference between conventional SQL statement and the Model clause is that the Model clause supports inter-row references, multi-cell references, and cell aggregation. It is easier to understand the Model clause with examples, so I will introduce the Model clause with examples. Then I'll discuss the advanced features in the Model clause.

Spreadsheets

Let's consider the spreadsheet in Listing 9-1. In this spreadsheet, the inventory for a region and week is calculated using a formula: current inventory is the sum of last week's inventory and the quantity received in this week minus the quantity sold in this week. This formula is shown in the example using Excel spreadsheet notation. For example, the formula for week 2's inventory would be =B5+C4-C3, where B5 is the prior week's inventory, C4 is the current week's receipt_qty and C3 is the current week's sales_qty. Essentially, this formula uses an inter-row reference to calculate the inventory.

Listing 9-1. *Spreadsheet Formula to Calculate Inventory*

Product = Xtend Memory, Country ='Australia'

	A	B	C	D	E	F	G ...
	Year=2001	Week→					
		1	2	3	4	5	6
	Sale	92.26	118.38	47.24	256.70	93.44	43.17
	Receipts	96.89	149.17	49.60	259.10	98.66	20.20
	Inventory	4.63	35.42	37.78	40.18	45.41	22.44
			=B5+C4-C3				

While it's easy to calculate this formula for a few dimensions using a spreadsheet, it's much more difficult to perform these calculations with more dimensions. Performance suffers as the amount of data increases in the spreadsheet. These issues can be remedied by using the Model clause that the Oracle Database provides. Not only does the Model clause provide for efficient formula calculations, but the writing of multi-dimensional, multi-variate analysis also becomes much more practical.

Inter-Row Referencing via the Model clause

In a conventional SQL statement, emulating the spreadsheet described in Listing 9-1 is achieved by a multitude of self-joins. With the advent of the Model clause, you can implement the spreadsheet without self-joins because the Model clause provides inter-row referencing ability.

Example Data

To begin your investigation of the Model clause, you will create a de-normalized fact table using the script in Listing 9-2. All the tables referred in this chapter refer to the objects in SH Schema supplied by the Oracle Corporation Example scripts.

■**NOTE** To install the Example schema, you can download software from Oracle Corporation at http://
download.oracle.com/otn/solaris/oracle11g/R2/solaris.sparc64_11gR2_examples.zip for the 11gR2
Solaris platform. Refer to the Readme document in the unzipped software directories for installation instructions.
Zip files for other platforms and versions are available in this Oracle site.

Listing 9-2. *Denormalized sales_fact Table*

```
drop table sales_fact;
CREATE table sales_fact AS
SELECT country_name country,country_subRegion region, prod_name product,
        calendar_year year, calendar_week_number week,
        SUM(amount_sold) sale,
        sum(amount_sold*
```

```
            ( case
                    when mod(rownum, 10)=0 then 1.4
                    when mod(rownum, 5)=0 then 0.6
                    when mod(rownum, 2)=0 then 0.9
                    when mod(rownum,2)=1 then 1.2
                    else 1
            end )) receipts
FROM sales, times, customers, countries, products
WHERE sales.time_id = times.time_id AND
sales.prod_id = products.prod_id AND
sales.cust_id = customers.cust_id AND
customers.country_id = countries.country_id
GROUP BY
country_name,country_subRegion, prod_name, calendar_year, calendar_week_number;
```

Anatomy of a Model Clause

Listing 9-3 shows a SQL statement using the Model clause and emulating the functionality of the spreadsheet discussed earlier. Let's explore this SQL statement in detail. I'll look at the columns declared in the Model clause and then I'll discuss rules.

In the Listing 9-3, line 3 declares that this statement is using the Model clause with the keywords Model return updated rows. In a SQL statement using the Model clause, there are three groups of columns: partitioning columns, dimension columns, and measures columns. Partitioning columns are analogous to a sheet in the spreadsheet. Dimension columns are analogous to row tags (A,B,C..) and column tags (1,2,3..). The measures columns are analogous to cells with formulas.

Line 5 identifies the columns Product and Country as partitioning columns with the clause partition by (product, country. Line 6 identifies columns Year and Week as dimension columns with the clause dimension by (year, week. Line 7 identifies columns Inventory, Sales, and, Receipts as measures columns with the clause measures (0 inventory, sale, receipts). A rule is similar to a formula, and one such rule is defined in lines 8 through 13.

Listing 9-3. *Inventory Formula Calculation using Model Clause*

```
col product format A30
col country format A10
col region format A10
col year format 9999
col week format 99
col sale format 999999
set lines 120 pages 100

1    select product, country, year, week, inventory, sale, receipts
2    from sales_fact
3    model return updated rows
4    where country in ('Australia') and product ='Xtend Memory'
5    partition by (product, country)
6    dimension by (year, week)
```

```
 7    measures ( 0 inventory , sale, receipts)
 8    rules automatic order(
 9        inventory [year, week ] =
10                            nvl(inventory [cv(year), cv(week)-1 ] ,0)
11                            - sale[cv(year), cv(week) ] +
12                            + receipts [cv(year), cv(week) ]
13    )
14*   order by product, country,year, week
/
PRODUCT        COUNTRY      YEAR WEEK  INVENTORY       SALE  RECEIPTS
-----------    ----------   ----- ----  ----------  ----------  ----------

..
Xtend Memory Australia    2001    1      4.634      92.26      96.89
Xtend Memory Australia    2001    2     35.424     118.38     149.17
Xtend Memory Australia    2001    3     37.786      47.24      49.60
...
Xtend Memory Australia    2001    9     77.372      92.67     108.64
Xtend Memory Australia    2001   10     56.895      69.05      48.57
..
```

In a mathematical sense, the Model clause is implementing partitioned arrays. Dimension columns are indices into array elements. Each array element, also termed as a cell, is a measures column.

All rows with the same value for the partitioning column(s) are considered to be in a partition. In this example, all rows with the same value for product and country are in a partition. Within a partition, the dimension columns uniquely identify a row. Rules implement formulas to derive the measures columns and they operate within a partition boundary, so partitions are not mentioned explicitly in a rule.

■**NOTE** It is important to differentiate between partitioning columns in the Model clause and the object partitioning feature. While you can use the keyword `partition` in the Model clause also, it's different from the object partitioning scheme used to partition large tables.

Rules

Let's revisit the rules section from Listing 9-3. You can see both the rule and the corresponding formula together in Listing 9-4. The formula is accessing the prior week's inventory to calculate current week's inventory, so it requires an inter-row reference. You can see that there is a great similarity between the formula and the rule.

The SQL statement in Listing 9-4 introduces a useful function named CV. CV stands for Current Value and can be used to refer to a column value in the right hand side of the rule from the left hand side of the rule. For example, cv(year) refers to the value of the Year column from the left hand side of the rule. If you think of a formula when it is being applied to a specific cell in a spreadsheet, the CV function allows you to reference the index values for that cell.

Listing 9-4. *Rule and Formula*

```
Formula for inventory:

Inventory for (year, week)  = Inventory (year, prior week)
                            - Quantity sold in this week
                              + Quantity received in this week


Rule from the SQL:

 8          inventory [year, week ] =
 9                              nvl(inventory [cv(year), cv(week)-1 ] ,0)
10                                  - sale[cv(year), cv(week) ] +
11                                  + receipts [cv(year), cv(week) ]
```

Let's discuss rules with substituted values, as in Listing 9-5. Let's say that a row with (year, week) column values of (2001, 3) is being processed. The left hand side of the rule will have the values of (2001, 3) for the year and column. The cv(year) clause in the right hand side of the rule refers to the value of the Year column from the left hand side of the rule, that is 2001. Similarly, the clause cv(week) refers to the value of the Week column from the left hand side of the rule, that is 3. So, the clause inventory [cv(year), cv(week)-1] will return the value of the inventory measures for the year equal to 2001 and the prior week, i.e. week equal 2.

Similarly, clauses sale[cv(year), cv(week)] and receipts[cv(year), cv(week)] are referring to the Sale and Receipts column values for the Year equal to 2001 and Week equal to 3 using CV function.

Notice that the partitioning columns Product and Country are not specified in these rules. Rules implicitly refer to the column values for the Product and Country column in the current partition.

Listing 9-5. *Rule Example*

```
Rule example:
1  rules (
2       inventory [2001 , 3] = nvl(inventory [cv(year), cv(week)-1 ] ,0)
3                               - sale [cv(year), cv(week) ] +
4                               + receipts [cv(year), cv(week) ]
5  )

  rules (
       inventory [2001 , 3] = nvl(inventory [2001, 3-1 ] ,0)
                              - sale [2001, 3 ] +
                              + receipts [2001, 3 ]
                        = 35.42  - 47.24 + 49.60
                        = 37.78
  )
```

Positional and Symbolic References

As discussed previously, the CV function provides the ability to refer to a single cell. It is also possible to refer to an individual cell or group of cells using positional or symbolic notations. In addition, you can write FOR loops as a way to create or modify many sells in an array-like fashion.

Positional Notation

Positional notation provides the ability to insert a new cell or update an existing cell in the result set. If the referenced cell exists in the result set, then the cell value is updated; if the cell doesn't exist, then a new cell will be added. This concept of "update if exists, insert if not" is termed as an UPSERT feature, a fused version of the Update and Insert facilities. Positional notation provides UPSERT capability.

Suppose that you need to add new cells to initialize the column values for the year equal to 2002 and week equal to 1. You could achieve that with a rule defined using a positional notation. In the Listing 9-6, line 13 and line 14 are adding new cells for the Year equal to 2002 and Week equal to 1 using the positional notation with the clause sale[2002,1]=0. Within the square brackets, the position of the value refers to the column order declared in the dimension clause. In this case, column order is (year, week, hence the clause sale[2002,1] refers to the Sale column value for the row satisfying the predicate year=2002 and week=1. There are no rows with a column value of year equal to 2002 and week equal to 1, and a new row was inserted with a zero value for the Sale column for the year =2002 and week=1. The last row in the output was inserted by this rule.

Listing 9-6. *Positional Reference to Initialize for Year 2002 - UPSERT*

```
1     select product, country, year, week, inventory, sale, receipts
2     from sales_fact
3     where country in ('Australia') and product ='Xtend Memory'
4     model return updated rows
5     partition by (product, country)
6     dimension by (year, week)
7     measures ( 0 inventory , sale, receipts)
8     rules automatic order(
9         inventory [year, week ] =
10                             nvl(inventory [cv(year), cv(week)-1 ] ,0)
11                             - sale[cv(year), cv(week) ] +
12                             + receipts [cv(year), cv(week) ],
13         sale [2002, 1] = 0,
14         receipts [2002,1] =0
15     )
16*   order by product, country,year, week
...
```

PRODUCT	COUNTRY	YEAR	WEEK	INVENTORY	SALE	RECEIPTS
...						
Xtend Memory	Australia	2001	49	2.519	45.26	47.33
Xtend Memory	Australia	2001	50	11.775	23.14	32.40
Xtend Memory	Australia	2001	51	-20.617	114.82	82.43
Xtend Memory	Australia	2001	52	-22.931	23.14	20.83
Xtend Memory	Australia	2002	1	0	.00	.00

...

Symbolic Notation

Symbolic notation provides the ability to specify a range of values in the left hand side of a rule. Let's say that you want to update the sales column values to 110% of their actual value for the weeks 1, 52, and 53 for the years 2000 and 2001. The SQL in the Listing 9-7 does that. The clause `year in (2000,2001)` in line 9 uses an `IN` operator to specify a list of values for the Year column. Similarly, the clause `week in (1,52,53)` specifies a list of values for the week column.

Note that the output in the Listing 9-7 is not a partial output and that there are no rows for the week equal to 53. Even though you specified 53 in the list of values for the week column in line 9, there are no rows returned for that week. The reason is that symbolic notation can *only update the existing cells*; it does not allow new cells to be added.

■**NOTE** I will discuss a method to insert an array of cells in the upcoming section "For Loops."

There is no data with a Week column value equal to 53 and no new row was added or updated in the result set for the week=53. The ability to generate rows is a key difference between symbolic and positional notations. Symbolic notation provides UPDATE-only facility and positional notation provides UPSERT facility.

Listing 9-7. *Symbolic Reference – UPDATE*

```
1    select product, country, year, week, sale
2    from sales_fact
3    where country in ('Australia') and product ='Xtend Memory'
4    model return updated rows
5    partition by (product, country)
6    dimension by (year, week)
7    measures ( sale )
8    rules(
9          sale [ year in (2000,2001), week in (1,52,53) ] order by year, week
10                 = sale [cv(year), cv(week)] * 1.10
11   )
12*  order by product, country,year, week

PRODUCT         COUNTRY      YEAR WEEK       SALE
----------- ---------- ----- ---- ----------
Xtend Memory Australia   2000    1     51.37
Xtend Memory Australia   2000   52     74.20
Xtend Memory Australia   2001    1    101.49
Xtend Memory Australia   2001   52     25.45
```

There are a few subtle differences between the SQL statement in Listing 9-7 and prior SQL statements. For example, the statement in Listing 9-7 is missing `automatic order` in line 8. I'll discuss the implication of that in the "Rule Evaluation Order" section later in this chapter.

FOR Loops

FOR loops allow you to specify list of values in the left hand side of a rule. FOR loops can be defined in the left hand side of the rule only to add new cells to the output; they can't be used in the right hand side of the rule. Syntax for the FOR loop is:

```
FOR dimension FROM <value1> TO <value2>
         [INCREMENT | DECREMENT] <value3>
```

For example, say you want to add cells for the weeks ranging from 1 to 53 for the year 2002 and initialize those cells with a value of 0. Line 13 in Listing 9-8 inserts new rows for the year 2002 and weeks ranging from 1 to 53 using a FOR loop. Clause Increment 1 increments the week column values to generate weeks from 1 to 53. Similarly, the receipts column is initialized using the clause receipts [2002, for week from 1 to 53 increment 1] =0.

Listing 9-8. *Positional Reference, Model and FOR Loops*

```
1     select product, country, year, week, inventory, sale, receipts
2     from sales_fact
3     where country in ('Australia') and product ='Xtend Memory'
4     model return updated rows
5     partition by (product, country)
6     dimension by (year, week)
7     measures ( 0 inventory , sale, receipts)
8     rules automatic order(
9         inventory [year, week ] =
10                             nvl(inventory [cv(year), cv(week)-1 ] ,0)
11                              - sale[cv(year), cv(week) ] +
12                              + receipts [cv(year), cv(week) ],
13        sale [2002, for week from 1 to 53 increment 1] = 0,
14        receipts [ 2002,for week from 1 to 53 increment 1] =0
15     )
16*   order by product, country,year, week
```

PRODUCT	COUNTRY	YEAR	WEEK	INVENTORY	SALE	RECEIPTS
...						
Xtend Memory	Australia	2001	52	-22.931	23.14	20.83
Xtend Memory	Australia	2002	1	0	.00	.00
...						
Xtend Memory	Australia	2002	52	0	.00	.00
Xtend Memory	Australia	2002	53	0	.00	.00
...						

Returning Updated Rows

In Listing 9-7, just four rows were returned even though there are rows for other weeks. The clause RETURN UPDATED ROWS controls this behavior and provides the ability to limit the cells returned by the SQL statement. Without this clause, all rows are returned regardless of whether the rules updates the cells or not. The rule in Listing 9-7 updates only four cells and other cells are untouched, and so just four rows are returned.

What happens if you don't specify the clause return updated rows? Listing 9-9 shows the output *without* the return updated rows clause. The output in this listing shows that both updated and non-updated rows are returned from the SQL statement. The rule updates cells for the weeks 1, 52, and 53 only, but the output rows in Listing 9-9 shows rows with other column values such as 2, 3, 4, too.

Listing 9-9. *SQL without RETURN UPDATED ROWS*

```
1    select product, country, year, week, sale
2    from sales_fact
3    where country in ('Australia') and product ='Xtend Memory'
4    model
5    partition by (product, country)
6    dimension by (year, week)
7    measures ( sale)
8    rules(
9            sale [ year in (2000,2001), week in (1,52,53) ] order by year, week
10                   = sale [cv(year), cv(week)] * 1.10
11    )
12*  order by product, country,year, week

PRODUCT       COUNTRY     YEAR WEEK     SALE
------------  ----------  ----- ---- ----------
...
Xtend Memory Australia    2000   50    21.19
Xtend Memory Australia    2000   52    74.20
Xtend Memory Australia    2001    1   101.49
Xtend Memory Australia    2001    2   118.38
Xtend Memory Australia    2001    3    47.24
Xtend Memory Australia    2001    4   256.70
...
```

The clause RETURN UPDATED ROWS is applicable to statements using positional notation also. In the Listing 9-10, a rule using a positional notation is shown, inserting a row. Note that there are more rows in the table matching with the predicate country in ('Australia') and product ='Xtend Memory'. But, just one row is returned as only one cell is inserted by the rule in line 9. Essentially, RETURN UPDATED ROWS clause is a limiting clause—it only fetches the rows modified by the rule.

Listing 9-10. *RETURN UPDATED ROWS and UPSERT*

```
1    select product, country, year, week, sale
2    from sales_fact
3    where country in ('Australia') and product ='Xtend Memory'
4    model return updated rows
5    partition by (product, country)
6    dimension by (year, week)
7    measures ( sale)
8    rules(
9                  sale [2002, 1] = 0
```

```
10    )
11*   order by product, country,year, week
/
PRODUCT       COUNTRY    YEAR WEEK       SALE
-----------   ---------- ----- ---- ----------
Xtend Memory Australia   2002    1        .00
```

Evaluation Order

Multiple rules can be specified in the rules section, and the rules can be specified with dependencies between them. The rule evaluation sequence can affect the functional behavior of the SQL statement, as you will see in this section. Furthermore, even within a single rule, the evaluation of the rule must adhere to a logical sequence. You will look at intra-rule valuation order first and then at inter-rule evaluation.

Row Evaluation Order

Let's look at row evaluation order *within* a rule. Listing 9-11 is copied from the Listing 9-3. However, this time I've commented out the keywords AUTOMATIC ORDER in line 8. By commenting those keywords, I force the default behavior of SEQUENTIAL ORDER.

The rule has an inter-row reference with the clause inventory [cv(year), cv(week)-1]. Inventory column values must be calculated in ascending order of the week. For example, the inventory rule for the week 40 must be evaluated before evaluating the inventory rule for the week 41. With AUTOMATIC ORDER, the database engine identifies the row dependencies and evaluates the rows in strict dependency order. Without the AUTOMATIC ORDER clause, row evaluation order is undetermined. That leads to ORA-32637 errors, as shown in Listing 9-11.

Listing 9-11. *Sequential with Error ORA-32637*

```
1     select product, country, year, week, inventory, sale, receipts
2     from sales_fact
3     where country in ('Australia')
4     model return updated rows
5     partition by (product, country)
6     dimension by (year, week)
7     measures ( 0 inventory , sale, receipts)
8     rules -- Commented: automatic order
9     (
10         inventory [year, week ] =
11                              nvl(inventory [cv(year), cv(week)-1 ] ,0)
12                              - sale[cv(year), cv(week) ] +
13                              + receipts [cv(year), cv(week) ]
14     )
15*   order by product, country,year, week
        *
ERROR at line 2:
ORA-32637: Self cyclic rule in sequential order MODEL
```

It is a better practice to specify the row evaluation order explicitly to avoid this error. Listing 9-12 provides an example. In the rule section, you specify the order of row evaluation using an ORDER BY year, week clause. This clause specifies that rules must be evaluated in the ascending order of Year, Week column values. That is inventory rule for the Year=2000 and Week=40 must be evaluated before evaluating the inventory rule for the Year=2000 and Week=41.

Listing 9-12. *Evaluation Order at Cell Level*

```
1     select product, country, year, week, inventory, sale, receipts
2     from sales_fact
3     where country in ('Australia')
4     model return updated rows
5     partition by (product, country)
6     dimension by (year, week)
7     measures ( 0 inventory , sale, receipts)
8     rules (
9         inventory [year, week ] order by year, week =
10                          nvl(inventory [cv(year), cv(week)-1 ] ,0)
11                          - sale[cv(year), cv(week) ] +
12                          + receipts [cv(year), cv(week) ]
13     )
14*   order by product, country,year, week
```

PRODUCT	COUNTRY	YEAR	WEEK	INVENTORY	SALE	RECEIPTS
...						
Xtend Memory	Australia	2001	49	2.519	45.26	47.33
Xtend Memory	Australia	2001	50	11.775	23.14	32.40
...						

Note that there is no consistency check performed to see if this specification of row evaluation order is logically consistent or not. It is up to the coder—to you!—to understand the implications of evaluation order. For example, the row evaluation order in Listing 9-13 is specified with the DESC keyword. While the rule is syntactically correct, semantic correctness is only known to the coder. Semantic correctness might well require the specification of ASC for an ascending sort. Only the person writing the SQL statement can know which order meets the business problem being addressed.

Notice that Inventory column values are different between the Listings 9-12 and 9-13. You need to ensure that the order of row evolution is consistent with the requirements.

Listing 9-13. *Evaluation Order using the DESC Keyword*

```
1     select product, country, year, week, inventory, sale, receipts
2     from sales_fact
3     where country in ('Australia') and product in ('Xtend Memory')
4     model return updated rows
5     partition by (product, country)
6     dimension by (year, week)
7     measures ( 0 inventory , sale, receipts)
8     rules (
```

```
 9          inventory [year, week ] order by year, week desc  =
10                              nvl(inventory [cv(year), cv(week)-1 ] ,0)
11                              - sale[cv(year), cv(week) ] +
12                              + receipts [cv(year), cv(week) ]
13      )
14*   order by product, country,year, week
```

PRODUCT	COUNTRY	YEAR	WEEK	INVENTORY	SALE	RECEIPTS
...						
Xtend Memory	Australia	2001	49	2.068	45.26	47.33
Xtend Memory	Australia	2001	50	9.256	23.14	32.40
...						

Rule Evaluation Order

In addition to the order in which rows are evaluated, you also have the question of the order in which the rules are applied. In Listing 9-14, there are two rules with inter-dependency between them. The first rule is evaluating the rule and refers to the Receipts column, which is calculated by the second rule. These two rules can be evaluated in any order and the results will depend upon the order of rule evaluation. It is important to understand the order of rule evaluation because the functional behavior of the SQL statement can change with the rule evaluation order.

To improve clarity, you will filter on rows with week > 50. In Listing 9-14, line 9 specifies sequential order. Sequential order specifies that the rules are evaluated in the order in which they are listed. In this example, the rule for the Inventory column is evaluated, followed by the rule for the Receipts column. Since the receipts rule is evaluated after the inventory rule, the inventory rule uses the unaltered values before the evaluation of the receipts rule. Essentially, changes from the receipts rule for the Receipts column calculation are not factored in to the Inventory calculation.

The situation with rule evaluation is the same as with rows. Only a coder will know what order of evaluation is appropriate for the business problem being solved. Only the coder will know whether the inventory rule should use altered values from execution of the receipts rule, or otherwise.

Listing 9-14. *Rule Evaluation Order – Sequential Order*

```
 1    select * from  (
 2    select product, country, year, week, inventory, sale, receipts
 3    from sales_fact
 4    where country in ('Australia') and product in ('Xtend Memory')
 5    model return updated rows
 6    partition by (product, country)
 7    dimension by (year, week)
 8    measures ( 0 inventory , sale, receipts)
 9    rules sequential order (
10        inventory [year, week ] order by year, week  =
11                        nvl(inventory [cv(year), cv(week)-1 ] ,0)
12                      - sale[cv(year), cv(week) ] +
13                      + receipts [cv(year), cv(week) ],
14        receipts [ year in (2000,2001), week in (51,52,53) ]
15                   order by year, week
```

```
16                        = receipts [cv(year), cv(week)] * 10
17           )
18      order by product, country,year, week
19*   ) where week >50
```

```
PRODUCT       COUNTRY     YEAR WEEK  INVENTORY      SALE  RECEIPTS
------------  ----------  ---- ----  ---------- ---------- ----------
...
Xtend Memory  Australia   2000   52     -6.037     67.45    614.13
Xtend Memory  Australia   2001   51    -20.617    114.82    824.28
Xtend Memory  Australia   2001   52    -22.931     23.14    208.26
```

Another method of evaluating the order employed by Oracle database is automatic order. In Listing 9-15, the evaluation order is changed to automatic order. With automatic order, dependencies between the rules are automatically resolved by Oracle and the order of rule evaluation depends upon the dependencies between the rules.

The results from Listing 9-15 and Listing 9-14 do not match. For example, inventory for week 52 is -22.931 in Listing 9-14, and it is 906.355 in Listing 9-15. By specifying automatic order, you allow the database engine to identify a dependency between the rules. Thus, the engine evaluates the receipts rule first, followed by the inventory rule.

Clearly, the order of rule evaluation can be quite important. If there are complex inter-dependencies, then you might want to specify sequential order and list the rules in a strict evaluation sequence. That way, you are in full control and nothing is left to doubt.

Listing 9-15. *Rule Evaluation Order- Automatic Order*

```
...
9    rules automatic order  (
...
```

```
PRODUCT       COUNTRY     YEAR WEEK  INVENTORY      SALE  RECEIPTS
------------  ----------  ---- ----  ---------- ---------- ----------
...
Xtend Memory  Australia   2000   52     546.68     67.45    614.13
Xtend Memory  Australia   2001   51    721.235    114.82    824.28
Xtend Memory  Australia   2001   52    906.355     23.14    208.26
```

Aggregation

Data aggregation is commonly used in the data warehouse queries. The Model clause provides the ability to aggregate the data using aggregate functions over the range of dimension columns.

Many different aggregation function calls such as sum, max, avg, stddev, and OLAP function calls can be used to aggregate the data in a rule. It is easier to understand aggregation with an example.

In Listing 9-16, the rule in lines 9 to 12 is calculating average inventory by Year using the clause avg_inventory[year,ANY] = avg(inventory) [cv(year), week]. In the left hand side of the rule, avg_invntory is the rule name. The first dimension in this rule is Year column. As the dimension clause is specifying the Week column as the second dimension, specifying ANY in the second position of the rule argument matches with any value of week column including nulls. In the right hand side of the rule, the clause avg(inventory) applies the avg function on the Inventory column. The first dimension is cv(year). The second dimension is specified as week. There is no need for the use of CV in the second dimension, as the function must be applied on all weeks in the year as computed by the clause cv(year).

Line 13 shows the use of avg. Line 14 shows an example of using the max function.

Listing 9-16. *Aggregation*

```
1    select product, country, year, week, inventory, avg_inventory, max_sale
2        from sales_fact
3        where country in ('Australia') and product ='Xtend Memory'
4        model return updated rows
5        partition by (product, country)
6        dimension by (year, week)
7        measures ( 0 inventory ,o avg_inventory , o max_sale, sale, receipts)
8        rules automatic order(
9            inventory [year, week ] =
10                                  nvl(inventory [cv(year), cv(week)-1 ] ,0)
11                                  - sale[cv(year), cv(week) ] +
12                                  + receipts [cv(year), cv(week) ],
13            avg_inventory [ year,ANY ] = avg (inventory) [ cv(year), week ],
14            max_Sale [ year, ANY ]   = max( sale) [ cv(year), week ]
15        )
16*      order by product, country,year, week
```

PRODUCT	COUNTRY	YEAR	WEEK	INVENTORY	AVG_INVENTORY	MAX_SALE
...						
Xtend Memory	Australia	2001	42	17.532	28.60	278.44
Xtend Memory	Australia	2001	43	24.511	28.60	278.44
Xtend Memory	Australia	2001	44	29.169	28.60	278.44
...						
Xtend Memory	Australia	2001	52	-22.931	28.60	278.44

Iteration

Iteration provides another facility to implementing complex business requirements using a concise Model SQL statement. A block of rules can be executed in a loop a certain number of times or while a condition remains true. The syntax for the iteration is:

```
[ITERATE (n) [UNTIL <condition>] ]
( <cell_assignment> = <expression> ... )
```

Use the syntax ITERATE (n) to execute an expression n times. Use the expression ITERATE UNTIL <condition> to iterate while the given condition remains true.

An Example

Suppose the goal is to show five weeks of sale column values in a comma-separated list format. This requirement is implemented in Listing 9-17.

■**NOTE** Conversion of rows to columns is termed as *pivoting*. Oracle database 11g introduces syntax to implement pivoting function natively. In Oracle database 10g, you could use the Model clause to implement pivoting.

Line 8 specifies that the rules block is to be iterated five times for each row. That's done through the clause rules iterate(5). In line 10, you use Iteration_number, which is a variable available within the rules section, to access the current iteration count of the loop. Iteration_number starts with a value of 0 for the first iteration in the loop and ends at n-1 where n is the number of loops as specified in the iterate(n) clause. In this example, the Iteration_number variable value ranges from 0 to 4. With Iteration_number and bit of arithmetic, you can access the prior two weeks and the next two weeks' values using the clause CV(week)-ITERATION_NUMBER +2. The CASE statement adds a comma for each element in the list, except for the first element.

For example, let's assume the current row in the process has a value of year=2001 and week=23. In the first iteration of the loop, iteration_number will be zero, and the clause cv(week)-ITERATION_NUMBER +2 will access the row with week=23-0+2=25. In the next iteration, week 24 will be accessed, and so on. The FOR loop is repeated for every row in the model output.

Let's review the output rows in Listing 9-17. For the year 2001, week 23, column Sale_list has the following list of values: 233.7, 141.78, 22.38, 136.92, 139.28. You can see how those values are centered on the current week. The first two come from sales column for the immediately preceding weeks. Then you have the current week's sales, and then the values from the following two weeks.

Listing 9-17. *Iteration*

```
1    select year, week,sale, sale_list
2        from sales_fact
3        where country in ('Australia') and product ='Xtend Memory'
4        model return updated rows
5        partition by (product, country)
6        dimension by (year, week)
7        measures ( cast(' ' as varchar2(50) ) sale_list, sale)
8        rules  iterate (5) (
9            sale_list [ year, week ] order by year, week =
10                sale [cv(year), CV(week)-ITERATION_NUMBER +2 ]        ||
11                case when iteration_number=0 then '' else ', ' end  ||
12                sale_list [cv(year) ,cv(week)]
13       )
14*   order by year, week
```

```
YEAR WEEK        SALE SALE_LIST
----- ----  ---------- -------------------------------------------------
2001   20      118.03 22.37, , 118.03, 233.7, 141.78
2001   21      233.70 , 118.03, 233.7, 141.78, 22.38
2001   22      141.78 118.03, 233.7, 141.78, 22.38, 136.92
2001   23       22.38 233.7, 141.78, 22.38, 136.92, 139.28
2001   24      136.92 141.78, 22.38, 136.92, 139.28,
2001   25      139.28 22.38, 136.92, 139.28, , 94.48
```

PRESENTV and NULLs

If a rule is accessing a non-existent row, the rule will return a null value. Notice that in the output of Listing 9-17, Sale_list column in the first row has two commas consecutively. The reason is that the row for the week=19 does not exist in the data, so accessing that non-existent cell returns a null value. You can correct this double comma issue using a function to check for cell existence using a PRESENTV function. This function accepts three parameters and the syntax for the function is:

```
PRESENTV (cell_reference, expr1, expr2)
```

If cell_reference references an existing cell, then the PRESENTV function returns expr1. If the Cell_reference references a non-existing cell, then the second argument expr2 is returned. In Listing 9-18, line 10 performs this existence check on the Sale column for the year and week combination using a clause sale [cv(year), CV(week)-iteration_number + 2]. If the cell exists, then the function adds the value of the cell and comma to the returned string (lines 11 to 13). If the cell does not exist, the function returns the Sale_list column without altering the string (line 14). This solution eliminates the double comma in the Sale_list column value.

Listing 9-18. *Iteration and presntv*

```
1     select year, week,sale, sale_list
2        from sales_fact
3        where country in ('Australia') and product ='Xtend Memory'
4        model return updated rows
5        partition by (product, country)
6        dimension by (year, week)
7        measures ( cast(' ' as varchar2(120) ) sale_list, sale, 0 tmp)
8        rules  iterate (5) (
9           sale_list [ year, week ] order by year, week =
10              presentv ( sale [cv(year), CV(week)-iteration_number + 2 ],
11                  sale [cv(year), CV(week)-iteration_number +2 ]           ||
12                     case when iteration_number=0 then '' else ', ' end  ||
13                     sale_list [cv(year) ,cv(week)]   ,
14                  sale_list [cv(year) ,cv(week)] )
15     )
16*    order by year, week
```

```
YEAR WEEK      SALE SALE_LIST
----- ----  ---------- -------------------------------------------------
2001   20     118.03 22.37, 118.03, 233.7, 141.78
2001   21     233.70 118.03, 233.7, 141.78, 22.38
2001   22     141.78 118.03, 233.7, 141.78, 22.38, 136.92
...
2001   29     116.85 94.48, 116.85, 162.91, 92.21
```

The PRESENTNNV function is similar to PRESENTV, but provides the additional ability to differentiate between references to non-existent cells and null values in existing cells. The syntax for the function PRESENTNNV is

```
PRESENTNNV (cell_reference, expr1, expr2).
```

If the first argument cell_reference references an existing cell and if that cell contains non-null value, then the first argument expr1 is returned, or else the second argument expr2 is returned. In contrast, the PRESENTV function checks for just the existence of a cell, whereas the PRESENTNNV function checks for both the existence of a cell and Null values in that cell. Table 9-1 lists shows the values returned from these two functions in four different cases.

Table 9-1. *Presentv and presentnnv Comparison*

Cell exists?	Null?	Presentv	Presentnnv
Y	Not null	expr1	expr1
Y	Null	expr1	expr2
N	Not null	expr2	expr2
N	Null	expr2	expr2

Lookup Tables

You can define a lookup table and refer to that lookup table in the rules section. Such a lookup table is sometimes termed a *reference table*. Reference tables are defined in the initial section of the SQL statement and then referred in the rules section of the SQL statement.

In Listing 9-19, lines 5 to 9 define a lookup table ref_prod using a Reference clause. Line 5 REFERENCE ref_prod is specifying ref_prod as a lookup table. Column Prod_name is a dimension column as specified in line 8 and column Prod_list_price is a measures column. Note that the reference table must be unique on dimension column and should retrieve exactly one row per dimension column's value.

Line 10 specifies the main model section starting with the keyword MAIN. This section is named as main_section for ease of understanding, although any name can be used. In the line 15, a rule for the column Prod_list_price is specified and populated from the lookup table ref_prod. Line 16 shows that the reference table that measures columns is accessed using the clause ref_prod.prod_list_price [cv(product)]. The current value of the Product column is passed as a lookup key in the lookup table using the clause cv(product).

In summary, you define a lookup table using a REFERENCE clause, and then access that lookup table using the syntax look_table_name.measures column. For example, the syntax in this example is ref_prod.prod_list_price [cv(product)]. To access a specific row in the lookup table, you pass the current value of the dimension column from the left hand side of the rule, in this example, using the cv(product) clause. You might be able to understand better if you imagine ref_prod as a table, cv(product) as primary key in to that table, and prod_list_price as a column to fetch from that lookup table.

Listing 9-19. *Reference Model*

```
1     select year, week,sale, prod_list_price
2        from sales_fact
3        where country in ('Australia') and product ='Xtend Memory'
4        model return updated rows
5        REFERENCE ref_prod on
6          (select prod_name, max(prod_list_price) prod_list_price from products
7             group by prod_name)
8           dimension by (prod_name)
9           measures (prod_list_price)
10       MAIN main_section
11         partition by (product, country)
12         dimension by (year, week)
13         measures ( sale, receipts, 0 prod_list_price )
14         rules   (
15            prod_list_price[year,week] order by year, week =
16                            ref_prod.prod_list_price [ cv(product) ]
17         )
18*   order by year, week;
```

YEAR	WEEK	SALE	PROD_LIST_PRICE
2000	31	44.78	20.99
2000	33	134.11	20.99
2000	34	178.52	20.99

...

More lookup tables can be added if needed. Suppose you also need to retrieve the country_iso_code column values from another table. You achieved that by adding a lookup table ref_country as shown in Listing 9-20 lines 10 to 13. Column Country_name is the dimension column and Country_iso_code is a measures column. Lines 22 and 23 refer to the lookup table using a new rule Iso_code. This rule is accessing the lookup table ref_country using the Current Value of the Country column as the lookup key.

Listing 9-20. *More Lookup Tables*

```
1     select year, week,sale,  prod_list_price, iso_code
2        from sales_fact
3        where country in ('Australia') and product ='Xtend Memory'
4        model return updated rows
```

```
5        REFERENCE ref_prod on
6          (select prod_name, max(prod_list_price) prod_list_price from
7              products group by prod_name)
8            dimension by (prod_name)
9            measures (prod_list_price)
10       REFERENCE ref_country on
11         (select country_name, country_iso_code from countries)
12           dimension by (country_name )
13           measures (country_iso_code)
14       MAIN main_section
15         partition by (product, country)
16         dimension by (year, week)
17         measures (  sale, receipts, 0 prod_list_price ,
18                            cast(' ' as varchar2(5)) iso_code)
19         rules   (
20            prod_list_price[year,week] order by year, week =
21                        ref_prod.prod_list_price [ cv(product) ],
22            iso_code [year, week] order by year, week =
23                        ref_country.country_iso_code [ cv(country)]
24         )
25*   order by year, week
```

YEAR	WEEK	SALE	PROD_LIST_PRICE	ISO_C
2000	31	44.78	20.99	AU
2000	33	134.11	20.99	AU
2000	34	178.52	20.99	AU
2000	35	78.82	20.99	AU
2000	36	118.41	20.99	AU

...

NULLs

In SQL statements using Model SQL, values can be null for two reasons: null values in the existing cells and references to non-existent cells. I will discuss the later scenario in this section.

By default, the reference to non-existent cells will return null values. In Listing 9-21, the rule in line 10 is accessing the Sale column for the year =2002 and the week =1 using the clause sale[2002,1]. There is no data in the sales_fact table for the year 2002 and so sale[2002,1] is accessing a non-existent cell. Output in this listing is null due to the arithmetic operation with a null value.

In Line 4, I added a KEEP NAV clause after the Model keyword explicitly even though KEEP NAV is the default value. NAV stands for Non Available Values and reference to a non-existent cell returns a null value by default.

Listing 9-21. *KEEP NAV Example*

```
1    select product, country, year, week,  sale
2    from sales_fact
3    where country in ('Australia') and product ='Xtend Memory'
4    model KEEP NAV return updated rows
5    partition by (product, country)
6    dimension by (year, week)
7    measures ( sale)
8    rules sequential  order(
9      sale[2001,1] order by year, week= sale[2001,1],
10     sale [ 2002, 1] order by year, week = sale[2001,1] + sale[2002,1]
11     )
12*  order by product, country,year, week
```

PRODUCT	COUNTRY	YEAR	WEEK	SALE
Xtend Memory	Australia	2001	1	92.26
Xtend Memory	Australia	2002	1	

This default behavior can be modified using the IGNORE NAV clause. Listing 9-22 shows an example. If the non-existent cells are accessed, then 0 is returned for numeric columns and an empty string is returned for text columns instead of null values. You can see that the output in Listing 9-22 shows that a value of 92.26 is returned for the clause sale[2001,1] + sale[2002,1] as zero is retuned for the non existing cell sale[2002,1].

Listing 9-22. *IGNORE NAV*

```
1    select product, country, year, week,  sale
2    from sales_fact
3    where country in ('Australia') and product ='Xtend Memory'
4    model IGNORE NAV return updated rows
5    partition by (product, country)
6    dimension by (year, week)
7    measures ( sale)
8    rules sequential  order(
9      sale[2001,1] order by year, week= sale[2001,1],
10     sale [ 2002, 1] order by year, week = sale[2001,1] + sale[2002,1]
11     )
12*  order by product, country,year, week
```

PRODUCT	COUNTRY	YEAR	WEEK	SALE
Xtend Memory	Australia	2001	1	92.26
Xtend Memory	Australia	2002	1	92.26

The functions PRESENTV and PRESNTNNV are also useful in handling NULL values. Refer to the earlier section called "Iteration" for discussion and examples of these two functions.

Performance Tuning with the Model Clause

As with all SQL, sometimes you need to tune statements using the Model clause. To that end, it helps to know how to read execution plans involving the clause. It also helps to know about some of the issues you'll encounter—such as predicate pushing and partitioning—when working with Model clause queries.

Execution Plans

In the Model clause, rule evaluation is the critical step. Rule evaluation can use one of five algorithm types: ACYCLIC, ACYCLIC FAST, CYCLIC, ORDERED, and ORDERED FAST. The algorithm chosen depends upon the complexity and dependency of the rules themselves. The algorithm chosen also affects the performance of the SQL statement. But details of these algorithms are not well documented.

ACYCLIC FAST and ORDERED FAST algorithms are more optimized algorithms that allow cells to be evaluated efficiently. However, the algorithm chosen depends upon the type of the rules that you specify. For example, if there is a *possibility* of a cycle in the rules, then the algorithm that can handle cyclic rules is chosen.

The algorithms of type ACYCLIC and CYCLIC are used if the SQL statement specifies the rules automatic order clause. An ORDERED type of the rule evaluation algorithm is used if the SQL statement specifies rules sequential order. If a rule is accessing individual cells without any aggregation, then either the ACYCIC FAST or ORDERED FAST algorithm is used.

ACYCLIC

In Listing 9-23, a Model SQL statement and its execution plan is shown. Step 2 in the execution plan shows that this SQL is using the SQL MODEL ACYCLIC algorithm for rule evaluation. The keyword ACYCLIC indicates that there are no possible CYCLIC dependencies between the rules. In this example, with the order by year, week clause you control the dependency between the rules, avoiding cycle dependencies,

Listing 9-23. *Automatic order and ACYCLIC*

```
1    select product, country, year, week, inventory, sale, receipts
2    from sales_fact
3    where country in ('Australia') and product='Xtend Memory'
4    model return updated rows
5    partition by (product, country)
6    dimension by (year, week)
7    measures ( 0 inventory , sale, receipts)
8    rules automatic order(
9        inventory [year, week ] order by year, week   =
10                            nvl(inventory [cv(year), cv(week)-1 ] ,0)
11                            - sale[cv(year), cv(week) ] +
12                            + receipts [cv(year), cv(week) ]
13     )
14*    order by product, country,year, week
```

```
-------------------------------------------------
| Id  | Operation          | Name     | E-Rows |
-------------------------------------------------
|   0 | SELECT STATEMENT   |          |        |
|   1 |  SORT ORDER BY     |          |    147 |
|   2 |   SQL MODEL ACYCLIC|          |    147 |
|*  3 |    TABLE ACCESS FULL| SALES_FACT|   147 |
-------------------------------------------------
```

ACYCLIC FAST

If a rule is a simple rule accessing just one cell, the ACYCLIC FAST algorithm can be used. The execution plan in Listing 9-24 shows that the ACYCLIC FAST algorithm is used to evaluate the rule in this example.

Listing 9-24. *Automatic Order and ACYCLIC FAST*

```
 1     select distinct product, country, year,week, sale_first_Week
 2     from sales_fact
 3     where country in ('Australia') and product='Xtend Memory'
 4     model return updated rows
 5     partition by (product, country)
 6     dimension by (year,week)
 7     measures ( 0 sale_first_week     ,sale )
 8     rules automatic order(
 9        sale_first_week [2000,1] = 0.12*sale [2000, 1]
10     )
11*    order by product, country,year, week
```

```
-----------------------------------------------
| Id  | Operation          | Name     |
-----------------------------------------------
|   0 | SELECT STATEMENT   |          |
|   1 |  SORT ORDER BY     |          |
|   2 |   SQL MODEL ACYCLIC FAST|     |
|*  3 |    TABLE ACCESS FULL | SALES_FACT |
-----------------------------------------------
```

CYCLIC

The execution plan in Listing 9-25 shows the use of CYCLIC algorithm to evaluate the rules. The SQL in Listing 9-25 is the copy of Listing 9-23 except for that the clause order by year, week is removed from the rule in line 9. Without the order-by clause, row evaluation can happen in any order, and so the CYCLIC algorithm is chosen.

Listing 9-25. *Automatic Order and CYCLIC*

```
1     select product, country, year, week, inventory, sale, receipts
2     from sales_fact
3     where country in ('Australia') and product='Xtend Memory'
4     model return updated rows
5     partition by (product, country)
6     dimension by (year, week)
7     measures ( 0 inventory , sale, receipts)
8     rules automatic order(
9          inventory [year, week ] =
10                              nvl(inventory [cv(year), cv(week)-1 ] ,0)
11                              - sale[cv(year), cv(week) ] +
12                              + receipts [cv(year), cv(week) ]
13     )
14*    order by product, country,year, week
```

```
-------------------------------------------
| Id | Operation          | Name      |
-------------------------------------------
|  0 | SELECT STATEMENT   |           |
|  1 |  SORT ORDER BY      |           |
|  2 |   SQL MODEL CYCLIC  |           |
|* 3 |    TABLE ACCESS FULL| SALES_FACT |
-------------------------------------------
```

Sequential

If the rule specifies sequential order, then the evaluation algorithm of the rules is shown as ORDERED. Listing 9-26 shows an example.

Listing 9-26. *Sequential Order*

```
1     select product, country, year, week, inventory, sale, receipts
2     from sales_fact
3     where country in ('Australia') and product='Xtend Memory'
4     model return updated rows
5     partition by (product, country)
6     dimension by (year, week)
7     measures ( 0 inventory , sale, receipts)
8     rules sequential order(
9          inventory [year, week ] order by year, week =
10                              nvl(inventory [cv(year), cv(week)-1 ] ,0)
11                              - sale[cv(year), cv(week) ] +
12                              + receipts [cv(year), cv(week) ]
13     )
14*    order by product, country,year, week
```

```
-------------------------------------------
| Id  | Operation          | Name          |
-------------------------------------------
|   0 | SELECT STATEMENT   |               |
|   1 |  SORT ORDER BY     |               |
|   2 |   SQL MODEL ORDERED |              |
|*  3 |    TABLE ACCESS FULL| SALES_FACT   |
-------------------------------------------
```

In a nutshell, the complexity and inter-dependency of the rules plays a critical role in the algorithm chosen. ACYCLIC FAST and ORDERED FAST algorithms are more scalable. This becomes important as the amount of data increases.

Predicate Pushing

Conceptually, the Model clause is a variant of analytical SQL and is typically implemented in a view or inline view. Predicates are specified outside the view, and these predicates must be pushed in to the view for acceptable performance. In fact, predicate pushing is critical to performance of the Model clause. Unfortunately, not all predicates can be pushed safely into the view due to the unique nature of the Model clause. If predicates are not pushed, then the Model clause will execute on the larger set of rows and can result in poor performance.

In Listing 9-27, an inline view is defined from lines 2 to 14 and then predicates on columns Country and Product are added. Step 4 in the execution plan shows that both predicates are pushed into the view, rows are filtered applying these two predicates, and then the Model clause executes on the result set. This is good, as the Model clause is operating on a smaller set of rows than it would otherwise—just 147 rows in this case.

Listing 9-27. *Predicate Pushing*

```
 1   select * from (
 2    select product, country, year, week, inventory, sale, receipts
 3    from sales_fact
 4    model return updated rows
 5    partition by (product, country)
 6    dimension by (year, week)
 7    measures ( 0 inventory , sale, receipts)
 8    rules automatic order(
 9         inventory [year, week ] =
10                                  nvl(inventory [cv(year), cv(week)-1 ] ,0)
11                                   - sale[cv(year), cv(week) ] +
12                                   + receipts [cv(year), cv(week) ]
13     )
14   ) where country in ('Australia') and product='Xtend Memory'
15*  order by product, country,year, week
...
```

```
select * from table (dbms_xplan.display_cursor('','','ALLSTATS LAST'));
-------------------------------------------------------------------------
| Id  | Operation            | Name       | E-Rows |  OMem |  1Mem | Used-Mem |
-------------------------------------------------------------------------
|   0 | SELECT STATEMENT     |            |        |       |       |          |
|   1 |  SORT ORDER BY       |            |    147 | 18432 | 18432 |16384  (0)|
|   2 |   VIEW               |            |    147 |       |       |          |
|   3 |    SQL MODEL CYCLIC  |            |    147 |  727K |  727K | 358K  (0)|
|*  4 |     TABLE ACCESS FULL| SALES_FACT |    147 |       |       |          |
-------------------------------------------------------------------------

Predicate Information (identified by operation id):
---------------------------------------------------
   4 - filter(("PRODUCT"='Xtend Memory' AND "COUNTRY"='Australia'))
```

Listing 9-28 enumerates an example in which the predicates are not pushed into the view. In this example, predicate year=2000 is specified, but not pushed into the inline view. The optimizer estimates show that the Model clause needs to operate on some 111,000 (110K) rows.

Predicates can be pushed into a view only if it's safe to do so. The SQL in Listing 9-28 uses both the Year and Week column as dimension columns. Generally, *predicates on the partitioning columns can be pushed in to a view safely*, but not all predicates on the dimension column can be pushed.

Listing 9-28. *Predicate not Pushed*

```
1    select * from (
2    select product, country, year, week, inventory, sale, receipts
3    from sales_fact
4    mod el return updated rows
5    partition by (product, country)
6    dimension by (year, week)
7    measures ( 0 inventory , sale, receipts)
8    rules automatic order(
9        inventory [year, week ] =
10                            nvl(inventory [cv(year), cv(week)-1 ] ,0)
11                            - sale[cv(year), cv(week) ] +
12                            + receipts [cv(year), cv(week) ]
13    )
14   ) where year=2000
15*  order by product, country,year, week
```

```
-------------------------------------------------------------------------
| Id  | Operation            | Name       | E-Rows |  OMem |  1Mem | Used-Mem |
-------------------------------------------------------------------------
|   0 | SELECT STATEMENT     |            |        |       |       |          |
|   1 |  SORT ORDER BY       |            |   111K | 2604K |  733K | 2314K (0)|
|*  2 |   VIEW               |            |   111K |       |       |          |
|   3 |    SQL MODEL CYCLIC  |            |   111K |   12M | 1886K |  12M  (0)|
|   4 |     TABLE ACCESS FULL| SALES_FACT |   111K |       |       |          |
-------------------------------------------------------------------------
```

```
Predicate Information (identified by operation id):
---------------------------------------------------
   2 - filter("YEAR"=2000)
```

Materialized Views

Typically, SQL statements using the Model clause access very large tables. Oracle's query Rewrite feature and Materialized views can be combined to improve performance of such statements.

In Listing 9-29, a materialized view mv_model_inventory is created with the enable query rewrite clause. Subsequent SQL in the listing executes the SQL statement accessing the Sales_fact table with the Model clause. The execution plan for the statement shows that the query rewrite feature rewrote the query redirecting access to the materialized view instead of the base table. The rewrite improves the performance of the SQL statement since the materialized view has pre-evaluated the rules and stored the results.

■**NOTE** The fast incremental refresh is not available for materialized views involving the Model clause.

Listing 9-29. *Materialized View and Query Rewrite*

```
create materialized view mv_model_inventory
enable query rewrite as
  select product, country, year, week, inventory, sale, receipts
  from sales_fact
  model return updated rows
  partition by (product, country)
  dimension by (year, week)
  measures ( 0 inventory , sale, receipts)
  rules sequential order(
      inventory [year, week ] order by year, week =
                          nvl(inventory [cv(year), cv(week)-1 ] ,0)
                          - sale[cv(year), cv(week) ] +
                          + receipts [cv(year), cv(week) ]
  )
/
Materialized view created.

select * from (
 select product, country, year, week, inventory, sale, receipts
  from sales_fact
  model return updated rows
  partition by (product, country)
  dimension by (year, week)
  measures ( 0 inventory , sale, receipts)
```

```
 rules sequential order(
      inventory [year, week ] order by year, week =
                         nvl(inventory [cv(year), cv(week)-1 ] ,0)
                           - sale[cv(year), cv(week) ] +
                           + receipts [cv(year), cv(week) ]
   )
 )
where country in ('Australia') and product='Xtend Memory'
order by product, country,year, week
/
```

```
---------------------------------------------------------------
| Id | Operation                       | Name                 |
---------------------------------------------------------------
|  0 | SELECT STATEMENT                |                      |
|  1 |  SORT ORDER BY                  |                      |
|* 2 |   MAT_VIEW REWRITE ACCESS FULL  | MV_MODEL_INVENTORY|
---------------------------------------------------------------

Predicate Information (identified by operation id):
---------------------------------------------------
  2 - filter(("MV_MODEL_INVENTORY"."COUNTRY"='Australia' AND
             "MV_MODEL_INVENTORY"."PRODUCT"='Xtend Memory'))
```

Parallelism

Model-based SQL works seamlessly with Oracle's parallel execution features. Queries against partitioned tables benefit greatly from parallelism and Model-based SQL statements.

An important concept with parallel query execution and Model SQL is that parallel query execution needs to respect the partition boundaries. Rules defined in the Model clause-based SQL statement might access another row. After all, accessing another row is the primary reason to use Model SQL statements. So, a parallel query slave must receive all rows from a Model data partition so that the rules can be evaluated. This distribution of rows to parallel query slaves is taken care of seamlessly by the database engine. The first set of parallel slaves reads row pieces from the table and distributes the row pieces to second set of slaves. That distribution is such that one slave receives all rows of a given model partition.

Listing 9-30 shows an example of Model and parallel queries. Two set of parallel slaves are allocated to execute the statement shown. The first set of slaves is read from the table. The second set of slaves evaluates the Model rule.

Listing 9-30. *Model and Parallel Queries*

```
select  /*+ parallel ( sf 4) */
   product, country, year, week, inventory, sale, receipts
   from sales_fact sf
   where country in ('Australia') and product='Xtend Memory'
   model return updated rows
   partition by (product, country)
```

```
    dimension by (year, week)
    measures ( 0 inventory , sale, receipts)
    rules automatic order(
        inventory [year, week ] order by year, week =
                            nvl(inventory [cv(year), cv(week)-1 ] ,0)
                             - sale[cv(year), cv(week) ] +
                             + receipts [cv(year), cv(week) ]
    )
/
```

```
----------------------------------------------...-------------------------
| Id | Operation            | Name     |    TQ |IN-OUT| PQ Distrib |
----------------------------------------------------------------------------
|   0 | SELECT STATEMENT     |          |...    |      |            |
|   1 |  PX COORDINATOR      |          |       |      |            |
|   2 |   PX SEND QC (RANDOM)| :TQ10001 | Q1,01 | P->S | QC (RAND)  |
|   3 |    BUFFER SORT       |          | Q1,01 | PCWP |            |
|   4 |     SQL MODEL ACYCLIC|          | Q1,01 | PCWP |            |
|   5 |      PX RECEIVE      |          | Q1,01 | PCWP |            |
|   6 |       PX SEND HASH   | :TQ10000 | Q1,00 | P->P | HASH       |
|   7 |        PX BLOCK ITERATOR |      | Q1,00 | PCWC |            |
|*  8 |         TABLE ACCESS FULL| SALES_FACT | Q1,00 | PCWP |     |
----------------------------------------------------------------------------
Predicate Information (identified by operation id):
---------------------------------------------------
   8 - access(:Z>=:Z AND :Z<=:Z)
       filter(("PRODUCT"='Xtend Memory' AND "COUNTRY"='Australia'))
```

Partitioning in Model Clause Execution

Table partitioning can be used to improve the performance of Model SQL statements. Generally, if the partitioning column(s) in the Model SQL matches the partitioning keys of the table, partitions are pruned. Partition pruning is a technique for performance improvement to limit scanning few partitions.

In Listing 9-31, the table sales_fact_part is list-partitioned by year using the script Listing_9_31_partition.sql (part of the example download for this book). The partition with partition_id=3 contains rows with the value of 2000 for the Year column. Since the Model SQL is using Year as the partitioning column and since a year=2000 predicate is specified, partition pruning lead to scanning partition 3 alone. The execution plan shows that both Pstart and Pstop columns have a value of 3, indicating that the range of partitions to be processed begins and ends with the single partition having id=3.

Listing 9-31. *Partition Pruning*

```
select * from (
  select product, country, year, week, inventory, sale, receipts
  from sales_fact_part sf
  model return updated rows
  partition by (year, country )
```

```
dimension by (product, week)
measures ( 0 inventory , sale, receipts )
rules automatic order(
    inventory [product, week ] order by product,  week =
                        nvl(inventory [cv(product),  cv(week)-1 ] ,0)
                        - sale[cv(product),  cv(week) ] +
                        + receipts [cv(product), cv(week) ]
  )
)   where year=2000 and country='Australia' and product='Xtend Memory'
/
```

```
-------------------------------------------------...----------------
| Id | Operation           | Name             |... Pstart| Pstop |
-------------------------------------------------...----------------
|   0 | SELECT STATEMENT    |                  |        |       |
|   1 |  SQL MODEL ACYCLIC  |                  |        |       |
|   2 |   PARTITION LIST SINGLE|               |    KEY |   KEY |
|*  3 |    TABLE ACCESS FULL | SALES_FACT_PART |      3 |     3 |
-------------------------------------------------...----------------
```

```
Predicate Information (identified by operation id):
---------------------------------------------------
   1 - filter("PRODUCT"='Xtend Memory')
   4 - filter("COUNTRY"='Australia')
```

In Listing 9-32, columns Product and County are used as partitioning columns, but the table Sales_fact_part has the Year column as the partitioning key. Step 1 in the execution plan indicates that predicate year=2000 was not pushed into the view since the rule can access other partitions (as Year is a dimension column). Because the partitioning key is not pushed into the view, partition pruning is not allowed, and all partitions are scanned. You can see that Pstart and Pstop are 1 and 5, respectively, in the execution plan.

Listing 9-32. *No Partition Pruning*

```
select * from (
select product, country, year, week, inventory, sale, receipts
from sales_fact_part sf
model return updated rows
partition by (product, country)
dimension by (year, week)
measures ( 0 inventory , sale, receipts)
rules automatic order(
    inventory [year, week ] order by year,  week =
                        nvl(inventory [cv(year),  cv(week)-1 ] ,0)
                        - sale[cv(year),  cv(week) ] +
                        + receipts [cv(year), cv(week) ]
  )
)   where year=2000 and country='Australia' and product='Xtend Memory'
/
```

```
-------------------------------------------------...-------------
| Id  | Operation            | Name           | Pstart| Pstop |
-------------------------------------------------...-------------
|   0 | SELECT STATEMENT     |                |       |       |
|*  1 |  VIEW                |                |       |       |
|   2 |   SQL MODEL ACYCLIC  |                |       |       |
|   3 |    PARTITION LIST ALL|                |    1  |     5 |
|*  4 |     TABLE ACCESS FULL| SALES_FACT_PART |   1  |     5 |
-------------------------------------------------...-------------
Predicate Information (identified by operation id):
---------------------------------------------------
 1 - filter("YEAR"=2000)
 4 - filter(("PRODUCT"='Xtend Memory' AND "COUNTRY"='Australia'))
```

Indexes

Choosing indexes to improve the performance of SQL statements using a Model clause is no different from choosing indexes for any other SQL statements. You use the access and filter predicates to determine the optimal indexing strategy.

As an example, Listing 9-32's execution plan shows that the filter predicates PRODUCT"='Xtend Memory' AND "COUNTRY"='Australia' were applied at step 4. Indexing on the two columns Product and Country will be helpful if there are many executions with these column predicates.

In the Listing 9-33, I added an index to the columns Country and Product. The resulting execution plan shows table access via the index, possibly improving performance.

Listing 9-33. *Indexing with SQL Access in Mind*

```
 create index sales_fact_part_i1 on sales_fact_part (country, product) ;
 select * from (
 select product, country, year, week, inventory, sale, receipts
 from sales_fact_part sf
 model return updated rows
 partition by (product, country)
 dimension by (year, week)
 measures ( 0 inventory , sale, receipts)
 rules automatic order(
     inventory [year, week ] order by year,  week =
                         nvl(inventory [cv(year),  cv(week)-1 ] ,0)
                          - sale[cv(year),  cv(week) ] +
                          + receipts [cv(year), cv(week) ]
  )
 )   where year=2000 and country='Australia' and product='Xtend Memory'
 /
```

```
--------------------------------------------------------------------------------
| Id  | Operation                           | Name                | Pstart| Pstop |
--------------------------------------------------------------------------------
|   0 | SELECT STATEMENT                    |                     |       |       |
|*  1 |  VIEW                               |                     |       |       |
|   2 |   SQL MODEL ACYCLIC                 |                     |       |       |
|   3 |    TABLE ACCESS BY GLOBAL INDEX ROWID| SALES_FACT_PART    | ROWID | ROWID |
|*  4 |     INDEX RANGE SCAN                | SALES_FACT_PART_I1  |       |       |
--------------------------------------------------------------------------------

Predicate Information (identified by operation id):
---------------------------------------------------
   1 - filter("YEAR"=2000)
   4 - access("COUNTRY"='Australia' AND "PRODUCT"='Xtend Memory')
```

Subquery Factoring

In a business setting, requirements are complex and multiple levels of aggregation are often needed. When writing complex queries, you can often combine subquery factoring with the Model clause to prevent a SQL statement from becoming unmanageably complex.

Listing 9-34 provides one such example. Two Model clauses are coded in the same SQL statement. The first Model clause is embedded within a view that is the result of a subquery being factored into the WITH clause. The main query uses that view to pivot the value of the Sale column from the prior year. The output shows that prior week sales are pivoted into the current week's row.

Listing 9-34. *More Indexing with SQL Access in Mind*

```
with t1 as (
  select  product, country, year, week, inventory, sale, receipts
  from sales_fact sf
  where country in ('Australia') and product='Xtend Memory'
  model return updated rows
  partition by (product, country)
  dimension by (year, week)
  measures ( 0 inventory , sale, receipts)
  rules automatic order(
      inventory [year, week ] order by year, week =
                            nvl(inventory [cv(year), cv(week)-1 ] ,0)
                            - sale[cv(year), cv(week) ] +
                            + receipts [cv(year), cv(week) ]
  )
)
select product, country, year, week , inventory, sale,receipts,
                  prev_sale
```

```
from t1
model return updated rows
partition by (product, country)
dimension by (year, week)
measures (inventory, sale, receipts,0 prev_sale)
rules sequential order (
  prev_sale [ year, week ] order by year, week =
                         nvl (sale [ cv(year) -1, cv(week)],0 )
)
order by 1,2,3,4
/
```

PRODUCT	COUNTRY	YEAR	WEEK	INVENTORY	SALE	RECEIPTS	PREV_SALE
Xtend Memory	Australia	1998	50	11.504	28.76	40.264	0
...							
Xtend Memory	Australia	2000	50	12.714	21.19	25.428	0
...							
Xtend Memory	Australia	2001	50	11.775	23.14	32.396	21.19

Summary

I can't stress enough the importance of thinking in terms of sets when writing SQL statements. Many SQL statements can be rewritten concisely using the Model clause discussed in this chapter. As an added bonus, rewritten queries such as Model or analytic functions can perform much better than traditional SQL statements. A combination of subquery factoring, Model, and analytic functions features can be used effectively to implement complex requirements.

CHAPTER 10

■ ■ ■

Subquery Factoring

Jared Still

You may not be familiar with the term *subquery factoring*. Prior to the release of Oracle 11gR2, the official Oracle documentation barely mentions it, providing just a brief synopsis of its use, a couple of restrictions, and a single example. If I instead refer to the WITH clause of the SELECT statement, you will probably know immediately what I mean as this term is more recognizable. Both terms will be used in this chapter.

With the release of Oracle 11gR2 (version 11.2), the WITH clause was enhanced with the ability to recurse; that is, the factored subquery is allowed to call itself within some limitation. The value of this may not be readily apparent. If you have used the CONNECT BY clause to create hierarchical queries, you will appreciate that recursive subqueries allow the same functionality to be implemented in an ANSI standard format.

If the term *subquery factoring* is not known to you, perhaps you have heard of the ANSI Standard term *common table expression* (commonly called CTE). Common table expressions were first specified in the 1999 ANSI SQL Standard. For some reason, Oracle has chosen to obfuscate this name. Other database vendors refer to common table expressions, so perhaps Oracle chose subquery factoring just to be different.

Standard Usage

One of the most useful features of the WITH clause when it was first introduced was to cleanup complex SQL queries. When a large number of tables and columns are involved in a query, it can become difficult to follow the flow of data through the query. Via the use of subquery factoring, a query can be made more understandable by moving some of the complexity away from the main body of the query.

The query in Listing 10-1 generates a crosstab report using the PIVOT operator. The formatting helps make the SQL somewhat readable, but there is quite a bit going on here. The innermost query is creating a set of aggregates on key sales columns, while the next most outer query simply provides column names that are presented to the PIVOT operator, where the final values of sales by channel and quarter for each product are generated.

Listing 10-1. *Crosstab without Subquery Factoring*

```
select *
from (
   select /*+ gather_plan_statistics */
       product
       , channel
       , quarter
```

```
      , country
      , quantity_sold
   from
   (
      select
         prod_name product
         , country_name country
         , channel_id channel
         , substr(calendar_quarter_desc, 6,2) quarter
         , sum(amount_sold) amount_sold
         , sum(quantity_sold) quantity_sold
      from
         sh.sales
         join sh.times on times.time_id = sales.time_id
         join sh.customers on customers.cust_id = sales.cust_id
         join sh.countries on countries.country_id = customers.country_id
         join sh.products on products.prod_id = sales.prod_id
      group by
         prod_name
         , country_name
         , channel_id
         , substr(calendar_quarter_desc, 6, 2)
   )
) PIVOT (
   sum(quantity_sold)
   FOR (channel, quarter) IN
   (
      (5, '02') AS CATALOG_Q2,
      (4, '01') AS INTERNET_Q1,
      (4, '04') AS INTERNET_Q4,
      (2, '02') AS PARTNERS_Q2,
      (9, '03') AS TELE_Q3
   )
)
order by product, country;
```

Now let's use the WITH clause to break the query in byte-sized chunks that are easier to comprehend. The SQL has been rewritten in Listing 10-2 using the WITH clause to create three subfactored queries, named sales_countries, top_sales, and sales_rpt. Notice that both the top_sales and sales_rpt subqueries are referring to other subqueries by name, as if they were a table or a view. By choosing names that make the intent of each subquery easy to follow, the readability of the SQL is improved. For instance, the subquery name sales_countries refers to the countries in which the sales took place, top_sales collects the sales data, and the sales_rpt subquery aggregates the data. The results of the sales_rpt subquery are used in the main query which answers the question, "What is the breakdown of sales by product and country per quarter?" If you were not told the intent of the SQL in Listing 10-1, it would take some time to discern its purpose; on the other hand, the structure of the SQL in Listing 10-2 with subfactored queries makes it easier to understand the intent of the code.

In addition, the statements directly associated with the PIVOT operator are in the same section of the SQL statement at the bottom, further enhancing readability.

Listing 10-2. *Crosstab with Subquery Factoring*

```
with sales_countries as (
   select /*+ gather_plan_statistics */
      cu.cust_id
      , co.country_name
   from  sh.countries co, sh.customers cu
   where cu.country_id = co.country_id
),
top_sales as (
   select
      p.prod_name
      , sc.country_name
      , s.channel_id
      , t.calendar_quarter_desc
      , s.amount_sold
      , s.quantity_sold
   from
      sh.sales s
      join sh.times t on t.time_id = s.time_id
      join sh.customers c on c.cust_id = s.cust_id
      join sales_countries sc on sc.cust_id = c.cust_id
      join sh.products p on p.prod_id = s.prod_id
),
sales_rpt as (
   select
      prod_name product
      , country_name country
      , channel_id channel
      , substr(calendar_quarter_desc, 6,2) quarter
      , sum(amount_sold) amount_sold
      , sum(quantity_sold) quantity_sold
   from top_sales
   group by
      prod_name
      , country_name
      , channel_id
      , substr(calendar_quarter_desc, 6, 2)
)
select * from
(
   select product, channel, quarter, country, quantity_sold
   from sales_rpt
) pivot (
   sum(quantity_sold)
```

```
    for (channel, quarter) in
    (
        (5, '02') as catalog_q2,
        (4, '01') as internet_q1,
        (4, '04') as internet_q4,
        (2, '02') as partners_q2,
        (9, '03') as tele_q3
    )
)
order by product, country;
```

While this is not an extremely complex SQL example, it does serve to illustrate the point of how the WITH clause can be used to make a statement more readable and easier to maintain. Large complex queries can be made more understandable by using this technique.

Optimizing SQL

When a SQL query is designed or modified to take advantage of subquery factoring, there are some not-so-subtle changes that may take place when the optimizer creates an execution plan for the query. The following quote comes from the Oracle 11gR2 documentation in the *Oracle Database SQL Language Reference* for SELECT, under the subquery_factoring_clause heading:

> *The* WITH query_name *clause lets you assign a name to a subquery block. You can then reference the subquery block multiple places in the query by specifying* query_name. *Oracle Database optimizes the query by treating the query name as either an inline view or as a temporary table.*

Notice that Oracle may treat the factored subquery as a temporary table. In queries where a table is referenced more than once, this could be a distinct performance advantage, as Oracle can materialize result sets from the query, thereby avoiding performing some expensive database operations more than once. The caveat here is that it "could be" a distinct performance advantage. Keep in mind that materializing the result set requires creating a temporary table and inserting the rows into it. Doing so may be of value if the same result set is referred to many times, or it may be a big performance penalty.

Testing Execution Plans

When examining the execution plans for subfactored queries, it may not be readily apparent if Oracle is choosing the best execution plan. It may seem that the use of the INLINE or MATERIALZE[1] hint would result in better performing SQL. In some cases it may, but the use of these hints needs to be tested and considered in the context of overall application performance.

The need to test for optimum query performance can be illustrated by a report that management has requested. The report must show the distribution of customers by country and income level,

---

[1] Though well known in the Oracle community for some time now, the INLINE and MATERIALIZE hints remain undocumented by Oracle.

showing only those countries and income levels that make up 1% or more of the entire customer base. A country and income level should also be reported if the number of customers in an income level bracket is greater than or equal to 25% of all customers in that income bracket[2].

The query in Listing 10-3 is the end result[3]. The cust factored subquery has been retained from previous queries. New are the subqueries in the HAVING clause; these are used to enforce the rules stipulated for the report.

Listing 10-3. *WITH and MATERIALIZE*

```
 1  with cust as (
 2   select /*+ materialize gather_plan_statistics */
 3     b.cust_income_level,
 4     a.country_name
 5   from sh.customers b
 6   join sh.countries a on a.country_id = b.country_id
 7  )
 8  select country_name, cust_income_level, count(country_name) country_cust_count
 9  from cust c
10  having count(country_name) >
11   (
12     select count(*) * .01
13     from cust c2
14   )
15   or count(cust_income_level) >=
16   (
17     select median(income_level_count)
18     from (
19       select cust_income_level, count(*) *.25 income_level_count
20       from cust
21       group by cust_income_level
22     )
23   )
24  group by country_name, cust_income_level
25  order by 1,2;
```

COUNTRY	INCOME LEVEL	CUSTOMER COUNT
France	E: 90,000 - 109,999	585
France	F: 110,000 - 129,999	651
...		
United States of America	H: 150,000 - 169,999	1857
United States of America	I: 170,000 - 189,999	1395
...		

---

[2] If you run these examples on a version of Oracle other then 11gR2, the output may appear differently, as the test data sometimes changes with versions of Oracle.

[3] The MATERIALIZE hint was used to ensure that the example would work as expected, given that you may be testing on a different version or patch level of Oracle. On the test system used by the author, this was the default action by Oracle.

35 rows selected.
Elapsed: 00:00:01.37

Statistics

      1854 recursive calls
       307 db block gets
      2791 consistent gets
      1804 physical reads
       672 redo size
      4609 bytes sent via SQL*Net to client
       700 bytes received via SQL*Net from client
        18 SQL*Net roundtrips to/from client
        38 sorts (memory)
         0 sorts (disk)
        35 rows processed

Id	Operation	Name	Starts	E-Rows	A-Rows	A-Time
0	SELECT STATEMENT		1		35	00:00:11.74
1	TEMP TABLE TRANSFORMATION		1		35	00:00:11.74
2	LOAD AS SELECT		1		0	00:00:09.87
* 3	HASH JOIN		1	55500	55500	00:03:30.11
4	TABLE ACCESS FULL	COUNTRIES	1	23	23	00:00:00.04
5	TABLE ACCESS FULL	CUSTOMERS	1	55500	55500	00:03:29.77
* 6	FILTER		1		35	00:00:01.88
7	SORT GROUP BY		1	18	209	00:00:01.84
8	VIEW		1	55500	55500	00:00:30.87
9	TABLE ACCESS FULL	SYS_TEMP_OF	1	55500	55500	00:00:30.73
10	SORT AGGREGATE		1	1	1	00:00:00.01
11	VIEW		1	55500	55500	00:00:00.21
12	TABLE ACCESS FULL	SYS_TEMP_OF	1	55500	55500	00:00:00.07
13	SORT GROUP BY		1	1	1	00:00:00.03
14	VIEW		1	11	13	00:00:00.03
15	SORT GROUP BY		1	11	13	00:00:00.03
16	VIEW		1	55500	55500	00:00:00.21
17	TABLE ACCESS FULL	SYS_TEMP_OF	1	55500	55500	00:00:00.07

When executing[4] the SQL, all appears as you expect. Then you check the execution plan and find that the join of the CUSTOMERS and COUNTRIES tables underwent a TEMP TABLE TRANSFORMATION, and the rest of the query was satisfied by using the temporary table SYS_TEMP_OF[5]. At this point, you might rightly wonder if the execution plan chosen was a reasonable one. That can easily be tested, thanks to the MATERIALIZED and INLINE hints.

---

[4] Initial executions are executed after first flushing the shared_pool and buffer_cache.
[5] The actual table name was SYS_TEMP_0FD9D66A2_453290, but was shortened in the listing for formatting purposes.

By using the INLINE hint, Oracle can be instructed to satisfy all portions of the query without using a TEMP TABLE TRANSFORMATION. The results of doing so are shown in Listing 10-4. Only the relevant portion of the SQL that has changed is shown here, the rest of it being identical to that in Listing 10-3.

Listing 10-4. *WITH and INLINE Hint*

```
1  with cust as (
2     select /*+ inline gather_plan_statistics */
3        b.cust_income_level,
4        a.country_name
5     from sh.customers b
6     join sh.countries a on a.country_id = b.country_id
7  )
...
```

```
COUNTRY                    INCOME LEVEL             COUNT
------------------------   --------------------   --------
France                     E: 90,000 - 109,999       585
France                     F: 110,000 - 129,999      651
...
United States of America   I: 170,000 - 189,999     1395
United States of America   J: 190,000 - 249,999     1390
...
35 rows selected.
```

Elapsed: 00:00:00.62

```
Statistics
----------------------------------------------------------
       1501  recursive calls
          0  db block gets
       4758  consistent gets
       1486  physical reads
          0  redo size
       4609  bytes sent via SQL*Net to client
        700  bytes received via SQL*Net from client
         18  SQL*Net roundtrips to/from client
         34  sorts (memory)
          0  sorts (disk)
         35  rows processed
```

Id	Operation	Name	Starts	E-Rows	A-Rows	A-Time
0	SELECT STATEMENT		1		35	00:00:09.65
* 1	FILTER		1		35	00:00:09.65
2	SORT GROUP BY		1	20	236	00:00:09.53
* 3	HASH JOIN		1	55500	55500	00:03:09.16

4	TABLE ACCESS FULL	COUNTRIES	1	23	23	00:00:00.03
5	TABLE ACCESS FULL	CUSTOMERS	1	55500	55500	00:03:08.83
6	SORT AGGREGATE		1	1	1	00:00:00.07
* 7	HASH JOIN		1	55500	55500	00:00:00.41
8	INDEX FULL SCAN	COUNTRIES_PK	1	23	23	00:00:00.03
9	TABLE ACCESS FULL	CUSTOMERS	1	55500	55500	00:00:00.09
10	SORT GROUP BY		1	1	1	00:00:00.06
11	VIEW		1	12	13	00:00:00.06
12	SORT GROUP BY		1	12	13	00:00:00.06
* 13	HASH JOIN		1	55500	55500	00:00:00.38
14	INDEX FULL SCAN	COUNTRIES_PK	1	23	23	00:00:00.01
15	TABLE ACCESS FULL	CUSTOMERS	1	55500	55500	00:00:00.08

From the execution plan in Listing 10-4, you can see that three full scans were performed on the CUSTOMERS table and one full scan on the COUNTRIES table. Two of the executions against the cust subquery required only the information in the COUNTRIES_PK index, so a full scan of the index was performed rather than a full scan of the table, saving a small bit of time and resources.

What may be surprising is that the execution using full table scans was .75 seconds, or about 100%, faster than when a temporary table was used. Of course, the cache was cold for both queries, as both the buffer cache and shared pool were flushed prior to running each query.

Testing Over Multiple Executions

What would happen if each query were run multiple times simultaneously from several different database sessions? Using a modified version of Tom Kyte's run_stats[6] queries, each query was run in twenty sessions, each session running the query twenty times. The results seem to indicate that using the INLINE hint may offer a performance advantage. Of course, making such a judgment would require testing in your own test environment, preferably while the application in question is running a normal load.

In this case, the tests were run both without and with a load running on the database server. The load consisted of 10 other sessions executing queries against another set of tables in the database. While the runtimes did increase for both MATERIALIZED and INLINE, the ratios remained about the same, so keeping the INLINE hint in this query seems to be a good idea.

Listing 10-5 shows some significant differences in the statistics reported for the two tests. Total elapsed time for 400 executions by 20 sessions using 20 database sessions required 68.4 seconds when the MATERIALIZED hint was used. When the INLINE hint was used, the elapsed time of 30.8 seconds was an improvement in elapsed time of over 100%.

The physical IO rates between the two tests stand in stark contrast to each other. While the tests using the INLINE hint performed approximately 1GB of physical IO, the test using the MATERIALIZE hint performed nearly twice as much. That could certainly account for the few extra seconds of time. Possibly even more telling are the values shown by the statistics gathered from v$session_event. The queries with the MATERIALIZED hint spent 1308 seconds in wait time compared to 306 seconds for INLINE.

---

[6] Available at www.oracle-developer.net/content/utilities/runstats.zip. The modified version used here is available with the source code for this chapter. It does require a UNIX or Linux environment to operate.

Listing 10-5. *Run_stats Comparison*

NO LOAD TEST

```
SQL> @test_harness_m
```

MATERIALIZE

```
68.446 secs
avg response time:    0.171115
```

INLINE

```
30.774 secs
avg response time:    0.076935
```

```
SQL> @sr
```

NAME	MATERIALIZE	INLINE	DIFF
STAT...user I/O wait time	122,096	8,687	-113,409
...			
STAT...physical writes direct temporary tablespace	118,000	0	-118,000
...			
STAT...physical writes	118,040	0	-118,040
STAT...db block gets	122,460	104	-122,356
STAT...DB time	0	147,349	147,349
STAT...free buffer requested	166,475	2	-166,473
LATCH.cache buffers lru chain	215,377	1	-215,376
LATCH.object queue header operation	340,352	27	-340,325
STAT...file io wait time	588,347,559	36,628	-588,310,931
STAT...physical read bytes	966,656,000	8,192	-966,647,808
STAT...physical write bytes	966,983,680	0	-966,983,680
STAT...physical read total bytes	967,491,584	499,712	-966,991,872
STAT...physical write total bytes	967,976,960	400,896	-967,576,064
STAT...cell physical IO interconnect bytes	1,935,468,544	900,608	-1,934,567,936

```
71 rows selected.
SQL> @mse
```

EVENT	RUN 1 TIME WAITED SECONDS	RUN 2 TIME WAITED SECONDS	TIME DIFF
enq: TM - contention	74.63	175.72	-101.09
latch: cache buffers chains	.00	38.89	-38.89
Disk file operations I/O	60.97	86.83	-25.86

```
SQL*Net message to client          .00         .00        -.00
library cache: mutex X             .00         .00         .00
cursor: pin S wait on X            .21         .00         .21
SQL*Net message from client       5.57        4.96         .62
buffer busy waits                 2.24         .00        2.24
events in waitclass Other         3.90         .01        3.90
db file sequential read           8.32         .00        8.32
direct path write temp          572.13         .00      572.13
db file scattered read          579.60         .00      579.60
                              --------- --------- ---------
sum                             1307.59      306.41     1001.18
```

12 rows selected.

LOAD TEST
SQL> @test_harness_m

MATERIALIZE
310.908 secs
avg response time: 0.777270

INLINE
144.683 secs
avg response time: 0.361708

Run Stats omitted – they are very similar to NO LOAD TEST.

SQL> @mse

| | RUN 1 TIME WAITED | RUN 2 TIME WAITED | TIME |
EVENT	SECONDS	SECONDS	DIFF
enq: TM - contention	721.66	989.28	-267.62
latch: cache buffers chains	22.04	34.70	-12.66
SQL*Net message to client	.00	.00	-.00
SQL*Net message from client	.80	.77	.03
buffer busy waits	4.61	.00	4.61
events in waitclass Other	21.05	8.69	12.36
db file sequential read	33.71	.00	33.71
direct path write temp	95.53	.00	95.53
Disk file operations I/O	1995.29	814.54	1180.76
db file scattered read	1418.30	.00	1418.30
sum	4313.00	1847.97	2465.02

From these tests you might feel safe using the INLINE hint in this bit of code, convinced that it will perform well. The amount of physical IO required in the first test outweighs the memory usage and logical IO required for the second test. If you know for sure that the size of the data sets will not grow and that the system load will remain fairly constant, using the INLINE hint in this query is probably a good idea. The problem, however, is that data is rarely static; often, data grows to a larger size than what was originally intended when developing a query. In that event, re-testing these queries would be in order to see if the use of the INLINE hint is still valid.

Testing the Effects of Query Changes

Even as data does not remain static, SQL is not always static. Sometimes requirements change, so code must be modified. What if the requirements changed for the examples in Listings 10-3 and 10-4? Would minor changes invalidate the use of the hints embedded in the SQL? This is probably something worth investigating, so let's do so.

Previously, you were reporting on income brackets when the count of them for any country was greater than or equal to 25% of the total global count for that bracket. Now you are asked to include an income bracket if it is among those income brackets the number of which is greater than the median, based on the number of customers per bracket. This SQL is seen in Listing 10-6. Notice that the INLINE hint has been left in. So now there's an additional full table scan and index scan as compared to the execution plan in Listing 10-4. While the elapsed time has increased, it still seems reasonable.

Now that there's an additional table scan and index scan, how do you think the performance of this query will fare if temporary table transformations are allowed to take place? The results can be seen in Listing 10-7.

Because there's that additional scan taking place in the modified version of the query, the overhead of logical IO becomes more apparent. It is significantly more efficient with this query to allow Oracle to perform table transformations, writing the results of the hash join to a temporary table on disk where they can be reused throughout the query.

Listing 10-6. *Modified Income Search - INLINE*

```
1   with cust as (
2   select /*+ inline gather_plan_statistics */
3     b.cust_income_level,
4     a.country_name
5   from sh.customers b
6   join sh.countries a on a.country_id = b.country_id
7   ),
8   median_income_set as (
9   select /*+ inline */ cust_income_level, count(*) income_level_count
10  from cust
11  group by cust_income_level
12  having count(cust_income_level) > (
13     select median(income_level_count) income_level_count
14     from (
15        select cust_income_level, count(*) income_level_count
16        from cust
17        group by cust_income_level
18     )
19  )
20  )
```

```
21  select country_name, cust_income_level, count(country_name) country_cust_count
22  from cust c
23  having count(country_name) >
24  (
25    select count(*) * .01
26    from cust c2
27  )
28  or cust_income_level in ( select mis.cust_income_level from median_income_set mis)
29  group by country_name, cust_income_level;
```

COUNTRY	INCOME LEVEL	CUSTOMER COUNT
Argentina	D: 70,000 - 89,999	25
Argentina	E: 90,000 - 109,999	39
...		
United States of America	K: 250,000 - 299,999	1062
United States of America	L: 300,000 and above	982

123 rows selected.

Elapsed: 00:00:01.26

Statistics

```
     1524  recursive calls
        0  db block gets
    23362  consistent gets
     1486  physical reads
        0  redo size
    15570  bytes sent via SQL*Net to client
     1195  bytes received via SQL*Net from client
       63  SQL*Net roundtrips to/from client
        3  sorts (memory)
        0  sorts (disk)
      123  rows processed
```

```
----------------------------------------------------------------------------
| Id | Operation            | Name      |Starts|E-Rows|A-Rows |  A-Time    |
----------------------------------------------------------------------------
|  0 | SELECT STATEMENT     |           |    1|      |   123 |00:00:00.37|
|* 1 |  FILTER              |           |    1|      |   123 |00:00:00.37|
|  2 |   SORT GROUP BY      |           |    1|   20|   236 |00:00:00.08|
|* 3 |    HASH JOIN         |           |    1|55500| 55500 |00:00:00.38|
|  4 |     TABLE ACCESS FULL| COUNTRIES |    1|   23|    23 |00:00:00.01|
|  5 |     TABLE ACCESS FULL| CUSTOMERS |    1|55500| 55500 |00:00:00.08|
|  6 |   SORT AGGREGATE     |           |    1|    1|     1 |00:00:00.04|
```

```
|* 7 |     HASH JOIN         |              |  1| 55500| 55500 |00:00:00.43|
|  8 |       INDEX FULL SCAN  | COUNTRIES_PK|  1|    23|    23 |00:00:00.01|
|  9 |       TABLE ACCESS FULL| CUSTOMERS    |  1| 55500| 55500 |00:00:00.10|
|* 10 |    FILTER             |              | 13|      |     6 |00:00:00.65|
|  11 |     HASH GROUP BY      |              | 13|     1|   133 |00:00:00.59|
|* 12 |      HASH JOIN         |              | 13| 55500|  721K |00:00:05.18|
|  13 |        INDEX FULL SCAN | COUNTRIES_PK| 13|    23|   299 |00:00:00.01|
|  14 |        TABLE ACCESS FULL| CUSTOMERS   | 13| 55500|  721K |00:00:01.10|
|  15 |    SORT GROUP BY       |              |  1|     1|     1 |00:00:00.06|
|  16 |     VIEW               |              |  1|    12|    13 |00:00:00.06|
|  17 |      SORT GROUP BY     |              |  1|    12|    13 |00:00:00.06|
|* 18 |       HASH JOIN        |              |  1| 55500| 55500 |00:00:00.42|
|  19 |         INDEX FULL SCAN| COUNTRIES_PK|  1|    23|    23 |00:00:00.01|
|  20 |         TABLE ACCESS FULL| CUSTOMERS |  1| 55500| 55500 |00:00:00.08|
-----------------------------------------------------------------------
```

Listing 10-7. *Modified Income Search - MATERIALIZE*

```
1  with cust as (
2  select /*+ materialize gather_plan_statistics */
3    b.cust_income_level,
4    a.country_name
5  from sh.customers b
6  join sh.countries a on a.country_id = b.country_id
7  ),
...
```

COUNTRY	INCOME LEVEL	CUSTOMER COUNT
Argentina	D: 70,000 - 89,999	25
Argentina	E: 90,000 - 109,999	39
...		
United States of America	K: 250,000 - 299,999	1062
United States of America	L: 300,000 and above	982

123 rows selected.

Elapsed: 00:00:00.87

Statistics
```
-------------------------------------------------------------
      2001  recursive calls
       324  db block gets
      3221  consistent gets
      1822  physical reads
```

```
    1244  redo size
   15570  bytes sent via SQL*Net to client
    1195  bytes received via SQL*Net from client
      63  SQL*Net roundtrips to/from client
      38  sorts (memory)
       0  sorts (disk)
     123  rows processed
```

Id	Operation	Name	Starts	E-Rows	A-Rows	A-Time
0	SELECT STATEMENT		1		123	00:00:00.54
1	TEMP TABLE TRANSFORMATION		1		123	00:00:00.54
2	LOAD AS SELECT		1		0	00:00:00.37
* 3	HASH JOIN		1	55500	55500	00:00:03.21
4	TABLE ACCESS FULL	COUNTRIES	1	23	23	00:00:00.01
5	TABLE ACCESS FULL	CUSTOMERS	1	55500	55500	00:00:02.91
6	LOAD AS SELECT		1		0	00:00:00.10
* 7	FILTER		1		6	00:00:00.09
8	HASH GROUP BY		1	1	13	00:00:00.06
9	VIEW		1	55500	55500	00:00:00.24
10	TABLE ACCESS FULL	SYS_TEMP_OF	1	55500	55500	00:00:00.11
11	SORT GROUP BY		1	1	1	00:00:00.03
12	VIEW		1	12	13	00:00:00.03
13	SORT GROUP BY		1	12	13	00:00:00.03
14	VIEW		1	55500	55500	00:00:00.21
15	TABLE ACCESS FULL	SYS_TEMP_OF	1	55500	55500	00:00:00.07
* 16	FILTER		1		123	00:00:00.06
17	SORT GROUP BY		1	20	236	00:00:00.05
18	VIEW		1	55500	55500	00:00:00.21
19	TABLE ACCESS FULL	SYS_TEMP_OF	1	55500	55500	00:00:00.07
20	SORT AGGREGATE		1	1	1	00:00:00.01
21	VIEW		1	55500	55500	00:00:00.21
22	TABLE ACCESS FULL	SYS_TEMP_OF	1	55500	55500	00:00:00.07
* 23	VIEW		13	1	6	00:00:00.01
24	TABLE ACCESS FULL	SYS_TEMP_OF	13	1	63	00:00:00.01

Seizing Other Optimization Opportunities

There are other opportunities where subquery factoring may be used to your advantage. If you are working on applications that were originally written several years ago, you may find that some of SQL could use a bit of improvement based on the features offered by Oracle versions 9i and later. The query in Listing 10-8, for example, does exactly what it was asked to do, which is to find the average, minimum, and maximum costs for each product that was produced in the year 2000, with the costs calculated for each of the sale channels the product was sold in. This SQL is not only difficult to read and hard to modify, but is also somewhat inefficient.

Listing 10-8. *Old SQL to Calculate Costs*

```
1   select /*+ gather_plan_statistics */
2       substr(prod_name,1,30) prod_name
3     , channel_desc
4     , (
5         select avg(c2.unit_cost)
6         from sh.costs c2
7         where c2.prod_id = c.prod_id and c2.channel_id = c.channel_id
8         and c2.time_id between to_date('01/01/2000','mm/dd/yyyy')
9          and to_date('12/31/2000')
10        ) avg_cost
11    , (
12        select min(c2.unit_cost)
13        from sh.costs c2
14        where c2.prod_id = c.prod_id and c2.channel_id = c.channel_id
15        and c2.time_id between to_date('01/01/2000','mm/dd/yyyy')
16         and to_date('12/31/2000')
17        ) min_cost
18    , (
19        select max(c2.unit_cost)
20        from sh.costs c2
21        where c2.prod_id = c.prod_id and c2.channel_id = c.channel_id
22        and c2.time_id between to_date('01/01/2000','mm/dd/yyyy')
23         and to_date('12/31/2000')
24        ) max_cost
25  from (
26      select distinct pr.prod_id, pr.prod_name, ch.channel_id, ch.channel_desc
27      from sh.channels ch
28        , sh.products pr
29        , sh.costs co
30      where ch.channel_id = co.channel_id
31        and co.prod_id = pr.prod_id
32        and co.time_id between to_date('01/01/2000','mm/dd/yyyy')
33         and to_date('12/31/2000')
34  ) c
35  order by prod_name, channel_desc;
```

PRODUCT	CHANNEL_DESC	AVG COST	MIN COST	MAX COST
1.44MB External 3.5" Diskette	Direct Sales	8.36	7.43	9.17
1.44MB External 3.5" Diskette	Internet	8.59	7.42	9.55
...				
Y Box	Internet	266.73	245.00	282.30
Y Box	Partners	272.62	242.79	293.68
sum		27,961.39	24,407.85	34,478.10

216 rows selected.

COLD CACHE Elapsed: 00:00:02.30
WARM CACHE Elapsed: 00:00:01.09

```
---------------------------------------------------------------------------------
| Id  | Operation                            |Name          |Sta|E-Rows|A-Rows |  A-Time   |
|     |                                      |              |rts|      |       |           |
---------------------------------------------------------------------------------
|   0 | SELECT STATEMENT                     |              |  1|      |   216 |00:00:01.13|
|   1 |  SORT AGGREGATE                      |              |216|     1|   216 |00:00:00.33|
|*  2 |   FILTER                             |              |216|      | 17373 |00:00:00.37|
|   3 |    PARTITION RANGE ITERATOR          |              |216|    96| 17373 |00:00:00.33|
|*  4 |     TABLE ACCESS BY LOCAL INDEX ROWID|COSTS         |864|    96| 17373 |00:00:00.36|
|   5 |      BITMAP CONVERSION TO ROWIDS     |              |864|      | 52119 |00:00:00.31|
|   6 |       BITMAP AND                     |              |864|      |   840 |00:00:00.23|
|   7 |        BITMAP MERGE                  |              |864|      |   864 |00:00:00.20|
|*  8 |         BITMAP INDEX RANGE SCAN      |COSTS_TIME_BIX|864|      | 79056 |00:00:00.13|
|*  9 |        BITMAP INDEX SINGLE VALUE     |COSTS_PROD_BIX|864|      |   840 |00:00:00.01|
|  10 |  SORT AGGREGATE                      |              |216|     1|   216 |00:00:00.33|
|* 11 |   FILTER                             |              |216|      | 17373 |00:00:00.32|
|  12 |    PARTITION RANGE ITERATOR          |              |216|    96| 17373 |00:00:00.28|
|* 13 |     TABLE ACCESS BY LOCAL INDEX ROWID|COSTS         |864|    96| 17373 |00:00:00.35|
|  14 |      BITMAP CONVERSION TO ROWIDS     |              |864|      | 52119 |00:00:00.30|
|  15 |       BITMAP AND                     |              |864|      |   840 |00:00:00.22|
|  16 |        BITMAP MERGE                  |              |864|      |   864 |00:00:00.20|
|* 17 |         BITMAP INDEX RANGE SCAN      |COSTS_TIME_BIX|864|      | 79056 |00:00:00.13|
|* 18 |        BITMAP INDEX SINGLE VALUE     |COSTS_PROD_BIX|864|      |   840 |00:00:00.01|
|  19 |  SORT AGGREGATE                      |              |216|     1|   216 |00:00:00.37|
|* 20 |   FILTER                             |              |216|      | 17373 |00:00:00.35|
|  21 |    PARTITION RANGE ITERATOR          |              |216|    96| 17373 |00:00:00.31|
|* 22 |     TABLE ACCESS BY LOCAL INDEX ROWID|COSTS         |864|    96| 17373 |00:00:00.39|
|  23 |      BITMAP CONVERSION TO ROWIDS     |              |864|      | 52119 |00:00:00.34|
|  24 |       BITMAP AND                     |              |864|      |   840 |00:00:00.26|
|  25 |        BITMAP MERGE                  |              |864|      |   864 |00:00:00.22|
|* 26 |         BITMAP INDEX RANGE SCAN      |COSTS_TIME_BIX|864|      | 79056 |00:00:00.16|
|* 27 |        BITMAP INDEX SINGLE VALUE     |COSTS_PROD_BIX|864|      |   840 |00:00:00.02|
|  28 | SORT ORDER BY                        |              |  1| 20640|   216 |00:00:01.13|
|  29 |  VIEW                                |              |  1| 20640|   216 |00:00:00.10|
|  30 |   HASH UNIQUE                        |              |  1| 20640|   216 |00:00:00.10|
|* 31 |    FILTER                            |              |  1|      | 17373 |00:00:00.33|
|* 32 |     HASH JOIN                        |              |  1| 20640| 17373 |00:00:00.28|
|  33 |      TABLE ACCESS FULL               |PRODUCTS      |  1|    72|    72 |00:00:00.01|
|* 34 |      HASH JOIN                       |              |  1| 20640| 17373 |00:00:00.18|
|  35 |       TABLE ACCESS FULL              |CHANNELS      |  1|     5|     5 |00:00:00.01|
|  36 |       PARTITION RANGE ITERATOR       |              |  1| 20640| 17373 |00:00:00.08|
|* 37 |        TABLE ACCESS FULL             |COSTS         |  4| 20640| 17373 |00:00:00.04|
---------------------------------------------------------------------------------
```

Examining the output of Listing 10-8, you see that the elapsed execution time on a cold cache is 2.30 seconds and 1.09 seconds on a warm cache. These times don't seem all that bad at first. But when you examine the execution plan, you find that this query can be improved upon from a performance perspective as well as a readability perspective.

The Starts column is telling. Each execution against the COSTS table is executed 864 times. This is due to there being 216 rows produced by a join between CHANNELS, PRODUCTS, and COSTS. Also, the COSTS table is queried in four separate places for the same information. By using subquery factoring, not only can this SQL be cleaned up and made easier to read, it can also be made more efficient.

As seen in Listing 10-9, you can start by putting the begin_date and end_date columns in a separate query bookends, leaving only one place that the values need to be set. The data for products is placed in the prodmaster subquery. While this bit of the SQL worked fine as subquery in the FROM clause, the readability of the SQL statement as a whole is greatly improved by moving it to a factored subquery.

The calculations for the average, minimum, and maximum costs are replaced with a single subquery called cost_compare. Finally, the SQL that joins the prodmaster and cost_compare subqueries is added. The structure of the SQL is now much easier on the eyes and the overworked Developer's brain. It's also simpler for the DBA to understand. The DBA will be especially happy with the execution statistics.

Where the old SQL queried the COSTS table and COSTS_TIME_BIX index several hundred times, the new SQL queries each only eight times. That is quite an improvement, and it shows in the elapsed times. The query time on a cold cache is 1.48 seconds, about 25% better than the old SQL. On a warm cache, however, the re-factored SQL really shines, running at 0.17 seconds whereas the old SQL managed only 1.09 seconds.

Listing 10-9. *Old SQL Refactored Using WITH Clause*

```
1   with bookends as (
2      select
3       to_date('01/01/2000','mm/dd/yyyy') begin_date
4          ,to_date('12/31/2000','mm/dd/yyyy') end_date
5      from dual
6   ),
7   prodmaster as (
8      select distinct pr.prod_id, pr.prod_name, ch.channel_id, ch.channel_desc
9      from sh.channels ch
10       , sh.products pr
11       , sh.costs co
12     where ch.channel_id = co.channel_id
13        and co.prod_id = pr.prod_id
14        and co.time_id between (select begin_date from bookends)
15         and (select end_date from bookends)
16  ),
17  cost_compare as (
18      select
19          prod_id
20        , channel_id
21        , avg(c2.unit_cost) avg_cost
22        , min(c2.unit_cost) min_cost
23        , max(c2.unit_cost) max_cost
24      from sh.costs c2
25      where c2.time_id between (select begin_date from bookends)
26        and (select end_date from bookends)
```

```
27          group by c2.prod_id, c2.channel_id
28  )
29  select /*+ gather_plan_statistics */
30     substr(pm.prod_name,1,30) prod_name
31     , pm.channel_desc
32     , cc.avg_cost
33     , cc.min_cost
34     , cc.max_cost
35  from prodmaster pm
36  join cost_compare cc on cc.prod_id = pm.prod_id
37     and cc.channel_id = pm.channel_id
38  order by pm.prod_name, pm.channel_desc;
```

PRODUCT	CHANNEL_DESC	AVG COST	MIN COST	MAX COST
1.44MB External 3.5" Diskette	Direct Sales	8.36	7.43	9.17
1.44MB External 3.5" Diskette	Internet	8.59	7.42	9.55
Y Box	Internet	266.73	245.00	282.30
Y Box	Partners	272.62	242.79	293.68
sum		27,961.39	24,407.85	34,478.10

216 rows selected.

COLD CACHE Elapsed: 00:00:01.48
WARM CACHE Elapsed: 00:00:00.17

Id	Operation	Name	Sta rts	E-Rows	A-Rows	A-Time
0	SELECT STATEMENT		1		216	00:00:00.09
1	SORT ORDER BY		1	17373	216	00:00:00.09
* 2	HASH JOIN		1	17373	216	00:00:00.09
3	VIEW		1	216	216	00:00:00.04
4	HASH GROUP BY		1	216	216	00:00:00.04
5	PARTITION RANGE ITERATOR		1	17373	17373	00:00:00.18
6	TABLE ACCESS BY LOCAL INDEX ROWID	COSTS	4	17373	17373	00:00:00.13
7	BITMAP CONVERSION TO ROWIDS		4		17373	00:00:00.02
* 8	BITMAP INDEX RANGE SCAN	COSTS_TIME_BIX	4		366	00:00:00.01
9	FAST DUAL		1	1	1	00:00:00.01
10	FAST DUAL		1	1	1	00:00:00.01
11	VIEW		1	17373	216	00:00:00.05
12	HASH UNIQUE		1	17373	216	00:00:00.05
* 13	HASH JOIN		1	17373	17373	00:00:00.19
14	TABLE ACCESS FULL	PRODUCTS	1	72	72	00:00:00.01
15	MERGE JOIN		1	17373	17373	00:00:00.10

```
|  16|       TABLE ACCESS BY INDEX ROWID     |CHANNELS      |  1|     5|     4|00:00:00.01|
|  17|         INDEX FULL SCAN               |CHANNELS_PK   |  1|     5|     4|00:00:00.01|
|* 18|     SORT JOIN                         |              |  4| 17373| 17373|00:00:00.05|
|  19|       PARTITION RANGE ITERATOR        |              |  1| 17373| 17373|00:00:00.17|
|  20|        TABLE ACCESS BY LOCAL INDEX RO|COSTS          |  4| 17373| 17373|00:00:00.13|
|  21|         BITMAP CONVERSION TO ROWIDS   |              |  4|      | 17373|00:00:00.03|
|* 22|          BITMAP INDEX RANGE SCAN      |COSTS_TIME_BIX|  4|      |   366|00:00:00.01|
|  23|           FAST DUAL                   |              |  1|     1|     1|00:00:00.01|
|  24|           FAST DUAL                   |              |  1|     1|     1|00:00:00.01|
--------------------------------------------------------------------------------------------
```

Applying Subquery Factoring to PL/SQL

Even PL/SQL can present golden opportunities for optimization using subquery factoring. Something that most of us have done at one time or another is to write a PL/SQL routine when we cannot figure out how to do what we want in a single SQL query. Sometimes it can be very difficult to capture everything in a single statement. It's often just easier to think procedurally rather than in sets of data, and just write some code to do what we need. As you gain experience, you will rely less and less on thinking in terms of "How would I code this in PL/SQL?" and more along the lines of "How do I capture this problem in a single SQL statement?" The more advanced features that Oracle has packed into SQL can help as well.

Here's an example. You've been asked to create a report with the following criteria:

- Only include customers that have purchased products in at least three different years.
- Compute total aggregate sales per customer, broken down by product category.

At first, this doesn't seem too difficult. But you may struggle for a bit trying to capture this in one SQL statement, so you decide to use a PL/SQL routine to get the needed data. The results may be similar to those in Listing 10-10. The logic is simple. Find all customers that fit the criteria and store their IDs in a temporary table. Then loop through the newly saved customer IDs and find all their sales, sum them up, and add them to another temporary table. The results are then joined to the CUSTOMERS and PRODUCTS tables to generate the report.

Listing 10-10. *PL/SQL to Generate Customer Report*

```
SQL> create global temporary table cust3year ( cust_id number );
Table created.

SQL> create global temporary table sales3year(
  2      cust_id number ,
  3      prod_category varchar2(50),
  4      total_sale number
  5  )
  6  /
Table created.

SQL> begin
  2      execute immediate 'truncate table cust3year';
  3      execute immediate 'truncate table sales3year';
  4
```

```
 5      insert into cust3year
 6      select cust_id --, count(cust_years) year_count
 7      from (
 8              select distinct cust_id, trunc(time_id,'YEAR') cust_years
 9              from sh.sales
10      )
11      group by cust_id
12      having count(cust_years) >= 3;
13
14      for crec in ( select cust_id from cust3year)
15      loop
16              insert into sales3year
17              select s.cust_id,p.prod_category, sum(co.unit_price * s.quantity_sold)
18              from sh.sales s
19              join sh.products p on p.prod_id = s.prod_id
20              join sh.costs co on co.prod_id = s.prod_id
21                      and co.time_id = s.time_id
22              join sh.customers cu on cu.cust_id = s.cust_id
23              where s.cust_id = crec.cust_id
24              group by s.cust_id, p.prod_category;
25      end loop;
26 end;
27 /
PL/SQL procedure successfully completed.
```

Elapsed: 00:01:17.48

```
SQL> break on report
SQL> compute sum of total_sale on report

SQL> select c3.cust_id, c.cust_last_name, c.cust_first_name, s.prod_category, s.total_sale
  2  from cust3year c3
  3  join sales3year s on s.cust_id = c3.cust_id
  4  join sh.customers c on c.cust_id = c3.cust_id
  5  order by 1,4;
```

CUST ID	LAST NAME	FIRST NAME	PRODUCT CATEGORY	TOTAL SALE
6	Charles	Harriett	Electronics	2,838.57
6	Charles	Harriett	Hardware	19,535.38
...				
50833	Gravel	Grover	Photo	15,469.64
50833	Gravel	Grover	Software/Other	9,028.87
sum				167,085,605.71

16018 rows selected.

The code in Listing 10-10 is fairly succinct, and it only takes 1:17 minutes to run. That's not too bad, is it? While this is a nice little chunk of PL/SQL, take another look at it and think in terms of subfactored subqueries. The section that determines the correct customer IDs can be captured in a WITH clause fairly easily. Once the customers are identified, it is a fairly easy job to then use the results of the subquery to lookup the needed sales, product, and customer information to create the report.

Listing 10-11 has a single SQL statement that captures what is done with the PL/SQL routine from Listing 10-10—without the need to manually create temporary tables or use PL/SQL loops. Should the use of temporary tables make for a more efficient query, Oracle will do so automatically, or you can choose how Oracle preserves the subquery results via the INLINE and MATERIALIZE hints. It is somewhat more efficient, too, with an elapsed time of 6.13 seconds.

The WITH clause in Listing 10-11 actually uses two subqueries. These could be combined into a single query, but I thought it easier to read broken out into two queries. Notice the use of the EXTRACT() function—it simplifies comparing years by extracting the year from a date and converting it to an integer.

Listing 10-11. *Use WITH Clause to Generate Customer Report*

```
1   with custyear as (
2     select cust_id, extract(year from time_id) sales_year
3     from sh.sales
4     where extract(year from time_id) between 1998 and 2002
5     group by cust_id,  extract(year from time_id)
6   ),
7   custselect as (
8     select distinct cust_id
9     from (
10        select cust_id, count(*) over ( partition by cust_id) year_count
11        from custyear
12    )
13    where  year_count >= 3 -- 3 or more years as a customer during period
14  )
15  select cu.cust_id, cu.cust_last_name, cu.cust_first_name, p.prod_category,
sum(co.unit_price * s.quantity_sold) total_sale
16  from custselect cs
17  join sh.sales s on s.cust_id = cs.cust_id
18  join sh.products p on p.prod_id = s.prod_id
19  join sh.costs co on co.prod_id = s.prod_id
20   and co.time_id = s.time_id
21  join sh.customers cu on cu.cust_id = cs.cust_id
22  group by cu.cust_id, cu.cust_last_name, cu.cust_first_name, p.prod_category
23  order by cu.cust_id;
```

CUST ID	LAST NAME	FIRST NAME	PRODUCT CATEGORY	TOTAL SALE
6	Charles	Harriett	Electronics	2,838.57
6	Charles	Harriett	Hardware	19,535.38

...

50833	Gravel	Grover	Photo		15,469.64
50833	Gravel	Grover	Software/Other		9,028.87
					---------------
sum					167,085,605.71

16018 rows selected.

Elapsed: 00:00:06.13

The SQL examples in this section of the chapter are not meant to be tuning exercises, but merely demonstrations showing how subquery factoring may be used. When refactoring legacy SQL to take advantage of the WITH clause, be sure to test the results. Subquery factoring can be used to better organize some queries, and in some cases can even be used as an optimization tool. Learning to use it adds another tool to your Oracle toolbox.

EXPERIMENT WITH SUBQUERY FACTORING

Included in this chapter are two scripts in the Exercises folder that you may want to experiment with. These scripts both run against the SH demo schema.

- Exercises/l_10_exercise_1.sql

- Exercises/l_10_exercise_2.sql

Run these scripts with both the MATERIALIZE and INLINE hints to compare performance. In the tsales subquery, a WHERE clause limits the data returned to a single year. Comment out the WHERE clause and run the queries again. How does the efficiency of the two hints compare now? Would you feel comfortable using these hints when the size of the data set is set at runtime by user input?

Recursive Subqueries

New to Oracle 11.2 is *recursive subquery factoring* (RSF for the remainder of this chapter). As you can probably guess, the ANSI name for this feature is *recursive common table expression*. Regardless of what you call it, Oracle has had a similar feature for a very long time in the form of the CONNECT BY[7] clause of the SELECT statement. This feature has been enhanced in Oracle 11gR2.

A CONNECT BY Example

Let's begin by looking at a traditional CONNECT BY query such as in Listing 10-12. The emp inline view is used to join the EMPLOYEE and DEPARTMENT tables, and then the single data set is presented to the SELECT ... CONNECT BY statement. The PRIOR operator is used to match the current EMPLOYEE_ID to rows where this value is in the MANAGER_ID column. Doing so iteratively creates a recursive query.

---

[7] CONNECT BY was first available in Oracle Version 2, or in others words, from the very beginning.

Listing 10-12 contains a number of extra columns in the output to help explain how the PRIOR operator works. Let's take a look at the output beginning with the row for Lex De Haan. You can see that the EMPLOYEE_ID for Lex is 102. The PRIOR operator will find all rows for which the MANAGER_ID is 102 and include them under the hierarchy for Lex De Haan. The only row that meets these criteria is the one for Alexander Hunold, with an EMPLOYEE_ID of 103. The process is then repeated for Alexander Hunold: are there any rows for which the MANAGER_ID is 103? There are four rows found with a MANAGER_ID of 103: those are for the employees Valli Pattaballa, Diana Lorentz, Bruce Ernst, and David Austin, so these are included in the output below Alexander Hunold. As there were no rows for which any of the EMPLOYEE_ID values for these four employees appears as a MANAGER_ID, Oracle moves back up to a level for which the rows have not yet been processed (in this case, for Alberto Errazuriz) and continues on to the end until all rows have been processed.

The START WITH clause is instructed to begin with a value for which MANAGER_ID is null. As this is an organizational hierarchy with a single person at the top of the hierarchy, this causes the query to start with Stephen King. As the CEO, Mr. King does not have a manager, so the MANAGER_ID column is set to NULL for his row.

The LEVEL pseudocolumn holds the value for the depth of the recursion, allowing for a simple method to indent the output so that the organizational hierarchy is visible.

Listing 10-12. *Basic CONNECT BY*

```
 1  select lpad(' ', level*2-1,' ') || emp.emp_last_name emp_last_name
 2    , emp.emp_first_name
 3    , emp.employee_id
 4    , emp.mgr_last_name, emp.mgr_first_name
 5    , emp.manager_id
 6    , department_name
 7  from (
 8  select /*+ inline gather_plan_statistics */
 9     e.last_name emp_last_name, e.first_name emp_first_name
10    , e.employee_id, d.department_id
11    , e.manager_id, d.department_name
12    , es.last_name mgr_last_name, es.first_name mgr_first_name
13  from hr.employees e
14  left outer join hr.departments d on d.department_id = e.department_id
15  left outer join hr.employees es on es.employee_id = e.manager_id
16  ) emp
17  connect by prior emp.employee_id = emp.manager_id
18  start with emp.manager_id is null
19 order siblings by emp.emp_last_name;
```

EMP_LAST_NAME	EMP_FIRST_NAME	EMP ID	MGR_LAST_NAME	MGR_FIRST_NAME	MGR ID	DEPARTMENT
King	Steven	100				Executive
Cambrault	Gerald	148	King	Steven	100	Sales
Bates	Elizabeth	172	Cambrault	Gerald	148	Sales
Bloom	Harrison	169	Cambrault	Gerald	148	Sales
Fox	Tayler	170	Cambrault	Gerald	148	Sales
Kumar	Sundita	173	Cambrault	Gerald	148	Sales

```
    Ozer       Lisa           168 Cambrault    Gerald      148 Sales
    Smith      William        171 Cambrault    Gerald      148 Sales
  De Haan      Lex            102 King         Steven      100 Executive
    Hunold     Alexander      103 De Haan      Lex         102 IT
      Austin   David          105 Hunold       Alexander   103 IT
      Ernst    Bruce          104 Hunold       Alexander   103 IT
      Lorentz  Diana          107 Hunold       Alexander   103 IT
      Pataballa Valli         106 Hunold       Alexander   103 IT
   Errazuriz   Alberto        147 King         Steven      100 Sales
     Ande      Sundar         166 Errazuriz    Alberto     147 Sales
     Banda     Amit           167 Errazuriz    Alberto     147 Sales
...

107 rows selected.
```

The Example Using an RSF

The example query on the EMPLOYEES table has been rewritten in Listing 10-13 to use RSF, where the main subquery is emp_recurse. The anchor member in this case simply selects the top most row in the hierarchy by selecting the only row where MANAGER_ID IS NULL. This is equivalent to START WITH EMP.MANAGER_ID IS NULL in Listing 10-12. The recursive member references the defining query emp_recurse by joining it to emp query. This join is used to locate the row corresponding to each employee's manager, which is equivalent to CONNECT BY PRIOR EMP.EMPLOYEE_ID = EMP.MANAGER_ID in Listing 10-12. The results in Listing 10-13 are identical to those in Listing 10-12.

Listing 10-13. *Basic Recursive Subquery Factoring*

```
 1  with emp as (
 2   select /*+ inline gather_plan_statistics */
 3      e.last_name, e.first_name, e.employee_id, e.manager_id, d.department_name
 4   from hr.employees e
 5   left outer join hr.departments d on d.department_id = e.department_id
 6  ),
 7  emp_recurse (last_name,first_name,employee_id,manager_id,department_name,lvl) as (
 8   select e.last_name, e.first_name
 9     , e.employee_id, e.manager_id
10     , e.department_name, 1 as lvl
11   from emp e where e.manager_id is null
12  union all
13   select emp.last_name, emp.first_name
14   , emp.employee_id, emp.manager_id
15   ,emp.department_name, empr.lvl + 1 as lvl
16   from emp
17   join emp_recurse empr on empr.employee_id = emp.manager_id
18  )
19   search depth first by last_name set order1
20  select lpad(' ', lvl*2-1,' ') || er.last_name last_name
```

306

```
21    , er.first_name
22    , er.department_name
23 from emp_recurse er;
```

```
LAST_NAME                 FIRST_NAME            DEPARTMENT
------------------------  --------------------  -----------
King                      Steven                Executive
  Cambrault               Gerald                Sales
    Bates                 Elizabeth             Sales
    Bloom                 Harrison              Sales
    Fox                   Tayler                Sales
    Kumar                 Sundita               Sales
    Ozer                  Lisa                  Sales
    Smith                 William               Sales
  De Haan                 Lex                   Executive
    Hunold                Alexander             IT
      Austin              David                 IT
      Ernst               Bruce                 IT
      Lorentz             Diana                 IT
      Pataballa           Valli                 IT
  Errazuriz               Alberto               Sales
    Ande                  Sundar                Sales
    Banda                 Amit                  Sales
    ...

107 rows selected.
```

While the new RSF method may at first appear verbose, the basis of how it works is simpler to understand than CONNECT BY and allows for more complex queries. The recursive WITH clause requires two query blocks, the anchor member and the recursive member. These two query blocks must be combined with the UNION ALL set operator. The anchor member is the query prior to the UNION ALL, while the recursive member is the query following. The recursive member must reference the defining subquery— by doing so, it is recursive.

Restrictions on RSF

As you might imagine, the use of RSF is quite a bit more flexible than CONNECT BY. There are some restrictions on its use, however. As per the 11gR2 documentation for the SELECT statement, the following elements cannot be used in the recursive member of an RSF:

- The DISTINCT keyword or a GROUP BY clause

- The model_clause

- An aggregate function. However, analytic functions are permitted in the select list.

- Subqueries that refer to query_name.

- Outer joins that refer to query_name as the right table.

Differences from CONNECT BY

There are several differences when using RSF as compared to CONNECT BY, and some of them are apparent in Listing 10-13. You may have wondered what happened to the LEVEL pseudocolumn, as it is missing in this query, replaced by the LVL column. I'll get to that one a little later on. Also notice that the columns returned by an RSF query must be specified in the query definition as seen in line 7 of Listing 10-13. One more new feature is the SEARCH DEPTH FIRST seen on line 19. The default search is BREADTH FIRST, which is not usually the output you want from a hierarchical query. Listing 10-14 shows the output when the SEARCH clause is not used or it is set to BREADTH FIRST. This search returns rows of all siblings at each level before returning any child rows. Specifying SEARCH DEPTH FIRST will return the rows in hierarchical order. The SET ORDER1 portion of the SEARCH clause sets the value of the ORDER1 pseudocolumn to the value of the order the rows are returned in, similar to what you might see with ROWNUM, but you get to name the column. This will also be used in later examples.

Listing 10-14. *Default BREADTH FIRST Search*

```
...
        search breadth first by last_name set order1
select lpad(' ', lvl*2-1,' ') || er.last_name last_name
...
```

LAST_NAME	FIRST_NAME	DEPARTMENT_NAME
King	Steven	Executive
Cambrault	Gerald	Sales
De Haan	Lex	Executive
Errazuriz	Alberto	Sales
Fripp	Adam	Shipping
Hartstein	Michael	Marketing
Kaufling	Payam	Shipping
Kochhar	Neena	Executive
Mourgos	Kevin	Shipping
Partners	Karen	Sales
Raphaely	Den	Purchasing
Russell	John	Sales
Vollman	Shanta	Shipping
Weiss	Matthew	Shipping
Zlotkey	Eleni	Sales
Abel	Ellen	Sales
Ande	Sundar	Sales

...

Notice that the SEARCH clause as it is used in Figures 10-13 and 10-14 specifies that the search be by LAST_NAME. This could also be by FIRST_NAME, or by a column list, such as LAST_NAME,FIRST_NAME. Doing so controls the order of the rows within each level. The SEARCH clause ends with SET ORDER1. This effectively adds the ORDER1 pseudocolumn to the column list returned by the recursive subquery. You will see it used more in some of the following examples.

Duplicating CONNECT BY Functionality

As the Oracle database has progressed through several versions, the functionality of the CONNECT BY clause has progressed as well. There are a number of hierarchical query operators, pseudocolumns, and one function available to CONNECT BY that are not natively available to RSF. The functionality these provide, however, can be duplicated in RSF. The functionality may not mimic exactly what occurs when CONNECT BY is used, but it can likely be made to do what you need. The trick to getting what you want from RSF sometimes requires stepping away from the keyboard and thinking about the results you want to achieve, rather than thinking about how you are going to code it. It is amazing how the change in perspective will help you easily achieve the desired output from the SQL you write.

The operators and pseudocolumns for CONNECT BY are listed in Table 10-1. I will go through each of these as needed, showing example usages for CONNECT BY, and then duplicating that functionality with RSF. Keep in mind that RSF is quite versatile, so TMTOWTDI[8] is definitely in force. Feel free to experiment and find other methods to achieve the same results.

Table 10-1. *CONNECT BY Functions, Operators, and Pseudocolumns*

Type	Name	Purpose
Function	SYS_CONNECT_BY_PATH	Returns all ancestors for the current row.
Operator	CONNECT_BY_ROOT	Returns the value from a root row.
Operator	PRIOR	Used to indicate hierarchical query. Not needed in a recursive subquery.
Pseudocolumn	CONNECT_BY_ISCYCLE	Detects cycles in the hierarchy.
Parameter	NOCYCLE	Parameter for CONNECT BY. Used with CONNECT_BY_ISCYCLE.
Pseudocolumn	CONNECT_BY_ISLEAF	Identifies leaf rows.
Pseudocolumn	LEVEL	Used to indicate level of depth in the hierarchy.

I will also cover the SEARCH clause of RSF as it is instrumental in solving some problems.

The LEVEL Pseudocolumn

Let's start with the LEVEL pseudocolumn. This is frequently used in hierarchical queries to indent the output, creating a visual representation of the hierarchy. Listing 10-15 contains a simple examples showing how LEVEL is generated. As the hierarchy increases in depth, LEVEL in incremented. Likewise, LEVEL is decremented when the hierarchy goes back a level.

---

[8] There's More Than One Way To Do It

Listing 10-15. *The LEVEL Pseudocolumn*

```
 1  select lpad(' ', level*2-1,' ') || e.last_name last_name, level
 2  from hr.employees e
 3  connect by prior e.employee_id = e.manager_id
 4  start with e.manager_id is null
 5  order siblings by e.last_name;
```

```
LAST_NAME                     LEVEL
------------------------- ----------

King                            1
   Cambrault                    2
      Bates                     3
      Bloom                     3
      Fox                       3
      Kumar                     3
      Ozer                      3
      Smith                     3
   De Haan                      2
...

107 rows selected.
```

This can also be accomplished in RSF, though it does require a little effort on your part. It's detailed in Listing 10-16. It may be somewhat surprising to see that this actually works. The value for LVL is never decremented, only incremented. Recall that the default search method for RSF is BREADTH FIRST. It is apparent that Oracle is processing the rows in sibling order, with the top of the hierarchy (King), followed by the child rows at the next level, continuing until the last row is reached. This behavior will allow you to solve some other problems as well.

Listing 10-16. *Create A LVL Column*

```
 1  with emp_recurse(employee_id,manager_id,last_name,lvl) as (
 2    select e.employee_id, null, e.last_name, 1 as lvl
 3    from hr.employees e
 4    where e.manager_id is null
 5    union all
 6    select e1.employee_id, e1.manager_id, e1.last_name, e2.lvl + 1 as lvl
 7    from hr.employees e1
 8    join emp_recurse e2 on e2.employee_id= e1.manager_id
 9  )
10  search depth first by last_name set last_name_order
11  select lpad(' ', r.lvl*2-1,' ') || r.last_name last_name, r.lvl
12  from emp_recurse r
13  order by last_name_order;
```

```
LAST_NAME                        LVL
------------------------ ----------
 King                              1
   Cambrault                       2
     Bates                         3
     Bloom                         3
     Fox                           3
     Kumar                         3
     Ozer                          3
     Smith                         3
   De Haan                         2
...

107 rows selected.
```

The SYS_CONNECT_BY_PATH Function

This function is used to return the values that comprise the hierarchy up to the current row. It's best explained with an example, such as the one seen in Listing 10-17. The SYS_CONNECT_BY_PATH function here is used to build a colon delimited list of the hierarchy, complete from root to node.

Listing 10-17. *SYS_CONNECT_BY_PATH*

```
1  select lpad(' ',2*(level-1)) || e.last_name last_name
2    , sys_connect_by_path(last_name,':') path
3  from hr.employees e
4  start with e.manager_id is null
5  connect by prior e.employee_id = e.manager_id
6  order siblings by e.last_name;
```

```
LAST_NAME                PATH
------------------------ -------------------------------------------------------
King                     :King
   Cambrault             :King:Cambrault
     Bates               :King:Cambrault:Bates
     Bloom               :King:Cambrault:Bloom
     Fox                 :King:Cambrault:Fox
     Kumar               :King:Cambrault:Kumar
     Ozer                :King:Cambrault:Ozer
     Smith               :King:Cambrault:Smith
   De Haan               :King:De Haan
...
107 rows selected.
```

Though the SYS_CONNECT_BY_PATH function is not available to RSF queries, this function can be duplicated using much the same method that was used to reproduce the LEVEL pseudocolumn. Rather than incrementing a counter, however, you will now be appending to a string value. Listing 10-18 shows how this is done.

Listing 10-18. *Build Your Own SYS_CONNECT_BY_PATH*

```
1  with emp_recurse(employee_id,manager_id,last_name,lvl,path) as (
2   select e.employee_id, null, e.last_name
3      , 1 as lvl
4      ,':' || to_char(e.last_name) as path
5   from hr.employees e
6   where e.manager_id is null
7   union all
8   select e1.employee_id, e1.manager_id, e1.last_name
9      ,e2.lvl + 1 as lvl
10     ,e2.path || ':' || e1.last_name as path
11  from hr.employees e1
12  join emp_recurse e2 on e2.employee_id= e1.manager_id
13  )
14  search depth first by last_name set last_name_order
15  select lpad(' ', r.lvl*2-1,' ') || r.last_name last_name, r.path
16  from emp_recurse r
17  order by last_name_order;
```

```
LAST_NAME                 PATH
------------------------  ------------------------------------------------------------
King                      :King
  Cambrault               :King:Cambrault
    Bates                 :King:Cambrault:Bates
    Bloom                 :King:Cambrault:Bloom
    Fox                   :King:Cambrault:Fox
    Kumar                 :King:Cambrault:Kumar
    Ozer                  :King:Cambrault:Ozer
    Smith                 :King:Cambrault:Smith
  De Haan                 :King:De Haan
...
107 rows selected.
```

The output of the SYS_CONNECT_BY_PATH as seen in Listing 10-17 is duplicated by the roll-your-own version using RSF in Listing 10-18. Take another look at this SQL; you may notice that there's something here that SYS_CONNECT_BY_PATH cannot do. Consider, for instance, if you wanted the hierarchy to be displayed as a comma delimited list. That is accomplished simply enough by changing the colon ":" to comma ",". The problem with SYS_CONNECT_BY_PATH is that the first character in the output will always be a comma.

Using the RFS method, you can simply remove the delimiter in the anchor member, and then change the delimiter in the recursive member to a comma. This is shown in Listing 10-19, along with a sample of the output. Should you feel inclined, the first character of the path could remain a colon and the values delimited by commas.

Listing 10-19. *Comma Delimited PATH*

```
 1  with emp_recurse(employee_id,manager_id,last_name,lvl,path) as (
 2    select e.employee_id, null, e.last_name
 3       , 1 as lvl
 4       ,e.last_name as path
 5    from hr.employees e
 6    where e.manager_id is null
 7    union all
 8    select e1.employee_id, e1.manager_id, e1.last_name
 9       ,e2.lvl + 1 as lvl
10       ,e2.path || ',' || e1.last_name as path
11    from hr.employees e1
12    join emp_recurse e2 on e2.employee_id= e1.manager_id
13  )
14  search depth first by last_name set last_name_order
15  select lpad(' ', r.lvl*2-1,' ') || r.last_name last_name, r.path
16  from emp_recurse r
17  order by last_name_order;
```

```
LAST_NAME                 PATH
------------------------  --------------------------------------------------------------
King                      King
   Cambrault              King,Cambrault
      Bates               King,Cambrault,Bates
      Bloom               King,Cambrault,Bloom
      Fox                 King,Cambrault,Fox
      Kumar               King,Cambrault,Kumar
      Ozer                King,Cambrault,Ozer
      Smith               King,Cambrault,Smith
   De Haan                King,De Haan
...
107 rows selected.
```

The CONNECT_BY_ROOT Operator

This operator enhances the CONNECT BY syntax by returning the root node of the current row. In the example of the HR.EMPLOYEES table, all rows will return "King" as the root. You can change it up a bit, however, by temporarily modifying the row for Neena Kochhar, putting her on the same level as the company president, Steven King. Then the hierarchy can be shown for Ms. Kochhar by using the CONNECT_BY_ROOT operator to restrict the output. You can see the results in Listing 10-20.

Listing 10-20. *CONNECT_BY_ROOT*

```
1* update hr.employees set manager_id= null where last_name ='Kochhar';
1 row updated.

 1  select /*+ inline gather_plan_statistics */
 2    level
 3    , lpad(' ',2*(level-1)) || last_name last_name
 4    , first_name
 5    , CONNECT_BY_ROOT last_name as root
 6    , sys_connect_by_path(last_name,':') path
 7  from hr.employees
 8  where connect_by_root last_name = 'Kochhar'
 9  connect by prior employee_id = manager_id
10  start with manager_id is null;
```

```
LEVEL LAST_NAME    FIRST_NAME   ROOT         PATH
----- ------------ ------------ ------------ ------------------------------
    1 Kochhar      Neena        Kochhar      :Kochhar
    2   Greenberg  Nancy        Kochhar      :Kochhar:Greenberg
    3     Faviet   Daniel       Kochhar      :Kochhar:Greenberg:Faviet
    3     Chen     John         Kochhar      :Kochhar:Greenberg:Chen
    3     Sciarra  Ismael       Kochhar      :Kochhar:Greenberg:Sciarra
    3     Urman    Jose Manuel  Kochhar      :Kochhar:Greenberg:Urman
    3     Popp     Luis         Kochhar      :Kochhar:Greenberg:Popp
    2   Whalen     Jennifer     Kochhar      :Kochhar:Whalen
    2   Mavris     Susan        Kochhar      :Kochhar:Mavris
    2   Baer       Hermann      Kochhar      :Kochhar:Baer
    2   Higgins    Shelley      Kochhar      :Kochhar:Higgins
    3     Gietz    William      Kochhar      :Kochhar:Higgins:Gietz
```

```
12 rows selected.
1 rollback;
```

This functionality can be duplicated in RSF, but it does require a little more SQL. The code in Listing 10-21 is based on the SYS_CONNECT_BY_PATH example, with some minor changes and additions. The delimiting character is now prepended and appended to the value for PATH in the anchor member. In the recursive member, the delimiter is appended to the PATH, whereas previously it was prepended to the LAST_NAME column. Doing so ensures that the root records will always have a delimiting character at the end of the value, allowing the SUBSTR() function in the emps subquery to correctly parse the root from the string when the path comes from the anchor member only, such as the rows for King and Kochar. This is probably better explained by examining the output from the query.

Listing 10-21. *Duplicate CONNECT_BY_ROOT*

```
1 update hr.employees set manager_id= null where last_name ='Kochhar';
1 row updated.
```

```
 1  with emp_recurse(employee_id,manager_id,last_name,lvl,path) as (
 2   select /*+ gather_plan_statistics */
 3      e.employee_id
 4      , null as manager_id
 5      , e.last_name
 6      , 1 as lvl
 7      , ':' || e.last_name || ':' as path
 8   from hr.employees  e
 9   where e.manager_id is null
10   union all
11   select
12      e.employee_id
13      , e.manager_id
14      , e.last_name
15      , er.lvl + 1 as lvl
16      , er.path || e.last_name  || ':' as path
17   from hr.employees e
18   join emp_recurse er on er.employee_id = e.manager_id
19   join hr.employees e2 on e2.employee_id = e.manager_id
20  )
21  search depth first by last_name set order1 ,
22  emps as (
23   select lvl
24      , last_name
25      , path
26      , substr(path,2,instr(path,':',2)-2) root
27   from emp_recurse
28  )
29  select
30   lvl
31  , lpad(' ',2*(lvl-1)) || last_name last_name
32  , root
33  , path
34  from emps
35  where root = 'Kochhar';
```

```
    LVL LAST_NAME       ROOT            PATH
---------- --------------- --------------- ------------------------------
      1 Kochhar         Kochhar         :Kochhar:
      2   Baer          Kochhar         :Kochhar:Baer:
      2   Greenberg     Kochhar         :Kochhar:Greenberg:
      3     Chen        Kochhar         :Kochhar:Greenberg:Chen:
      3     Faviet      Kochhar         :Kochhar:Greenberg:Faviet:
```

```
    3      Popp       Kochhar        :Kochhar:Greenberg:Popp:
    3      Sciarra    Kochhar        :Kochhar:Greenberg:Sciarra:
    2      Urman      Kochhar        :Kochhar:Greenberg:Urman:
    2      Higgins    Kochhar        :Kochhar:Higgins:
    3      Gietz      Kochhar        :Kochhar:Higgins:Gietz:
    2      Mavris     Kochhar        :Kochhar:Mavris:
    2      Whalen     Kochhar        :Kochhar:Whalen:

12 rows selected.
1* rollback;
```

This is not a perfect duplication of the CONNECT_BY_ROOT operator. In this case, it does exactly what is needed. The built-in operator, however, does allow some flexibility in specifying the level and returning the root at that level. The example given would need more modification to match that ability. However, you may find that this example works well for most cases.

The CONNECT_BY_ISCYCLE Pseudocolumn and NOCYCLE Parameter

The CONNECT_BY_ISCYCLE pseudocolumn makes it easy to detect loops in a hierarchy. This is illustrated by the SQL in Listing 10-22. Here, an intentional error has been introduced by updating the HR.EMPLOYEES row for the President, assigning Smith as King's manager. This will cause an error in the CONNECT BY.

Listing 10-22. *Cycle Error in CONNECT BY*

```
1 update hr.employees set manager_id = 171 where employee_id = 100;
1 row updated.
Elapsed: 00:00:00.02

  1   select lpad(' ',2*(level-1)) || last_name last_name
  2    ,first_name, employee_id, level
  3   from hr.employees
  4   start with employee_id = 100
  5*  connect by prior employee_id = manager_id
```

```
LAST_NAME                    FIRST_NAME    EMPLOYEE_ID  LEVEL
------------------------     ------------  -----------  -----
King                         Steven                100      1
   Kochhar                   Neena                 101      2
      Greenberg             Nancy                 108      3
...
      Smith                  William               171      3
         King                Steven                100      4
...
ERROR:
ORA-01436: CONNECT BY loop in user data
```

316

```
187 rows selected.
 1 rollback;
```

In the output, Smith appears as the Manager of King, which you know to be incorrect. But if you didn't already know what the problem was, how would you find it? That's where the NOCYCLE parameter and CONNECT_BY_ISCYCLE operator come in to play. These are used to detect a cycle in the hierarchy. The NOCYCLE parameter prevents the ORA-1436 error from occurring, allowing all rows to be output. The CONNECT_BY_ISCYCLE operator allows you to easily find the row causing the error.

As seen in Listing 10-23, the value of CONNECT_BY_ISCYCLE is 1, indicating that the row for Smith is somehow causing the error. The next query looks up the data for Smith, and all appears normal. Finally, you query the table again, this time using Smith's employee ID to find all employees that he manages. The error becomes apparent—the President of the company does not have a manager, so the solution is to set the MANAGER_ID back to NULL for this row.

Listing 10-23. *Detect the Cycle with CONNECT_BY_ISCYCLE*

```
1* update hr.employees set manager_id = 171 where employee_id = 100
1 row updated.

1  select lpad(' ',2*(level-1)) || last_name last_name
2   ,first_name, employee_id, level
3   , connect_by_iscycle
4  from hr.employees
5  start with employee_id = 100
6  connect by nocycle prior employee_id = manager_id;
```

```
LAST_NAME                FIRST_NAME   EMPLOYEE_ID LEVEL CONNECT_BY_ISCYCLE
------------------------ ------------ ----------- ----- ------------------
King                     Steven               100     1                  0
  Kochhar                Neena                101     2                  0
...
    Smith                William              171     3                  1
...
107 rows selected.

Elapsed: 00:00:00.03
  1  select last_name, first_name, employee_id, manager_id
  2  from hr.employees
  3* where employee_id = 171

LAST_NAME                FIRST_NAME   EMPLOYEE_ID MANAGER_ID
------------------------ ------------ ----------- ----------
Smith                    William              171        148

  1  select last_name, first_name, employee_id, manager_id
  2  from hr.employees
  3* where manager_id = 171
```

```
LAST_NAME                 FIRST_NAME   EMPLOYEE_ID MANAGER_ID
------------------------- ------------ ----------- ----------
King                      Steven               100        171
```

```
  1  rollback;
```

So, how do you do this with RSF? It's really quite simple, as Oracle has provided the built-in CYCLE clause that will make short work of detecting cycles in recursive queries. It is somewhat more robust than the CONNECT_BY_ISCYCLE pseudocolum in that it lets you determine what values will be used to indicate a cycle, as well as providing a column name at the same time. Listing 10-24 uses the same data error as in Listing 10-23, but this time you will use a recursive subfactored query.

Listing 10-24. *Detect Cycles in Recursive Queries*

```
1 update hr.employees set manager_id = 171 where employee_id = 100;
1 row updated.
Elapsed: 00:00:00.00

  1  with emp(employee_id,manager_id,last_name,first_name,lvl) as (
  2  select e.employee_id
  3    , null as manager_id
  4    , e.last_name
  5    , e.first_name
  6    , 1 as lvl
  7  from hr.employees  e
  8  where e.employee_id =100
  9  union all
 10  select e.employee_id
 11    , e.manager_id
 12    , e.last_name
 13    , e.first_name
 14    , emp.lvl + 1 as lvl
 15  from hr.employees e
 16  join emp on emp.employee_id = e.manager_id
 17  )
 18  search depth first by last_name set order1
 19  CYCLE employee_id SET is_cycle TO '1' DEFAULT '0'
 20  select lpad(' ',2*(lvl-1)) || last_name last_name
 21    , first_name
 22    , employee_id
 23    , lvl
 24    , is_cycle
 25  from emp
 26  order by order1;
```

```
LAST_NAME                 FIRST_NAME   EMPLOYEE_ID        LVL I
------------------------- ------------ ----------- ---------- -
King                      Steven               100          1 0
  Cambrault               Gerald               148          2 0
    Bates                 Elizabeth            172          3 0
    Bloom                 Harrison             169          3 0
    Fox                   Tayler               170          3 0
    Kumar                 Sundita              173          3 0
    Ozer                  Lisa                 168          3 0
    Smith                 William              171          3 0
        King                  Steven               100          4 1
...

108 rows selected.

Elapsed: 00:00:00.04
  1  select last_name, first_name, employee_id, manager_id
  2  from hr.employees
  3  where employee_id = 100;

LAST_NAME                 FIRST_NAME   EMPLOYEE_ID MANAGER_ID
------------------------- ------------ ----------- ----------
King                      Steven               100        171
1 row selected.

  1  rollback;
```

Notice how the CYCLE clause lets you set the two possible values for the IS_CYCLE column to 0 or 1. Only single value characters are allowed here. The name of the column is also user defined, and is set to IS_CYCLE in this example. Examining the output, it appears that the CYCLE clause in RSF does a somewhat better job of identifying the row that causes the data cycle. The row with the error is identified clearly as that of King, so you can query that row and immediately determine the error.

The CONNECT_BY_ISLEAF Pseudocolumn

Finally, there is the CONNECT_BY_ISLEAF pseudocolumn. This permits easy identification of leaf[9] nodes in hierarchical data. You can see that leaf nodes are identified in the output of Listing 10-25 when the value of CONNECT_BY_ISLEAF is 1.

Listing 10-25. *CONNECT_BY_ISLEAF*

```
  1  select lpad(' ',2*(level-1)) || e.last_name last_name, connect_by_isleaf
  2  from hr.employees e
  3  start with e.manager_id is null
  4  connect by prior e.employee_id = e.manager_id
  5  order siblings by e.last_name;
```

---

[9] A leaf node is a node in the hierarchical tree that has no children.

```
LAST_NAME                 CONNECT_BY_ISLEAF
------------------------- ------------------
King                                      0
  Cambrault                               0
    Bates                                 1
    Bloom                                 1
    Fox                                   1
    Kumar                                 1
    Ozer                                  1
    Smith                                 1
  De Haan                                 0
    Hunold                                0
      Austin                              1
      Ernst                               1
      Lorentz                             1
      Pataballa                           1
...

107 rows selected.
```

```
---------------------------------------------------------------------------
| Id  | Operation                             |  Name      |  E-Rows  |
---------------------------------------------------------------------------
|   0 |  SELECT STATEMENT                     |            |          |
|*  1 |    CONNECT BY NO FILTERING WITH START-WITH |       |          |
|   2 |      TABLE ACCESS FULL                |  EMPLOYEES |    107   |
---------------------------------------------------------------------------
```

Duplicating this in RSF is somewhat of a challenge. There are probably many methods that can be used to accomplish this, with some limitations. This is one of those problems that may require a little extra thought to solve, where "solve" means you get the output you desire, but you won't necessarily completely duplicate the functionality of CONNECT_BY_ISLEAF.

In this case, you want to identify the leaf nodes in the employee hierarchy. By definition, none of the leaf nodes can be managers, so one way to accomplish this is to determine which rows are those of managers. All rows that are not those of managers are then leaf nodes.

Listing 10-26 uses this approach to solve the problem. The cost of solving it is two more extra scans of the HR.EMPLOYEES table and three index scans, but if RSF must be used, this is one way to get the desired results. The LEAVES subquery is used find the leaf nodes. This is then left outer joined to the EMPLOYEES table, and the value (or lack of a value) of LEAVES.EMPLOYEE_ID column indicates if the current row is a leaf.

Listing 10-26. *Finding Leaf Nodes in a Recursive Query*

```
1  with leaves as (
2   select employee_id
3   from hr.employees
4   where employee_id not in (
5      select manager_id
6      from hr.employees
```

```
 7       where manager_id is not null
 8   )
 9   ),
10   emp(manager_id,employee_id,last_name,lvl,isleaf) as (
11   select e.manager_id, e.employee_id, e.last_name, 1 as lvl, 0 as isleaf
12   from hr.employees e
13   where e.manager_id is null
14   union all
15   select e.manager_id,nvl(e.employee_id,null) employee_id,e.last_name,emp.lvl + 1 as lvl
16     , decode(l.employee_id,null,0,1) isleaf
17   from hr.employees e
18   join emp on emp.employee_id = e.manager_id
19   left outer join leaves l on l.employee_id = e.employee_id
20   )
21   search depth first by last_name set order1
22   select lpad(' ',2*(lvl-1)) || last_name last_name, isleaf
23   from emp;
```

```
LAST_NAME                    ISLEAF
------------------------- ----------
King                             0
  Cambrault                      0
    Bates                        1
    Bloom                        1
    Fox                          1
    Kumar                        1
    Ozer                         1
    Smith                        1
  De Haan                        0
    Hunold                       0
      Austin                     1
      Ernst                      1
      Lorentz                    1
      Pataballa                  1
...
107 rows selected.
```

```
---------------------------------------------------------------------
| Id  | Operation                             | Name      | E-Rows |
---------------------------------------------------------------------
|   0 | SELECT STATEMENT                      |           |        |
|   1 |  VIEW                                 |           |      7 |
|   2 |   UNION ALL (RECURSIVE WITH) DEPTH FIRST|         |        |
|*  3 |    TABLE ACCESS FULL                  | EMPLOYEES |      1 |
|   4 |    NESTED LOOPS OUTER                 |           |      6 |
|   5 |     NESTED LOOPS                      |           |      6 |
|   6 |      RECURSIVE WITH PUMP              |           |        |
```

```
|    7 |       TABLE ACCESS BY INDEX ROWID      | EMPLOYEES      |    6 |
|*   8 |         INDEX RANGE SCAN               | EMP_MANAGER_IX |    6 |
|    9 |       VIEW PUSHED PREDICATE            |                |    1 |
|   10 |        NESTED LOOPS ANTI               |                |    1 |
|*  11 |          INDEX UNIQUE SCAN             | EMP_EMP_ID_PK  |    1 |
|*  12 |          INDEX RANGE SCAN              | EMP_MANAGER_IX |    6 |
-----------------------------------------------------------------------------
```

Another way to accomplish this is seen in Listing 10-27. Here the analytic function LEAD() uses the value of the LVL column to determine if a row is a leaf node. While it does avoid two of the index scans that were seen in Listing 10-26, correctly determining if a row is a leaf node is dependent on the order of the output, as seen in line 16. The LEAD() function depends on the value of the LAST_NAME_ORDER column that is set in the SEARCH clause.

Listing 10-27. *Using LEAD() to Find Leaf Nodes*

```
 1  with emp(manager_id,employee_id,last_name,lvl) as (
 2    select e.manager_id, e.employee_id, e.last_name, 1 as lvl
 3    from hr.employees e
 4    where e.manager_id is null
 5    union all
 6    select e.manager_id, nvl(e.employee_id,null) employee_id
 7       , e.last_name, emp.lvl + 1 as lvl
 8    from hr.employees e
 9    join emp on emp.employee_id = e.manager_id
10  )
11  search depth first by last_name set last_name_order
12  select lpad(' ',2*(lvl-1)) || last_name last_name,
13    lvl,
14    lead(lvl) over (order by last_name_order) leadlvlorder,
15    case
16    when ( lvl - lead(lvl) over (order by last_name_order) ) < 0
17    then 0
18    else 1
19    end isleaf
20  from emp;
```

LAST_NAME	LVL	LEADLVLORDER	ISLEAF
King	1	2	0
Cambrault	2	3	0
Bates	3	3	1
Bloom	3	3	1
Fox	3	3	1
Kumar	3	3	1
Ozer	3	3	1
Smith	3	2	1
De Haan	**2**	**3**	**0**

```
     Hunold                      3            4            0
       Austin                    4            4            1
       Ernst                     4            4            1
       Lorentz                   4            4            1
       Pataballa                 4            2            1
...
107 rows selected.
```

```
-------------------------------------------------------------------------
| Id  | Operation                                | Name          | E-Rows |
-------------------------------------------------------------------------
|   0 | SELECT STATEMENT                         |               |        |
|   1 |  WINDOW BUFFER                           |               |      7 |
|   2 |   VIEW                                   |               |      7 |
|   3 |    UNION ALL (RECURSIVE WITH) DEPTH FIRST|               |        |
|*  4 |     TABLE ACCESS FULL                    | EMPLOYEES     |      1 |
|   5 |     NESTED LOOPS                         |               |        |
|   6 |      NESTED LOOPS                        |               |      6 |
|   7 |       RECURSIVE WITH PUMP                |               |        |
|*  8 |       INDEX RANGE SCAN                   | EMP_MANAGER_IX|      6 |
|   9 |      TABLE ACCESS BY INDEX ROWID         | EMPLOYEES     |      6 |
-------------------------------------------------------------------------
```

What might happen if the SEARCH clause is changed from DEPTH FIRST to BREADTH first? The results are shown in Listing 10-28. The use of the LEAD() function appears at first an elegant solution, but it is somewhat fragile in its dependency on the order of the data. The example in Listing 10-26 will work regardless of the SEARCH clause parameters. It is readily apparent that the output in Listing 10-28 is incorrect.

Listing 10-28. *LEAD() with BREADTH FIRST*

```
 1  with emp(manager_id,employee_id,last_name,lvl) as (
 2   select e.manager_id, e.employee_id, e.last_name, 1 as lvl
 3   from hr.employees e
 4   where e.manager_id is null
 5   union all
 6   select e.manager_id, nvl(e.employee_id,null) employee_id
 7      , e.last_name, emp.lvl + 1 as lvl
 8   from hr.employees e
 9   join emp on emp.employee_id = e.manager_id
10  )
11  search breadth first by last_name set last_name_order
12  select lpad(' ',2*(lvl-1)) || last_name last_name,
13   lvl,
14   lead(lvl) over (order by last_name_order) leadlvlorder,
15   case
16   when ( lvl - lead(lvl) over (order by last_name_order) ) < 0
17   then 0
```

```
18    else 1
19    end isleaf
20  from emp;
```

LAST_NAME	LVL	LEADLVLORDER	ISLEAF
King	1	2	0
Cambrault	2	2	1
De Haan	**2**	**2**	**1**
Errazuriz	2	2	1
Fripp	2	2	1
Hartstein	2	2	1
Kaufling	2	2	1

Summary

While the functionality of CONNECT BY can be duplicated for most practical purposes in recursive subfactored queries, the question is, should you do so? In many cases, the CONNECT BY syntax is simpler to use, though the syntax does take some getting used to. Doing the same things in RSF requires quite a bit more SQL in most cases. In addition, CONNECT BY may produce better execution plans than RSF, especially for relatively simple queries. Keep in mind, however, that RSF is a new feature, and will likely improve in later versions of Oracle.

Also, there may be good reasons to not use CONNECT BY. Perhaps you need to maintain ANSI compatibility in your application. Or perhaps the ability to write hierarchical queries that will work in other databases that support recursive common table expressions would simplify the code for an application that runs on databases from different vendors. In that circumstance, RSF is quite useful.

Whatever the need for hierarchical queries, with a little ingenuity you can write suitable queries on hierarchical data using recursive subfactored queries, and they will be capable of doing everything that can currently be done with CONNECT BY.

■ ■ ■

Semi-joins and Anti-joins

Kerry Osborne

Semi-joins and anti-joins are two closely related join methods (options of join methods, actually) that the Oracle optimizer can choose to apply when retrieving information. The SQL language is designed to specify the set of data that the user wishes to retrieve, but to leave the decisions as to how to actually navigate to the data up to the database itself. Therefore, there is no SQL syntax to specifically invoke a particular join method. Of course, Oracle does provide the ability to give the optimizer directives via hints. This chapter will cover these two join optimization options, the SQL syntax that can provoke them, requirements for and restrictions on their use, and finally, some guidance on when and how they should be used.

It is important to be aware that Oracle is constantly improving the optimizer code and that not all details of its behavior are documented. All examples were created on an Oracle 11gR2 database (11.2.0.1). My version of 11g currently has 2399 parameters, many of which affect the way the optimizer behaves. Where appropriate, I will mention parameter settings that have a direct bearing on the topics at hand. However, you should verify the behavior on your own system.

Semi-joins

A semi-join is a join between two sets of data (tables) where rows from the first set are returned, based on the presence or absence of at least one matching row in the other set. We'll come back to the "absence" of a matching row later—that is a special case of the semi-join called an anti-join. If you think back to your days in grade school math, you should be able to visualize this operation with a typical set theory picture such as the one shown in Figure 11-1.

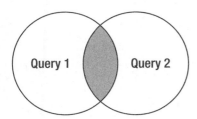

Figure 11-1. *Ilustration of a semi-join*

Figure 11-1 provides a basic idea of what a semi-join is but it's not detailed enough to describe the nuances. Diagrams of this sort are called Venn diagrams; this particular Venn diagram is commonly used to illustrate an inner join, which is essentially an intersection. Unfortunately, there is not a convenient way to fully describe a semi-join with a Venn diagram. The main difference between a normal inner join and a semi-join is that with a semi-join, each record in the first set (Query 1 in the diagram) is returned only once, regardless of how many matches there are in the second set (Query 2 in the diagram). This definition implies that the actual processing of the query can be optimized by stopping Query 2 as soon as the first match is found. And at its heart, that's what a semi-join is: the optimization that allows processing to stop before the Query 2 part is complete. This join technique is a choice that's available to Oracle's cost-based optimizer when the query contains a sub-query inside of an IN or EXISTS clause (or inside the rarely used =ANY clause which is synonymous with IN). The syntax should look pretty familiar. Listings 11-1 and 11-2 show examples of the two most common forms of semi-join queries using IN and EXISTS.

Listing 11-1. *Semi-join IN example*

```
SQL>
SQL> select /* using in */ department_name
  2   from hr.departments dept
  3   where department_id IN (select department_id from hr.employees emp);

DEPARTMENT_NAME
------------------------------
Administration
Marketing
Purchasing
Human Resources
Shipping
IT
Public Relations
Sales
Executive
Finance
Accounting

11 rows selected.
```

Listing 11-2. *Semi-join EXISTS example*

```
SQL> select /* using exists */ department_name
  2   from hr.departments dept
  3   where EXISTS (select null from hr.employees emp
  4                 where emp.department_id = dept.department_id);

DEPARTMENT_NAME
------------------------------
Administration
Marketing
Purchasing
Human Resources
Shipping
```

```
IT
Public Relations
Sales
Executive
Finance
Accounting

11 rows selected.
```

These two queries are functionally equivalent. That is to say that they will always return the same set of data, given the same inputs. There are several other forms that are closely related. Listings 11-3 through 11-6 show several examples of closely related alternatives.

Listing 11-3. *Alternatives to EXISTS and IN – Inner Join*

```
SQL> select /* inner join */ department_name
  2  from hr.departments dept, hr.employees emp
  3  where dept.department_id = emp.department_id;

DEPARTMENT_NAME
------------------------------
Administration
Marketing
Marketing
Purchasing
Purchasing
Shipping
IT
IT
Public Relations
Sales
Sales
. . .
Executive
Finance
Finance
Accounting

106 rows selected.
```

Obviously the inner join is not functionally equivalent to the semi-join due to the number of rows returned. You'll also notice that there are many repeating values. Let's try using a DISTINCT to eliminate the duplicates. Look at Listing 11-4.

Listing 11-4. *Alternatives to EXISTS and IN – Inner Join with Distinct*

```
SQL> select /* inner join with distinct */ distinct department_name
  2  from hr.departments dept, hr.employees emp
  3  where dept.department_id = emp.department_id;
```

```
DEPARTMENT_NAME
------------------------------
Administration
Accounting
Purchasing
Human Resources
IT
Public Relations
Executive
Shipping
Sales
Finance
Marketing

11 rows selected.
```

The inner join with DISTINCT looks pretty good. In this case, it actually returns the same exact set of records. As previously mentioned, the INTERSECT set operation is very close to a semi-join so let's try that next in Listing 11-5.

Listing 11-5. *Alternatives to EXISTS and IN – Ugly Intersect*

```
SQL> select /* ugly intersect */ department_name
  2  from hr.departments dept,
  3    (select department_id from hr.departments
  4      intersect
  5      select department_id from hr.employees) b
  6  where b.department_id = dept.department_id;

DEPARTMENT_NAME
------------------------------
Administration
Marketing
Purchasing
Human Resources
Shipping
IT
Public Relations
Sales
Executive
Finance
Accounting

11 rows selected.
```

The intersect also looks pretty good but the syntax is convoluted. Finally, let's try the somewhat obscure =ANY key word with a subquery in Listing 11-6.

Listing 11-6. *Alternatives to EXISTS and IN – =ANY Subquery*

```
SQL> select /* ANY subquery */ department_name
  2  from hr.departments dept
  3  where department_id = ANY (select department_id from hr.employees emp);

DEPARTMENT_NAME
------------------------------
Administration
Marketing
Purchasing
Human Resources
Shipping
IT
Public Relations
Sales
Executive
Finance
Accounting

11 rows selected.
```

There isn't much to say about the =ANY version since it is merely an alternate way of writing IN. So to recap, the query in Listing 11-3 (inner join) doesn't look promising as it obviously doesn't return the same set of data. Because it returns a row for each match, the total number of records returned is 106 instead of 11. Let's skip over the second one using the DISTINCT operator for a moment. Note that the query in Listing 11-5 (an ugly intersect), although it returns the correct set of records, doesn't look promising either because it uses convoluted syntax, even for the simple case I'm illustrating. Of course, the query in Listing 11-6 (using the =ANY syntax) is exactly the same as the IN version, since IN and =ANY are the same thing.

The query in Listing 11-4 (inner join with distinct) looks promising, but is it functionally equivalent to the queries in Listings 11-1 and 11-2? The short answer is no, it's not. In many situations the inner join with distinct query will return the same data as a semi-join (using IN or EXISTS), as it does in this case. But that's due to a convenient fluke of the data model and it does not make the query in Listing 11-3 equivalent to the semi-join queries in Listing 11-1 and 11-2. Consider the example in Listing 11-7 which shows a case where the two forms return different results.

Listing 11-7. *Semi-join and DISTINCT Are Not The Same*

```
SQL> select /* SEMI using IN */ department_id
  2  from hr.employees
  3  where department_id in (select department_id from hr.departments);

DEPARTMENT_ID
-------------
           10
           20
           20
           30
           30
```

```
                   30
                   30
                   30
                   30
                   40
                   50
                   50
                   50
                   . . .
                   80
                  110
                  110

106 rows selected.

SQL>
SQL> select /* inner join with distinct */ distinct emp.department_id
  2  from hr.departments dept, hr.employees emp
  3  where dept.department_id = emp.department_id;

DEPARTMENT_ID
-------------
           10
           20
           30
           40
           50
           60
           70
           80
           90
          100
          110

11 rows selected.
```

So it's clear from this example that the two constructs are not equivalent. The IN/EXISTS form takes each record in the first set and, if there is at least one match in the second set, returns the record. It does not apply a DISTINCT operator at the end of the processing (i.e. it doesn't sort and throw away duplicates). Therefore, it is possible to get repeating values, assuming that there are duplicates in the records returned by Query 1. The DISTINCT form, on the other hand, retrieves all the rows, sorts them, and then throws away any duplicate values. As you can see from the example, these are clearly not the same. And as you might expect from the description, the DISTINCT version can end up doing significantly more work, as it has no chance to bail out of the subquery early. We'll talk more about that shortly.

There is another common mistake that is made with the EXISTS syntax that should probably be mentioned. If you use EXISTS, you need to make sure you include a subquery that is correlated to the outer query. If the subquery does not reference the outer query, it's meaningless. Listing 11-8 shows an example from a web page that is currently number one on Google for the search term "Oracle EXISTS".

Listing 11-8. *Common Mistake with EXISTS – Non-Correlated Subquery*

```
Select
    book_key
from
    book
 where
    exists (select book_key from sales) ;
```

Because the subquery in this example is not related to the outer query, the end result will be to return every record in the BOOK table (as long as there is at least one record in the SALES table). This is probably not what the author of this statement intended. Listing 11-9 shows a few examples demonstrating the difference between using correlated and non-correlated subqueries: the first two showing EXISTS with a proper correlated subquery, and the last two showing EXISTS with non-correlated subqueries.

Listing 11-9. *Common Mistake with EXISTS – Correlated vs. Non-Correlated Subquery*

```
SQL> select /* correlated */ department_id
  2      from hr.departments dept
  3      where exists (select department_id from hr.employees emp
  4                        where emp.department_id = dept.department_id);

DEPARTMENT_ID
-------------
           10
           20
           30
           40
           50
           60
           70
           80
           90
          100
          110

11 rows selected.

SQL>
SQL> select /* not correlated */ department_id
  2      from hr.departments dept
  3      where exists (select department_id from hr.employees emp );

DEPARTMENT_ID
-------------
           10
           20
           30
```

```
                    40
                    50
                    60
                    70
                    80
                    90
                   100
                   110
                   120
                   130
                   140
                   150
                   160
                   170
                   180
                   190
                   200
                   210
                   220
                   230
                   240
                   250
                   260
                   270

27 rows selected.

SQL>
SQL> select /* not correlated no nulls */ department_id
  2      from hr.departments dept
  3      where exists (select department_id from hr.employees emp where department_id↵
 is not null);

DEPARTMENT_ID
-------------
           10
           20
           30
           40
           50
           60
           70
           80
           90
          100
          110
          120
```

```
                130
                140
                150
                160
                170
                180
                190
                200
                210
                220
                230
                240
                250
                260
                270

27 rows selected.

SQL>
SQL> select /* non-correlated totally unrelated */ department_id
  2      from hr.departments dept
  3      where exists (select null from dual);

DEPARTMENT_ID
-------------
             10
             20
             30
             40
             50
             60
             70
             80
             90
            100
            110
            120
            130
            140
            150
            160
            170
            180
            190
            200
            210
            220
```

```
            230
            240
            250
            260
            270

27 rows selected.

SQL>
SQL> select /* non-correlated empty subquery */ department_id
  2       from hr.departments dept
  3       where exists (select 'anything' from dual where 1=2);

no rows selected
```

So the correlated queries get the records we expect (i.e. only the ones that have a match in the second query). Obviously, the non-correlated subqueries do not work as expected. They return every record from the first table, which is actually what you've asked for if you write a query that way. In fact, as you can see in the next-to-last example (having the non-correlated query against the dual table), no matter what you select in the subquery, all the records from the first table are returned. The last example shows what happens when no records are returned from the subquery. In that case, no records are returned at all. So, without a correlated subquery, you either get all the records in the outer query or none of the records in the outer query, without regard to what the inner query is actually doing.

Semi-join Plans

I mentioned in the introduction that semi-joins are not really a join method on their own, but rather an option of other join methods. The three most common join methods in Oracle are nested loops, hash joins, and merge joins. Each of these methods can have the semi option applied to it. Remember also that it is an optimization that allows processing to stop when the first match is found in the subquery. Let's use a little pseudo code to more fully describe the process. The outer query is Q1 and the inner (subquery) is Q2. What you see in Listing 11-10 is the basic processing of a nested loop semi-join.

Listing 11-10. *Pseudo Code for Nested Loop Semi-join*

```
open Q1
while Q1 still has records
   fetch record from Q1
   result = false
   open Q2
   while Q2 still has records
      fetch record from Q2
      if (Q1.record matches Q2.record) then    ←= semi-join optimization
         result = true
         exit loop
      end if
   end loop
   close Q2
```

```
    if (result = true) return Q1 record
end loop
close Q1
```

The optimization provided by the semi option is the IF statement that lets the code exit the inner loop as soon as it finds a match. Obviously, with large data sets, this technique can result in significant time savings when compared to a normal nested loops join that must loop through every record returned by the inner query for every row in the outer query. At this point, you may be thinking that this technique could save a lot of time with a nested loops join vs. the other two. And you'd be right because the other two have to get all the records from the inner query before they start checking for matches. So the nested loops joins generally have the most to gain from this technique. Keep in mind that the optimizer still picks which join method to use based on its costing algorithms, which include the various semi options.

Now let's re-run the queries from Listings 11-1 and 11-2 and look at the plans the optimizer generates (shown in Listing 11-11)..

Listing 11-11. *Semi-join Execution Plans*

```
SQL> -- semi_ex1.sql
SQL>
SQL> select /* in */ department_name
  2      from hr.departments dept
  3      where department_id in (select department_id from hr.employees emp);

DEPARTMENT_NAME
------------------------------
Administration
Marketing
Purchasing
Human Resources
Shipping
IT
Public Relations
Sales
Executive
Finance
Accounting

11 rows selected.


Execution Plan
----------------------------------------------------------
Plan hash value: 2605691773

---------------------------------------------------------------------------
|Id| Operation          | Name          |Rows|Bytes|Cost (%CPU)| Time      |
---------------------------------------------------------------------------
| 0| SELECT STATEMENT   |               | 10| 190|    3   (0)| 00:00:01 |
```

```
| 1|   NESTED LOOPS SEMI |                   |  10|  190|   3   (0)| 00:00:01 |
| 2|    TABLE ACCESS FULL|  DEPARTMENTS      |  27|  432|   3   (0)| 00:00:01 |
|*3|     INDEX RANGE SCAN |  EMP_DEPARTMENT_IX |  41|  123|   0   (0)| 00:00:01 |
---------------------------------------------------------------------------

Predicate Information (identified by operation id):
---------------------------------------------------

   3 - access("DEPARTMENT_ID"="DEPARTMENT_ID")


Statistics
----------------------------------------------------------
          0  recursive calls
          0  db block gets
         11  consistent gets
          0  physical reads
          0  redo size
        622  bytes sent via SQL*Net to client
        420  bytes received via SQL*Net from client
          2  SQL*Net roundtrips to/from client
          0  sorts (memory)
          0  sorts (disk)
         11  rows processed

SQL>
SQL> select /* exists */ department_name
  2      from hr.departments dept
  3      where exists (select null from hr.employees emp
  4                      where emp.department_id = dept.department_id);

DEPARTMENT_NAME
------------------------------
Administration
Marketing
Purchasing
Human Resources
Shipping
IT
Public Relations
Sales
Executive
Finance
Accounting

11 rows selected.
```

Execution Plan

Plan hash value: 2605691773

```
---------------------------------------------------------------------------
|Id|Operation              |Name             |Rows|Bytes|Cost (%CPU)|Time     |
---------------------------------------------------------------------------
| 0|SELECT STATEMENT       |                 |  10|  190|   3   (0)| 00:00:01 |
| 1| NESTED LOOPS SEMI     |                 |  10|  190|   3   (0)| 00:00:01 |
| 2|  TABLE ACCESS FULL|DEPARTMENTS          |  27|  432|   3   (0)| 00:00:01 |
|*3|  INDEX RANGE SCAN |EMP_DEPARTMENT_IX    |  41|  123|   0   (0)| 00:00:01 |
---------------------------------------------------------------------------
```

Predicate Information (identified by operation id):
----

   3 - access("EMP"."DEPARTMENT_ID"="DEPT"."DEPARTMENT_ID")

Statistics

```
          0  recursive calls
          0  db block gets
         11  consistent gets
          0  physical reads
          0  redo size
        622  bytes sent via SQL*Net to client
        420  bytes received via SQL*Net from client
          2  SQL*Net roundtrips to/from client
          0  sorts (memory)
          0  sorts (disk)
         11  rows processed
```

The autotrace statistics are included so that you can see that these statements are indeed processed the same way. The plans are identical and the statistics are identical. I make this point to dispel the long held belief that queries written with EXIST behave very differently than queries written with IN. This was an issue in the past (version 8i), but it has not been an issue for many years. The truth is that the optimizer can and does transform queries in both forms to the same statement.

Note that there is a way to get a better idea of the decision making process that the optimizer goes through when parsing a statement. You can have the optimizer log its actions in a trace file by issuing the following command:

```
alter session set events '10053 trace name context forever, level 1';
```

Setting this event will cause a trace file to be created in the USER_DUMP_DEST directory when a hard parse is performed. I call it "Wolfganging" because Wolfgang Breitling was the first guy to really analyze the content of these 10053 trace files and publish his findings. For further information, please refer to Wolfgang's paper called "A Look Under the Hood of CBO." At any rate, a close look at 10053 trace data for each statement will confirm that both statements are transformed into the same statement before the optimizer determines a plan. Listing 11-12 and 11-13 show excerpts of 10053 trace files generated for both the IN and the EXISTS versions.

Listing 11-12. *Excerpts from 10053 trace for IN version*

```
****************
QUERY BLOCK TEXT
****************
select /* using in */ department_name
    from hr.departments dept
    where department_id IN (select department_id from hr.employees emp)


****************************
Cost-Based Subquery Unnesting
****************************
SU: Unnesting query blocks in query block SEL$1 (#1) that are valid to unnest.
Subquery removal for query block SEL$2 (#2)
RSW: Not valid for subquery removal SEL$2 (#2)
Subquery unchanged.
Subquery Unnesting on query block SEL$1 (#1)SU: Performing unnesting that does not require
costing.
SU: Considering subquery unnest on query block SEL$1 (#1).
SU:   Checking validity of unnesting subquery SEL$2 (#2)
SU:   Passed validity checks.
SU:   Transforming ANY subquery to a join.

Final query after transformations:******* UNPARSED QUERY IS *******
SELECT "DEPT"."DEPARTMENT_NAME" "DEPARTMENT_NAME" FROM "HR"."EMPLOYEES"
"EMP","HR"."DEPARTMENTS" "DEPT" WHERE "DEPT"."DEPARTMENT_ID"="EMP"."DEPARTMENT_ID"
```

Listing 11-13. *Excerpts from 10053 trace for EXISTS version*

```
****************
QUERY BLOCK TEXT
****************
select /* using exists */ department_name
    from hr.departments dept
    where EXISTS (select null from hr.employees emp
                  where emp.department_id = dept.department_id)


****************************
Cost-Based Subquery Unnesting
****************************
SU: Unnesting query blocks in query block SEL$1 (#1) that are valid to unnest.
Subquery Unnesting on query block SEL$1 (#1)SU: Performing unnesting that does not↵
 require costing.
SU: Considering subquery unnest on query block SEL$1 (#1).
SU:   Checking validity of unnesting subquery SEL$2 (#2)
```

```
SU:    Passed validity checks.
SU:    Transforming EXISTS subquery to a join.

Final query after transformations:******* UNPARSED QUERY IS *******
SELECT "DEPT"."DEPARTMENT_NAME" "DEPARTMENT_NAME" FROM "HR"."EMPLOYEES"↵
 "EMP","HR"."DEPARTMENTS" "DEPT" WHERE "EMP"."DEPARTMENT_ID"="DEPT"."DEPARTMENT_ID"
```

As you can see in the trace file excerpts, subquery unnesting has occurred on both queries and they have both been transformed into the same statement (i.e. the "Final query after transformations" section is exactly the same for both versions). Oracle Database 10gR2 behaves the same way, by the way.

Controlling Semi-join Plans

Now let's look at some of the methods to control the execution plan, should the optimizer need a little help. There are two mechanisms at your disposal. One mechanism is a set of hints that you can apply to individual queries. The other is an instance-level parameter affecting all queries.

Controlling Semi-join Plans Using Hints

There are several hints that may be applied to encourage or discourage semi-joins. As of 11gR2, the following hints are available:

SEMIJOIN – perform a semi-join (the optimizer gets to pick which kind)

NO_SEMIJOIN – obviously means don't perform a semi-join

NL_SJ – perform a nested loops semi-join (deprecated as of 10g)

HASH_SJ – perform a hash semi-join (deprecated as of 10g)

MERGE_SJ – perform a merge semi-join (deprecated as of 10g)

The more specific hints (NL_SJ, HASH_SJ, MERGE_SJ) have been deprecated since 10g. Although they continue to work as in the past, even with 11gR2, be aware that the documentation says they may be going away at some point. All of the semi-join related hints need to be specified in the subquery as opposed to in the outer query. Listing 11-14 shows an example using the NO_SEMIJOIN hint.

Listing 11-14. *EXISTS with NO_SEMIJOIN Hint*

```
SQL> set autotrace trace
SQL> -- semi_ex5a.sql - no_semijoin hint
SQL>
SQL> select /* exists no_semijoin */ department_name
  2      from hr.departments dept
  3      where exists (select /*+ no_semijoin */ null from hr.employees emp
  4                          where emp.department_id = dept.department_id);

DEPARTMENT_NAME
------------------------------
Administration
Marketing
```

Purchasing
Human Resources
Shipping
IT
Public Relations
Sales
Executive
Finance
Accounting

11 rows selected.

Execution Plan

Plan hash value: 440241596

```
------------------------------------------------------------------------------
| Id|Operation           |Name           |Rows|Bytes|Cost (%CPU)|Time      |
------------------------------------------------------------------------------
|  0|SELECT STATEMENT    |               |   1|  16|   17   (0)|00:00:01|
|* 1| FILTER             |               |    |    |           |        |
|  2|  TABLE ACCESS FULL | DEPARTMENTS    |  27| 432|    3   (0)|00:00:01|
|* 3|  INDEX RANGE SCAN  | EMP_DEPARTMENT_IX|  2|   6|    1   (0)|00:00:01|
------------------------------------------------------------------------------
```

Predicate Information (identified by operation id):

```
   1 - filter( EXISTS (SELECT 0 FROM "HR"."EMPLOYEES" "EMP" WHERE
           "EMP"."DEPARTMENT_ID"=:B1))
   3 - access("EMP"."DEPARTMENT_ID"=:B1)
```


Statistics

```
          0  recursive calls
          0  db block gets
         35  consistent gets
          0  physical reads
          0  redo size
        622  bytes sent via SQL*Net to client
        419  bytes received via SQL*Net from client
          2  SQL*Net roundtrips to/from client
          0  sorts (memory)
          0  sorts (disk)
         11  rows processed
```

In this example we turned off the optimizer's ability to use semi-joins via the NO_SEMIJOIN hint. As expected, the query no longer does a semi-join, but instead uses a FILTER operation to combine the two row sources. Note that the Predicate Information section of the explain plan output shows the FILTER operation is to enforce the EXISTS clause. As a side note, this informative representation of the filter step is unique to EXPLAIN PLAN, which autotrace does behind the scenes. In general, I am not a fan of the EXPLAIN PLAN statement as it is a separate code path from the actual optimizer. The main reason I don't like it is that it occasionally comes up with a different plan than the optimizer. However, in this case it provides some additional information that is not available to us if we use DBMS_XPLAN to show the actual plan. Listing 11-15 shows the xplan output for the same statement.

Listing 11-15. *EXISTS with NO_SEMIJOIN Hint*

```
SQL> set echo on
SQL> -- semi_ex5b.sql
SQL>
SQL> select sql_id, sql_text from v$sqlarea
  2  where sql_text like 'select /* EXISTS NO_SEMIJOIN */ %';

SQL_ID        SQL_TEXT
------------- ---------------------------------------------------------------
b120fvtzr94an select /* EXISTS NO_SEMIJOIN */ department_name      from
              hr.departments dept    where exists (select /*+ no_semijoin
              */ null from hr.employees emp                      where
              emp.department_id = dept.department_id)


1 row selected.

SQL>
SQL> -- @dplan
SQL> set lines 150
SQL> select * from table(dbms_xplan.display_cursor('b120fvtzr94an',null,'typical'));

PLAN_TABLE_OUTPUT
------------------------------------------------------------------------
SQL_ID  b120fvtzr94an, child number 0
--------------------------------------
select /* EXISTS NO_SEMIJOIN */ department_name     from hr.departments
dept    where exists (select /*+ no_semijoin */ null from hr.employees
emp                 where emp.department_id = dept.department_id)

Plan hash value: 440241596
```

```
----------------------------------------------------------------------
|Id |Operation            |Name             |Rows|Bytes|Cost (%CPU)|Time      |
----------------------------------------------------------------------
|  0|SELECT STATEMENT     |                 |    |     |   17 (100)|          |
|* 1| FILTER              |                 |    |     |           |          |
|  2|  TABLE ACCESS FULL  |DEPARTMENTS      | 27| 432|    3  (0)|00:00:01 |
|* 3|  INDEX RANGE SCAN   |EMP_DEPARTMENT_IX|  2|   6|    1  (0)|00:00:01 |
----------------------------------------------------------------------

Predicate Information (identified by operation id):
---------------------------------------------------

   1 - filter( IS NOT NULL)
   3 - access("EMP"."DEPARTMENT_ID"=:B1)


23 rows selected.
```

As you can see, the filter step in the predicate section is not nearly as informative as it is in the EXPLAIN PLAN output.

Controlling Semi-join Plans at the Instance Level

There is also a hidden parameter that exerts control over the optimizer's semi-join choices: _always_semi_join was a normal parameter originally but was changed to a hidden parameter in 9i. Listing 11-16 shows a list of the valid values for the parameter.

Listing 11-16. *Valid Values for_always_semi_join*

```
SYS@LAB112> select NAME_KSPVLD_VALUES name, VALUE_KSPVLD_VALUES value
  2  from X$KSPVLD_VALUES
  3  where NAME_KSPVLD_VALUES like nvl('&name',NAME_KSPVLD_VALUES);
Enter value for name: _always_semi_join

NAME                VALUE
------------------- -------------------------------------------------
_always_semi_join   HASH
_always_semi_join   MERGE
_always_semi_join   NESTED_LOOPS
_always_semi_join   CHOOSE
_always_semi_join   OFF
```

The parameter has a somewhat misleading name as it does not force semi-joins at all. The default value is CHOOSE, which allows the optimizer to evaluate all the SEMI join methods and choose the one it thinks will be the most efficient. Setting the parameter to HASH, MERGE, or NESTED_LOOPS appears to reduce the optimizer's choices to the specified join method. Setting the parameter to OFF disables semi-joins. The parameter can be set at the session level. Listing 11-17 contains an example showing how the parameter can be used to change the optimizer's choice from NESTED_LOOPS semi to MERGE semi.

Listing 11-17. *Using _always_semi_join to Change Plan to Merge Semi-join*

```
SQL> @semi_ex1a
SQL> -- semi_ex1a.sql
SQL>
SQL> select /* using in */ department_name
  2       from hr.departments dept
  3       where department_id IN (select department_id from hr.employees emp);

DEPARTMENT_NAME
------------------------------
Administration
Marketing
Purchasing
Human Resources
Shipping
IT
Public Relations
Sales
Executive
Finance
Accounting

11 rows selected.


Execution Plan
----------------------------------------------------------
Plan hash value: 2605691773
```

Id	Operation	Name	Rows	Bytes	Cost (%CPU)	Time
0	SELECT STATEMENT		10	190	3 (0)	00:00:01
1	NESTED LOOPS SEMI		10	190	3 (0)	00:00:01
2	TABLE ACCESS FULL	DEPARTMENTS	27	432	3 (0)	00:00:01
* 3	INDEX RANGE SCAN	EMP_DEPARTMENT_IX	41	123	0 (0)	00:00:01

```
Predicate Information (identified by operation id):
---------------------------------------------------

   3 - access("DEPARTMENT_ID"="DEPARTMENT_ID")
```

```
Statistics
----------------------------------------------------------
          0  recursive calls
          0  db block gets
         11  consistent gets
          0  physical reads
          0  redo size
        622  bytes sent via SQL*Net to client
        419  bytes received via SQL*Net from client
          2  SQL*Net roundtrips to/from client
          0  sorts (memory)
          0  sorts (disk)
         11  rows processed

SQL> alter session set "_always_semi_join"=MERGE;

Session altered.

SQL> @semi_ex1a
SQL> -- semi_ex1a.sql
SQL>
SQL> select /* using in */ department_name
  2      from hr.departments dept
  3      where department_id IN (select department_id from hr.employees emp);

DEPARTMENT_NAME
------------------------------
Administration
Marketing
Purchasing
Human Resources
Shipping
IT
Public Relations
Sales
Executive
Finance
Accounting

11 rows selected.


Execution Plan
----------------------------------------------------------
Plan hash value: 954076352
```

```
--------------------------------------------------------------------------
|Id|Operation            |Name             |Rows|Bytes|Cost (%CPU)|Time    |
--------------------------------------------------------------------------
| 0|SELECT STATEMENT     |                 | 10| 190|    4  (25)|00:00:01|
| 1| MERGE JOIN SEMI     |                 | 10| 190|    4  (25)|00:00:01|
| 2|  TABLE ACCESS BY    |DEPARTMENTS      | 27| 432|    2   (0)|00:00:01|
  |   INDEX ROWID        |                 |   |    |           |        |
| 3|   INDEX FULL SCAN   |DEPT_ID_PK       | 27|    |    1   (0)|00:00:01|
|*4|  SORT UNIQUE        |                 |107| 321|    2  (50)|00:00:01|
| 5|   INDEX FULL SCAN   |EMP_DEPARTMENT_IX|107| 321|    1   (0)|00:00:01|
--------------------------------------------------------------------------

Predicate Information (identified by operation id):
---------------------------------------------------

   4 - access("DEPARTMENT_ID"="DEPARTMENT_ID")
       filter("DEPARTMENT_ID"="DEPARTMENT_ID")


Statistics
----------------------------------------------------------
          0  recursive calls
          0  db block gets
          5  consistent gets
          0  physical reads
          0  redo size
        622  bytes sent via SQL*Net to client
        419  bytes received via SQL*Net from client
          2  SQL*Net roundtrips to/from client
          1  sorts (memory)
          0  sorts (disk)
         11  rows processed
```

Semi-join Restrictions

There is only one major documented restriction controlling when the optimizer can use a semi-join (in 11gR2). The optimizer will not choose a semi-join for any subqueries inside of an OR branch. In previous versions of Oracle, the inclusion of the DISTINCT key word would also disable semi-joins, but that restriction no longer exists. Listing 11-18 contains an example showing a semi-join being disabled inside an OR branch.

Listing 11-18. *Using _always_semi_join to Change Plan to Merge Semi-join*

```
SQL> select /* exists with or */ department_name
  2      from hr.departments dept
  3      where 1=2 or exists (select null from hr.employees emp
  4                    where emp.department_id = dept.department_id);
```

```
DEPARTMENT_NAME
------------------------------
Administration
Marketing
Purchasing
Human Resources
Shipping
IT
Public Relations
Sales
Executive
Finance
Accounting

11 rows selected.


Execution Plan
------------------------------------------------------------
Plan hash value: 440241596

---------------------------------------------------------------------------
|Id|Operation          |Name             |Rows|Bytes|Cost (%CPU)|Time     |
---------------------------------------------------------------------------
| 0|SELECT STATEMENT    |                 | 27| 432|    4  (0)|00:00:01|
|*1| FILTER             |                 |   |    |          |         |
| 2|  TABLE ACCESS FULL |DEPARTMENTS      | 27| 432|    3  (0)|00:00:01|
|*3|  INDEX RANGE SCAN  |EMP_DEPARTMENT_IX|  2|   6|    1  (0)|00:00:01|
---------------------------------------------------------------------------

Predicate Information (identified by operation id):
---------------------------------------------------

   1 - filter( EXISTS (SELECT 0 FROM "HR"."EMPLOYEES" "EMP" WHERE
          "EMP"."DEPARTMENT_ID"=:B1))
   3 - access("EMP"."DEPARTMENT_ID"=:B1)


Statistics
------------------------------------------------------------
          1  recursive calls
          0  db block gets
         35  consistent gets
          0  physical reads
          0  redo size
        622  bytes sent via SQL*Net to client
        420  bytes received via SQL*Net from client
```

```
 2  SQL*Net roundtrips to/from client
 0  sorts (memory)
 0  sorts (disk)
11  rows processed
```

Semi-join Requirements

Semi-joins are an optimization that can dramatically improve performance of some queries. They are not used that often, however. Here, briefly, are the requirements for Oracle's cost based optimizer to decide to use a semi-join:

- The statement must use either the keyword IN (= ANY) or the keyword EXISTS

- The statement must have a subquery in the IN or EXISTS clause

- If the statement uses the EXISTS syntax, it must use a correlated subquery (to get the expected results)

- The IN or EXISTS clause may not be contained inside an OR branch

Many systems have queries with massive numbers of literals (thousands sometimes) inside IN clauses. These are often generated statements that get populated by doing a query to find the list in the first place. These statements can occasionally benefit from being rewritten to let the optimizer take advantage of a semi-join. That is, taking the query that populated the literals in the IN clause and combining it with the original, instead of running them as two separate queries.

One of the reasons that developers avoid this approach is fear of the unknown. The IN and EXISTS syntax was at one time processed very differently, leading to situations where performance could vary considerably depending on the method chosen. The good news is that the optimizer is smart enough now to transform either form into a semi-join, or not, depending on the optimizer costing algorithms. The question of whether to implement a correlated subquery with EXISTS or the more simple IN construct is now pretty much a mute point from a performance standpoint. And with that being the case, there seems to be little reason to use the more complicated EXISTS format. No piece of software is perfect, though; occasionally, the optimizer makes incorrect choices. Fortunately, when the optimizer does make a mistake, there are tools available to "encourage" it to do the right thing.

Anti-joins

Anti-joins are basically the same as semi-joins in that they are an optimization option that can be applied to nested loop, hash, and merge joins. However, they are the opposite of semi-joins in terms of the data they return. Those mathematician types familiar with relational algebra would say that anti-joins can be defined as the complement of semi-joins.

Figure 11-2 shows a Venn diagram that is commonly used to illustrate a MINUS operation (all the records from table A, MINUS the records from table B).

The diagram in Figure 11-2 is a reasonable representation of an anti-join as well. The *Oracle Database SQL Language Reference, 11g Release 2* describes the anti-join this way:

> *An anti-join returns rows from the left side of the predicate for which there are no corresponding rows on the right side of the predicate. It returns rows that fail to match (NOT IN) the subquery on the right side.*

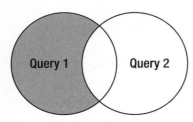

Figure 11-2. *Illustration of an anti-join*

The Oracle manual also provides this example of an anti-join:

```
SELECT * FROM employees
   WHERE department_id NOT IN
   (SELECT department_id FROM departments
       WHERE location_id = 1700)
   ORDER BY last_name;
```

As with semi-joins, there is no specific SQL syntax that invokes an ANTI join. They are one of several choices that the optimizer may use when the SQL statement contains the key words NOT IN or NOT EXISTS. By the way, NOT IN is much, much more common than NOT EXISTS, probably because it is easier to understand.

So let's take a look at our standard queries, now altered to anti form (i.e. using NOT IN and NOT EXISTS instead of IN and EXISTS) in Listing 11-19.

Listing 11-19. *Standard NOT IN and NOT EXISTS Examples*

```
SQL> -- anti_ex1.sql
SQL>
SQL> select /* NOT IN */ department_name
  2      from hr.departments dept
  3      where department_id NOT IN
  4      (select department_id from hr.employees emp);

no rows selected

SQL>
SQL> select /* NOT EXISTS */ department_name
  2      from hr.departments dept
  3      where NOT EXISTS (select null from hr.employees emp
  4                          where emp.department_id = dept.department_id);

DEPARTMENT_NAME
------------------------------
Treasury
Corporate Tax
Control And Credit
Shareholder Services
```

```
Benefits
Manufacturing
Construction
Contracting
Operations
IT Support
NOC
IT Helpdesk
Government Sales
Retail Sales
Recruiting
Payroll

16 rows selected.
```

Clearly NOT IN and NOT EXISTS do not return the same data in this example, and are therefore not functionally equivalent. The reason for this behavior has to do with how the queries deal with null values being returned by the subquery. If a null value is returned to a NOT IN operator, then no records will be returned by the overall query. This seems counter intuitive, but if you think about it for a minute it should make a little more sense. In the first place, the NOT IN operator is just another way of saying !=ANY. So you can think of it as a loop comparing values. If it finds a match, the record is discarded. If it doesn't, the record gets returned to the user. But what if is doesn't know whether the records match or not? Remember that a null is not equal to anything, even another null. In this case, Oracle has chosen to return a value of false, even though the theoretical answer is unknown. C.J. Date would probably argue that this is a shortcoming of Oracle's implementation of relation theory, as it should provide for all three potential answers. At any rate, this is the way it works in Oracle.

Assuming that your requirements are to return records even in the case of nulls being returned by the subquery, you have the following options:

- Apply an NVL function to the column(s) returned by the subquery

- Add an IS NOT NULL predicate to the subquery

- Implement NOT NULL constraint(s)

- Don't use NOT IN (use the NOT EXISTS form, which doesn't care about nulls)

In many cases a NOT NULL constraint is the best option, but there are situations where there are valid arguments against them. Listing 11-20 shows two examples of dealing with the null issue.

Listing 11-20. *Avoiding Nulls with NOT IN*

```
SQL> select /* IN with NVL */ department_name
  2      from hr.departments dept
  3      where department_id NOT IN
  4      (select nvl(department_id,-10) from hr.employees emp);

DEPARTMENT_NAME
------------------------------
Treasury
Corporate Tax
Control And Credit
```

```
Shareholder Services
Benefits
Manufacturing
Construction
Contracting
Operations
IT Support
NOC
IT Helpdesk
Government Sales
Retail Sales
Recruiting
Payroll

16 rows selected.

SQL>
SQL> select /* IN with NOT NULL */ department_name
  2        from hr.departments dept
  3        where department_id NOT IN (select department_id from hr.employees emp
  4                                    where department_id is not null);

DEPARTMENT_NAME
-------------------------------
Treasury
Corporate Tax
Control And Credit
Shareholder Services
Benefits
Manufacturing
Construction
Contracting
Operations
IT Support
NOC
IT Helpdesk
Government Sales
Retail Sales
Recruiting
Payroll

16 rows selected.
```

So as you can see, while an unconstrained NOT IN statement is not the same as a NOT EXISTS, applying an NVL function or adding an IS NOT NULL clause to the subquery predicate solves the issue.

While NOT IN and NOT EXISTS are the most commonly chosen syntax options for producing an anti-join, there are at least two other options that can return the same data. The MINUS operator can obviously be used for this purpose. A clever trick with an outer join can also be used. Listing 11-21 shows examples of both techniques.

Listing 11-21. *Alternative Syntax to NOT IN and NOT EXISTS*

```
SQL> select /* MINUS */ department_name
  2      from hr.departments
  3      where department_id in
  4        (select department_id from hr.departments
  5         minus
  6         select department_id from hr.employees);

DEPARTMENT_NAME
------------------------------
Treasury
Corporate Tax
Control And Credit
Shareholder Services
Benefits
Manufacturing
Construction
Contracting
Operations
IT Support
NOC
IT Helpdesk
Government Sales
Retail Sales
Recruiting
Payroll

16 rows selected.

SQL> select /* LEFT OUTER */ department_name
  2      from hr.departments dept left outer join
  3          hr.employees emp on dept.department_id = emp.department_id
  4      where emp.department_id is null;

DEPARTMENT_NAME
------------------------------
Treasury
Corporate Tax
Control And Credit
Shareholder Services
Benefits
Manufacturing
Construction
Contracting
```

```
Operations
IT Support
NOC
IT Helpdesk
Government Sales
Retail Sales
Recruiting
Payroll

16 rows selected.


SQL> select /* LEFT OUTER OLD (+) */ department_name
  2      from hr.departments dept, hr.employees emp
  3      where dept.department_id = emp.department_id(+)
  4      and emp.department_id is null;

DEPARTMENT_NAME
------------------------------
Treasury
Corporate Tax
Control And Credit
Shareholder Services
Benefits
Manufacturing
Construction
Contracting
Operations
IT Support
NOC
IT Helpdesk
Government Sales
Retail Sales
Recruiting
Payroll

16 rows selected.
```

So the MINUS is slightly convoluted but it returns the right data and is functionally equivalent to the NOT EXISTS form and the null constrained NOT IN form. The LEFT OUTER statement probably needs a little discussion. It makes use of the fact that an outer join creates a dummy record on the right side for each record on the left that doesn't have an actual match. Since all the columns in the dummy record will be null, we can get the records without matches by adding the EMP.DEPARTMENT_ID IS NULL clause to the outer join. This statement is also functionally equivalent to the NOT EXISTS statement and the null constrained NOT IN form. There is a myth that this form performs better than NOT EXISTS, and maybe that was true at some point, but it is not the case now. Therefore, there appears to be little reason to use it as it is considerably less clear in its intent.

Anti-join Plans

As with semi-joins, anti-joins are an optimization option that may be applied to NESTED LOOP JOINS, HASH JOINS or MERGE JOINS. Also remember that it is an optimization that allows processing to stop when the first match is found in the subquery. Listing 11-22 shows the pseudo code that should help to more fully describe the process. Note that the outer query is Q1 and the inner (subquery) is Q2.

Listing 11-22. *Pseudo Code for Nested Loop Anti-join*

```
open Q1
while Q1 still has records
   fetch record from Q1
   result = true
   open Q2
   while Q2 still has records
      fetch record from Q2
      if (Q1.record matches Q2.record) then    ⬅= anti-join optimization
         result = false                        ⬅= Difference from semi-join
         exit loop
      end if
   end loop
   close Q2
   if (result = true) return Q1 record
end loop
close Q1
```

This example is basically a nested loop anti-join. The optimization provided by the anti option is the IF statement that lets the code bail out of the inner loop as soon as it finds a match. Obviously, with large data sets, this technique can result in significant time saving when compared to a normal nested loops join that must loop through every record returned by the inner query.

Now let's re-run our first two anti-join examples (i.e. the standard NOT IN and NOT EXISTS queries) in Listing 11-23 and look at the plans the optimizer generates:

Listing 11-23. *Anti-join Execution Plans*

```
SQL> select /* NOT IN */ department_name
  2      from hr.departments dept
  3      where department_id NOT IN (select department_id from hr.employees emp);

no rows selected


Execution Plan
----------------------------------------------------------
Plan hash value: 4201340344
```

```
-------------------------------------------------------------------
|Id|Operation            |Name       |Rows|Bytes|Cost (%CPU)|Time     |
-------------------------------------------------------------------
| 0|SELECT STATEMENT     |           |  17|  323|   6  (17)|00:00:01|
| 1| MERGE JOIN ANTI NA  |           |  17|  323|   6  (17)|00:00:01|
| 2|  SORT JOIN          |           |  27| 432 |   2   (0)|00:00:01|
| 3|   TABLE ACCESS BY   |DEPARTMENTS|  27| 432|   2   (0)|00:00:01|
|  |     INDEX ROWID     |           |    |     |          |        |
| 4|    INDEX FULL SCAN  |DEPT_ID_PK |  27|     |   1   (0)|00:00:01|
|*5|  SORT UNIQUE        |           | 107|  321|   4  (25)|00:00:01|
| 6|   TABLE ACCESS FULL |EMPLOYEES  | 107|  321|   3   (0)|00:00:01|
-------------------------------------------------------------------
```

Predicate Information (identified by operation id):

```
   5 - access("DEPARTMENT_ID"="DEPARTMENT_ID")
       filter("DEPARTMENT_ID"="DEPARTMENT_ID")
```

```
SQL>
SQL> select /* NOT EXISTS */ department_name
  2     from hr.departments dept
  3     where NOT EXISTS (select null from hr.employees emp
  4                    where emp.department_id = dept.department_id);

DEPARTMENT_NAME
------------------------------
Treasury
Corporate Tax
Control And Credit
Shareholder Services
Benefits
Manufacturing
Construction
Contracting
Operations
IT Support
NOC
IT Helpdesk
Government Sales
Retail Sales
Recruiting
Payroll

16 rows selected.
```

```
Execution Plan
-----------------------------------------------------------
Plan hash value: 3082375452

------------------------------------------------------------------------
|Id|Operation          |Name             |Rows|Bytes|Cost (%CPU)|Time     |
------------------------------------------------------------------------
| 0|SELECT STATEMENT   |                 |  17|  323|   3  (0)|00:00:01 |
| 1| NESTED LOOPS ANTI |                 |  17|  323|   3  (0)|00:00:01 |
| 2|  TABLE ACCESS FULL|DEPARTMENTS      |  27|  432|   3  (0)|00:00:01 |
|*3|  INDEX RANGE SCAN |EMP_DEPARTMENT_IX|  41|  123|   0  (0)|00:00:01 |
------------------------------------------------------------------------

Predicate Information (identified by operation id):
---------------------------------------------------

   3 - access("EMP"."DEPARTMENT_ID"="DEPT"."DEPARTMENT_ID")
```

Notice that the NOT EXISTS statement generated a NESTED LOOPS ANTI plan while the NOT IN statement generated a MERGE JOIN ANTI NA plan. The NESTED LOOPS ANTI is the standard anti-join that has been available since version 7 or thereabouts. The ANTI NA that was applied to the MERGE JOIN, however, is a new optimization that was introduced in 11g. (NA stands for Null Aware.) This new optimization allows the optimizer to deal with NOT IN queries where the optimizer doesn't know if nulls can be returned by the subquery. Prior to 11g, anti-joins could not be performed on NOT IN queries unless the optimizer was sure the nulls would not be returned. Note that this optimization technique has nothing at all to do with the "unintuitive" behavior of NOT IN clauses with respect to nulls that was mentioned previously. The query still returns no records if a null is returned by the subquery, but it does it a lot faster with the ANTI NA option. Listing 11-24 provides another example showing how the various ways of handling nulls in the subquery affect the optimizer's choices (note: the fsp.sql script shows some execution statistics from v$sql along with the operation and options from v$sql_plan if a semi- or anti-join is used).

Listing 11-24. *Anti-join Execution Plans*

```
SYS@LAB112> set echo on
SYS@LAB112> @flush_pool
SYS@LAB112> alter system flush shared_pool;

System altered.

SYS@LAB112> @anti_ex2
SYS@LAB112> set echo on
SYS@LAB112> -- anti_ex2.sql
SYS@LAB112>
SYS@LAB112> select /* IN */ department_name
  2      from hr.departments dept
  3      where department_id not in
  4      (select department_id from hr.employees emp);

no rows selected
```

```
SYS@LAB112>
SYS@LAB112> select /* IN with NVL */ department_name
  2      from hr.departments dept
  3      where department_id not in
  4      (select nvl(department_id,-10) from hr.employees emp);

DEPARTMENT_NAME
------------------------------
Treasury
Corporate Tax
Control And Credit
Shareholder Services
Benefits
Manufacturing
Construction
Contracting
Operations
IT Support
NOC
IT Helpdesk
Government Sales
Retail Sales
Recruiting
Payroll

16 rows selected.

SYS@LAB112>
SYS@LAB112> select /* IN with NOT NULL */ department_name
  2      from hr.departments dept
  3      where department_id not in (select department_id from hr.employees emp
  4                                  where department_id is not null);

DEPARTMENT_NAME
------------------------------
Treasury
Corporate Tax
Control And Credit
Shareholder Services
Benefits
Manufacturing
Construction
Contracting
Operations
IT Support
NOC
IT Helpdesk
```

Government Sales
Retail Sales
Recruiting
Payroll

16 rows selected.

SYS@LAB112>
SYS@LAB112> select /* EXISTS */ department_name
  2   from hr.departments dept
  3   where not exists (select null from hr.employees emp
  4   where emp.department_id = dept.department_id);

DEPARTMENT_NAME

Treasury
Corporate Tax
Control And Credit
Shareholder Services
Benefits
Manufacturing
Construction
Contracting
Operations
IT Support
NOC
IT Helpdesk
Government Sales
Retail Sales
Recruiting
Payroll

16 rows selected.

SYS@LAB112>
SYS@LAB112> set echo off
SYS@LAB112> set echo on
SYS@LAB112> @fsp
SYS@LAB112> select distinct s.sql_id,
  2 -- s.child_number,
  3 s.plan_hash_value plan_hash,
  4   sql_text,
  5 -- decode(options,'SEMI',operation||' '||options,null) join
  6 case when options like '%SEMI%' or options like '%ANTI%' then
  7 operation||' '||options end join
  8   from v$sql s, v$sql_plan p
  9   where s.sql_id = p.sql_id

```
10    and s.child_number = p.child_number
11    and upper(sql_text) like upper(nvl('&sql_text','%department%'))
12    and sql_text not like '%from v$sql where sql_text like nvl(%'
13    and s.sql_id like nvl('&sql_id',s.sql_id)
14    order by 1, 2, 3
15    /
Enter value for sql_text:
Enter value for sql_id:


SQL_ID         PLAN_HASH  SQL_TEXT                                         JOIN
-------------  ---------  ----------------------------------------------   --------------------
0pcrmdk1tw0tf  4201340344 select /* IN */ department_name    from hr.de    MERGE
JOIN ANTI NA

                          partments dept    where department_id not in
                          (select department_id from hr.employees emp)


56d82nhza8ftu  3082375452 select /* IN with NOT NULL */ department_name    NESTED
LOOPS ANTI

                              from hr.departments dept    where departm
                          ent_id not in (select department_id from hr.e
                          mployees emp                              w
                          here department_id is not null)


5c77dgzy60ubx  3082375452 select /* EXISTS */ department_name    from h    NESTED
LOOPS ANTI

                          r.departments dept    where not exists (selec
                          t null from hr.employees emp
                              where emp.department_id = dept.department
                          _id)


a71yzhpc0n2uj  3822487693 select /* IN with NVL */ department_name    f    MERGE
JOIN ANTI

                          rom hr.departments dept    where department_i
                          d not in (select nvl(department_id,-10) from
                          hr.employees emp)
```

As you can see, the EXISTS, NOT IN with NOT NULL, and NOT IN with NVL all use the normal anti-join, while the NOT IN that ignores the handling of nulls must use the new null aware anti-join (ANTI NA). Now, let's rerun our examples of LEFT OUTER and MINUS and see what plans they come up with. Listing 11-25 shows the results that the optimizer comes up with for several alternative syntax variations.

Listing 11-25. *Alternate Anti-join Syntax Execution Plans*

```
SYS@LAB112> set echo on
SYS@LAB112> @flush_pool
SYS@LAB112> alter system flush shared_pool;

System altered.

SYS@LAB112> @anti_ex3
SYS@LAB112> set echo on
SYS@LAB112> -- anti_ex3.sql
SYS@LAB112>
SYS@LAB112> select /* NOT EXISTS */ department_name
  2      from hr.departments dept
  3      where not exists (select null from hr.employees emp
  4                         where emp.department_id = dept.department_id);

DEPARTMENT_NAME
------------------------------
Treasury
Corporate Tax
Control And Credit
Shareholder Services
Benefits
Manufacturing
Construction
Contracting
Operations
IT Support
NOC
IT Helpdesk
Government Sales
Retail Sales
Recruiting
Payroll

16 rows selected.

SYS@LAB112>
SYS@LAB112> select /* NOT IN NOT NULL */ department_name
  2      from hr.departments dept
  3      where department_id not in (select department_id from hr.employees emp
  4                                  where department_id is not null);
```

```
DEPARTMENT_NAME
------------------------------
Treasury
Corporate Tax
Control And Credit
Shareholder Services
Benefits
Manufacturing
Construction
Contracting
Operations
IT Support
NOC
IT Helpdesk
Government Sales
Retail Sales
Recruiting
Payroll

16 rows selected.

SYS@LAB112>
SYS@LAB112> select /* LEFT OUTER */ department_name
  2      from hr.departments dept left outer join
  3          hr.employees emp on dept.department_id = emp.department_id
  4      where emp.department_id is null;

DEPARTMENT_NAME
------------------------------
Treasury
Corporate Tax
Control And Credit
Shareholder Services
Benefits
Manufacturing
Construction
Contracting
Operations
IT Support
NOC
IT Helpdesk
Government Sales
Retail Sales
Recruiting
Payroll

16 rows selected.
```

```
SYS@LAB112>
SYS@LAB112> select /* LEFT OUTER OLD (+) */ department_name
  2      from hr.departments dept, hr.employees emp
  3      where dept.department_id = emp.department_id(+)
  4      and emp.department_id is null;

DEPARTMENT_NAME
------------------------------
Treasury
Corporate Tax
Control And Credit
Shareholder Services
Benefits
Manufacturing
Construction
Contracting
Operations
IT Support
NOC
IT Helpdesk
Government Sales
Retail Sales
Recruiting
Payroll

16 rows selected.

SYS@LAB112>
SYS@LAB112> select /* MINUS */ department_name
  2      from hr.departments
  3      where department_id in
  4        (select department_id from hr.departments
  5         minus
  6         select department_id from hr.employees);

DEPARTMENT_NAME
------------------------------
Treasury
Corporate Tax
Control And Credit
Shareholder Services
Benefits
Manufacturing
Construction
Contracting
Operations
IT Support
NOC
```

```
IT Helpdesk
Government Sales
Retail Sales
Recruiting
Payroll

16 rows selected.

SYS@LAB112>
SYS@LAB112> set echo off
SYS@LAB112> @fsp
Enter value for sql_text:
Enter value for sql_id:


SQL_ID        PLAN_HASH SQL_TEXT                                         JOIN
------------- ---------- ------------------------------------------------ ---------------------
6tt0zwazv6my9 3082375452 select /* NOT EXISTS */ department_name      fr NESTED LOOPS ANTI
                         om hr.departments dept    where not exists (s
                         elect null from hr.employees emp
                                 where emp.department_id = dept.depart
                         ment_id)


as34zpj5n5dfd 3082375452 select /* LEFT OUTER */ department_name      fr NESTED LOOPS ANTI
                         om hr.departments dept left outer join
                           hr.employees emp on dept.department_id = em
                         p.department_id    where emp.department_id is
                          null


czsqu5txh5tyn 3082375452 select /* NOT IN NOT NULL */ department_name  NESTED LOOPS ANTI
                                 from hr.departments dept    where departme
                         nt_id not in (select department_id from hr.em
                         ployees emp                              wh
                         ere department_id is not null)


dcx0kqhwbuv6r 3082375452 select /* LEFT OUTER OLD (+) */ department_na NESTED LOOPS ANTI
                         me    from hr.departments dept, hr.employees
                         emp    where dept.department_id = emp.departm
                         ent_id(+)    and emp.department_id is null


gvdsm57xf24jv 2972564128 select /* MINUS */ department_name      from hr
                         .departments    where department_id in      (
                         select department_id from hr.departments
                           minus        select department_id from hr.em
                         ployees)
```

362

While all these statements return the same data, the MINUS does not use the anti-join optimization. If you look closely, you'll notice that all the other statements have the same plan hash value, meaning they have exactly the same plan.

Controlling Anti-join Plans

Not surprisingly, the mechanisms for controlling anti-join plans are similar to those available for controlling semi-joins. As before, you have both hints and parameters to work with.

Controlling Anti-join Plans Using Hints

There are several hints:

ANTIJOIN – perform an anti-join (the optimizer gets to pick which kind)

USE_ANTI – older version of ANTIJOIN hint

NL_AJ – perform a NESTED LOOPS anti-join (deprecated as of 10g)

HASH_AJ – perform a HASH anti-join (deprecated as of 10g)

MERGE_AJ – perform a MERGE anti-join (deprecated as of 10g)

As with the hints controlling semi-joins, several of the anti-join hints (NL_AJ, HASH_AJ, MERGE_AJ) have been documented as being deprecated. Nevertheless, they continue to work in 11gR2. However, it should be noted that these specific hints do not work in situations where the optimizer must use the new null aware version of anti-join (more on that in a moment). All of the anti-join hints should be specified in the subquery as opposed to in the outer query. Also note that there is not a NO_ANTIJOIN hint, which is a bit unusual. Listing 11-26 shows an example of using the NL_AJ hint.

Listing 11-26. *Controlling Anti-join Execution Plans with Hints*

```
SQL> set autotrace traceonly exp
SQL> @anti_ex4
SQL> -- anti_ex4.sql
SQL>
SQL> select /* IN */ department_name
  2      from hr.departments dept
  3      where department_id not in (select /*+ nl_aj */ department_id
  4                                  from hr.employees emp);

Execution Plan
----------------------------------------------------------
Plan hash value: 4201340344
```

Id	Operation	Name	Rows	Bytes	Cost (%CPU)	Time
0	SELECT STATEMENT		17	323	6 (17)	00:00:01
1	MERGE JOIN ANTI NA		17	323	6 (17)	00:00:01
2	SORT JOIN		27	432	2 (0)	00:00:01

```
| 3|    TABLE ACCESS BY          |DEPARTMENTS|  27|  432|     2  (0)|00:00:01|
         INDEX ROWID
| 4|      INDEX FULL SCAN        |DEPT_ID_PK |  27|     |     1  (0)|00:00:01|
|*5|   SORT UNIQUE               |           | 107|  321|     4 (25)|00:00:01|
| 6|    TABLE ACCESS FULL        |EMPLOYEES  | 107|  321|     3  (0)|00:00:01|
-------------------------------------------------------------------------------
```

Predicate Information (identified by operation id):

```
   5 - access("DEPARTMENT_ID"="DEPARTMENT_ID")
       filter("DEPARTMENT_ID"="DEPARTMENT_ID")
```

```
SQL>
SQL> select /* EXISTS */ department_name
  2      from hr.departments dept
  3      where not exists (select /*+ nl_aj */ null from hr.employees emp
  4                    where emp.department_id = dept.department_id);
```

Execution Plan

Plan hash value: 3082375452

```
-------------------------------------------------------------------------------
|Id |Operation          |Name            |Rows|Bytes|Cost (%CPU)|Time    |
-------------------------------------------------------------------------------
| 0 |SELECT STATEMENT   |                |  17|  323|    3  (0)|00:00:01|
| 1 | NESTED LOOPS ANTI |                |  17|  323|    3  (0)|00:00:01|
| 2 |  TABLE ACCESS FULL|DEPARTMENTS     |  27|  432|    3  (0)|00:00:01|
|*3 |  INDEX RANGE SCAN |EMP_DEPARTMENT_IX|  41|  123|    0  (0)|00:00:01|
-------------------------------------------------------------------------------
```

Predicate Information (identified by operation id):

```
   3 - access("EMP"."DEPARTMENT_ID"="DEPT"."DEPARTMENT_ID")
```

Controlling Anti-join Plans at the Instance Level

There are also a number of parameters (all hidden) that affect the optimizer's behavior with respect to anti-joins:

- _always_anti_
- _gs_anti_semi_join_allowed
- _optimizer_null_aware_antijoin
- _optimizer_outer_to_anti_enabled

The main parameter to be concerned about is _always_anti_join which is equivalent to _always_semi_join in its behavior (it has the same valid values and the options do the same things). Note that it's been documented as being obsolete for some time. Nevertheless, as with _always_semi_join, it appears to still work in 11gR2. Listing 11-27 shows an example of using a hint and turning off anti-joins altogether with the _optimizer_null_aware_antijoin parameter.

Listing 11-27. *Controlling Anti-join Execution Plans with Parameters*

```
SQL> -- anti_ex5.sql
SQL>
SQL> select /* EXISTS */ department_name
  2      from hr.departments dept
  3      where not exists (select null from hr.employees emp
  4                         where emp.department_id = dept.department_id);

DEPARTMENT_NAME
------------------------------
Treasury
Corporate Tax
Control And Credit
Shareholder Services
Benefits
Manufacturing
Construction
Contracting
Operations
IT Support
NOC
IT Helpdesk
Government Sales
Retail Sales
Recruiting
Payroll

16 rows selected.

SQL>
SQL> select /* EXISTS with hint */ department_name
  2      from hr.departments dept
  3      where not exists (select /*+ hash_aj */ null from hr.employees emp
  4                         where emp.department_id = dept.department_id);

DEPARTMENT_NAME
------------------------------
NOC
Manufacturing
Government Sales
IT Support
```

```
Benefits
Shareholder Services
Retail Sales
Control And Credit
Recruiting
Operations
Treasury
Payroll
Corporate Tax
Construction
Contracting
IT Helpdesk

16 rows selected.

SQL>
SQL> select /* IN */ department_name
  2      from hr.departments dept
  3      where department_id not in
  4      (select department_id from hr.employees emp);

no rows selected

SQL>
SQL> alter session set "_optimizer_null_aware_antijoin"=false;

Session altered.

SQL>
SQL> select /* IN with AAJ=OFF*/ department_name
  2      from hr.departments dept
  3      where department_id not in
  4      (select department_id from hr.employees emp);

no rows selected

SQL>
SQL> alter session set "_optimizer_null_aware_antijoin"=true;

Session altered.

SQL>
SQL> set echo off
SQL> @fsp
Enter value for sql_text:
Enter value for sql_id:
```

SQL_ID	PLAN_HASH	SQL_TEXT	JOIN
0kvb76bzacc7b	3587451639	select /* EXISTS with hint */ department_name from hr.departments dept where not exi sts (select /*+ hash_aj */ null from hr.emplo yees emp where emp.depart ment_id = dept.department_id)	HASH JOIN ANTI
0pcrmdk1tw0tf	4201340344	select /* IN */ department_name from hr.de partments dept where department_id not in (select department_id from hr.employees emp)	MERGE JOIN ANTI NA
5c77dgzy60ubx	3082375452	select /* EXISTS */ department_name from h r.departments dept where not exists (selec t null from hr.employees emp where emp.department_id = dept.department _id)	NESTED LOOPS ANTI
67u11c3rv1aag	3416340233	select /* IN with AAJ=OFF*/ department_name from hr.departments dept where departmen t_id not in (select department_id from hr.emp loyees emp)	

Anti-join Restrictions

As with semi-joins, anti-join transformations cannot be performed if the subquery is on an OR branch of a WHERE clause. I trust you will take my word for this one, as the behavior has already been demonstrated with semi-joins in the previous sections.

As of 11g, there are no major restrictions on the use of anti-joins. The major restriction in 10g was that any subquery that could return a null was not a candidate for anti-join optimization. The new ANTI NA (and ANTI SNA) provide the optimizer with the capability to apply the anti-join optimization even in those cases where a null may be returned by a subquery. Note that this does not change the somewhat confusing behavior causing no records to be returned from a subquery contained in a NOT IN clause if a null value is returned by the subquery.

Because 10g is still in wide use, a brief discussion of the restriction which has been removed in 11g by the Null Aware anti-join is warranted. When a NOT IN clause is specified in 10g, the optimizer checks to see if the column(s) being returned are guaranteed to not contain nulls. This is done by checking for NOT NULL constraints, IS NOT NULL predicates, or a function which translates null into a value (typically NVL). If all three of these checks fail, the 10g optimizer will not choose an anti-join. Furthermore, it will transform the statement by applying an internal function (LNNVL) that has the possible side affect of disabling potential index access paths. Listing 11-28 shows an example from a 10.2.0.4 database.

Listing 11-28. *10g NOT NULL Anti-join Behavior*

```
> !sql
sqlplus "/ as sysdba"

SQL*Plus: Release 10.2.0.4.0 - Production on Tue Jun 29 14:50:25 2010

Copyright (c) 1982, 2007, Oracle.  All Rights Reserved.


Connected to:
Oracle Database 10g Enterprise Edition Release 10.2.0.4.0 - Production
With the Partitioning, OLAP, Data Mining and Real Application Testing options

SYS@LAB1024> @anti_ex6
SYS@LAB1024> -- anti_ex6.sql
SYS@LAB1024>
SYS@LAB1024> set autotrace trace exp
SYS@LAB1024>
SYS@LAB1024> select /* NOT IN */ department_name
  2      from hr.departments dept
  3      where department_id not in (select department_id from hr.employees emp);

Execution Plan
----------------------------------------------------------
Plan hash value: 3416340233


--------------------------------------------------------------------
|Id|Operation             |Name        |Rows|Bytes|Cost (%CPU)|Time     |
--------------------------------------------------------------------
| 0|SELECT STATEMENT      |            |  26|  416|  29    (0)|00:00:01|
|*1| FILTER               |            |    |     |           |        |
| 2|  TABLE ACCESS FULL   |DEPARTMENTS |  27|  432|   2    (0)|00:00:01|
|*3|  TABLE ACCESS FULL   |EMPLOYEES   |   2|    6|   2    (0)|00:00:01|
--------------------------------------------------------------------

Predicate Information (identified by operation id):
---------------------------------------------------

   1 - filter( NOT EXISTS (SELECT /*+ */ 0 FROM "HR"."EMPLOYEES" "EMP"
              WHERE LNNVL("DEPARTMENT_ID"<>:B1)))
   3 - filter(LNNVL("DEPARTMENT_ID"<>:B1))
```

```
SYS@LAB1024> select /* NOT NULL */ department_name
  2       from hr.departments dept
  3       where department_id not in (select department_id from hr.employees emp
  4                                   where department_id is not null);

Execution Plan
----------------------------------------------------------
Plan hash value: 3082375452


---------------------------------------------------------------------------
|Id|Operation              |Name             |Rows|Bytes|Cost (%CPU)|Time    |
---------------------------------------------------------------------------
|  0|SELECT STATEMENT      |                 |  17|  323|    2   (0)|00:00:01 |
|  1| NESTED LOOPS ANTI    |                 |  17|  323|    2   (0)|00:00:01 |
|  2|  TABLE ACCESS FULL   |DEPARTMENTS      |  27|  432|    2   (0)|00:00:01 |
|*3|  INDEX RANGE SCAN    |EMP_DEPARTMENT_IX|  41|  123|    0   (0)|00:00:01 |
---------------------------------------------------------------------------

Predicate Information (identified by operation id):
---------------------------------------------------

   3 - access("DEPARTMENT_ID"="DEPARTMENT_ID")
       filter("DEPARTMENT_ID" IS NOT NULL)

SYS@LAB1024>
SYS@LAB1024> select /* NVL */ department_name
  2       from hr.departments dept
  3       where department_id not in (select nvl(department_id,'-10')
  4                                   from hr.employees emp);

Execution Plan
----------------------------------------------------------
Plan hash value: 2918349777


----------------------------------------------------------------------------
|Id|Operation              |Name            |Rows|Bytes|Cost (%CPU)|Time     |
----------------------------------------------------------------------------
|  0|SELECT STATEMENT      |                |  17|  323|    5  (20)|00:00:01 |
|*1| HASH JOIN ANTI       |                |  17|  323|    5  (20)|00:00:01 |
|  2|  TABLE ACCESS FULL   |DEPARTMENTS     |  27|  432|    2   (0)|00:00:01 |
|  3|  TABLE ACCESS FULL   |EMPLOYEES       | 107|  321|    2   (0)|00:00:01 |
----------------------------------------------------------------------------

Predicate Information (identified by operation id):
---------------------------------------------------

   1 - access("DEPARTMENT_ID"=NVL("DEPARTMENT_ID",(-10)))
```

The first statement in this example is the same old NOT IN query that we've run several times already in 11g. Note that in 10g, instead of doing an ANTI NA, it doesn't apply the anti optimization at all. This is due to the restriction regarding guaranteeing that nulls will not be returned from the subquery in 10g. The second statement (NOT NULL) applies the NOT NULL predicate to the where clause in the subquery which enables the optimizer to pick a standard anti-join. The third statement uses the NVL function to ensure that no nulls will be returned by the subquery. Notice that it also is able to apply the anti-join. Finally, notice the predicate section below the plan for the first statement (NOT IN). You will see that the optimizer has transformed the statement by adding the LNNVL function. This can have the unpleasant side affect of disabling index access paths. The other plans do not have this transformation applied. Listing 11-29 shows the same NOT IN statement run in 11g.

Listing 11-29. *11g NOT NULL Anti-join Behavior*

```
SQL> -- anti_ex6.sql
SQL>
SQL> set autotrace trace exp
SQL>
SQL> select /* NOT IN */ department_name
  2      from hr.departments dept
  3      where department_id not in (select department_id from hr.employees emp);

Execution Plan
----------------------------------------------------------
Plan hash value: 4201340344
```

Id	Operation	Name	Rows	Bytes	Cost (%CPU)	Time
0	SELECT STATEMENT		17	323	6 (17)	00:00:01
1	MERGE JOIN ANTI NA		17	323	6 (17)	00:00:01
2	SORT JOIN		27	432	2 (0)	00:00:01
3	TABLE ACCESS BY INDEX ROWID	DEPARTMENTS	27	432	2 (0)	00:00:01
4	INDEX FULL SCAN	DEPT_ID_PK	27		1 (0)	00:00:01
*5	SORT UNIQUE		107	321	4 (25)	00:00:01
6	TABLE ACCESS FULL	EMPLOYEES	107	321	3 (0)	00:00:01

```
Predicate Information (identified by operation id):
---------------------------------------------------

   5 - access("DEPARTMENT_ID"="DEPARTMENT_ID")
       filter("DEPARTMENT_ID"="DEPARTMENT_ID")
```

Notice that in 11g the optimizer generates the new Null Aware ANTI join (ANTI NA). Also notice that the internally applied LNNVL function which is used in 10g is no longer necessary.

Anti-join Requirements

"Requirements" is such a strong word. Oracle's optimizer is a very complex piece of software. Producing an exhaustive list of every possible way to get a specified result is a difficult task at best. With respect to anti-joins, Oracle has recently implemented some clever ways of making use of this join option that you would not normally expect. So please take these "requirements" as a list of the most probable ways to cause Oracle to produce an ANTI join, as opposed to an exhaustive list:

- The statement should use either the NOT IN (!= ALL) or NOT EXISTS phrases

- The statement should have a subquery in the NOT IN or NOT EXISTS clause

- The NOT IN or NOT EXISTS clause should not be contained inside an OR branch

- Subqueries in NOT EXISTS clauses should be correlated to the outer query

- Note: 10g requires NOT IN subqueries to be coded to not return nulls (11g doesn't)

Anti-joins are a powerful optimization option that can be applied by the optimizer. They can provide impressive performance improvements, particularly when large data volumes are involved. While the NOT IN syntax is more intuitive, it also has some counter-intuitive behavior when it comes to dealing with nulls. The NOT EXISTS syntax is better suited to handling subqueries that may return nulls, but is generally a little harder to read—and probably for that reason—not used as often. The outer join trick is even less intuitive than the NOT EXISTS syntax and generally provides no advantage over it. The MINUS operator does not appear to offer any advantages over the other forms and does not currently use the anti-join optimization. It is apparent that Oracle's intent is to allow the optimizer to use the anti-join option wherever possible because of the dramatic performance enhancement potential that it provides.

Summary

Anti-joins and Semi-joins are options that the optimizer can apply to many of the common join methods. The basic idea of these optimization options is to cut short the processing of the normal Hash, Merge, or Nested Loop joins. In some cases, anti-joins and semi-joins can provide dramatic performance improvements. There are multiple ways to construct SQL statements that will result in the optimizer using these options. The most common are the IN and EXISTS key words. When these optimizations were first released, the processing of the statements varied significantly depending on whether you used IN or EXISTS. Over the years, the optimizer has been enhanced to allow many statement transformations; the result is that in 11g there is little difference between using one form or the other. In many cases, the statements get transformed into the same form anyway. In this chapter you've seen how this optimization technique works, when it can be used, and how to verify whether it is being used or not. You've also seen some mechanisms for controlling the optimizer's use of this feature.

CHAPTER 12

■ ■ ■

Indexes

Riyaj Shamsudeen

Indexes are critical structures needed for efficient retrieval of rows, for uniqueness enforcement, and for the efficient implementation of referential constraints. Oracle Database provides many index types suited for different needs of application access methods. Effective choice of index type and critical choice of columns to index are of paramount importance for optimal performance. Inadequate or incorrect indexing strategy can lead to performance issues. In this chapter, I will discuss basic implementation of indexes, various index types, their use cases, and strategy to choose optimal index type. Indexes available in Oracle Database as of version 11gR2 can be broadly classified in to one of three categories based upon the algorithm they use: B-tree indexes, bitmap indexes, and index organized tables.

Implementation of Bitmap indexes are suitable for columns with infrequent Update, Insert, and Delete activity. They are better fit for static columns with lower distinct values, a typical case in the data warehouse applications. Gender column in a table holding population data is a good example as there are only few distinct values for this column. I will discuss this in more detail later in this chapter.

■NOTE All tables referred in this chapter refer to the objects in SH Schema supplied by Oracle Corporation Example scripts.

B-tree indexes are commonly used in all applications. There are many index types such as partitioned indexes, compressed indexes, and function-based indexes implemented as B-tree indexes. Special index types such as index organized tables and secondary indexes on index organized tables also are implemented as B-tree indexes.

THE IMPORTANCE OF CHOOSING CORRECTLY

I have a story to share about the importance of indexing choice. During an application upgrade, an application designer chose bitmap indexes on few key tables which were modified heavily. After the application upgrade, the application response time was not acceptable. As this application was a warehouse management application, performance issues were affecting the shipping and order fulfillment process of this U.S. retail giant.

We were called in to troubleshoot the issue. We reviewed the database performance metrics and quickly realized that the poor choice of index type was the root cause of the performance issue. Database metrics were showing that the application was suffering from locking contention, too. These bitmap indexes used to grow from about 100MB in the morning to around 4-5GB in the mid-afternoon. The designer even introduced a job to rebuild the index at regular intervals. We resolved the issue converting the bitmap indexes to B-tree indexes. This story tells you the importance of choosing optimal indexing strategy.

Understanding Indexes

Is full table scan access path always bad? Not necessarily. Efficiency of an access path is very specific to the construction of the SQL statement, application data, distribution of data, and the environment. No one access path is suitable for all execution plans. In some cases, a full table scan access path is better than index based access path. I will discuss choice of index usage, considerations for choosing columns to index, and special consideration for null clause.

When to use Indexes

Generally, index based access paths will perform better if the predicates specified in the SQL statement is selective, meaning that few rows are fetched applying the specified predicates. Typical index based access path usually involves following three steps:

1. Traversing the index tree and collecting the rowids from the leaf block after applying the SQL predicates on indexed columns.

2. Fetching the rows from the table blocks using the rowids.

3. Applying the remainder of the predicates on the rows fetched to derive final result set.

The second step of accessing the table block is costlier if numerous rowids are returned at step 1. For every rowid from the index leaf blocks, table blocks need to be accessed, and this might result in multiple physical I/Os leading to performance issues. Further, table blocks are accessed one block at a time physically and can magnify the performance issues. For example, consider the SQL statement in Listing 12-1 accessing the Sales table with just one predicate country='Spain' and the number of rows returned from step 5 estimated to be 7985. So, 7985 rowids estimated to be retrieved from that execution step and table blocks must be accessed at least 7985 times to retrieve the row pieces. Some of these table block accesses might result in physical I/O if the block is not in the buffer cache already. So, the index based access path might perform worse for this specific case.

In Listing 12-1, in the first SELECT statement, you force an index based access path using a hint index (s sales_fact_c2) and the optimizer estimates the cost of the index based access plan as 723. The execution plan for the next SELECT statement without the hint shows that the optimizer estimates the cost of the full table Scan access path as 316. Evidently, the full table scan access path is estimated to be cheaper and more suited for this SQL statement.

Listing 12-1. *Index Access Path*

```
drop index sales_fact_c2;
create index sales_fact_c2 on sales_fact ( country);
set head off

select /*+ index ( s sales_fact_c2) */ count(distinct(region)) from sales_fact s where
country='Spain'   ;
@x
```

```
------------------------------------------------------------..----------
| Id  | Operation                      | Name          | Rows  |  |Cost(%CPU|
------------------------------------------------------------..----------
|   0 | SELECT STATEMENT               |               |       |  |723 (100)|
|   1 |  SORT AGGREGATE                |               |     1 |  |         |
|   2 |   VIEW                         | VW_DAG_0      |     7 |  |723   (1)|
|   3 |    HASH GROUP BY               |               |     7 |  |723   (1)|
|   4 |     TABLE ACCESS BY INDEX ROWID| SALES_FACT    |  6185 |  |721   (0)|
|*  5 |      INDEX RANGE SCAN          | SALES_FACT_C2 |  6185 |  | 21   (0)|
------------------------------------------------------------..----------
```

```
select count(distinct(region)) from sales_fact s where country='Spain'   ;
@x
```

```
--------------------------------------------------------------...-
| Id  | Operation             |Name        | Rows  |Bytes |Cost (%CPU)|   |
--------------------------------------------------------------...-
|   0 | SELECT STATEMENT      |            |       |      | 316 (100)|   |
|   1 |  SORT AGGREGATE       |            |     1 |   17 |          |   |
|   2 |   VIEW                |VW_DAG_0    |     7 |  119 | 316   (1)|   |
|   3 |    HASH GROUP BY      |            |     7 |  175 | 316   (1)|   |
|*  4 |     TABLE ACCESS FULL |SALES_FACT  |  6185 | 151K | 315   (1)|   |
--------------------------------------------------------------
```

■**NOTE** In Listing 12-1, a Script x.sql is used to fetch the execution plan of the SQL statement executed recently in this session. This script uses dbms_xplan package to fetch the execution plan using the SQL statement:

```
select * from table (dbms_xplan.display_cursor('','','ALL'));
```

Let's consider another SELECT statement. In Listing 12-2, all three columns are specified in the predicate of the SQL statement. As the predicates are more selective, the optimizer estimates that 9 rows will be retrieved from this SELECT statement and the cost of the execution plan as 3. You force the full table scan execution plan in the subsequent SELECT statement execution and the cost of this execution plan is 315. Index based access is more optimal for this SQL statement.

Listing 12-2. *Index Access Path 2*

```
alter session set statistics_level=all;
select product, year, week from sales_fact where
product='Xtend Memory' and  year=1998 and week=1;
@x
```

```
-------------------------------------------------------------------------
| Id  | Operation        | Name         | Rows  | Bytes | Cost (%CPU)|
-------------------------------------------------------------------------
|   0 | SELECT STATEMENT |              |       |       |   3 (100)|
|*  1 |   INDEX RANGE SCAN| SALES_FACT_C1 |    9 |   306 |   3   (0)|
-------------------------------------------------------------------------
```

```
select /*+ full(sales_fact) */ product, year, week from sales_fact where product='Xtend
Memory'and  year=1998 and week=1;
@x
```

```
----------------------------------------------------------------------
| Id  | Operation        | Name        | Rows  | Bytes | Cost (%CPU)|
----------------------------------------------------------------------
|   0 | SELECT STATEMENT |             |       |       | 315 (100)|
|*  1 |   TABLE ACCESS FULL| SALES_FACT |    9 |   306 | 315   (1)|
----------------------------------------------------------------------
```

Evidently, no single execution plan is better for all SQL statements. Even for the same statement, depending upon the data distribution and the underlying hardware, execution plans can behave differently. If the data distribution changes, the execution plans can have different costs. This is precisely why you need to collect statistics reflecting the distribution of data so that the optimizer can choose optimal plan.

Furthermore, full table scans and fast full scans perform multi block read calls, whereas index range scans or index unique scans do single block reads. Multi block reads are much more efficient then single block reads on a block-by-block basis. Optimizer calculations factor this difference and can choose index based access path or full table access path as appropriate. Generally speaking, an OLTP application will use index based access paths predominantly and the data warehouse application will use full table access paths predominantly.

A final consideration is parallelism. Queries can be tuned to execute faster using parallelism when the predicates are not selective enough. The cost of an execution plan using a parallel full table scan can be cheaper than the cost of serial index range scan, leading to an optimizer choice of a parallel execution plan.

Choice of Columns

Choosing optimal columns for indexing is essential to improve SQL access performance. The choice of columns to index should match the predicates used by the SQL statements. The following are considerations for choosing an optimal indexing column:

- If the application code uses the equality or range predicates on a column while accessing a table, it's a good strategy to consider indexing that column. For multi-column indexes, the leading column should be the column used in most predicates. For example, if you have a choice to index the columns c1 and c2, then the leading column should be the column used in most predicates.

- It is also important to consider the cardinality of the predicates and the selectivity of the columns. For example, if a column has just two distinct values with a uniform distribution, then that column is probably not a good candidate for the B-tree indexes as fifty percent of the rows will be fetched by equality predicates on the column value. On the other hand, if the column has two distinct values with non-uniform distribution, i.e. one value occurs in few rows *and* the application accesses that table with the infrequently occurring column value, it is preferable to index that column.

- An example is a processed column in a work-in-progress table with three distinct values (P, N, and E). The application accesses that table with Processed='N' predicate. Only few unprocessed rows are left with a status of 'N' in the processed_column, so access through the index will be optimal. But queries with the predicate Processed='Y' should not use the index as nearly all rows will be fetched by this predicate. Histograms can be utilized so that optimizer can choose the optimal execution plan depending upon the literal or bind variables.

■**NOTE** Cardinality is defined as the number of rows expected to be fetched by a predicate or execution step. Consider a simple equality predicate on the column assuming uniform distribution in the column values. Cardinality is calculated as the number of rows in the table divided by the number of distinct values in the column. For example, inr the Sales table, there are 918K rows in the table and the Prod_id column has 72 distinct values, so the cardinality of the equality predicate on Prod_id column is 918K/72 =12,750. So, in other words, the predicate Prod_id=:b1 expects to fetch 12,750 rows. Columns with lower cardinality are better candidate for indexing as the index selectivity will be better. For unique columns, cardinality of equality predicate is 1. Selectivity is a measure ranging between 0 and 1, simplistically defined as 1/NDV where NDV stands for Number of Distinct Values. So, the cardinality of a predicate can be defined as the selectivity times the number of rows in the table.

- Think about column ordering, and arrange the column order in the index to suite the application access patterns. For example, in the Sales table@SH schema, the selectivity of the Prod_id column is 1/72 and the selectivity of the Cust_id column is 1/7059. It might appear that column Cust_id is a better candidate for indexes as the selectivity of that column is lower. However, if the application specifies equality predicates on Prod_id column and does not specify Cust_id column in the predicate, then Cust_id column need not be indexed even though Cust_id column has better selectivity. If the application uses the predicates on both Prod_id and Cust_id columns, then it is preferable to index both columns with Cust_id column as the leading column. Consideration should be given to the column usage in the predicates instead of relying upon the selectivity of the columns.

- You should also consider the cost of an index. Inserts, deletes, and updates (updating the indexed columns) will maintain the indexes, meaning, if a row is inserted in to the Sales table, then a new value pair will be added to the index matching with the new value. This index maintenance is costlier if the columns are updated heavily, as the indexed column update results in a delete and insert at the index level internally. This could introduce additional contention points, too.

- Consider the length of the column. If the indexed column is longer, then the index will be bigger. The cost of that index may be higher than the overall gain from the index. A bigger index also will increase undo and redo size.

- In a multi-column index, if the leading column has few distinct values, consider creating that index as a compressed index. The size of these indexes will be smaller as repeating values are not stored in a compressed index. Compressed indexes are discussed later in this chapter.

- If the predicates use functions on indexed columns, the index on that column may not be chosen. For example, the predicate to_char(prod_id) =:B1 is applying a to_char function on the Prod_id column. A conventional index on Prod_id column might not be chosen for this predicate and a function based index needs to be created on to_char(prod_id) column.

- Do not create bitmap indexes on columns modified aggressively. Internal implementation of a bitmap index is more suitable for read-only columns with few distinct values. The size of the bitmap index will grow rapidly if the indexed columns are updated. Excessive modification to a bitmap index can lead to enormous locking contention, too. Bitmap indexes are more prevalent in data warehouse applications.

The Null Issue

It is common practice for a SQL statement to specify IS NULL predicate. Null values are not stored in the single column indexes, so the predicate IS NULL clause will not use a single column index. But null values are stored in a multi column index. By creating a multi column index with a dummy second column, you can enable the use of index for the IS NULL clause

In Listing 12-3, a single column index T1_N1 was created on column n1. The optimizer does not choose the index access path for the SELECT statement with the predicate n1 is null. Another index t1_n10 was created on the expression (n1, 0) and the optimizer chose the access path utilizing the index, as the null values are stored in this multi column index. The size of the index is kept smaller by adding a dummy value of zero to the index.

Listing 12-3. *NULL Handling*

```
drop table t1;
create table  t1 (n1 number, n2 varchar2(100) );
insert into t1 select object_id, object_name from dba_objects where rownum<101;
commit;
create index t1_n1 on t1(n1);
select * from t1 where n1 is null;
@x
```

```
-----------------------------------------------------------------
| Id | Operation          | Name | Rows | Bytes | Cost (%CPU)|
-----------------------------------------------------------------
|  0 | SELECT STATEMENT   |      |      |       |   3 (100)|
|* 1 |  TABLE ACCESS FULL | T1   |   1  |  11   |   3   (0)|
-----------------------------------------------------------------
```

```
create index t1_n10 on t1(n1,0);
select * from t1 where n1 is null;
@x
```

```
-----------------------------------------------------------
| Id  | Operation                    | Name   | Rows | Bytes |
-----------------------------------------------------------
|   0 | SELECT STATEMENT             |        |      |       |
|   1 |   TABLE ACCESS BY INDEX ROWID| T1     |    1 |    11 |
|*  2 |     INDEX RANGE SCAN         | T1_N10 |    1 |       |
-----------------------------------------------------------
```

Index Structural Types

Oracle database provides various types of indexes to suite application access paths. These index types can be loosely classified in to three broad categories based upon the structure of an index.

B-tree indexes

B-tree indexes implement a structure similar to an inverted tree with a root node, branch nodes, and leaf nodes and they use tree traversal algorithms to search for a column value. The leaf node holds the (value, rowid) pair for that index key column and the rowids refers to the physical location of a row in the table block. The branch block holds the directory of leaf blocks and the value ranges stored in those leaf blocks. The root block holds the directory of branch blocks and the value ranges addressed in those branch blocks.

Figure 12-1 shows the B-tree index structure for a column of number data type. This figure is a generalization of the index structure to improve the understanding; the actual index structures are far more complex. The root block of the index holds branch block addresses and the range of values addressed in the branch blocks. The branch blocks hold the leaf block addresses and the range of values stored in the leaf blocks.

A search for a column value using an index usually results in an index range scan or an index unique scan. Such a search starts at the root block of the index tree, traverses to the branch block, and then traverses to the leaf block. Rowids are fetched from the leaf blocks from the (column value, rowid) pairs, and each row piece is fetched from the table block using the rowid. Without the indexes, searching for a key would inevitably result in a full table scan of the table.

In Figure 12-1, if the SQL statement is searching for a column value of 12000 with a predicate n1=12000, the index range scan will start at the root block, traverse to the second branch block as the second branch block holds the range of values between 11001 to 22000, and then traverse to the fourth leaf block as that leaf block holds the column value range between 11001 and 16000. As the index stores the sorted column values, the range scan quickly accesses the column value matching with n1=12000 from the leaf block entries, reads the rowids associated with that column value, and accesses the rows from the table using those rowid. Rowids are pointers to the physical location of a row in the table block.

B-tree indexes are suitable for columns with lower selectivity. If the columns are not selective enough, the index range scan will be slower. Further, less selective columns will retrieve numerous rowids from the leaf blocks leading to excessive single block access to the table.

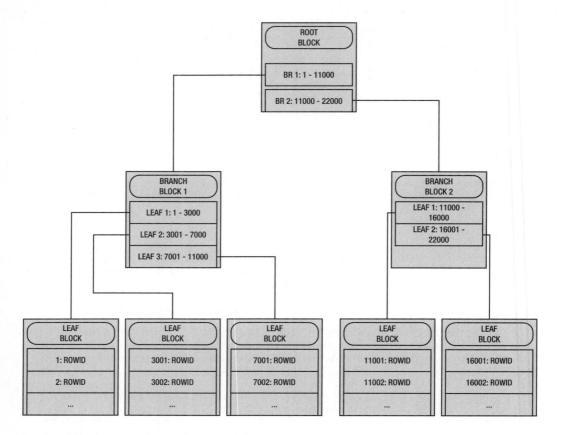

Figure 12-1. *B-tree Index Structure*

Bitmap Indexes

Bitmap indexes are organized and implemented differently than B-tree indexes, bitmaps are employed to indicate the rowids with the column value. Bitmap indexes are not suitable for columns with higher number of updates or tables with heavy DML activity. Bitmap indexes are suitable for data warehouse tables with mostly read only operations on columns with lower distinct values. If the tables are loaded regularly, as in the case of a typical data warehouse table, it is important to drop the bitmap index before the load, then load data and recreate the bitmap index.

Bitmap indexes can be created on partitioned tables, too, but they must be created as local indexes. As of Oracle Database release 11gR2, bitmap indexes cannot be created as global indexes. Bitmap indexes cannot be created as unique indexes either.

In Listing 12-4, two new bitmap indexes are added on columns Country and Region. The SELECT statement specifies predicates on columns Country and Region. The execution plan shows three major operations: bitmaps from the bitmap index sales_fact_part_bm1 were fetched applying the predicate country='Spain'; the bitmaps from the bitmap index sales_fact_part_bm2 were fetched applying the predicate region='Western Europe'; and then those two bitmaps were ANDed to calculate the final bitmap using the BITMAP AND operation. This resultant bitmap was converted to rowids and the table rows were accessed using those rowids.

Listing 12-4. *Bitmap Indexes*

```
drop index sales_fact_part_bm1;
drop index sales_fact_part_bm2;

create bitmap index sales_fact_part_bm1 on sales_fact_part ( country ) Local;
create bitmap index sales_fact_part_bm2 on sales_fact_part ( region )  Local ;

set termout off
select * from sales_fact_part where country='Spain' and region='Western Europe' ;
set termout on
@x
-----------------------------------------------------------...--------------
| Id | Operation                          | Name                 | | Pstart| Pstop
----------------------------------------------------------------------------
|  0 | SELECT STATEMENT                   |                      | |      |
|  1 |  PARTITION HASH ALL                |                      | |    1 |    32
|  2 |   TABLE ACCESS BY LOCAL INDEX ROWID| SALES_FACT_PART      | |    1 |    32
|  3 |    BITMAP CONVERSION TO ROWIDS     |                      | |      |
|  4 |     BITMAP AND                     |                      | |      |
|* 5 |      BITMAP INDEX SINGLE VALUE     | SALES_FACT_PART_BM1  | |    1 |    32
|* 6 |      BITMAP INDEX SINGLE VALUE     | SALES_FACT_PART_BM2  | |    1 |    32
----------------------------------------------------------------------------
```

Bitmap indexes can introduce severe locking issues if the index was created on column modified heavily by DML activity. Updates to a column with bitmap index must update a bitmap, and the bitmaps usually cover a set of rows. So, an update to one row can lock a set of rows in that bitmap. Bitmap indexes are used predominantly in data warehouse applications and it is of limited use in OLTP applications.

Index Organized Tables

Conventional tables are organized as heap tables as the table rows can be stored in any table block. Fetching a row from a conventional table using a primary key would involve primary key index traversal, followed by a table block access using the rowid. In index organized tables (IOTs), the table itself is organized as an index, all columns are stored in the index tree itself, and the access to a row using a primary key would involve index access only. This access using IOT is better since all columns can be fetched accessing the index structure, thereby avoiding the table access. This is an efficient access pattern as the number of accesses is minimized.

With conventional tables, every row has a rowid. Once the row is created in a conventional table, they do not move (row chaining and row migration possible, but the head piece of the row will not move). However, IOT rows are stored in the index structure itself. So, rows can be migrated to different leaf blocks due to DML operations, resulting in index leaf block splitting and merging. In a nutshell, rows in the IOTs do not have physical rowids, whereas rows in the heap tables always will have a fixed rowid.

IOTs are appropriate for tables with the following properties:

- **Tables with shorter row length**: Tables with fewer short columns are appropriate for IOTs. If the row length is longer, the size of index structure can be unduly large, leading to more resource usage then the heap tables.

- **Tables accessed mostly through primary key columns**: While secondary indexes can be created on IOTs, secondary indexes can be resource intensive if the primary key is longer. Secondary indexes will be covered later in this section.

In Listing 12-5, an IOT Sales_iot is created by specifying the keywords organization index. Notice the SELECT statement specifies few columns in the primary key and the execution plan shows that columns are retrieved by an index range scan, thereby avoiding a table access. Had this been a conventional heap table, you would see INDEX UNIQUE SCAN access path followed by a rowid based table access.

Listing 12-5. *Index Organized Tables*

```
drop table sales_iot;
create table sales_iot
  ( prod_id number not null,
    cust_id number not null,
    time_id date not null,
    channel_id number not null,
    promo_id number not null,
    quantity_sold number (10,2) not null,
    amount_sold number(10,2) not null,
    primary key ( prod_id, cust_id, time_id, channel_id, promo_id)
 )
organization index ;
insert into sales_iot select * from sales;
commit;

@analyze_table

select quantity_sold, amount_sold from sales_iot where
prod_id=13 and cust_id=2 and channel_id=3 and promo_id=999;
@x
```

```
----------------------------------------------------------------------
| Id  | Operation         | Name       | Rows | Bytes | Cost (%CPU)|
----------------------------------------------------------------------
|   0 | SELECT STATEMENT  |            |      |       |   2 (100)|
|*  1 |  INDEX RANGE SCAN | SYS_IOT_PK |    1 |    78 |   2   (0)|
----------------------------------------------------------------------
```

A secondary index can be created on an IOT, too. Conventional indexes store the (column value, rowid) pair. But, in IOT, rows do not have physical rowid, instead a (column value, logical rowid) pair is stored in the secondary index. This logical rowid is essentially a primary key column with the values of the row stored efficiently. Access through the secondary index fetches the logical rowid using the secondary index, then uses the logical rowid to access the row piece using the primary key IOT structure.

In the Listing 12-6, a secondary index Sales_iot_sec is created on an IOT Sales_iot. The SELECT statement specifies the predicates on secondary index columns. The execution plan shows an all index access, where logical rowids are fetched from the secondary index Sales_iot_sec with an INDEX RANGE SCAN access method, and then rows are fetched from the IOT primary key using the logical rowids fetched with an INDEX UNIQUE SCAN access method. Also, note that size of the secondary index is nearly one-half of the size of the primary index and the secondary indexes can be resource intensive if the primary key is longer.

Listing 12-6. *Secondary Indexes on IOT*

```
drop index sales_iot_sec ;
create index sales_iot_sec on
 sales_iot (channel_id, time_id, promo_id, cust_id) ;

select quantity_sold, amount_sold from sales_iot where
channel_id=3 and promo_id=999 and cust_id=12345 and time_id='30-JAN-00';
@x
-------------------------------------------------------------------------
| Id  | Operation          | Name          | Rows  | Bytes | Cost (%CPU)|
-------------------------------------------------------------------------
|   0 | SELECT STATEMENT   |               |       |       |   7 (100)|
|*  1 |  INDEX UNIQUE SCAN | SALES_IOT_PK  |     4 |   112 |   7   (0)|
|*  2 |   INDEX RANGE SCAN | SALES_IOT_SEC |     4 |       |   3   (0)|
-------------------------------------------------------------------------

col segment_name format A30
select segment_name, sum( bytes/1024/1024) sz from dba_segments
where segment_name in ('SALES_IOT_PK','SALES_IOT_SEC')
group by segment_name
/
SEGMENT_NAME                           SZ
------------------------------ ----------
SALES_IOT_SEC                          36
SALES_IOT_PK                           72
```

Index organized tables are special structures that are useful to eliminate additional indexes on tables with short rows that undergo heavy DML and SELECT activity. But adding secondary indexes on IOT can cause increase in index size, redo size, and undo size if the primary key is longer.

Partitioned Indexes

Indexes can be partitioned similar to table partitioning scheme. There are varieties of ways to partition the indexes. Indexes can be created on partitioned tables as local or global indexes, too. Further, there are various partitioning schemes available such as range partitioning, hash partitioning, list partitioning, and composite partitioning schemes. From Oracle Database version 10g onwards, partitioned indexes also can be created on non-partitioned tables.

Local Indexes

Locally partitioned indexes are created with the LOCAL keyword and have the same partition boundaries as the table. In a nutshell, there is an index partition associated with each table partition. Availability of the table is better since the maintenance operations can be performed at individual partition level. Maintenance operations on the index partitions lock only the corresponding table partitions, not the whole table.

If the local index includes the partitioning key columns *and* if the SQL statement specifies predicates on the partitioning key columns, the execution plan needs to access just one or few index partitions. This concept is known as partition elimination. Performance improves if the execution plan searches in minimal number of partitions. In the Listing 12-6, a partitioned table Sales_fact_part is created with a partitioning key on Year column. A local index Sales_fact_part_n1 is created on Product and Year column. First, the SELECT statement specifies the predicates on just the Product column without specifying any predicate on the partitioning key column. In this case, all five index partitions must be accessed using the predicates product = 'Xtend Memory'. Columns PStart and PStop in the execution plan indicate that all partitions are accessed to execute this SQL statement.

Next, the SELECT statement in Listing 12-7 specifies the predicates on columns Product and Year. Using the predicate Year=1998, the optimizer determines that only the second partition is to be accessed, eliminating access to all other partitions, as only the second partition stores the Year column 1998 as indicated by the PStart and PStop columns in the execution plan. Also, the keywords in the execution plan TABLE ACCESS BY LOCAL INDEX ROWID indicate that row is accessed using a local index.

Listing 12-7. *Local Indexes*

```
drop table sales_fact_part;
CREATE table sales_fact_part
partition by range ( year )
( partition p_1997 values less than ( 1998) ,
  partition p_1998 values less than ( 1999),
  partition p_1999 values less than (2000),
  partition p_2000 values less than (2001),
  partition p_max values less than (maxvalue)
)
AS SELECT * from sales_fact;

create index sales_fact_part_n1 on sales_fact_part( product, year) local;

set lines 120 pages 100
set serveroutput off

select * from  (
 select * from sales_fact_part where product = 'Xtend Memory'
) where rownum <21 ;

@x
```

```
-------------------------------------------------- . . .---------------
| Id  | Operation                            | Name            |   |Pstart|Pstop
-------------------------------------------------- . . .---------------
|   0 | SELECT STATEMENT                     |                 |   |      |
|*  1 |  COUNT STOPKEY                       |                 |   |      |
|   2 |   PARTITION RANGE ALL                |                 |   |    1 |     5
|   3 |    TABLE ACCESS BY LOCAL INDEX ROWID| SALES_FACT_PART  |   |    1 |     5
|*  4 |     INDEX RANGE SCAN                 | SALES_FACT_PART_N1 |  |    1 |     5
-------------------------------------------------- . . .---------------
```

```
select * from  (
 select * from sales_fact_part where product = 'Xtend Memory' and year=1998
) where rownum <21 ;
@x
```

```
-------------------------------------------------- . . .---------------
| Id  | Operation                            | Name            |   |Pstart|Pstop
-------------------------------------------------- . . .---------------
|   0 | SELECT STATEMENT                     |                 |   |      |
|*  1 |  COUNT STOPKEY                       |                 |   |      |
|   2 |   PARTITION RANGE SINGLE             |                 |   |    2 |     2
|   3 |    TABLE ACCESS BY LOCAL INDEX ROWID| SALES_FACT_PART  |   |    2 |     2
|*  4 |     INDEX RANGE SCAN                 | SALES_FACT_PART_N1 |  |    2 |     2
-------------------------------------------------- . . .---------------
```

While the application availability is important, you should consider another point: if the predicate does not specify partitioning key column, then all index partitions must be accessed to identify the candidate rows in the case of LOCAL indexes. This could lead to a performance issue if the partition count is very high, in the order of 1000s. Even then, you want to measure the impact of creating the index as a LOCAL instead of a GLOBAL index.

Creating local indexes will improve the concurrency, too. I will discuss this concept while discussing hash partitioning schemes.

Global Indexes

Global indexes are created with the keyword GLOBAL. In global indexes, partition boundaries of the index and the table do not need to match, and the partition keys can be different between the table and the index.

In Listing 12-8, a global index Sales_fact_part_n1 is created on Year column. The partition boundaries are different between the table and the index, even though the partitioning column is the same. The subsequent SELECT statement specifies the predicate year=1998 to access the table and the execution plan shows that partition 1 of the index and partition 2 of the table is accessed. Partition pruning was performed both at table and index level.

Any maintenance on the global index will lead to acquiring a higher level lock on the table, thereby reducing application availability. In contrast, maintenance can be done at the partition level in the local indexes affecting only the corresponding table partition. In this example, rebuilding the index Sales_fact_part_n1 will acquire a table level lock in exclusive mode, leading to application down time.

Listing 12-8. *Global Indexes*

```
create index sales_fact_part_n1 on sales_fact_part (year)
global partition by range ( year)
  (partition p_1998 values less than (1999),
   partition p_2000 values less than (2001),
   partition p_max values less than  (maxvalue)
);

select * from  (
 select * from sales_fact_part where product = 'Xtend Memory' and year=1998
) where rownum <21 ;
@x
```

```
--------------------------------------------------------------------------------
|Id| Operation                          | Name             |..Pstart| Pstop |
--------------------------------------------------------------------------------
| 0| SELECT STATEMENT                   |                  |        |       |
|*1|   COUNT STOPKEY                    |                  |        |       |
| 2|    PARTITION RANGE SINGLE          |                  |    1 |     1 |
|*3|     TABLE ACCESS BY GLOBAL INDEX ROWID| SALES_FACT_PART  |    2 |     2 |
|*4|      INDEX RANGE SCAN              | SALES_FACT_PART_N1|    1 |     1 |
--------------------------------------------------------------------------------
```

Unique indexes can be created as global indexes without including partitioning columns. But the partitioning key of the table should be included in the case of LOCAL indexes to create a unique LOCAL index.

The partitioning scheme discussed so far is known as a *range partitioning scheme*. In this scheme, each partition stores rows with a range of partitioning column values. For example, clause partition p_2000 values less than (2001) specifies the upper boundary of the partition, so the partition p_2000 will store rows with Year column values less than 2001. The lower boundary of this partition is determined by the prior partition specification partition p_1998 values less than (1999). So, partition p_2000 will store the Year column value range between 1999 and 2000.

Hash Partitioning vs. Range Partitioning

In the hash partitioning scheme, the partitioning key column values are hashed using a hashing algorithm to identify the partition to store the row. This type of partitioning scheme is appropriate for partitioning columns populated with artificial keys such as rows populated with sequence generated values. If the distribution of column value is uniform, then all partitions will store nearly equal number of rows.

There are few added advantages with the hash partitioning scheme. There is an administration overhead with range partitioning scheme since new partitions need to be added regularly to accommodate future rows. For example, if the partitioning key is order date_column, then the new partitions must be added (or the partition with maxvalue specified must be split) to accommodate rows with future date values. With the hash partitioning scheme, that overhead is avoided as the rows are distributed equally among the partitions using a hashing algorithm. All partitions will have nearly equal number of rows if the distribution of column value is uniform and there is no reason to add more partitions regularly.

■**NOTE** Due to the nature of hashing algorithms, it is better to use a partition count of binary powers, i.e. 2, 4, 8, etc. If you are splitting the partitions, it's better to double the number of partitions to keep near equal sized partitions.

Hash partitioned tables and indexes are effective in combating concurrency related performance associated with unique and primary key indexes. It is typical of primary key columns to be populated using a sequence of generated values. Since the indexes store the column values in a sorted order, the column values for new rows will go into the right most leaf block of the index. After that leaf block is full, subsequently inserted rows will go in to the new right most leaf block, the contention point moving from one leaf block to another leaf block. As the concurrency of the insert into the table increases, sessions will be modifying the right most leaf block of the index aggressively. Essentially, the current right most leaf block of that index will be a major contention point. Sessions will be seen waiting for block contention wait events such as buffer busy waits. In RAC, this problem is magnified due to global cache communication overhead and the event gc buffer busy will be the top wait event. This type of index growing rapidly on the right hand is called *right hand growth indexes*.

Concurrency issues associated with the right hand growth indexes can be eliminated by hash partitioning the index with many partitions. For example, if the index is partitioned by a hash with 32 partitions, then inserts will be effectively spread among the 32 right most leaf blocks as there are 32 index trees (an index tree for an index partition). Partitioning the table using a hash partitioning scheme and then creating local index on that partitioned table also will have the same effect.

In Listing 12-9, a hash partitioned table Sales_fact_part is created and the primary key id column is populated from the sequence Sfseq. There are 32 partitions in this table with 32 matching index partitions for the Sales_fact_part_n1 index, as the index is defined as a local index. The subsequent SELECT statement is accessing the table with the predicate id=1000. Pstart and Pstop columns in the execution plan show that partition pruning took place and only partition 25 was being accessed. The optimizer identified partition 25 by applying a hash function on the column value 1000.

Listing 12-9. *Hash Partitioning Scheme*

```
drop sequence sfseq;
create sequence sfseq cache 200;

drop table sales_fact_part;
CREATE table sales_fact_part
partition by hash ( id )
partitions 32
AS SELECT sfseq.nextval id , f.* from sales_fact f;

create unique index sales_fact_part_n1 on sales_fact_part( id ) local;

set lines 120 pages 100
set serveroutput off

select * from sales_fact_part where id =1000;
@x
```

```
---------------------------------------------------------------------------
| Id  | Operation                          | Name              |...| Pstart| Pstop
---------------------------------------------------------------------------
|   0 | SELECT STATEMENT                   |                   |   |       |
|   1 |  PARTITION HASH SINGLE             |                   |   |   25  |   25
|   2 |   TABLE ACCESS BY LOCAL INDEX ROWID| SALES_FACT_PART   |   |   25  |   25
|*  3 |    INDEX UNIQUE SCAN               | SALES_FACT_PART_N1|   |   25  |   25
---------------------------------------------------------------------------
```

If the data distribution is uniform in the partitioning key, as in the case of values generated from a sequence, then the rows will be distributed uniformly to all partitions. You can use dbms_rowid package to measure the data distribution in a hash partitioned table. In Listing 12-10, you use dbms_rowid.rowid_object call to derive the object_id of the partition. As every partition has its own object_id, you can aggregate the rows by object_id to measure the distribution of rows among the partitions. The output shows that all partitions have nearly equal number of rows.

Listing 12-10. *Hash Partitioning Distribution*

```
select dbms_rowid.rowid_object(rowid) obj_id, count(*) from sales_fact_part
group by dbms_rowid.rowid_object(rowid);

    OBJ_ID   COUNT(*)
---------- ----------
     75427       3575
     75437       3478
     75441       3512
...
     75435       3453
     75445       3420
     75447       3470

32 rows selected.
```

Rows are uniformly distributed between partitions using the hashing algorithm. In few cases, you might need to pre-calculate the partition where a row will be stored. This knowledge is useful to improve massive loading of data into a hash partitioned table. As of Oracle Database version 11gR2, the ora_hash function can be used to derive the partition id if supplied with a partition key value. For example, for a table with 32 partitions, ora_hash(column_name, 31, 0) will return the partition id. The second argument to the ora_hash function is the partition count minus 1. In Listing 12-11, you use both ora_hash and dbms_rowid.rowid_object to show the mapping between the object_id and hashing algorithm output. A word of caution, though: in future releases of Oracle Database, you need to test this before relying upon this strategy as the internal implementation of hash partitioned tables may change.

Listing 12-11. *Hash Partitioning Algorithm*

```
select dbms_rowid.rowid_object(rowid) obj_id, ora_hash ( id, 31, 0) part_id ,count(*) from
sales_fact_part
group by dbms_rowid.rowid_object(rowid), ora_hash(id,31,0)
order by 1;
```

```
    OBJ_ID     PART_ID     COUNT(*)
---------- ---------- ----------
     75418          0        3505
     75419          1        3492
...
     75446         28        3424
     75447         29        3470
     75448         30        3555
     75449         31        3527
...
```

In essence, concurrency can be increased by partitioning the table and creating the right hand growth indexes as local indexes. If the table cannot be partitioned, then that index alone can be partitioned to hash partitioning schema to resolve the performance issue.

Solutions to Match Application Characteristics

Oracle Database also provides indexing facilities to match the application characteristics. For example, some application might be using function calls heavily and SQL statements from those applications can be tuned using function based indexes. I will discuss a few special indexing options available in Oracle Database.

Compressed Indexes

Compressed indexes are variation of the conventional B-tree indexes. This type of index is more suitable for columns with repeating values in the leading columns. Compression is achieved by storing the repeating values in the leading columns once in the index leaf block. Pointers from the row area points to these prefix rows, avoiding explicit storage of these repeating values in the row area. Compressed indexes can be smaller compared to conventional indexes if the column has many repeating values. There is a minor increase in CPU usage in the processing of compressed indexes; this can be ignored safely.

The simplified syntax for the compressed index specification clause is:

```
Create index <index name> on <schema.table_name>
( col1 [,col2... coln] )
Compress N Storage-parameter-clause
;
```

The number of leading columns to compress can be specified while creating a compressed index using the syntax compress N. For example, to compress two leading columns in a three column index, the clause compress 2 can be specified. Repeating values in the first two columns are stored in the prefix area just once. You can only compress the leading columns; for example, you can't compress columns 1 and 3.

In Listing 12-12, a compressed index Sales_fact_c1 is created on columns Product, Year, and Week with a compression clause compress 2 specified to compress the two leading columns. In this example, the repeating values of Product and Year columns are stored once in the leaf blocks as the compress 2 clause is specified. As there is higher amount of repetition in these two column values, the index size is reduced from 6MB (conventional index) to 2MB (compressed index) by compressing these two leading columns.

Listing 12-12. *Compressed Indexes*

```
select * from  (
  select product, year,week, sale from sales_fact
  order by product, year,week
) where rownum <21;
```

```
PRODUCT                           YEAR  WEEK       SALE
------------------------------- ---------- ----- ----------
1.44MB External 3.5" Diskette     1998    1        9.71
1.44MB External 3.5" Diskette     1998    1       38.84
1.44MB External 3.5" Diskette     1998    1        9.71
...
create index sales_fact_c1 on sales_fact ( product, year, week);

select 'Compressed index size (MB) :' ||trunc(bytes/1024/1024, 2)
from user_segments where segment_name='SALES_FACT_C1';

Compressed index size (MB) :6
...
create index sales_fact_c1 on sales_fact ( product, year, week) compress 2;

select 'Compressed index size (MB) :' ||trunc(bytes/1024/1024,2)
from user_segments where segment_name='SALES_FACT_C1';

Compressed index size (MB) :2
```

In Figure 12-2, a high level overview of a compressed index leaf block is shown. This compressed index is a two column index on Continent and Country columns. Repeating values of Continent columns are stored once in the prefix area of the index leaf blocks as the index is created with the clause compress 1. Pointers are used from the row area pointing to the prefix rows. For example, the Continent column value ASIA occurs in three rows [(Asia, HongKong), (Asia, India), and (Asia, Indonesia)] but is stored once in the prefix area, and these three rows are reusing the continent column value, avoiding explicit storage of the value three times. This reuse of column values reduces the size of index.

It is evident that data properties play critical role in the compression ratio. If the repetition count of the column values is higher, then the compressed indexes will provide greater benefit. If there is no repetition, then the compressed index might be bigger than the conventional index. So, compressed indexes are suitable for indexes with fewer distinct values in the leading columns. Columns Compression and Prefix_length in the dba_indexes/user_indexes view shows the compression attributes of the indexes.

The number of columns to choose for compression depends upon the column value distribution. To identify the optimal number of columns to compress, the analyze index/validate structure statement can be used. In Listing 12-5, an uncompressed index SALES_FACT_C1 is analyzed with validate structure clause. This analyze statement populates the Index_stats view. The column Index_stats.opt_cmpr_count displays the optimal compression count; for this index, it's 2. The column Index_stats.Cmpr_pctsave displays the index size savings compressing with Opt_cmpr_count columns. In this example, there will be a saving of 67% in the index space usage; so, the size of the compressed index with compress 2 clause will be of 33% of the conventional uncompressed index size. This size estimate computes to 1.98MB and is close enough to actual index size.

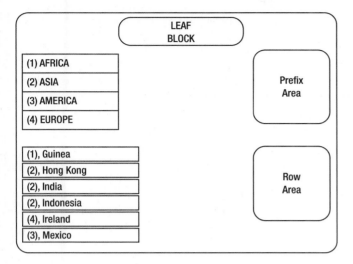

Figure 12-2. *Compressed index*

Beware that `analyze index validate structure` statement will acquire a share level lock on the table and might induce application downtime.

Listing 12-13. *Optimal Compression Count*

```
analyze index sales_fact_c1 validate structure;
Index analyzed.

select opt_cmpr_count, opt_cmpr_pctsave from index_stats
where name ='SALES_FACT_C1';

OPT_CMPR_COUNT OPT_CMPR_PCTSAVE
-------------- ----------------
             2               67
             3
```

There are few restrictions on compressed indexes, though. For example, all columns can be compressed in the case of non-unique indexes; and all but the last column can be compressed in the case of unique indexes.

Function Based Indexes

If a predicate applies a function on an indexed column, then the index on that column might not be chosen by the optimizer. For example, the index on id column may not be chosen for the predicate `to_char(id)='1000'` since `to_char` function is applied on the indexed column. This restriction can be overcome by creating a function based index on the expression `to_char(id)`. Function based indexes pre-store the results of functions. Expression specified in the predicate must match with the expression specified in the function based index, though.

A function based index can be created on user defined functions, but that function must be defined as a deterministic function, meaning the function must always return a consistent value for every execution of the function. User defined functions that do not adhere to this rule can't be used to create the function based indexes.

In the Listing 12-14, a SELECT statement accesses the Sales_fact_part table using the clause to_char(id)='1000'. Without a function based index, the optimizer chose a full table scan access plan. A function based index fact_part_fbi1 with the expression to_char(id) was added, and the optimizer chooses an index based access path for the SELECT statement.

Listing 12-14. *Function Based Index*

```
drop index sales_fact_part_fbi1;
select * from sales_fact_part where to_char(id)='1000';
@x
```

```
----------------------------------------------...-----------------
| Id  | Operation          | Name         |    | Pstart| Pstop |
-------------------------------------------------------------------
|   0 | SELECT STATEMENT   |              |    |       |       |
|   1 |  PARTITION HASH ALL|              |    |    1  |   32  |
|*  2 |   TABLE ACCESS FULL| SALES_FACT_PART |  |   1  |   32  |
-------------------------------------------------------------------
```

```
create index sales_fact_part_fbi1 on sales_fact_part( to_char(id)) ;
@analyze_table_sfp
select * from sales_fact_part where to_char(id)='1000';
@x
```

```
-----------------------------------------------------------...-
| Id  | Operation                          | Name              |  |
-----------------------------------------------------------------
|   0 | SELECT STATEMENT                   |                   |  |
|   1 |  TABLE ACCESS BY GLOBAL INDEX ROWID| SALES_FACT_PART   |  |
|*  2 |   INDEX RANGE SCAN                 | SALES_FACT_PART_FBI1|  |
-----------------------------------------------------------------
```

```
Predicate Information (identified by operation id):
---------------------------------------------------
2 - access("SALES_FACT_PART"."SYS_NC00009$"='1000')
```

Note the access predicates printed at the end of the Listing 12-14 "SYS_NC00009$" = '1000'. A few implementation details of the function based indexes are listed in the Listing 12-5. Function based indexes add a virtual column with the specified expression as default value and then indexes that virtual column. This virtual column is visible in the dba_tab_cols view, and the dba_tab_cols.data_default column shows that expression used to populate the virtual column. Further View dba_ind_columns show that the virtual column is indexed.

Listing 12-15. *Virtual Columns and Function Based Index*

```
select data_default, hidden_column, virtual_column from dba_tab_cols
where table_name='SALES_FACT_PART' and virtual_column='YES'
;
DATA_DEFAULT                      HID VIR
------------------------------    --- ---
TO_CHAR("ID")                     YES YES

select index_name,column_name from dba_ind_columns
where index_name='SALES_FACT_PART_FBI1'
;
INDEX_NAME                        COLUMN_NAME
------------------------------    -------------
SALES_FACT_PART_FBI1              SYS_NC00009$
```

It is important to collect statistics on the *table* after adding a function based index. If not, that new virtual column will not have statistics, which might lead to performance anomalies. Script analyze_table_sfp.sql is used to collect statistics on the table with cascade=>true and the Listing 12-16 shows the contents of the script analyze_table_sfp.sql.

Listing 12-16. *Analyze_table_sfp.sql*

```
begin
    dbms_stats.gather_table_stats (
    ownname =>user,
    tabname=>'SALES_FACT_PART',
    estimate_percent=>30,
    cascade=>true);
end;
/
```

Function based indexes can be implemented using virtual columns explicitly, too. An index can be added over that virtual column optionally. The added advantage with this method is that you can also employ partitioning scheme with a virtual column as the partitioning key. In Listing 12-17, a new virtual column id_char is added to the table using the virtual keyword. Then a globally partitioned index on id_char virtual column is created. The execution plan of the SELECT statement shows that table is accessed using the new index and the predicate to_char(id)='1000' is rewritten to use the virtual column with the predicate id_char='1000'.

Listing 12-17. *Virtual Columns and Function Based Index*

```
alter table sales_fact_part add
 ( id_char varchar2(40) generated always as (to_char(id) ) virtual )
/
create index sales_fact_part_c1 on sales_fact_part ( id_char)
global partition by hash (id_char)
partitions 32
/
```

```
@analyze_table_sfp
select * from sales_fact_part where to_char(id)='1000'
/
@x

-----------------------------------------------------------------
| Id  | Operation                            | Name              |
-----------------------------------------------------------------
|   0 | SELECT STATEMENT                     |                   |
|   1 |  PARTITION HASH SINGLE               |                   |
|   2 |   TABLE ACCESS BY GLOBAL INDEX ROWID | SALES_FACT_PART   |
|*  3 |    INDEX RANGE SCAN                  | SALES_FACT_PART_C1 |
-----------------------------------------------------------------

Predicate Information (identified by operation id):
---------------------------------------------------
   3 - access("SALES_FACT_PART"."ID_CHAR"='1000')
```

Reverse Key Indexes

Reverse key indexes were introduced as another option to combat performance issues associated with right-hand growth indexes discussed in the section titled "Hash Partitioning vs. Range Partitioning." In the reverse key indexes, column values are stored in the reverse order, character by character. For example, column value 12345 is stored as 54321 in the index. As the column values are stored in reverse order, consecutive column values will be stored in different leaf blocks of the index, thereby avoiding the contention issues with right hand growth indexes. In the table blocks, these column values are stored as 12345, though.

There are two issues with reverse key indexes:

- The range scan on reverse key indexes is not possible for range operators such as between, <, >, etc. This is understandable as the underlying assumption of an index range scan is that column values are stored in ascending or descending logical key order. Reverse key indexes break that assumption as the column values are stored in the reverse order, no logical key order is maintained, and so index range scans are not possible with reverse key indexes.

- Reverse key indexes can artificially increase physical reads as the column values are stored in numerous leaf blocks and those leaf blocks might need to be read in to buffer cache to modify the block. But, cost of this increase in I/O should be measured against the concurrency issues associated with right hand growth indexes.

In the Listing 12-18, a reverse key index Sales_fact_part_n1 is created with a reverse keyword. First, the SELECT statement with the predicate id=1000 is using the reverse key index, as equality predicates can use the reverse key indexes. But, the next SELECT statement with the predicate id between 1000 and 1001 is using the Full Table Scan access path, as the Index Range Scan access path is not possible with reverse key indexes.

Listing 12-18. *Reverse Key Indexes*

```
drop index sales_fact_part_n1;
create unique index sales_fact_part_n1 on sales_fact_part ( id ) global  reverse ;
select * from sales_fact_part where id=1000;
@x
```

```
------------------------------------------------------------...-------------
| Id | Operation                        | Name               |  |Pstart|Pstop
------------------------------------------------------------...-------------
|  0 | SELECT STATEMENT                 |                    |  |      |
|  1 |   TABLE ACCESS BY GLOBAL INDEX ROWID| SALES_FACT_PART |  |  25  |   25
|* 2 |    INDEX UNIQUE SCAN             | SALES_FACT_PART_N1 |  |      |
------------------------------------------------------------...-------------
```

```
set termout off

select * from sales_fact_part where id between 1000 and 1001;
set termout on
@x
```

```
---------------------------------------------...------------------
| Id | Operation          | Name          |  | Pstart| Pstop |
---------------------------------------------...------------------
|  0 | SELECT STATEMENT   |               |  |       |       |
|  1 |  PARTITION HASH ALL|               |  |   1   |   32  |
|* 2 |    TABLE ACCESS FULL| SALES_FACT_PART |  |   1   |   32  |
-----------------------------------------------------------------
```

Especially in RAC, right-hand growth indexes can cause intolerable performance issues. Reverse key indexes were introduced to combat that performance problem. But you should probably consider hash partitioned indexes instead of reverse key indexes.

Descending Indexes

Indexes store column values in ascending order by default; this can be switched to descending order using descending indexes. If your application fetches the data in a specific order, then the rows need to be sorted before the rows are sent to the application. These sorts can be avoided using the descending indexes. These indexes are useful if the application is fetching the data millions of times in a specific order, for example, customer data fetched from the customer transaction table in the reverse chronological order.

In the Listing 12-19, an index Sales_fact_c1 added with the column list as product desc, year desc, week desc specifying a descending order for these three columns. The SELECT statement accesses the table specifying an order by clause with the sort order product desc, year desc, week desc matching with index sort order. The execution plan shows that there is no sort step even though there is an order by clause in the SELECT statement.

Descending indexes are implemented as a function based index as of Oracle Database release 11gR2.

Listing 12-19. *Descending Indexes*

```
drop index sales_fact_c1;
create index sales_fact_c1 on sales_fact ( product desc, year desc, week desc ) ;
@analyze_sf.sql
set termout off
select year, week from sales_fact s where year in ( 1998,1999,2000) and week<5
and product='Xtend Memory'
order by product desc,year desc, week desc ;
set termout on
@x
```

```
-------------------------------------------------------------------------
| Id | Operation          | Name          | Rows  | Bytes | Cost (%CPU)|...|
-------------------------------------------------------------------------
|  0 | SELECT STATEMENT |              |       |       |    13 (100)|   |
|* 1 |   INDEX RANGE SCAN| SALES_FACT_C1 |   105 |  3570 |    13   (0)|   |
-------------------------------------------------------------------------
```

```
select index_name, index_type from dba_indexes
where index_name='SALES_FACT_C1';
Index
Name                              INDEX_TYPE
-----------------------------     --------------------------
SALES_FACT_C1                     FUNCTION-BASED NORMAL
```

Solutions to Management Problems

Indexes can be used to resolve operational problems faced in the real world. For example, to see the effects of a new index on a production application, you can employ invisible indexes. You can also use invisible indexes to *safely* drop the indexes.

Invisible Indexes

In certain scenarios, you might want to add an index to tune the performance of a SQL statement, but you are not sure about the negative impact of the index. Invisible indexes are useful to measure the impact of a new index with less risk. An index can be added to the database marked as invisible and the optimizer will not choose that index. It can be marked as invisible after confirming that there is no negative impact or no negative execution plan regression due to that index.

After adding the index to the database, you could set a parameter optimizer_use_invisible_indexes to true in your session without affecting the application performance and then review the execution plan of the SQL statement. In Listing 12-20, first SELECT statement uses the index sales_fact_c1 in the execution plan. The next SQL statement is marking the Sales_fact_c1 index as invisible and the second execution plan of the same SELECT statement shows that the index is ignored by the optimizer.

Listing 12-20. *Invisible Indexes*

```
select * from  (
 select * from sales_fact where product = 'Xtend Memory' and year=1998 and week=1
) where rownum <21
;
@x
```

```
-------------------------------------------------------------------
| Id  | Operation                   | Name          | Rows | Bytes |
-------------------------------------------------------------------
|   0 | SELECT STATEMENT            |               |      |       |
|*  1 |  COUNT STOPKEY              |               |      |       |
|   2 |   TABLE ACCESS BY INDEX ROWID| SALES_FACT   |    7 |   490 |
|*  3 |    INDEX RANGE SCAN         | SALES_FACT_C1 |    7 |       |
-------------------------------------------------------------------
```

```
alter index sales_fact_c1 invisible;
select * from  (
 select * from sales_fact where product = 'Xtend Memory' and year=1998 and week=1
) where rownum <21
;
@x
```

```
---------------------------------------------------------
| Id  | Operation          | Name       | Rows | Bytes |
---------------------------------------------------------
|   0 | SELECT STATEMENT   |            |      |       |
|*  1 |  COUNT STOPKEY     |            |      |       |
|*  2 |   TABLE ACCESS FULL| SALES_FACT |    7 |   490 |
---------------------------------------------------------
```

In Listing 12-21, the execution plan shows that the optimizer chose the Sales_fact_c1 index after setting the parameter to true at session level.

There is another use case for the invisible indexes. These indexes are useful to reduce the risk while dropping unused indexes. It is not a pleasant experience to drop unused indexes from a production database, only to realize later that the dropped index is used in *that* important report. Even after performing extensive analysis, it is possible that the dropped index might be needed for a business process and recreating indexes might lead to application downtime. From Oracle Database version 11g onwards, you can mark the index as invisible, wait for few weeks, and then drop the index if no process is affected with less risk. If the index is needed after marking them as invisible, then that index can be reverted back to visible state with just a SQL statement quickly.

Listing 12-21. *Optimizer_use_invisible_indexes*

```
alter session set optimizer_use_invisible_indexes =true;
select * from  (
 select * from sales_fact where product = 'Xtend Memory' and year=1998 and week=1
) where rownum <21
;
@x
```

```
--------------------------------------------------------------------------
| Id  | Operation                       | Name         | Rows  | Bytes |
--------------------------------------------------------------------------
|   0 | SELECT STATEMENT                |              |       |       |
|*  1 |  COUNT STOPKEY                  |              |       |       |
|   2 |   TABLE ACCESS BY INDEX ROWID   | SALES_FACT   |    7  |   490 |
|*  3 |    INDEX RANGE SCAN             | SALES_FACT_C1|    7  |       |
--------------------------------------------------------------------------
```

Invisible indexes are maintained during DML activity similar to any other indexes. This operational feature is useful in reducing the risk associated with dropping indexes.

Virtual Indexes

Have you ever added an index only to realize later that the index is not chosen by the optimizer due to data distribution or some statistics issue? Virtual indexes are useful to review the effectiveness of an index. Virtual indexes do not have storage allocated and so can be created quickly. Virtual indexes are different from invisible indexes in that the invisible indexes have storage associated with them, just the optimizer cannot choose them and the virtual indexes do not have storage segment associated with them. For that reason, virtual indexes are also termed as *nosegment* indexes.

A session modifiable underscore parameter _use_nosegment_indexes controls whether the optimizer can consider a virtual index or not. This parameter is false by default and the application will not choose virtual indexes. You can test the virtual index without affecting other application functionality with this method: create index, enable the parameter to true in your session, and verify the execution plan of the SQL statement. In Listing 12-22, a virtual index Sales_virt was created with nosegment clause. After modifying the parameter to true in the current session, the execution plan of the SELECT statement is checked. The execution plan shows that this index will be chosen by the optimizer for this SQL statement. After reviewing the plan, this index can be dropped and recreated as conventional index.

Listing 12-22. *Virtual Indexes*

```
create index sales_virt on sales ( cust_id, promo_id) nosegment;
alter session set "_use_nosegment_indexes"=true;

explain plan for select * from sales where cust_id=:b1 and promo_id=:b2;

select * from table(dbms_xplan.display(null,'','all'))'
```

```
--------------------------------------------------------------------------
| Id  | Operation                         | Name       |  | Cost (%CPU)|
--------------------------------------------------------------------------
|   0 | SELECT STATEMENT                  |            |  |    9   (0)|
|   1 |  TABLE ACCESS BY GLOBAL INDEX ROWID| SALES     |  |    9   (0)|
|*  2 |   INDEX RANGE SCAN                | SALES_VIRT |  |    1   (0)|
--------------------------------------------------------------------------
```

Virtual indexes do not have storage associated with them and so these indexes are not maintained. But you could collect statistics on these indexes as if they are conventional indexes. Virtual indexes can be used to improve the cardinality estimates of predicates without incurring the storage overhead associated with the conventional indexes.

Bitmap Join Indexes

Bitmap join indexes are useful in data warehouse applications to materialize the joins between fact and dimension tables. In data warehouse tables, fact tables are typically much larger than the dimension tables, and the dimension and fact tables are joined using primary key—with a foreign key relationship between them. These joins are costlier due to the size of the fact tables, and the performance can be improved for these queries if the join results can be pre-stored. Materialized views are one option to pre-calculate the join results and the bitmap join indexes are another option.

In Listing 12-23, a typical data warehouse query and its execution plan is shown. Table Sales is a fact table and other tables are dimension tables in this query. The Sales table is joined to other dimension tables by primary key columns on the dimension tables. The execution plan shows Sales table is the leading table in this join processing and other dimension tables are joined to derive the final result set. These are the four join operations in this execution plan. This execution plan can be very costly if the fact table is huge.

Listing 12-23. *A Typical DW Query*

```
select sum(s.quantity_sold), sum(s.amount_sold)
  from sales s, products p, customers c, channels ch
where s.prod_id = p.prod_id and
      s.cust_id = c.cust_id and
      s.channel_id = ch.channel_id and
      p.prod_name='Y box' and
      c.cust_first_name='Abigail' and
      ch.channel_desc = 'Direct_sales'
/
```

Id	Operation	Name	Rows	Bytes
0	SELECT STATEMENT			
1	SORT AGGREGATE		1	75
* 2	HASH JOIN		20	1500
* 3	TABLE ACCESS FULL	CUSTOMERS	43	516
4	NESTED LOOPS			
5	NESTED LOOPS		3235	199K
6	MERGE JOIN CARTESIAN		1	43
* 7	TABLE ACCESS FULL	CHANNELS	1	13
8	BUFFER SORT		1	30
* 9	TABLE ACCESS FULL	PRODUCTS	1	30
10	PARTITION RANGE ALL			
11	BITMAP CONVERSION TO ROWIDS			
12	BITMAP AND			
* 13	BITMAP INDEX SINGLE VALUE	SALES_PROD_BIX		
* 14	BITMAP INDEX SINGLE VALUE	SALES_CHANNEL_BIX		
15	TABLE ACCESS BY LOCAL INDEX ROWID	SALES	3190	63800

In the Listing 12-24, a bitmap join index Sales_bji1 is created to pre-calculate the join results. Notice the index creation statement is joining Sales and the dimension tables similar to the join predicates specified in the query. The SELECT statement is re-executed after creating the index, and the execution plan of the SELECT statement shows access to the bitmap join index, followed by access to the Sales table without any join processing. Internally, three new virtual columns are added to this table and an index is created on these three virtual columns. In a nutshell, the bitmap join index materializes the result set with the indexes on the virtual columns, thereby avoiding costly join processing.

There are few restrictions on bitmap join index, all dimensions need to have validated primary or unique constraints defined, the index must be local, etc. The first three statements in Listing 12-24 is modifying the constraint state to validated to enable creation of bitmap join index.

Listing 12-24. *Bitmap Join Index*

```
alter table products modify primary key validate;
alter table customers modify primary key validate;
alter table channels modify primary key validate;

create bitmap index sales_bji1 on sales ( p.prod_name, c.cust_first_name, ch.channel_desc)
from sales s, products p, customers c, channels ch
where s.prod_id = p.prod_id and
      s.cust_id = c.cust_id and
      s.channel_id = ch.channel_id
LOCAL
/

select sum(s.quantity_sold), sum(s.amount_sold)
  from sales s, products p, customers c, channels ch
where s.prod_id = p.prod_id and
      s.cust_id = c.cust_id and
      s.channel_id = ch.channel_id and
      p.prod_name='Y box' and
      c.cust_first_name='Abigail' and
      ch.channel_desc = 'Direct sales'
/
@x
```

```
---------------------------------------------------------------------
| Id  | Operation                        | Name       | Rows | Bytes |
---------------------------------------------------------------------
|   0 | SELECT STATEMENT                 |            |    1 |    20 |
|   1 |  SORT AGGREGATE                  |            |    1 |    20 |
|   2 |   PARTITION RANGE ALL            |            |   19 |   380 |
|   3 |    TABLE ACCESS BY LOCAL INDEX ROWID| SALES   |   19 |   380 |
|   4 |     BITMAP CONVERSION TO ROWIDS  |            |      |       |
|*  5 |      BITMAP INDEX SINGLE VALUE   | SALES_BJI1 |      |       |
---------------------------------------------------------------------
```

Bitmap join indexes are useful in data warehouse environments, adhering to a good data model. These indexes are not useful in OLTP applications, though.

Summary

A good choice of index type and an optimal choice of indexed columns are essential to maintaining application performance. Armed with knowledge about various index types, you should focus on matching index types to application access paths. As Oracle Database provides rich index functionality, it is best to employ optimal index types to suit your application access patterns. It's also vitally important to add indexes only when necessary. Unnecessary indexes not only waste space, they also waste valuable CPU cycles and memory. Further, excessive indexes will increase redo size and undo size.

■ ■ ■

Beyond the SELECT

Kerry Osborne

This chapter is a collection of topics involving SQL statements that are not straight SELECTs. These statements are often referred to as Data Manipulation Language (or DML) statements. My intention is to provide some information on some of the less well known options to the standard DML commands, namely INSERT, UPDATE, DELETE, and MERGE. The chapter will also focus on alternate approaches with an eye towards improving performance.

INSERT

INSERT is the primary command used in the SQL language to load data. If you are reading this book, you probably already have a pretty good handle on the INSERT command. In this section, I'll talk about some of the less often used options, some of which I rarely, if ever, see in the wild. I believe this is due to lack of familiarity more than lack of functionality.

There are two basic methods that Oracle uses for inserts. For simplicity, let's call them the *slow way* and the *fast way*. The slow way is usually called *conventional*. With this mechanism, the data goes through the buffer cache, empty space in existing blocks is reused, undo is generated for all data and metadata changes, and redo is generated for all changes by default. This is a lot of work. That's why I call it the slow way. The fast way is also called *direct path*. This method does not look for space in existing blocks, it just starts inserting data above the high water mark. It protects the data dictionary with undo and redo for metadata changes but it generates no undo for data changes. It can also avoid redo generation for data changes in some cases (i.e. nologging operations). Keep in mind that by default indexes on tables loaded with direct path inserts will still generate both undo and redo.

Direct Path Inserts

Direct path inserts can be invoked by using the APPEND hint (parallel inserts do this by default, by the way). In Oracle Database 11g Release 2, there is a new APPEND_VALUES hint that can be used for inserts that specify a values clause as opposed to using a SELECT to provide the values for inserting. Listing 13-1 shows a simple example of both forms.

Listing 13-1. *Simple Insert APPEND and APPEND_VALUES*

```
insert /*+ append */ into kso.big_emp select * from hr.employees nologging;

insert /*+ append_values */ into dual (dummy) values ('Y');
```

There are a few issues with the fast approach, however.

- Only one direct path write can be occurring on a table at any given time.

- Data will be inserted above the high water mark, so any available space in the blocks below the high water mark will not be used by the direct path inserts.

- The session that performs the insert append can't do anything with the table (even select from it) after the insert until a commit or rollback is issued.

- Some of the less frequently used data structures (object types, indexed organized tables, etc.) are not supported.

- Referential constraints are not supported (i.e. they cause the insert to be executed using the conventional method)

The first item in the list is the biggest issue. In an OLTP type system with many small inserts occurring frequently, the direct path mechanism will just not work. The second bulleted item is also a big issue. It makes no sense for small inserts to be applied in empty blocks above the high water mark. This would result in a huge waste of space. In fact, in Oracle Database 11g, the behavior of the APPEND hint was modified to allow it to be used in insert statements using the Values clause (prior to 11g, it would be ignored unless the insert statement had a Select clause). This behavior change resulted in a bug being logged because it was using so much space for small inserts. The eventual resolution was to return the APPEND hint to its original behavior and introduce the APPEND_VALUES hint in Oracle Database 11gR2. At any rate, you should note that the direct path inserts are designed for large "bulk" inserts only.

Note also that, as with most hints, the APPEND hint will be silently ignored if for any reason it is not possible for Oracle to obey the hint. When this occurs with the APPEND hint, the insert will be done using the conventional mechanism. Listing 13-2 shows an example of the APPEND hint being ignored due to a foreign key constraint.

Listing 13-2. *Disabled APPEND Hint*

```
KSO@LAB112> @constraints
Enter value for owner: KSO
Enter value for table_name: BIG_EMP
Enter value for constraint_type:

TABLE_NAME   CONSTRAINT_NAME      C SEARCH_CONDITION                      STATUS
-----------  -------------------  - ------------------------------------  --------
BIG_EMP      BIG_EMP_MANAGER_FK   R                                       ENABLED
BIG_EMP      SYS_C0026608         C "JOB_ID" IS NOT NULL                  ENABLED
BIG_EMP      SYS_C0026607         C "HIRE_DATE" IS NOT NULL               ENABLED
BIG_EMP      SYS_C0026606         C "EMAIL" IS NOT NULL                   ENABLED
BIG_EMP      SYS_C0026605         C "LAST_NAME" IS NOT NULL               ENABLED

SYS@LAB112> @mystats
Enter value for name: write direct

NAME                                                     VALUE
-------------------------------------------------------  -------
physical writes direct                                   0
```

```
SYS@LAB112>
SYS@LAB112>
SYS@LAB112> insert /*+ append */ into kso.big_emp select * from hr.employees;

107 rows created.

SYS@LAB112> @mystats
Enter value for name: direct

NAME                                                     VALUE
-------------------------------------------------------- -------
physical writes direct                                   0

SYS@LAB112> select count(*) from kso.big_emp;

COUNT(*)
--------
     107
```

The APPEND hint definitely did not do what it was intended to do in this case. The inserts were not done with direct path writes, as shown by the physical direct writes statistic and the fact that you could select from the table after the insert. (If the insert had been done with direct path writes, you would have had to issue a commit or rollback before you could select from the table). Listing 13-3 shows the expected behavior if you disable the foreign key constraint that was responsible for disabling the APPEND hint.

Listing 13-3. *Disabling Constraint Enables APPEND Hint*

```
SYS@LAB112> alter table kso.big_emp disable constraint BIG_EMP_MANAGER_FK;

Table altered.

SYS@LAB112> insert /*+ append */ into kso.big_emp select * from hr.employees;

107 rows created.

SYS@LAB112> @mystats
Enter value for name: direct

NAME                                                              VALUE
----------------------------------------------------------------- ---------------
physical writes direct                                            2

SYS@LAB112> select count(*) from kso.big_emp;
select count(*) from kso.big_emp
                        *
ERROR at line 1:
ORA-12838: cannot read/modify an object after modifying it in parallel
```

The direct path method was clearly used in this example as can be seen from the statistics and the fact that you could not select from the table without issuing a commit first. By the way, the error message is a bit of a red herring. It says that the object was modified in parallel, which in this case is not true. This is a hangover from an earlier version where a parallel insert was the only way to do an insert above the high water mark. Now I'll discuss a couple of unusual variants on the insert statement.

Multi-Table Inserts

The multi-table insert is rarely used even though it has been around since at least version 9i. This construct can be useful for ETL type processing when data is staged and then rearranged as it is loaded into permanent structures. In these cases, it is fairly common to stage data in a non-normalized format that is later split into multiple tables or some other more normalized structure. The multi-table insert is a convenient way to accomplish this type of work without having to write a bunch of procedural code. The syntax is very straight forward: just use INSERT ALL and then supply multiple INTO clauses.

These clauses can specify the same or different tables. Only one set of input values can be used (either via a Values clause or a subquery), but the individual values can be reused or not used at all. Listing 13-4 shows an example of the syntax inserting into a single table. (Note that the scripts are provided in the online code suite to create the PEOPLE and DENORMALIZED_PEOPLE tables).

Listing 13-4. *Basic Multi-Table Insert into a Single Table*

```
INSERT ALL
  INTO people (person_id, first_name, last_name) -- the parent
    VALUES (person_id, first_name, last_name)
  INTO people (first_name, last_name, parent_id) -- the child
    VALUES (child1, last_name, person_id)
  INTO people (first_name, last_name, parent_id) -- the child
    VALUES (child2, last_name, person_id)
  INTO people (first_name, last_name, parent_id) -- the child
    VALUES (child3, last_name, person_id)
  INTO people (first_name, last_name, parent_id) -- the child
    VALUES (child4, last_name, person_id)
  INTO people (first_name, last_name, parent_id) -- the child
    VALUES (child5, last_name, person_id)
  INTO people (first_name, last_name, parent_id) -- the child
    VALUES (child6, last_name, person_id)
  SELECT person_id, first_name, last_name,
         child1, child2, child3, child4, child5, child6
FROM denormalized_people;
```

The previous example shows that multiple INTO clauses can be used, although in this case all the INTO clauses referenced the same table. You could just as easily insert into multiple tables (hence the term multi-table insert), as shown in Listing 13-5.

Listing 13-5. *Basic Multi-Table Insert*

```
INSERT ALL
  INTO parents (person_id, first_name, last_name)
    VALUES (person_id, first_name, last_name)
```

```
  INTO children (first_name, last_name, parent_id)
    VALUES (child1, last_name, person_id)
  INTO children (first_name, last_name, parent_id)
    VALUES (child1, last_name, person_id)
  INTO children (first_name, last_name, parent_id)
    VALUES (child1, last_name, person_id)
  INTO children (first_name, last_name, parent_id)
    VALUES (child1, last_name, person_id)
  INTO children (first_name, last_name, parent_id)
    VALUES (child1, last_name, person_id)
  INTO children (first_name, last_name, parent_id)
    VALUES (child1, last_name, person_id)
SELECT person_id, first_name, last_name,
       child1, child2, child3, child4, child5, child6
FROM denormalized_people;
```

Conditional Insert

The INSERT command also has the ability to do conditional processing. It's like having a CASE statement embedded in the INSERT statement.

In the previous example, you inserted a record for every child, but most likely some of the child columns would be null in that kind of a repeating column layout. So it would be nice if you could avoid creating those records without having to write procedural code. That's exactly the situation this feature was built for. By the way, this type of data layout is often seen when loading files from external systems. Creating external tables on files is an excellent way to load them, and it allows these less common insert options to be applied directly to the data loading process, rather than after they have been staged in an Oracle table. Listing 13.6 shows an example of the conditional insert where the parent fields are always loaded, but the child fields are only loaded if they have data in them.

Listing 13-6. *Conditional Insert*

```
INSERT ALL
WHEN 1=1 THEN -- always insert the parent
  INTO people (person_id, first_name, last_name)
    VALUES (person_id, first_name, last_name)
WHEN child1 is not null THEN -- only insert non-null children
  INTO people (first_name, last_name, parent_id)
    VALUES (child1, last_name, person_id)
WHEN child2 is not null THEN
  INTO people (first_name, last_name, parent_id)
    VALUES (child2, last_name, person_id)
WHEN child3 is not null THEN
  INTO people (first_name, last_name, parent_id)
    VALUES (child3, last_name, person_id)
```

```
WHEN child4 is not null THEN
  INTO people (first_name, last_name, parent_id)
    VALUES (child4, last_name, person_id)
WHEN child5 is not null THEN
  INTO people (first_name, last_name, parent_id)
    VALUES (child5, last_name, person_id)
WHEN child6 is not null THEN
  INTO people (first_name, last_name, parent_id)
    VALUES (child6, last_name, person_id)
SELECT person_id, first_name, last_name,
  child1, child2, child3, child4, child5, child6
FROM denormalized_people;
```

DML Error Logging

And now for something really cool: DML error logging. This feature provides a mechanism for preventing your one million row insert from failing because a few rows had problems. This feature was introduced in 10gR2 and it's similar to the SQL*Loader error logging feature. It basically diverts any records that would otherwise cause the statement to fail, placing them instead in an Errors table. This is an extremely useful feature that is rarely used, which is a little surprising because it's very easy to implement. It also provides excellent performance and saves a lot of coding. Without this feature you would have to create a bad records table, write procedural code to handle any exceptions raised by any single record, insert the problem records into the bad records table, and preserve the integrity of the transaction by handling the errors records in an autonomous transaction. That's a lot of work. By the way, the LOG ERRORS clause works with the other DML statements as well (UPDATE, DELETE and MERGE).

1. Create the Error Log table using DBMS_ERRLOG.CREATE_ERROR_LOG

2. Specify the LOG ERRORS clause on the INSERT

That's it. Listing 13-7 shows how the CREATE_ERROR_LOG procedure works.

Listing 13-7. *CREATE_ERROR_LOG*

```
SQL> EXECUTE DBMS_ERRLOG.CREATE_ERROR_LOG('big_emp', 'big_emp_bad');

PL/SQL procedure successfully completed.

SQL> desc big_emp
 Name                                      Null?    Type
 ----------------------------------------- -------- ----------------
 EMPLOYEE_ID                                        NUMBER(6)
 FIRST_NAME                                         VARCHAR2(20)
 LAST_NAME                                 NOT NULL VARCHAR2(25)
 EMAIL                                     NOT NULL VARCHAR2(25)
 PHONE_NUMBER                                       VARCHAR2(20)
 HIRE_DATE                                 NOT NULL DATE
 JOB_ID                                    NOT NULL VARCHAR2(10)
 SALARY                                             NUMBER(8,2)
```

```
COMMISSION_PCT                                          NUMBER(2,2)
MANAGER_ID                                              NUMBER(6)
DEPARTMENT_ID                                           NUMBER(4)

SQL> desc big_emp_bad
 Name                                      Null?    Type
 ---------------------------------------- -------- ------------------
 ORA_ERR_NUMBER$                                    NUMBER
 ORA_ERR_MESG$                                      VARCHAR2(2000)
 ORA_ERR_ROWID$                                     ROWID
 ORA_ERR_OPTYP$                                     VARCHAR2(2)
 ORA_ERR_TAG$                                       VARCHAR2(2000)
 EMPLOYEE_ID                                        VARCHAR2(4000)
 FIRST_NAME                                         VARCHAR2(4000)
 LAST_NAME                                          VARCHAR2(4000)
 EMAIL                                              VARCHAR2(4000)
 PHONE_NUMBER                                       VARCHAR2(4000)
 HIRE_DATE                                          VARCHAR2(4000)
 JOB_ID                                             VARCHAR2(4000)
 SALARY                                             VARCHAR2(4000)
 COMMISSION_PCT                                     VARCHAR2(4000)
 MANAGER_ID                                         VARCHAR2(4000)
 DEPARTMENT_ID                                      VARCHAR2(4000)
```

As you can see, all the columns in the Errors table were created as VARCHAR2(4000). This allows columns of most datatypes to be inserted into the Errors table, even if records are failing due to data being too large to fit into a column or because of inconsistent datatype issues, such as number columns that contain non-numeric data. There are also a few extra columns for the error number, the error message, and the row_id. Finally, there is a column called ORA_ERR_TAG$ that allows user defined data to be placed in the row for debugging purposes (i.e. what step the ETL process was on, or something of that nature).

The syntax is very straightforward. You simply add the keywords LOG ERRORS INTO and specify the name of your errors table. Optionally, you can tell Oracle how many errors to allow before giving up and canceling the statement. This is done with the Reject Limit clause. You should note that by default, the Reject Limit is set to 0, so if you hit one error, the statement will abort and rollback (just the statement, not the transaction). The single error will be preserved in the Errors table, though. In most cases, you will probably want to set Reject Limit to UNLIMITED, which allows the insert statement to complete regardless of how many records were diverted to the Errors table. It is somewhat surprising that UNLIMITED is not the default as this is the most common usage. Listing 13-8 shows a simple example.

Listing 13-8. *Insert Error Logging*

```
SQL>
SQL> insert into big_emp
  2      (employee_id, first_name, last_name,
  3       hire_date, email, department_id)
  4    values (300,'Bob', 'Loblaw',
  5           '01-jan-10', 'bob@yourfavoritelawyer.com', 12345)
```

```
  6    log errors into big_emp_bad;
         '01-jan-10', 'bob@yourfavoritelawyer.com', 12345)
                                                      *
ERROR at line 5:
ORA-12899: value too large for column "KSO"."BIG_EMP"."EMAIL" (actual: 26, maximum: 25)


SQL> insert into big_emp
  2      (employee_id, first_name, last_name,
  3       hire_date, email, department_id)
  4    values (301,'Bob', 'Loblaw',
  5           '01-jan-10', 'bob@yflawyer.com', 12345)
  6    log errors into big_emp_bad;
         '01-jan-10', 'bob@yflawyer.com', 12345)
                                          *
ERROR at line 5:
ORA-01400: cannot insert NULL into ("KSO"."BIG_EMP"."JOB_ID")


SQL> insert into big_emp
  2      (employee_id, first_name, last_name,
  3       hire_date, email, department_id,job_id)
  4    values (302,'Bob', 'Loblaw',
  5           '01-jan-10', 'bob@yflawyer.com', 12345, 1)
  6    log errors into big_emp_bad;
         '01-jan-10', 'bob@yflawyer.com', 12345, 1)
                                          *
ERROR at line 5:
ORA-01438: value larger than specified precision allowed for this column


SQL> insert into big_emp
  2      (employee_id, first_name, last_name,
  3       hire_date, email, department_id,job_id)
  4    values (303,'Bob', 'Loblaw',
  5           '01-jan-10', 'bob@yflawyer.com', '2A45', 1)
  6    log errors into big_emp_bad;
         '01-jan-10', 'bob@yflawyer.com', '2A45', 1)
                                          *
ERROR at line 5:
ORA-01722: invalid number


SQL>
SQL> SELECT ORA_ERR_MESG$, ORA_ERR_TAG$, employee_id FROM big_emp_bad;
```

```
ORA_ERR_MESG$
--------------------------------------------------------------------------------
ORA_ERR_TAG$
--------------------------------------------------------------------------------
EMPLOYEE_ID
--------------------------------------------------------------------------------
ORA-01438: value larger than specified precision allowed for this column

302

ORA-01722: invalid number

303

ORA-12899: value too large for column "KSO"."BIG_EMP"."EMAIL" (actual: 26, maximum: 25)

300

ORA-01400: cannot insert NULL into ("KSO"."BIG_EMP"."JOB_ID")

301
```

The example in Figure 13-8 shows several insert statements, all of which failed. The records that failed to be inserted into the table, regardless of the error that caused the failure, were automatically inserted into the Errors table. Since I didn't specify a value for Reject Limit, each of the statements was rolled back when it encountered the first error. Therefore, no records were actually inserted into the BIG_EMP table. All the Error records were preserved, though. This was done to demonstrate that a single Errors table can be reused for multiple loads, preserving the records across multiple insert statements. Note that Error logging would rarely be used in this manner in real life. In real life, the Reject Limit would generally be set to UNLIMITED. Listings 13-9 and 13-10 show better examples of using a multi-row insert statement. Listing 13-9 shows what happens to an insert when a record fails without the Error Logging clause and Listing 13-10 shows how it works with the Error Logging clause.

Listing 13-9. *Better Insert Error Logging*

```
SQL> set echo on
SQL> create table test_big_insert as select * from dba_objects where 1=2;

Table created.

SQL>
SQL> desc test_big_insert
 Name                                      Null?    Type
 ----------------------------------------- -------- ----------------------
 OWNER                                              VARCHAR2(30)
 OBJECT_NAME                                        VARCHAR2(128)
 SUBOBJECT_NAME                                     VARCHAR2(30)
 OBJECT_ID                                          NUMBER
 DATA_OBJECT_ID                                     NUMBER
```

```
    OBJECT_TYPE                            VARCHAR2(19)
    CREATED                                DATE
    LAST_DDL_TIME                          DATE
    TIMESTAMP                              VARCHAR2(19)
    STATUS                                 VARCHAR2(7)
    TEMPORARY                              VARCHAR2(1)
    GENERATED                              VARCHAR2(1)
    SECONDARY                              VARCHAR2(1)
    NAMESPACE                              NUMBER
    EDITION_NAME                           VARCHAR2(30)

SQL>
SQL> alter table test_big_insert modify object_id number(2);

Table altered.

SQL>
SQL> insert into test_big_insert
  2     select * from dba_objects
  3     where object_id is not null;
  select * from dba_objects
         *
ERROR at line 2:
ORA-01438: value larger than specified precision allowed for this column
```

Since I've set up the situation, I have a pretty good idea which column is causing the problem. It's the object_id column that was modified in the listing. But in real life, the troublesome column will not usually be so obvious. In fact, without the Error Logging clause, it can be quite difficult to determine which row caused the problem.

The error message doesn't give me any information about which column or which record caused the failure. I could determine which column was causing the problem by manually specifying the column names in the select. However, there is no way to know which rows are causing the problem. The Error Logging clause in Listing 13-10 solves both problems. Remember that all the column's values will be saved in the Errors table along with the error messages, making it easy to determine where the problem lies.

Listing 13-10. *Better Insert Error Logging (con't)*

```
SQL>
SQL> EXECUTE DBMS_ERRLOG.CREATE_ERROR_LOG('test_big_insert', 'tbi_errors');

PL/SQL procedure successfully completed.

SQL>
SQL> insert into test_big_insert
  2     select * from dba_objects
  3     where object_id is not null
  4     log errors into tbi_errors
  5     reject limit unlimited;
```

```
98 rows created.

SQL>
SQL> select count(*) from dba_objects
  2  where object_id is not null
  3  and length(object_id) < 3;

  COUNT(*)
----------
        98

SQL> select count(*) from test_big_insert;

  COUNT(*)
----------
        98

SQL>
SQL> select count(*) from dba_objects
  2  where object_id is not null
  3  and length(object_id) > 2;

  COUNT(*)
----------
     73276

SQL> select count(*) from tbi_errors;

  COUNT(*)
----------
     73276

SQL> rollback;

Rollback complete.

SQL> select count(*) from test_big_insert;

  COUNT(*)
----------
         0

SQL> select count(*) from tbi_errors;

  COUNT(*)
----------
     73282
```

This example showed the Error Logging clause with the Reject Limit at UNLIMITED, which allows the statement to complete despite the fact that most of the records failed to be inserted. In addition, you can see that while a rollback removed the records from the base table, the error records remained.

While DML error logging is extremely robust, you should be aware of the following caveats:

- The LOG ERRORS clause does not cause implicit commits. The insert of error records is handled as an autonomous transaction, meaning that you can commit or rollback the entire set of records inserted into the base table (along with other pending changes), even if errors are returned and bad records are inserted into the Errors table. The records loaded into the Errors table will be preserved, even if the transaction is rolled back.

- The LOG ERRORS clause does not disable the APPEND hint. Inserts into the base table will be done using the direct path write mechanism if the APPEND hint is used. However, any inserts into the Errors table will not use direct path writes. This is generally not a problem since you rarely expect to load a lot of data into an Errors table.

- Direct path insert operations that violate a unique constraint or index will cause the statement to fail and rollback.

- Any update operation that violates a unique constraint or index will cause the statement to fail and rollback.

- Any operation that violates a deferred constraint will cause the statement to fail and rollback.

- The LOG ERRORS clause does not track the values of LOBs, LONGs, or object type columns. It can be used with tables that contain these unsupported types of columns, but the unsupported columns will not be added to the Errors table. In order to create the Errors table for a table that contains unsupported column types, you must use the SKIP_UNSUPPORTED parameter of the CREATE_ERROR_LOG procedure. The default for this parameter is FALSE, which causes the procedure to fail when attempting to create an Errors table for a table with unsupported column types. Listing 13.11 shows the proper syntax for creating an Errors table when there are unsupported column types in the base table.

Listing 13-11. *DBMS_ERRLOG.CREATE_ERROR_LOG Parameters*

```
exec DBMS_ERRLOG.CREATE_ERROR_LOG(err_log_table_owner => '&owner', -
                                  dml_table_name => '&table_name', -
                                  err_log_table_name => '&err_log_table_name', -
                                  err_log_table_space => NULL, -
                              skip_unsupported => TRUE);
```

As you've seen, the INSERT statement has several options that are rarely used. The most useful of these features, in my opinion, is the DML error logging (which can also be used with the other DML commands). It allows very difficult problems such as corruption issues to be identified fairly easily, and it provides excellent performance compared to the row-by-row processing that would be required without it. Note also the fairly extreme performance improvement provided by direct path inserts vs. conventional inserts; there are drawbacks with regards to recoverability and serialization, but for bulk loading of data, the positives generally far outweigh the negatives.

UPDATE

Massive updates are almost always a bad idea. I recently reviewed a system that updates a billion+ rows in a single table every night—a full year forecast and every single value is recalculated every night. Aside from the observation that forecasting that far in the future is not necessary for items that have a 90-day turnaround time, it's much faster to load a billion records from scratch than to update a billion records.

The traditional method when doing this type of processing is to do a truncate and then a reload. But what if the truncate and reload method just won't work? One alternative is using Create Table As Select (CTAS) to create a new table and then just replacing the original table with the newly created one. It sounds easy if you say it fast. Of course, there are many details that must be addressed. Listing 13-12 shows a quick demonstration of the potential difference in performance between these two approaches.

Listing 13-12. *Performance Delta Between UPDATE and CTAS*

```
SYS@LAB112> set autotrace on
SYS@LAB112> set timing on
SYS@LAB112> update skew2 set col1 = col1*1;

32000004 rows updated.

Elapsed: 00:27:56.41

Execution Plan
----------------------------------------------------------
Plan hash value: 1837483169
```

```
--------------------------------------------------------------------------
| Id  | Operation          | Name  | Rows  | Bytes | Cost (%CPU)| Time     |
--------------------------------------------------------------------------
|   0 | UPDATE STATEMENT   |       |   32M |  793M | 28370   (1)| 00:05:41 |
|   1 |  UPDATE            | SKEW2 |       |       |            |          |
|   2 |   TABLE ACCESS FULL| SKEW2 |   32M |  793M | 28370   (1)| 00:05:41 |
--------------------------------------------------------------------------
```

```
Statistics
----------------------------------------------------------
      1908  recursive calls
  32743098  db block gets
    163363  consistent gets
    317366  physical reads
8187521328  redo size
      1373  bytes sent via SQL*Net to client
      1097  bytes received via SQL*Net from client
         5  SQL*Net roundtrips to/from client
         1  sorts (memory)
         0  sorts (disk)
  32000004  rows processed
```

```
SYS@LAB112> create table skew_temp as
  2   select pk_col, col1*1 col1, col2, col3, col4 from kso.skew2;

Table created.

Elapsed: 00:00:44.30

SYS@LAB112> set timing off
SYS@LAB112>
SYS@LAB112> select count(*) from skew_temp;

  COUNT(*)
----------
  32000004

SYS@LAB112> @find_sql_stats
Enter value for sql_text: %skew2%
Enter value for sql_id:

SQL_ID          ROWS_PROCESSED  AVG_ETIME  AVG_PIO    AVG_LIO SQL_TEXT
-------------   --------------  ---------  --------   ------------ --------------
2aqsvr3h3qrrg        32000004   1,676.78   928,124   65,409,243 update skew2
                                                                set col1 = col

4y4dquf0mkhup        32000004      44.30   162,296      492,575 create table
                                                                skew_temp as s
```

As you can see, the update took almost 30 minutes (1,676.78 seconds) while the CTAS table took less than a minute (44.30 seconds). So it's clear that there are significant performance benefits to be had by recreating the table vs. updating all the records. And as you might already expect from the previous example, recreating a table can also be more efficient than updating a relatively small portion of the rows. Listing 13-13 shows a comparison of the two methods when updating approximately 10% of the rows.

Listing 13-13. *Performance Delta Between Update and CTAS – 10%*

```
SYS@LAB112> select count(*) from skew2 where col1 = 1;

  COUNT(*)
----------
   3199971

Elapsed: 00:00:10.90
SYS@LAB112> select 3199971/32000004 from dual;

3199971/32000004
----------------
      .099999081
```

```
Elapsed: 00:00:00.01
SYS@LAB112> -- about 10% of the rows col1=1
SYS@LAB112>
SYS@LAB112> update skew2 set col1=col1*1 where col1 = 1;

3199971 rows updated.

Elapsed: 00:03:11.63
SYS@LAB112> drop table skew_temp;

Table dropped.

Elapsed: 00:00:00.56
SYS@LAB112> create table skew_temp as
  2  select pk_col, case when col1 = 1 then col1*1 end col1,
  3  col2, col3, col4 from skew2;

Table created.

Elapsed: 00:01:23.62

KSO@LAB112> alter table skew2 rename to skew_old;

Table altered.

Elapsed: 00:00:00.06
KSO@LAB112> alter table skew_temp rename to skew2;

Table altered.

Elapsed: 00:00:00.05
```

In this example, I recreated a table using CTAS in less than half the time it took to update about 10% of the records. Obviously, there are many details that are ignored in the previous two examples. These examples had no constraints or indexes or grants to deal with, making them considerably less complicated than most real life situations. Each of these complications can be dealt with in an automated fashion, however.

Listing 13-14 shows a more realistic example of using this technique to replace an UPDATE statement. For this example, I'll use a script from the online code suite called recreate_table.sql. It uses the DBMS_METADATA package to generate a script with the necessary DDL to recreate a table and its dependent objects. It then uses an INSERT APPEND in place of the UPDATE to move the data. The last step is to use ALTER TABLE RENAME to swap the new table for the original one. Once the script is generated, it should be edited to customize how the steps are performed. For example, you may want to comment out the swap of the tables via the RENAME at the end until you're sure everything worked as expected. Note that the particulars of the INSERT APPEND will also have to be built when editing the script. Note also that the script renames all existing indexes due to the fact that you cannot have duplicate index names, even if they are on different tables.

Listing 13-14. *INSERT APPEND Instead of Mass Update*

```
SYS@LAB112>
SYS@LAB112> @recreate_table
Enter value for owner: KSO
Enter value for table_name: SKEW2

… Output supressed for readability


SYS@LAB112> @recreate_SKEW2.sql
SYS@LAB112> set timing on
SYS@LAB112>
SYS@LAB112> ALTER INDEX KSO.SYS_C0029558 RENAME TO SYS_C0029558_OLD;

Index altered.

Elapsed: 00:00:00.02
SYS@LAB112> ALTER INDEX KSO.SKEW2_COL1 RENAME TO SKEW2_COL1_OLD;

Index altered.

Elapsed: 00:00:00.02
SYS@LAB112> ALTER INDEX KSO.SKEW2_COL4 RENAME TO SKEW2_COL4_OLD;

Index altered.

Elapsed: 00:00:00.02
SYS@LAB112>
SYS@LAB112>
SYS@LAB112>    CREATE TABLE "KSO"."SKEW2_TEMP"
  2      (    "PK_COL" NUMBER,
  3           "COL1" NUMBER,
  4           "COL2" VARCHAR2(30),
  5           "COL3" DATE,
  6           "COL4" VARCHAR2(1)
  7      ) SEGMENT CREATION IMMEDIATE
  8      PCTFREE 10 PCTUSED 40 INITRANS 1 MAXTRANS 255 NOCOMPRESS LOGGING
  9      STORAGE(INITIAL 1483735040 NEXT 1048576
                   MINEXTENTS 1 MAXEXTENTS 2147483645
 10      PCTINCREASE 0 FREELISTS 1 FREELIST GROUPS 1 BUFFER_POOL
 11      DEFAULT FLASH_CACHE DEFAULT CELL_FLASH_CACHE DEFAULT)
 12      TABLESPACE "USERS" ;

Table created.

Elapsed: 00:00:00.10
```

```
SYS@LAB112>
SYS@LAB112>
SYS@LAB112>    INSERT /*+APPEND*/ INTO KSO.SKEW2_TEMP SELECT /*+PARALLEL(a 4)*/
  2  PK_COL,
  3  COL1,
  4  case when COL1 = 2 then 'ABC' else COL2 end,
  5  COL3,
  6  COL4
  7  FROM KSO.SKEW2 a;

32000004 rows created.

Elapsed: 00:00:52.87
SYS@LAB112>
SYS@LAB112>    CREATE INDEX "KSO"."SKEW2_COL1" ON "KSO"."SKEW2_TEMP" ("COL1")
  2    PCTFREE 10 INITRANS 2 MAXTRANS 255 NOLOGGING COMPUTE STATISTICS
  3    STORAGE(INITIAL 595591168 NEXT 1048576 MINEXTENTS 1 MAXEXTENTS 2147483645
  4    PCTINCREASE 0 FREELISTS 1 FREELIST GROUPS 1 BUFFER_POOL DEFAULT
  5    FLASH_CACHE DEFAULT CELL_FLASH_CACHE DEFAULT)
  6    TABLESPACE "USERS"
  7    PARALLEL 8 ;

Index created.

Elapsed: 00:01:40.16
SYS@LAB112>
SYS@LAB112>
SYS@LAB112>
SYS@LAB112>    CREATE INDEX "KSO"."SKEW2_COL4" ON "KSO"."SKEW2_TEMP" ("COL4")
  2    PCTFREE 10 INITRANS 2 MAXTRANS 255 COMPUTE STATISTICS
  3    STORAGE(INITIAL 65536 NEXT 1048576 MINEXTENTS 1 MAXEXTENTS 2147483645
  4    PCTINCREASE 0 FREELISTS 1 FREELIST GROUPS 1 BUFFER_POOL DEFAULT
  5    FLASH_CACHE DEFAULT CELL_FLASH_CACHE DEFAULT)
  6    TABLESPACE "USERS"
  7    PARALLEL 8 ;

Index created.

Elapsed: 00:01:11.05
SYS@LAB112>
SYS@LAB112>
SYS@LAB112>
SYS@LAB112>    CREATE UNIQUE INDEX "KSO"."SYS_C0029558"
  2           ON "KSO"."SKEW2_TEMP" ("PK_COL")
  3    PCTFREE 10 INITRANS 2 MAXTRANS 255 NOLOGGING COMPUTE STATISTICS
  4    STORAGE(INITIAL 865075200 NEXT 1048576
  5           MINEXTENTS 1 MAXEXTENTS 2147483645
```

```
  6     PCTINCREASE 0 FREELISTS 1 FREELIST GROUPS 1 BUFFER_POOL DEFAULT
  7     FLASH_CACHE DEFAULT CELL_FLASH_CACHE DEFAULT)
  8     TABLESPACE "USERS"
  9     PARALLEL 8 ;

Index created.

Elapsed: 00:01:34.26
SYS@LAB112>
SYS@LAB112>
SYS@LAB112>     -- Note: No Grants found!
SYS@LAB112>     -- Note: No Triggers found!
SYS@LAB112>
SYS@LAB112>
SYS@LAB112>    ALTER TABLE "KSO"."SKEW2_TEMP" ADD PRIMARY KEY ("PK_COL")
  2     USING INDEX PCTFREE 10 INITRANS 2 MAXTRANS 255 NOLOGGING
  3     COMPUTE STATISTICS
  4     STORAGE(INITIAL 865075200 NEXT 1048576
  5           MINEXTENTS 1 MAXEXTENTS 2147483645
  6     PCTINCREASE 0 FREELISTS 1 FREELIST GROUPS 1 BUFFER_POOL DEFAULT
  7     FLASH_CACHE DEFAULT CELL_FLASH_CACHE DEFAULT)
  8     TABLESPACE "USERS"   ENABLE;

Table altered.

Elapsed: 00:00:15.16
SYS@LAB112>
SYS@LAB112>
SYS@LAB112>
SYS@LAB112>    ALTER TABLE KSO.SKEW2 RENAME TO SKEW2_ORIG;

Table altered.

Elapsed: 00:00:00.04
SYS@LAB112>
SYS@LAB112>    ALTER TABLE KSO.SKEW2_TEMP RENAME TO SKEW2;

Table altered.

Elapsed: 00:00:00.03
```

The order of the steps is very important: it is generally much faster to defer the creation of indexes and the enabling of constraints until after loading the data. You should also be aware that you will need to manually drop the old table (maybe after a day or two when everyone is quite sure that the operation worked correctly). By the way, I think it's a really bad idea to drop objects in a script. As a matter of fact, I would recommend commenting out the last two statements that do the RENAME. It's safer to run them interactively after you make sure everything worked as planned. For comparison, Listing 13-15 shows the timing of the same change made by using a standard UPDATE statement.

Listing 13-15. *Mass Update Timings for Comparison*

```
SYS@LAB112> select my_rows, total_rows,
  2  100*my_rows/total_rows row_percent from
  3  (select sum(decode(col1,1,1,0)) my_rows, count(*) total_rows
  4* from kso.skew2)


   MY_ROWS TOTAL_ROWS ROW_PERCENT
---------- ---------- -----------
   8605185   32000004        26.9

1 row selected.

Elapsed: 00:00:01.29
SYS@LAB112> update /*+ parallel 4 */ kso.skew2 set col2 = 'ABC' where col1 = 2;

8605185 rows updated.

Elapsed: 00:12:37.53
```

To sum up this example, when modifying roughly 27% of the rows in the table, the straight UPDATE took about 12.5 minutes and the rebuild with INSERT APPEND took about 5.5 minutes. Keep in mind that there are many variables that I have not covered in detail. Every situation will have differences in the number of dependent objects and the percentage of rows affected by the update. These factors will have a large affect on the outcome, so test thoroughly in your environment with your specific data.

In this section, you learned that it can be considerably faster to rebuild tables than to update a large percentage of the rows. Obviously, making use of the direct path write via the APPEND hint is an important part of that. The biggest negative to this approach is that the table must be offline for the entire time that the rebuild is taking place—or at least protected in some manner from concurrent modifications. This does not usually present a major obstacle because these types of mass updates are rarely done while users are accessing the table. In cases where concurrent access is required, partitioning or materialized views can provide the necessary isolation.

DELETE

Just like massive updates, massive deletes are almost always a bad idea. It is generally faster (if somewhat more complicated) to recreate a table or partition (without the rows you wish to eliminate) than it is to delete a large percentage of the rows. The biggest downside to the approach of recreating is that the object must be protected from other changes while it is being rebuilt. It's basically the same approach as I used in the previous section with the UPDATE command, but DELETEs can be even more time consuming.

The basic idea is pretty much the same as with the mass updates.

1. Create a temporary table.
2. Insert the records that are not to be deleted into the temporary table.
3. Recreate the dependent objects (indexes, constraints, grants, triggers).
4. Rename the tables.

I'll use the recreate_table.sql script again to create a script that I can edit. Then I'll modify the INSERT statement to give me the records that would be left behind after my DELETE. Listing 13-16 shows an example of how a DELETE statement compares to a rebuild using a reciprocal INSERT statement.

Listing 13-16. *Mass DELETE*

```
SYS@LAB112> delete from kso.skew2 where col1=1;

3199972 rows deleted.

Elapsed: 00:04:12.64

SYS@LAB112> rollback;

Rollback complete.

Elapsed: 00:01:48.59

KSO@LAB112> @recreate_SKEW3.sql
KSO@LAB112> set timing on
KSO@LAB112>
KSO@LAB112> ALTER INDEX KSO.SYS_C0029558 RENAME TO SYS_C0029558_OLD;

Index altered.

Elapsed: 00:00:00.03
KSO@LAB112> ALTER INDEX KSO.SKEW2_COL1 RENAME TO SKEW2_COL1_OLD;

Index altered.

Elapsed: 00:00:00.04
KSO@LAB112> ALTER INDEX KSO.SKEW2_COL4 RENAME TO SKEW2_COL4_OLD;

Index altered.

Elapsed: 00:00:00.02
KSO@LAB112>
KSO@LAB112>
KSO@LAB112>   CREATE TABLE "KSO"."SKEW2_TEMP"
  2    (    "PK_COL" NUMBER,
```

```
  3          "COL1" NUMBER,
  4          "COL2" VARCHAR2(30),
  5          "COL3" DATE,
  6          "COL4" VARCHAR2(1)
  7     ) SEGMENT CREATION IMMEDIATE
  8    PCTFREE 10 PCTUSED 40 INITRANS 1 MAXTRANS 255 NOCOMPRESS LOGGING
  9    STORAGE(INITIAL 1483735040 NEXT 1048576
 10    MINEXTENTS 1 MAXEXTENTS 2147483645
 11    PCTINCREASE 0 FREELISTS 1 FREELIST GROUPS 1 BUFFER_POOL DEFAULT
 12    FLASH_CACHE DEFAULT CELL_FLASH_CACHE DEFAULT)
 13    TABLESPACE "USERS" ;

Table created.

Elapsed: 00:00:00.11
KSO@LAB112>
KSO@LAB112>
KSO@LAB112>    INSERT /*+APPEND*/ INTO KSO.SKEW2_TEMP SELECT /*+PARALLEL(a 4)*/
  2    PK_COL,
  3    COL1,
  4    COL2,
  5    COL3,
  6    COL4
  7    FROM KSO.SKEW2 a where col1 != 1;

28800032 rows created.

Elapsed: 00:00:42.30
KSO@LAB112>
KSO@LAB112>    CREATE INDEX "KSO"."SKEW2_COL1" ON "KSO"."SKEW2_TEMP" ("COL1")
  2     PCTFREE 10 INITRANS 2 MAXTRANS 255 NOLOGGING COMPUTE STATISTICS
  3     STORAGE(INITIAL 595591168 NEXT 1048576
  4            MINEXTENTS 1 MAXEXTENTS 2147483645
  5     PCTINCREASE 0 FREELISTS 1 FREELIST GROUPS 1 BUFFER_POOL DEFAULT
  6     FLASH_CACHE DEFAULT CELL_FLASH_CACHE DEFAULT)
  7     TABLESPACE "USERS"
  8     PARALLEL 8 ;

Index created.

Elapsed: 00:01:36.50
KSO@LAB112>
KSO@LAB112>
KSO@LAB112>
KSO@LAB112>    CREATE INDEX "KSO"."SKEW2_COL4" ON "KSO"."SKEW2_TEMP" ("COL4")
  2     PCTFREE 10 INITRANS 2 MAXTRANS 255 COMPUTE STATISTICS
  3     STORAGE(INITIAL 65536 NEXT 1048576 MINEXTENTS 1 MAXEXTENTS 2147483645
```

```
  4      PCTINCREASE 0 FREELISTS 1 FREELIST GROUPS 1 BUFFER_POOL DEFAULT
  5      FLASH_CACHE DEFAULT CELL_FLASH_CACHE DEFAULT)
  6      TABLESPACE "USERS"
  7      PARALLEL 8 ;

Index created.

Elapsed: 00:01:09.43
KSO@LAB112>
KSO@LAB112>
KSO@LAB112>
KSO@LAB112>    CREATE UNIQUE INDEX "KSO"."SYS_C0029558"
  2             ON "KSO"."SKEW2_TEMP" ("PK_COL")
  3      PCTFREE 10 INITRANS 2 MAXTRANS 255 NOLOGGING COMPUTE STATISTICS
  4      STORAGE(INITIAL 865075200 NEXT 1048576
  5              MINEXTENTS 1 MAXEXTENTS 2147483645
  6      PCTINCREASE 0 FREELISTS 1 FREELIST GROUPS 1 BUFFER_POOL DEFAULT
  7      FLASH_CACHE DEFAULT CELL_FLASH_CACHE DEFAULT)
  8      TABLESPACE "USERS"
  9      PARALLEL 8 ;

Index created.

Elapsed: 00:01:26.30
KSO@LAB112>
KSO@LAB112>
KSO@LAB112>    -- Note: No Grants found!
KSO@LAB112>    -- Note: No Triggers found!
KSO@LAB112>
KSO@LAB112>
KSO@LAB112>    ALTER TABLE "KSO"."SKEW2_TEMP" ADD PRIMARY KEY ("PK_COL")
  2      USING INDEX PCTFREE 10 INITRANS 2 MAXTRANS 255
  3      NOLOGGING COMPUTE STATISTICS
  4      STORAGE(INITIAL 865075200 NEXT 1048576
  5              MINEXTENTS 1 MAXEXTENTS 2147483645
  6      PCTINCREASE 0 FREELISTS 1 FREELIST GROUPS 1 BUFFER_POOL DEFAULT
  7      FLASH_CACHE DEFAULT CELL_FLASH_CACHE DEFAULT)
  8      TABLESPACE "USERS"  ENABLE;

Table altered.

Elapsed: 00:00:20.42
```

As with the comparison to the UPDATE statement, the rebuild provides a viable alternative. In this example, I deleted roughly 10% or the records. The DELETE took about 4.25 minutes and the rebuild took about 5.25 minutes. In this case, the straight DELETE was actually faster. But as the number of records goes up, the time to rebuild will remain basically flat while the time to run the DELETE will go up. Eventually, there will be a point where the rebuild becomes much cheaper than the delete.

Truncate

I am sure you are aware of the truncate command, but I should mention it here anyway. If you need to delete all the rows from a table or a partition, the TRUNCATE command is the way to do it. Truncating a table moves the high water mark rather than actually changing all the blocks that hold records. It is blazingly fast compared to using the DELETE command. There are only a few very minor negatives.

- It is a DDL command so it issues an implicit commit (once a table is truncated, there is no going back).

- You cannot flash back to the state of the table prior to the truncate.

- It is the whole table or nothing.

In addition to completing extremely quickly, the TRUNCATE command can make a big difference for future queries on the table. Since full table scans read every block to the highwater mark, and the DELETE command has no affect on the highwater mark, you may be giving up performance gains for future statements.

MERGE

The MERGE statement was introduced in Oracle Database 9i. It provides the classic UPSERT functionality. MERGE will update the record if one already exists or insert a new record if one doesn't already exist. (Oracle Database 10g enhanced the MERGE command to allow it to delete records as well.) The idea is to eliminate the extra code necessary to do error checking and the additional round trips to the database when it's necessary to issue additional SQL statements (i.e. write a piece of code that attempts an update, check the status of the update, and if the update fails then issue the insert). The MERGE statement does all this at the database level without all the additional code. Obviously, it will perform better than the procedural code version.

Syntax and Usage

The syntax of the typical MERGE statement is relatively easy to follow. The following is the basic syntax of a MERGE statement:

```
MERGE INTO table_name
USING (subquery) ON (subquery.column = table.column)
WHEN MATCHED THEN UPDATE …
WHEN NOT MATCHED THEN INSERT …
```

The first part of the MERGE statement looks just like an INSERT, specifying the table (or view) that will be the target of the inserted, updated, or deleted data. The USING keyword specifies a data source (usually a subquery, although it could be a staging table as well) and a join condition that tells Oracle how to determine if a record already exists in the target table. In addition, you must add an Update clause or an Insert clause or both. In most cases, you see both since there is little value in using the

MERGE statement without both clauses. Now let's move on to the Update and Insert clauses (they probably should have called these the When Matched and When Not Matched clauses instead).

The Update clause tells Oracle what to do when a matching record is found. In most cases, finding a matching record results in an update to that record. There is also an optional Where clause that can be used to limit which records are updated, even if there is a match. Alternatively, you can delete matching records using yet another Where clause. Note that the records to be deleted must pass the criteria in the main Where clause AND the criteria in the Delete Where clause. The Delete clause is not actually used that often. It can be handy, though, for a job that needs to do more than just load data. For example, some ETL processes also perform cleanup tasks. For the Delete portion of the Update clause to kick in, a matching record must be found that passes the Where clause in the Update clause as well as the Where clause associated with the Delete. Listing 13-17 shows the MERGE command with an Update clause that contains a Delete.

Listing 13-17. *MERGE with Update Clause*

```
MERGE INTO kso.big_emp t
USING (select * from hr.employees) s
ON (t.employee_id = s.employee_id)
WHEN MATCHED THEN UPDATE SET
--  t.employee_id = s.employee_id, -- ON clause columns not allowed
  t.first_name = t.first_name,
  t.last_name = s.last_name ,
  t.email = s.email ,
  t.phone_number = s.phone_number ,
  t.hire_date = s.hire_date ,
  t.job_id = s.job_id ,
  t.salary = s.salary ,
  t.commission_pct = s.commission_pct ,
  t.manager_id = s.manager_id ,
  t.department_id = s.department_id
    WHERE (S.salary <= 3000)
DELETE WHERE (S.job_id = 'FIRED');
```

The Insert clause tells Oracle what to do when a matching record is not found. Generally, this means "do an insert." However, the Insert clause can be left off altogether. There is also an optional Where clause that can be applied so it is not always the case that an insert will be done if a match is not found. Listing 13-18 shows two versions of a MERGE statement with an Insert clause.

Listing 13-18. *MERGE with Insert Clause*

```
MERGE INTO big_emp t
USING (select * from hr.employees) s
ON (t.employee_id = s.employee_id)
WHEN NOT MATCHED THEN INSERT
(t.employee_id ,
 t.first_name ,
 t.last_name ,
 t.email ,
 t.phone_number ,
 t.hire_date ,
```

```
 t.job_id ,
 t.salary ,
 t.commission_pct ,
 t.manager_id ,
 t.department_id)
VALUES
(s.employee_id ,
 s.first_name ,
 s.last_name ,
 s.email ,
 s.phone_number ,
 s.hire_date ,
 s.job_id ,
 s.salary ,
 s.commission_pct ,
 s.manager_id ,
 s.department_id)
    WHERE (S.job_id != 'FIRED');


MERGE INTO big_emp t
USING (select * from hr.employees where job_id != 'FIRED') s
ON (t.employee_id = s.employee_id)
WHEN NOT MATCHED THEN INSERT
(t.employee_id ,
 t.first_name ,
 t.last_name ,
 t.email ,
 t.phone_number ,
 t.hire_date ,
 t.job_id ,
 t.salary ,
 t.commission_pct ,
 t.manager_id ,
 t.department_id)
VALUES
(s.employee_id ,
 s.first_name ,
 s.last_name ,
 s.email ,
 s.phone_number ,
 s.hire_date ,
 s.job_id ,
 s.salary ,
 s.commission_pct ,
 s.manager_id ,
 s.department_id);
```

The statements accomplish the same thing but are using a slightly different mechanism. One qualifies the set of records to be merged in the subquery in the USING clause, while the other qualifies the statements to be merged in the Where clause inside of the Insert clause. Be aware that these two forms can have different performance characteristics and may even result in different plans. Listing 13-19 shows a more realistic example with both the Insert clause and the Update clause. Note that the Update clause also contains a Delete Where clause that cleans up records of employees that have been fired.

Listing 13-19. *Full MERGE*

```
KSO@LAB112>
KSO@LAB112> -- delete from big_emp where employee_id > 190;
KSO@LAB112> -- insert into hr.jobs select 'FIRED', 'Fired', 0, 0 from dual;
KSO@LAB112> -- update hr.employees set job_id = 'FIRED' where employee_id=197;
KSO@LAB112> MERGE /*+ APPEND */ INTO kso.big_emp t
  2  USING (select * from hr.employees) s
  3  ON (t.employee_id = s.employee_id)
  4  WHEN MATCHED THEN UPDATE SET
  5  --  t.employee_id = s.employee_id,
  6    t.first_name = t.first_name,
  7    t.last_name = s.last_name ,
  8    t.email = s.email ,
  9    t.phone_number = s.phone_number ,
 10    t.hire_date = s.hire_date ,
 11    t.job_id = s.job_id ,
 12    t.salary = s.salary ,
 13    t.commission_pct = s.commission_pct ,
 14    t.manager_id = s.manager_id ,
 15    t.department_id = s.department_id
 16       WHERE (S.salary <= 3000)
 17       DELETE WHERE (S.job_id = 'FIRED')
 18  WHEN NOT MATCHED THEN INSERT
 19  (t.employee_id ,
 20    t.first_name ,
 21    t.last_name ,
 22    t.email ,
 23    t.phone_number ,
 24    t.hire_date ,
 25    t.job_id ,
 26    t.salary ,
 27    t.commission_pct ,
 28    t.manager_id ,
 29    t.department_id)
 30  VALUES
 31  (s.employee_id ,
 32    s.first_name ,
 33    s.last_name ,
 34    s.email ,
```

```
35   s.phone_number ,
36   s.hire_date ,
37   s.job_id ,
38   s.salary ,
39   s.commission_pct ,
40   s.manager_id ,
41   s.department_id)
42       WHERE (S.job_id != 'FIRED');

88140 rows merged.

Elapsed: 00:00:06.51
```

Performance Comparison

So how does the MERGE statement compare to a straight INSERT or CTAS operation? Obviously, there is some inherent overhead in the MERGE statement that makes such a comparison an unfair test. But MERGE is no slouch. Keep in mind that just like with the INSERT command, the fastest way to load a lot of data is to make sure it uses the direct path mechanism by using the APPEND hint. Listing 13-20 compares the performance of INSERT, MERGE, and CTAS. It also demonstrates that all are capable of doing direct path writes.

Listing 13-20. *INSERT, MERGE, CTAS Performance Comparison*

```
KSO@LAB112> @compare_insert_merge_ctas.sql

Table dropped.

Elapsed: 00:00:00.69
KSO@LAB112> @flush_pool
KSO@LAB112> alter system flush shared_pool;

System altered.

Elapsed: 00:00:00.46
KSO@LAB112> select name, value from v$mystat s, v$statname n
  2  where n.statistic# = s.statistic# and name = 'physical writes direct';

NAME                                                             VALUE
---------------------------------------------------------------- ----------
physical writes direct                                               0

Elapsed: 00:00:00.03
KSO@LAB112> create /* compare_insert_merge_ctas.sql */ table skew3
  2  as select * from skew;

Table created.
```

```
Elapsed: 00:00:32.92
KSO@LAB112> select name, value from v$mystat s, v$statname n
  2  where n.statistic# = s.statistic# and name = 'physical writes direct';

NAME                                                                  VALUE
---------------------------------------------------------------- ----------
physical writes direct                                               163031

Elapsed: 00:00:00.03
KSO@LAB112>
KSO@LAB112> truncate table skew3 drop storage;

Table truncated.

Elapsed: 00:00:01.01
KSO@LAB112> INSERT /*+ APPEND */ /* compare_insert_merge_ctas.sql */
  2  INTO skew3 select * from skew;

32000004 rows created.

Elapsed: 00:00:31.23
KSO@LAB112> select name, value from v$mystat s, v$statname n
  2  where n.statistic# = s.statistic# and name = 'physical writes direct';

NAME                                                                  VALUE
---------------------------------------------------------------- ----------
physical writes direct                                               326062

Elapsed: 00:00:00.03
KSO@LAB112>
KSO@LAB112> truncate table skew3 drop storage;

Table truncated.

Elapsed: 00:00:00.84
KSO@LAB112> MERGE /*+ APPEND */ /* compare_insert_merge_ctas.sql */
  2  INTO skew3 t
  3  USING (select * from skew) s
  4  ON (t.pk_col = s.pk_col)
  5  WHEN NOT MATCHED THEN INSERT
  6  (t.pk_col, t.col1, t.col2, t.col3, t.col4)
  7      VALUES (s.pk_col, s.col1, s.col2, s.col3, s.col4);

32000004 rows merged.
```

```
Elapsed: 00:00:49.07
KSO@LAB112> select name, value from v$mystat s, v$statname n
  2  where n.statistic# = s.statistic# and name = 'physical writes direct';

NAME                                                             VALUE
---------------------------------------------------------------- ----------
physical writes direct                                          489093

Elapsed: 00:00:00.01

KSO@LAB112> @fss2
Enter value for sql_text: %compare_insert%
Enter value for sql_id:

SQL_ID          AVG_ETIME AVG_CPU  AVG_PIO  AVG_LIO SQL_TEXT
--------------- --------- -------  -------- -------- --------------------
6y6ms28kzzb5z       49.07   48.48  162,294  490,664 MERGE /*+ APPEND */
g1pf9b564j7yn       31.22   30.93  162,296  489,239 INSERT /*+ APPEND */
g909cagdbs1t5       32.91   31.25  162,294  494,480 create /* compare_in
```

In this very simple test, you can see that all three approaches were able to use the direct path writes and that CTAS and INSERT were very similar in performance. The MERGE statement was considerably slower, as you would expect due to its additional capabilities and the necessary overhead associated with those capabilities. But the MERGE statement provides the most flexibility, so don't overlook the fact that this single statement can perform multiple types of DML with a single execution.

Summary

There are four SQL commands for modifying data: INSERT, UPDATE, DELETE, and MERGE (and the latter is actually capable of performing all three functions). This chapter briefly discussed these commands and focused on one key performance concept: direct path inserts are much, much faster than conventional inserts. There is a good reason for this difference in performance—it's because direct path inserts do a lot less work. There are a number of drawbacks with using the technique, however. The biggest drawback is that it is a serial operation; only one process can be engaging in a direct path insert on a table at any given time and any other process that wishes to do the same will simply have to wait. Another big drawback is that available space that's already allocated to the table will not be used by direct path inserts. For these reasons, it's only applicable for large batch type loading operations. Nevertheless, it is the fastest way to insert data into a table, and as such, should be considered whenever performance is among the most important decision-making criteria. Techniques have been developed for using direct path inserts in the place of updates and deletes. You have explored a couple of these techniques in this chapter as well. Finally, you learned about several of the lesser known options of the DML commands, including the extremely powerful Error Logging clause that can be applied to all four of them.

CHAPTER 14

■ ■ ■

Transaction Processing

Robyn Sands

After you have been using the Oracle database for a while, you might have certain expectations of how the database will behave. When you enter a query, you expect a consistent results set to be returned. If you enter a SQL statement to update several hundred records and the update of one of those rows fails, you expect the entire update to fail, and all rows to be returned to their prior state. If your update succeeds and you commit your work to the database, you expect your changes to become visible to other users and remain in the database, at least until the data is updated again by someone else. You expect that when you are reading data, you will never block a session from writing, and you also expect that the reverse to be true. These are fundamental truths about how the Oracle database operates and once you've become comfortable working with Oracle, you tend to take them for granted.

However, when you begin to write code for applications, you need to be keenly aware of how Oracle provides the consistency and concurrency you've learned to rely on. Relational databases are intended to process transactions, and in this author's opinion, the Oracle database is exceptional at keeping transaction data consistent, accurate and available. However, you must design and implement transactions correctly if the protections you receive automatically at the statement level are to be extended to your transactions. How you design and code a transaction impacts the integrity and consistency of the application data, and if you do not clearly define the transaction boundaries, your application may behave in some unexpected ways. Transaction design also influences how well the system performs when multiple users are retrieving and altering the information within it. Scalability can be severely limited when transactions are poorly designed.

Although there are only few transaction control statements, understanding how a transaction will be processed requires an understanding of some of the more complex concepts and architectural components in the Oracle database. In the next few sections, I'll briefly cover a few transaction basics, the ACID properties, ISO/ANSI SQL transaction isolation levels and multi-version read consistency. For a more thorough treatment of these topics, please read the *Oracle Concepts Manual* and then follow up with Tom Kyte's *Expert Oracle Database Architecture Oracle Database 9i, 10g and 11g Programming Techniques and Solutions*, Chapters 6, 7, and 8. The goal for this chapter is to provide a basic understanding of how to design a sound transaction, and how to ensure that Oracle processes your transactions exactly as you intend for them to be processed.

What is a Transaction?

Let's start by making sure we're all on the same page when it comes to the word *transaction*. The definition of a transaction is a *single, logical unit of work*: it is comprised of a specific set of SQL statements that *must succeed or fail as a whole*. Every transaction has a distinct beginning with the first executable SQL statement and a distinct ending, when the work of the transaction is either committed or rolled back. Transactions that have started but not yet committed or rolled back their work are *active* transactions, and all changes within an active transaction are considered pending until they are committed. If the transaction fails or is rolled back, then those pending changes never existed in the database at all.

The most common example of a transaction is a banking transfer. For example, a customer would like to transfer $500 from a checking account to a savings account. This requires a two step process: a $500 debit from checking and a $500 credit to savings. Both updates must complete successfully in order to guarantee the accuracy of the data. If both updates cannot be completed, then both updates must roll back. Transactions are an all-or-nothing proposition, as a partial transaction may corrupt the data's integrity. Consider the bank transfer: if the funds are removed from the checking account but the credit to the savings account fails, the data is no longer consistent and the bank's financial reporting is inaccurate. The bank would also have a very unhappy customer on their hands since the customer's $500 has mysteriously disappeared.

It is also necessary to ensure that both updates are committed to the database as a single unit. Committing after each statement increases the possibility of one statement succeeding and the other statement failing, it also results in a point in time when the data is inconsistent. From the moment the first commit succeeds until the second commit completes, the bank records would not represent reality. If the bank manager happened to execute a report summarizing all account balances during that space of time in between the two commits, the total in the deposited accounts would be short by $500. In this case, the customer would be fine since the $500 does eventually end up in their savings account. Instead, there would be a very frustrated accountant working late into the night to balance the books. By allowing the statements to process independently, the integrity of the data provided to the users becomes questionable.

A transaction should not include any extraneous work. Using the banking example again, it would be wrong to add the customer's order for new checks in the transfer transaction. Adding unrelated work violates the definition of a transaction: there is no logical reason why a check order should depend on the success of a transfer. Nor should the transfer depend on the check order. Maybe if a customer was opening a new account, it could be appropriate to include the check order with the transaction. The bank wouldn't want to issue checks on a non-existent account. But then again, is the customer required to get checks for the account? Probably not. The most important element of coding a sound transaction is accurately setting the transaction boundaries around a logical unit of work and ensuring that all operations within that transaction are processed as a whole. In order to know where those boundaries should be, you need to understand the application requirements and the business process.

A transaction can be comprised of multiple data manipulation language (DML) statements, but it can only contain one data definition language (DDL) statement. This is because every DDL statement creates an implicit commit, which will also commit any previously uncommitted work. Be very cautious when including DDL statements in a transaction. Since a transaction must encompass a complete logical unit of work, you want to be certain that a DDL statement either is issued prior to the DML statements as a separate transaction, or after all DML statements have processed successfully. If a DDL statement occurs in the middle of a transaction, then your "logical unit of work" will end up divided into two not-so-logical partial updates.

ACID Properties of a Transaction

Transaction processing is a defining characteristic of a data management system; it's what makes a database different from a file system. There are four required properties for all database transactions: *Atomicity*, *Consistency*, *Isolation* and *Durability*. These four properties are known as *ACID* properties. The ACID properties have been used to define the key characteristics of database transactions across all brands of database systems since Jim Gray first wrote about them in 1976, and clearly he defined those characteristics very well, as no one has done it better in the 35 years since that time. Every transactional database must comply with ACID but *how* they choose to implement their compliance has created some of the more interesting differences in database software products.

All Oracle transactions comply with the ACID properties, which are described in the Oracle Concepts Manual as follows:

Atomicity: All tasks of a transaction are performed or none of them are. There are no partial transactions.

Consistency: The transaction takes the database from one consistent state to another consistent state.

Isolation: The effect of a transaction is not visible to other transactions until the transaction is committed.

Durability: Changes made by committed transactions are permanent.

Think for a moment about the fundamental behaviors of the individual SQL statements you issue to the Oracle database and compare them to the ACID properties listed above. These properties represent the behaviors you expect at the statement level, as Oracle provides atomicity, consistency, isolation and durability for SQL statements automatically without you having to expend any additional effort. Essentially, when you design a transaction to be processed by the database, your goal is to communicate the entire set of changes as a single operation. As long as you use transaction control statements to correctly convey the contents of an individual transaction and set your transactions to the appropriate isolation level when the default behavior is not what you need, the Oracle database will provide the atomicity, consistency, isolation and durability required to protect your data.

Transaction Isolation Levels

And now for a little more depth on one particular ACID property: isolation. The definition of isolation in the Oracle Concepts Manual referenced above states that the effects of your transaction cannot be visible until you have committed your changes. This also means that your changes should not influence the behavior of other active transactions in the database.

In the banking transaction, I discussed the importance of protecting (isolating) the financial report from your changes until the entire transaction was complete. If you committed the credit to checking before you committed the debit to savings, the total bank funds would be overstated (briefly) by $500. This would violate the isolation property as any users or transactions could see that the checking account balance had been reduced before the funds were added to the savings account.

However there are two sides to the requirement for transaction isolation. In addition to isolating other transactions from your updates, you need to be aware of how isolated your transaction needs to be from updates made by other transactions. To some extent, the answer to this question depends on those business requirements, but it also depends on how sensitive your transaction is to changes made by other users and how likely the data is to change while your transaction is processing. To appreciate the need for isolation, you need to understand how isolation, or the lack thereof, impacts transactions on a multi-user database.

The ANSI/ISO SQL standard defines four distinct levels of transaction isolation: read uncommitted, read committed, repeatable read, and serializable. Within these four levels, the standard defines three phenomena that are either permitted or not permitted at a specific isolation level: dirty reads, non-repeatable reads, and phantom reads. Each of the three phenomena is a specific type of inconsistency that can occur in data that is read by one transaction while another transaction is processing updates. As the isolation level increases, there is a greater degree of separation between transactions, which results in increasingly consistent data.

The ANSI/ISO SQL standard does not tell you how a database should achieve these isolation levels, nor does it define which kinds of reads should or should not be permitted. The standard simply defines the impact one transaction may have on another at a given level of isolation. Table 14-1 lists the four isolation levels and notes whether a given phenomena is permitted or not permitted.

Table 14-1. *ANSI Isolation Levels*

Isolation Level	Dirty Read	Non-repeatable Read	Phantom Read
Read Uncommitted	Permitted	Permitted	Permitted
Read Committed	X	Permitted	Permitted
Repeatable Read	X	X	Permitted
Serializable	X	X	X

The definitions of each phenomenon are:

- **Dirty Read** Reading an uncommitted transaction is called a dirty read, and it's a very appropriate name. Dirty reads have not been committed, which means that data has not yet been verified against any constraints set in the database. Uncommitted data may never be committed, and if this happens, the data was never really part of the database at all. Result sets built from dirty reads should be considered highly suspect as they can represent a view of the information that never actually existed.

- **Non-Repeatable Read** A non-repeatable read occurs when a transaction executes a query a second time and receives a different result due to committed updates by another transaction. In this case, the updates by the other transaction have been verified and made durable, so the data is valid; it's just been altered since the last time your transaction read it.

- **Phantom Read** If a query is executed a second time within a transaction, and additional records matching the filter criteria are returned, it is considered a phantom read. Phantom reads result when another transaction has inserted more data and committed its work.

By default, transactions in Oracle are permitted to read the committed work of other users immediately after the commit. This means that it is possible to get non-repeatable and phantom reads unless you specifically set the isolation level for your transaction to either read-only or serializable. The important question is "Will either phenomenon prevent my transaction from applying its changes correctly and taking the database from one consistent state to the next?" If your transaction will not issue the same query more than once in a single transaction or it does not need the underlying data to remain consistent for the duration of your transaction, then the answer is "No" and the transaction can be processed safely at the default read committed isolation level.

Only a serializable transaction completely removes the possibility of all three phenomena while still allowing for updates, thus providing the most consistent view of the data even as it is changing. However, serializable transactions can reduce the level of concurrency in the database, as there is a greater risk of transactions failing due to conflicts with other updates. If you require repeatable reads AND you need to update data in the transaction, setting your transaction to execute in serializable mode is your only option. If your transaction requires repeatable reads but it will not update data, then you can set your transaction to read only mode, which will guarantee repeatable reads until your transaction completes or until the system exceeds its undo retention period. I'll talk about how to accomplish serializable and repeatable read transactions shortly.

Oracle does not support the read uncommitted isolation level, nor is it possible to alter the database to do so. Reading uncommitted data is permitted in other databases to prevent writers from blocking readers and readers from blocking writers. Oracle prevents such blocks from occurring with multi-version read consistency, which provides each transaction with its own read consistent view of the data. Thanks to multi-version read consistency, dirty reads are something Oracle users and developers never need to worry about.

Multi-Version Read Consistency

As mentioned earlier, the ACID properties do not determine how the database should provide data consistency for transactions. Nor do the ANSI/ISO SQL transaction isolation levels define how to achieve transaction isolation, or even specify the levels of isolation a database product must provide. Each individual vendor determines how to comply with ACID and the levels of isolation they will support. If you develop applications that operate on multiple database platforms, it is crucial for you to understand the different implementations provided by each vendor and how those differences can impact the results of a given transaction.

Fortunately, you only have to worry about one approach in this chapter. Oracle provides data consistency and concurrency with the multi-version read consistency model. This can be a fairly complex concept to grasp, although it's transparent to users. Oracle is able to simultaneously display multiple versions of the data, based on the specific point in time a transaction requested the information and the transaction's isolation level. The database accomplishes this amazing feat by retaining the before and after condition of altered data blocks, so that the database can recreate a consistent view of the data for multiple sessions at a single point in time. If a transaction is running in the default read committed mode, then a "consistent view of the data" means the results are based on the committed data as of when a query or update was initiated. When a transaction is executing in serializable mode, the read consistent view is based on the committed data as of when the transaction began. There is a limit to how far Oracle can reach into the past to create this consistent view of the data, and that limit depends on the allocation of undo space configured for the database. If Oracle cannot reach back far enough into the past to support a given statement, that statement will fail with a "snapshot too old" error.

Undo blocks retain the before condition of the data, while the redo information is stored in the online redo logs in the system global area (SGA). The redo logs contain both the change to the data block and the change to the undo block. The same structures that provide the means to roll back your changes also provide read consistent views of the data to multiple users and multiple transactions. Because a transaction should always encompass a complete logical unit of work, the undo storage and retention level should be configured to support transactions at the required level of concurrency. If you are considering dividing your logical unit of work to prevent "snapshot too old" errors, you need to revisit your code or talk with your DBA. Maybe do both.

The database buffers of the SGA are updated with changes for a committed transaction, but the changes are not necessarily written immediately to the data files. Oracle uses the system change number (SCN) to keep a sequential record of changes occurring throughout the instance and to connect changes to a particular point in time. Should the database fail, all pending transactions are rolled back so that when the database is restarted, the data will be at a consistent state once again, reflecting only the committed work as of the time of failure. You would get the exact same result if the database administrator issued a command to flash the database back to a specific SCN. The database returns to the point in time marked by the SCN, and any transactions committed after that will no longer exist in the database. This is necessary to prevent partial transactions from being stored in the database.

So how does multi-version read consistency impact individual transactions? If Transaction B requests data that has been altered by Transaction A, but Transaction A has not committed its changes, Oracle will read the before condition of the data, and return that view to Transaction B. If Transaction C begins after Transaction A commits its changes, the results returned to Transaction C will include the changes committed by Transaction A. This means that Transaction C receives a different result than Transaction B, but the results are consistent with the point in time when each session requested the information.

Transaction Control Statements

There are only five transaction control statements: commit, savepoint, rollback, set transaction, and set constraints. There are relatively few variants of these statements, so learning the syntax and the options for controlling your transactions is not too difficult. The challenge of coding a transaction is understanding how and where to use the appropriate combination of statements to ensure your transaction complies with ACID and that it will be processed by the database exactly as you expected.

Commit

Commit, or the SQL standard compliant version *commit work*, ends your transaction by making your changes durable and visible to other users. With the commit write extensions now available, you have the option to change the default behavior of a commit. Changes can be committed asynchronously with the *write nowait* extension, and you can also choose to allow Oracle to write commits in batches. The default behavior processes a commit as *commit write wait immediate*, which is how commits were processed in earlier versions of Oracle. This will still be the correct behavior for the majority of applications.

So when might you choose to not wait for Oracle to confirm your work has been written? By choosing an asynchronous commit, you are allowing the database to confirm that your changes have been received before those changes are made durable. If the database fails before the commit is written, your transaction will be gone yet your application and your users will expect it to be there. While this behavior may be acceptable for applications that process highly transitive data, for most of us, ensuring the data has indeed been committed is essential. A nowait commit should be carefully considered before being implemented. You need to be certain that your application can function when committed transactions seem to disappear.

Savepoint

Savepoints allow you to mark specific points within your transaction and roll your transaction back to the specified savepoint. You then have the option to continue your transaction rather than starting a brand new one. Savepoints are sequential so if you have five savepoints and you rollback to the second savepoint, all changes made for savepoints three through five are rolled back.

Rollback

Rollback is the other option for ending a transaction. If you choose to rollback, your changes will be reversed and the data returns to its previously consistent state. As noted above, you have the option to rollback to a specific savepoint but rolling back to a savepoint does not end a transaction. Instead, the transaction remains active until either a complete rollback or commit is issued.

Set Transaction

The *set transaction command* provides multiple options to alter default transaction behavior. *Set transaction read only* will provide repeatable reads but you cannot alter data. You also use the set transaction command to specify serializable isolation. Set transaction can be used to choose a specific rollback segment for a transaction, but this is no longer recommended by Oracle; in fact, if you are using automatic undo management, this command will be ignored. You can also use set transaction to name your transaction, but the DBMS.Application_Info package is a better option for labeling your transactions as it provides additional functionality.

Set Constraints

Constraints can be deferred during a transaction with the *set constraint(s)* command. The default behavior is to check the constraints after each statement, but in some transactions, it may be that the constraints will not be met until all the updates within the transaction are complete. In these cases, you can defer constraint verification, as long as the constraints were created as deferrable. This command can defer a single constraint, or it can defer all constraints.

As far as the SQL language goes, transaction control statements may be some of the simplest and clearest language options you have. Commit, rollback, and rollback to savepoint will be the transaction control commands you use most often. You may need to set the isolation level with set transaction occasionally, while deferring constraints is likely to be a rare occurrence. If you want more information about the transaction control statements, referring to the SQL statement documentation is likely to give you enough information to execute the commands, but before you use one of the less common commands, be sure to research and test extensively so you know absolutely what the effect non-default behavior will have on your data.

Grouping Operations into Transactions

By now, you should be well aware that understanding the business requirements is central to designing a good transaction. However, what is considered a logical unit of work in one company may be very different at another company. For example, when an order is placed, is the customer's credit card charged immediately or is the card charged when the order ships? If payment is required to place the order, then the procuring the funds should be part of the order transaction. If payments are processed when product is shipped, then payment may be authorized with the order, but processed just before shipment. Neither option is more correct than the other, it just depends on how the business has decided to manage their orders. If a company is selling a very limited product, then expecting payment at the time of order is perfectly reasonable as the company is making that rare item unavailable to other customers. If the product is common, then customers generally don't expect to pay until the product has shipped and choosing to process payments earlier may cost the company some business.

In addition to understanding the business requirements, there are some general rules for designing a sound transaction:

- Process each logical unit of work as an independent transaction. Do not include extraneous work.

- Ensure the data is consistent when your transaction begins and that it will remain consistent when the transaction is complete.

- Get the resources you need to process your transaction and then release the resources for other transactions. Hold shared resources for as long as you need them, but no longer. By the same token, do not commit during your transaction to just to release locks that you still need. Adding commits breaks up the logical unit of work and does not benefit the database.

- Consider other transactions likely to be processing at the same time. Do they need to be isolated from your transaction? Does your transaction need to be isolated from other updates?

- Use savepoints to mark specific SQL statements that may be appropriate for mid-transaction rollbacks.

- Transactions should always be explicitly committed or rolled back. Do not rely on the default behavior of the database or a development tool to commit or rollback. Default behavior can change.

- Once you've designed a solid transaction, consider wrapping it in a procedure or package. As long as a procedure does not contain any commits or rollbacks within it, it will be provided with the same default atomicity level Oracle provides to all statements. This means that the protections automatically afforded to statements will also apply to your procedure, and therefore, your transaction.

- Exception handling can have a significant impact on a transaction's integrity. Exceptions should be handled with relevant application errors, and any unhandled exceptions should always raise the database error. Using the When Others clause to bypass an error condition is a serious flaw in your code.

- Consider using the DBMS.Application_Info package to label your transactions. This will help identify specific sections of code quickly and accurately when troubleshooting errors or tuning performance. I'll talk more about DBMS.Application_Info and instrumentation in the next chapter.

The Order Entry Schema

Before I move on to talking about active transactions, let's talk about the sample schema you'll be using for your transaction examples. The Order Entry (OE) schema contains a product set that is available for orders, and it is associated with the Human Resources (HR) schema you may already be familiar with. In this case, some of those employees are sales representatives who will take orders on behalf of your customers. Listing 14-1 shows the names of the tables in the default Order Entry schema.

Listing 14-1. *Order Entry (OE) Schema Tables*

```
TABLE_NAME
------------------------------
CATEGORIES
CUSTOMERS
INVENTORIES
ORDERS
ORDER_ITEMS
PRODUCT_DESCRIPTIONS
PRODUCT_INFORMATION
WAREHOUSES
```

The OE schema may be missing a few critical components; there are no warehouses in the WAREHOUSES table and there is no inventory in the INVENTORIES table, so you are out of stock on everything and you have no place to store the stock if you did have any. It's hard to create orders without any inventory, so you'll need to add data to the existing tables first.

You'll start by adding a warehouse to the company's Southlake, Texas location where there should be plenty of real estate, and then you'll add lots of inventory to be sold. I've used the DBMS.RANDOM procedure to generate over 700,000 items, so if you choose to follow along, your actual inventory may vary. But you should end up with enough products in stock to experiment with a few transactions, and you can always add more. As you create your orders, you will notice the PRODUCT_INFORMATION table contains some very old computing equipment. If it helps, consider the equipment vintage and pretend you're selling collectibles.

The ORDERS table contains an ORDER_STATUS column, but the status is represented by a numeric value. You will create a lookup table for the order status values, and since the existing orders use a range of one through 10, your ORDER_STATUS table will contain ten records. Although this is not a PL/SQL book, I have created a few functions and a procedure to provide some necessary functionality without having to show a lot extra code that might detract from primary purpose of an example. You will see functions to get the list price from the PRODUCT_INFORMATION table, one to get a count of number of line items added to an order, and another one to calculate the order total using the sum of the line items. The contents of the functions are not important to your transactions, but the code to create them is included in the download available at the Apress website, along with the rest of the schema updates.

You will also create a billing schema and a credit authorization procedure. The procedure accepts a customer id number and order total, and then returns a randomly generated number to simulate the process of ensuring payment for the products. In the real world, billing would likely represent an entire accounting system and possibly a distributed transaction, but for your purposes, you simply need to represent the customer's promise to pay for the items they wish to order. Remember, the most important rule for any transaction is that it should contain a complete logical unit of work. The credit authorization represents the exchange of funds for the product. You're not in business to give your products away, and the customer isn't going to send you cash unless they receive something in return. It's this exchange that represents a transaction. Listing 14-2 shows the rest of the OE schema changes.

Listing 14-2. *Order Entry (OE) Schema Changes*

```
-- create 'billing' user to own a credit authorization procedure

conn / as sysdba
create user billing identified by &passwd ;

grant create session to billing ;
grant create procedure to billing ;

--- add warehouses and inventory using a random number to populate inventory quantities

connect oe

insert into warehouses values (1, 'Finished Goods', 1400) ;

insert into inventories
select product_id, 1, round(dbms_random.value(2, 5000),0)
  from product_information;

commit;

--- check total quantity on hand

select sum(quantity_on_hand) from inventories;

--- create a sequence for the order id

create sequence order_id start with 5000;
```

```
--- create a table for order status

create table oe.order_status
 (
  order_status          number(2, 0) not null,
  order_status_name     varchar2(12) not null,
  constraint order_status_pk order_status)
 );


--- add values for order status 1 through 10 to match existing sample data

insert into order_status (order_status, order_status_name) values (0, 'Pending');
insert into order_status (order_status, order_status_name) values (1, 'New');
insert into order_status (order_status, order_status_name) values (2, 'Cancelled');
insert into order_status (order_status, order_status_name) values (3, 'Authorized');
insert into order_status (order_status, order_status_name) values (4, 'Processing');
insert into order_status (order_status, order_status_name) values (5, 'Shipped');
insert into order_status (order_status, order_status_name) values (6, 'Delivered');
insert into order_status (order_status, order_status_name) values (7, 'Returned');
insert into order_status (order_status, order_status_name) values (8, 'Damaged');
insert into order_status (order_status, order_status_name) values (9, 'Exchanged');
insert into order_status (order_status, order_status_name) values (10, 'Rejected');


--- create a function to get the list prices of order items

@get_listprice.fnc

--- create a function to get the order total

@get_ordertotal.fnc

--- create a function to get the order count

@get_orderitemcount.fnc

--- create order detail views

@order_detail_views.sql

--- Create credit_request procedure

connect billing

@credit_request.sql
```

Now that you know what you're selling and you've got a CUSTOMERS table to tell you who you might be selling it to, let's take a look at an order transaction. Your longstanding customer, Maximilian Henner of Davenport, Iowa has contacted the sales manager, John Russell, and placed an order for five 12GB hard drives, five 32GB RAM sticks, and 19 boxes of business cards containing 1,000 cards per box. Mr. Henner has a credit authorization of $50,000, although your customers table does not tell you how much he may already owe for prior purchases. That would be stored in your imaginary billing system. John enters Mr. Henner's order in the order entry screen of your sales system, and creates order number 2459 for customer 141. The order is a direct order entered into the system by your employee, id number 145. When your sales manager sends a copy of this order to his customer, the order should look something like this:

Order No: 2459

Customer: Maximilian Henner
2102 E Kimberly Rd
Davenport, IA 52807

Sold by: John Russell

No	Product	Description	Qty	Price	Sale Price	Total
1	2255	HD 12GB @7200 /SE	5	775.00	658.75	3,293.75
2	2274	RAM - 32MB	5	161.00	136.85	684.25
3	2537	Business Cards Box – 1000	19	200.00	170.00	3230.00

The customer would like to purchase multiple quantities of three different products, so you need to add three items to the ORDER_ITEM table. Each item needs a product id, a quantity, and a list price. There is a discount percentage that is applied to the entire order, and it will be used to calculate the discounted price. The discounted priced is multiplied by the item quantity to produce the line item total.

As you add the items to the order, you also must reduce the on-hand inventory for those items so that another sales person will not commit to delivering a product that is no longer available. Next, you need to calculate the order total as a sum of the line items and then call the credit authorization procedure to verify that Mr. Henner has the required amount available in his credit line. Once you have the authorization, you will set the order total to equal the amount charged and the transaction is complete. All of these steps are required for the order to exist and therefore, these steps comprise your logical unit of work for an order.

Before you enter the order, you'll check the inventory for the products the customer has requested as shown in listing 14-3.

Listing 14-3. *Verify Available Inventory*

```
SQL> select product_id, quantity_on_hand
        from inventories
      where product_id in (2255, 2274, 2537)
      order by product_id ;
```

```
PRODUCT_ID QUANTITY_ON_HAND
---------- ----------------
      2255              672
      2274              749
      2537             2759
```

If you look at the statements as they would be received by the database to create this order, reduce the inventory, and obtain a credit authorization, they might look something like the transaction shown in Listing 14-4.

Listing 14-4. *Order Transaction in a Procedure*

```
SQL> begin

    savepoint create_order;

    insert into orders
          (order_id, order_date, order_mode, order_status, customer_id, sales_rep_id)
      values
          (2459, sysdate, 'direct', 1, 141, 145) ;

  --- Add first ordered item and reduce inventory

    savepoint detail_item1;

    insert into order_items
          (order_id, line_item_id, product_id, unit_price, discount_price, quantity)
      values
          (2459, 1, 2255, 775, 658.75, 5) ;

    update inventories set quantity_on_hand = quantity_on_hand - 5
      where product_id = 2255 and warehouse_id = 1 ;

  --- Add second ordered item and reduce inventory

    savepoint detail_item2;

    insert into order_items
          (order_id, line_item_id, product_id, unit_price, discount_price, quantity)
      values
          (2459, 2, 2274, 161, 136.85, 5) ;

    update inventories set quantity_on_hand = quantity_on_hand - 5
      where product_id = 2274 and warehouse_id = 1 ;

  --- Add third ordered item and reduce inventory

    savepoint detail_item3;
```

```
   insert into order_items
          (order_id, line_item_id, product_id, unit_price, discount_price, quantity)
   values
          (2459, 3, 2537, 200, 170, 19) ;

   update inventories set quantity_on_hand = quantity_on_hand - 19
    where product_id = 2537 and warehouse_id = 1 ;

   --- Request credit authorization

   savepoint credit_auth;

   begin billing.credit_request(141,7208); end;

   savepoint order_total;

   --- Update order total

   savepoint order_total;

   update orders set order_total = 7208 where order_id = 2459;

   exception
    when others then RAISE;
   end;
   /

Customer ID = 141
Amount = 7208
Authorization = 3452

PL/SQL procedure successfully completed.
```

You see the output from the credit authorization and get a confirmation that your procedure completed. You have not yet ended your transaction as you haven't issued a commit or a rollback. First, you'll query the data to confirm your updates, including the update to reduce the on-hand inventory. The confirmation queries are shown in listing 14-5.

Listing 14-5. *Confirm Transaction Updates*

```
SQL> select order_id, customer, mobile, status, order_total, order_date
       from order_detail_header
      where order_id = 2459 ;
```

ORDER_ID	CUSTOMER	MOBILE	STATUS	ORDER_TOTAL	ORDER_DATE
2459	Maximilian Henner	+1 319 123 4282	New	7,208.00	04 Jul 2010

1 row selected.

```
SQL> select line_item_id ITEM, product_name, unit_price,
            discount_price, quantity, line_item_total
      from order_detail_line_items
     where order_id = 2459
     order by line_item_id ;
```

ITEM	PRODUCT_NAME	UNIT_PRICE	DISCOUNT_PRICE	QUANTITY	LINE_ITEM_TOTAL
1	HD 12GB @7200 /SE	775.00	658.75	5	3,293.75
2	RAM - 32 MB	161.00	136.85	5	684.25
3	Business Cards Box - 1000	200.00	170.00	19	3,230.00

3 rows selected.

```
SQL> select product_id, quantity_on_hand
      from inventories
     where product_id in (2255, 2274, 2537)
     order by product_id ;
```

PRODUCT_ID	QUANTITY_ON_HAND
2255	667
2274	744
2537	2740

All required operations within your transaction have been confirmed. The order has been created, three products have been added, the inventory was reduced, and your order total was updated to reflect the sum of the individual line items. Your transaction is complete, and you can commit the changes. But instead you're going to roll them back and use this transaction again.

■**NOTE** The most important rule for transaction processing is to ensure the transaction is ACID compliant. The transaction in Listing 14-4 has been wrapped in a procedure with an exception clause to illustrate the atomicity principal. The remainder of the examples may be shown as independently entered SQL statements, and in some cases, only a portion of the transaction will be shown, but that is only to keep the examples to a reasonable length. If there is one message you take away from this chapter, it is the importance of ensuring that the entire transaction succeeds as a whole or fails as a whole.

The Active Transaction

As soon as you issue the first SQL statement that alters data, the database recognizes an active transaction and creates a transaction id. The transaction id will remain the same whether you have one DML statement in your transaction or twenty, and the transaction id will only exist as long as your transaction is active and your changes are still pending. In the order example from the previous section, the transaction id is responsible for tracking only one transaction, the new order for Mr. Henner. Once you rolled the entire transaction back, your transaction ended and the transaction id was gone. You would see the same result if you committed your work.

The SCN number, on the other hand, continues to increment regardless of where you are in your transaction process. The SCN number identifies a specific point in time for the database, and it can be used to return the database to a prior point in time while still ensuring the data is consistent. Committed transactions will remain committed (durability) and any pending transactions will be rolled back (atomicity).

If you were to check the transaction id and SCN number while executing the individual statements that comprised the order procedure shown earlier, you would see something like the results in Listing 14-6.

Listing 14-6. *Order Transaction with Transaction ID and SCN Shown*

```
SQL> insert into orders
        (order_id, order_date, order_mode, order_status, customer_id, sales_rep_id)
     values
        (2459, sysdate, 'direct', 1, 141, 145) ;

1 row created.

SQL> select current_scn from v$database;

CURRENT_SCN
-----------
   83002007

SQL> select xid, status from v$transaction ;

XID              STATUS
---------------- ----------------
0A001800CE8D0000 ACTIVE
.......

SQL> --- Update order total

SQL> update orders set order_total = 7208 where order_id = 2459;

1 row updated.

SQL> select order_id, customer, mobile, status, order_total, order_date
        from order_detail_header
     where order_id = 2459;
```

ORDER_ID	CUSTOMER	MOBILE	STATUS	ORDER_TOTAL	ORDER_DATE
2459	Maximilian Henner	+1 319 123 4282	New	7,208.00	04 Jul 2010

```
SQL> select line_item_id, product_name, unit_price,
            discount_price, quantity, line_item_total
       from order_detail_line_items
      where order_id = 2459
      order by line_item_id ;
```

ITEM	PRODUCT_NAME	UNIT_PRICE	DISCOUNT_PRICE	QUANTITY	LINE_ITEM_TOTAL
1	HD 12GB @7200 /SE	775.00	658.75	5	3,293.75
2	RAM - 32 MB	161.00	136.85	5	684.25
3	Business Cards Box - 1000	200.00	170.00	19	3,230.00

```
SQL> select current_scn from v$database;

CURRENT_SCN
-----------
   83002012

SQL> select xid, status from v$transaction ;

XID              STATUS
---------------- ----------------
0A001800CE8D0000 ACTIVE

SQL> rollback;

Rollback complete.

SQL> select current_scn from v$database;

CURRENT_SCN
-----------
   83002015

SQL> select xid, status from v$transaction ;

no rows selected
```

If the database were flashed back to SCN 83002012, none of the operations in your order would exist. Since any changes you had made were pending at that point in time, the only way Oracle can guarantee data consistency is to roll back all non-committed work. Whether you committed the transaction or rolled it back is immaterial. The updates were not committed at SCN 830020012, and pending changes are always reversed.

Using Savepoints

In the initial order transaction, you included savepoints but did not make use of them. Instead, you executed your transaction, confirmed the order information with two queries, and then rolled the entire transaction back. In the example shown in Listing 14-7, you will roll back to savepoint item_detail1, which is recorded prior to adding any product to the order. When you re-execute the queries to check the order data, notice in Listing 14-8 that all changes occurring after the savepoint are reversed, yet the order itself still exists. Your sales rep would have the option of continuing with Mr. Henner's order by adding new line items or rolling it back completely to end the transaction. Let's take a look at your data after the returning to a savepoint.

Listing 14-7. *Returning to a Savepoint*

```
SQL> savepoint create_order;

Savepoint created.

SQL> insert into orders
            (order_id, order_date, order_mode, order_status, customer_id, sales_rep_id)
      values
            (2459, sysdate, 'direct', 1, 141, 145) ;

1 row created.

SQL> --- Add first ordered item and reduce inventory

SQL> savepoint detail_item1;

Savepoint created.

SQL> insert into order_items
            (order_id, line_item_id, product_id, unit_price, discount_price, quantity)
      values
            (2459, 1, 2255, 775, 658.75, 5) ;

1 row created.

SQL> update inventories set quantity_on_hand = quantity_on_hand - 5
      where product_id = 2255 and warehouse_id = 1 ;

1 row updated.

SQL> --- Add second ordered item and reduce inventory

SQL> savepoint detail_item2;

Savepoint created.
```

```
SQL> insert into order_items
          (order_id, line_item_id, product_id, unit_price, discount_price, quantity)
      values
          (2459, 2, 2274, 161, 136.85, 5) ;

1 row created.

SQL> update inventories set quantity_on_hand = quantity_on_hand - 5
      where product_id = 2274 and warehouse_id = 1 ;

1 row updated.

SQL> --- Add third ordered item and reduce inventory

SQL> savepoint detail_item3;

Savepoint created.

SQL> insert into order_items
          (order_id, line_item_id, product_id, unit_price, discount_price, quantity)
      values
          (2459, 3, 2537, 200, 170, 19) ;

1 row created.

SQL> update inventories set quantity_on_hand = quantity_on_hand - 19
      where product_id = 2537 and warehouse_id = 1 ;

1 row updated.

SQL> --- Request credit authorization

SQL> savepoint credit_auth;

Savepoint created.

SQL> exec billing.credit_request(141,7208) ;
Customer ID = 141
Amount = 7208
Authorization = 1789

PL/SQL procedure successfully completed.

SQL> savepoint order_total;

Savepoint created.
```

```
SQL> --- Update order total

SQL> savepoint order_total;

Savepoint created.

SQL> update orders set order_total = 7208 where order_id = 2459;

1 row updated.

SQL> select order_id, customer, mobile, status, order_total, order_date
       from order_detail_header
       where order_id = 2459;

  ORDER_ID CUSTOMER                      MOBILE           STATUS         ORDER_TOTAL ORDER_DATE
---------- ----------------------------- ---------------- ------------- ------------ -----------
      2459 Maximilian Henner             +1 319 123 4282  New              7,208.00 04 Jul 2010

SQL> select line_item_id, product_name, unit_price, discount_price,
            quantity, line_item_total
        from order_detail_line_items
        where order_id = 2459
        order by line_item_id ;

ITEM PRODUCT_NAME               UNIT_PRICE DISCOUNT_PRICE   QUANTITY LINE_ITEM_TOTAL
---- ------------------------- ---------- -------------- ---------- ---------------
   1 HD 12GB @7200 /SE             775.00         658.75          5        3,293.75
   2 RAM - 32 MB                   161.00         136.85          5          684.25
   3 Business Cards Box - 1000     200.00         170.00         19        3,230.00

SQL> rollback to savepoint detail_item1;

Rollback complete.
```

Listing 14-8. *Verifying Data After Rollback to a Savepoint*

```
SQL> select order_id, customer, mobile, status, order_total, order_date
       from order_detail_header
       where order_id = 2459;

  ORDER_ID CUSTOMER                      MOBILE           STATUS         ORDER_TOTAL ORDER_DATE
---------- ----------------------------- ---------------- ------------- ------------ -----------
      2459 Maximilian Henner             +1 319 123 4282  New                       04 Jun 2010

SQL> select line_item_id, product_name, unit_price, discount_price,
            quantity, line_item_total
```

```
         from order_detail_line_items
      where order_id = 2459
      order by line_item_id ;
```

no rows selected

```
SQL> select product_id, quantity_on_hand
       from inventories
      where product_id in (2255, 2274, 2537)
      order by product_id ;
```

```
PRODUCT_ID QUANTITY_ON_HAND
---------- ----------------
      2255              672
      2274              749
      2537             2759
```

Notice how in the first set of queries selects, both the order and the three products are added to the ORDER_ITEMS table. After you've rolled back to the item_detail1 savepoint, there are no products associated with the order, the inventory has returned to its previous level, and while the order header still exists, the order total field is now null.

Serializing Transactions

When a transaction is executed in serializable mode, Oracle's multi-version read consistency model provides a view of the data as it existed at the start of the transaction. No matter how many other transactions may be processing updates at the same time, a serializable transaction will only see its own changes. This creates the illusion of a single user database, as changes committed by other users after the start of the transaction remain invisible. Serializable transactions are used when a transaction needs to update data and requires repeatable reads. Listings 14-8, 14-9 and 14-10 will demonstrate when a serialized transaction or repeatable read may be required.

Executing transactions in serializable mode does not mean that updates are processed sequentially. If a serializable transaction attempts to update a record that has been changed since the transaction began, the update will not be permitted and Oracle will return this error:

```
ORA-08177: can't serialize access for this transaction
```

At this point, the transaction could be rolled back and repeated. For a serializable transaction to be successful there needs to be a strong possibility that no one else will update the same data while the transaction is executing. You can increase the odds of success by completing any changes that may conflict with other updates early in your transaction, and by keeping the serialized transaction as short and quick as possible.

This makes the need for serializable updates somewhat contrary to their usage. If the data is unlikely to be updated by another user, then why would you need serializable isolation? Yet if the data is changeable enough to require serializable isolation, it may be difficult to achieve.

For the next example, you will open two sessions. Session A will initiate a serializable transaction and add an additional product to an existing order. After the item has been added, and before the order total has been updated, you'll pause the transaction to make a change to the same order in another session. In

Session B, you'll update the status of the order to "Processing" and commit your changes. Then you'll return to Session A to update the order. This will result in an ORA-08177 error, as shown in Listing 14-9.

Listing 14-9. *Serialized Transaction and ORA-08177*

```
Session A: Serialized transaction to add an additional item

SQL> set transaction isolation level serializable;

Transaction set.

SQL> variable o number
SQL> execute :o := &order_id
Enter value for order_id: 5006

PL/SQL procedure successfully completed.

SQL> variable d number
SQL> execute :d := &discount
Enter value for discount: .1

PL/SQL procedure successfully completed.

SQL> --- Add new ordered item and reduce on-hand inventory

SQL> variable i number
SQL> execute :i := &first_item
Enter value for first_item: 1791

PL/SQL procedure successfully completed.

SQL> variable q number
SQL> execute :q := &item_quantity
Enter value for item_quantity: 15

PL/SQL procedure successfully completed.

SQL> variable p number
SQL> execute :p := get_ListPrice(:i)

PL/SQL procedure successfully completed.

SQL> insert into order_items
            (order_id, line_item_id, product_id, unit_price, discount_price, quantity)
     values
            (:o, 1, :i, :p, :p-(:p*:d), :q) ;

1 row created.
```

```
SQL> update inventories set quantity_on_hand = quantity_on_hand - :q
       where product_id = :i and warehouse_id = 1 ;

1 row updated.

SQL> pause Pause  ...
Pause  ...

Session B: Order Status Update

SQL> variable o number
SQL> execute :o := &order_id
Enter value for order_id: 5006

PL/SQL procedure successfully completed.

SQL> variable s number
SQL> execute :s := &status
Enter value for status: 4

PL/SQL procedure successfully completed.

SQL> update orders
        set order_status = :s
      where order_id = :o ;

1 row updated.

SQL> select order_id, customer, mobile, status, order_total, order_date
       from order_detail_header
      where order_id = :o;
```

ORDER_ID CUSTOMER	MOBILE	STATUS	ORDER_TOTAL ORDER_DATE
5006 Harry Mean Taylor	+1 416 012 4147	Processing	108.00 04 Jul 2010

```
SQL> select line_item_id, product_name, unit_price, discount_price,
     quantity, line_item_total
       from order_detail_line_item
      where order_id = :o
      order by line_item_id ;
```

ITEM PRODUCT_NAME	UNIT_PRICE	DISCOUNT_PRICE	QUANTITY	LINE_ITEM_TOTAL
1 Cable RS232 10/AM	6	5.40	20	108.00

```
SQL> commit;
```

```
Session A: Return to the serializable transaction

SQL> --- Get New Order Total

SQL> variable t number
SQL> execute :t := get_OrderTotal(:o)

PL/SQL procedure successfully completed.

SQL> --- Update order total

SQL> update orders set order_total = :t where order_id = :o ;
update orders set order_total = :t where order_id = :o
*
ERROR at line 1:
ORA-08177: can't serialize access for this transaction
```

Since Session B had already committed changes to order 5006, Session A was not permitted to update the order total. This is necessary to prevent a lost update. Session A could not see that the order status had changed; its serialized view of the data still considered the order to be "New." If Session A had replaced the record in the order table with its version of the data, changes made by Session B would be overwritten by the previous version of the data even though they were committed changes.

In this case, the order total would have to be updated earlier in Session A's transaction for this transaction to be successful. However, since the order total is a sum of the individual line items, that number is unknown until the new line item is added. This is also a case where serializable isolation might really be required. If two sessions were attempting to add line items to the same order at the same time, the calculated order total might end up inaccurate.

■**NOTE** I have switched from hard-coded data values to user variables in the transactions. This makes it easier to execute the order transactions repeatedly for testing and view the results at each step. The code to process orders with prompts, variables, and functions is available on the Apress web site.

Isolating Transactions

Using the same pair of transactions, let's take a quick look at what can happen when you don't properly isolate a transaction. In this case, Session A will commit the additional items to order 5007 before pausing, which means the product has been added to the order and made durable, but order total does not include the additional product. Listing 14-10 shows how permitting other sessions to see partial transactions can jeopardize data integrity.

Listing 14-10. *Inappropriate Commits and Transaction Isolation Levels*

```
Session A: Serializable transaction to add an additional item

SQL> set transaction isolation level serializable;
```

Transaction set.

```
SQL> variable o number
SQL> execute :o := &order_id
Enter value for order_id: 5007

PL/SQL procedure successfully completed.

SQL> variable d number
SQL> execute :d := &discount
Enter value for discount: .2

PL/SQL procedure successfully completed.

SQL> --- Add new ordered item and reduce on-hand inventory

SQL> variable i number
SQL> execute :i := &first_item
Enter value for first_item: 3127

PL/SQL procedure successfully completed.

SQL> variable q number
SQL> execute :q := &item_quantity
Enter value for item_quantity: 5

PL/SQL procedure successfully completed.

SQL> variable p number
SQL> execute :p := get_ListPrice(:i)

PL/SQL procedure successfully completed.

SQL> insert into order_items
        (order_id, line_item_id, product_id, unit_price, discount_price, quantity)
     values
        (:o, 1, :i, :p, :p-(:p*:d), :q) ;

1 row created.

SQL> update inventories set quantity_on_hand = quantity_on_hand - :q
        where product_id = :i and warehouse_id = 1 ;

1 row updated.

SQL> commit;
```

```
Commit complete.

SQL> pause Pause ...
Pause ...


Session B: Order Status Update

SQL> variable o number
SQL> execute :o := &order_id
Enter value for order_id: 5007

PL/SQL procedure successfully completed.

SQL> variable s number
SQL> execute :s := &status
Enter value for status: 4

PL/SQL procedure successfully completed.

SQL> update orders
        set order_status = :s
      where order_id = :o ;

1 row updated.

SQL> select order_id, customer, mobile, status, order_total, order_date
        from order_detail_header
      where order_id = :o;

  ORDER_ID CUSTOMER                 MOBILE          STATUS       ORDER_TOTAL ORDER_DATE
---------- ------------------------ --------------- ------------ ------------- -----------
      5007 Alice Oates              +41 4 012 3563  Processing     16,432.00 04 Jul 2010

SQL> select line_item_id, product_name, unit_price, discount_price,
          quantity, line_item_total
        from order_detail_line_item
      where order_id = :o
      order by line_item_id ;

ITEM PRODUCT_NAME                   UNIT_PRICE DISCOUNT_PRICE  QUANTITY LINE_ITEM_TOTAL
---- ----------------------------- ---------- -------------- ---------- ---------------
   1 Monitor 21/HR/M                   889.00         711.20          5        3,556.00
   2 Laptop 128/12/56/v90/110        3,219.00       2,575.20          5       12,876.00
   3 LaserPro 600/6/BW                 498.00         398.40          5        1,992.00

SQL> commit;
```

Notice in the output above that the LaserPro 600 printer has been added to the order, but the order total does not reflect the additional $1,992. The status update transaction is able to view changes made by the partial transaction. Since Session A issued a commit, its serializable transaction has ended. Either session will now be able to record their view of the order table, and the statement that is recorded last gets to determine the data in the order header. If Session A completes first, Session B will alter the order status to "Processing" but the order total will remain wrong. If Session B completes first, Session A will set the correct order total, but the order will be returned to an order status of 'New." Either option results in a lost update, which demonstrates why it's so critical to ensure that transaction completes a single logical unit of work. Due to Session A's partial transaction, data consistency has been jeopardized.

What if Session B was running a report instead of updating the order's status? Session A would eventually result in a consistent update, but Session B may end up reporting inaccurate data. This is a slightly less serious infraction, as the data in the database will be accurate. However, end users make decisions based on reports, and the impact of a poorly placed commit will depend on the decisions to be made. The best solution to this issue is two-fold. First, the code executed in Session A should be corrected to removed the ill-placed commit and ensure the entire transaction will commit or fail as a single unit. Second, if data is changing quickly and the reports are not bound by date or time ranges, setting the report transaction to ensure a repeatable read may also be advisable.

Autonomous Transactions

Within your main transaction, you have the option of calling an autonomous transaction, which is an independent transaction that can be called from within another transaction. The autonomous transaction is able to commit or rollback its changes without impacting the calling, or main, transaction. Autonomous transactions are very useful if you have information that you need to store, regardless of the final resolution of the main transaction. Error logging is possibly the best example of a good use of autonomous transactions, and in some cases auditing is an appropriate use as well, although overusing autonomous transactions is not a good idea. For most of us, there are better tools available in the database for auditing, and any attempts to circumvent normal database or transaction behavior is likely to create problems eventually.

So when would you want to use an autonomous transaction? I can think of a few examples in your ordering system, and in both cases, the goal would be to retain information to prevent lost sales opportunities. For example, you might want to record the customer id and a timestamp in an ORDER_LOG table in case the order failed. If the transaction was successful, the entry in ORDER_LOG could note that order was created successfully. This would allow you to provide your sales team with a report on any attempted orders that were not completed. If you've done much shopping online, you may have received one of those e-mail reminders that you have left items in your shopping cart. Maybe you were shopping, but something came up, or perhaps you decided that you didn't really need to purchase that item after all. Either way, the vendor knows you were interested enough in the items to think about buying them, and they don't want to miss an opportunity to sell products to an interested customer. I've been browsing Amazon lately for diving equipment, in part because I'm still learning about the gear and in part to do a little price comparison with my local dive shop. Within a day or two, Amazon will send an e-mail to let me know about a special sale on one of the products I was browsing. I find this a little disconcerting, especially when I haven't even logged in while browsing, but I have to admit that it can be awfully tempting when you receive the news that the shiny, expensive piece of equipment you really wanted is now 20% less.

Another possibility for an autonomous transaction would be to record customer information when a new customer places their first order. Creating a new customer can be considered a separate logical unit of work so you're not breaking any of the transaction design rules by committing the customer information outside of the order. If the order is interrupted for any reason, it would be advantageous to retain the contact data so someone can follow up with the customer to make sure the order has been placed correctly.

In Listing 14-11, you'll create an ORDER_LOG table with four fields: customer_id, order_id, order_date, and order_status. Next, you'll create autonomous transaction in a procedure. The record_new_order procedure will log the customer id, the order id, and the current date, committing the information immediately. You'll add a call to the procedure in the order transaction as soon as the order id and customer id are known.

Listing 14-11. *Creating the Autonomous Order Logging Transaction*

```
SQL> @autonomous_transaction
SQL> create table order_log
     (
         customer_id              number not null,
         order_id                 number not null,
         order_date               date    not null,
         order_outcome            varchar2(10),
       constraint order_log_pk primary key (customer_id, order_id, order_date)
     );

Table created.

SQL> create or replace procedure record_new_order (p_customer_id  IN NUMBER,
                                                   p_order_id     IN NUMBER)
       as
     pragma autonomous_transaction;
     begin
       insert into order_log
         (customer_id, order_id, order_date)
       values
         (p_customer_id, p_order_id, sysdate);

     commit;
     end;
     /

Procedure created.
```

Listing 14-12 shows the execution of a new order transaction containing the autonomous transaction to log the customer information. The main transaction is rolled back, yet when you query the order_log table, the customer information is stored. This is because the write to the order_log table is an autonomous transaction and does not depend on the successful completion of the calling transaction.

Listing 14-12. *Executing an Order Transaction with the Order Logging Autonomous Transaction*

```
SQL> @order_transaction

SQL> WHENEVER SQLERROR EXIT SQL.SQLCODE ROLLBACK;
SQL> variable o number
SQL> execute :o := order_id.nextval

PL/SQL procedure successfully completed.

SQL> variable c number
SQL> execute :c := &customer_id
Enter value for customer_id: 264

PL/SQL procedure successfully completed.

SQL> execute oe.record_new_order(:c,:o);

PL/SQL procedure successfully completed.

SQL> variable s number
SQL> execute :s := &salesperson_id
Enter value for salesperson_id: 145

PL/SQL procedure successfully completed.

SQL> variable d number
SQL> execute :d := &discount
Enter value for discount: .1

PL/SQL procedure successfully completed.

SQL> savepoint create_order;

Savepoint created.

SQL> insert into orders
        (order_id, order_date, order_mode, order_status, customer_id, sales_rep_id)
     values
        (:o, sysdate, 'direct', 1, :c, :s) ;

1 row created.
```

```
SQL> --- Add first ordered item and reduce on-hand inventory

SQL> savepoint detail_item1;

Savepoint created.

SQL> variable i number
SQL> execute :i := &first_item
Enter value for first_item: 2335

PL/SQL procedure successfully completed.

SQL> variable q number
SQL> execute :q := &item_quantity
Enter value for item_quantity: 1

PL/SQL procedure successfully completed.

SQL> variable p number
SQL> execute :p := get_ListPrice(:i)

PL/SQL procedure successfully completed.

SQL> insert into order_items
        (order_id, line_item_id, product_id, unit_price, discount_price, quantity)
     values
        (:o, 1, :i, :p, :p-(:p*:d), :q) ;

1 row created.

SQL> update inventories set quantity_on_hand = quantity_on_hand - :q
     where product_id = :i and warehouse_id = 1 ;

1 row updated.

SQL> --- Get Order Total

SQL> variable t number
SQL> execute :t := get_OrderTotal(:o)

PL/SQL procedure successfully completed.

SQL> -- Request credit authorization

SQL> savepoint credit_auth;

Savepoint created.
```

```
SQL> execute billing.credit_request(:c,:t);
Customer ID = 264
Amount = 90
Authorization = 99

PL/SQL procedure successfully completed.

SQL> --- Update order total

SQL> savepoint order_total;

Savepoint created.

SQL> update orders set order_total = :t where order_id = :o ;

1 row updated.

SQL> select order_id, customer, mobile, status, order_total, order_date
       from order_detail_header
     where order_id = :o ;

  ORDER_ID CUSTOMER                     MOBILE          STATUS        ORDER_TOTAL ORDER_DATE
---------- --------------------------- --------------- ------------ ------------- -----------
      5020 George Adjani                +1 215 123 4702     New             90.00 05 Jul 2010

SQL> select line_item_id ITEM, product_name, unit_price, discount_price, quantity,
line_item_total
        from order_detail_line_items
      where order_id = :o
      order by line_item_id ;

 ITEM PRODUCT_NAME            UNIT_PRICE DISCOUNT_PRICE   QUANTITY LINE_ITEM_TOTAL
----- ----------------------- ---------- -------------- ---------- ---------------
    1 Mobile phone                100.00          90.00          1           90.00

SQL> rollback;

Rollback complete.

SQL> select * from order_log;

CUSTOMER_ID ORDER_ID ORDER_DATE          ORDER_STATUS
----------- -------- ------------------- ------------
        264     5020 2010-07-05 00:45:56
```

The order log retains a committed record of the attempted order. As for the order status, there are several ways you could handle that. You could create another procedure that would set the order status in the ORDER_LOG table when the order was committed by the application. If the order status was not populated in the ORDER_LOG, you would know the order had not been committed. You could also schedule a process to compare the ORDER_LOG table to the ORDERS table. If no record was found in the ORDERS table, then you would update the ORDER_LOG table to note the order had failed.

When using autonomous transactions, you want to be certain that you are not attempting to divide a transaction or circumvent normal database behavior. You also want to think carefully about the effect you are creating when you allow the autonomous transaction to commit while rolling the main transaction back. The work in the autonomous transaction should clearly be its own logical unit of work.

Summary

Transactions are the heart of the database. You create databases to store information and if that information is going to be useful, the data must be protected and it must remain consistent. If you jeopardize the integrity of the data, you have significantly devalued the system. Data integrity is an all or nothing proposition: either you have it or you don't. Although I've heard people use percentage values to describe a database's level of accuracy, that seems to be a downward spiral into increasing uncertainty. Once you know part of the data is wrong, how do you know any of the data is accurate? And how do you know which part of the data you can trust?

If your data is going to remain trustworthy, you need to ensure that each transaction complies with the ACID properties. Transactions must be atomic, containing one logical unit of work that will succeed or fail as a whole. Transactions must be consistent: they need to ensure the data is consistent when they begin, and that the data will remain consistent when the transaction ends. Transactions should occur in isolation: uncommitted changes should not be visible to users or other transactions, and some transactions require higher levels of isolation than others. Transactions must be durable: once the changes have been committed to the database and the database has responded that the changes exist, users should be able to count on the fact that there is a record of their changes.

Fortunately, Oracle makes it fairly easy for you to build ACID compliant transactions as long as you define the boundaries of your transaction carefully and accurately. Oracle does not require you to specify that you are starting a new transaction; instead the database knows which kinds of statements begin a transaction, and it creates a transaction id to track the operations within it. You should always specifically commit or rollback your transactions, as failing to do so can make those transaction boundaries a little fuzzy. Relying on the default behavior of software tools is risky, as the behavior may change in a future release.

Building sound transactions requires both technical skills and functional knowledge, and having both of those is a rare and valuable commodity in the IT industry. This book will provide a solid foundation for the development of your technical skill. You can further develop those skills by following up with the reference material mentioned earlier, but learning to apply those skills requires practice. Start by downloading the changes I made to the Order Entry schema and build a few transactions of your own. Deliberately introduce some bad choices just to see what happens. (But you don't leave that code lying around—it can be dangerous!) Experimenting with isolation levels can be particularly interesting. Practice building a few more complex transactions, and make sure that the transaction will fail if any part of it fails. Then add some custom exception handling and savepoints so that you don't have to lose the entire transaction if you need to revert part of it. Once you've got something you're proud of, wrap it up in a procedure and be sure to share what you've learned with someone else.

CHAPTER 15

■ ■ ■

Testing and Quality Assurance

Robyn Sands

As you've worked through the chapters of this book, you may have written some code to test the examples. And since you chose this particular book instead of a "Welcome to SQL" style book, it's likely that you had written quite a few SQL statements before you ever picked this book up. As you've read this book, did some of the chapters remind you of your prior work? If so, how did you feel about the code you've written in the past?

If you're like most developers, there were times when you thought, "Hey, considering how little I knew about this functionality back then, I did pretty well." And there may have been a few times when you cringed a bit, realizing that something you were very proud of at the time wasn't such a great approach after all. Don't worry; we all have applications that we would write completely differently if we only knew then what we know now. Besides, it's always easier to write better code with hindsight vision or as an armchair code jockey.

If the code you write today is better than the code you wrote yesterday, you're continuing to grow and learn, and that is commendable. Realizing our older work could have been done better is an inevitable part of the learning process. As long as we learn from our mistakes and do it a little better with the next application or the next bit of code, we're moving in the right direction.

It's also true that we need to be able to measure the quality of our current code now, not five years from now when we've grown even wiser. We want to find the problems in our code before those problems affect our users. Most of us want to find all the errors or performance issues before anyone else even sees our work. However, while that kind of attitude may indicate an admirable work ethic, it's not an advisable or even achievable goal. What we can achieve is a clear definition what a specific piece of code needs to accomplish and how we will prove that the code meets the defined requirements. Code should have measurable indicators of success that can prove or disprove the fact that we have met our goal.

So what are those measurable factors? While the target measurement will vary depending on the application, there are several basic requirements for all application code. First and foremost, the code needs to return accurate results and we need to know that results will continue to be accurate throughout the system's life cycle. If end users cannot count on the data returned by a database application, that's a pretty serious failure.

Performance is another measurable attribute of our code. The target run times will be highly dependent on the application in question: a database used by the home owner's association to track who has paid their annual fees is not required to perform at the same level as a database containing the current stock quotes, but the methods used to compare execution plans and measure run time can be the same. Code quality requires that we understand the application requirements, the function being performed, and the strengths and weaknesses of the specific system. Testing should focus on verifying functionality, pushing the weakest links to their breaking point, and recording all measurements along the way.

Test Cases

For the examples in this chapter, you will be working with the same Order Entry sample schema that you used for the transaction processing examples in Chapter 14. You will make more changes to your schema, adding new data and altering views and reports. You will begin by defining the changes to be made and the tests you will use to verify the success of those changes.

So here is the backstory: one of your suppliers, identified only as "Supplier 103089" in the database, is changing their product numbers for the software you purchase from them to resell to your customers. The new identifiers are appended with a '-' and a two character value to identify the software package language. For example, the supplier's product identifier for all English software packages will end in "-EN". The supplier will require their product identifier to be referenced for ordering, software updates, and warranty support. The new product identifiers have an effective date of October 10, 2010. This change presents the following challenges for your company:

- The Order Entry schema includes the supplier's identifier in the PRODUCT_INFORMATION table, but the supplier *product* identifier is not stored in the sample schema database at all. You will alter the order entry schema to add this field and create a numerical value to serve as the current supplier product id. These changes can be considered a prerequisite to the changes instituted by your supplier.

- Once you have added an initial supplier product identifier for all the products you sell, you need to determine how you will add the modified product identifiers for this one supplier. You also need to have a method of controlling the effective date of the new identifiers.

- The purchasing department uses an inventory report to determine which products are getting low on stock. This report will need to reflect the current supplier product identifier until October 10, 2010. After that date, the report should print the new supplier product identifier so the purchasing agent can place and verify orders easily.

- The order entry system will continue to use your internal product identifier when orders are received from your customers. Orders and invoices must show your product identifier and name, plus the supplier product identifier.

- You have inventory on hand that is packaged with the current supplier product identifier. You can continue to sell those products as-is but your customer invoices must show the actual supplier product ID found on the packaging. This means your inventory system must treat the items labeled with the new numbering scheme as a distinct product.

As you make these changes, there are several basic tests and quality issues to consider. The points that follow are not intended to be all-inclusive as every system will have its own unique test requirements; however, there are some quality checks that can be applied to all systems. You'll use the following points as a starting point:

- All objects that were valid before your changes should be valid when your changes are complete. Views, functions, procedures, and packages can be invalidated by a table change, depending on how the code for those objects was originally written. You will check for invalid schema objects both before and after you make your changes. Objects that are invalidated as an indirect result of your planned modifications should recompile successfully without further changes.

- All data changes and results output must be accurate. Verifying data can be one of the more tedious tasks when developing or altering a database application, and the more data in the system, the more tedious the work will be. It's also the most critical test your code must past: if the data is not accurate, it doesn't matter if the other requirements have been met or how fast the code executes. If the data being stored or returned cannot be trusted, your code is wrong and you've failed the most basic requirement. The simplest approach is to break data verification into manageable components, beginning by verifying the core data set, and then gradually expanding the test to the more unique use cases (the "edge cases") until you are certain all data is correct.

- Query performance can be verified by comparing the before and after versions of the execution plan. If the execution plan indicates the process has to work harder after your modifications, you want to be sure that additional work is, in fact, required and not the result of a mistake. Use of execution plans was addressed in detail in Chapter 6 so refer back to that chapter for more information on the topic plus tips on making the best use of the information found in the execution plan.

Later in this chapter, I will discuss code instrumentation and the Instrumentation Library for Oracle (ILO). ILO uses Oracle's DBMS_APPLICATION_INFO procedures. While it is possible to use the DBMS_APPLICATION_INFO procedures on their own, ILO makes it very easy and straightforward to add instrumentation to your code. I've added some additional functionality to the ILO package; the updates are available for download at Apress. Once your code is instrumented, these additional modules make it possible to build test systems that record processing times as you make iterative changes to your code or system configuration. This performance data will make it very clear when your changes have had a positive impact on processing times and when you might want to consider another approach.

Testing Methods

There are as many different approaches to software testing as there are software development—and there have quite possibly been an equal number of battles fought over both topics. Although it may be slightly controversial in a database environment, I'm going to advocate an approach known as *Test Driven Development* (TDD). Test Driven Development originated in the realm of extreme programming so you will need to make some modifications to the process to make it effective for database development, but it offers some very genuine benefits for both new development and modification efforts.

In TDD, the developer begins by creating simple, repeatable tests that will fail in the existing system but will succeed once the change is implemented correctly. This approach has the following benefits:

- In order to write the test that will fail, you will have to thoroughly understand the requirements and the current implementation before you even begin to write application code.

- Building the unit test script first ensures that you start by working through the logic of the necessary changes, thereby decreasing the odds that your code will have bugs or need a major rewrite.

- By creating small, reusable unit tests to verify the successful implementation of a change, you build a library of test scripts that can be used both to test the initial implementation of the change and to confirm that the feature is still operating as expected as other system changes are made.

- These small unit test scripts can be combined to create larger integration-testing scripts or become part of an automated test harness to simplify repetitive testing.

- TDD assists in breaking changes or new development into smaller, logical units of work. The subsets may be easier to understand and explain to other developers, which can be especially important when project members are not co-located.

- When test design is delayed until after development, testing frequently ends up being shortchanged, with incomplete or poorly written tests due to schedule constraints. Including test development efforts in the code development phases results in higher quality tests that are more accurate.

As acknowledged earlier, TDD needs some adjustments in a database environment or you run the risk of building yet another black box database application that is bound to fail performance and scalability testing. Whenever you are developing or modifying an application that stores or retrieves information from a database, as you are preparing those first unit tests, you must consider the data model or work with the individual(s) responsible for that task. In my (sometimes) humble opinion, *the data model is the single most important indicator of a database application's potential to perform*. The schema design is crucial to the application's ability to scale for more users, more data, or both. This does not mean that development cannot begin until there is a flawless entity-relationship model, but it does mean that the core data elements must be understood and the application tables should be well designed for at least those core elements. And if the database model is not fully developed, then build the application using code that will not result in extensive changes as the data model is refactored.

So what exactly am I suggesting? To put it bluntly, if your application schema will continue to be developed progressively, use procedures and packages for your application code. This will allow the database to be refactored as data elements are moved or added, without requiring major front end code rewrites.

■**NOTE** This has been far from a complete explanation of Test Driven Development or database refactoring. I strongly recommend the book *Refactoring Databases: Evolutionary Database Design* by Scott W. Ambler and Pramodkumar J. Sadalage for a look at database development using Agile methods. If you are interested in information specifically on TDD, you are welcome to contact me directly for additional references.

But let's get back to your application changes, shall we? In the case of the changing supplier product identifier, you begin by asking some questions. How will this new data element be used by your company and your employees? How will this change impact your order entry and inventory data? Will this change impact systems or processes beyond your order entry system? At minimum, your purchasing agents need the supplier's current product identifier to place an order for new products. Depending on how well recognized the component is, the supplier's product identifier could be used more widely than one might expect. A specific product or component may even be a selling point with your customers. A great example is CPUs: the make and the model of the processor in the laptop can be far more important than the brand name on the case. If this is true for the products you are reselling, the supplier's product id may be represented throughout multiple systems beyond the ordering system, so it would be necessary to extend your evaluation to include additional systems and processes.

Unit Tests

As noted in the previous section, your first goal will be to write the unit tests you need to demonstrate that your application modifications are successful. However, since this is a database application, you need to determine where this data element belongs before you can even begin to write the first unit test. Although the Oracle-provided sample schemas are far from perfect, you cannot refactor the entire schema in this chapter, so there will be many data design compromises in the examples. This can also be true in the real world: it is seldom possible to make all the corrections we know should be made. This is why correcting problems in the schema design can be a long, iterative process requiring very careful management.

■**NOTE** Reminder: The focus for this chapter is testing methods. I'll keep the examples as short as possible to avoid detracting from the core message. This means the examples do not represent production ready code, nor do the sample schemas represent production ready data models.

Considering the primary Order Entry functions that will make use of the supplier product identifier, you decide to store the supplier product id in the PRODUCT_INFORMATION table. This table contains other descriptive attributes about the product, and it is already used in the output reports that will now need to include your newest data element. These are not the sole considerations when deciding where and how to store data, but for your purposes in this chapter, it will do. In the real world, the amount of data to be stored and accessed, which data values will read most frequently, and how often specific data values will be updated should all be considered prior to making decisions about where the data belongs.

Once you've decided where you will keep the data, you can begin preparing the necessary unit tests for your change. So, what are the unit tests that will fail before you've added the supplier's product id to your schema? Here's a list of the unit tests you will complete in this chapter:

- Include the supplier's product id on individual orders and invoices.

- Print the supplier's product id on the open order summary report.

- Print a purchasing report that shows the current supplier's product id.

If you have been using a TDD process throughout development, then there are likely to be several generic unit tests that have already been written and may be appropriate to include in this round of tests. Typical verification tests may focus on the following tasks:

- Confirm that all objects are valid before and after your changes.

- Confirm that an insert will fail if required constraints are not met.

- Verify that default values are populated when new data records are added.

- Execute a new order transaction with and without products from this specific supplier.

If you have been thorough in your initial evaluation and unit test development work, you will know which tests are expected to fail. Other operations, such as the new order transaction I covered in the last chapter, you would expect to succeed, as you did not note that any changes are required for a new order. Should the existing unit tests for creating a new order fail after your changes, it would indicate that you did not analyze the impact of this latest change as thoroughly as you should have.

Before you make any changes to the database objects, you should confirm the state of the existing objects. Preferably, all objects will be valid before you start making changes. This is important as it ensures that you are aware of any objects that were invalid prior to your changes, and it helps you to recognize when you are responsible for invalidating the objects. Listing 15-1 shows a query to check for invalid objects and the result of the query.

Listing 15-1. *Checking for Invalid Objects Prior to Altering Database Objects*

```
SQL> select object_name, object_type, last_ddl_time, status
        from user_objects where status != 'VALID';

no rows selected
```

Listing 15-2 shows your three unit test scripts. Each of these scripts represents a report that must include the correct supplier product identifier as related to your internal product number. The first test creates a report for a single order, which is essentially the customer's invoice. The second test is the purchasing report, which must print the correct supplier product identifier plus the inventory on hand. The third unit test is a complete listing of all open orders; it has been built using several views.

Listing 15-2. *Unit Test Scripts*

```
--- order_report.sql

set linesize 115
column order_id new_value v_order noprint
column order_date new_value v_o_date noprint
column line_no format 99
column order_total format 999,999,999.99

BREAK ON order_id SKIP 2 PAGE
BTITLE OFF

compute sum of line_item_total on order_id

ttitle left 'Order ID: ' v_order         -
       right 'Order Date: ' v_o_date      -
       skip 2

spool logs/order_report.txt

select h.order_id ORDER_ID, h.order_date, li.line_item_id LINE_NO,
       li.supplier_product_id SUPP_PROD_ID, li.product_name, li.unit_price,
       li.discount_price, li.quantity, li.line_item_total
  from order_detail_header h, order_detail_line_items li
 where h.order_id = li.order_id
   and h.order_id = '&Order_Number'
 order by h.order_id, line_item_id ;

spool off

--- purchasing_report.sql
```

```
break on supplier skip 1
column target_price format 999,999.99
set termout off

spool logs/purchasing_report.txt

select p.supplier_id SUPPLIER, p.supplier_product_id SUPP_PROD_ID,
       p.product_name PRODUCT_NAME, i.quantity_on_hand QTY_ON_HAND,
       (p.min_price * .5) TARGET_PRICE
  from product_information p, inventories i
 where p.product_id = i.product_id
   and p.product_status = 'orderable'
   and i.quantity_on_hand < 1000
 order by p.supplier_id, p.supplier_product_id ;

spool off

set termout on

--- order_reports_all.sql

set linesize 115
column order_id new_value v_order noprint
column order_date new_value v_o_date noprint
column line_no format 99
column order_total format 999,999,999.99

BREAK ON order_id SKIP 2 PAGE
BTITLE OFF

compute sum of line_item_total on order_id

ttitle left 'Order ID: ' v_order        -
       right 'Order Date: ' v_o_date     -
       skip 2

select h.order_id ORDER_ID, h.order_date,
       li.line_item_id line_no, li.product_name, li.supplier_product_id ITEM_NO,
       li.unit_price, li.discount_price, li.quantity, li.line_item_total
  from order_detail_header h, order_detail_line_item li
 where h.order_id = li.order_id
 order by h.order_id, li.line_item_id ;
```

Listing 15-3 shows execution of your unit test scripts and the resulting (expected) failures.

Listing 15-3. *Initial Unit Test Results*

```
SQL> @ order_report.sql
      li.supplier_product_id,
      *
ERROR at line 2:
ORA-00904: "LI"."SUPPLIER_PRODUCT_ID": invalid identifier


SQL> @purchasing_report.sql
 order by p.supplier_id, p.supplier_product_id
                  *
ERROR at line 6:
ORA-00904: "P"."SUPPLIER_PRODUCT_ID": invalid identifier


SQL> @order_report_all.sql
 li.line_item_id line_no, li.product_name, li.supplier_product_id ITEM_NO,
                  *
ERROR at line 2:
ORA-00904: "LI"."SUPPLIER_PRODUCT_ID": invalid identifier
```

Unit tests are typically created for and executed from the application interface but it's extremely helpful to create database-only unit tests as well. Having a set of scripts that you can run independently of the application code outside of the database will allow you to check database functionality before you hand new code over to the test team. And if the front-end application tests result in unexpected errors, you will already have information about a successful database level execution, which will help both teams troubleshoot problems more efficiently.

Regression Tests

The goal of regression testing is to confirm that all prior functionality continues to work as expected. You also must be certain that you do not re-introduce old issues (bugs) into your code as you implement new functionality. Regression tests are most likely to fail when there has not been adequate source code control so someone has inadvertently used an obsolete piece of code as their starting point.

If unit tests were written for the existing functionality as the first step when the functionality was developed, those unit tests become the regression tests to confirm that each component of the system is still working as expected. In your case, the tests used to verify the order transaction process can be used to verify that orders will still be processed as expected. Although I'm cheating a bit, I'll skip the re-execution of the order entry transactions as I spent many pages on this topic in the last chapter.

Schema Changes

As a prerequisite to executing your examples, you need to make several changes to your schema to support storing a supplier product number at all. You'll add a new varchar2 column in the PRODUCT_INFORMATION table to store the SUPPLIER_PRODUCT_ID field for each item you sell. You'll populate the new column with a value to represent the current supplier product ids for all the products you sell, and you'll use the DBMS_RANDOM package to generate these numbers. Once this data exists, your basic unit tests referencing the supplier product identifier should succeed.

However, to support the concept of effective product ids, you will add new records to the PRODUCT_INFORMATION table using your supplier's new identification values, a new internal product number with the same product description and pricing. While you could update the existing records, this would violate the requirement to accurately reflect the supplier's product identifier shown on the product packaging in your warehouses. It would also result in changing historical data, since you've already sold copies of this software to other customers. Although the software in the package is unchanged, the fact that your supplier has relabeled it essentially creates a brand new product, which is why you need these new product records. The new records will be entered with a product status of "planned," since the effective date is in the future. On the October 10, 2010, the new parts will be marked as "orderable" and the current parts will become "obsolete."

In order to manage the effective dates for the changing internal product identifiers, you will create a new table, PRODUCT_ID_EFFECTIVITY. You'll also create a PRODUCT_ID sequence to generate your new internal identifiers, making certain that your sequence begins at a higher value that any of your existing product records. Although I won't cover it in this chapter, this table could be used by a scheduled process that would update the PRODUCT_STATUS field in the PRODUCT_INFORMATION table to reflect whether a product was planned, orderable, or obsolete. It is the change in product status that will trigger which supplier's product id is shown on the purchasing report so the purchasing agent can reference the correct number when placing new orders. Listing 15-4 shows the schema changes as they are processed.

Listing 15-4. *Schema Changes and New Product Data*

```
SQL> alter table product_information add supplier_product_id varchar2(15);

Table altered.

SQL> update product_information
        set supplier_product_id = round(dbms_random.value(100000, 80984),0) ;

288 rows updated.

SQL> commit;

Commit complete.

SQL> create sequence product_id start with 3525 ;

Sequence created.

SQL> create table product_id_effectivity (
        product_id              number,
        new_product_id          number,
        supplier_product_id     varchar(15),
        effective_date          date) ;

Table created.

SQL> insert into product_id_effectivity
```

```
        (select product_id, product_id.nextval,
              round(dbms_random.value(100000, 80984),0)||'-'||
              substr(product_name, instr(product_name,'/',-1,1)+1), '10-oct-10'
          from product_information, dual
        where supplier_id = 103089
          and product_name like '%/%') ;

9 rows created.

SQL> select * from product_id_effectivity ;

PRODUCT_ID NEW_PRODUCT_ID SUPPLIER_PRODUC EFFECTIVE_DATE
---------- -------------- --------------- -------------------
      3170           3525 93206-SP        0010-10-10 00:00:00
      3171           3526 84306-EN        0010-10-10 00:00:00
      3176           3527 89127-EN        0010-10-10 00:00:00
      3177           3528 81889-FR        0010-10-10 00:00:00
      3245           3529 96987-FR        0010-10-10 00:00:00
      3246           3530 96831-SP        0010-10-10 00:00:00
      3247           3531 85011-DE        0010-10-10 00:00:00
      3248           3532 88474-DE        0010-10-10 00:00:00
      3253           3533 82876-EN        0010-10-10 00:00:00

9 rows selected.

SQL> commit ;

Commit complete.

SQL>  insert into product_information (
            product_id, product_name, product_description, category_id,
            weight_class, supplier_id, product_status, list_price, min_price,
            catalog_url, supplier_product_id)
        (select e.new_product_id,
              p.product_name,
              p.product_description,
              p.category_id,
              p.weight_class,
              p.supplier_id,
              'planned',
              p.list_price,
              p.min_price,
              p.catalog_url,
              e.supplier_product_id
```

```
        from product_information p, product_id_effectivity e
      where p.product_id = e.product_id
        and p.supplier_id = 103089) ;
```

9 rows created.

```
SQL> select product_id, product_name, product_status, supplier_product_id
        from product_information
      where supplier_id = 103089
      order by product_id ;
```

```
PRODUCT_ID PRODUCT_NAME                       PRODUCT_STATUS       SUPPLIER_PRODUC
---------- --------------------------------- -------------------- ---------------
      3150 Card Holder - 25                  orderable            3150
      3170 Smart Suite - V/SP                orderable            3170
      3171 Smart Suite - S3.3/EN             orderable            3171
      3175 Project Management - S4.0         orderable            3175
      3176 Smart Suite - V/EN                orderable            3176
      3177 Smart Suite - V/FR                orderable            3177
      3245 Smart Suite - S4.0/FR             orderable            3245
      3246 Smart Suite - S4.0/SP             orderable            3246
      3247 Smart Suite - V/DE                orderable            3247
      3248 Smart Suite - S4.0/DE             orderable            3248
      3253 Smart Suite - S4.0/EN             orderable            3253
      3525 Smart Suite - V/SP                planned              93206-SP
      3526 Smart Suite - S3.3/EN             planned              84306-EN
      3527 Smart Suite - V/EN                planned              89127-EN
      3528 Smart Suite - V/FR                planned              81889-FR
      3529 Smart Suite - S4.0/FR             planned              96987-FR
      3530 Smart Suite - S4.0/SP             planned              96831-SP
      3531 Smart Suite - V/DE                planned              85011-DE
      3532 Smart Suite - S4.0/DE             planned              88474-DE
      3533 Smart Suite - S4.0/EN             planned              82876-EN
```

20 rows selected.

Once you've completed the necessary schema updates, your next step will be to check for invalid objects again. All objects were valid when you ran your initial check, but now you have altered a table that is likely to be referenced by several other code objects in your schema. If those objects were coded properly, you will be able to recompile them as-is and they'll become valid again. If the code is sloppy (perhaps someone used a 'select * from PRODUCT_INFORMATION' clause to populate an object that does not have the new field), then the recompile will fail and you'll need to plan for more application modifications. The unit test to look for invalid objects, plus the two recompiles that are required after your changes are shown in Listing 15-5.

Listing 15-5. *Invalid Objects Unit Test and Object Recompile*

```
SQL> select object_name, object_type, last_ddl_time, status
     from user_objects
     where status != 'VALID';

OBJECT_NAME                         OBJECT_TYPE          LAST_DDL_ STATUS
----------------------------------- -------------------- --------- -------
GET_ORDER_TOTAL                     PROCEDURE            04-jul-10 INVALID
GET_LISTPRICE                       FUNCTION             04-jul-10 INVALID

SQL> alter function GET_LISTPRICE compile ;

Function altered.

SQL> alter procedure GET_ORDER_TOTAL compile ;

Procedure altered.

SQL> select object_name, object_type, last_ddl_time, status
     from user_objects
     where status != 'VALID';

no rows selected
```

Repeating the Unit Tests

Once you've confirmed that your planned schema changes have been successfully implemented and all objects are valid, it's time to repeat the remaining unit tests. This time, each of the tests should execute and you should be able to verify that the supplier's product id is accurately represented in the data results. Results from the second execution of the unit test are shown in Listing 15-6. To minimize the number of trees required to print this book, output from the reports will be abbreviated.

Listing 15-6. *Second Execution of Unit Tests*

```
SQL> @order_report

Order ID:5041 Order Date: 13 Jul 2010

 NO SUP_PROD_ID PRODUCT_NAME              UNIT_PRICE DISC_PRICE  QTY ITEM_TOTAL
--- ----------- ------------------------- ---------- ---------- ---- ----------
  1 98811       Smart Suite - S4.0/DE         222.00     199.80    5     999.00

SQL> @purchasing_report
```

```
SUPPLIER S_PRODUCT    PRODUCT_NAME             QTY_ON_HAND TARGET_PRICE
---------- ------------ ------------------------ ----------- ------------
   103086 96102        IC Browser Doc - S               623        50.00

   103088 83069        OSI 1-4/IL                        76        36.00

   103089 86151        Smart Suite - S4.0/EN            784        94.00
          89514        Smart Suite - V/DE              290        48.00
          92539        Smart Suite - V/EN              414        51.50
          93275        Smart Suite - V/FR              637        51.00
          95024        Smart Suite - S4.0/SP           271        96.50
          95857        Smart Suite - V/SP              621        66.00
          98796        Smart Suite - S3.3/EN           689        60.00
          98811        Smart Suite - S4.0/DE           114        96.50
          99603        Smart Suite - S4.0/FR           847        97.50
.......

SQL> @order_report_all.sql

Order ID: 2354                            Order Date: 14 Jul 2002
ID PRODUCT_NAME           ITEM_NO UNIT_PRICE DISCOUNT_PRICE   QTY LINE_ITEM_TOTAL
--- ---------------------- -------- ---------- -------------- ----- ---------------
  1 KB 101/EN               94979     48.00          45.00    61        2,745.00
  1 KB 101/EN               98993     48.00          45.00    61        2,745.00
  1 KB 101/EN               85501     48.00          45.00    61        2,745.00
.......

Order ID: 5016                            Order Date: 06 Jul 2010
 ID PRODUCT_NAME           ITEM_NO UNIT_PRICE DISCOUNT_PRICE   QTY LINE_ITEM_TOTAL
--- ---------------------- -------- ---------- -------------- ----- ---------------
  1 Inkvisible Pens         86030      6.00           5.40  1000        5,400.00

Order ID: 5017                            Order Date: 06 Jul 2010
 ID PRODUCT_NAME           ITEM_NO UNIT_PRICE DISCOUNT_PRICE   QTY LINE_ITEM_TOTAL
--- ---------------------- -------- ---------- -------------- ----- ---------------
  1 Compact 400/DQ          87690    125.00         118.75    25        2,968.75

Order ID: 5041                            Order Date: 13 Jul 2010
 ID PRODUCT_NAME           ITEM_NO UNIT_PRICE DISCOUNT_PRICE   QTY LINE_ITEM_TOTAL
--- ---------------------- -------- ---------- -------------- ----- ---------------
  1 Smart Suite - S4.0/DE   98811    222.00         199.80     5          999.00
```

Take note that in each case where the product name shows a product that will be affected by your supplier's new identifiers, your reports are still showing the current supplier identifier. That's because these reports have all been executed as of a date prior to the October 10, 2010 effective date. What you have not yet addressed in your testing is a mechanism to set products referencing the old supplier product identifiers to "obsolete" and to make your new products referencing the new supplier product identifier "orderable." After the effective date has passed, you need the purchasing report in particular to reference the new IDs. Order data should continue to represent the item ordered and shipped, which would not necessarily be determined by the effective date for the part number change. Instead, you want your sales team to sell the older product first, so you would only begin to see the new product identifiers on orders and invoices after the existing inventory was depleted. This thought process should trigger the development of a few more unit tests, such as testing the process to alter product status after a product change effectivity date had passed and confirming that the Order Entry system will not make the new product identifiers available for purchase until the old stock has been depleted.

Execution Plan Comparison

One of the best tools available for evaluating the impact of the changes you make to database objects and code is the execution plan. By recording the execution plan both before and after your changes, you have a detailed measurement of exactly how much work the database needs to complete in order to process requests for the data in the past and how much work will be required to process those same requests in the future. If the comparison of the before and after versions of the execution plan indicates that a significant amount of additional work is required, it may be necessary to reevaluate the code to see if you can optimize it. If you find the process is already as optimized as it can be, you can then use the information to nicely explain to the users that their report may take longer in the future due to the additional functionality. Once you express your findings in those terms, you will discover exactly how much the users value that new functionality, and it will be up to them to decide if the changes are important enough to move to production.

Comparing the execution plans can also make it very clear when there is something wrong with a query. If you find that a process is working much harder to get the data, but the new changes don't justify the additional work, there is a strong possibility that there is an error in the code somewhere.

For the next example, you will review the execution plans of the complete order report from your unit testing. The execution plan recorded before you made any changes to the database is shown in Listing 15-7. The scripts to gather the execution plans are based on the approach demonstrated in Chapter 6.

Listing 15-7. *Order Report Execution Plan (Before)*

```
alter session set statistics_level = 'ALL';

set linesize 105
column order_id new_value v_order noprint
column order_date new_value v_o_date noprint
column ID format 99
column order_total format 999,999,999.99

BREAK ON order_id SKIP 2 PAGE
BTITLE OFF

compute sum of line_item_total on order_id

ttitle left 'Order ID: ' v_order          -
      right 'Order Date: ' v_o_date     -
      skip 2

spool logs/order_report_all_pre.txt
```

```
select /* OrdersPreChange */ h.order_id ORDER_ID, order_date,
       li.line_item_id ID, li.product_name, li.product_id ITEM_NO,
       li.unit_price, li.discount_price, li.quantity, li.line_item_total
  from order_detail_header h, order_detail_line_items li
 where h.order_id = li.order_id
 order by h.order_id, li.line_item_id ;

spool off

set lines 150
spool logs/OrdersPreChange.txt

@pln.sql OrdersPreChange

PLAN_TABLE_OUTPUT
-------------------------------------------------------------------------------------
SQL_ID  ayucrh1mf6v4s, child number 0
-------------------------------------
select /* OrdersPreChange */ h.order_id ORDER_ID, order_date,
li.line_item_id ID, li.product_name, li.product_id ITEM_NO,
li.unit_price, li.discount_price, li.quantity, li.line_item_total
from order_detail_header h, order_detail_line_items li  where
h.order_id = li.order_id  order by h.order_id, li.line_item_id

Plan hash value: 3662678147
```

Id	Operation	Name	Starts	E-Rows	A-Rows	Buffers
0	SELECT STATEMENT		1		417	29
1	SORT ORDER BY		1	474	417	29
* 2	HASH JOIN		1	474	417	29
3	TABLE ACCESS FULL	PRODUCT_INFORMATION	1	297	297	16
4	NESTED LOOPS		1	474	417	13
5	MERGE JOIN		1	474	417	9
* 6	TABLE ACCESS BY INDEX ROW	ORDERS	1	79	79	2
7	INDEX FULL SCAN	ORDER_PK	1	114	114	1
* 8	SORT JOIN		79	678	417	7
9	TABLE ACCESS FULL	ORDER_ITEMS	1	678	678	7
* 10	INDEX UNIQUE SCAN	ORDER_STATUS_PK	417	1	417	4

```
Predicate Information (identified by operation id):
---------------------------------------------------

   2 - access("OI"."PRODUCT_ID"="PI"."PRODUCT_ID")
   6 - filter("O"."SALES_REP_ID" IS NOT NULL)
```

```
  8 - access("O"."ORDER_ID"="OI"."ORDER_ID")
      filter("O"."ORDER_ID"="OI"."ORDER_ID")
 10 - access("O"."ORDER_STATUS"="OS"."ORDER_STATUS")
```

35 rows selected.

The order report is generated by joining two views: the order header information and the order line item details. You'll assume the report is currently running fast enough to meet user requirements and that there are no indicators that the quantity of data in the underlying tables is expected to increase dramatically in the future. The report is deemed as meeting requirements and the execution plan shall be saved for future reference.

This order report was executed as one of your first unit tests to verify that your unit tests work as expected. After you made the required database changes, you executed the order report again and confirmed that it completed. The report also seems to complete in about the same amount of time as it did in the past. But let's take a look at the latest execution plan to see how the report is really performing. The post-change execution plan is shown in Listing 15-8.

Lising 15-8. *Order Report Execution Plan (After)*

```
alter session set statistics_level = 'ALL';

set linesize 115
column order_id new_value v_order noprint
column order_date new_value v_o_date noprint
column ID format 99
column order_total format 999,999,999.99

BREAK ON order_id SKIP 2 PAGE
BTITLE OFF

compute sum of line_item_total on order_id

ttitle left 'Order ID: ' v_order          -
       right 'Order Date: ' v_o_date      -
       skip 2

spool logs/order_report_all_fail.txt

select /* OrdersChangeFail */ h.order_id ORDER_ID, order_date,
       li.line_item_id ID, li.product_name, p.supplier_product_id ITEM_NO,
       li.unit_price, li.discount_price, li.quantity, li.line_item_total
  from order_detail_header h, order_detail_line_items li, product_information p
 where h.order_id = li.order_id
   and li.product_id = p.product_id
 order by h.order_id, li.line_item_id ;

spool off

set lines 150
```

```
spool logs/OrdersChangeFail.log

@pln.sql OrdersChangeFail

PLAN_TABLE_OUTPUT
----------------------------------------------------------------------------------
SQL_ID  avhuxuj0d23kc, child number 0
----------------------------------------
select /* OrdersChangeFail */ h.order_id ORDER_ID, order_date,
li.line_item_id ID, li.product_name, p.supplier_product_id ITEM_NO,
   li.unit_price, li.discount_price, li.quantity, li.line_item_total
from order_detail_header h, order_detail_line_items li,
product_information p  where h.order_id = li.order_id     and
li.product_id = p.product_id  order by h.order_id, li.line_item_id

Plan hash value: 1984333101
```

Id	Operation	Name	Starts	E-Rows	A-Rows	Buffers
0	SELECT STATEMENT		1		417	45
1	SORT ORDER BY		1	474	417	45
* 2	HASH JOIN		1	474	417	45
3	TABLE ACCESS FULL	PRODUCT_INFORMATION	1	297	297	16
* 4	HASH JOIN		1	474	417	29
5	TABLE ACCESS FULL	PRODUCT_INFORMATION	1	297	297	16
6	NESTED LOOPS		1	474	417	13
7	MERGE JOIN		1	474	417	9
* 8	TABLE ACCESS BY INDEX RO	ORDERS	1	79	79	2
9	INDEX FULL SCAN	ORDER_PK	1	114	114	1
* 10	SORT JOIN		79	678	417	7
11	TABLE ACCESS FULL	ORDER_ITEMS	1	678	678	7
* 12	INDEX UNIQUE SCAN	ORDER_STATUS_PK	417	1	417	4

```
Predicate Information (identified by operation id):
---------------------------------------------------

   2 - access("PI"."PRODUCT_ID"="P"."PRODUCT_ID")
   4 - access("OI"."PRODUCT_ID"="PI"."PRODUCT_ID")
   8 - filter("O"."SALES_REP_ID" IS NOT NULL)
  10 - access("O"."ORDER_ID"="OI"."ORDER_ID")
       filter("O"."ORDER_ID"="OI"."ORDER_ID")
  12 - access("O"."ORDER_STATUS"="OS"."ORDER_STATUS")

39 rows selected.
```

Looking at this latest plan, the database is doing much more work after your changes, even though the report is not taking any appreciable amount of extra time to complete. You know there is no good reason for this to be so: you've only added one additional column to a table that was already the central component of the query. Furthermore, the table in question already required a full table scan, as most of the columns are needed for the report. But the execution plan shows that your report is now doing two full table scans of the PRODUCT_INFORMATION table. Why?

In this case, I've made a common error deliberately to illustrate how an execution plan can help find quality problems in changed code. Rather than simply add the new column to the existing ORDER_DETAIL_LINE_ITEM view that is built on the PRODUCT_INFORMATION table, the PRODUCT_INFORMATION table has been joined to the ORDER_DETAIL_LINE_ITEM view, resulting in a second full table scan of the central table.

This probably seems like a really foolish mistake to make, but it can be easily done. I've seen many developers add a new column to a query by adding a new join to a table or view that was already part of the existing report. This error will have a clear and visible impact on an execution plan, especially if the query is complex (and it usually is when this type of error is made). Listing 15-9 shows the execution plan for the same query once the additional join is removed and the column is added to the existing ORDER_DETAIL_LINE_ITEM view instead.

Listing 15-9. *Order Report Execution Plan (Corrected)*

```
alter session set statistics_level = 'ALL';

set linesize 115
column order_id new_value v_order noprint
column order_date new_value v_o_date noprint
column ID format 99
column order_total format 999,999,999.99

BREAK ON order_id SKIP 2 PAGE
BTITLE OFF

compute sum of line_item_total on order_id

ttitle left 'Order ID: ' v_order          -
       right 'Order Date: ' v_o_date      -
       skip 2

spool logs/order_report_all_corrected.txt

select /* OrdersCorrected */ h.order_id ORDER_ID, order_date,
       li.line_item_id ID, li.product_name, li.supplier_product_id ITEM_NO,
       li.unit_price, li.discount_price, li.quantity, li.line_item_total
  from order_detail_header h, order_detail_line_items li
 where h.order_id = li.order_id
 order by h.order_id, li.line_item_id ;

spool off

set lines 150
```

```
spool logs/OrdersCorrected_plan.txt

@pln.sql OrdersCorrected

PLAN_TABLE_OUTPUT
--------------------------------------------------------------------------------
SQL_ID  901nkw7f6fg4r, child number 0
-------------------------------------
select /* OrdersCorrected */ h.order_id ORDER_ID, order_date,
li.line_item_id ID, li.product_name, li.supplier_product_id ITEM_NO,
    li.unit_price, li.discount_price, li.quantity, li.line_item_total
from order_detail_header h, order_detail_line_items li  where
h.order_id = li.order_id  order by h.order_id, li.line_item_id

Plan hash value: 3662678147
```

Id	Operation	Name	Starts	E-Rows	A-Rows	Buffers
0	SELECT STATEMENT		1		417	29
1	SORT ORDER BY		1	474	417	29
* 2	HASH JOIN		1	474	417	29
3	TABLE ACCESS FULL	PRODUCT_INFORMATION	1	297	297	16
4	NESTED LOOPS		1	474	417	13
5	MERGE JOIN		1	474	417	9
* 6	TABLE ACCESS BY INDEX ROW	ORDERS	1	79	79	2
7	INDEX FULL SCAN	ORDER_PK	1	114	114	1
* 8	SORT JOIN		79	678	417	7
9	TABLE ACCESS FULL	ORDER_ITEMS	1	678	678	7
* 10	INDEX UNIQUE SCAN	ORDER_STATUS_PK	417	1	417	4

```
Predicate Information (identified by operation id):
---------------------------------------------------

   2 - access("OI"."PRODUCT_ID"="PI"."PRODUCT_ID")
   6 - filter("O"."SALES_REP_ID" IS NOT NULL)
   8 - access("O"."ORDER_ID"="OI"."ORDER_ID")
       filter("O"."ORDER_ID"="OI"."ORDER_ID")
  10 - access("O"."ORDER_STATUS"="OS"."ORDER_STATUS")


35 rows selected.
```

You can see by this latest execution plan that your report is now performing as expected, with no additional impact to performance or use of system resources.

Instrumentation

One of my favorite Oracle features is instrumentation. The database itself is fully instrumented, which is why you can see exactly when the database is waiting and what it is waiting for. Without this instrumentation, a database would be something of a black box, providing little information about where resources are spending, or not spending, their time.

Oracle also provides the DBMS_APPLICATION_INFO package that you can use to instrument the code that you write. This package allows you to label the actions and modules within your code so that you can more easily identify which processes in your application are active. You can also combine your instrumentation data with Oracle's Active Session History (ASH), Active Workload Repository (AWR), and other performance management tools to gain further insight into your application's performance while easily filtering out other unrelated processes.

The simplest method I know of for adding instrumentation to application code is the Instrumentation Library for Oracle (ILO), which is available at http://sourceforge.net/projects/ilo/. ILO is open source software written and supported by my friends at Method-R. Method-R also offers the option to purchase a license for ILO so that it can be used in commercial software products. I've been using ILO to instrument code for several years and have added functionality to the 2.3 version. The enhancements allow me to record the exact start and stop time of an instrumented process using the database's internal time references. This data can then be used to calculate statistical indicators on process execution times, which helps to highlight potential performance issues before they become major problems. I've also added code to enable 10044 tracing for a specific process by setting an On/Off switch in a table. So if I determine that I need trace data for a specific application process, I can set tracing to On for that process by its instrumented process name and it will be traced every time it executes until tracing is set to Off again. The configuration module can also be used to set the elapsed time collection On or Off, but I usually prefer to leave elapsed time recording on and purge older data when it is no longer useful.

If you'd like to test the ILO instrumentation software as you go through the next few sections, start by downloading ILO 2.3 from SourceForge.net and install it per the instructions. You can then download the code to store elapsed time and set the trace and timing configuration from the Apress download site. Instructions to add the updates are included in the ZIP file.

Adding Instrumentation to Code

Once you've installed the ILO schema, adding instrumentation to your application is easily done. There are several ways to accomplish this. Of course, you'll need to determine the best method and the appropriate configuration based on your environment and requirements, but here are a few general guidelines:

- Within your own session, you can turn timing and tracing on or off at any time. You can also instrument any of your SQL statements by executing the ILO call to begin a task before you execute your SQL statement and executing the call to end the task after the statement. This approach is shown in Listing 15-10.

- You can encapsulate your code within a procedure and include the calls to ILO within the procedure itself. This has the added advantage of ensuring that every call to the procedure is instrumented and that the ILO action and module are labeled consistently. Consistent labeling will be very important if you want to aggregate your timing data in a meaningful way, or track trends in performance. We will look at the billing.credit_request procedure from Chapter 14 with added calls to ILO in Listing 15-11.

- You can create an application-specific wrapper to call the ILO procedures. One benefit of using a wrapper is that you can make sure a failure in ILO does not result in a failure for the application process. While you do want good performance data, you don't want to prevent the application from running because ILO isn't working. A simple wrapper is included with the ILO update download at Apress.

Listing 15-10. *ILO Execution in a Single Session*

```
SQL> exec ilo_timer.set_mark_all_tasks_interesting(TRUE,TRUE);

PL/SQL procedure successfully completed.

SQL> exec ilo_task.begin_task('Month-end','Purchasing');

PL/SQL procedure successfully completed.

SQL> @purchasing_report

SQL> exec ilo_task.end_task;

PL/SQL procedure successfully completed.

    Selected from ILO_ELAPSED_TIME table:

    INSTANCE: TEST
    SPID: 21509
    ILO_MODULE: Month-end
    ILO_ACTION: Purchasing
    START_TIME: 14-JUL-10 06.08.19.000000 AM
    END_TIME: 14-JUL-10 06.09.06.072642 AM
    ELAPSED_TIME: 46.42
    ELAPSED_CPUTIME: .01
    ERROR_NUM: 0
```

Listing 15-11. *Incorporating ILO into a Procedure*

```
create or replace procedure credit_request(p_customer_id     IN    NUMBER,
                                           p_amount          IN    NUMBER,
                                           p_authorization   OUT   NUMBER,
                                           p_status_code     OUT   NUMBER,
                                           p_status_message  OUT   VARCHAR2)

  IS

  /****************************************************************************
      status_code values
        status_code  status_message
        ===========  =========================================================
                  0  Success
            -20105  Customer ID must have a non-null value.
            -20110  Requested amount must have a non-null value.
            -20500  Credit Request Declined.
  ****************************************************************************/

  v_authorization NUMBER;
```

```
BEGIN
  ilo_task.begin_task('New Order', 'Credit Request');

  SAVEPOINT RequestCredit;

  IF ( (p_customer_id) IS NULL ) THEN
    RAISE_APPLICATION_ERROR(-20105, 'Customer ID must have a non-null value.', TRUE);
  END IF;

  IF ( (p_amount) IS NULL ) THEN
    RAISE_APPLICATION_ERROR(-20110, 'Requested amount must have a non-null value.', TRUE);
  END IF;

   v_authorization := round(dbms_random.value(p_customer_id, p_amount), 0);

  IF ( v_authorization between 324 and 342 ) THEN
    RAISE_APPLICATION_ERROR(-20500, 'Credit Request Declined.', TRUE);
  END IF;

  p_authorization:= v_authorization;
  p_status_code:= 0;
  p_status_message:= NULL;

  ilo_task.end_task;

EXCEPTION
  WHEN OTHERS THEN
    p_status_code:= SQLCODE;
    p_status_message:= SQLERRM;

    BEGIN
      ROLLBACK TO SAVEPOINT RequestCredit;
    EXCEPTION WHEN OTHERS THEN NULL;
    END;

    ilo_task.end_task(error_num => p_status_code);

END credit_request;
/

Execution Script:

set serveroutput on

DECLARE
  P_CUSTOMER_ID       NUMBER;
  P_AMOUNT            NUMBER;
```

```
  P_AUTHORIZATION     NUMBER;
  P_STATUS_CODE       NUMBER;
  P_STATUS_MESSAGE    VARCHAR2(200);

BEGIN
  P_CUSTOMER_ID := '&customer';
  P_AMOUNT := '&amount';

  billing.credit_request(
    P_CUSTOMER_ID => P_CUSTOMER_ID,
    P_AMOUNT => P_AMOUNT,
    P_AUTHORIZATION => P_AUTHORIZATION,
    P_STATUS_CODE => P_STATUS_CODE,
    P_STATUS_MESSAGE => P_STATUS_MESSAGE
  );
commit;

  DBMS_OUTPUT.PUT_LINE('P_CUSTOMER_ID = ' || P_CUSTOMER_ID);
  DBMS_OUTPUT.PUT_LINE('P_AMOUNT = ' || P_AMOUNT);
  DBMS_OUTPUT.PUT_LINE('P_AUTHORIZATION = ' || P_AUTHORIZATION);
  DBMS_OUTPUT.PUT_LINE('P_STATUS_CODE = ' || P_STATUS_CODE);
  DBMS_OUTPUT.PUT_LINE('P_STATUS_MESSAGE = ' || P_STATUS_MESSAGE);

END;
/

Execution:

SQL> @exec_CreditRequest
Enter value for customer: 237
Enter value for amount: 10000

P_CUSTOMER_ID = 237
P_AMOUNT = 10000
P_AUTHORIZATION = 8302
P_STATUS_CODE = 0
P_STATUS_MESSAGE =

PL/SQL procedure successfully completed.

SQL> @exec_CreditRequest
Enter value for customer: 334
Enter value for amount: 500

P_CUSTOMER_ID = 237
P_AMOUNT = 500
P_AUTHORIZATION =
```

```
P_STATUS_CODE = -20500
P_STATUS_MESSAGE = ORA-20500: Credit Request Declined.

PL/SQL procedure successfully completed.

    Selected from ILO_ELAPSED_TIME table:

    INSTANCE: TEST
    SPID: 3896
    ILO_MODULE: New Order
    ILO_ACTION: Request Credit
    START_TIME: 14-JUL-10 01.43.41.000000 AM
    END_TIME: 14-JUL-10 01.43.41.587155 AM
    ELAPSED_TIME: .01
    ELAPSED_CPUTIME: 0
    ERROR_NUM: 0
```

The level of granularity you decide to implement with your instrumentation depends on your goals. For some tasks, it will be perfectly acceptable to include multiple processes in a single ILO module or action. For critical code, I recommend that you instrument the individual processes with their own action and module values, which will give you more visibility into complex procedures. If you are supporting an application that is not instrumented and it seems like too big a task to go back and instrument all the existing code, consider adding the instrumentation just to the key processes.

Again, how you decide to implement will depend on your needs. Instrumentation is exceptionally useful for testing code and configuration changes during development and performance testing. Once the calls to ILO have been built into the code, you can turn timing/tracing on or off in production to provide definitive performance data. Overhead is exceedingly low and being able to enable tracing easily will help you find the problems much more quickly.

Using the ILO_ELAPSED_TIME table to store performance data will typically allow you to retain critical performance data for longer periods of time. While it is possible to set longer retention values for AWR data, some sites may not have the resources available to keep as much data as they would like. Since the ILO data is not part of the Oracle product itself, you have the option to customize the retention levels to your needs without endangering any Oracle delivered capabilities.

■**NOTE** Keep the ILO code in its own schema and allow other schemas to use the same code base. This will keep the instrumentation code and data consistent, which will allow you to roll performance data up to the server level or across other multiple servers when appropriate.

Testing for Performance

Once you've added instrumentation to your code, you open the door to all kinds of potential uses for the instrumentation and the data you collect. Earlier in this chapter, I talked about building test harnesses by automating many small unit test scripts and then replaying those tasks to confirm that new and old functionality are working as expected and that old bugs have not been reintroduced. If your code is instrumented, you can record the timing for each execution of the test harness and you will have complete information on the exact amount of elapsed time and CPU time required for each labeled module and action.

The ILO package includes an ILO_COMMENT field in addition to the ILO_MODULE and ILO_ACTION labels. In some cases, this field can be used to record some identifying piece of information about a specific process execution. For example, if you were to add instrumentation to the order transaction from the last chapter, you could record the order number in the ILO_COMMENT field. Then if you found an exceptionally long execution in your ILO_ELAPSED_TIME table, you could connect that execution time with an order number, which then connects you to a specific customer and a list of ordered items. Combining this information with the very specific timestamp recorded in your table can help you troubleshoot the problem, ensure the transaction did process correctly, and determine the cause of the unusually long execution time.

In other cases, you may want to use the comment field to label specific set of test results for future reference. When testing changes to an application or instance configuration, it's always better to make one change and measure the results before making additional adjustments. Otherwise, how will you know which change was responsible for the results you obtained? This can be very difficult to do, unless you've created a test harness and measurement tool that can be easily and consistently re-executed multiple times. By making a single change, re-executing the complete test package while recording timing data, and labeling the results set of that test execution, you create a series of data sets, each showing the impact of a specific change, test dataset, or stress factor. Over time, this information can be used to evaluate the applications ability to perform under a wide range of conditions.

A sample of data retained from one such test harness is shown in Table 15-1 (times are shown in seconds).

Table 15-1. *Repetitive Test Results*

ILO ACTION	COUNT	MIN	AVG	MAX	VAR	CPU MIN	CPU AVG	CPU MAX	CPU VAR
process 1	46	0	.01	.09	0	0	.008	.03	0
process 2	2	.12	.125	.13	0	.12	.125	.13	0
process 3	2772526	0	.382	4.44	.078	0	.379	2.6	.074
child 3a	2545208	.01	.335	2.26	.058	.01	.332	1.77	.055
child 3b	2752208	0	.065	2.24	.011	0	.065	1.39	.01
child 3c	2153988	0	0	.21	0	0	0	.02	0
child 3d	2153988	0	0	.36	0	0	0	.07	0
child 3e	2153988	0	0	.16	0	0	0	.02	0
child 3f	2153988	0	0	.42	0	0	0	.02	0
process 4	1564247	0	.001	.18	0	0	.001	.02	0
process 5	2873236	0	.043	6.2	.013	0	.041	.49	.006
process 6	149589	0	.018	5.53	.002	0	.013	.11	0
process 7	2395999	0	.001	6	0	0	.001	.03	0

While the numbers shown above aren't particularly meaningful on their own, if you have this set of numbers representing code executions prior to a change and you have another set of numbers from the same server with the same data set representing code execution after the code has been changed, you have definitive information regarding the impact your code changes have had on the database. Imagine being able to quickly and painlessly repeat this test for subsequent code changes and configuration adjustments, and you'll begin to appreciate the potential of code instrumentation combined with repeatable, automated test processes.

Testing to Destruction

Testing a system to its breaking point can be one of the more entertaining aspects of software testing, and meetings to brainstorm all the possible ways to break the database are seldom dull. Early in my career, I developed and managed an Oracle database application built using client/server technology. (Yes, this was long ago and far away.) The application itself was a problem tracking tool that allowed manufacturing workers to record issues they found and send those problems to Engineering for review and correction. The initial report landed in Quality Engineering, where it would be investigated and assigned to the appropriate Engineering group. As each Engineering department signed off on their work, the request would move on to the next group. The application was reasonably successful so it ended up on many workstations throughout a very large facility.

If you ever want to see "testing to destruction" in action, try supporting a database application installed on the workstations of hundreds of electrical, hydraulic, and structural engineers. In a fairly short period of time, I learned that engineers will do everything in their power to learn about the computers on their desks, and they considered breaking those computers and the applications on them to be an educational experience. I can't say that I disagree with them: sometimes taking something apart just so you can build it again really is the best way to understand the guts of the tool.

However, after several months of trying to support this very inquisitive group of people, I developed a new approach to discourage excessive tampering. By keeping a library of ghosted drives containing the standard workstation configuration with all the approved applications, I could replace the hard drive on a malfunctioning computer in under 10 minutes and the engineer and I could both get back to work. Since everyone was expected to store their work on the server, no one could really object to my repair method. However, most engineers did not like losing their customized desktops, so they soon quit trying quite so hard to break things.

Although I loved to grumble at those engineers, I really owe them a very big thank you, for now whenever I need to think about how to test a server or application to destruction, all I need to do is think about those engineers and wonder what they would do. And never discount even the craziest ideas: if you can think of it, someone is likely to try it. As you work to identify your system's weak links, consider everything on the following list, and then think of some more items:

Data Entry: What happens when a user or program interface sends the wrong kind of data or too much data?

Task Sequences: What happens when a user skips a step or performs the tasks out of order?

Repeating/Simultaneous Executions: Can the user run the same process simultaneously? Will that action corrupt data or will it just slow the process down?

Unbounded Data Ranges: Can the user request an unreasonable amount of data? What happens if the user enters an end range that is prior to the start range (such as requesting a report on sales from July 1, 2010 to June 30, 2010)?

Resource usage: Excessive use of CPU, memory, temporary storage and undo space can impact many users at the same time. Your DBA should limit usage with resource caps appropriately, but you still need to identify all the potential ways users and processes can grab more than their fair share.

I bet some of you could add some very interesting options for other ways to break systems. Can you also identify the ways to prevent those problems? While finding the best correction is a bit harder and not as entertaining, every time you can make it difficult for a user to break your code, you create a more robust system—one that will need less support and less maintenance over the long run.

Every system will have its own weakest links. Once you've identified those weaknesses, assemble your unit tests into a test harness that will push that resource beyond its limits so you can see how the system responds. In general, it seems that memory and I/O usage are the primary stressors for a databases system. However, lately I've been working on an Oracle 11g database with spatial functionality, and in this case, CPU processing is the system's bottleneck. When we designed the system capacity tests, we made certain that the spatial processes would be tested to the extreme and we measured the internal database performance using the ILO data as shown in the last section. We also had external measurements of the total application and system performance, but having the ILO elapsed time data provided some unique advantages over other test projects I've participated in.

First and foremost, the ILO data provides specific measurements of the time spent in the database. This makes it easier to troubleshoot performance issue that do show up, as you can quickly tell when the process is slow in the database and when it is not. A second advantage is that the recorded timestamps give a very specific indicator of exactly when a problem occurred, what other processes were running at the same time, and the specific sequencing of the application processes. With this information, you can easily identify the point when the system will hit the knee in its performance curve. And since the elapsed time module in ILO uses DBMS_UTILITY.get_time and DBMS_UTLITITY.get_cpu_time, you can record exactly how much time your process spent active in the database and what portion of that time was spent on CPU.

This detailed performance data is also useful for troubleshooting, as the low level timestamps assist in narrowing down the timeframe for the problem. Once you know the specific timeframe you need to research, you can review a much smaller quantity of AWR or StatsPack data to see what happened and find the answers quickly. Once the window is small enough, any problem will be almost immediately visible. We will look at a specific case in the next section.

Troubleshooting through Instrumentation

Sometimes it can be difficult to identify the cause of small problems. When you don't know the source of the problem, you also don't know the potential impact the problem could have on your application. In one such case, developers had noticed timeouts from the database at random intervals, yet the process they suspected of causing the issue showed no sign of the errors and the database appeared to be working well below its potential.

About a week after a new test server was installed, a review of the ILO_ELAPSED_TIME table showed that most tasks were performing well, except there were two processes that had overrun the 30 second timeout clock on the application. The error numbers recorded on the tasks showed the front end application had ended the connection: this message was consistent with a possible timeout, but it was not very helpful. The captured ILO data is shown in Table 15-2.

If you take a look at process 7, you will note that the maximum completion time does exceed 30 seconds and the variance in processing times is relatively high when compared to other processes in the application. The process spends almost no time on CPU, so this is a problem worth investigating. Where is this time going? It's also interesting to note that this was not a process that anyone would have expected to have a performance issue. Process 3 had been the target of previous timeout investigations; it has to perform considerably more work than process 7.

Table 15-2. *Timeout Errors*

ILO ACTION	COUNT	MIN	AVG	MAX	VAR	CPU MIN	CPU AVG	CPU MAX	CPU VAR
process 1	4	0.01	0.015	0.03	0	0	0.01	0.03	0
process 2	2	0	0	0	0	0	0	0	0
process 3	56	0.01	0.112	0.8	0.015	0.01	0.109	0.62	0.011
child 3a	36	0.04	0.078	0.15	0	0.03	0.078	0.15	0.001
child 3b	56	0	0.01	0.09	0	0	0.009	0.07	0
child 3c	36	0	0	0.01	0	0	0.001	0.01	0
child 3d	36	0	0.001	0.01	0	0	0	0.01	0
child 3e	36	0	0.001	0.01	0	0	0.001	0.01	0
child 3f	36	0	0.001	0.01	0	0	0.001	0.01	0
process 4	8	0	0.01	0.02	0	0	0.008	0.02	0
process 5	1	0.01	0.01	0.01	0	0.01	0.01	0.01	0
process 6	152	0	0.002	0.1	0	0	0.002	0.09	0
process 7	90	0	**0.681**	**30.57**	**20.449**	0	0.002	0.02	0
process 8	1	0	0	0	0	0.01	0.01	0.01	0
process 9	77	0	0.001	0.01	0	0	0.001	0.01	0
process 10	8	0	0.008	0.01	0	0	0.008	0.01	0

Next, let's take a look at Table 15-3, which contains the results of a query looking for all cases in which process 7 exceeded 30 seconds.

Table 15-3. *Processes Exceeding 30 Seconds*

SPID	ILO ACTION	START TIME	END TIME	ELAPSED TIME	ERROR
28959	process 7	22-JUL-10 05.40.00.000000 PM	22-JUL-10 09.40.31.234635 PM	30.45	−1013
29221	process 7	22-JUL-10 05.55.30.000000 PM	22-JUL-10 09.56.00.619850 PM	30.57	−1013

The start and stop times shown in Table 15-3 reflect the connection pool start and stop times, which is a much wider window than you need in order to troubleshoot this problem. You also record internal database and CPU clock times in the ILO_ELAPSED_TIME table: it is these values that are used to calculate the elapsed times as shown in Table 15-4. Table 15-4 also shows the sequential execution of the processes, and you'll notice that process 7 was executed repeatedly within intervals of just a few seconds.

Table 15-4. *Sequential Listing of Processes with Internal Clock Times*

SPID	ILO ACTION	GO TIME	STOP TIME	ELAPSED TIME	CPU TIME	ERROR
29221	process 7	498854690	498854690	0	0	0
28959	**process 7**	**498856045**	**498859090**	**30.45**	**0**	**-1013**
29047	process 7	498862109	498862109	0	0	0
29309	process 3	498862111	498862121	0.1	0.11	0
29309	child 3a	498862113	498862121	0.08	0.07	0
29309	child 3b	498862113	498862113	0	0	0
29309	child 3c	498862121	498862121	0	0	0
29309	child 3d	498862121	498862121	0	0	0
29309	child 3e	498862121	498862121	0	0	0
29309	child 3f	498862121	498862121	0	0	0
28959	process 7	498947571	498947571	0	0	0
29221	**process 7**	**498948957**	**498952014**	**30.57**	**0**	**-1013**

continued

Table 15-4. *Sequential Listing of Processes with Internal Clock Times*

SPID	ILO ACTION	GO TIME	STOP TIME	ELAPSED TIME	CPU TIME	ERROR
29047	process 7	498957717	498957717	0	0	0
29309	process 3	498957718	498957728	0.1	0.1	0
29309	assign_child1	498957720	498957728	0.08	0.07	0
29309	assign_child2	498957720	498957720	0	0	0
29309	assign_child3	498957728	498957728	0	0	0
29309	assign_child4	498957728	498957728	0	0.01	0
29309	assign_child5	498957728	498957728	0	0	0
29309	assign_child6	498957728	498957728	0	0	0

Looking at the two processes that exceeded thirty seconds, you have a very small timeframe when both errors occurred. Your next step will be to check the Active Workload Repository (AWR) for that particular timeframe. Reviewing the AWR data shown in Listing 15-12, the problem is immediately clear.

Listing 15-12. *AWR Output for One Hour Timeframe*

```
Top 5 Timed Foreground Events
~~~~~~~~~~~~~~~~~~~~~~~~~~~~~~~

                                                Avg
                                                wait   % DB
Event                          Waits    Time(s) (ms)   time Wait Class
------------------------------ -------- -------- ------ ------ ----------
enq: TX - row lock contention         2       61 30511  78.6 Application
DB CPU                                        12         15.0
SQL*Net break/reset to client    21,382        5     0   6.6 Application
log file sync                        32        0     1    .1 Commit
SQL*Net message to client        10,836        0     0    .0 Network
```

Between the series of events shown in Table 15-2 and the AWR output shown in Listing 15-20, the cause of the timeouts becomes clear. Process 7 had been called two or even three times, when only one execution should be necessary. If those calls came in fast enough, the second process would attempt to update the same row, creating a lock and preventing the first process from committing. When process 1 could not commit in 30 seconds, the process would terminate and the second (or third) process would be able to save its changes successfully. Since the application has a built-in timeout, this problem is a minor one, and a self correcting one at that.

The tables above show data from a newly installed server with only a few executions. I've selected this particular data set as it is easy to use as an example, but it does make it appear as if it would have been possible to spot this problem with almost any other troubleshooting tool. However, consider this:

when this same data is reviewed on more active test servers over longer periods of time, timeouts for this process may occur on one day in any given month, and there are likely to be no more the four to six processes that exceed 30 seconds on that day. This process may execute hundreds of thousands of times over two or three months on a busy test server. And then there are test results like those shown in Table 15-1. In that case, the process is executed millions of times without a single timeout. Trying to spot this problem from an AWR report and then identifying the process that caused the application lock would take a bit more time with that many executions. And while this problem is not significant right now, it has the potential to cause the application to miss required performance targets. Due to the data recorded by the instrumentation, the problem can be monitored and addressed before that happens.

Although this is a simple example, identifying these kinds of problems can be difficult, especially during typical development test cycles. Early in unit testing, tests are not normally executed in rapid succession, so some problems may not appear until later. And once testing has moved on to load testing, an occasionally longer running process or two may not be noticed among millions of executions. Yet by using the ILO execution times to abbreviate the amount of AWR performance data that must be reviewed, problems like this can be identified and diagnosed in just a few moments. And while access to AWR and ASH data may not be available to you in all development environments, the instrumentation data you create will be.

Summary

I've covered a wide range of information in this chapter, including execution plans and instrumentation, performance and failures, testing theory and practical application. Each of these topics could have been a chapter or even an entire book on their own, which is why there are already many, many books out there.

What I hope you will take away from this chapter is the recognition that each system has its own strengths and limitations, so any testing and measurement approach should be customized to some extent for the specific system needs and performance requirements. No single testing method can be perfectly effective for all systems, but the basic approach is fairly straightforward. Break the work down into measurable test modules, measure, adjust. and measure again. Whenever possible, minimize the changes between test iterations but keep the test realistic. You can test the functionality of your code with unit tests on a subset of the data, but testing performance requires a comparable amount of data on a comparably configured system. Verifying that a report runs exceptionally fast on a development server with little data and no other users doesn't prove anything if that report will be run on a multiuser data warehouse. Understanding what you need to measure and confirm is crucial to preparing an appropriate test plan. And be sure to consider testing and performance early in the process. That does not necessarily mean that you need to write a perfectly optimized piece of code right out of the gate, but you should be aware of the limitations your code is likely to face in production and write the code accordingly. It also doesn't hurt to have a few alternatives in your back pocket, so you are prepared to optimize the code and measure it once again.

Plan Stability and Control

Kerry Osborne

One of the most frustrating things about Oracle's Cost Based Optimizer (CBO) is its tendency to change plans for statements at seemingly random intervals. Of course, these changes are not random at all. But because the optimizer code is so complex, it's often difficult to determine why a plan changed. Oracle recognized this issue years ago and has been working to improve the situation for at least a decade. They have provided many tools for identifying when plans change and why they changed. They have also provided numerous tools that allow you to exert varying degrees of control over the execution plans that the optimizer chooses.

This chapter is made up of two main focus areas. The first focus area concerns itself with plan instability. It is concerned with issues that cause you to not experience the stability you expect. You'll learn how to identify when and why plans have changed, how to locate plan changes that have created a significant performance impact, and gain some insight into common causes of plan instability issues. The second focus area, as you've probably guessed by now, covers various techniques for controlling execution plans. I probably should say "influencing" instead of "controlling," because there is really no foolproof method of locking an execution plan (at least as of release 11.2.0.1 of the Oracle database).

In this chapter, I will use a number of scripts, but for readability purposes, in most cases, I will not show the source of these scripts in the listings. The scripts can be found in the example download for this book.

Plan Instability: Understanding The Problem

Oracle's CBO is an extremely complex piece of software. Its job is basically to work out the fastest way to retrieve a given set of data as specified by a SQL statement. Generally speaking, it must do this in an extremely short period of time using pre-calculated statistical information about the objects involved (tables, indexes, partitions, etc.). The optimizer usually doesn't have the time to verify any of the information. The tight time constraints are imposed because parsing is a serialized operation. Therefore, the database needs to do it as quickly as possible and as infrequently as possible; otherwise, parsing can become a severe bottleneck to scalability. I should note here that my comments are basically aimed at what I would typically call an OLTP type environment—an environment with many users, executing lots of relatively quick SQL statements. Of course, in environments with relatively few but long running statements, it's much more important to get the correct plan than to get a decent plan quickly. These types of systems though don't suffer from plan stability issues nearly as often (partly because they tend to use literals as opposed to bind variables, but I'll talk about that more later).

So why do plans change? Well there are three main inputs to the CBO:

- Statistics - associated with the objects that are referenced by the SQL statement
- Environment - optimizer related parameter settings for example
- SQL - the statement itself

So, unless one of those three things changes, the plan should not change. Period. I believe that the frustration with plan instability arises primarily from the belief that "nothing has changed," when in fact something has changed. I can't even count the number of times that I have heard that phrase. The story usually goes something like this:

Them:	"Everything was working fine and then all of a sudden, the system just started crawling."
Me:	"When did this happen?"
Them:	"12:00 noon on Thursday"
Me:	"What changed around that time?"
Them:	"Nothing changed!"

Of course, they are not intentionally trying to lie to me. What they really mean is, "Nothing has changed… that I think could have anything to do with this particular issue." But regardless of whether someone thinks an event is relevant or not, or if they even know about it or not, there was a change that precipitated the issue.

So the first thing I want you to get out of this chapter is that performance doesn't just magically get worse (or better). If a SQL statement gets a new plan, there is a reason. Something changed!

Let's briefly go over the possibilities for why a plan can change.

Changes to Statistics

This is a rather obvious place to look for changes that can cause new plans to be generated. Object level statistics are gathered frequently on most systems. By default, 10g and 11g both have a job that runs on a nightly basis to calculate new statistics. If these jobs are running on your system, it means that every day you have an opportunity to get a new plan. While a thorough discussion of statistics gathering is outside the scope of this chapter, you should be aware of what mechanisms are in play in your environment. You should also know that you can quickly check to see when stats were last gathered on an object and that you can restore a previous version of an objects statistics in a matter of seconds. Finally, you should be aware that by default the standard stats gathering jobs in 10g and 11g allow statements to stay in the shared pool for some period of time after new stats have been gathered. This feature is called *rolling invalidation*. By default in 10g and 11g, the dbms_stats procedures set the no_invalidate parameter to dbms_stats.auto_invalidate. This means that cursors will not automatically be invalidated when statistics are gathered. Existing cursors will be invalidated at some random time during the next five hours. This is a feature designed to prevent parsing storms that can occur if all statements referencing a specific object are invalidated at the same time. Generally speaking, this feature is a good thing, but you should be aware that a plan change can be due to a statistics change, even though the statistics change occurred several hours before the new plan showed up. Listing 16-1 is an example of checking for a tables last statistics gathering and for restoring a previous version (all scripts are in the example download for the book).

Listing 16-1. *Table Statistics Setting and Restoring*

```
SYS@LAB112> exec dbms_stats.set_table_stats(ownname => 'KSO', tabname => 'SKEW', -
                                            numrows => 1234, numblks => 12, -
                                            avgrlen => 123, no_invalidate => false);

PL/SQL procedure successfully completed.

SYS@LAB112> @set_col_stats
Enter value for owner: KSO
Enter value for table_name: SKEW
Enter value for col_name: PK_COL
Enter value for ndv: 1234
Enter value for density: 1/1234
Enter value for nullcnt: 0

PL/SQL procedure successfully completed.

SYS@LAB112> @dba_tables
Enter value for owner: KSO
Enter value for table_name: SKEW

OWNER       TABLE_NAME               STATUS    LAST_ANAL   NUM_ROWS    BLOCKS
----------  -----------------------  --------  ---------   ----------  ----------
KSO         SKEW                     VALID     12-AUG-10   1234        12

SYS@LAB112> @col_stats
Enter value for owner: KSO
Enter value for table_name: SKEW
Enter value for column_name:

COLUMN_NAME  DATA_TYPE    DENSITY        NDV HISTOGRAM        BUCKETS LAST_ANAL
-----------  ----------   -----------   ------------ ---------------  ------- ---------
PK_COL       NUMBER       .000810373      1,234 NONE                  1 12-AUG-10
COL1         NUMBER       .000002568    902,848 HEIGHT BALANCED      75 02-AUG-10
COL2         VARCHAR2     .500000000          2 NONE                  1 03-AUG-10
COL3         DATE         .000002581  1,000,512 HEIGHT BALANCED      75 02-AUG-10
COL4         VARCHAR2     .000000016          3 FREQUENCY             2 02-AUG-10

SYS@LAB112> @tab_stats_history
Enter value for owner: KSO
Enter value for table_name: SKEW

OWNER         TABLE_NAME               STATS_UPDATE_TIME
-------------  -----------------------  ---------------------------------
KSO           SKEW                     31-JUL-10 09.06.42.785067 PM -05:00
KSO           SKEW                     02-AUG-10 07.14.04.486871 PM -05:00
KSO           SKEW                     02-AUG-10 09.29.48.761056 PM -05:00
```

```
KSO             SKEW                      02-AUG-10 09.31.11.788522 PM -05:00
KSO             SKEW                      02-AUG-10 09.38.00.524266 PM -05:00
KSO             SKEW                      12-AUG-10 08.27.17.497396 PM -05:00

6 rows selected.

SYS@LAB112> @restore_table_stats.sql

Note: No_Invalidate=false - means invalidate all cursors now (stupid triple negatives)

Enter value for owner: KSO
Enter value for table_name: SKEW
Enter value for as_of_date: 03-aug-10
Enter value for no_invalidate: false

PL/SQL procedure successfully completed.

SYS@LAB112> @dba_tables
Enter value for owner: KSO
Enter value for table_name: SKEW

OWNER       TABLE_NAME                STATUS    LAST_ANAL   NUM_ROWS    BLOCKS
----------  ------------------------  --------  ---------   ----------  ----------
KSO         SKEW                      VALID     02-AUG-10   32000004    162294

SYS@LAB112> @col_stats
Enter value for owner: KSO
Enter value for table_name: SKEW
Enter value for column_name:

COLUMN_NAME  DATA_TYPE    DENSITY          NDV  HISTOGRAM        BUCKETS  LAST_ANAL
-----------  ----------   ------------  ------------  ---------------  -------  ---------
PK_COL       NUMBER       .000000032  32,000,004  HEIGHT BALANCED       75  02-AUG-10
COL1         NUMBER       .000002568     902,848  HEIGHT BALANCED       75  02-AUG-10
COL2         VARCHAR2     .000000016           2  FREQUENCY              1  02-AUG-10
COL3         DATE         .000002581   1,000,512  HEIGHT BALANCED       75  02-AUG-10
COL4         VARCHAR2     .000000016           3  FREQUENCY              2  02-AUG-10
```

Changes to the Environment

There are many parameters that affect the optimizer's calculations. Some of the optimizer parameters have values that are calculated automatically based on the values of other parameters or the physical characteristics of the machine the database is running on, such as the number of CPUs. If any of these environmental values change, the optimizer may come up with a new plan. This is also one of the reasons that it is sometimes difficult to get the plans in Development and Test environments to match the plans that are generated in Production.

The settings in affect when a statement is parsed can be obtained by enabling a 10053 trace. Oracle also keeps track of the settings for each of the optimizer-related parameters in an X$ table called X$KQLFSQCE. This is the structure that underlays the V$SQL_OPTIMZER_ENV view, which (much like v$parameter) doesn't display the hidden parameters (unless they have been altered). The optim_parms.sql script shows all the parameters, including the so-called hidden parameters that start with an underscore (this is the complete list of parameters that affect the optimizer's calculations and the same ones that are dumped in a 10053 trace file). In Listing 16-2, you see the optimizer parameter values for SQL statement 84q0zxfzn5u6s in a 10.2.04 instance. Note that these are the values that were set when the statement was parsed.

Listing 16-2. *Optimizer Parameter Values*

```
SYS@LAB1024> @optim_parms
Enter value for sql_id: 84q0zxfzn5u6s
Enter value for child_no: 0
Enter value for isdefault:
Enter value for show_hidden: Y
```

NAME	VALUE	ISDEFAUL
_pga_max_size	330540 KB	NO
optimizer_mode_hinted	false	YES
optimizer_features_hinted	0.0.0	YES
parallel_execution_enabled	true	YES
parallel_query_forced_dop	0	YES
parallel_dml_forced_dop	0	YES
parallel_ddl_forced_degree	0	YES
parallel_ddl_forced_instances	0	YES
_query_rewrite_fudge	90	YES
optimizer_features_enable	10.2.0.4	YES
_optimizer_search_limit	5	YES
cpu_count	16	YES
active_instance_count	1	YES
...		
_first_k_rows_dynamic_proration	true	YES
_px_ual_serial_input	true	YES
_optimizer_native_full_outer_join	off	YES
_optimizer_star_trans_min_cost	0	YES
_optimizer_star_trans_min_ratio	0	YES
_optimizer_fkr_index_cost_bias	10	YES
_optimizer_connect_by_combine_sw	true	YES
_optimizer_use_subheap	true	YES
_optimizer_or_expansion_subheap	true	YES
_optimizer_sortmerge_join_inequality	true	YES
_optimizer_use_histograms	true	YES
_optimizer_enable_density_improvements	false	YES

```
204 rows selected.
```

Changes to the SQL

This one may not make much sense at first blush. How can the SQL statement change? When I talk about plan instability, I am talking about the optimizer coming up with different plans for a single statement (i.e. the same SQL text and therefore the same sql_id). However, there are a couple of reasons that the text of a statement (and its sql_id or hash_value) remains fixed but the actual SQL statement that the optimizer evaluates may change. These are:

- If a statement references views and an underlying view changes, the statement has changed.

- If a statement uses bind variables and the values passed via the variables change, the statement has changed.

The first situation is easy to understand and rarely a point of confusion. The second situation, though, can be confusing. We have been trained over the years to use variables in our SQL statements so that Oracle can reuse the statements without having to reparse them. So instead of writing a statement like this:

```
select avg(col1) from skew where col1 > 1;
```

We would typically write it like this:

```
select avg(col1) from skew where col1 > :X;
```

That way, we can pass any value we want to our program via variable X and Oracle would not have to reparse the statement. This is a very good thing when it comes to scalability, particularly for systems where many users execute many statements concurrently. However, unless the bind variables always contain the same data, the optimizer is basically evaluating a different SQL statement every time it undergoes a hard parse. This is due to the fact that Oracle introduced a feature in 9i that allows the optimizer to "peek" at the values of bind variables during the part of the parsing process where the execution plan is determined. This is the infamous Bind Variable Peeking that you've probably already heard about. And it is one of the major contributors to plan stability issues.

Bind Variable Peeking

When Oracle introduced histograms in 8i, they provided a mechanism for the optimizer to recognize that the values in a column were not distributed evenly. That is, in a table with 100 rows and 10 distinct values, the default assumption the optimizer would make, in the absence of a histogram, would be that no matter which value you picked, you would always get 100/10 or 10 rows back. Histograms let the optimizer know if that was not the case. The classic example would be 100 records with 2 distinct values where value "Y" occurred 99 times and the value "N" occurred only 1 time. Without a histogram, the optimizer would always assume that whether you requested records with a "Y" or an "N" you would get half the records back (100/2 = 50). Therefore, you always want to do a full table scan as opposed to using an index on the column. A histogram, assuming it was accurate (I'll come back to that later), would let the optimizer know that the distribution was not normal (i.e. not spread out evenly—also commonly called *skewed*) and that a "Y" would get basically the whole table, while an "N" would get only 1%. This would allow the optimizer to pick an appropriate plan regardless of which value was specified in the Where Clause.

So let's consider the implications of that. Would that improve the response time for the query where the value was "Y"? The answer is no. In this simple case, the default costing algorithm is close enough and produces the same plan that the histogram produces. The full table scan takes just as long whether the optimizer thought it was getting 50 rows or 99 rows. But what about the case where you specified the value of "N"? In this case, with a histogram you would pick up the index on that column and presumably get a much better response time than the plan with the full table scan. This is an important point.

Generally speaking, it is only the outliers—the exceptional cases, if you will—where the histogram really makes a difference.

So at first glance, it looked like a pretty good idea. But there was a fly in the ointment. You had to use literals in your SQL statements for the optimizer to be able use the histograms. So you had to write your statements like this:

```
SELECT XYZ FROM TABLE1 WHERE COLUMN1 = 'Y';
SELECT XYZ FROM TABLE1 WHERE COLUMN1 = 'N';
```

This is not a problem in this simple example because you only have two possibilities. But consider a statement with two or three skewed columns, each with a couple hundred distinct values. The possible combinations could quickly grow into the millions. Not a good thing for the shared pool or scalability of your system.

Enter the star: bind variable peeking, a new feature introduced in 9i that was added to allow the optimizer to peek at the value of bind variables and then use a histogram to pick an appropriate plan, just like it would do with literals. The problem with the new feature was that it only looked at the variables once, when the statement was parsed. So let's make that simple example a little more realistic by assuming you have a table with 10 million rows where 99% have a value of "Y" and 1% have a value of "N". In this example, if the first time the statement was executed it was passed a "Y", the full table scan plan would be locked in and it would be used until the statement had to be re-parsed, even if the value "N" was passed to it in subsequent executions.

Let's consider the implication of that. When you get the full table scan plan (because you passed a "Y" the first time) it behaves the same way no matter what which value you pass subsequently. Oracle always performs a full table scan, always does the same amount of work, and usually results in the same basic elapsed time. From a user standpoint, that seems reasonable. The performance is consistent. (This is the way it would work without a histogram, by the way.) On the other hand, if the index plan gets picked because the first execution that caused the parse occurs with a value of "N", the executions where the value is "N" will almost certainly be faster than they were before (maybe considerably faster) , but the execution with a value of "Y" will be incredibly slow. That's because using an index to read virtually every row in a table is incredibly slow. This is not at all what the users expect. They expect the response time to be about the same every time they execute a piece of code. And this is the problem with bind variable peeking. It's basically just Russian Roulette. It just depends on what value you happen to pass the statement when it's parsed (which could be any execution, by the way).

So is bind variable peeking a feature or a bug? Figure 16-1 illustrates how that can sometimes be a tricky question to answer.

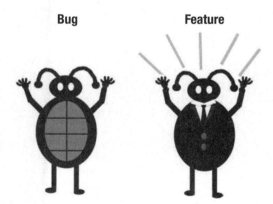

Figure 16-1. *Feature or Bug? (Figure by Noah Osborne)*

Well technically it's not a bug because it works the way it's designed. I just happen to believe that it was not a good decision to implement it that way. But what other choices did the optimizer development group have?

- They could have evaluated the bind variables and re-parsed for every execution of every statement using bind variables. This would eliminate the advantage of having bind variables in the first place and would never work for high transaction systems. So it was basically not an option.

- They could have just said no, and made us use literals in order to get the benefit of histograms. This is probably not a bad option in retrospect; the fact that they added _optim_peek_user_binds, which allows us to turn off bind variable peeking altogether, probably means that they decided later to give us that option via setting this hidden parameter.

- They could have implemented a system where they could identify statements that might benefit from different plans based on the values of bind variables. Then peek at those variables for every execution of those "bind sensitive" statements (Sound familiar? It's what they finally did in 11g with Adaptive Cursor Sharing).

So why is it such a pervasive problem? (And I do believe it is a pervasive problem with 10g in particular.)

1. We've been taught to always use bind variables. It's a "best practice" which allows SQL statements to be shared, thus eliminating a great deal of work/contention. Using bind variables is an absolute necessity when building scalable high transaction rate systems. Of course, just because it's a "best practice" doesn't mean you have to follow it blindly. There are situations where literals work better.

2. In 10g, the default stats gathering method was changed to automatically gather histograms. So in a typical 10g database, there are a huge number of histograms, many of them inappropriate (i.e. on columns that don't have significantly skewed distributions) and many of them created with very small sample sizes causing the histograms to be less than accurate. Note that 11g does a better job on both counts. That is to say, 11g seems to create fewer inappropriate histograms and appears to create much more accurate histograms, even with relatively small sample sizes.

3. In my humble opinion, Bind Variable Peeking is not that well understood. When I talk to people about the issue, they usually have heard of it and have a basic idea what the problem is, but their behavior (in terms of the code they write and how they manage their databases) indicates that they don't really have a good handle on the issue.

So what's the best way to deal with this issue? Well, recognizing that you have a problem is the first step to recovery. In other words, being able to identify that you have a problem with plan stability is an appropriate first step. Direct queries against the Statspack or AWR tables are probably the best way to identify the issue. What you're looking for is statements that flip flop back and forth between two or more plans. Note that there are other reasons for statements to change plans, but bind variable peeking is high on the list of usual suspects.

■**NOTE** Adaptive Cursor Sharing is a new feature of 11g that is aimed at fixing performance issues due to bind variable peeking. The basic idea is to try to automatically recognize when a statement might benefit from multiple plans. If a statement is found that the optimizer thinks is a candidate, it is marked as bind aware. Subsequent executions will peek at the bind variables and new cursors with new plans may result. The feature does work, although it has a few quirks. The two biggest drawbacks are that it must execute a statement badly before it will notice that an additional plan is needed, and that the information regarding bind sensitivity is not persistent (i.e. if the statement gets flushed from the shared pool, all information about bind sensitivity is lost). As a result, we continue to see bind variable peeking issues in 11g.

Identifying Plan Instability

Sometimes it's painfully obvious when a plan has changed for the worse. A quick look at Enterprise Manager or a query against gv$session will show dozens of sessions executing the same statement. Other times the problem is not as obvious. One of the best ways to identify the problem is to look for statements with multiple plans that have very different performance characteristics depending on which plan they use. AWR is extremely handy for this as it keeps copies of execution statistics as well as plans used for the most "important" statements. Note that not all statements are captured by AWR. Those that rank high in number of executions, logical i/o, physical i/o, elapsed time, CPU time, or parses will be there, but if you have a statement that is very efficient which later becomes very inefficient, the very efficient version may not be captured by AWR. Regardless of the fact that AWR does not represent a complete record of every statement executed, it does provide data on most statements that are of interest.

Capturing Data on Currently-Running Queries

One of my most used diagnostic scripts queries v$session for all sessions that have a status of ACTIVE. This can be used to see what is actually running at any give point in time. It is not perfect because really fast statements may not show up very often, even if they are dominating the workload. So I often use Tanel Poder's snapper script for this same purpose. His script has many advantages but one of the most useful is that runs many times in a tight loop and aggregates the data so that very fast statements still show up in the output. Listing 16-3 shows both scripts in action.

Listing 16-3. *Two Diagnostic Scripts, as.sql and Session Snapper*

```
SYS@LAB112> @as

 SID PROG        SQL_ID         CHILD PLAN_HASH_VALUE      EXECS   AVG_ETIME SQL_TEXT
 ---- ---------- -------------- ------ --------------- ---------- ----------- --------------
  24 sqlplus@ho gf5nnx0pyfqq2      0      4072605661         55       86.18 select a.col2,
  42 sqlplus@ho gf5nnx0pyfqq2      0      4072605661         55       86.18
 100 sqlplus@ho gf5nnx0pyfqq2      0      4072605661         55       86.18
  83 sqlplus@ho gf5nnx0pyfqq2      0      4072605661         55       86.18
  61 sqlplus@ho gf5nnx0pyfqq2      0      4072605661         55       86.18
```

```
SYS@LAB112> @snapper ash=sid+event+wait_class,ash1=sql_id 5 1 all
Sampling with interval 5 seconds, 1 times...

-- Session Snapper v3.11 by Tanel Poder @ E2SN ( http://tech.e2sn.com )


-----------------------------------------------------------------
Active% |   SID | EVENT                   | WAIT_CLASS
-----------------------------------------------------------------
   100% |    83 | ON CPU                  | ON CPU
    98% |    42 | ON CPU                  | ON CPU
    98% |    61 | ON CPU                  | ON CPU
    93% |    24 | ON CPU                  | ON CPU
    88% |   100 | ON CPU                  | ON CPU
    12% |   100 | direct path read temp   | User I/O
     7% |    24 | direct path read temp   | User I/O
     5% |   248 | control file parallel wri | System I/O
     2% |    42 | direct path read temp   | User I/O
     2% |    61 | direct path read temp   | User I/O


-------------------------
Active% | SQL_ID
-------------------------
   500% | gf5nnx0pyfqq2
     5% |

--  End of ASH snap 1, end=2010-08-12 22:23:17, seconds=5, samples_taken=42
```

The scripts have very different output formats. My as.sql script has one line per session and shows the SQL_ID that is being executed by the session, along with the Average Elapsed Time for that statement. Keep in mind that this represents a single instant in time. So you should run it several times in succession to get a feel for what is actually happening. Tanel's snapper, on the other hand, doesn't require repeated running. Just give it a length of time to run and it automatically samples repeatedly for that length of time. It is also considerably more flexible than my simple script. The format is quite different, too. The top section shows the activity percentage by SID and Event. Notice that the same SID may have multiple entries if it spends significant time on more than one thing during the sample period. The second section shows a break down of the work by SQL statement.

In the case shown, both snapper and my `as.sql` scripts show different views of the same situation. There are five sessions all running the same statement. Any time you are asked to look at a system and you see that many sessions are all running the same long running SQL statement, you have a pretty good idea where to start your investigation into the problem.

Reviewing the History of a Statement's Performance

When the problem is obvious (as in the previous example where several sessions were all running the same long running query), it is often instructive to see what the performance of the statement of interest has looked like over time. This can easily be done by directly querying the AWR or Statspack tables. Listing 16-4 shows an example.

Listing 16-4. *The awr_plan_change.sql Script*

```
SYS@LAB112> @awr_plan_change
Enter value for sql_id: 3dhwvfmkjzwtv
```

SNAP_ID	NODE	BEGIN_INTERVAL_TIME	PLAN_HASH_VALUE	EXECS	AVG_ETIME	AVG_LIO
1785	3	24-APR-09 05.00 PM	1093407144	6	1.102	2,872.7
1786	2	24-APR-09 06.00 PM		158	0.024	2,873.0
1786	3	24-APR-09 06.00 PM		223	0.023	2,873.0
1787	2	24-APR-09 07.00 PM		749	0.020	2,873.0
1787	3	24-APR-09 07.00 PM		873	0.019	2,873.0
1788	2	24-APR-09 08.00 PM		726	0.020	2,873.9
1788	3	24-APR-09 08.00 PM		871	0.020	2,873.9
1789	2	24-APR-09 09.00 PM		373	0.016	2,874.0
1789	3	24-APR-09 09.00 PM		566	0.016	2,874.0
1892	2	29-APR-09 04.00 AM		1	2.613	3,811.0
1897	2	29-APR-09 09.00 AM		2	8.179	8,529.0
1918	3	30-APR-09 06.00 AM		2	0.421	485.5
1919	2	30-APR-09 07.00 AM		1	1.152	1,242.0
1920	2	30-APR-09 08.00 AM		4	3.273	3,200.3
1920	3	30-APR-09 08.00 AM		12	2.491	3,314.2
1921	2	30-APR-09 09.00 AM		5	3.947	3,333.4
1921	3	30-APR-09 09.00 AM		2	2.416	1,769.5
1922	3	30-APR-09 10.00 AM	4076066623	2	54.237	2,291,432.5
1923	2	30-APR-09 11.00 AM	1093407144	2	0.812	975.0
1923	3	30-APR-09 11.00 AM	4076066623	3	134.031	933,124.3
1924	3	30-APR-09 12.00 PM		3	227.009	6,987,169.3
1926	2	30-APR-09 02.00 PM	1093407144	8	0.818	1,574.5
1926	3	30-APR-09 02.00 PM	4076066623	2	175.709	8,963,417.0
1927	2	30-APR-09 03.00 PM	1093407144	4	1.344	1,068.8
1927	3	30-APR-09 03.00 PM	4076066623	5	156.378	10,059,992.0
1928	2	30-APR-09 04.00 PM	1093407144	6	0.923	1,225.8
1928	3	30-APR-09 04.00 PM	4076066623	1	180.488	2,150,190.0
1930	3	30-APR-09 06.00 PM		2	180.371	8,255,881.5
1934	3	30-APR-09 10.00 PM		1	180.491	3,002,577.0
1939	2	01-MAY-09 03.00 AM	1093407144	21	0.825	1,041.8
1939	3	01-MAY-09 03.00 AM		4	0.575	1,211.8
1944	3	01-MAY-09 08.00 AM		6	1.328	1,788.3
1946	2	01-MAY-09 10.00 AM		1	1.170	2,411.0
1946	3	01-MAY-09 10.00 AM		4	2.041	2,414.3
1947	3	01-MAY-09 11.00 AM		10	1.725	2,937.1
1948	3	01-MAY-09 12.00 PM		3	2.232	3,415.7
1987	2	03-MAY-09 03.00 AM		7	1.029	901.0
1990	3	03-MAY-09 06.00 AM		3	1.225	1,465.7
1991	3	03-MAY-09 07.00 AM		26	0.370	710.5
1992	2	03-MAY-09 08.00 AM		6	0.213	685.7
1992	3	03-MAY-09 08.00 AM		3	0.658	883.0

1993	2	03-MAY-09 09.00 AM		8	0.769	950.9
1996	2	03-MAY-09 12.00 PM		2	0.101	861.5
2015	3	04-MAY-09 07.00 AM		4	0.376	854.5
2016	3	04-MAY-09 08.00 AM		6	0.143	571.0
2019	2	04-MAY-09 11.00 AM		12	0.937	1,352.1
2019	3	04-MAY-09 11.00 AM		10	1.612	1,341.9
2019	3	04-MAY-09 11.00 AM	4076066623	1	41.592	3,942,672.0
2020	2	04-MAY-09 12.00 PM	1093407144	15	1.037	1,734.6
2020	3	04-MAY-09 12.00 PM	4076066623	1	181.044	1,764,007.0
2022	2	04-MAY-09 02.00 PM	1093407144	2	2.214	2,780.5

The awr_plan_change.sql script simply queries DBA_HIST_SQLSTAT for a list of snapshots that contain information about the statement in question (based on its sql_id) and then prints out the relevant statistical information. In this output, I have shown the plan_hash_value, the average logical i/o, and the average elapsed time. (This sort of a report could also be generated from data collected by Statspack, by the way) One of the most interesting features of this kind of a historical view of a statement is the history of the plan(s) being used. The output in the example shows a classic case of plan instability. As you can see, the plan changes fairly often (note that the script uses the SQL*Plus break feature on the plan_hash_value column, so if the value does not change from row to row, the value is not printed). This is not a situation where something changed in the environment that caused a plan to change, but rather a situation where the plans are constantly in a state of flux. This is classic plan instability. If you had seen a single plan being used for many days and then an abrupt change to another plan, you would be looking for a change to statistics or some other environmental change such as an optimizer setting.

You can also clearly see that the performance characteristics are wildly different between the two plans. In the sample output, you can see that plan 1093407144 does only a couple of thousand lios, while plan 4076066623 does a few million. Consequently, the average elapsed time is several minutes for the "bad" plan and a couple of seconds for the "good" plan. This is another characteristic of classic plan instability. There is often a single plan that, while not the absolute best performance you can get for any combination of bind variables, is good enough to be acceptable and provides the desired stability.

Aggregating Statistics by Plan

Generally speaking, you don't care much about the optimizer changing its mind and picking a different plan unless the execution times vary widely from one plan to the other. When you have a lot of snapshots or a lot of plans, it's often helpful to aggregate the statistics by plan. The awr_plan_stats.sql script does just that (Note: I've cut some of the rows from the above output so the averages won't exactly match, but they are close enough to get the point across):

```
SQL> @awr_plan_stats
Enter value for sql_id: 3dhwvfmkjzwtv
```

SQL_ID	PLAN_HASH_VALUE	EXECS	ETIME	AVG_ETIME	AVG_LIO
3dhwvfmkjzwtv	1093407144	207	100.0	.935	2,512.5
3dhwvfmkjzwtv	4076066623	22	1,236.5	154.559	4,072,416.3

The output from the awr_plan_stats.sql script clearly shows that in this example there are two plans with very different performance characteristics. This is a fairly common situation (although there are often more than two plans). But it is nevertheless a common occurrence where one plan is fairly consistent with a reasonable amount of work and a reasonable average elapsed time. Although you should be aware that averages can hide a lot of important details (such as a few very fast executions with the plan that has the horrible averages). But again, the goal is generally to get stability at a reasonable performance level. So finding a plan that you can stick with is often all you're after. (I'll talk about how you get the optimizer to stick with a single plan shortly.)

■**NOTE** The default retention period for both AWR and Statspack are woefully inadequate for this type of diagnosis. The default is seven days for AWR. I've been involved in many cases where the necessary data has scrolled out of the retention window and been purged before a proper diagnosis was done. AWR (and Statspack) data does not take up that much space, so I routinely set the retention to several months (and I know of sites where they retain multiple years of AWR data). There is even a supplied script that will allow you to estimate the storage requirements for AWR based on the workload in your system: $ORACLE_HOME/rdbms/admin/utlsyxsz.sql.

Looking for Statistical Variance by Plan

When the problem is not obvious but you suspect plan instability is an issue, it's often helpful to look for statements that have run with more than one plan that have a large statistical variance in their execution times or the amount of work they do (logical i/os, for example). Listing 16-5 shows the header of a script (unstable_plans.sql) that can help identify statements that are suffering from plan instability along with an example of it usage.

Listing 16-5. *The.unstable_plans.sql Script*

```
-----------------------------------------------------------------------------------
--
-- File name:    unstable_plans.sql
--
-- Purpose:      Attempts to find SQL statements with plan instability.
--
-- Author:       Kerry Osborne
--
-- Usage:        This scripts prompts for two values, both of which can be left blank.
--
--               min_stddev: the minimum "normalized" standard deviation between plans
--                           (the default is 2)
--
--               min_etime:  only include statements that have an avg. etime > this value
--                           (the default is .1 second)
--
-- See http://kerryosborne.oracle-guy.com/2008/10/unstable-plans/ for more info.
-----------------------------------------------------------------------------------


SQL> @unstable_plans
Enter value for min_stddev:
```

```
Enter value for min_etime:

SQL_ID          SUM(EXECS)   MIN_ETIME   MAX_ETIME   NORM_STDDEV
-------------   ----------   ---------   ---------   -----------
4fc7tprp1x3uj        43212         .18         .84        2.0222
47s01ypztkmn6            6       54.46      210.28        2.0230
3rx5cnvua3myj         8126         .03         .12        2.0728
80tb4vmrsag5j        29544         .78        3.16        2.1433
cahnk07yj55st           17       26.35      113.09        2.3272
2azfw6wnqn01s          388        1.39        6.20        2.4522
a31u2rn7zup46            4       30.38      183.82        2.5271
607twnwf0ym10           30      146.50      728.15        2.8075
7y3w2mnqnp8jn           65         .56        3.05        3.1227
82rq0xvp6u1t2           34       12.34      119.20        3.4625
9cp3tujh0z4mt        42455         .02         .15        3.5998
6ykn5wq4jmu91        58584         .01         .21        3.7001
cvfj7g4fub5kn          116         .43        3.76        5.4863
26nrsfgurpgpm       427450         .07        1.08        5.5286
brntkgfqa9u1u            2      261.26    2,376.86        5.7258
d9ddsn04krw9d           99         .43        5.66        5.9018
fnwxd5kmnp6x9         2227         .47        4.46        6.0031
96567x1dqvzw1           23       27.02      311.04        7.4330
5wwnfumndntbq           10       98.58    1,481.40        7.7765
dm4hyyyxyay5t         1368         .03         .36        7.8945
5ub7xd1pn57by      1118281         .04        1.23       10.8031
870uasttnradg       441864         .12        2.07       11.3099
2p86vc476bvht           34       14.66      297.76       13.6548
2gz0c5c3vw59b           30       53.45    1,197.24       15.1320
4g22whjx1ycnu          818         .55       22.02       15.3194
48k8mu4mt68pw         1578       13.58    2,002.27       81.6759
1ct9u20mx6nnf        25782         .00         .93      287.5165

27 rows selected.
```

The output in Listing 16-5 shows that there are several SQL statements in this system that are most likely suffering from plan instability issues. The script pulls the info from the AWR tables and displays the total executions, the average elapsed time for the fastest plan, the average elapsed time for the slowest plan, and a calculated normalized standard deviation. As you can see, statement 1ct9u20mx6nnf is the worst offender. However, it may not be all that noticeable to the users because the delta between the slowest and the fastest plan is still less than a second. If it is executed many times in succession, the users will almost certainly suffer, but otherwise they may not notice. On the other hand, SQL_ID 48k8mu4mt68pw varies from 14 seconds to over 30 minutes. Anyone that runs this statement will certainly notice the difference. And seeing that it was executed over 1500 times certainly makes this one appear as a significant contributor to perceived inconsistency. Finally, after identifying the suspects, I usually use the awr_plan_stats.sql and awr_plan_change.sql to get a better idea of what's going with specific statements.

Checking for Variations Around a Point in Time

The other thing I occasionally do is to look for variations around a point in time. My `whats_changed.sql` script computes a normalized variance for elapsed time around a specific point in time. In fact, it computes the average elapsed time before a reference time and the average elapsed time after the reference time for every statement in the AWR tables. It then displays all statements whose average elapsed times are significantly different (2x by default). It's similar to the `unstable_plans.sql` script, but it looks for variance around a point in time as opposed to variance between plans. It is most useful when new code is rolled out or a new index is created or basically whenever you want to see which statements have been affected either for the better or the worse. Listing 16-6 shows the script's header and an example of its use.

Listing 16-6. *The* `whats_changed.sql` *Script*

```
-----------------------------------------------------------------------------------------
--
-- File name:    whats_changed.sql
--
-- Purpose:      Find statements that have significantly different elapsed time than before.
-
-- Author:       Kerry Osborne
--
-- Usage:        This scripts prompts for four values.
--
--                 days_ago: how long ago was the change made that you wish to evaluate
--                           (this could easily be changed to a snap_id for more precision)
--
--                 min_stddev: the minimum "normalized" standard deviation between plans
--                             (the default is 2 - which means twice as fast/slow)
--
--                 min_etime:  only include statements that have an avg. etime > this value
--                             (the default is .1 second)
--
--                 faster_slower: a flag to indicate if you want only Faster or Slower SQL
--                                (the default is both - use S% for slower and F% for faster)
--
-- Description: This script attempts to find statements with significantly different
--              average elapsed times per execution. It uses AWR data and computes a
--              normalized standard deviation between the average elapsed time per
--              execution before and after the date specified by the days_ago parameter.
--
--              The ouput includes the following:
--
--              SQL_ID - the sql_id of a statement that is in the shared pool (v$sqlarea)
--
--              EXECS - the total number of executions in the AWR tables
--
```

```
--              AVG_ETIME_BEFORE - the average elapsed time per execution before the
--                          REFERENCE_TIME specified by days_ago
--
--              AVG_ETIME_AFTER - the average elapsed time per execution after the
--                          REFERENCE_TIME specified by days_ago
--
--              NORM_STDDEV - this is a normalized standard deviation
--                          (i.e. how many times slower/faster is it now)
--
-- See http://kerryosborne.oracle-guy.com/2009/06/what-did-my-new-index-mess-up
-- for additional information.
-----------------------------------------------------------------------------------------
```

```
SQL> @whats_changed
Enter Days ago: 30
Enter value for min_stddev:
Enter value for min_etime:
Enter value for faster_slower:
```

SQL_ID	EXECS	AVG_ETIME_BEFORE	AVG_ETIME_AFTER	NORM_STDDEV	RESULT
5ub7xd1pn57by	1,118,281	0.18	0.05	2.0827	Faster
03rhvyrhjxgg9	3,838	0.10	0.38	2.0925	Slower
cahnk07yj55st	17	113.09	26.35	2.3272	Faster
4bf2kzg2h1sd0	148	0.60	0.13	2.6403	Faster
9cp3tujh0z4mt	42,455	0.12	0.02	2.7272	Faster
fnwxd5kmnp6x9	2,227	0.92	4.47	2.7283	Slower
607twnwf0ym10	30	146.50	728.15	2.8075	Slower
akm80a52q4qs9	649	6.16	1.21	2.9014	Faster
4g22whjx1ycnu	818	0.48	2.44	2.9272	Slower
14mxyzzjzjvpq	1,537	33.08	191.20	3.3800	Slower
6zncujjc43gsm	1,554	22.53	168.79	4.5894	Slower
6zt6cu6upnm8y	3,340	0.62	0.08	4.8153	Faster
870uasttnradg	441,864	0.98	0.12	4.9936	Faster
d9ddsn04krw9d	99	5.66	0.68	5.1708	Faster
cvfj7g4fub5kn	116	3.76	0.43	5.4863	Faster
2p86vc476bvht	34	14.66	297.76	13.6548	Slower
2gz0c5c3vw59b	30	53.45	1,197.24	15.1320	Slower

17 rows selected.

That wraps up the first portion of this chapter on identifying the problem. I've discussed a couple of primary causes for plans changing (statistics gathering and bind variable peeking) and I've covered some techniques for identifying the issue. In the next section, I'll turn the discussion towards how to improve the situation.

Plan Control: Solving the Problem

When you have access to the code (and the change control requirements are not too stringent) you can make changes to get the plan you want. Mechanisms such as hints, changing the structure of the query itself, or using literals in key locations to avoid bind variable peeking issues are all viable options.

■**NOTE**   See the next section "Plan Control: Without Access to the Code" for help in exerting control over execution plans when you do not have the luxury of being able to modify the code that is being executed.

Discussions about controlling execution plans can turn into a religious debate. Questions concerning the degree and mechanism of control can all degenerate from spirited debate into questioning our rival's ancestry. There is a strong argument for letting the optimizer do what it was written to do. After all, it's one of the most complex pieces of software in existence with countless man-hours invested in its programming. In many (I dare say, most) situations the optimizer is capable of coming up with very serviceable execution plans. However, that assumes that the database is configured correctly, and that the statistics are accurate, and that the data model is reasonable, and that the SQL is written correctly, etc… That's a lot of assumptions and rarely are they all true.

So one camp says fix the configuration, the stats, the data model, or whatever else is leading the optimizer astray. On the surface, this seems like a perfectly reasonable position that would be hard to argue. If the statistics are not accurate, there will most likely be numerous issues even if they aren't readily apparent. So fixing inaccurate statistics can improve things in many areas at the same time.

The flip side is that fixing some things is almost an insurmountable task. Changing the data model, for example, presents a substantial challenge even in a small application, and it is certainly not something that can be done with any degree of expediency. Likewise, changing configuration parameters can have sweeping effects that often require other adjustments. Because of those issues, there is a group that says, "Let's just focus on fixing the slow running process." People in this camp tend to want to zero in on a SQL statement and fix it. This argument is also hard to argue with since we are often under the gun to provide relief to the users of the system.

The key, in my mind, is to weigh the cost (time to implement and risk) against the potential benefit. I tend to be a pragmatist and therefore rarely get into religious debates about which approach is "right." I am quite comfortable with making a decision to implement a solution that provides quick relief, even if there is a long term solution that needs to be implemented at some point in the future. I consider myself akin to an emergency room doctor. When a patient's heart stops, I expect the doctor to break out the defibrillator and get the patient stabilized, not lecture him on proper lifestyle and put him on a diet and new exercise regime. There's plenty of time for that later. On the other hand, once the guy has had the triple bypass, it would be foolish for his cardiologist to tell him that he should keep doing what he's always been doing, just because the technology exists to give him another jump start in the emergency room and put in a couple more stents if necessary.

The bottom line is that even when you have a system that is configured well with accurate statistics, you still occasionally run across plan stability issues. So let's put the philosophical issues aside and talk about the basic tools you have at your disposal for controlling execution plans.

Modifying Query Structure

Prior to version 8, changing the structure of a query was basically the only tool available for influencing execution plans (other than making physical changes to the database objects like adding or dropping indexes). Modifying SQL structure is still a valid technique, but since the optimizer has become so adept at transforming queries, it is not nearly as useful as it once was. Nevertheless, being aware of alternative forms that will return the same set of rows can give you an advantage when you are trying to get the optimizer to pick a certain plan. Alternative forms can open up or close off options that the optimizer has to choose from.

Making Appropriate Use of Literals

Although it's been drummed into your head for years that you should use bind variables, they are not appropriate in every situation. In fact, anywhere you have skewed data distributions and need histograms to get the best plans, you should use literals as opposed to bind variables, at least for the special cases (i.e. the values that you want to make sure the optimizer is aware of). It is not necessary to choose one approach or the other for each statement, either. It is perfectly reasonable to code conditional logic that branches to a SQL construct which uses literals when the values are highly selective (or highly unselective). All of the other values can be covered by a single version of the statement that uses a bind variable. Of course, if the number of very popular (or very unpopular) values is high, you'll have to weigh the cost of the coding effort, the impact on the shared pool, and the additional impediment to scalability caused by the additional parsing for all these unique SQL statements. As my Grand Dad used to say, "There's no such thing as a free puppy."

Giving the Optimizer some Hints

One of the oldest and most basic methods of controlling execution plans is embedding optimizer instructions directly into the statement. Unfortunately, the name of this feature, HINT, is somewhat misleading. The word "hint" makes it sound like it is a mild suggestion that the optimizer can consider or ignore as it pleases. Nothing could be further from the truth. Hints are actually directives to the optimizer. As long as the hint is valid, the optimizer will obey it. In general, hints are not well understood. One reason is that they are not particularly well documented. But worse than that, they return no error or warning message when an invalid hint is specified. In cases where there is a syntax error, or object names are mistyped, or the combination of hints cannot be applied together, they are simply silently ignored. So it is difficult to know if a hint is even recognized as valid, much less whether it is doing what it is supposed to do. This lack of error or warning messages is probably the biggest reason for confusion about what they do.

Hints can be used to tell Oracle to do a full table scan instead of using an index, or to do a nested loops join, or to use a specific index, or all of the above. Each of these access path oriented hints effectively reduces the universe of possible options that the optimizer can consider when coming up with an execution plan for a statement. Hints can also be used to alter optimizer settings, object statistics, and even internal optimizer calculations. These kinds of hints alter the way the optimizer does its work or the calculations that it makes, but do not directly limit the choices the optimizer has in terms of access paths. By the way, 11g provides a list of valid hints along with the version in which they were introduced via the V$SQL_HINT view. Listing 16-7 shows the valid_hints.sql script.

Listing 16-7. *The valid_hints.sql Script*

```
SYS@LAB112> @valid_hints
Enter value for hint: index
Enter value for version:
```

```
NAME                                                            VERSION
--------------------------------------------------------------  ------------------------
CHANGE_DUPKEY_ERROR_INDEX                                       11.1.0.7
DOMAIN_INDEX_FILTER                                             11.1.0.6
DOMAIN_INDEX_NO_SORT                                            8.1.5
DOMAIN_INDEX_SORT                                               8.1.5
IGNORE_ROW_ON_DUPKEY_INDEX                                      11.1.0.7
INDEX                                                           8.0.0
INDEX_ASC                                                       8.1.0
INDEX_COMBINE                                                   8.1.0
INDEX_DESC                                                      8.1.0
INDEX_FFS                                                       8.1.0
INDEX_JOIN                                                      8.1.5
INDEX_RRS                                                       9.0.0
INDEX_RS_ASC                                                    11.1.0.6
INDEX_RS_DESC                                                   11.1.0.6
INDEX_SS                                                        9.0.0
INDEX_SS_ASC                                                    9.0.0
INDEX_SS_DESC                                                   9.0.0
INDEX_STATS                                                     10.1.0.3
LOCAL_INDEXES                                                   9.0.0
NO_DOMAIN_INDEX_FILTER                                          11.1.0.6
NO_INDEX                                                        8.1.5
NO_INDEX_FFS                                                    10.1.0.3
NO_INDEX_SS                                                     10.1.0.3
NO_PARALLEL_INDEX                                               8.1.0
NO_USE_INVISIBLE_INDEXES                                        11.1.0.6
NO_XMLINDEX_REWRITE                                             11.1.0.6
NO_XMLINDEX_REWRITE_IN_SELECT                                   11.1.0.6
NUM_INDEX_KEYS                                                  10.2.0.3
PARALLEL_INDEX                                                  8.1.0
USE_INVISIBLE_INDEXES                                           11.1.0.6
USE_NL_WITH_INDEX                                               10.1.0.3
XMLINDEX_REWRITE                                                11.1.0.6
XMLINDEX_REWRITE_IN_SELECT                                      11.1.0.6
XMLINDEX_SEL_IDX_TBL                                            11.2.0.1

34 rows selected.
```

Hints can be applied to individual statements by embedding them inside comments that begin with a plus sign (+). Any comment immediately following a select, update, insert, or delete keyword that begins with a (+) will be evaluated by the optimizer. The comment can contain multiple hints. The documentation also states that comment text can be interspersed with hints. I would not recommend this technique, however, as not all hints are documented and you may inadvertently put in a word that that has significance to the optimizer. There can only be one hint-comment per query block. Subsequent comments that start with a (+) will not be evaluated by the optimizer. If you use an alias for an object name in your SQL statement, all hints must refer to the object by its alias. Also note that if you specify an owner name in your statement, the hint should not include the owner name (use an alias, it will make it easier). Listing 16-8 shows a couple of examples

Listing 16-8. *Examples of Hints*

Valid:

```
select /* real comment */ /*+ gather_plan_statistics full (a) */ avg(col1)
from kso.skew a where col1 = 1234234;

select /*+ gather_plan_statistics full (a) */ /* real comment */ avg(col1)
from kso.skew a where col1 = 1234234;

select /*+ gather_plan_statistics full (skew) */ /* real comment */ avg(col1)
from kso.skew where col1 = 1234234;
```

Invalid

```
-- don't use owner in hint
select /*+ gather_plan_statistics full (kso.skew) */ /* real comment */ avg(col1)
from kso.skew  where col1 = 1234234;

-- if you use a table alias it must be used in the hint
select /*+ gather_plan_statistics full (skew) */ /* real comment */ avg(col1)
from kso.skew a where col1 = 1234234;

-- apparently the word comment has a special meaning - disabling the hints
select /*+ real comment gather_plan_statistics more comment full (a) */ avg(col1)
from kso.skew a where col1 = 1234234;

-- the 2nd hint will not be evaluated as a hint
select /*+ gather_plan_statistics */ /*+ full (kso.skew) */ /* real comment */ avg(col1)
from kso.skew  where col1 = 1234234;
```

The format of hints is actually more complicated than the abbreviated version you usually see. The simplified format you normally see is used to specify tables where the hints are embedded directly in the query blocks where the table occurs. This is not always desirable or even possible, so Oracle has a way of declaring hints that specify where the table is located in the SQL structure. This becomes important when specifying hints that affect objects inside of views, for example, and as you'll see later on, for the hint based mechanisms that Oracle uses to try to improve plan stability. The documentation refers to a "global hint format," which basically means the query block an object resides is specified within the hint. Any hint that applies to one or more tables can make use of this global format. The query block names can be manually specified with a hint (QB_NAME) or can be assigned automatically by the system. The system generated names are not always intuitive. In simple statements, they often take the form of SEL$1, SEL$2, etc. (or UPD$1 or DEL$1 for update and delete statements). Here are some examples using the FULL hint:

```
select /*+ full (a) */ avg(col1)
from kso.skew a where col1 = 1234234;

select /*+ full (@SEL$1 a@SEL$1) */ avg(col1)
from kso.skew a where col1 = 1234234;

select /*+ full (a@SEL$1) */ avg(col1)
from kso.skew a where col1 = 1234234;

select /*+ full (@SEL$1 a) */ avg(col1)
from kso.skew a where col1 = 1234234;

select /*+ qb_name (MYQB) full (a@MYQB) */ avg(col1)
from kso.skew a where col1 = 1234234;
```

All five of the above statements are equivalent. The first @SEL$1 is the query block where the hint should be applied. The term a@SEL$1 is the fully qualified table alias. In this case, the whole query block name is redundant. There is only one table and one query block. In general, even when there are multiple query blocks, specifying the query block and then fully qualifying the alias is not necessary. There are situations, though, where you may need both.

There are a couple of ways to determine the correct query block name when system assigned Query Block names are in play. One is to use dbms_xplan with the ALIAS parameter. The other is to look at the data in the OTHER_XML column of V$SQL that contains all the hints that Oracle thinks would be necessary to recreate the plan. These hints are fully qualified. Listing 16-9 shows examples of both techniques.

Listing 16-9. *Examples of Determining the Correct Query Block Name*

```
SYS@LAB112> @sql_hints
SYS@LAB112> select
  2  extractvalue(value(d), '/hint') as outline_hints
  3  from
  4  xmltable('/*/outline_data/hint'
  5  passing (
  6  select
  7  xmltype(other_xml) as xmlval
  8  from
  9  v$sql_plan
 10  where
 11  sql_id like nvl('&sql_id',sql_id)
 12  and child_number = &child_no
 13  and other_xml is not null
 14  )
 15  ) d;
Enter value for sql_id: 14swym6ry0x99
Enter value for child_no: 0
```

```
OUTLINE_HINTS
--------------------------------------------------------------------------------
IGNORE_OPTIM_EMBEDDED_HINTS
OPTIMIZER_FEATURES_ENABLE('11.2.0.1')
DB_VERSION('11.2.0.1')
ALL_ROWS
OUTLINE_LEAF(@"SEL$5DA710D3")
UNNEST(@"SEL$2")
OUTLINE(@"SEL$1")
OUTLINE(@"SEL$2")
INDEX(@"SEL$5DA710D3" "DEPARTMENTS"@"SEL$1" ("DEPARTMENTS"."DEPARTMENT_ID"))
FULL(@"SEL$5DA710D3" "EMPLOYEES"@"SEL$2")
LEADING(@"SEL$5DA710D3" "DEPARTMENTS"@"SEL$1" "EMPLOYEES"@"SEL$2")
USE_MERGE(@"SEL$5DA710D3" "EMPLOYEES"@"SEL$2")

12 rows selected.


SYS@LAB112> select * from table(dbms_xplan.display_cursor('&sql_id','&child_no','alias'))
  2  /
Enter value for sql_id: 14swym6ry0x99
Enter value for child_no:

PLAN_TABLE_OUTPUT
--------------------------------------------------------------------------------
SQL_ID  14swym6ry0x99, child number 0
-------------------------------------
select /* not in */ department_name    from hr.departments    where
department_id not in (select department_id from hr.employees)

Plan hash value: 4201340344
```

Id	Operation	Name	Rows	Bytes	Cost (%CPU)	Time
0	SELECT STATEMENT				6 (100)	
1	MERGE JOIN ANTI NA		17	323	6 (17)	00:00:01
2	SORT JOIN		27	432	2 (0)	00:00:01
3	TABLE ACCESS BY INDEX ROWID	DEPARTMENTS	27	432	2 (0)	00:00:01
4	INDEX FULL SCAN	DEPT_ID_PK	27		1 (0)	00:00:01
* 5	SORT UNIQUE		107	321	4 (25)	00:00:01
6	TABLE ACCESS FULL	EMPLOYEES	107	321	3 (0)	00:00:01

```
Query Block Name / Object Alias (identified by operation id):
---------------------------------------------------------------

   1 - SEL$5DA710D3
   3 - SEL$5DA710D3 / DEPARTMENTS@SEL$1
   4 - SEL$5DA710D3 / DEPARTMENTS@SEL$1
   6 - SEL$5DA710D3 / EMPLOYEES@SEL$2

Predicate Information (identified by operation id):
---------------------------------------------------

   5 - access("DEPARTMENT_ID"="DEPARTMENT_ID")
       filter("DEPARTMENT_ID"="DEPARTMENT_ID")


33 rows selected.
```

Notice that the query block names in this example are more complex than the simple SEL$1 although the aliases still use the SEL$1 format referencing their original position in the statement. The complex Query Block names are due to transformations done by the optimizer. Listing 16-10 shows what happens when you run the same query with query transformation turned off .

Listing 16-10. *The Same Query with Query Transformation Turned Off.*

```
SYS@LAB112> @dplan_alias
Enter value for sql_id: 5nz6s5j41rsrt
Enter value for child_no: 0

PLAN_TABLE_OUTPUT
--------------------------------------------------------------------------------------------
SQL_ID  5nz6s5j41rsrt, child number 0
-------------------------------------
select /* NOT IN */ /*+ no_query_transformation */ department_name
from hr.departments dept   where department_id not in (select
department_id from hr.employees emp)

Plan hash value: 3416340233
```

Id	Operation	Name	Rows	Bytes	Cost (%CPU)	Time
0	SELECT STATEMENT				30 (100)	
* 1	FILTER					
2	TABLE ACCESS FULL	DEPARTMENTS	27	432	3 (0)	00:00:01
* 3	TABLE ACCESS FULL	EMPLOYEES	2	6	2 (0)	00:00:01

```
Query Block Name / Object Alias (identified by operation id):
-----------------------------------------------------------------

   1 - SEL$1
   2 - SEL$1 / DEPT@SEL$1
   3 - SEL$2 / EMP@SEL$2

Predicate Information (identified by operation id):
----------------------------------------------------

   1 - filter( IS NULL)
   3 - filter(LNNVL("DEPARTMENT_ID"<>:B1))
```

Notice that the more complicated Query Block names have disappeared. Furthermore, when you specify your own query block names, you still get a generated name if a transformation takes place. This makes sense if you think about it. Transformations can completely change the structure of the query, turning a statement with a subquery (like this example) into a join, for example. This combines two query blocks into a single new block. It is for this reason that I prefer to use the fully qualified alias rather than the hint format that includes a Query Block name as the first element of the hint. For comparison, Listing 16-11 shows another plan dump where transformations were allowed and the Query Blocks were explicitly named.

Listing 16-11. *Explicitly Named Query Blocks*

```
SYS@LAB112> @dplan_alias
Enter value for sql_id: 3fmskpabbf8y9
Enter value for child_no:

PLAN_TABLE_OUTPUT
-------------------------------------------------------------------------------------------
SQL_ID  3fmskpabbf8y9, child number 0
-------------------------------------
select /* NOT IN */ /*+ qb_name(outer) */ department_name    from
hr.departments dept    where department_id not in (select /*+
qb_name(inner) */ department_id from hr.employees emp)

Plan hash value: 4201340344
```

```
-------------------------------------------------------------------------------------
| Id  | Operation                      | Name        | Rows  | Bytes | Cost (%CPU)| Time     |
-------------------------------------------------------------------------------------
|   0 | SELECT STATEMENT               |             |       |       |   6 (100)|          |
|   1 |  MERGE JOIN ANTI NA            |             |    17 |   323 |   6  (17)| 00:00:01|
|   2 |   SORT JOIN                    |             |    27 |   432 |   2   (0)| 00:00:01|
|   3 |    TABLE ACCESS BY INDEX ROWID | DEPARTMENTS |    27 |   432 |   2   (0)| 00:00:01|
|   4 |     INDEX FULL SCAN            | DEPT_ID_PK  |    27 |       |   1   (0)| 00:00:01|
|*  5 |   SORT UNIQUE                  |             |   107 |   321 |   4  (25)| 00:00:01|
|   6 |    TABLE ACCESS FULL           | EMPLOYEES   |   107 |   321 |   3   (0)| 00:00:01|
-------------------------------------------------------------------------------------
```

```
Query Block Name / Object Alias (identified by operation id):
-------------------------------------------------------------

   1 - SEL$F38A2936
   3 - SEL$F38A2936 / DEPT@OUTER    ⬅== The alias remains in tact
   4 - SEL$F38A2936 / DEPT@OUTER        even though a Query Block Name has
   6 - SEL$F38A2936 / EMP@INNER         been generated due to transformation.

Predicate Information (identified by operation id):
---------------------------------------------------

   5 - access("DEPARTMENT_ID"="DEPARTMENT_ID")
       filter("DEPARTMENT_ID"="DEPARTMENT_ID")


34 rows selected.
```

Notice that the aliases retained their original names even though the Query Block was renamed due to the transformation. The transformation can be verified by a 10053 trace, which details the decision making process that the optimizer goes through when determining an execution plan. Listing 16-12 shows an excerpt from the trace file for the above statement.

Listing 16-12. *An excerpt from the Trace File*

```
Registered qb: OUTER 0xf64c3e34 (HINT OUTER)
---------------------
QUERY BLOCK SIGNATURE
---------------------
  signature (): qb_name=OUTER nbfros=1 flg=0
    fro(0): flg=4 objn=73928 hint_alias="DEPT"@"OUTER"

Registered qb: INNER 0xf64c1df0 (HINT INNER)
---------------------
QUERY BLOCK SIGNATURE
---------------------
  signature (): qb_name=INNER nbfros=1 flg=0
    fro(0): flg=4 objn=73933 hint_alias="EMP"@"INNER"


. . .


JPPD: Applying transformation directives
query block OUTER transformed to SEL$F38A2936 (#1)


. . .
```

```
Final query after transformations:******* UNPARSED QUERY IS *******
SELECT /*+ QB_NAME ("OUTER") */ "DEPT"."DEPARTMENT_NAME" "DEPARTMENT_NAME" FROM
"HR"."EMPLOYEES" "EMP","HR"."DEPARTMENTS" "DEPT" WHERE
"DEPT"."DEPARTMENT_ID"="EMP"."DEPARTMENT_ID" AND  NOT EXISTS (SELECT /*+ QB_NAME ("INNER")
*/ 0 FROM "HR"."EMPLOYEES" "EMP" WHERE "EMP"."DEPARTMENT_ID" IS NULL)

. . .

Dumping Hints
=============
atom_hint=(@=0xf6473d1c err=0 resol=1 used=1 token=1003 org=1 lvl=2 txt=QB_NAME ("OUTER") )
====================== END SQL Statement Dump ======================
```

The trace file shows the original query blocks along with the objects in them. It shows that the first Query Block (named OUTER) was transformed into SEL$F38A2936. And it shows the final version of the statement that was executed. Notice that in the final version the original subquery is gone. It has been merged (unnested) into the OUTER query as a join, and a new subquery has been introduced that checks to see if DEPARTMENT_ID is null. Finally, there is a section at the bottom of every 10053 trace that shows hints that have been evaluated. I'd like to think that the err=0 means that there was not an error and the used=1 means that the hint was used, but I have not found these values to be consistent with my observations of whether a hint was actually used or not, although I think you can assume that the optimizer at least recognized the hint if it shows up in this section of the trace file.

Plan Control: Without Access to the Code

One of the most frustrating problems you face as DBAs is not being able to fix bad code. Your inability to change the code occurs for many reasons. In some cases, you are dealing with packaged applications where the code is just not available. In other cases, the politics of an organization can dictate lengthy delays in making changes to code. Regardless of the reasons, Oracle specialists often find themselves in the unenviable position of being asked to make things better without touching the code.

Fortunately, Oracle provides many options for doing just that.

Both changing statistics and modifying database parameters come to mind as effective techniques for affecting execution plan changes. These techniques can cause sweeping changes that affect many SQL statements. Obviously, the statistics need to be as accurate as possible. It will be very difficult to get reasonable performance if the statistics are not correct. The database also needs to be configured correctly, although from a stability standpoint, it is not imperative that every parameter be set to an "optimal" value. In fact, there are often trade offs that must be made. But the good news is that stability can usually be accomplished regardless of the configuration as long as it stays consistent.

Changing access paths (i.e. adding or removing indexes) can also be an effective tool. Of course, this is also a sweeping change that can affect many SQL statements (maybe for the better, maybe not). Certainly adding an index will impose additional overhead to DML operations. This approach generally requires a fair amount of testing to be assured that statements other than the one you are attempting to fix are not negatively impacted.

Among the most effective approaches, though, are techniques that focus on modifying execution plans of individual statements. Oracle has provided various mechanisms for accomplishing this over the years such as Stored Outlines, SQL Profiles, and Baselines. These techniques provide laser-like specificity by limiting their effect to a single statement (or in some cases, a set of statements). While these constructs are extremely powerful, they are not well documented and therefore not particularly well understood. They also suffer from some quirkiness. For example, despite what the documentation implies regarding Outlines locking execution plans, there are situations where creating an Outline on an existing statement, instead of locking in the current plan, will actually cause the plan to change. This quirk is not limited to the older Outline construct. It has been carried forward to the newer SQL Profiles and SQL Baselines as well. And if you think about it, the basic mechanism of these constructs (applying hints) is somewhat suspect. The more complicated a SQL statement is, the more options the optimizer has and the more difficult it becomes to narrow down the choices to a single plan. Nevertheless, it is a widely used technique and probably the best tool at your disposal for controlling the plan of a single statement. So let's discuss each of these options in a little more detail.

Option 1: Change the Statistics

If statistics are inaccurate, they should be fixed. In order for the optimizer to do its job, you must give it the information it needs in order to make good decisions. Karen Morton wrote an excellent paper on the very complicated subject of gathering appropriate object statistics in 2009 called *Managing Statistics for Optimal Query Performance*. It can be found at http://method-r.com/downloads/doc_download/11-managing-statistics-for-optimal-query-performance-karen-morton.

I highly recommend that you review Karen's paper. In terms of plan stability, just changing the stats is not sufficient. Generally, it's the method of gathering them that needs to be addressed. While a complete discussion of statistics gathering is out of the scope of this chapter, there are a few things that I believe are important to know:

- The default stats gathering job in 10g will generate histograms on most columns. This is usually not a good thing. 11g does a much better job of gathering histograms where they are appropriate.

- Histograms generated in 10g with small sample sizes are often not very accurate (dbms_stats.auto_sample_size often chooses very small sample sizes that result in inaccurate histograms).

- Histograms are most useful for columns where the values are not evenly distributed.

- Bind variables and histograms do not work well together if the data distribution is uneven.

- Statistics should be gathered (or set) often enough to make sure that max and min values are close to reality. This is especially important with large tables where it takes a while for the default stats job to determine it's time to re-gather (more than 10% of the rows have been modified). Plans can change radically (and unexpectedly) when the values specified in Where clauses are above or below the range that the optimizer thinks is there.

- Partitions should be pre-populated with representative stats if they will be queried before the normal statistics gathering job has had a chance to run; otherwise, you may get the dreaded "Why do my jobs always run slow on Mondays?" syndrome.

- Most importantly, you should be intimately familiar with how statistics are generated on your systems.

The bottom line is that object statistics need to be accurate. If they are way out of whack, there may be little choice but to address the issue before attempting any other measures. Of course, as in all triage situations, you may have to take some expedient actions in order to save the patient.

One last thing on stats: Oracle provides the ability to manually set the values for the object statistics that the optimizer uses. Manually setting statistics for an object is a perfectly valid technique in some situations. For example, manually setting a maximum value for a frequently queried column that is constantly increasing and running ahead of the standard statistics gathering might be a perfectly reasonable thing to do. Building your own histogram with the values that are important to your application is also possible and may be a reasonable approach if you can't get the normal stats gathering procedures to do what you want. Listing 16-13 shows a couple of scripts that manually set column statistics.

Listing 16-13. *Scripts that Manually Set Column Statistics*

```
SYS@LAB112> @col_stats
Enter value for owner: KSO
Enter value for table_name: LITTLE_SKEW
Enter value for column_name:

COLUMN_NAME DATA_TYPE AVG_LEN    DENSITY    NDV ... LAST_ANAL LOW_VALUE   HIGH_VALUE
----------- --------- ------- ----------- ------- ... --------- ----------- -----------
PK_COL      NUMBER          5 .000010000  99,999 ... 03-AUG-10 1           1000002
COL1        NUMBER          4 .000005000       2 ... 03-AUG-10 1           999999
COL2        VARCHAR2        8 .000005000       1 ... 03-AUG-10 TESTING     TESTING
COL3        DATE            8 .000005000       1 ... 03-AUG-10 08-nov-2008 08-nov-2008
COL4        VARCHAR2        2 .000005000       2 ... 03-AUG-10 N           Y

SYS@LAB112> @set_col_stats_max
Enter value for owner: KSO
Enter value for table_name:
Enter value for column_name:
Enter value for minimum:
Enter value for maximum XXXXXXX

PL/SQL procedure successfully completed.
SYS@LAB112> @col_stats
Enter value for owner: KSO
Enter value for table_name: LITTLE_SKEW
Enter value for column_name:

COLUMN_NAME DATA_TYPE AVG_LEN    DENSITY    NDV ... LAST_ANAL LOW_VALUE   HIGH_VALUE
----------- --------- ------- ----------- ------- ... --------- ----------- -----------
PK_COL      NUMBER          5 .000010000  99,999 ... 03-AUG-10 1           1000002
COL1        NUMBER          4 .000005000       2 ... 03-AUG-10 1           999999
COL2        VARCHAR2        8 .000005000       1 ... 13-AUG-10 TESTING     XXXXXXX
COL3        DATE            8 .000005000       1 ... 03-AUG-10 08-nov-2008 08-nov-2008
COL4        VARCHAR2        2 .000005000       2 ... 03-AUG-10 N           Y

SYS@LAB112> @set_col_stats
Enter value for owner: KSO
Enter value for table_name: LITTLE_SKEW
Enter value for col_name: COL1
Enter value for ndv: 10
Enter value for density: 1/10
Enter value for nullcnt: 0

PL/SQL procedure successfully completed.

SYS@LAB112> @col_stats
Enter value for owner: KSO
```

```
Enter value for table_name: LITTLE_SKEW
Enter value for column_name:
```

COLUMN_NAME	DATA_TYPE	AVG_LEN	DENSITY	NDV	...	LAST_ANAL	LOW_VALUE	HIGH_VALUE
PK_COL	NUMBER	5	.000010000	99,999	...	03-AUG-10	1	1000002
COL1	NUMBER	4	.100000000	10	...	13-AUG-10	1	999999
COL2	VARCHAR2	8	.000005000	1	...	13-AUG-10	TESTING	XXXXXXX
COL3	DATE	8	.000005000	1	...	03-AUG-10	08-nov-2008	08-nov-2008
COL4	VARCHAR2	2	.000005000	2	...	03-AUG-10	N	Y

These scripts make use of the dbms_stats.set_column_stats procedure to manually set the column level statistics. The set_col_stats_max.sql script is probably the more useful of the two. Notice also that the call to the procedure modifies the LAST_ANALYZED field.

Don't be afraid of this technique. Remember, you know your data and how your applications use it (often better than Oracle does). Oracle has provided you the tools to set the statistics as you see fit. Keep in mind, though, that if you do decide to make manual changes to statistics, you will have to decide how to integrate those changes into the normal statistics gathering routine in place on your systems. Don't make the mistake of manually fixing some statistics issue and then have the standard stats gathering job come along and wipe out your work a week later.

Option 2: Change Database Parameters

This is a SQL book so I won't discuss this technique in depth. In general, I am very hesitant to attempt to modify plans by manipulating database parameters at the system level except in situations where something is completely misconfigured and I have a reasonable amount of time to test. There are a few parameters that show up on the frequent offenders list such as optimizer_index_cost_adj, optimizer_index_caching, optimizer_mode, cursor_sharing, and db_file_multiblock_read_count. Basically, anything with a non-default value is suspect in my mind, particularly if there is not a well defined reason why it's set to a non-default value. The biggest problem with changing parameters is that they affect the optimizer's calculations for every single statement in the system. That means that every single statement will be re-evaluated and the optimizer may come up with a new plan. Maybe that's what you want, but changing parameters certainly provides the opportunity for many plans to change, which is by definition the opposite of increasing stability.

Option 3: Add or Remove Access Paths

There are definitely times when a new index will significantly improve performance of a query. And occasionally the statement is important enough to create one in a production system. But the problem with adding an index is that a single index can change the execution plans of a number of statements. Assuming that the statistics are in good shape, adding an index should rarely have a significant negative affect on a query. Nevertheless, indexes should be tested with a representative workload prior to introduction into production. Also, don't forget that adding an index will most definitely add overhead to DML that affects the columns you index.

And while I'm on the subject, removing unneeded indexes can significantly improve DML statements. It's actually more common to see tables that are over-indexed than ones that are under-indexed. That's because it's scarier to remove an index than to create one. As a result, it usually takes an Act of Congress to get one removed from a production system. One of the main reasons for this is that it can take a lot of time to re-create an index on a large table. 11g has a great new feature that makes this process more palatable, by the way. Indexes can now be marked as invisible, which means that the optimizer doesn't consider them when determining execution plans. So you can see how your application behaves in production minus the index that you intend to drop, without actually dropping it. Invisible indexes continue to be maintained so you won't see any improvement in DML speed due to making an index invisible, but you will be to make it visible again by simply issuing an alter index statement should dropping the index turn out to have been a bad idea.

So adding (or removing) an index is a technique that can be used to modify execution plans, but it is not a particularly useful one when it comes to plan stability issues. If plans change, you need to solve the issue that is causing them to change or prevent them from changing. So while I hate to say never, adding or removing an index is unlikely to do that.

Option 4: Apply Hint Based Plan-Control Mechanisms

Oracle Database 11g implements three plan-control mechanisms that rely upon optimizer hints. These mechanisms are so important and useful that they deserve a top-level section of their own.

Plan Control: With Hint-Based Mechanisms

The three hint-based mechanisms supported in Oracle Database 11g are:

- Outlines
- SQL Profiles
- SQL Baselines

These mechanisms are each designed with slightly different goals in mind, but they use the same basic approach of giving the application of a set of hints that is named and associated with a SQL statement. The hints are then applied behind the scenes to any matching statement that is executed.

Outlines

Outlines, or Stored Outlines as they are sometimes called, were introduced shortly after the CBO. They are the oldest of the hint-based mechanisms. The documentation and marketing material also referred to the new feature as "Plan Stability." The design goal was to "lock" a specific plan for a statement. This was done by using the CREATE OUTLINE statement to parse a SQL statement (including coming up with an execution plan), determine a set of hints that should be sufficient to force the optimizer to pick that plan, and then store the hints. The next time a matching SQL statement was processed by the database, the hints would be applied behind the scenes before the execution plan was determined. The intention was that the set of hints would be sufficient to allow one and only one plan for the given statement, regardless of the optimizer settings, statistics, etc. By the way, "matching" basically means that the text of the statement matches. Originally, outlines had to match character for character just like the normal rules for sharing SQL statements, but for some reason, Oracle later decided that the matching algorithm should be somewhat relaxed. What that means is that in any version you're likely to run into today, whitespace is collapsed and differences in case are ignored. So (at least as far as Outlines are concerned) "select * from dual" is the same as "SELECT   *   FROM DuAl". You'll still get two different statements in the shared pool, but they will use the same Outline, if one exists.

With 9i, Oracle started to enhance this feature by adding the ability to edit the outlines themselves, but they never really completed the job. In fact, they pretty much quit doing anything with the feature after 10gR1. The script that creates the DBMS_OUTLN package ($ORACLE_HOME/rdbms/admin/dbmsol.sql), for example, has not been updated since early in 2004 (with the exception of a tweak to keep it working in 11g). At any rate, the feature has worked pretty well over the years; in fact, it still works in 11g, although the documentation has been warning us for the last several years that the feature has been deprecated and is no longer being maintained.

The first version of the feature required you to create an Outline by specifying the statement inline in a CREATE OUTLINE statement. Here's an example:

```
SYS@LAB112> create or replace outline junk for category test on
  2  select avg(pk_col) from kso.skew a where col1 > 0;

Outline created.
```

This syntax was a bit unwieldy due to having to specify the complete SQL statement as part of the command. Fortunately, a way to create an Outline was later introduced that allowed an outline to be created on a statement that already existed in the shared pool. The CREATE_OUTLINE procedure was added to the DBMS_OUTLN package to do this. In general, it was a better approach because it was much easier to identify a cursor (with a hash_value) than to cut and paste a long SQL statement on to the command line. It also allowed you to see the plan that had been arrived at by the optimizer prior to creating the Outline. Listing 16-14 shows the definition of the procedure and an example of its use.

Listing 16-14. *CREATE_OUTLINE*

```
PROCEDURE CREATE_OUTLINE
 Argument Name                  Type                      In/Out Default?
 ------------------------------ ------------------------- ------ --------
 HASH_VALUE                     NUMBER                    IN
 CHILD_NUMBER                   NUMBER                    IN
 CATEGORY                       VARCHAR2                  IN     DEFAULT


SYS@LAB112> select sql_id, hash_value, child_number from v$sql
  2  where sql_text like 'select avg(pk_col) from kso.skew where col1 = 136133'
  3  /

SQL_ID        HASH_VALUE CHILD_NUMBER
------------- ---------- ------------
fh70fkqr78zz3 2926870499            0


SYS@LAB112> exec dbms_outln.create_outline(2926870499,0,'DEFAULT');

PL/SQL procedure successfully completed.


SYS@LAB112> select category, ol_name, hintcount hints, sql_text from outln.ol$;
```

```
CATEGORY    OL_NAME                            HINTS SQL_TEXT
----------  ---------------------------------  -------------------------------------------------
DEFAULT     OUTLINE_11.2.0.1                       6 select /*+ index(a SKEW_COL2_COL1) */
DEFAULT     SYS_OUTLINE_10081416353513714          6 select avg(pk_col) from kso.skew where col1=
TEST        JUNK                                   6 select avg(pk_col) from kso.skew a where
```

So you can see that the Outline was created in the DEFAULT category with a very ugly name and that it has 6 hints assigned to it. Let's have a quick look at the hints:

```
SYS@LAB112> @outline_hints
Enter value for name: SYS_OUTLINE_10081416353513714
Enter value for hint:

NAME                            HINT
------------------------------  ------------------------------------------------------------------------
SYS_OUTLINE_10081416353513714   IGNORE_OPTIM_EMBEDDED_HINTS
SYS_OUTLINE_10081416353513714   OPTIMIZER_FEATURES_ENABLE('11.2.0.1')
SYS_OUTLINE_10081416353513714   DB_VERSION('11.2.0.1')
SYS_OUTLINE_10081416353513714   ALL_ROWS
SYS_OUTLINE_10081416353513714   OUTLINE_LEAF(@"SEL$1")
SYS_OUTLINE_10081416353513714   INDEX_RS_ASC(@"SEL$1" "SKEW"@"SEL$1" ("SKEW"."COL1"))

6 rows selected.
```

In 10g and 11g, v$sql_plan has a column called other_xml. This column is a clob and all the rows are null except the top record in the plan, which contains a mishmash of stuff including the database version, the parsing schema name, the plan_hash_value, etc. But the most interesting bit is that the complete set of hints that will be assigned to an Outline if one is created using the DBMS_OUTLN.CREATE_OUTLINE procedure, also contained in that column. Of course, it's all in XLM format so you'll have to do an XML type query to get it to come out nicely (or you can just use the sql_hints.sql script):

```
SYS@LAB112> @sql_hints
Enter value for sql_id: fh70fkqr78zz3
Enter value for child_no: 0

OUTLINE_HINTS
------------------------------------------------------------------------------------------
IGNORE_OPTIM_EMBEDDED_HINTS
OPTIMIZER_FEATURES_ENABLE('11.2.0.1')
DB_VERSION('11.2.0.1')
ALL_ROWS
OUTLINE_LEAF(@"SEL$1")
INDEX_SS(@"SEL$1" "SKEW"@"SEL$1" ("SKEW"."COL2" "SKEW"."COL1"))

6 rows selected.
```

Outlines definitely suffer from some quirkiness. In fact, I have previously described them as "half baked."

Here are a few of things you should be aware of:

- Outlines aren't used unless you set the USE_STORED_OUTLINES pseudo parameter. This can be set at the session or the system level. Setting this at the session level only makes sense to me for testing purposes. The value can be TRUE, FALSE, or a category name. (More about categories in a minute.) The default value for 9i, 10g, and 11g is FALSE. This means that even if an Outline is created, it won't be used. The really irritating thing about USE_STORED_OUTLINES is that it is not a full-fledged parameter, so you can't see what it's set to by selecting from the v$parameter view or it's underlying X$ views (where the hidden parameters are exposed). Fairlie Rego has a post on his blog about using oradebug to see whether it has been set or not. More importantly, this quirk means that the USE_STORED_OUTLINES setting is not persisted across instance bounces. This prompted an official bug and enhancement request (see Oracle Support Note:560331.1). The official response was to suggest a database trigger to set the value when an instance is started (see outline_startup_trigger.sql in the example download for the recommended trigger).

- The DBMS_OUTLN.CREATE_OUTLINE procedure uses the old HASH_VALUE identifier as opposed to the newer SQL_ID that was introduced in 10g. While most of the internal structures were updated to use SQL_ID, Outlines never were. This is just a slight irritation as it means you have to find the hash value to use the DBMS_OUTLN.CREATE_OUTLINE procedure. (See the create_outline.sql script in the example download for a way to get around this.)

- The DBMS_OUTLN.CREATE_OUTLINE procedure is a bit buggy. It often results in error 1330 that disconnects your session from Oracle. There is a Oracle Support note describing this issue (Note:463288.1) that references a bug (Bug 5454975) that is supposed to be fixed in 10.2.0.4. Anyway, the bottom line is that you should execute the command to enable stored Outlines at the session level (i.e. ALTER SESSION SET USE_STORED_OUTLINES=TRUE) before attempting to create an Outline with the DBMS_OUTLN.CREATE_OUTLINE procedure (again, see the create_outline.sql script).

- The DBMS_OUTLN.CREATE_OUTLINE procedure does not allow a name to be specified for an Outline. Instead, it creates a system generated name. This is another minor irritation as Outlines can be renamed easily enough with the ALTER OUTLINE command (see the create_outline.sql script yet again for a way to do this when creating an outline).

- Outlines are grouped together into categories. Each Outline is assigned to a single category. The default category is DEFAULT. If USE_STORED_OUTLINES is set to TRUE, Outlines in the DEFAULT category will be used. If USE_STORED_OUTLINES is set to some other text string, only Outlines in the category that matches the value of USE_STORED_OUTLINES will be used.

- As with all hints, Outline hints are directives that will be obeyed unless they are invalid. Invalid hints will be silently ignored. An invalid hint does not necessarily cause other hints in the Outline to be ignored or disabled however.

Listing 16-15 shows an example of creating an Outline the old fashioned way (using the Create Outline statement):

Listing 16-15. *Using the Create Outline statement*

```
SYS@LAB112> @outlines
Enter value for category:
Enter value for name:

CATEGORY NAME              USED      ENABLED  HINTS SQL_TEXT
-------- ---------------- --------  -------- ----- -------------------------------------------
DEFAULT  OUTLINE_11.2.0.1 UNUSED    ENABLED      6 select /*+ index(a SKEW_COL2_COL1) */
TEST     JUNK             UNUSED    ENABLED      6 select avg(pk_col) from kso.skew a where

2 rows selected.

SYS@LAB112> create or replace outline junk2 on select avg(pk_col)
  2  from kso.skew a where col1 > 1;

Outline created.

SYS@LAB112> @outlines
Enter value for category:
Enter value for name:

CATEGORY NAME              USED      ENABLED  HINTS SQL_TEXT
-------- ---------------- --------  -------- ----- -------------------------------------------
DEFAULT  JUNK2            UNUSED    ENABLED      6 select avg(pk_col) from kso.skew a where
DEFAULT  OUTLINE_11.2.0.1 UNUSED    ENABLED      6 select /*+ index(a SKEW_COL2_COL1) */
TEST     JUNK             UNUSED    ENABLED      6 select avg(pk_col) from kso.skew a where

3 rows selected.

SYS@LAB112> select avg(pk_col) from kso.skew a where col1 > 0;

AVG(PK_COL)
-----------
 16093749.3

SYS@LAB112> @find_sql
Enter value for sql_text: select avg(pk_col) from kso.skew a where col1 > 0
Enter value for sql_id:

SQL_ID        CHILD  PLAN_HASH  EXECS AVG_ETIME AVG_LIO  SQL_TEXT
------------- ------ ---------- ----- --------- -------- --------------------------------
05cq2hb1r37tr     0  568322376     1      9.74  162,310  select avg(pk_col) from kso.skew
                                                         a where col1 > 0

1 row selected.
```

```
SYS@LAB112> @dplan
Enter value for sql_id: 05cq2hb1r37tr
Enter value for child_no:

PLAN_TABLE_OUTPUT
----------------------------------------------------------------------------------------
SQL_ID  05cq2hb1r37tr, child number 0
-------------------------------------
select avg(pk_col) from kso.skew a where col1 > 0

Plan hash value: 568322376

-----------------------------------------------------------------------------
| Id  | Operation          | Name | Rows  | Bytes | Cost (%CPU)| Time     |
-----------------------------------------------------------------------------
|   0 | SELECT STATEMENT   |      |       |       | 28420 (100)|          |
|   1 |  SORT AGGREGATE    |      |     1 |    24 |            |          |
|*  2 |   TABLE ACCESS FULL| SKEW |   32M |  732M | 28420  (2)| 00:05:42 |
-----------------------------------------------------------------------------

Predicate Information (identified by operation id):
---------------------------------------------------

   2 - filter("COL1">0)


19 rows selected.
```

Notice that there is no indication that the statement is using an Outline. The outlines.sql script queries the outln.ol$ table that holds the outline definitions and it reports your new Outline as being UNUSED. Also, the xplan output would include a note stating that an Outline was used if it had been used. The reason that the Outline hasn't been used is because Outlines are not enabled by default. Listing 16-16 shows the command to enable them and then what you should expect to see when a statement is using an Outline.

Listing 16-16. *Enabling Outlines*

```
SYS@LAB112> alter session set use_stored_outlines=true;

Session altered.

SYS@LAB112> select avg(pk_col) from kso.skew a where col1 > 1;

AVG(PK_COL)
-----------
 16049999.5

1 row selected.
```

```
SYS@LAB112> @find_sql
Enter value for sql_text: select avg(pk_col) from kso.skew a where col1 > 1
Enter value for sql_id:

SQL_ID        CHILD  PLAN_HASH  EXECS  AVG_ETIME   VG_LIO SQL_TEXT
------------- ------ ---------- ----- ----------- -------- ----------------------------------------
3u57q0vkbag55      0 568322376      1        9.97  162,527 select avg(pk_col)
                                                           from kso.skew a where col1
> 1


1 row selected.

SYS@LAB112> @dplan
Enter value for sql_id: 3u57q0vkbag55
Enter value for child_no:

PLAN_TABLE_OUTPUT
---------------------------------------------------------------------------------------------
SQL_ID  3u57q0vkbag55, child number 0
-------------------------------------
select avg(pk_col) from kso.skew a where col1 > 1

Plan hash value: 568322376

----------------------------------------------------------------------------
| Id  | Operation            | Name | Rows  | Bytes | Cost (%CPU)| Time     |
----------------------------------------------------------------------------
|   0 | SELECT STATEMENT     |      |       |       | 28414 (100)|          |
|   1 |  SORT AGGREGATE      |      |     1 |    24 |            |          |
|*  2 |   TABLE ACCESS FULL| SKEW |   29M|  664M| 28414   (2)| 00:05:41 |
----------------------------------------------------------------------------

Predicate Information (identified by operation id):
---------------------------------------------------

   2 - filter("COL1">1)

Note
-----
   - outline "JUNK2" used for this statement


23 rows selected.
```

```
SYS@LAB112> @outlines
Enter value for category:
Enter value for name:

CATEGORY NAME               USED      ENABLED  HINTS SQL_TEXT
-------- ---------------- -------- --------  ---------------------------------------------
DEFAULT  JUNK2               USED      ENABLED      6 select avg(pk_col) from kso.skew a where
DEFAULT  OUTLINE_11.2.0.1 UNUSED    ENABLED      6 select /*+ index(a SKEW_COL2_COL1) */
TEST     JUNK             UNUSED    ENABLED      6 select avg(pk_col) from kso.skew a where

3 rows selected.
```

Notice that the Note section of the xplan output clearly shows that Outline JUNK2 was used for this statement. Also notice that the outlines.sql script now reports that the Outline has been USED. Listing 16-17 shows an example of getting the optimizer to use Outline JUNK which is not in the DEFAULT category.

Listing 16-17. *DEFAULT Category Outline Example*

```
SYS@LAB112> select avg(pk_col) from kso.skew a where col1 > 0;

AVG(PK_COL)
-----------
 16093749.3

1 row selected.

SYS@LAB112> @find_sql
Enter value for sql_text: select avg(pk_col) from kso.skew a where col1 > 0
Enter value for sql_id:

SQL_ID         CHILD  PLAN_HASH EXECS AVG_ETIME AVG_LIO SQL_TEXT
------------- ------ ---------- ----- --------- ------- --------------------------------
05cq2hb1r37tr      0  568322376     1      9.89 162,304 select avg(pk_col) from kso.skew a
                                                        where col1 > 0

1 row selected.
SYS@LAB112> @dplan
Enter value for sql_id: 05cq2hb1r37tr
Enter value for child_no: 1

PLAN_TABLE_OUTPUT
--------------------------------------------------------------------------------------
SQL_ID  05cq2hb1r37tr, child number 1
-------------------------------------
select avg(pk_col) from kso.skew a where col1 > 0
```

Plan hash value: 568322376

```
---------------------------------------------------------------------
| Id  | Operation          | Name | Rows  | Bytes | Cost (%CPU)| Time     |
---------------------------------------------------------------------
|   0 | SELECT STATEMENT   |      |       |       | 28420 (100)|          |
|   1 |  SORT AGGREGATE    |      |     1 |    24 |            |          |
|*  2 |   TABLE ACCESS FULL| SKEW |   32M |  732M | 28420  (2)| 00:05:42 |
---------------------------------------------------------------------
```

Predicate Information (identified by operation id):
----

   2 - filter("COL1">0)

19 rows selected.

SYS@LAB112> @outlines
Enter value for category:
Enter value for name:

```
CATEGORY NAME              USED      ENABLED   HINTS SQL_TEXT
-------- ---------------   --------  --------  -------------------------------------------
DEFAULT  JUNK2             USED      ENABLED       6 select avg(pk_col) from kso.skew a where
DEFAULT  OUTLINE_11.2.0.1  UNUSED    ENABLED       6 select /*+ index(a SKEW_COL2_COL1) */
TEST     JUNK              UNUSED    ENABLED       6 select avg(pk_col) from kso.skew a where
```

3 rows selected.

SYS@LAB112> -- JUNK not used (because it's not in the DEFAULT Category)
SYS@LAB112> -- let's set the category to test
SYS@LAB112>
SYS@LAB112> alter session set use_stored_outlines=test;

Session altered.

SYS@LAB112> select avg(pk_col) from kso.skew a where col1 > 0;

AVG(PK_COL)

 16093749.3

1 row selected.

```
SYS@LAB112> @find_sql
Enter value for sql_text: select avg(pk_col) from kso.skew a where col1 > 0
Enter value for sql_id:

SQL_ID          CHILD  PLAN_HASH EXECS AVG_ETIME  AVG_LIO SQL_TEXT
------------- ------ ---------- ----- --------- -------- ------------------------------------
05cq2hb1r37tr      0  568322376     2     10.35  162,865 select avg(pk_col) from kso.skew a
                                                         where col1 > 0

1 row selected.

SYS@LAB112> @dplan
Enter value for sql_id: 05cq2hb1r37tr
Enter value for child_no:

PLAN_TABLE_OUTPUT
-------------------------------------------------------------------------------------------
SQL_ID  05cq2hb1r37tr, child number 0
-------------------------------------
select avg(pk_col) from kso.skew a where col1 > 0

Plan hash value: 568322376

--------------------------------------------------------------------------
| Id  | Operation          | Name | Rows  | Bytes | Cost (%CPU)| Time     |
--------------------------------------------------------------------------
|   0 | SELECT STATEMENT   |      |       |       | 28420 (100)|          |
|   1 |  SORT AGGREGATE    |      |     1 |    24 |            |          |
|*  2 |   TABLE ACCESS FULL| SKEW |   32M|  732M| 28420   (2)| 00:05:42 |
--------------------------------------------------------------------------

Predicate Information (identified by operation id):
---------------------------------------------------

   2 - filter("COL1">0)

Note
-----
   - outline "JUNK" used for this statement


23 rows selected.

SYS@LAB112> -- now it's working
SYS@LAB112>
SYS@LAB112> @outlines
Enter value for category:
```

```
Enter value for name:

CATEGORY NAME               USED     ENABLED  HINTS SQL_TEXT
-------- ---------------- -------- -------- ---------------------------------------------
DEFAULT  JUNK2              USED     ENABLED      6 select avg(pk_col) from kso.skew a where
DEFAULT  OUTLINE_11.2.0.1 UNUSED   ENABLED      6 select /*+ index(a SKEW_COL2_COL1) */
TEST     JUNK               USED     ENABLED      6 select avg(pk_col) from kso.skew a where

3 rows selected.
```

After using the alter session command to set the category to TEST, the Outline was used. In the final example on Outlines, Listing 16-18 demonstrates the use of the create_outline.sql script which, as mentioned earlier, uses the DBMS_OUTLN.CREATE_OUTLINE procedure to create an Outline.

Listing 16-18. *The create_outline.sql script*

```
SYS@LAB112> -- finally – let's create an outline using the create_outline.sql script
SYS@LAB112>
SYS@LAB112> alter system flush shared_pool;

System altered.

SYS@LAB112> select avg(pk_col) from kso.skew where col1 = 136133;

AVG(PK_COL)
-----------
   15636133

1 row selected.
SYS@LAB112> @find_sql
Enter value for sql_text: %skew%
Enter value for sql_id:

SQL_ID         CHILD  PLAN_HASH EXECS AVG_ETIME  AVG_LIO SQL_TEXT
------------- ------ ---------- ----- --------- --------------------------------------------
84q0zxfzn5u6s      0 2650913906     1       .08      687 select avg(pk_col) from kso.skew where
                                                         col1 = 136133

1 row selected.

SYS@LAB112> @create_outline

Session altered.

Enter value for sql_id: 84q0zxfzn5u6s
Enter value for child_number: 0
Enter value for outline_name (OL_sqlid_planhash): OL_84q0zxfzn5u6s
Enter value for category (DEFAULT):
```

```
Outline OL_84q0zxfzn5u6s created.

PL/SQL procedure successfully completed.

SYS@LAB112> @outlines
Enter value for category:
Enter value for name:

CATEGORY NAME              USED      ENABLED   HINTS SQL_TEXT
-------- ----------------  --------  --------  ----------------------------------------------
DEFAULT  JUNK2             USED      ENABLED   6 select avg(pk_col) from kso.skew a where
DEFAULT  OL_84q0zxfzn5u6s  UNUSED    ENABLED   6 select avg(pk_col) from kso.skew where
DEFAULT  OUTLINE_11.2.0.1  UNUSED    ENABLED   6 select /*+ index(a SKEW_COL2_COL1) */
TEST     JUNK              USED      ENABLED   6 select avg(pk_col) from kso.skew a where
col1

4 rows selected.

SYS@LAB112> select avg(pk_col) from kso.skew a where col1 > 1;

AVG(PK_COL)
-----------
 16049999.5

SYS@LAB112> select avg(pk_col) from kso.skew where col1 = 136133;

1 row selected.

AVG(PK_COL)
-----------
   15636133

1 row selected.

SYS@LAB112> -- now let's check for SQL using Outlines in the shared pool
SYS@LAB112> -- we could also use the find_sql_using_outline.sql script
SYS@LAB112>
SYS@LAB112> select sql_id, sql_text, outline_category
  2  from v$sql where outline_category is not null;

SQL_ID         SQL_TEXT                                                    OUTLINE_CATEGORY
-------------  ----------------------------------------------------------  ----------------
fh70fkqr78zz3 select avg(pk_col) from kso.skew where col1 = 136133         DEFAULT
3u57q0vkbag55 select avg(pk_col) from kso.skew a where col1 > 1            DEFAULT

2 rows selected.
```

There are several things to note in the previous examples:

- The `outlines.sql` script queries the outln.ol$ table that holds the outline definitions.

- Only one category can be used at a time by a single session. In general, if an Outline is not in the DEFAULT category, it will not be used. This means you can create an Outline in some other category for testing without affecting other users.

- The `dplan.sql` script uses DMS_XPLAN.DISPLAY_CURSOR that provides a note section at the bottom of its plan output showing whether an Outline (or Profile or Baseline for that matter) was used.

- The `create_outline.sql` script provides an easier way to create an Outline using the dbms_outln.create_outline procedure. This allows you to see the plan (and the hints) that will be used prior to creating the Outline. It prompts for a sql_id (instead of a hash_value) and renames the outline to something meaningful as opposed to the system generated name that it would normally create.

- The v$sql view has a column (outline_category) that indicates whether a particular SQL statement is using an Outline (although it doesn't tell you which Outline).

Despite their minor flaws, Outlines have been a standard method for influencing execution plans for the last decade, and prior to 10g, they were the only option available. They also work with RAC, so if you create an Outline (or Profile or Baseline, for that matter), it will be picked up across all the nodes in the cluster. So, if you find yourself working on a 9i database, don't discount their usefulness. If you're working on 10g or 11g, read on, as there are other options available.

■**NOTE** I find it useful to include the SQL_ID and the PLAN_HASH_VALUE of a statement in the name of Outlines (and SQL Profiles and Baselines). For Outlines, I have used a convention of OL_sqlid_planhash. This makes it very easy to track the object back to a SQL statement and to see what the original plan was that I was trying to "lock in." See the `create_outline.sql` script for an example.

SQL Profiles

SQL Profiles were introduced in 10g. They are the second iteration of Oracle's hint-based mechanisms for influencing execution plans. SQL Profiles are only documented as a part of the SQL Tuning Advisor, so the only documented way to create a SQL Profile is to run a SQL Tuning Advisor (STA) job. In some cases, STA will offer to create a SQL Profile for you. The task of STA is to analyze a SQL statement and determine if there is a better plan. Since it is allowed as much time as it needs, the advisor can sometimes find better execution plans than the optimizer. That's because it can actually validate the optimizer's original estimates by running various steps in a plan and comparing the actual results to the estimates. When it's all done, if it has found a better plan, it offers to implement a SQL Profile that will hopefully cause the optimizer to generate a new and better plan.

Those offered SQL Profiles are simply a collection of hints (much like Outlines) and they almost always contain a lightly documented hint (OPT_ESTIMATE) that allows the optimizer to scale its estimates for various operations. Essentially, it's a fudge factor. The problem with this hint is that, far from locking a plan in place, it is locking an empirically derived fudge factor in place. This still leaves the optimizer with a lot of flexibility when it comes to choosing a plan. It also sets up a commonly occurring situation where the fudge factors stop making sense as things change over time. It is common for SQL

Profiles generated by STA to work well for a while and then lose their effectiveness, thus the observation that SQL Profiles tend to sour over time.

Regardless of their intended purpose, the fact remains that SQL Profiles provide a mechanism for applying hints to SQL statements behind the scenes in the same basic manner as Outlines. In fact, it appears that the code is actually based on the earlier Outline code. Of course, SQL Profiles have some additional features that provide some distinct advantages, such as:

- SQL Profiles are turned on by default in 10g and 11g. They can be disabled by setting SQLTUNE_CATEGORY to false. This parameter behaves in much the same way as the USE_STORED_OUTLINE parameter. However, it is a real parameter that is exposed via v$parameter and it retains its value across bounces. The value can be TRUE, FALSE, or a category name.

- SQL Profiles are assigned to Categories just like Outlines. Each SQL Profile is assigned to a single category. The default category is DEFAULT. If SQLTUNE_CATEGORY is set to TRUE, outlines in the DEFAULT category will be used. If SQLTUNE_CATEGORY is set to some other text string, only SQL Profiles in the category that matches the value of SQLTUNE_CATEGORY will be used. As with Outlines, this parameter can be changed with an ALTER SESSION statement allowing SQL Profiles to be tested without enabling them for the whole database (more on this later).

- DBMS_SQLTUNE.IMPORT_SQL_PROFILE procedure creates a SQL Profile for a given SQL statement. Any set of hints may be passed to the procedure. While this procedure is not mentioned in the documentation (at least as of 11.2.0.1), it is used by the SQL Tuning Advisor and migration procedures. It is also referenced by at least one Oracle Support document as a way of creating what I call a Manual SQL Profile. This is a giant leap forward from Outlines. With the IMPORT_SQL_PROFILE procedure you can create any hints you want and apply them to any statement you want.

- SQL Profiles have the ability to ignore literals when it comes to matching SQL statements. Think of it as being similar to the cursor_sharing parameter. This means you can have a SQL Profile that will match multiple statements that differ only in their use of literals—without having to set the cursor_sharing parameter for the whole instance. This attribute of a SQL Profile is called FORCE_MATCHING. When you create a SQL Profile you tell it whether you want to set this attribute or not. If the attribute is set to TRUE, the Profile will apply to all statements that have the same signature, regardless of the literals used in the statement.

- There is a view (DBA_SQL_PROFILES) that exposes the SQL profiles that have been created.

- As with all hints, SQL Profile hints are directives that will be obeyed unless they are invalid. Invalid hints will be silently ignored. An invalid hint does not necessarily cause other hints in the SQL Profile to be ignored or disabled, however.

- SQL Profiles appear to be able to apply most, if not all, valid hints.

SQL TUNING ADVISOR

SQL Tuning Advisor is not the answer to plan stability issues. However, it is occasionally capable of finding a better plan than the one the optimizer came up with for the reasons I have already discussed. I occasionally create a tuning task for a problem statement to see what suggestions the Tuning Advisor might have. The example download for this book contains a number of scripts to help with that task (look for `create_tuning_task.sql` and `accept_sql_profile.sql`).

If the Tuning Advisor recommends a SQL Profile, do yourself a favor and create it in an alternate category (TEST, for example). This will allow you to review the hints and test the performance before making your users the guinea pigs in your experiment.

The hints can provide valuable information as to where the optimizer is having problems. Remember that the OPT_ESTIMATE hint applies a scaling factor to various calculations based on its more thorough analysis.

Anywhere that the Advisor comes up with very large or very small scaling factor is a direct pointer to a place in the plan where the optimizer is having trouble. Such a scaling factor can often point out a problem with statistics or in some cases a shortcoming of the optimizer itself. If it is an optimizer shortcoming and if the optimizer is going to keep making the same error no matter how the data changes, then leaving an STA SQL Profile in place may be perfectly reasonable.

If, on the other hand, you're looking for a way to lock in a specific plan, then you may want to consider creating another hint-based object (Outline, Profile, or Baseline) that contains directive hints instead of the OPT_ESITMATE hint. This is fairly easy to accomplish, as all three of these mechanisms can exist on the same statement. For example, you could accept the STA SQL Profile and then create an Outline on the same statement. You could also use the `lock_STA_profile.sql` script from the example download to do away with the OPT_ESTIMATE-based Profile and replace it with a SQL Profile using directive type hints. For further information see this blog post: `http://kerryosborne.oracle-guy.com/2008/09/sql-tuning-advisor`.

Listing 16-19 shows an example of a couple of scripts for finding SQL Profiles and statements that are using them.

Listing 16-19. *Scripts for finding SQL Profiles*

```
SYS@LAB112> @sql_profiles.sql
Enter value for sql_text:
Enter value for name:

NAME                             CATEGORY   STATUS    SQL_TEXT                                      FORCE
-------------------------------- ---------- --------- --------------------------------------------- -----
PROFILE_fgn6qzrvrjgnz            DEFAULT    DISABLED  select /*+ index(a SKEW_COL1) */ av           NO
PROFILE_8hjn3vxrykmpf            DEFAULT    DISABLED  select /*+ invalid_hint (doda) */ a           NO
PROFILE_69k5bhm12sz98            DEFAULT    DISABLED  SELECT dbin.instance_number,                  NO
PROFILE_8js5bhfc668rp            DEFAULT    DISABLED  select /*+ index(a SKEW_COL2_COL1)            NO
PROFILE_bxd77v75nynd8            DEFAULT    DISABLED  select /*+ parallel (a 4) */ avg(pk           NO
PROFILE_7ng34ruy5awxq            DEFAULT    DISABLED  select i.obj#,i.ts#,i.file#,i.block           NO
SYS_SQLPROF_0126f1743c7d0005     SAVED      ENABLED   select avg(pk_col) from kso.skew              NO
PROF_6kymwy3guu5uq_1388734953    DEFAULT    ENABLED   select 1                                      YES
PROFILE_cnpx9s9na938m_MANUAL     DEFAULT    ENABLED   select /*+ opt_param('statistics_le          NO
PROF_79m8gs9wz3ndj_3723858078    DEFAULT    ENABLED   /* SQL Analyze(252,1) */ select avg           NO
PROFILE_9ywuaagwscbj7_GPS        DEFAULT    ENABLED   select avg(pk_col) from kso.skew              NO
PROF_arcvrg5na75sw_3723858078    DEFAULT    ENABLED   select /*+ index(skew@sel$1 skew_co          NO
SYS_SQLPROF_01274114fc2b0006     DEFAULT    ENABLED   select i.table_owner, i.table_name,          NO

18 rows selected.
```

```
SYS@LAB112> @find_sql_using_profile.sql
Enter value for sql_text:
Enter value for sql_id:
Enter value for sql_profile_name:

SQL_ID          PLAN_HASH SQL_PROFILE                    SQL_TEXT
------------- ---------- ------------------------------ ------------------------------------
bqfx5q2jas08u 3755463150 SYS_SQLPROF_01281e513ace0000   SELECT TASK_LIST.TASK_ID FROM (SELE
                                                        CT /*+ NO_MERGE(T) ORDERED */ T.TAS
                                                        K_ID FROM (SELECT * FROM DBA_ADVISO
                                                        R_TASKS ORDER BY TASK_ID DESC) T, D
                                                        BA_ADVISOR_PARAMETERS_PROJ P1, DBA_
                                                        ADVISOR_PARAMETERS_PROJ P2 WHERE T.
                                                        ADVISOR_NAME='ADDM' AND T.STATUS =
                                                        'COMPLETED' AND T.EXECUTION_START >
                                                        = (SYSDATE - 1) AND T.HOW_CREATED =
                                                        'AUTO' AND T.TASK_ID = P1.TASK_ID
                                                        AND P1.PARAMETER_NAME = 'INSTANCE'
                                                        AND P1.PARAMETER_VALUE = SYS_CONTEX
                                                        T('USERENV','INSTANCE') AND T.TASK_
                                                        ID = P2.TASK_ID AND P2.PARAMETER_NA
                                                        ME = 'DB_ID' AND P2.PARAMETER_VALUE
                                                        = TO_CHAR(:B1 ) ORDER BY T.TASK_ID
                                                        DESC) TASK_LIST WHERE ROWNUM = 1
```

The `sql_profiles.sql` script queries DBA_SQL_PROFILES and the `fnd_sql_using_profile.sql` queries V$SQL. The SQL Profiles with names that begin with SYS_SQLPROF are generated by the SQL Tuning Advisor. The others are manually created using the DBMS_SQLTUNE.IMPORT_SQL_PROFILE procedure. Now, let's create a couple of SQL Profiles. To do this, you'll use a script called `create_1_hint_profile.sql` that simply prompts for a SQL_ID and a hint and then creates a SQL Profile for the statement containing the hint (see Listing 16-20).

Listing 16-20. *The create_1_hint_profile.sql Script*

```
SYS@LAB112> select /* test 1 hint */ avg(pk_col) from kso.skew a where col1 = 222222;

AVG(PK_COL)
-----------
   15722222

1 row selected.

SYS@LAB112> @find_sql
Enter value for sql_text: select /* test 1 hint */ avg(pk_col) from kso.skew % 222222
Enter value for sql_id:
```

```
SQL_ID         CHILD  PLAN_HASH EXECS AVG_ETIME  AVG_LIO SQL_TEXT
------------- ------ ---------- ----- --------- ------------------------------------------------
0pvj94afp6faw      0 2650913906     1       .10      876 select /* test 1 hint */ avg(pk_col)
                                                         from kso.skew a where col1 = 222222
```

1 row selected.

```
SYS@LAB112>
SYS@LAB112> @dplan
Enter value for sql_id: 0pvj94afp6faw
Enter value for child_no:

PLAN_TABLE_OUTPUT
-------------------------------------------------------------------------------------------------
SQL_ID  0pvj94afp6faw, child number 0
-------------------------------------
select /* test 1 hint */ avg(pk_col) from kso.skew a where col1 = 222222

Plan hash value: 2650913906
```

```
-------------------------------------------------------------------------------------------
| Id  | Operation                    | Name         | Rows  | Bytes | Cost (%CPU)| Time     |
-------------------------------------------------------------------------------------------
|   0 | SELECT STATEMENT             |              |       |       |  34 (100)|          |
|   1 |  SORT AGGREGATE              |              |     1 |    24 |          |          |
|   2 |   TABLE ACCESS BY INDEX ROWID| SKEW         |    32 |   768 |  34   (0)| 0:00:01 |
|*  3 |    INDEX SKIP SCAN           | SKEW_COL2_COL1 |  32 |       |   5   (0)| 00:00:01|
-------------------------------------------------------------------------------------------
```

```
Predicate Information (identified by operation id):
---------------------------------------------------

   3 - access("COL1"=222222)
       filter("COL1"=222222)
```

21 rows selected.

```
SYS@LAB112> -- So it's using an index skip scan
SYS@LAB112>
SYS@LAB112> -- Now lets create a SQL Profile with a FULL hint
SYS@LAB112>
SYS@LAB112> @create_1_hint_sql_profile
Enter value for sql_id: 0pvj94afp6faw
Enter value for profile_name (PROFILE_sqlid_MANUAL): PROF_0pvj94afp6faw_FULL
Enter value for category (DEFAULT):
```

```
Enter value for force_matching (false):
Enter value for hint:                               FULL( A@SEL$1 )

Profile PROF_0pvj94afp6faw_FULL created.

SYS@LAB112> select /* test 1 hint */ avg(pk_col) from kso.skew a where col1 = 222222;

AVG(PK_COL)
-----------
   15722222

1 row selected.

SYS@LAB112> @find_sql
Enter value for sql_text: select /* test 1 hint */ avg(pk_col) from kso.skew a where col1 %
Enter value for sql_id:

SQL_ID          CHILD  PLAN_HASH EXECS AVG_ETIME  AVG_LIO SQL_TEXT
------------- ------ ---------- ----- --------- -------------------------------------------
0pvj94afp6faw      0  568322376     1      6.34  162,309 select /* test 1 hint */ avg(pk_col)
                                                         from kso.skew a where col1 = 222222

1 row selected.

SYS@LAB112> -- Well it has a different plan hash value and it took a lot longer
SYS@LAB112>
SYS@LAB112> @dplan
Enter value for sql_id: 0pvj94afp6faw
Enter value for child_no:

PLAN_TABLE_OUTPUT
---------------------------------------------------------------------------------------------
SQL_ID  0pvj94afp6faw, child number 0
-------------------------------------
select /* test 1 hint */ avg(pk_col) from kso.skew a where col1 = 222222

Plan hash value: 568322376

--------------------------------------------------------------------------------
| Id  | Operation          | Name | Rows  | Bytes | Cost (%CPU)| Time     |
--------------------------------------------------------------------------------
|   0 | SELECT STATEMENT   |      |       |       | 28360 (100)|          |
|   1 |  SORT AGGREGATE    |      |     1 |    24 |            |          |
|*  2 |   TABLE ACCESS FULL| SKEW |    32 |   768 | 28360   (1)| 00:05:41 |
--------------------------------------------------------------------------------
```

```
Predicate Information (identified by operation id):
---------------------------------------------------

   2 - filter("COL1"=222222)

Note
-----
   - SQL profile PROF_0pvj94afp6faw_FULL used for this statement


23 rows selected.

SYS@LAB112> -- So it is using the SQL Profile and it did change to a FULL SCAN
SYS@LAB112>
SYS@LAB112> -- Let's check the hints in the SQL Profile
SYS@LAB112>
SYS@LAB112> @sql_profile_hints
Enter value for profile_name: PROF_0pvj94afp6faw_FULL


HINT
----------------------------------------------------------------------------------------
                    FULL( A@SEL$1 )

1 rows selected.

SYS@LAB112> -- Let's check the hints in the OTHER_XML field of V$SQL_PLAN
SYS@LAB112>
SYS@LAB112> @sql_hints
Enter value for sql_id: 0pvj94afp6faw
Enter value for child_no: 0


OUTLINE_HINTS
----------------------------------------------------------------------------------------
IGNORE_OPTIM_EMBEDDED_HINTS
OPTIMIZER_FEATURES_ENABLE('11.2.0.1')
DB_VERSION('11.2.0.1')
ALL_ROWS
OUTLINE_LEAF(@"SEL$1")
FULL(@"SEL$1" "A"@"SEL$1")

6 rows selected.
```

Notice that the hint was specified using the fully qualified alias for the SKEW table, FULL (A@SEL$1). This was done on purpose because Outlines, Profiles, and Baselines are more picky about object identification than those normal hints that are embedded in the SQL statement text. For example, it would be perfectly acceptable to use FULL (A) in the text of the SQL statement. But if you put that into a SQL Profile, the optimizer will not know what to do with it (and so it will silently ignore it). Notice also that the complete syntax for the FULL hint would also include the Query Block (QB) name as shown in the output from the sql_hints.sql script. Remember that this is the set of hints that Oracle thinks would be necessary to recreate the plan and thus is the set of hints that would be used if you created an Outline on the statement. You may wonder how I knew that SEL$1 was the correct QB name to use. The answer is experience. And you know how I got the experience? By making lots of mistakes! Actually, since I know that the default QB names are SEL$1, UPD$1, and DEL$1, and this is a very simple query with only one QB and very little (if any) way that the optimizer could transform it to something else, it was a pretty good guess. But why guess when you can know? If you use DBMS_XPLAN.DISPLAY_CURSOR with the alias option, you can see exactly what the QB name and fully qualified aliases are (see Listing 16-21).

Listing 16-21. *DBMS_XPLAN.DISPLAY_CURSOR with the Alias Option*

```
SYS@LAB112> @dplan_alias
Enter value for sql_id: 0pvj94afp6faw
Enter value for child_no:

PLAN_TABLE_OUTPUT
-------------------------------------------------------------------------------------------
SQL_ID  0pvj94afp6faw, child number 0
-------------------------------------
select /* test 1 hint */ avg(pk_col) from kso.skew a where col1 = 222222

Plan hash value: 568322376

-------------------------------------------------------------------------
| Id  | Operation          | Name | Rows  | Bytes | Cost (%CPU)| Time     |
-------------------------------------------------------------------------
|   0 | SELECT STATEMENT   |      |       |       | 28360 (100)|          |
|   1 |  SORT AGGREGATE    |      |     1 |    24 |            |          |
|*  2 |   TABLE ACCESS FULL| SKEW |    32 |   768 | 28360   (1)| 00:05:41 |
-------------------------------------------------------------------------

Query Block Name / Object Alias (identified by operation id):
-------------------------------------------------------------

   1 - SEL$1
   2 - SEL$1 / A@SEL$1

Predicate Information (identified by operation id):
---------------------------------------------------

   2 - filter("COL1"=222222)

Note
-----
   - SQL profile PROF_0pvj94afp6faw_FULL used for this statement


29 rows selected.
```

SQL Profiles can also duplicate the functionality of Outlines, but without all the quirks, so you can create a SQL Profile using the same hints that an Outline would use (i.e. the ones in the OTHER_XML column). The goal would be to have all the hints necessary to "lock" the plan. There is no way to guarantee that the plan will never be able to change, but the technique works fairly well. It is actually quite easy to create a SQL Profile using the hints that an Outline would use, and of course there is a script in the example download to help you out (`create_sql_profile.sql`). Listing 16-22 shows an example.

Listing 16-22. *The create_sql_profile.sql Script*

```
SYS@LAB112> select /* NOT IN */ department_name
  2      from hr.departments dept
  3      where department_id not in (select department_id from hr.employees emp);

no rows selected

SYS@LAB112> @find_sql
Enter value for sql_text: select /* NOT IN */ department_name%
Enter value for sql_id:

SQL_ID        CHILD  PLAN_HASH EXECS AVG_ETIME  AVG_LIO SQL_TEXT
------------- ------ ---------- ----- --------- ------------------------------------------
875qbqc2gw2qz      0 4201340344     3       .00        9 select /* NOT IN */ department_name

1 row selected.


SYS@LAB112> @dplan
Enter value for sql_id: 875qbqc2gw2qz
Enter value for child_no:

PLAN_TABLE_OUTPUT
-------------------------------------------------------------------------------------------
SQL_ID  875qbqc2gw2qz, child number 0
-------------------------------------
select /* NOT IN */ department_name     from hr.departments dept
where department_id not in (select department_id from hr.employees emp)

Plan hash value: 4201340344
```

Id	Operation	Name	Rows	Bytes	Cost (%CPU)	Time
0	SELECT STATEMENT				6 (100)	
1	MERGE JOIN ANTI NA		17	323	6 (17)	00:00:01
2	SORT JOIN		27	432	2 (0)	00:00:01
3	TABLE ACCESS BY INDEX ROWID	DEPARTMENTS	27	432	2 (0)	00:00:01
4	INDEX FULL SCAN	DEPT_ID_PK	27		1 (0)	00:00:01
* 5	SORT UNIQUE		107	321	4 (25)	00:00:01
6	TABLE ACCESS FULL	EMPLOYEES	107	321	3 (0)	00:00:01

```
Predicate Information (identified by operation id):
---------------------------------------------------

   5 - access("DEPARTMENT_ID"="DEPARTMENT_ID")
       filter("DEPARTMENT_ID"="DEPARTMENT_ID")


25 rows selected.

SYS@LAB112> @create_sql_profile
Enter value for sql_id: 875qbqc2gw2qz
Enter value for child_no (0):
Enter value for profile_name (PROF_sqlid_planhash):
Enter value for category (DEFAULT):
Enter value for force_matching (FALSE):

SQL Profile PROF_875qbqc2gw2qz_4201340344 created.

SYS@LAB112> select /* NOT IN */ department_name
  2      from hr.departments dept
  3      where department_id not in (select department_id from hr.employees emp);

no rows selected

SYS@LAB112> @find_sql
Enter value for sql_text: select /* NOT IN */ department_name%
Enter value for sql_id:

SQL_ID          CHILD  PLAN_HASH  EXECS  AVG_ETIME  AVG_LIO SQL_TEXT
-------------  ------  ---------  -----  ---------- ------------------------------------------
875qbqc2gw2qz      1 4201340344      1        .01       17 select /* NOT IN */ department_name

1 row selected.

SYS@LAB112> @dplanEnter value for sql_id: 875qbqc2gw2qz
Enter value for child_no:

PLAN_TABLE_OUTPUT
---------------------------------------------------------------------------------------------
SQL_ID  875qbqc2gw2qz, child number 1
-------------------------------------
select /* NOT IN */ department_name     from hr.departments dept
where department_id not in (select department_id from hr.employees emp)

Plan hash value: 4201340344
```

```
-----------------------------------------------------------------------------
| Id  | Operation                   | Name         | Rows  | Bytes | Cost (%CPU)| Time     |
-----------------------------------------------------------------------------
|   0 | SELECT STATEMENT            |              |       |       |   6 (100)|           |
|   1 |  MERGE JOIN ANTI NA         |              |    17 |   323 |   6  (17)| 00:00:01|
|   2 |   SORT JOIN                 |              |    27 |   432 |   2   (0)| 00:00:01|
|   3 |    TABLE ACCESS BY INDEX ROWID| DEPARTMENTS |    27 |   432 |   2   (0)| 00:00:01|
|   4 |     INDEX FULL SCAN         | DEPT_ID_PK   |    27 |       |   1   (0)| 00:00:01|
|*  5 |   SORT UNIQUE               |              |   107 |   321 |   4  (25)| 00:00:01|
|   6 |    TABLE ACCESS FULL        | EMPLOYEES    |   107 |   321 |   3   (0)| 00:00:01|
-----------------------------------------------------------------------------
```

Predicate Information (identified by operation id):

```
   5 - access("DEPARTMENT_ID"="DEPARTMENT_ID")
       filter("DEPARTMENT_ID"="DEPARTMENT_ID")
```

Note

   - SQL profile PROF_875qbqc2gw2qz_4201340344 used for this statement

29 rows selected.

```
SYS@LAB112> @sql_profile_hints
Enter value for profile_name: PROF_875qbqc2gw2qz_4201340344

HINT
-----------------------------------------------------------------------------
IGNORE_OPTIM_EMBEDDED_HINTS
OPTIMIZER_FEATURES_ENABLE('11.2.0.1')
DB_VERSION('11.2.0.1')
ALL_ROWS
OUTLINE_LEAF(@"SEL$5DA710D3")
UNNEST(@"SEL$2")
OUTLINE(@"SEL$1")
OUTLINE(@"SEL$2")
INDEX(@"SEL$5DA710D3" "DEPT"@"SEL$1" ("DEPARTMENTS"."DEPARTMENT_ID"))
FULL(@"SEL$5DA710D3" "EMP"@"SEL$2")
LEADING(@"SEL$5DA710D3" "DEPT"@"SEL$1" "EMP"@"SEL$2")
USE_MERGE(@"SEL$5DA710D3" "EMP"@"SEL$2")

12 rows selected.
```

So that's handy if you have a SQL statement in the Shared Pool with a plan that you like. But what if you have a statement that goes bad and there is no longer a copy of the good plan in the shared pool? No problem, as long as your AWR retention allows you to get back to a previous execution that used a plan you like, because all the hints will be stored in the OTHER_XML column of the DBA_HIST_SQL_PLAN table along with the rest of the plan data. So it is a relatively simple matter to create a SQL Profile using those hints in order to restore your previous plan (while you go looking for the reason it went south in the first place). Of course there is a script for that one as well (create_sql_profile_awr.sql). Listing 16-23 shows an example of its use (note that this example was run in 10g as it's easier to get the optimizer to behave badly in 10g than in 11g).

Listing 16-23. *The create_sql_profile_awr.sql Script*

```
SYS@LAB1024> @awr_plan_change
Enter value for sql_id: 05cq2hb1r37tr

SNAP_ID NODE BEGIN_INTERVAL_TIME          PLAN_HASH_VALUE  EXECS   AVG_ETIME        AVG_LIO
------- ---- --------------------------   ---------------  ------  ------------   ----------
9532    1    12-AUG-10 03.00.09.212 PM    68322376         1       90.339         162,298.0
9534    1    12-AUG-10 10.00.08.716 AM                     1       51.715         162,298.0
9535    1    13-AUG-10 06.00.10.280 PM                     4       23.348         162,298.0
9536    1    15-AUG-10 04.00.05.439 PM    3723858078       1       622.170      9,218,284.0

SYS@LAB1024>
SYS@LAB1024> -- statement 05cq2hb1r37tr has taken a turn for the worse
SYS@LAB1024> -- let's get it back to plan 568322376
SYS@LAB1024>
SYS@LAB1024> @create_sql_profile_awr
Enter value for sql_id: 05cq2hb1r37tr
Enter value for plan_hash_value: 568322376
Enter value for profile_name (PROF_sqlid_planhash):
Enter value for category (DEFAULT):
Enter value for force_matching (FALSE):

SQL Profile PROF_05cq2hb1r37tr_568322376 created.

SYS@LAB1024> @sql_profile_hints
Enter value for profile_name: PROF_05cq2hb1r37tr_568322376

HINT
------------------------------------------------------------------------------------------
IGNORE_OPTIM_EMBEDDED_HINTS
OPTIMIZER_FEATURES_ENABLE('10.2.0.4')
ALL_ROWS
OUTLINE_LEAF(@"SEL$1")
FULL(@"SEL$1" "A"@"SEL$1")

5 rows selected.
```

This approach is very handy if you have a statement that ran well at some point and AWR captured it. But what if you need to tune a statement from scratch, but you don't have access to the code? Well, SQL Profiles have one more trick up their sleeve. Since you have already demonstrated that you can build SQL Profiles with any set of hints and associate them with any SQL statement and since you have shown you can use OTHER_XML as a source of hints, why not move a set of hints from one statement to another? This would allow you to take a statement and manipulate it to get the plan you want (via hints, alter session statements, etc.) and then create a SQL Profile on your un-manipulated statement using the hints from your manipulated statement. And of course there is a script in the example download to do that (`move_sql_profile.sql`). There are several steps to this process. First, you need to identify the statement and get it's SQL_ID, then you need to make a copy of it to manipulate, then you need to create a SQL Profile on the new manipulated version, and finally, you need to move the hints to the original statement. Listing 16-24 shows an example.

Listing 16-24. *The move_sql_profile.sql Script*

```
SYS@LAB112> select count(*) from kso.skew where col3 = '01-jan-10';

  COUNT(*)
----------
         0

1 row selected.

SYS@LAB112> @find_sql
Enter value for sql_text: select count(*) from kso.skew where col3 = %
Enter value for sql_id:

SQL_ID          CHILD  PLAN_HASH EXECS AVG_ETIME  AVG_LIO SQL_TEXT
-------------  ------ ---------- ----- --------- --------------------------------------------
4cp821ufcwvgc      0 3438766830     1       .39      675 select count(*) from kso.skew where
                                                         col3 = '01-jan-10'

1 row selected.

SYS@LAB112> @dplan
Enter value for sql_id: 4cp821ufcwvgc
Enter value for child_no:

PLAN_TABLE_OUTPUT
--------------------------------------------------------------------------------------------
SQL_ID  4cp821ufcwvgc, child number 0
-------------------------------------
select count(*) from kso.skew where col3 = '01-jan-10'

Plan hash value: 3438766830
```

```
-------------------------------------------------------------------------
| Id  | Operation          | Name       | Rows  | Bytes | Cost (%CPU)| Time     |
-------------------------------------------------------------------------
|   0 | SELECT STATEMENT   |            |       |       |   3 (100)|          |
|   1 |  SORT AGGREGATE    |            |     1 |    26 |          |          |
|*  2 |   INDEX RANGE SCAN | COL3_INDEX |     1 |    26 |   3  (0)| 00:00:01 |
-------------------------------------------------------------------------

Predicate Information (identified by operation id):
---------------------------------------------------

   2 - access("COL3"='01-jan-10')
```

19 rows selected.

So you have identified your statement and found the SQL_ID. Now let's create another version of the statement and force it to use a different index. You'll do this by adding an inline hint to the select statement text (Listing 16-25).

Listing 16-25. *Adding an Inline Hint to the Select Statement Text*

```
SYS@LAB112> -- let's create a statement that does the same thing but uses a different index
SYS@LAB112>
SYS@LAB112> select /*+ index (skew skew_col3_col2_col1) */ count(*)
  2 from kso.skew where col3 = '01-jan-10';

  COUNT(*)
----------
         0

1 row selected.

SYS@LAB112> @find_sql
Enter value for sql_text: select /*+ index (skew skew_col3_col2_col1) */ count(*)%
Enter value for sql_id:

SQL_ID         CHILD  PLAN_HASH EXECS AVG_ETIME  AVG_LIO SQL_TEXT
-------------- ------ ---------- ----- --------- -------- -------------------------------------------
09gdkwq1bs48h      0  167097056     1       .06        8 select /*+ index (skew
                                                         skew_col3_col2_col1)
                                                         */ count(*) from kso.skew where
                                                         '01- jan-10'

1 row selected.

SYS@LAB112> @dplan
Enter value for sql_id: 09gdkwq1bs48h
Enter value for child_no:
```

```
PLAN_TABLE_OUTPUT
---------------------------------------------------------------------------------------------
SQL_ID  09gdkwq1bs48h, child number 0
-------------------------------------
select /*+ index (skew skew_col3_col2_col1) */ count(*) from kso.skew
where col3 = '01-jan-10'

Plan hash value: 167097056

---------------------------------------------------------------------------------------------
| Id  | Operation          | Name              | Rows  | Bytes | Cost (%CPU)| Time     |
---------------------------------------------------------------------------------------------
|   0 | SELECT STATEMENT   |                   |       |       |     4 (100)|          |
|   1 |  SORT AGGREGATE    |                   |     1 |    26 |            |          |
|*  2 |   INDEX RANGE SCAN | SKEW_COL3_COL2_COL1 |   1 |    26 |     4   (0)| 00:00:01 |
---------------------------------------------------------------------------------------------

Predicate Information (identified by operation id):
---------------------------------------------------

   2 - access("COL3"='01-jan-10')

20 rows selected.
```

In Listing 16-25, you created a new statement (SQL_ID: 09gdkwq1bs48h) that has the same structure but uses a different execution plan (because of the hint). The next step is to create a SQL Profile on the new statement. You'll do this with the create_sql_profile.sql script as shown in Listing 16-26.

Listing 16-26. *The create_sql_profile.sql Script*

```
SYS@LAB112> -- now let's create a profile on our new statement
SYS@LAB112>
SYS@LAB112> @create_sql_profile
Enter value for sql_id: 09gdkwq1bs48h
Enter value for child_no (0):
Enter value for profile_name (PROF_sqlid_planhash):
Enter value for category (DEFAULT):
Enter value for force_matching (FALSE):

SQL Profile PROF_09gdkwq1bs48h_167097056 created.

SYS@LAB112> select /*+ index (skew skew_col3_col2_col1) */ count(*)
  2 from kso.skew where col3 = '01-jan-10';

  COUNT(*)
----------
         0

1 row selected.
```

```
SYS@LAB112> @find_sql
Enter value for sql_text: select /*+ index (skew skew_col3_col2_col1) */ count(*)%
Enter value for sql_id:

SQL_ID         CHILD  PLAN_HASH EXECS AVG_ETIME  AVG_LIO SQL_TEXT
-------------  ------ ---------- ----- ---------  -------------------------------------------------
09gdkwq1bs48h      0  167097056     1       .01  16 select /*+ index (skew
                                                     skew_col3_col2_col1
                                                     */ count(*) from kso.skew where col3 =
                                                     '01- jan-10'


1 row selected.
SYS@LAB112> @dplan
Enter value for sql_id: 09gdkwq1bs48h
Enter value for child_no:

PLAN_TABLE_OUTPUT
---------------------------------------------------------------------------------------------
SQL_ID  09gdkwq1bs48h, child number 0
-------------------------------------
select /*+ index (skew skew_col3_col2_col1) */ count(*) from kso.skew
where col3 = '01-jan-10'

Plan hash value: 167097056


---------------------------------------------------------------------------------------------
| Id  | Operation          | Name               | Rows  | Bytes | Cost (%CPU)| Time     |
---------------------------------------------------------------------------------------------
|   0 | SELECT STATEMENT   |                    |       |       |      4 (100)|          |
|   1 |  SORT AGGREGATE    |                    |     1 |    26 |            |          |
|*  2 |   INDEX RANGE SCAN | SKEW_COL3_COL2_COL1 |    1 |    26 |      4   (0)| 00:00:01 |
---------------------------------------------------------------------------------------------

Predicate Information (identified by operation id):
-------------------------------------------------

   2 - access("COL3"='01-jan-10')

Note
-----
   - SQL profile PROF_09gdkwq1bs48h_167097056 used for this statement


24 rows selected.
```

The last step is to move the newly created SQL Profile on to the original statement. You'll do this with the move_sql_profile.sql script in Listing 16-27. Then you'll verify that the SQL Profile is being used and having the desired effect.

Listing 16-27. *The move_sql_profile.sql Script*

```
SYS@LAB112> -- let's attach that same SQL Profile on to our original statement
SYS@LAB112>
SYS@LAB112> @move_sql_profile
Enter value for profile_name: PROF_09gdkwq1bs48h_167097056
Enter value for sql_id: 4cp821ufcwvgc
Enter value for category (DEFAULT):
Enter value for force_matching (false):

PL/SQL procedure successfully completed.

SYS@LAB112> select count(*) from kso.skew where col3 = '01-jan-10';

  COUNT(*)
----------
         0

1 row selected.

SYS@LAB112> @find_sql
Enter value for sql_text: select count(*) from kso.skew where col3 = %
Enter value for sql_id:

SQL_ID          CHILD  PLAN_HASH EXECS AVG_ETIME  AVG_LIO SQL_TEXT
-------------  ------ ---------- ----- --------- -------------------------------------------
4cp821ufcwvgc       0  167097056     1       .12 16 select count(*) from kso.skew where
                                                     col3 = '01-jan-10'


1 row selected.

SYS@LAB112> @dplan
Enter value for sql_id: 4cp821ufcwvgc
Enter value for child_no:

PLAN_TABLE_OUTPUT
---------------------------------------------------------------------------------------------
SQL_ID  4cp821ufcwvgc, child number 0
---------------------------------------
select count(*) from kso.skew where col3 = '01-jan-10'
```

Plan hash value: 167097056

```
-------------------------------------------------------------------------------
| Id | Operation           | Name               | Rows | Bytes | Cost (%CPU)| Time     |
-------------------------------------------------------------------------------
|  0 | SELECT STATEMENT    |                    |      |       |   4 (100)|          |
|  1 |  SORT AGGREGATE     |                    |    1 |    26 |          |          |
|* 2 |   INDEX RANGE SCAN  | SKEW_COL3_COL2_COL1 |    1 |    26 |   4   (0)| 00:00:01 |
-------------------------------------------------------------------------------
```

Predicate Information (identified by operation id):

```
   2 - access("COL3"='01-jan-10')
```

Note

   - SQL profile PROFILE_4cp821ufcwvgc_moved used for this statement

23 rows selected.

As you can see, the move worked and the new plan is in effect for the original statement. Moving SQL Profiles from one statement to another is a very useful technique and very easy to do. It basically allows you to manipulate a SQL statement until you get the plan you want and then attach the plan to a statement that you can't touch. There are a few restrictions you should be aware of, however:

- You cannot change the structure of the statement. Remember that SQL Profile hints are very specific when it comes to QB names. So anything that would change the Query Blocks will not work.

- You cannot change any object aliases. Remember that all hints must reference objects by alias names (if aliases exist in the statement). Adding, removing, or changing an alias name in your manipulated statement will create hints that won't match the original, and so they will be silently ignored.

So to wrap up the section on SQL Profiles, I believe they provide a very powerful tool for controlling execution plans. The ability to match multiple statements via the FORCE_MATCHING attribute and the ability to attach any set of hints to a statement via the IMPORT_SQL_PROFILE procedure sets SQL Profiles apart as one of the most useful tools in our tool belt.

SQL Plan Baselines

Oracle Database 11g has provided a new method of dealing with plan instability. The third iteration of Oracle's hint based mechanisms for influencing execution plans is called a SQL Plan Baseline (Baseline, for short). With Baselines, the design goal has morphed into eliminating backwards movement ("performance regressions" as the Oracle documentation calls them)—in other words, not allowing a statement to switch to a plan that is significantly slower than the one it has already been executing. This new mechanism depends on Baselines, which look very much like SQL Profiles; in fact, they are actually stored in the same structure in the data dictionary.

Baselines are at their core a set of hints that are given a name and attached to a specific SQL statement. They are associated with a SQL statement using the same "normalized" text matching as Outlines and SQL Profiles. Here are some key features of Baselines:

- Baselines will be used by default in 11g if they exist. There is a parameter to control whether they are used or not (OPTIMIZER_USE_SQL_PLAN_BASELINE). It is set to TRUE by default.

- In 11g, Baselines will not be created by default. So, like the older Outlines or SQL Profiles, you must do something to create them. This also means that by default, 11g plan management does not look very different from 10g.

- The concept of Categories has disappeared from Baselines.

- Unlike Outlines and Profiles, you can have multiple Baselines per SQL statement. In an even more confusing twist, there's a concept of a preferred set of Baselines called the "Fixed" set.

- One of the key features of Baselines is that they are the first hint-based mechanism to have knowledge of the plan that was used to create them. That is to say, they store a plan_hash_value along with the hints. So if a Baseline is applied to a statement and the optimizer doesn't come up with the same plan_hash_value that it had when the Baseline was created, all the hints are thrown out and the optimization is re-done without any of the hints. (Note: It doesn't actually happen in this order but the point is that this mechanism is very different from Outlines and Profiles where the optimizer has no idea what plan the hints were trying generate. With Baselines, it does.)

- There is a view called DBA_SQL_PLAN_BASELINES that exposes the Baselines that have been created.

- Just like Outlines and SQL Profiles, Baselines apply to all instances in a RAC environment. They are not localized to a specific instance.

SQL PLAN MANAGEMENT INFRASTRUCTURE

Baselines are a part of the new SQL Plan Management (SPM) infrastructure in 11g. The concept of SPM is to have a Baseline associated with every statement that runs through the database. The optimizer then uses the Baselines to attempt to recreate the original plans they were created from.

Every time a statement is parsed in 11g, the optimizer goes through its normal process including coming up with an execution plan. It then checks to see if the plan it just came up with is already stored in a Baseline. If it is, the optimizer will use that plan. If it's not, the optimizer will use the Baseline plan and store the alternate plan in the history for later evaluation with the DBMS_SPM.EVOLVE_SQL_PLAN_BASELINE function (assuming that the database is configured to do that).

The approach of saving plans for later evaluation sounds like a great plan to limit instability due to unexpected plan changes. The only real downside to that approach is that seeding the Baselines can be a difficult task and it is not done by default. The result is that most shops have not embraced this feature yet. I expect we'll see more of this feature as people become more familiar with it, at least for key SQL statements.

You can do pretty much the same things with Baselines that you can do with Outlines and SQL Profiles. For example, you can find a list of them, see what hints are contained by them, see what their status is, see which SQL statements are using them, etc. Listing 16-28 shows a quick example using a few scripts from the example download.

Listing 16-28. *Using Baselines*

```
SYS@LAB112> @find_sql_using_baseline
Enter value for sql_text:
Enter value for sql_id:
Enter value for plan_hash_value:
```

SQL_ID	PLAN_HASH	SQL_PLAN_BASELINE	AVG_ETIME SQL_TEXT
04s94zftphcgb	2650913906	SQL_PLAN_3mmrpt1hutfzs7456d135	.00 select sum(pk_col) from k
12417fbdsfaxt	2333976600	SQL_PLAN_0j493a65j2bamc0e39d1a	.01 SELECT SQL_HANDLE FROM DB
2us663zxp440c	329476029	SQL_PLAN_6dny19g5cvmaj059cc611	.04 /* OracleOEM */ select at
3972rvxu3knn3	3007952250	SQL_PLAN_05a32329hrft07347ab53	.00 delete from sdo_geor_ddl_
	3007952250	SQL_PLAN_05a32329hrft07347ab53	.00 delete from sdo_geor_ddl_
62m44bym1fdhs	3137838658	SQL_PLAN_2jvcuyb2j5t1g4d67c3d9	.00 SELECT ID FROM WWV_FLOW_M
	3137838658	SQL_PLAN_2jvcuyb2j5t1g4d67c3d9	.00 SELECT ID FROM WWV_FLOW_M
6abthk1u14yb7	2848324471	SQL_PLAN_5y7pbdmj87bz3ea394c8e	.00 SELECT VERSION FROM V$INS
	2848324471	SQL_PLAN_5y7pbdmj87bz3ea394c8e	.00 SELECT VERSION FROM V$INS
9xw644rurr1nk	2848324471	SQL_PLAN_ba7pvw56m6m1cea394c8e	.00 SELECT REGEXP_REPLACE(VER
aukfj0ur6962z	2366097979	SQL_PLAN_adx60prqvaaqhf8e55c8a	.00 SELECT VALUE V FROM WWV_F
	2366097979	SQL_PLAN_adx60prqvaaqhf8e55c8a	.00 SELECT VALUE V FROM WWV_F
b1um9gxnf22a3	1475283301	SQL_PLAN_1kj53db9w5gzga4a6b425	.00 select count(*) from sqll
d56r760yr1tgt	2650913906	SQL_PLAN_dn32tuq14sj5q7456d135	.01 select sum(pk_col) from k
f1b04310fhv7a	2650913906	SQLID_AR5DZ1STDPFC6_2650913906	.00 select sum(pk_col) from
fg5u3ydzcqzvw	3291240065	SQL_PLAN_3ndjuqr0f58a716c3d523	.03 select spb.sql_handle, sp
	3291240065	SQL_PLAN_3ndjuqr0f58a716c3d523	.03 select spb.sql_handle, sp

```
17 rows selected.

SYS@LAB112> @baselines
Enter value for sql_text: %skew%
Enter value for name:
Enter value for plan_name:
```

SQL_HANDLE	PLAN_NAME	SQL_TEXT	ENABLED	ACC	FIX
SYS_SQL_17fbdf9452045c7d	SQL_PLAN_1gyyzkj908r3x6c55a992	select avg(pk_col)	YES	NO	NO
	SQL_PLAN_1gyyzkj908r3x7b89d948	select avg(pk_col)	YES	NO	NO
SYS_SQL_36bf1c88f777e894	SQL_PLAN_3dgswj3vrgu4n11d25c67	select avg(pk_col)	YES	NO	NO
	SQL_PLAN_3dgswj3vrgu4ned88b4f4	select avg(pk_col)	NO	YES	NO
SYS_SQL_39cef5c861acbbf8	SQL_PLAN_3mmrpt1hutfzs7456d135	select sum(pk_col)	YES	YES	NO
SYS_SQL_3a363ab5c0e2a147	SQL_PLAN_3ndjuqr0f58a716c3d523	select spb.sql_hand	YES	YES	NO
SYS_SQL_3c55382b2b2a4d5f	SQL_PLAN_3sp9s5cpknmaz7456d135	select sum(pk_col)	YES	YES	NO

```
SYS_SQL_94dc89c011141f02 SQL_PLAN_99r49s08j87s255381d08 select avg(pk_col)  YES    NO  NO
                         SQL_PLAN_99r49s08j87s27456d135 select avg(pk_col)  YES    NO  NO
SYS_SQL_d0686c14959cbf64 SQL_PLAN_d0u3c2kattgv48b1420d2 select avg(pk_col)  YES    YES NO
SYS_SQL_da0c59d5824c44b6 SQL_PLAN_dn32tuq14sj5q7456d135 select sum(pk_col)  YES    YES NO
SYS_SQL_f1140cddb13082df DODA                           select sql_id, chil YES    YES NO
SYS_SQL_f5cd6b7b73c7a1f7 SQLID_F1B04310FHV7A_2650913906 select sum(pk_col)  YES    YES NO

13 rows selected.

SYS@LAB112> @baseline_hints
Enter value for baseline_plan_name: SQLID_F1B04310FHV7A_2650913906

OUTLINE_HINTS
--------------------------------------------------------------------------------
IGNORE_OPTIM_EMBEDDED_HINTS
OPTIMIZER_FEATURES_ENABLE('11.2.0.1')
DB_VERSION('11.2.0.1')
ALL_ROWS
OUTLINE_LEAF(@"SEL$1")
INDEX_SS(@"SEL$1" "SKEW"@"SEL$1" ("SKEW"."COL2" "SKEW"."COL1"))

6 rows selected.
```

The naming of baselines is not particularly friendly. The sql_handle is a unique identifier for a SQL statement while the sql_plan_name is a unique identifier for a plan. By the way, the sql_plan_name is also called sql_plan_baseline in the v$sql view.

There are many ways to create Baselines. They can be automatically created for every statement that is excuted by setting the OPTIMIZER_CAPTURE_SQL_PLAN_BASELINES parameter to true. They can also be created for statements in a SQL Tuning Set using the LOAD_PLANS_FROM_SQLSET function or migrated from Outlines using the MIGRATE_STORED_OUTLINE function. These mechanisms are primarily designed for seeding Baselines when doing migrations.

Creating a baseline for an individual statement that is already in the cursor cache can be accomplished via the DBMS_SPM.LOAD_PLANS_FROM_CURSOR_CACHE function. All the function needs is a SQL_ID and a PLAN_HASH_VALUE. Optionally, a parameter can be used to define the baseline as FIXED. If it's FIXED then it gets priority over any other Baselines for that statement, except other FIXED Baselines. Confused? Well it's not exactly the most straightforward setup. I'm a simple guy, so at this point I'm thinking one FIXED Baseline is plenty. After all, you're looking to minimize plan changes. So with that said, let's look an example of creating a baseline for a single statement in Listing 16-29.

Listing 16-29. *Creating a Baseline for a Single Statement*

```
SYS@LAB112> select sum(pk_col) from kso.skew where col1=666666;

SUM(PK_COL)
-----------
  517333312

SYS@LAB112> @find_sql
Enter value for sql_text: %66666%
```

```
Enter value for sql_id:

SQL_ID        CHILD PLAN_HASH EXECS AVG_ETIME  AVG_LIO SQL_TEXT
------------- ------ ---------- ----- --------- --------------------------------------------
dv1qm9crkf281     0 2650913906     1       .08      45 select sum(pk_col) from kso.skew
                                                       col1=666666

SYS@LAB112> @create_baseline
Enter value for sql_id: dv1qm9crkf281
Enter value for plan_hash_value: 2650913906
Enter value for fixed (NO):
Enter value for enabled (YES):
Enter value for plan_name (ID_sqlid_planhashvalue):

Baseline SQLID_DV1QM9CRKF281_2650913906 created.

SYS@LAB112> select sql_handle, plan_name, sql_text
  2  from dba_sql_plan_baselines where sql_text like '%66666%';

SQL_HANDLE              PLAN_NAME                     SQL_TEXT
---------------------- ----------------------------- ------------------------------------
SYS_SQL_8a22ceb091365064 SQLID_DV1QM9CRKF281_2650913906 select sum(pk_col) from kso.skew

1 row selected.

SYS@LAB112> select sum(pk_col) from kso.skew where col1=666666;

SUM(PK_COL)
-----------
  517333312

1 row selected.

SYS@LAB112> /
SUM(PK_COL)
-----------
  517333312

1 row selected.

SYS@LAB112> @dplan
Enter value for sql_id: dv1qm9crkf281
Enter value for child_no:
```

```
PLAN_TABLE_OUTPUT
---------------------------------------------------------------------------------------------
SQL_ID  dv1qm9crkf281, child number 1
-------------------------------------
select sum(pk_col) from kso.skew where col1=666666

Plan hash value: 2650913906

---------------------------------------------------------------------------------------------
| Id  | Operation                     | Name          | Rows  | Bytes | Cost (%CPU)| Time     |
---------------------------------------------------------------------------------------------
|   0 | SELECT STATEMENT              |               |       |       | 34  (100)|          |
|   1 |  SORT AGGREGATE               |               |     1 |    24 |          |          |
|   2 |   TABLE ACCESS BY INDEX ROWID | SKEW          |    32 |   768 | 34    (0)| 00:00:01 |
|*  3 |    INDEX SKIP SCAN            | SKEW_COL2_COL1|    32 |       |  5    (0)| 00:00:01 |
---------------------------------------------------------------------------------------------

Predicate Information (identified by operation id):
---------------------------------------------------

   3 - access("COL1"=666666)
       filter("COL1"=666666)

Note
-----
   - SQL plan baseline SQLID_DV1QM9CRKF281_2650913906 used for this statement

46 rows selected.
```

Listing 16-29 shows the use of the create_baseline.sql script that creates a Baseline on an existing statement in the shared pool. The script also renames the Baseline to something more meaningful (SQLID_sqlid_planhash by default). This renaming only works in 11gR2, by the way; 11gR1 allows you to rename a Baseline but there is a bug that causes a statement that uses a renamed Baseline to fail. Consequently, the create_baseline.sql script does not rename Baselines if the version is not 11.2 or higher.

Baselines can also be used to retrieve a plan from the AWR history although it's not quite a straight forward as getting the plan from the cursor cache. Listing 16-30 shows an of example of doing just that with the create_baseline_awr.sql script.

Listing 16-30. *The create_baseline_awr.sql Script*

```
SYS@LAB112> @find_sql_awr
Enter value for sql_text: %cursor%skew%
Enter value for sql_id:
```

```
SQL_ID        SQL_TEXT
------------- --------------------------------------------------------------------------------
3ggjbbd2varq2 select /*+ cursor_sharing_exact */ avg(pk_col) from kso.skew where col1 = 1
48up9g2j8dkct select /*+ cursor_sharing_exact */ avg(pk_col) from kso.skew where col1 = 136135
2z6s4zb5pxp9k select /*+ opt_param('cursor_sharing' 'exact') */ avg(pk_col) from kso.skew where
13krz9pwd6a88 select /*+ opt_param('cursor_sharing=force') */ avg(pk_col) from kso.skew

4 rows selected.

SYS@LAB112> @dplan_awr
Enter value for sql_id: 3ggjbbd2varq2
Enter value for plan_hash_value:

PLAN_TABLE_OUTPUT
--------------------------------------------------------------------------------------------
---
SQL_ID 3ggjbbd2varq2
--------------------
select /*+ cursor_sharing_exact */ avg(pk_col) from kso.skew where col1 = 1

Plan hash value: 568322376

-------------------------------------------------------------------------
| Id  | Operation          | Name | Rows  | Bytes | Cost (%CPU)| Time     |
-------------------------------------------------------------------------
|   0 | SELECT STATEMENT   |      |       |       | 28366 (100)|          |
|   1 |  SORT AGGREGATE    |      |     1 |    24 |            |          |
|   2 |   TABLE ACCESS FULL| SKEW | 3149K |   72M | 28366   (1)| 00:05:41 |
-------------------------------------------------------------------------


15 rows selected.
SYS@LAB112> @find_sql
Enter value for sql_text:
Enter value for sql_id: 3ggjbbd2varq2

no rows selected

SYS@LAB112> -- so it's not in the cursor cache
SYS@LAB112>
SYS@LAB112> @create_baseline_awr
Enter value for SQL_ID: 48up9g2j8dkct
Enter value for PLAN_HASH_VALUE: 568322376
Enter value for fixed (NO):
Enter value for enabled (YES):
Enter value for plan_name (ID_sqlid_planhashvalue):

Baseline SQLID_48UP9G2J8DKCT_568322376 created.
```

```
SYS@LAB112>
SYS@LAB112> select sql_handle, plan_name, sql_text
  2  from dba_sql_plan_baselines where plan_name like 'SQLID_48UP9G2J8DKCT_568322376';

SQL_HANDLE               PLAN_NAME                       SQL_TEXT
-----------------------  ------------------------------  -----------------------------------
SYS_SQL_d52c57087080269e SQLID_48UP9G2J8DKCT_568322376   select /*+ cursor_sharing_exact */
                                                         avg(pk_col)

1 row selected.
```

So Baselines are obviously the wave of the future, but at this point they are not quite as flexibile as SQL Profiles when it comes to applying custom controls to statements. They can attempt to lock in plans from the cursor cache or from AWR history, but they cannot import arbitrary hints or apply to many statements at a time like SQL Profiles can via the FORCE_MATCHING attribute. However, they can collect alternate plans for later evaluation and they are designed to store a large set of plans in an attempt to keep any plan from changing without warning.

Hint Based Plan Control Mechanisms Wrap Up

Of the three options availabe in 11g, I believe that SQL Profiles are the most straight forward and functional. They have the advantage of "force matching" which allows a single SQL Profile to apply to multiple SQL statements by ignoring literals (much like cursor_sharing=force , i.e. the "force" matching). They also have a built in procedure (dbms_sqltune.import_sql_profile) that allows any set of hints to be attached to any SQL statement. This is an extremely powerful tool that basically allows you to apply any hint to any statement, even if you have don't have access to the code. Neither Outlines nor Baselines have either one of these advantages. Baselines do store the original plan_hash_value, which means they can tell if the hints are still generating the original plan. But they have no way of getting back to the original plan in cases when the hints fail to do their job. Their only option at that point is to throw away the hints all together and try again. It would be nice if there was a way to just store the plan itself, instead of a set of hints that "should" get you back to the same plan. Maybe in the next release.

Conclusion

There are several things that contribute to plan instability. If you get one thing out of this chapter, I hope it is that plans do not change without a reason. Plans will remain static unless something else changes in the system. Changes in statistics and bind variable peeking are the most likely causes of plan instability. Oddly enough, failure of statistics to keep up with changing data is another common cause of instability. Of these three issues, though, bind variable peeking is probably the most prevalent and the most frustrating to deal with. While most shops are understandably reluctant to turn off the bind variable peeking "feature" turning it off altogether is in fact a viable option. There are many production systems that have taken this approach. Part of the standard configuration of SAP, for example, is to set the _optim_peek_user_binds parameter to false. This can prevent the optimizer from choosing the absolute best plan available for a certain set of queries, but the trade off is a more consistent environment. Short of turning off bind variable peeking altogether, using literals appropriately with columns that need histograms to deal with skewed data distributions is really the only effective way to deal with the issue while still providing the optimizer the ability to choose the absolute best execution plans. However, if circumstances prevent this approach, there are other techniques that can be applied.

SQL Profiles provide an extremely valuable tool in situations where the need is urgent and the ability to change the code is non-existent. They also have the advantage of being very specific in their scope (i.e. they can be targeted at a single statement without the possibility of having negative affects on other statements). Baselines can also be very useful if you are using 11g. Although they are not as flexible as SQL Profiles, they do have the advantage of knowing what plan they are trying to recreate. They also have the capability of keeping a list of alternate plans that can be evaluated later. SQL Tuning Advisor Profiles can be useful for identifying better plans and pointing out problem areas, but I am not a fan of implementing them in most cases. Generally speaking, I would rather have a mechanism that applies directive hints that list specific objects and join methods rather than fudge factors. All of these types of hint-based control mechanisms, though, should be considered temporary fixes. Although they may work well for an extended period of time while a more permenant solution is contemplated, they really should be considered a temporary fix while appropriate statistics gathering methodology is implemented or code is changed to make appropriate use of literals.

From a philosophical standpoint, I strongly believe that consistency is more important than absolute speed. So when a choice must be made, I always favor slightly reduced but consistent performance over anything that doesn't provide that consistency.

Index

■ ■ ■

■ S

You Need the Companion eBook

Your purchase of this book entitles you to buy the companion PDF-version eBook for only $10. Take the weightless companion with you anywhere.

We believe this Apress title will prove so indispensable that you'll want to carry it with you everywhere, which is why we are offering the companion eBook (in PDF format) for $10 to customers who purchase this book now. Convenient and fully searchable, the PDF version of any content-rich, page-heavy Apress book makes a valuable addition to your programming library. You can easily find and copy code—or perform examples by quickly toggling between instructions and the application. Even simultaneously tackling a donut, diet soda, and complex code becomes simplified with hands-free eBooks!

Once you purchase your book, getting the $10 companion eBook is simple:

1. Visit **www.apress.com/promo/tendollars/**.

2. Complete a basic registration form to receive a randomly generated question about this title.

3. Answer the question correctly in 60 seconds, and you will receive a promotional code to redeem for the $10.00 eBook.

233 Spring Street, New York, NY 10013

Offer valid through 6/11.